ELEVENTH EDITION  **W9-BPM-786**

LANGUAGE AWARENESS

Readings for College Writers

Paul Eschholz, *University of Vermont*
Alfred Rosa, *University of Vermont*
Virginia Clark, *late of University of Vermont*

BEDFORD / ST. MARTIN'S   Boston • New York

For Bedford/St. Martin's

DEVELOPMENTAL EDITOR: Sarah Macomber
SENIOR PRODUCTION EDITOR: Anne Noonan
PRODUCTION SUPERVISOR: Samuel Jones
EXECUTIVE MARKETING MANAGER: Molly Parke
EDITORIAL ASSISTANT: Daniel Schafer
COPYEDITOR: Marcy Ross
PERMISSIONS MANAGER: Kalina K. Ingham
SENIOR ART DIRECTOR: Anna Palchik
TEXT DESIGN: Jean Hammond
COVER DESIGN: Marine Miller
COVER ART: Adwaita (2008), 48 × 48 inches, oil on canvas. Copyright: Bratsa
Bonifacho
COMPOSITION: Cenveo Publisher Services
PRINTING AND BINDING: RR Donnelley and Sons

PRESIDENT, BEDFORD/ST. MARTIN'S: Denise B. Wydra
PRESIDENTS, MACMILLAN HIGHER EDUCATION: Joan E. Feinberg and Tom Scotty
EDITOR IN CHIEF: Karen S. Henry
DIRECTOR OF MARKETING: Karen R. Soeltz
PRODUCTION DIRECTOR: Susan W. Brown
ASSOCIATE PRODUCTION DIRECTOR: Elise S. Kaiser
MANAGING EDITOR: Elizabeth M. Schaaf

Manufactured in the United States of America

6 5 4
f e d

For information, write: Bedford/St. Martin's, 75 Arlington Street, Boston, MA
02116   (617-399-4000)

ISBN 978-1-4576-1078-3

Acknowledgments

Dedicated to our colleague, mentor, and friend
Virginia P. Clark (1929–2012).

PREFACE

Since the first edition of *Language Awareness* appeared in 1974, its purpose has been twofold: to foster an appreciation of the richness, flexibility, and vitality of the English language and to help students to use their language more responsibly and effectively in speech and particularly in writing. Because of these purposes, *Language Awareness* has been used successfully in a variety of courses over the years. Its primary use, however, has been and continues to be in college composition courses. Clearly, many instructors believe as we do—that the study of language and the study of writing go hand in hand.

Because the study of language is so multifaceted, we cover a broad spectrum of topics, including language acquisition, regional dialects of American English, the relationship between language and culture, the language of new technologies, the language of prejudice, and the power of language in influencing advertising, politics, the media, and gender roles. Opening students' eyes to the power of language—its ability to shape and influence perceptions and cultural attitudes—is, we believe, one of the worthiest goals a writing class can pursue.

NEW TO THE ELEVENTH EDITION

As in previous editions of *Language Awareness*, the selections in the eleventh edition are written primarily in nontechnical language on topics of current interest. Our questions and introductory material help students to understand those topics, providing clearly defined opportunities for thoughtful writing. Guided by comments and advice from hundreds of colleagues and students across the country who have used the previous editions, we have made some dramatic improvements in this eleventh edition.

New Organizational Structure

A new organization offers sharply focused chapters designed to be more manageable in today's classroom. Flexible and brief, each chapter still collects diverse perspectives on a given topic, while a wider variety of chapter topics gives instructors more choice and flexibility when deciding what to include in their syllabi. In addition, four chapters devoted to the tasks of reading and writing offer students time-tested advice on how to read and analyze texts, work with sources, conduct research, and write and revise their own polished essays.

New Selections

Almost half of the sixty-six professional selections in *Language Awareness* are new to this edition. We have retained many of the classic, informative, and well-written essays from earlier editions, such as Gordon Allport's "The Language of Prejudice," Helen Keller's "The Day Language Came into My Life," Martin Luther King Jr.'s "I Have a Dream," William Lutz's "The World of Doublespeak," Malcolm X's "Coming to an Awareness of Language," Gloria Naylor's "The Meanings of a Word," George Orwell's "Politics and the English Language," and Andrew Sullivan's "What's So Bad about Hate?"

The thirty new selections, chosen for their insight and clear, thought-provoking writing, also reflect the language issues of an increasingly complex, multicultural America. Representing a wide variety of voices, the readings address a range of language concerns from gay rights to deaf culture. New selections include Pat Conroy's "Letter to the Editor of the *Charleston Gazette*," Firoozeh Dumas's "The 'F Word,'" Joseph P. Kahn's "What Does 'Friend' Mean Now?" Martin Luther King Jr.'s "Letter from Birmingham Jail," Stephen King's "Reading to Write," Frank Luntz's "Be All That You Can Be: The Company Persona and Language Alignment," Wangari Maathai's "Planting the Seeds of Peace: 2004 Nobel Prize for Peace," Bharati Mukherjee's "Two Ways to Belong in America," and Ben Zimmer's "Chunking." We believe that the new selections will spark student interest and bring currency to the otherwise class-proven essays retained from earlier editions.

New Emphasis on Academic Writing

Throughout this edition of *Language Awareness* we have seized every opportunity to emphasize the kinds of writing that students will be called upon to do in their college courses. In Chapter 2, "Writing in College and Beyond," students will find advice on academic writing ranging from determining their topics and developing strong thesis statements to marshaling evidence, using discipline-specific prose, and achieving the appropriate level of formality. This academic advice is, in turn, bolstered by the new chapters "Writing with Sources" and "A Brief Guide to Writing a Research Paper."

New "Writing with Sources" Chapter

This chapter offers practical instruction on how to work with outside sources. One of the biggest challenges student writers face is incorporating supporting evidence from other writers into their essays. Chapter 3 models for students some effective strategies for taking effective notes from sources, avoiding plagiarism, and using signal phrases to integrate quotations, summaries, and paraphrases smoothly into the text of their papers. These strategies help students become more confident in starting and joining academic conversations through their writing. The chapter concludes with a student essay on the "Official English" controversy, using outside sources to serve as a model of both source-based writing and proper citation.

New Research Writing Chapter

Chapter 15, "A Brief Guide to Writing a Research Paper," provides students with all the essentials they need to undertake a research project. The chapter offers clear guidance on establishing a realistic schedule for a research project; conducting online research using directory and keyword searches; evaluating sources; analyzing sources; developing a working bibliography; taking useful notes; and using MLA citation style to fully document the paper. This chapter, in combination with Chapter 3, "Writing with Sources," gives students more practical help while building confidence in their academic writing skills.

New Thematic Chapter

Students and teachers, pleased with the relevancy of the thematic chapters in past editions of *Language Awareness*, asked us to provide more material on technology and how it has influenced our use of language. The result is Chapter 11, "Language and Technology," a thematic chapter that offers a collection of readings on texting and social media, a topic of special interest to our students today. Recent technological innovations have already changed the ways we interact with one another using language — texting information and ideas and updating our friends on our recent activities via *Facebook, Twitter, Foursquare,* or *Yelp,* for example — and certainly new modes of information transfer and entertainment will continue to capture our imaginations. The authors of the readings in this chapter have already begun to assess how we and the language we use are responding and adjusting to new forms of communication and the etiquette that accompanies them. Not surprisingly, these observers and experts prefer to focus on real and perceived problems with the new intersections of technology and language rather than praising them for their obvious gifts. This chapter challenges and questions some of our most widespread assumptions about technology and its effects on the language we use and the ways we communicate.

Arguing about Language

Chapter 14, "Arguing about Language," offers three debates on current language issues: "Should English Be the Law?" "Should Language Be Censored?" which has been updated with two new selections, and the new debate "How Do Words Hurt?," which concerns the use of the word *retard* and whether or not its use (whether casual, derogatory, or clinical) should be discouraged. While the first two debates begin with an introduction of the essential issue, together with an overview of how the multiple perspectives play off against one another, the third debate presents its selections in chronological order and shows students how the debate unfolds and how different voices complicate the issue with no clear resolution. We think that this organization offers a special opportunity for students to enter into the debate in a realistic and timely manner. The end-of-selection questions invite students to bring the language concepts and ideas they have learned in the earlier core chapters of *Language Awareness* to bear on the topics of the language debates. At the end of each debate, a set of Writing Suggestions offers students opportunities to join in the debate by extending their analyses of individual articles and making connections among the various perspectives of the writers.

e-Pages: Multimodal Readings for *Language Awareness* (bedfordstmartins.com/languageawareness/epages)

Some aspects of language are best experienced beyond the printed page—for instance, watching a video that demonstrates differences in regional accents, interacting with a Web site that encourages new modes of language learning, or listening to the cadences and pauses of a skilled orator. To help extend what students read and learn in *Language Awareness* to the kinds of media they are most familiar with and excited by, we have added a compelling multimodal selection to each reading chapter in *Language Awareness*. For a complete list of e-Pages, see the book's table of contents. Instructors can also use the free tools accompanying the e-Pages to upload a syllabus, readings, and assignments to share with the class.

You and your students can access the e-Pages from the *Student Site for Language Awareness* at **bedfordstmartins.com/languageawareness /epages.** Students receive access automatically with the purchase of a new book. If the activation code printed on the inside back cover of the student edition has already been revealed and is expired, students can purchase access at the *Student Site.* Instructors receive access information in a separate email with access to all of the resources on the *Student Site*. You can also log in or request access information at the *Student Site*.

KEY FEATURES OF *LANGUAGE AWARENESS*

Class-Tested Topics

Instructors have told us that the chapters on "Understanding the Power of Language," "Language Essentials," "Language Communities," "Writers on Writing," "Politics, Propaganda, and Doublespeak," "Language That Made a Difference," "Prejudice, Discrimination, and Stereotypes," "Language and Advertising," "Language and Gender," "Should English Be the Law?," and "Should Language Be Censored?" are indispensable in the courses they teach. Not only do the readings in these chapters represent essential areas of language study, but they also teach students useful ways to look at and write about the world around them. Each of these chapters has been updated with new essays that reflect recent trends, but they retain the spirit and purpose of their predecessors.

Introductory Chapters on Reading and Writing

To supplement the study of language with instruction in reading and writing, we have expanded our coverage of the twin tasks of reading and writing. Based on years of classroom experience, these opening two chapters provide students with the essentials of college reading and writing. The first chapter, "Reading Critically," provides students with guidelines for critical reading, demonstrates how they can get the most out of their reading by taking advantage of the apparatus accompanying each selection, and shows how they can generate their own writing from the reading they do. The second chapter, "Writing in College and Beyond," explores the world of academic writing. Here students learn how to master the core elements that all instructors expect in academic essays, starting with an understanding of the writing assignment itself, establishing a thesis, determining an organization, using evidence, and culminating with documenting sources and avoiding plagiarism. Each step in the process is illustrated with a student essay in progress.

Chapter Introductions

Brief, one- to two-page chapter introductions discuss the key elements of each chapter's topic and why the topic is important to study. In addition, the introductions briefly discuss individual readings, explaining how they connect to larger language issues and how they relate to each other.

Student-Tested Headnotes, Journal Prompts, Questions, Activities, and Writing Suggestions

INFORMATIVE HEADNOTES. Headnotes preceding each selection discuss the content of the essay and provide pertinent information about the author and where and when the selection was first published.

"WRITING TO DISCOVER" JOURNAL PROMPTS. Each selection begins with a journal prompt designed to get students writing—before they start reading—about their own experiences with the language issues discussed in the selection. Students are then more likely to approach the selection with a critical eye. From time to time, class activities or writing assignments ask students to return to these journal writings and to reflect on them before proceeding with more formal writing tasks.

END-OF-SELECTION QUESTIONS. The "Thinking Critically about the Reading" questions at the end of each selection emphasize content and writing strategies. Content questions challenge students to develop a deeper understanding of ideas contained in the essay, in some cases by drawing connections to other readings or analyzing their own experiences. Other questions ask students to explore and analyze the writer's strategies in developing the selection to determine how effective writing achieves its aims.

LANGUAGE IN ACTION ACTIVITIES. The "Language in Action" activities that follow every selection in Chapters 4 through 13 give students a chance to analyze real-world examples of the language issues discussed by the essayists, with poems, cartoons, parodies, advertisements, photographs, letters to the editor, syndicated columns, and more. Designed to be completed either in class or at home in about twenty minutes, these activities ask students to take a hands-on approach to what they are learning from the essays and to give them a chance to demonstrate their growing language aptitude.

END-OF-SELECTION WRITING ASSIGNMENTS. To give students more opportunities to practice thinking and writing, we provide several Writing Suggestions at the end of every selection in Chapters 4 through 14. Each assignment is designed to elicit a three- to five-page paper. Some assignments ask students to use their "Writing to Discover" journal entries as springboards for an extended essay; for others, students use their analytical skills to make critical connections among articles on the same topic; and some assignments ask students to do library or community-based research in order, for example, to examine the language used in local public documents, the language used in law offices, or campus slang.

Glossary of Rhetorical and Linguistic Terms

The Glossary of Rhetorical and Linguistic Terms includes definitions of key language terms and concepts as well as the standard terminology of rhetoric. References to glossary entries appear where needed in the questions that accompany each selection, allowing students to look up unfamiliar terms as they read.

Rhetorical Contents

At the end of the text, an alternate table of contents classifies the selections in *Language Awareness* according to the rhetorical strategies they exemplify (i.e., Comparison and Contrast, Definition, Illustration, Cause and Effect Analysis, and Argument), making it easier for instructors to assign readings that parallel the types of writing their students are doing.

HELPFUL SUPPLEMENTS

Instructor Resources

You have a lot to do in your course. Bedford/St. Martin's wants to make it easy for you to find the support you need — and to get it quickly.

The **Instructor's Manual for** *Language Awareness* is available as a PDF that can be downloaded from bedfordstmartins.com/languageawareness. Packed with teaching tips and suggested answers to end-of-selection questions, the new Instructor's Manual reflects all the features in the apparatus that accompanies each selection within the core chapters and the language debates. It also offers advice on how to approach each of the Language in Action activities.

Teaching Central (**bedfordstmartins.com/teachingcentral**) offers the entire list of Bedford/St. Martin's print and online professional resources in one place. You'll find landmark reference works, sourcebooks on pedagogical issues, award-winning collections, and practical advice for the classroom — all free for instructors.

Bits (**bedfordbits.com**) collects creative ideas for teaching a range of composition topics in an easily searchable blog. A community of teachers — leading scholars, authors, and editors — discuss revision, research, grammar and style, technology, peer review, and much more. Take, use, adapt, and pass the ideas around. Then, come back to the site to comment or share your own suggestions.

Bedford Course Packs allow you to easily integrate our most popular content into your own course management system. For details, visit bedfordstmartins.com/coursepacks.

Student Resources

The Student Site for *Language Awareness* (bedfordstmartins .com/languageawareness) provides students with easy-to-access reference materials, visual tutorials, reading quizzes, and support for working with sources.

- 3 free tutorials from *ix visual exercises* by Cheryl Ball and Kristin Arola
- *TopLinks* with reliable online sources
- *The Bedford Bibliographer*: a tool for collecting source information and making a bibliography in MLA, APA, and *Chicago* styles

VideoCentral is a growing collection of videos for the writing class that captures real-world, academic, and student writers talking about how and why they write. *VideoCentral* can be packaged for free with *Language Awareness*. An activation code is required. To order *VideoCentral* packaged with the print book, use ISBN 1-4576-4330-8 or 978-1-4576-4330-9.

Re: Writing Plus gathers all of the premium digital content for composition offered by Bedford/St. Martin's into one online collection. It includes hundreds of model documents, the first ever peer review game, and *VideoCentral*. *Re:Writing Plus* can be purchased separately or packaged with the print book at a significant discount. An activation code is required. To order *Re:Writing Plus* packaged with *Language Awareness,* use ISBN 1-4576-4329-4 or 978-1-4576-4329-3.

The Language Awareness E-book to Go allows students to purchase *Language Awareness* in several popular e-book formats for computers, tablets, and e-readers. For more details, visit bedfordstmartins.com /ebooks.

ACKNOWLEDGMENTS

We are grateful to the following reviewers, whose comments helped us shape this edition:

Dianne Armstrong, Columbus State University; Shavawn Berry, Arizona State University; Nicole Beveridge, Kingsborough Community College; Yvonne Bruce, University of Akron; Jonathan Campbell, Valdosta State University; Cindy Cochran, Illinois College; Lorna Condit, University of Missouri-Kansas City; Stacey Corbitt, Montana Tech of the University of Montana; Felicia Crittenden, Fayetteville State University; Joshua Dickinson, Jefferson Community College; Phyllis Dircks, C.W. Post College of Long Island University; Ann-Marie Dunbar, Winona State University; Wade Edwards, Longwood University; Geraldine Grunow, Henry Ford Community College; Cynthia Hess, Elizabethtown College; Beverly Holmes, Northwest Florida State College; Barbara Hunt, Columbus State University; Patrick Hunter, California State University-Northridge; Robert Lively, Truckee Meadows Community College; Ilka Luyt, Jefferson Community College; Louis Martin, Elizabethtown College; Marsha McSpadden, University of Alabama; Susan Miller, University of California-Merced; Susan Morris, Creighton University; Nancy Moore, Columbus State University; Cheryl Murray, Queens University of Charlotte; Julia Newcome, Robert Morris University; Daniel Roth, Contra Costa College; Guy Shebat, Youngstown State University; Kathryn Swanson, Augsburg College; Diane Todd, Robert Morris University; Carey Scott Wilkerson, Columbus State University; Judith Wootten, Kent State University; and Sara Yaklin, University of Toledo.

We would like to express our appreciation to the staff at Bedford/St. Martin's, especially Sarah Macomber for supporting us in our efforts to find innovative and engaging new readings and to update and energize our Language in Action activities so that they provide strong links between language study and real-world issues. Her assistant, Daniel Schafer, handled a number of important tasks and facilitated manuscript flow. Thanks go to Anne Noonan, our production editor; to Marcy Ross, our superlative copyeditor; and to Natalie Giboney Turner and Sheri Blaney-Nogg for clearing permissions. Without our students at the University of Vermont over the years, a book such as *Language Awareness* would not have been possible. Their enthusiasm for language study and writing and their responses to materials included in this book have proved invaluable.

Finally, we thank each other. Beginning in 1971 we have collaborated on many textbooks in language and writing, all of which have gone into multiple editions. With this eleventh edition of *Language Awareness*, we enter the forty-first year of working together. Ours must be one of the longest-running and most mutually satisfying writing partnerships in college textbook publishing. The journey has been invigorating and challenging as we have come to understand the complexities and joys of good writing and sought out new ways to help students become better writers.

PAUL ESCHHOLZ
ALFRED ROSA

CONTENTS

e **For readings that go beyond the printed page, see
bedfordstmartins.com/languageawareness/epages**

"I saw that the best thing I could do was get hold of a dictionary — to study, to learn some words."

The celebrated deaf and blind writer recalls her discovery of language.

This beginning writer describes life as a dyslexic high school student and how he met his language challenge.

"All writing is designed to change the world, at least a small part of the world, or in some small way, perhaps a change in a reader's mood or in his or her appreciation of a certain kind of beauty."

"For years now I have heard the word 'Wait!' It rings in the ear of every Negro with piercing familiarity. This 'Wait' has almost always meant 'Never.' We must come to see, with one of our distinguished jurists, that 'justice too long delayed is justice denied.'"

"It's true that speeches don't solve all problems, but what is also true is if we cannot inspire the country to believe again, then it doesn't matter how many policies and plans we have."

e bedfordstmartins.com/languageawareness/epages

🄴 bedfordstmartins.com/languageawareness/epages

7. WRITERS ON WRITING   177

bedfordstmartins.com/languageawareness/epages

Inaugural Address, JOHN F. KENNEDY   282

> "Let every nation know, whether it wishes us well or ill, that we shall
> pay any price, bear any burden, meet any hardship, support any friend,
> oppose any foe to assure the survival and success of liberty."

Second Inaugural Address, ABRAHAM LINCOLN   287

> "With malice toward none, with charity for all, with firmness in the
> right as God gives us to see the right, let us strive on to finish the work
> we are in, to bind up the nation's wounds, to care for him who shall
> have borne the battle and for his widow and his orphan, to do all which
> may achieve and cherish a just and lasting peace among ourselves and
> with all nations."

And Ain't I a Woman?, SOJOURNER TRUTH   291

> The celebrated nineteenth-century evangelist and activist demonstrates
> the rich power of the vernacular in rallying women to fight for their
> rights.

A Modest Proposal, JONATHAN SWIFT   295

> This well-known satirical essay clearly outlines a plan to end hunger in
> eighteenth-century Ireland.

10. THE LANGUAGE OF PREJUDICE, DISCRIMINATION, AND STEREOTYPES   305

What's So Bad about Hate?, ANDREW SULLIVAN   307

> Legislating against hate crimes has become more and more common
> in the past decades. But, what does hate mean in this context, and can
> legislation really be effective?

The Language of Prejudice, GORDON ALLPORT   324

> What causes prejudice? This famous psychologist points to the workings
> of language for the answer.

The Meanings of a Word, GLORIA NAYLOR   336

> An African American writer believes that "words themselves are
> innocuous; it is the consensus that gives them true power."

"FOBs" vs. "Twinkies": The New Discrimination Is Intraracial, GRACE HSIANG   342

> This writer notes that discrimination and generalization within cultures
> is as common as discrimination from the outside.

Black Men and Public Space, BRENT STAPLES   346

> Reflecting on the power of body language, Staples recounts his
> experiences moving through public spaces at night.

e bedfordstmartins.com/languageawareness/epages

bedfordstmartins.com/languageawareness/epages

e   bedfordstmartins.com/languageawareness/epages

1

READING CRITICALLY

The readings in *Language Awareness* emphasize the crucial role language plays in virtually every aspect of our lives, and they reveal the essential elements of the writer's craft. As you read and study the selections in this text, you will discover the power of language in our world: You will become more aware of your own language usage and how it affects others, and, at the same time, you will become more sensitive to how the language of others affects you. An additional benefit of close, critical reading is that you will become more familiar with different types of writing and learn how good writers make decisions about writing strategies and techniques. All of these insights will help you become a more thoughtful, discerning reader and, equally important, a better writer.

As the word *critical* suggests, reading critically means questioning what you read in a thoughtful, organized way and with an alert, inquiring mind. Critical reading is a skill you need if you are truly to engage and understand the content of a piece of writing as well as the craft that shapes the writer's ideas into an effective, efficient, and presentable form. Never accept what you read simply because it's in print. Instead, scrutinize it, challenge it, and think about its meaning and significance.

Critical reading is also a skill that takes time and practice to acquire. While most of us learned before we got to college how to read for content and summarize what a writer said, not all of us learned how to analyze what we were reading. Reading critically is like engaging a writer in a conversation—asking for the meaning of a particular statement, questioning the definition of a crucial term, or demanding more evidence to support a generalization. In addition, critical reading requires asking ourselves why we like one piece of writing and not another, or why one argument is more believable or convincing than another.

As you learn more about reading thoughtfully and purposefully, you will come to a better understanding of both the content and the craft of any piece of writing. As an added bonus, learning to read critically will help you read your own work with more insight and, as a result, write more persuasively.

GETTING THE MOST OUT OF YOUR READING

Critical reading requires, first of all, that you commit time and effort. Second, it requires that you apply goodwill and energy to understanding and appreciating what you are reading, even if the subject matter does not immediately appeal to you. Remember, your mission is twofold: You must analyze and comprehend the content of what you are reading; and then you must understand the writer's methods to see firsthand the kinds of choices a writer makes in his or her writing.

To help you grow as a critical reader and to get the most out of what you read, use the following classroom-proven steps:

1. Prepare yourself to read the selection.
2. Read the selection to get an overview of it.
3. Annotate the selection with marginal notes.
4. Summarize the selection in your own words.
5. Analyze the selection to come to an understanding of it.
6. Complete the "Language in Action" activity to discover the far-reaching connections between the selection and language in the real world.

To demonstrate how these steps can work for you, we've applied them to an essay by the popular nonfiction writer Natalie Goldberg. Like the other selections in *Language Awareness,* Goldberg's essay "Be Specific" is accessible and speaks to an important contemporary language issue. She points to the importance of using specific names in speaking and writing, and she demonstrates how we give things their proper dignity and integrity when we name them.

1. Prepare Yourself to Read the Selection

Instead of diving into any given selection in *Language Awareness* or any other book, there are a few things that you can do that will prepare you to get the most out of what you will read. It's helpful, for example, to get a context for what you'll read. What's the essay about? What do you know about the writer's background and reputation? Where was the essay first published? Who was the intended audience for the essay? And, finally, how much do you already know about the subject of the reading selection? We encourage you to consider carefully the materials that precede each selection in this book. Each selection begins with a title, headnote, and journal prompt. From the **title** you often discover the writer's position on an issue or attitude toward the topic. On occasion, the title can give clues about the intended audience and the writer's purpose in writing the piece. The **headnote** contains a biographical note about the author followed by publication information and rhetorical highlights about the selection. In addition to information on the person's life and work, you'll read about his or her reputation and authority to write on the subject of the piece. The

publication information indicates when the essay was published and in what book or magazine it first appeared. This information, in turn, gives you insight about the intended audience. The **rhetorical highlights** direct your attention to one or more aspects of how the selection was written. Finally, the Writing to Discover **journal prompt** encourages you to collect your thoughts and opinions about the topic or related issues before you commence reading. The journal prompt makes it easy to keep a record of your own knowledge or thinking on a topic before you see what the writer has to offer.

To understand how these context-building materials can work for you, carefully review the following informational materials that accompany Natalie Goldberg's essay "Be Specific."

Be Specific

NATALIE GOLDBERG

Born in 1948, author Natalie Goldberg is a teacher of writing who has conducted writing workshops across the country. In addition to her classes and workshops, Goldberg shares her love of writing in her books; she has made writing about writing her speciality. Her first and best-known work, *Writing Down the Bones: Freeing the Writer Within,* was published in 1986. Goldberg's advice to would-be writers is practical and pithy, on the one hand, and mystical or spiritual in its call to writers to know and become more connected to the environment. In short, as one reviewer observed, "Goldberg teaches us not only how to write better, but how to live better." *Writing Down the Bones* was followed by five more books about writing: *Wild Mind: Living the Writer's Life* (1990), *Living Color: A Writer Paints Her World* (1996), *Thunder and Lightning: Cracking Open the Writer's Craft* (2000), and *Old Friend from Far Away: The Practice of Writing Memoir* (2008). Altogether, more than a million copies of these books are now in print. Goldberg has also written fiction: the novel *Banana Rose* (1995), and the autobiography: *Long Quiet Highway: Waking Up in America* (1993) and *The Great Failure: A Bartender, a Monk, and My Unlikely Path to Truth* (2004).

"Be Specific" is taken from Goldberg's *Writing Down the Bones* and is representative of the book as a whole. Notice the ways in which Goldberg demonstrates her advice to be specific, to use names whenever possible. Which of her many examples resonates best with you?

Title

Headnote

Biographical information

Publication information

Rhetorical highlight

WRITING TO DISCOVER: *Suppose someone says to you, "I*   Journal
walked in the woods today."What do you envision? Write down what   prompt
*you see in your mind's eye. Now suppose someone says, "I walked in
the redwood forest today." Again, write what you see. What's different
about your two descriptions, and why?*

From reading these preliminary materials, what expectations do you
have for the selection itself? How does this knowledge equip you to engage
the selection before you actually read it? From the *title* you probably inferred
that Goldberg will explain what she means by the command "be specific"
and what is to be gained by following this advice. Her purpose clearly is
to give advice to writers. The *biographical note* reveals that Goldberg has
written a number of books detailing her own experiences with writing as
well as giving advice to aspiring writers of all ages, and that she has taught
writing courses and conducted writing workshops for many years. This
experience gives her the knowledge and authority to write on this topic.
The *publication information* indicates that the subject of Goldberg's essay
is an argument in favor of being specific in writing. Because the selection
was first published as part of her book *Writing Down the Bones: Freeing the
Writer Within,* Goldberg can anticipate that readers, who we can assume
are looking for writing advice, will be open to her argument. The *rhetorical highlight* alerts you to be mindful of how Goldberg practices what she's
preaching in her own writing and prompts you to consider her examples.
Finally, the *journal prompt*—a hands-on exercise in specificity—asks you to
describe in writing the visuals conjured up in your mind by two statements
and to draw conclusions about any differences you note in your responses.

It's always a good practice to take several minutes before reading a selection to reflect on what you already know about a particular issue and where
you stand on it and why. After reading Goldberg's essay, you can compare
your own experiences with being specific—or being unspecific—in writing
with those of Goldberg.

2. Read the Selection to Get an Overview of It

Always read the selection at least twice, no matter how long it is. The
first reading gives you a chance to get acquainted with the essay and to
form first impressions. With the first reading you want to get an overall
sense of what the writer is saying, keeping in mind the essay's title and
what you learned about the writer in the headnote. The essay will offer
you information, ideas, and arguments—some you may have expected;
some you may not have. As you read, you may find yourself questioning
or modifying your sense of what the writer is saying. Resist the urge to
annotate at this point; instead, concentrate on the content, on the main
points of what's being said. Now read Natalie Goldberg's essay.

Be Specific

NATALIE GOLDBERG

Be specific. Don't say "fruit." Tell what kind of fruit—"It is a pomegran-ate." Give things the dignity of their names. Just as with human beings, it is rude to say, "Hey, girl, get in line." That "girl" has a name. (As a matter of fact, if she's at least twenty years old, she's a woman, not a "girl" at all.) Things, too, have names. It is much better to say "the geranium in the window" than "the flower in the window." "Geranium"—that one word gives us a much more specific picture. It penetrates more deeply into the beingness of that flower. It immediately gives us the scene by the window—red petals, green circular leaves, all straining toward sunlight.

About ten years ago I decided I had to learn the names of plants and flow-ers in my environment. I bought a book on them and walked down the tree-lined streets of Boulder, examining leaf, bark, and seed, trying to match them up with their descriptions and names in the book. Maple, elm, oak, locust. I usually tried to cheat by asking people working in their yards the names of the flowers and trees growing there. I was amazed how few people had any idea of the names of the live beings inhabiting their little plot of land.

When we know the name of something, it brings us closer to the ground. It takes the blur out of our mind; it connects us to the earth. If I walk down the street and see "dogwood," "forsythia," I feel more friendly toward the environment. I am noticing what is around me and can name it. It makes me more awake.

If you read the poems of William Carlos Williams, you will see how specific he is about plants, trees, flowers—chicory, daisy, locust, poplar, quince, primrose, black-eyed Susan, lilacs—each has its own integrity. Williams says, "Write what's in front of your nose." It's good for us to know what is in front of our noses. Not just "daisy," but how the flower is in the season we are looking at it—"The dayseye hugging the earth/in August . . . brownedged,/green and pointed scales/armor his yellow."* Continue to hone your awareness: to the name, to the month, to the day, and finally to the moment.

Williams also says: "No idea, but in things." Study what is "in front of your nose." By saying "geranium" instead of "flower," you are penetrat-ing more deeply into the present and being there. The closer we can get to what's in front of our nose, the more it can teach us everything. "To see the World in a Grain of Sand, and a heaven in a Wild Flower . . . "** 5

In writing groups and classes too, it is good to quickly learn the names of all the other group members. It helps to ground you in the group and make you more attentive to each other's work.

---

* William Carlos Williams, "Daisy," in *The Collected Earlier Poems* (New York: New Directions, 1938). [Goldberg's note.]

** William Blake, "The Auguries of Innocence." [Goldberg's note.]

Learn the names of everything: birds, cheese, tractors, cars, buildings. A writer is all at once everything—an architect, French cook, farmer—and at the same time, a writer is none of these things.

Some students find it valuable to capture their first impressions, thoughts, or reactions immediately after they've finished reading a selection. If you keep a reading journal, record your ideas in a paragraph or two. You are now ready for the second reading of the essay, this time with pencil or pen in hand to annotate the text.

3. Annotate the Selection with Marginal Notes

As you read the essay a second time, engage it—highlight key passages and make marginal annotations. Your second reading will be quite different from your first, because you already know what the essay is about, where it is going, and how it gets there. Now you can relate the parts of the essay more accurately to the whole. Use the second reading to test your first impressions against the words on the page, developing and deepening your sense of the writer's argument. Because you already have a general understanding of the essay's content and structure, you can focus on the writer's purpose and means of achieving it. You can look for features of organization and style that you can learn from and adapt to your own work.

One question that students frequently ask us is "What should I annotate?" When you annotate a text, you should do more than simply underline or highlight what you think are the important points to remember. Instead, as you read, write down your thoughts, reactions, and questions in the margins or on a separate piece of paper. Think of your annotations as an opportunity to have a conversation with the writer of the essay.

Mark what you believe to be the selection's main point when you find it stated directly. Look for the pattern or patterns of development the author uses to explore and support that point, and record the information. If you disagree with a statement or conclusion, object in the margin: "No!" If you're not convinced by the writer's claims or evidence, indicate that response: "Why?" or "Who says?" or "Explain." If you are impressed by an argument or turn of phrase, compliment the writer: "Good point." If there are any words that you do not recognize or that seem to you to be used in a questionable way, circle them so that you can look them up in a dictionary.

Jot down whatever marginal notes come naturally to you. Most readers combine brief responses written in the margins with their own system of underlining, circling, highlighting, stars, vertical lines, and question marks.

Remember that there are no hard-and-fast rules for which elements you annotate. Choose a method of annotation that works best for you and that will make sense to you when you go back to recollect your thoughts and responses to the essay. When annotating a text, don't be

---

How to Annotate a Text

Here are some suggestions of elements you may want to mark to help you keep a record of your responses as you read:

- Memorable statements of important points
- Key terms or concepts
- Central issues or themes
- Examples that support a main point
- Unfamiliar words
- Questions you have about a point or passage
- Your responses to a specific point or passage

---

timid. Mark up your book as much as you like, or jot down as many responses in your notebook as you think will be helpful. Don't let annotating become burdensome. A word or phrase is usually as good as a sentence. Notice how one of our students used marginal annotations to record her responses to Goldberg's text.

Be specific. Don't say "fruit." Tell what kind of fruit—"It is a pomegranate." Give things the dignity of their names. Just as with human beings, it is rude to say, "Hey, girl, get in line." That "girl" has a name. (As a matter of fact, if she's at least twenty years old, she's a woman, not a "girl" at all.) Things, too, have names. It is much better to say "the geranium in the window" than "the flower in the window." "Geranium"—that one word gives us a much more specific picture. It penetrates more deeply into the beingness of that flower. It immediately gives us the scene by the window—red petals, green circular leaves, all straining toward sunlight.

About ten years ago I decided I had to learn the names of plants and flowers in my environment. I bought a book on them and walked down the tree-lined streets of Boulder, examining leaf, bark, and seed, trying to match them up with their descriptions and names in the book. Maple, elm, oak, locust. I usually tried to cheat by asking people working in their yards the names

I agree—tho my grandma calls her friends "the girls"—?

I think I do pay more attn. when people call me by name.

She's practicing what she preaches—but that's a LOT of work. . . .

I doubt I could tell the difference between a maple and an elm.

of the flowers and trees growing there. I was amazed how few people had any idea of the names of the live beings inhabiting their little plot of land.

THESIS

Interesting — wonder if it's true. (How could you test it?)

When we know the name of something, it brings us closer to the ground. It takes the blur out of our mind; it connects us to the earth. If I walk down the street and see "dogwood," "forsythia," I feel more friendly toward the environment. I am noticing what is around me and can name it. It makes me more awake.

Is Williams a really famous poet? LOOK THIS UP. Why does she keep quoting him?

If you read the poems of William Carlos Williams, you will see how specific he is about plants, trees, flowers — chicory, daisy, locust, poplar, quince, primrose, black-eyed Susan, lilacs — each has its own integrity. Williams says, "Write what's in front of your nose." It's good for us to know what is in front of our noses. Not just "daisy," but how the flower is in the season we are looking at it — "The dayseye hugging the earth/in August . . . brownedged,/green and pointed scales/armor his yellow." Continue to hone your awareness: to the name, to the month, to the day, and finally to the moment.

I know I couldn't name all the people in my writing class. (Wonder if it would make a difference.)

Williams also says: "No idea, but in things." Study what is "in front of your nose." By saying "geranium" instead of "flower," you are penetrating more deeply into the present and being there. The closer we can get to what's in front of our nose, the more it can teach us everything. "To see the World in a Grain of Sand, and a heaven in a Wild Flower . . . "

In writing groups and classes too, it is good to quickly learn the names of all the other group members. It helps to ground you in the group and make you more attentive to each other's work.

Not sure what she means here. How can a writer be "all" and "none" of these things??

Learn the names of everything: birds, cheese, tractors, cars, buildings. A writer is all at once everything — an architect, French cook, farmer — and at the same time, a writer is none of these things.

4. Summarize the Selection in Your Own Words

After carefully annotating the selection, you will find it worthwhile to summarize what the writer has said, to see how the main points work together to give support to the writer's thesis. An efficient way to do this is to make a simple paragraph-by-paragraph outline of what you've read. Try to capture the essence of each paragraph in a single sentence. Such an outline enables you to understand how the essay works, to see what the writer's position is and how he or she has structured the essay and organized the main ideas.

Consider the following paragraph-by-paragraph outline one of our students made after reading Goldberg's essay:

Paragraph 1: Goldberg announces her topic and demonstrates the power of names with the example of the geranium.

Paragraph 2: She recounts how she went about learning the names of plants and trees in her Colorado neighborhood.

Paragraph 3: She explains how knowing the names of things makes her feel connected to the world around her.

Paragraph 4: She uses the example of poet William Carlos Williams to support her point about the power of names.

Paragraph 5: She continues with the example of Williams to broaden the discussion of what it means to "penetrate more deeply" into the world that is "in front of your nose."

Paragraph 6: She says that knowing the names of people in your writing group or class creates community.

Paragraph 7: She advises writers to "learn the names of everything" as a way of being "at once everything" and "at the same time . . . none of these things."

With your paragraph-by-paragraph outline in hand, you are now ready to analyze the reading.

5. Analyze the Selection to Come to an Understanding of It

After reading the essay a second time and annotating it, you are ready to analyze it, to probe for a deeper understanding of and appreciation for what the writer has done. In analyzing an essay, you will examine its basic parts methodically to see the significance of each part and understand how they relate to one another. One of the best ways to analyze an essay is to answer a basic set of questions — questions that require you to do some critical thinking about the essay's content and form.

Each essay in *Language Awareness* is followed by a set of "Thinking Critically about the Reading" questions similar to the ones suggested here

Questions to Help You Analyze What You Read

1. What is the writer's main point or thesis?

2. To whom is the essay addressed? To a general audience with little or no background knowledge of the subject? To a specialized group familiar with the topic? To those who are likely to agree or disagree with the argument?

3. What is the writer's purpose in addressing this audience?

4. What is the writer's attitude toward the subject of the essay—positive, critical, objective, ironic, hostile?

5. What assumptions, if any, does the writer make about the subject and/or the audience? Are these assumptions explicit (stated) or implicit (unstated)?

6. What kinds of evidence does the writer use to support his or her thesis—personal experience, expert opinions, statistics? Does the writer supply enough evidence to support his or her position? Is the evidence reliable, specific, and up-to-date?

7. Does the writer address opposing views on the issue?

8. How is the essay organized and developed? Does the writer's strategy of development suit his or her subject and purpose?

9. How effective is the essay? Is the writer convincing about his or her position?

but more specific to the essay. These questions help you analyze both the content of an essay and the writer's craft. In answering each of these questions, always look for details from the selection itself to support your position.

Having read and reread Goldberg's essay and studied the student annotations to the text, consider the following set of student answers to the key questions listed above. Are there places where you would have answered the questions differently? Explain.

1. *What is the writer's main point or thesis?*

Goldberg wants to tell her readers why it's important for people, especially writers, to be specific and to learn the names of everything in their part of the world. She states her main point in paragraph 3: "When we know the name of something, it brings us closer to the ground. It takes the blur out of our mind; it connects us to the earth." In short, being specific in what we call things makes us see, think, and write more clearly.

2. *To whom is the essay addressed? To a general audience with little or no background knowledge of the subject? To a specialized group familiar with the topic? To those who are likely to agree or disagree with the argument?*

    Goldberg's intended audience seems to be writers who are looking for advice. In paragraph 4, she quotes William Carlos Williams: "Write what's in front of your nose." In paragraph 6, Goldberg stresses the importance of knowing classmates' or group members' names and how this knowledge "helps to ground you in the group and make you more attentive to each other's work." In her final paragraph Goldberg acknowledges her audience of writers by emphasizing the writer's duty to learn the names of everything.

3. *What is the writer's purpose in addressing this audience?*

    Goldberg's purpose is to give her readers some direct advice about writing and life: "Be specific." More specifically(!), she advises her readers to give people and things names and to create a specific time context (month, day, moment, etc.) for what they're describing ("Not just 'daisy,' but how the flower is in the season we are looking at it . . .").

4. *What is the writer's attitude toward the subject of the essay — positive, critical, objective, ironic, hostile?*

    Goldberg is enthusiastic and extremely positive about the importance of naming things. She believes that "[w]hen we know the name of something, it brings us closer to the ground. It takes the blur out of our mind; it connects us to the earth" and makes us more "awake" to the environment; it allows us to "[penetrate] more deeply" into what is in front of us and to learn from it; and it grounds us and makes us more attentive in a group. She's excited to share her own experiences with learning the names of things.

5. *What assumptions, if any, does the writer make about the subject and/ or the audience? Are these assumptions explicit (stated) or implicit (unstated)?*

    Goldberg makes several key assumptions in this essay:
    * The title assumes that readers will be comfortable with commands.
    * The examples of "pomegranate," "geranium," "maple," "elm," "oak," "locust," "dogwood," and "forsythia" assume that readers have a basic knowledge of fruits, flowers, and trees — or that they'll be motivated enough to look them up.
    * The reference to the poet William Carlos Williams assumes that the audience will know who he is and perhaps be familiar with his poetry — or, again, that they will be motivated enough to look him up. Goldberg's footnotes, however, show that she does not assume readers will recognize the poem "Daisy" (paragraph 4) or "The Auguries of Innocence," quoted in paragraph 5.
    * Goldberg assumes that readers, after learning the names of the plants, flowers, trees, and people in their environment, will have experiences similar to the ones she has had: "I feel more friendly toward the environment. I am noticing what is around me and can name it. It makes me more awake" (paragraph 3).

6. *What kinds of evidence does the writer use — personal experience, expert opinions, statistics? Does the writer supply enough evidence to support his or her position? Is the evidence reliable, specific, and up-to-date?*

To support her claim that writers need to be specific, Goldberg uses the examples of "fruit/pomegranate," "girl/[name]," and "flower/geranium" in her opening paragraph — hoping that her readers will agree that the specific terms are better than the general ones. She follows these examples with personal experience: She explains how she went about learning the names of plants and flowers in Boulder, Colorado, and shares what she felt as a result. In paragraphs 4 and 5, Goldberg cites the poetry of William Carlos Williams as evidence that specific language creates great poems.

It is difficult to say whether this evidence is enough. Assuming her readers are beginning writers eager to learn, as she seems to have intended, it is probably safe to say that her evidence will be convincing. If a less receptive audience or an audience of nonwriters were reading the essay, though, more evidence or a different kind (maybe examples of how being specific helps in everyday life) might be needed.

7. *Does the writer address opposing views on the issue?*

While Goldberg does not directly address opposing views, she does discuss what happens when writers or speakers are *not* specific. For example, in paragraph 1 she says that calling someone "girl" instead of calling her by name can be rude, which is another way of saying that it denies that person her dignity — a pretty serious charge. In addition, when she tells us how knowing the names of things brings us closer to our environment, she implies that not knowing these names actually makes us feel disconnected from the world around us — something no one wants to feel.

8. *How is the essay organized and developed? Does the writer's strategy of development suit his or her subject and purpose?*

Goldberg organizes her essay in a straightforward and logical manner. She introduces her topic with her central directive, "Be specific," and then immediately shows through three examples what happens when a writer is specific. She organizes the examples in the body of her essay — paragraphs 2 through 6 — by telling how she learned to be more specific, quoting William Carlos Williams's advice to "Write what's in front of your nose," and advising us that we should learn the names of people in the groups and classes we belong to. Goldberg concludes her essay where she began, by directing us to "Learn the names of everything." In learning the names of everything, she reminds us that "A writer is all at once everything — an architect, French cook, farmer — and at the same time, a writer is none of these things." Although it seems paradoxical at first, this statement, when you stop to think about it, is very empowering — you're not really an architect or a French cook or a farmer, but, when you write, you get to experience the world the way they do.

9. *How effective is the essay? Is the writer convincing about his or her position?*

Goldberg's essay is effective because it serves her purpose very well. She raises her readers' awareness of the value of names and demonstrates why it is so important to give things their names in order to understand our world and to write effectively about it. Her argument about being specific is convincing — after reading the essay, it's difficult to look at a flower and not wonder, at least, whether it's a tulip, poppy, daffodil, rose, or something else. Goldberg offers practical advice on how each of us can get started learning the names of things, be they the names of the other people in our class or the names of the plants, trees, and flowers on our campus.

6. Complete the "Language in Action" Activity to Discover the Far-Reaching Connections between the Selection and Language in the Real World

The "Language in Action" activities that accompany each selection in *Language Awareness* give you an opportunity to work with real world examples of language issues or concepts discussed in the selections, with exercises, cartoons, advertisements, photographs, poems, movie reviews, parodies, essay excerpts, syndicated columns, letters to the editor and more. Designed to be completed either in class or at home in about fifteen to twenty minutes, these activities invite you to take a hands-on approach to what you're learning from the essays and give you a chance to demonstrate your growing language aptitude. Consider the following activity that accompanied the Goldberg essay:

LANGUAGE IN ACTION

A useful exercise in learning to be more specific in our writing is to see the words we use for people, places, things, and ideas as being positioned somewhere on what might be called a "ladder of abstraction." In the following chart, notice how the words progress from more general to more specific.

More General	General	Specific	More Specific
Organism	Plant	Flower	Iris
Vehicle	Car	Chevrolet	1958 Chevrolet Impala

Using the examples above as models, try to fill in the missing parts of the following ladder of abstraction:

More General	General	Specific	More Specific
Writing instrument	_____	Fountain pen	Waterman fountain pen
_____	Sandwich	Corned beef sandwich	Reuben
Fruit	Dessert	Pie	_____
American	_____	Navaho	Laguna Pueblo

	Reference book	Dictionary	_____
School		Technical high school	_____
Medicine	Oral medicine	Gel capsule	_____

After filling in the blanks yourself, compare your answers with those of your classmates. Now compare them to those provided by one of our students and discuss the variety of possible answers:

Line 1: Pen

Line 2: Lunch food

Line 3: Blueberry pie

Line 4: Native American

Line 5: Book, *American Heritage Dictionary of the English Language*

Line 6: High school, Essex Junction Technical Education Center

Line 7: Tylenol Gel Caps

PRACTICE READING, ANNOTATING, AND ANALYZING

Before you read the following essay, think about its title, the biographical and rhetorical information in the headnote, and the journal prompt. Make some marginal notes of your expectations for the essay, and write out a response to the journal prompt. Then, as you read the essay itself for the first time, try not to stop; take it all in as if in one breath. The second time, however, pause to annotate key points in the text, using the marginal rules we have provided alongside each paragraph. As you read, remember the nine basic questions we listed earlier on page 10.

What's in a Name?

Title: _____

HENRY LOUIS GATES JR.

The preeminent African American scholar of our time, Henry Louis Gates Jr. is the Alphonse Fletcher University Professor and director of the W. E. B. Du Bois Institute for African and African American Research at Harvard University. Among his impressive list of publications are *Figures in Black: Words, Signs and the "Racial" Self* (1987), *The Signifying Monkey: A Theory of Afro-American Literary Criticism* (1988), *Loose Canons: Notes on Culture Wars* (1992), *The Future of the Race* (1997), and *Thirteen Ways*

Biographical note: _____

of Looking at a Black Man (1999). His most recent books
are *Mr. Jefferson and Miss Wheatley* (2003) and *Finding
Oprah's Roots: Finding Your Own* (2007). In 2010, Gates
published *Faces of America: How 12 Extraordinary Americans Reclaimed Their Pasts.* His *Colored People: A Memoir* (1994) recollects in a wonderful prose style his youth
growing up in Piedmont, West Virginia, and his emerging
sexual and racial awareness. Gates first enrolled at Potomac
State College and later transferred to Yale, where he studied history. With the assistance of an Andrew W. Mellon
Foundation Fellowship and a Ford Foundation Fellowship,
he pursued advanced degrees in English at Clare College
at the University of Cambridge. He has been honored
with a MacArthur Foundation Fellowship, inclusion on
Time magazine's "25 Most Influential Americans" list, a
National Humanities Medal, and election to the American
Academy of Arts and Letters.

Publication
information:
_____
_____
_____

   In "What's in a Name?," excerpted from a longer
article published in the fall 1989 issue of *Dissent* magazine, Gates tells the story of an early encounter with
the language of prejudice. In learning how one of the
"bynames" used by white people to define African
Americans robs them of their identity, he feels the sting
of racism firsthand. Notice how Gates's use of dialogue
gives immediacy and poignancy to his narration.

Rhetorical
highlight: ____
_____
_____
_____
_____
_____

WRITING TO DISCOVER: *Reflect on racially charged language
you have heard. For example, has anyone ever used a racial or ethnic epithet to refer to you? When did you first become aware that
such terms existed? How do you feel about being characterized or
defined by your race or ethnicity? If you yourself have ever used such
terms, what was your intent in using them? What was the response
of others?*

Journal
prompt: ____
_____
_____
_____
_____
_____

The question of color takes up much space in these pages,
but the question of color, especially in this country, operates to hide the graver questions of the self.
                               —JAMES BALDWIN, 1961

Epigraphs:____
_____
_____
_____
_____

...blood, darky, Tar Baby, Kaffir, shine...moor, blacka-
moor, Jim Crow, spooks....quadroon, meriney, red bone,
high yellow...Mammy, porch monkey, home, homeboy,
George spearchucker, schwarze, Leroy, Smokey...mouli,
buck, Ethiopian, brother, sistah...
                               —TREY ELLIS, 1989

I had forgotten the incident completely, until I read Para. 1. _____ Trey Ellis's essay, "Remember My Name," in a recent issue of the *Village Voice*[1] (June 13, 1989). But there, in the middle of an extended italicized list of the bynames of "the race" ("the race" or "our people" being the terms my parents used in polite or reverential discourse, "jigaboo" or "nigger" more commonly used in anger, jest, or pure disgust), it was: "George." Now the events of that very brief exchange return to mind so vividly that I wonder why I had forgotten it.

My father and I were walking home at dusk from his Para. 2. _____ second job. He "moonlighted" as a janitor in the evenings for the telephone company. Every day but Saturday, he would come home at 3:30 from his regular job at the paper mill, wash up, eat supper, then at 4:30 head downtown to his second job. He used to make jokes frequently about a union official who moonlighted. I never got the joke, but he and his friends thought it was hilarious. All I knew was that my family always ate well, that my brother and I had new clothes to wear, and that all of the white people in Piedmont, West Virginia, treated my parents with an odd mixture of resentment and respect that even we understood at the time had something directly to do with a small but certain measure of financial security.

He had left a little early that evening because I was with Para. 3. _____ him and I had to be in bed early. I could not have been more than five or six, and we had stopped off at the Cut-Rate Drug Store (where no black person in town but my father could sit down to eat, and eat off real plates with real silverware) so that I could buy some caramel ice cream, two scoops in a wafer cone, please, which I was busy licking when Mr. Wilson walked by.

Mr. Wilson was a very quiet man, whose stony, brood- Para. 4. _____ ing, silent manner seemed designed to scare off any overtures of friendship, even from white people. He was Irish, as was one-third of our village (another third being Italian), the more affluent among whom sent their children to "Catholic School" across the bridge in Maryland. He had white straight hair, like my Uncle Joe, whom he uncannily resembled, and he carried a black worn metal lunch pail, the kind that Riley[2] carried on the television show. My father always spoke to him, and for reasons that we never did understand, he always spoke to my father.

---

1. *Village Voice:* a nationally distributed weekly newspaper published in New York City.
2. A character on the U.S. television show *The Life of Riley,* a blue-collar, ethnic sitcom popular in the 1950s.

"Hello, Mr. Wilson," I heard my father say.   Para. 5–8
"Hello, George."
I stopped licking my ice cream cone, and asked my Dad
in a loud voice why Mr. Wilson had called him "George."
"Doesn't he know your name, Daddy? Why don't you
tell him your name? Your name isn't George."
For a moment I tried to think of who Mr. Wilson was
mixing Pop up with. But we didn't have any Georges among
the colored people in Piedmont; nor were there colored
Georges living in the neighboring towns and working at the
mill.
"Tell him your name, Daddy."   Para. 10–14
"He knows my name, boy," my father said after a long
pause. "He calls all colored people George."
A long silence ensued. It was "one of those things," as
my Mom would put it. Even then, that early, I knew when
I was in the presence of "one of those things," one of those
things that provided a glimpse, through a rent[3] curtain, at
another world that we could not affect but that affected us.
There would be a painful moment of silence, and you would
wait for it to give way to a discussion of a black superstar such
as Sugar Ray[4] or Jackie Robinson.[5]
"Nobody hits better in a clutch than Jackie Robinson."
"That's right. Nobody."
I never again looked Mr. Wilson in the eye.   Para. 15. ____

Once you have read and reread Gates's essay and annotated the text,
write out answers to the six Thinking Critically about the Reading questions as well as the Language in Action activity found below. Then compare your answers with those of the other students in class.

THINKING CRITICALLY ABOUT THE READING

1. In the epigraph to this essay, Gates presents two quotations, one by James
   Baldwin. What do you think Baldwin meant when he wrote, "The question
   of color, especially in this country [America], operates to hide the graver
   questions of self"? How does this statement relate to the theme of Gates's
   essay?

---

3. torn.
4. Walker Smith Jr. (1921–1989), American professional boxer and six-time world
champion.
5. (1919–1972): The first black baseball player in the National League.

2. In his opening paragraph, Gates refers to the other quotation in the epigraph—a list of bynames used to refer to African Americans that appeared in an article by Trey Ellis—and states that his reading of this article triggered a childhood memory for him. How did you first feel after reading Ellis's list of bynames for African Americans? What did you find offensive about these racial slurs? Explain.

3. Later in his opening paragraph Gates reveals that "'the race' or 'our people' [were] the terms my parents used in polite or reverential discourse, 'jigaboo' or 'nigger' more commonly used in anger, jest, or pure disgust." Why does Gates make so much of Mr. Wilson's use of "George" when his own parents used words so much more obviously offensive? What do you see as the essential difference between white people using Trey Ellis's list of terms to refer to people of color and African Americans using the same terms to refer to themselves? Explain.

4. Gates describes Mr. Wilson and provides some background information about him in paragraph 4. What do you think is Gates's purpose in providing this information? (Glossary: *Description*)

5. Explain what happens in paragraph 12. What is "one of those things," as Gates's mother put it? In what ways is "one of those things" really Gates's purpose in telling his story? Why does Gates say, "I never again looked Mr. Wilson in the eye" (15)?

6. In paragraphs 5 and 6, Gates uses dialogue to capture the key exchange between his father and Mr. Wilson. What does this dialogue add to his narration? (Glossary: *Narration*) What would have been lost if Gates had simply described the conversation between the two men?

LANGUAGE IN ACTION

Comment on the importance of one's name as revealed in the following Ann Landers column. Ann Landers is the pen name created for advice columnist Ruth Crowley in 1943 and later used by Eppie Lederer for her "Ask Ann Landers" syndicated lifestyle advice column that was featured in newspapers across the country from 1955 to 2002. Though fictional, Ann Landers became an institution and cultural icon for the era.

Refusal to Use Name Is the Ultimate Insult

DEAR ANN LANDERS: Boy, when you're wrong, you're really wrong. Apparently, you have never been the victim of a hostile, nasty, passive-aggressive person who refuses to address you by name. Well, I have.

My husband's mother has never called me by my name in the 21 years I've been married to her son. Nor has she ever said "please" or "thank you," unless someone else is within hearing distance. My husband's children by his first wife are the same way. The people they care about are always referred to by name, but the rest of us are not called anything.

> If you still think this is a "psychological glitch," as you said in
> a recent column, try speaking to someone across the room without
> addressing that person by name. To be nameless and talked at is the
> ultimate put-down, and I wish you had said so. — "Hey You" in Florida
>
> DEAR FLORIDA: Sorry I let you down. Your mother-in-law's
> refusal to call you by name is, I am sure, rooted in hostility. Many years
> ago, Dr. Will Menninger said, "The sweetest sound in any language is
> the sound of your own name." It can also be a valuable sales tool. My
> former husband, one of the world's best salesmen, said if you want to
> make a sale, get the customer's name, use it when you make your pitch,
> and he will be half sold. His own record as a salesman proved him right.

What is the meaning of Dr. Will Menninger's statement: "The sweetest
sound in any language is the sound of your own name"?

READING AS A WRITER

Reading and writing are the two sides of the same coin: Active critical
reading is a means to help you become a better writer. By reading we can
begin to see how other writers have communicated their experiences, ideas,
thoughts, and feelings in their writing. We can study how they have used
the various elements of the essay — thesis, unity, organization, beginnings
and endings, paragraphs, transitions, effective sentences, word choice, tone,
and figurative language — to say what they wanted to say. By studying the
style, technique, and rhetorical strategies of other writers we learn how we
might effectively do the same. The more we read and write, the more we
begin to read as writers and, in turn, to write knowing what readers expect.

What does it mean to read as a writer? Most of us have not been
taught to read with a writer's eye, to ask why we like one piece of writing
and not another. Likewise, most of us do not ask ourselves why one piece
of writing is more believable or convincing than another. When you learn
to read with a writer's eye, you begin to answer these important questions
and, in the process, come to appreciate what is involved in selecting and
focusing a subject as well as the craftsmanship involved in writing — how
a writer selects descriptive details, uses an unobtrusive organizational pattern, opts for fresh and lively language, chooses representative and persuasive examples, and emphasizes important points with sentence variety.

On one level, reading stimulates your thinking by providing you
with subjects to write about. After reading David Raymond's essay "On
Being 17, Bright, and Unable to Read," Helen Keller's "The Day Language Came into My Life," or Malcolm X's "Coming to an Awareness
of Language," you might, for example, be inspired to write about a
powerful language experience you have had and how that experience, in
retrospect, was a "turning point" in your life.

On a second level, reading provides you with information, ideas, and perspectives for developing your own paper. In this way, you respond to what you read, using material from what you've read in an essay. For example, after reading Richard Lederer's essay on regional language differences in America, you might want to elaborate on what he has written, drawing on your own experiences and either agreeing with his examples or generating better ones for the area of the country in which you were raised. You could also qualify his argument for the preservation of these language differences or take issue with it. The three mini-debates in Chapter 14 "Arguing about Language" offer you the opportunity to read extensively about focused topics — "Should English Be the Law?," "Should Language Be Censored?," and "How Do Words Hurt?" — and to use the information and opinions expressed in these essays as resources for your own thesis-driven paper.

On a third level, active reading can increase your awareness of how others' writing affects you, thus making you more sensitive to how your own writing will affect your readers. For example, if you have been impressed by an author who uses convincing evidence to support each of her claims, you might be more likely to back up your own claims carefully. If you have been impressed by an apt turn of phrase or absorbed by a writer's new idea, you may be less inclined to feed your readers dull, worn out, and trite phrases. More to the point, however, the active reading that you will be encouraged to do in *Language Awareness* will help you to recognize and analyze the essential elements of the essay. When you see, for example, how a writer like Susanne K. Langer uses a strong thesis statement, about how language separates humans from the rest of the animal kingdom, to control the parts of her essay, you can better appreciate the importance of having a clear thesis statement in your writing. When you see the way Deborah Tannen uses transitions to link key phrases with important ideas so that readers can recognize clearly how the parts of her essay are meant to flow together, you have a better idea of how to achieve such coherence in your own writing. And when you see the way Donna Woolfolk Cross uses a division and classification organizational plan to differentiate clearly the various categories of propaganda, you see a powerful way in which you too can organize an essay using this method of development.

Finally, another important reason to master the skills of critical reading is that you will be your own first reader and critic for everything you write. How well you are able to scrutinize your own drafts will powerfully affect how well you revise them, and revising well is crucial to writing well. Reading others' writing with a critical eye is a useful and important practice; the more you read, the more practice you will have in sharpening your skills. The more sensitive you become to the content and style decisions made by the writers in *Language Awareness,* the more skilled you will be at making similar decisions in your own writing.

2

WRITING IN COLLEGE AND BEYOND

Nothing is more important to your success in school and in the workplace than learning to write well. You've heard it so often you've probably become numb to the advice. Let's ask the big question, however. Why is writing well so important? The simple answer is that no activity develops your ability to think better than writing does. Writing allows you to develop your thoughts and to "see" and reflect critically on what you think: In that sense, writing also involves its twin sister, reading. Writing well often means organizing your thoughts into a compelling argument and engaging readers by using concise, specific language. Small wonder, then, that academic programs and employers in all fields are constantly looking for people who can read and write well. Simply put, the ability to read and write well is a strong indication of a good mind.

College is a practical training ground for learning to write and think well. Whenever you write in college, you are writing as a member of a community of scholars, teachers, and students. By questioning, researching, and writing in company with other members of the college community, you come both to understand college material and to demonstrate your knowledge of it. In college, with the help of instructors, you will write essays, analyses, term papers, reports, reviews of research, critiques, and summaries. What you learn now will be fundamental, not only to your education, but also to your later success, no matter what career you intend to pursue.

DEVELOPING AN EFFECTIVE WRITING PROCESS

Writers cannot rely on inspiration alone to produce effective writing. Good writers follow a writing *process*: They analyze their assignment, gather ideas, draft, revise, edit, and proofread. It is worth remembering, however, that the writing process is rarely as simple and straightforward as it might appear to be. Often the process is recursive, moving back and forth among different stages. Moreover, writing is personal — no two people go about it exactly the same way. Still, it is possible to describe basic guidelines for developing a writing process, thereby allowing you to devise your own reliable method for undertaking a writing task.

1. Understand Your Assignment

Much of your college writing will be done in response to specific assignments from your instructors or research questions that you develop in consultation with your teachers. Your environmental studies professor, for example, may ask you to write a report on significant new research on carbon dioxide emissions and global warming; your American history professor may ask you to write an analysis of the long-term effects of Japanese Americans' internment during World War II. From the outset you need to understand precisely what your instructor is asking you to do. The keys to understanding assignments such as these are *subject* words (words that focus on content) and *direction* words (words that indicate your purpose for and method of development in writing). For example, consider what you are being asked to do in each of the following assignments:

> Tell about an experience you have had that dramatically revealed to you the importance of being accurate and precise in your use of language.

> Many languages are lost over time because speakers of those languages die. When a language is lost, the particular culture embodied in the language is also lost. Using an extinct language and culture as an example, explain how the language embodies a culture and exactly what is lost when a language becomes extinct.

> Advocates of the English-only movement want to see English adopted as our country's official language. Argue for or against the philosophy behind this movement.

In the first example above, the subject words are *experience* and *importance of being accurate and precise in your use of language*. The direction word is *tell*, which means that you must share the details of the experience so that your readers can appreciate them as if they were there, sharing the experience. The content words in the second example are *languages, culture,* and *extinct language and culture*. The direction word is *explain*. In the third example, the content words are *English-only movement* and *our country's official language*. The direction word is *argue*. In each case the subject words limit and focus the content, and the direction words dictate how you will approach this content in writing.

The words *tell, explain,* and *argue* are only a few of the direction words that are commonly found in academic writing assignments. The following list of additional direction words and their meanings will help you better understand your writing assignments and what is expected of you.

Direction Words

Analyze: take apart and examine closely

Categorize: place into meaningful groups

Compare: look for differences, stress similarities

Contrast: look for similarities, stress differences

Critique: point out positive and negative features

Define: provide the meaning for a term or concept

Describe: give detailed sensory perceptions for a person, place, or event

Evaluate: judge according to some established standard

Identify: recognize or single out

Illustrate: show through examples

Interpret: explain the meaning of a document, action, event, or behavior

Prove: demonstrate truth by logic, fact, or example

Synthesize: bring together or make meaningful connections among elements

After reading an assignment several times, check with your instructor if you are still unsure about what is being asked of you. He or she will be glad to clear up any possible confusion before you start writing. Be sure, as well, that you understand any additional requirements of the assignment, such as length or format.

2. Find a Subject and Topic

Although your instructor will sometimes give you specific writing assignments, you will often be asked to choose your own subject and topic. In a course in which you are using *Language Awareness,* you would in this case first select a broad subject within the area of language studies that you think you may enjoy writing about, such as professional jargon, dialects, political speeches, advertising language, or propaganda. A language issue that you have experienced firsthand (discrimination, for example) or something you've read may bring other subjects to mind. In the student essay that concludes this chapter, Rebekah Sandlin revisits her own racial prejudices as an elementary school student and what she has learned from them. You might also consider a language-related issue that involves your career ambitions, such as the areas of business (avoiding exaggerated advertising claims), law (eliminating obscure legal language), nursing (communicating effectively with patients), or journalism (reporting the news objectively). Another option is to list some subjects you enjoy discussing with friends and that you can approach from a language perspective: music (gender bias in rap lyrics), work (decoding insurance policies and medical benefits), and college life (speech codes on campus).

Next, try to narrow your general subject until you arrive at a topic that you think will be both interesting to your readers and appropriate for the length of your paper (and the time you have to write it). The following chart shows how the general areas of jargon, journalism, and television commercials might be narrowed to a specific essay topic. (If you're having trouble coming up with general subjects or specific topics, try some of the discovery techniques discussed in Step 3 (pp. 27–30).

General Subject Area	Narrowed Topic	Specific Essay Topic
Jargon	Medical jargon	Medical jargon used between doctors and terminally ill patients
Journalism	Slanted language in newswriting	Slanted language in newspapers' coverage of international events
Television commercials	Hidden messages in television commercials	Hidden messages in television commercials on children's Saturday morning programs

USE THE WRITING SUGGESTIONS IN *LANGUAGE AWARENESS*. As far as writing about the subjects and topics discussed in *Language Awareness* is concerned, there is no shortage of ideas and approaches at your disposal. There are at least two Writing Suggestions at the end of every selection in the book. If you have the freedom to choose your own subject and topic, and the approach you take, you may want to use one of the suggestions as a springboard for your own creativity. If, on the other hand, you are assigned a Writing Suggestion, be sure you understand what is being asked of you. If you are unclear about the assignment or you want to widen or narrow its focus or change its intent in any way, be sure to do so in consultation with your instructor. You can and should be creative in using even an assigned suggestion, maybe even using it as a starting point for your own research and thesis, but again get your instructor's approval before starting your paper so no misunderstandings result.

DETERMINE YOUR PURPOSE. All effective writing springs from a clear purpose. Most good writing seeks specifically to accomplish any one of the following three purposes:

- To express thoughts and feelings about life experiences
- To inform readers by explaining something about the world around them
- To persuade readers to adopt some belief or take some action

In *expressive writing*, or writing from experience, you put your thoughts and feelings before all other concerns. When Malcolm X shows his frustration at not having appropriate language to express himself (Chapter 4) and when Amy Tan describes how her mother's use of English shaped her own approach to writing (Chapter 6), each one is writing from experience. In each case, the writer has clarified an important life experience and has conveyed what he or she learned from it.

Informative writing focuses on telling the reader something about the outside world. In informative writing, you report, explain, analyze, define, classify, compare, describe a process, or examine causes and effects. When Paul Roberts explains the formation of speech communities (Chapter 6) and when Deborah Tannen explores the fraught language of mother-daughter relationships (Chapter 13), each one is writing to inform.

Argumentative writing seeks to influence readers' thinking and attitudes toward a subject and, in some cases, to move them to a particular course of action. Such persuasive writing uses logical reasoning, authoritative evidence, and testimony, and it sometimes includes emotionally charged language and examples. In writing their arguments, Robert D. King (Chapter 14) uses numerous historical examples to make the case that a multilingual America does not threaten national unity and Kim Severson (Chapter 12) uses logical reasoning and evidence to debunk the healthy image of so-called "all natural" products.

KNOW YOUR AUDIENCE. The best writers always keep their audience in mind. Once they have decided on a topic and a purpose, writers present their material in a way that empathizes with their readers, addresses their difficulties and concerns, and appeals to their rational and emotional faculties. Based on knowledge of their audience, writers make conscious decisions on content, sentence structure, and word choice.

Writing for an Academic Audience   Academic writing most often employs the conventions of formal standard English, or the language of educated professionals. Rather than being heavy or stuffy, good academic writing is lively and engaging and holds the reader's attention by presenting interesting ideas supported with relevant facts, statistics, and detailed information. Informal writing, usually freer and simpler in form, is typically used in notes, journal entries, e-mail, text messages, instant messaging, and the like.

In order not to lessen the importance of your ideas and your credibility, be sure that informal writing does not carry over into your academic writing. Always keeping your audience and purpose in mind will help you achieve an appropriate style.

When you write, your audience might be an individual (your instructor), a group (the students in your class), a specialized group (art history majors), or a general readership (readers of your student newspaper). To help identify your audience, ask yourself the questions posed page 27.

Using Discipline-Specific Language   The point of discipline-specific language, sometimes referred to as professional language or even jargon, is not to make a speaker or writer sound like a scientist, or a humanities scholar, or a geologist. Rather, discipline-specific language provides a kind of "shorthand" means of expressing complex concepts. Its proper use will grow from your knowledge of the discipline, from the reading you have done in the field, and from the hours you have spent in the company of your teachers and peers.

While the meaning of some disciplinary language will become clear to you from context as you read and discuss course material, some of it, left undefined, will present a stumbling block to your understanding of the material. Glossaries of disciplinary terms exist for most disciplines: Make use of them. Also, never be shy about asking your instructor or more experienced classmates for help when you're unsure of the meaning of a term.

Considering Opposing Arguments   You will likely not have trouble convincing those who agree with your argument from the outset, but what about those who are skeptical or think differently from you? You need to discover who these people are by talking with them or by reading what they have written. Do your research, be reasonable, and find common ground where possible, but take issue where you must. To refute an opposing argument, you can present evidence showing that the opposition's data or evidence is incomplete or distorted, that its reasoning is faulty, or that its conclusions do not fit the evidence.

Formal versus Informal Writing

Formal Writing	*Informal Writing*
Uses standard English, the language of public discourse typical of newspapers, magazines, books, and speeches	Uses nonstandard English, slang, colloquial expressions (*anyways, dude, freaked out*), and shorthand (*OMG, IMHO, GR8*)
Uses mostly third person	Uses first and second person most often

Avoids most abbreviations (*Professor, brothers, miles per gallon, Internet, digital video recorder*)	Uses abbreviations and acronyms (*Prof., bros., mpg, Net, DVR*)
Uses an impersonal tone (*The speaker took questions from the audience at the end of her lecture.*)	Uses an informal tone (*It was great the way she answered questions at the end of her talk.*)
Uses longer, more complex sentences	Uses shorter, simpler sentences
Adheres to the rules and conventions of proper grammar	Takes a casual approach to the rules and conventions of proper grammar

Questions about Audience

- Who are my readers? Are they a specialized or a general group?
- What do I know about my audience's age, gender, education, religious affiliation, economic status, and political views?
- What does my audience know about my subject? Are they experts or novices?
- What does my audience need to know about my topic in order to understand my discussion of it?
- Will my audience be interested, open-minded, resistant, or hostile to what I have to say?
- Do I need to explain any specialized language so that my audience can understand my subject? Is there any language that I should avoid?
- What do I want my audience to do as a result of reading my essay?

3. Gather Ideas

Ideas and information (facts and details) lie at the heart of good prose. Ideas grow out of information; information supports ideas. Before you begin to draft, gather as many ideas as possible and as much information as you can about your topic in order to inform and stimulate your readers intellectually.

Most writers use one or more discovery techniques to help them gather information, zero-in on a specific topic, or find connections among ideas. In addition to your reading and discussing writing ideas with your classmates and friends, you may want to experiment with some of the discovery techniques explained below.

KEEPING A JOURNAL.   Many writers use a journal to record thoughts and observations that might be mined for future writing projects. They have learned not to rely on their memories to retain ideas, facts, and statistics they have heard or read about. Writers also use journals to keep all kinds of lists: lists of questions they would like answers to; lists of issues that concern them; lists of topics they would like to write about someday.

To aid your journal writing as you use this text, each reading selection in *Language Awareness* begins with a journal prompt called "Writing to Discover." The purpose of each prompt is to get you thinking and writing about your own experiences with the language issues discussed in the selection before you start reading. You thus have the opportunity to discover what you already know about a particular topic and to explore your observations, feelings, and opinions about it. The writing you do at this point is something you can always return to after reading each piece.

FREEWRITING.   Journals are also useful if you want to freewrite. *Freewriting* is simply writing for a brief uninterrupted period of time—say, ten or fifteen minutes—on anything that comes to your mind. It is a way to get your mind working and to ease into a writing task. Start with a blank sheet of paper or computer screen and write about the general subject you are considering. Write as quickly as you can, don't stop for any reason, and don't worry about punctuation, grammar, or spelling. Write as though you were talking to your best friend, and let your writing take you in any direction. If you run out of ideas, don't stop; just repeat the last few things you wrote over and over again, and you'll be surprised—more ideas will begin to emerge. Just as regular exercise gets you in shape, regular freewriting will help you feel more natural and comfortable when writing.

OPEN-ENDED WRITING.   A useful extension of freewriting is a discovery strategy called open-ended writing. Follow the same directions for freewriting but also stop every ten minutes or so to evaluate what you have written. Analyze your freewriting and identify ideas, issues, expressions, phrases, and terms that show relationships and themes, and that may also engender questions about your material. Copy only those related elements onto a new sheet of paper and begin freewriting again. By repeating the process at least several times, following your freewrites with analysis each time, you will inevitably deepen your thinking about your topic and get closer to being able to write your first draft.

BRAINSTORMING. Another good way to generate ideas and information about a topic is to *brainstorm*—to list everything you know about a topic, freely associating one idea with another. Don't worry about order or level of importance. Try to capture everything that comes to mind because you never know what might prove valuable later on. Write quickly, but if you get stalled, reread what you have written; doing so will help you move in new directions. Keep your list handy so that you can add to it over the course of several days. Here, for example, is a student's brainstorming list on why Martin Luther King Jr.'s speech, "I Have a Dream," has endured:

Why "I Have a Dream" Is Memorable

civil rights demonstration in Washington, D.C., delivered on steps of Lincoln Memorial

repetition of "I have a dream"

references to the Bible, spirituals

"bad check" metaphor

other memorable figures of speech

200,000 people

reminds me of other great American documents and speeches—Declaration of Independence and Gettysburg Address

refers to various parts of the country

embraces all races and religions

sermon format

displays energy and passion

ASKING QUESTIONS. *Asking questions* about a particular topic or experience may help you generate information before you start to write. If you are writing about a personal experience, for example, asking questions may refresh your memory about the details and circumstances of the incident or help you discover why the experience is still so memorable. The newspaper reporter's five Ws and an H—Who? What? Where? When? Why? and How?—are excellent questions to start with. One student, for example, developed the following questions to help her explore an experience of verbal abuse:

1. *Who was involved in the abusive situation?*
2. *What specific language was used?*
3. *Where did the abuse most often take place?*
4. *When did the verbal abuse first occur?*
5. *Why did the abusive situation get started? Why did it continue?*
6. *How did I feel about the abuse as it was happening? How do I feel about it now?*

As the student jotted down answers to these questions, other questions came to mind, such as, *What did I try to do after the verbal abuse occurred? Did I seek help from anyone else? How can I help others who are being verbally abused?* Before long, the student had recalled enough information for a rough draft about her experience.

CLUSTERING. Another strategy for generating ideas and gathering information is *clustering*. Put your topic, or a key word or phrase about your topic, in the center of a sheet of paper and draw a circle around it. (The student example below shows the topic "Hospital jargon at summer job" in the center.) Draw three or more lines out from this circle, and jot down main ideas about your topic, drawing a circle around each one. Repeat the process by drawing lines from the main-idea circles and adding examples, details, or questions you have. You may wind up pursuing one line of thought through many add-on circles before beginning a new cluster.

One advantage of clustering is that it allows you to sort your ideas and information into meaningful groups right from the start. As you carefully sort your ideas and information, you may begin to see an organizational plan for your writing. In the following example, the student's clustering is based on the experiences he had while working one summer in a hospital emergency room. Does the clustering provide any clues to how he might organize his essay?

4. Formulate a Thesis

The thesis of an essay is its main idea, the major point the writer is trying to make. A thesis should be

- The most important point you make about your topic
- More general than the ideas and facts used to support it
- Focused enough to be covered in the space allotted for the essay

The thesis is often expressed in one or two sentences called a *thesis statement*. Here's an example of a thesis statement about television news programs:

> The so-called serious news programs are becoming too like tabloid news shows in both their content and their presentation.

A thesis statement should not be a question but rather an assertion. If you find yourself writing a question for a thesis statement, answer the question first — this answer will be your thesis statement.

An effective strategy for developing a thesis statement is to begin by writing, "What I want to say is that . . ."

> *What I want to say is that* unless language barriers between patients and health care providers are bridged, many patients' lives in our most culturally diverse cities will be endangered.

Later you can delete the formulaic opening, and you will be left with a thesis statement.

To determine whether your thesis is too general or too specific, think hard about how easy it will be to present data — that is, facts, statistics, names, examples or illustrations, and opinions of authorities — to support it. If you stray too far in either direction, your task will become much more difficult. A thesis statement that is too general will leave you overwhelmed by the number of issues you must address. For example, the statement "Political attack speeches damage the American political system" would lead to the question "How?" To answer it, you would probably have to include information about national politics, free speech, libel, character assassination, abusive language, the fallacy of ad hominem arguments, and so on. To cover all of this in the time and space you have for a typical college paper would mean taking shortcuts, and your paper would be ineffective. On the other hand, too specific a thesis statement would leave you with too little information to present. "Governor Wright's speech implies that Senator Smith's personal life is a disgrace" does not leave you with any opportunity to develop an argument. An appropriate thesis statement like "Political attack speeches have harmed politicians' images and turned off voters in Big City's mayoral elections over the past decade" leaves room for argument but can still be proven by examining poll responses, voter turnout records, and other evidence.

The thesis statement is usually presented near the beginning of the essay. One common practice in shorter college papers is to position the thesis statement as the final sentence of the first paragraph.

Is Your Thesis Solid?

Once you have a possible thesis statement in mind, ask yourself the following questions:

- Does my thesis statement take a clear position on an issue? (Could I imagine someone agreeing or disagreeing with it? If not, it might be a statement of fact, instead of an arguable thesis.)
- Will I be able to find evidence that supports my position? Where? What kinds? (If you're unsure, it wouldn't hurt to take a look at a few secondary sources at this point.)
- Will I be able to make my claim and present sufficient evidence to support it in a paper of the assigned length, and by the due date? (If not, you might need to scale back your claim to something more manageable.)

---

5. Support Your Thesis with Evidence

The types of evidence you use in your academic writing will be determined to some extent by the discipline in which you are working. For example, for a research project in psychology on the prejudice shown toward people with unusual names, you will almost certainly rely heavily on published studies from peer-reviewed journals. Depending on the assignment, however, you might also devise an experiment of your own or interview people with unusual names to gather firsthand accounts of their experiences. For an argument essay on the same topic in a composition course, as in many courses in the humanities, languages, and literatures, you would cite a wide range of sources, perhaps including—but not limited to—peer-reviewed journals. Depending on the assignment, you might also include your own experience and informal observations.

To support her argument on book banning, one student derives most of her evidence from an array of experts, as in the following example, where she cites scholar Henry Reichman:

Henry Reichman writes that in 1990, Frank Mosca's *All-American Boys* (1983) and Nancy Garden's *Annie on My Mind* (1982), two books with gay themes, were donated to high schools in Contra Costa, California; at three of these high schools, the books were seized by administrators and then "lost" (53).

PRIMARY AND SECONDARY SOURCES. In general, researchers and writers work with two types of evidence: primary sources and secondary sources.

Primary sources in the humanities and languages/literatures are works that grow out of and are close to a time, place, or culture under study. These can include documents such as letters, speeches, interviews, manuscripts, diaries, treaties, maps; creative written works such as novels, plays, poems, songs, and autobiographies; and three-dimensional artifacts such as paintings, sculptures, pottery, weaving, buildings, tools, and furniture. Primary sources in the social, natural, and applied sciences are the factual reports and descriptions of discoveries, experiments, surveys, and clinical trials.

Secondary sources in the humanities and languages/literatures restate, analyze, and interpret primary sources. Common secondary sources include analyses, critiques, histories, and commentaries in the form of books, articles, encyclopedia entries, and documentaries. Secondary sources in the sciences analyze and interpret discoveries and experiments and often comment on the validity of the research models and methods and the value of those discoveries and experiments.

Writing in a specific discipline requires that you use the most authoritative and reliable source materials available for that discipline. Your instructors can help you in this regard by either providing you with a list of resources commonly used in their fields or directing you to such a list in your library or on the Internet. Many academic libraries include helpful subject study guides on their home pages as well.

For a brief guide to finding, evaluating, and documenting sources in print and online, see pages 548–551.

FACTS, STATISTICS, EXAMPLES, AND EXPERT TESTIMONY. The evidence you use in your academic writing should place a high value on facts and statistics, examples and illustrations, and the testimony of experts. You must be accurate in your use of facts and statistics, and you must check and double-check that you have cited them correctly. Be sure that you carefully consider the examples and illustrations you use to support your thesis: Use those that work best with your subject and the audience you have in mind. Finally, be selective in citing the works and comments of experts in your discipline. If you choose wisely, the works of respected scholars and experts will be immediately recognizable to others familiar with the subject area, and your argument will have a much better chance of succeeding.

The following passage illustrates how student Jake Jamieson uses examples in his paper on the Official English movement:

> Ed Morales, the author of *Living in Spanglish*, reports that the mayor of Bogota, New Jersey, called for a boycott of McDonald's restaurants after the "company displayed a billboard advertising a new iced coffee drink in Spanish," calling "the ad . . . 'offensive' and 'divisive' because it sends a message that Hispanic immigrants do not need to learn English" (par. 2–3).

6. Determine Your Organization

There are several organizational patterns you might follow in drafting an essay. Most of you are already familiar with the most common one — *chronological order*. In this pattern, which is often used to narrate a story, explain a process, or relate a series of events, you start with the earliest event or step and move forward in time.

In a comparison-and-contrast essay, you might follow a *block* pattern or a *point-by-point* organization. In a block pattern, a writer provides all the information about one subject, followed by a block of comparable information about the other subject. In a point-by-point comparison, on the other hand, the writer starts by comparing both subjects in terms of a particular point, then compares both on a second point, and so on. In an essay comparing two dialects of American English, for example, you could follow the block pattern, covering all the characteristics of one dialect and then all the characteristics of the other. Alternatively, you could organize your material in terms of defining characteristics (for example, geographical range; characteristics of speakers; linguistic traits), filling in the details for each dialect in turn.

Other patterns of organization include moving from *the general to the specific,* from *smallest to largest,* from *least important to most important,* or from *the usual to the unusual.* In an essay about medical jargon, for instance, you might cover its general characteristics first and then move to specifics, or you might begin with what is most usual (or commonly known) about doctors' language and then discuss what is unusual about it. Whatever order you choose, keep in mind that what you present first and last will probably stay in the reader's mind the longest.

After you choose an organizational pattern, jot down the main ideas in your essay. In other words, make a scratch outline. As you add more information and ideas to your scratch outline, you may want to develop a formal, more detailed outline of your paper. In writing a formal outline, follow these rules:

1. Include the title of your essay, a statement of purpose, and the thesis statement.
2. Write in complete sentences unless your meaning is immediately clear from a phrase.
3. If you divide any category, make sure there are at least two subcategories. The reason for this is simple: You cannot divide something into fewer than two parts.
4. Observe the traditional conventions of formal outlining. Notice how each new level of specificity is given a new letter or number designation.

Title:
Purpose:
Thesis:
  I.
    A.
    B.
      1.
      2.
        a.
        b.
        c.
  II.

7. Write Your First Draft

Sometimes we are so eager to get on with the writing of a first draft that we begin before we are ready, and the results are disappointing. Before beginning to write, therefore, ask yourself, "Have I done enough prewriting? Is there a point to what I want to say?" If you have done a thorough job of gathering ideas and information, if you think you can accomplish the purpose of your paper, and if you are comfortable with your organizational plan, your answers will be "yes."

If, however, you feel uneasy, review the various prewriting steps to try to resolve the problem. Do you need to gather more information? Sharpen your thesis? Rethink your purpose? Refine your organization? Now is the time to think about these issues, to evaluate and clarify your writing plan. Time spent at this juncture is time well spent because it will not only improve your paper but will save you time and effort later on.

As you write, don't be discouraged if you do not find the most appropriate language for your ideas or if your ideas do not flow easily. Push ahead with the writing, realizing that you will be able to revise the material later, adding information and clarifications wherever necessary. Be sure to keep your audience in mind as you write, so that your diction and coverage stay at the appropriate level. Remember also to bridge all the logical and emotional leaps for your audience. Rereading what you have already written as you go along will help you to further develop your ideas and tie them together. Once completed, a first draft will give you a sense of accomplishment. You will see that you have something to work with, something to build on and improve during the revision process.

8. Revise

After you complete your first draft, you will need to revise it. During the revision stage of the writing process, you will focus on the large issues of thesis, purpose, evidence, organization, and paragraph structure to make sure that your writing says what you want it to say. First, though, it is crucial that you set your draft aside for a while. Then you can come back to it with a fresh eye and some objectivity. When you do, resist the temptation to plunge immediately into a second draft: Scattered changes will not necessarily improve the piece. Instead, try to look at your writing as a whole and to tackle your writing problems systematically. Use the following guidelines:

- Make revisions on a hard copy of your paper. (Triple-space your draft so that you can make changes more easily.)
- Read your paper aloud, listening for parts that do not make sense.
- Ask a fellow student to read your essay and critique it.

A Brief Guide to Peer Critiquing

When critiquing someone else's paper:

- Read the essay carefully. Read it to yourself first, and then, if possible, have the writer read it to you at the beginning of the session. Some flaws become obvious when read aloud.
- Ask the writer to state his or her purpose for writing and to identify the thesis statement within the paper itself.
- Be positive, but be honest. Never denigrate the paper's content or the writer's effort, but do your best to identify how the writer can improve the paper through revision.
- Try to address the most important issues first. Think about the thesis and the organization of the paper before moving on to more specific topics like word choice.
- Do not be dismissive, and do not dictate changes. Ask questions that encourage the writer to reconsider parts of the paper that you find confusing or ineffective.

When someone critiques your work:

- Give your reviewer a copy of your paper before your meeting.
- Listen carefully to your reviewer, and try not to discuss or argue each issue. Record comments, and evaluate them later.

- Do not get defensive or explain what you wanted to say if the reviewer misunderstands what you meant. Try to understand the reviewer's point of view, and learn what you need to revise to clear up the misunderstanding.
- Consider every suggestion, but only use the ones that make sense to you in your revision.
- Be sure to thank your reviewer for his or her effort on your behalf.

One way to begin the revision process is to compare the earlier outline of your first draft to an outline of how it actually came out. This will help you see, in abbreviated form, the organization and flow of the essential components of your essay and perhaps detect flaws in reasoning.

Another method you can use in revising is to start with large-scale issues, such as your overall structure, and then concentrate on finer and finer points. As you examine your essay, ask yourself about what you have written and address the large elements of your essay: thesis, purpose, organization, paragraphs, and evidence.

Revising the Large Elements of an Essay

- Is my topic specific enough?
- Does my thesis statement identify my topic and make an assertion about it?
- Is my essay organized the best way, given my purpose?
- Are my paragraphs adequately developed, and does each support my thesis?
- Have I accomplished my purpose?
- How effective is my beginning? My ending?
- Is my title effective?

Once you have addressed the major problems in your essay by writing a second draft, you should be ready to turn your attention to the finer elements of sentence structure, word choice, and usage.

Revising Sentence-Level Elements

- Do my sentences convey my thoughts clearly, and do they emphasize the most important parts of my thinking?
- Are my sentences stylistically varied?
- Is my choice of words fresh and forceful, or is my writing weighed down by clichés and unnecessary wordiness?
- Have I made any errors of usage?

Finally, if you find yourself dissatisfied with specific elements of your draft, look at several essays in *Language Awareness* to see how other writers have dealt with the particular situation you are confronting. For example, if you don't like the way the essay starts, find some beginnings you think are particularly effective; if your paragraphs don't seem to flow into one another, examine how various writers use transitions; if an example seems unconvincing, examine the way other writers include details, anecdotes, facts, and statistics to strengthen their illustrations. Remember that the readings in the text are there as a resource for you as you write.

9. Edit and Proofread

Now that you have revised in order to make your essay "right," it is time to think about making it "correct." During the editing stage of the writing process, check your writing for errors in grammar, punctuation, capitalization, spelling, and manuscript format. Both your dictionary and your college handbook will help you answer specific editing questions about your paper.

Addressing Common Editing Problems and Errors

- Do my verbs agree in number with their subjects?
- Do my pronouns have clear antecedents—that is, do they clearly refer to specific nouns earlier in my sentences?
- Do I have any sentence fragments, comma splices, or run-on sentences?
- Have I made any unnecessary shifts in person, tense, or number?
- Have I used the comma properly in all instances?
- Have I checked for misspellings, mistakes in capitalization, and typos?

- Have I inadvertently confused words like *their, they're,* and *there* or *it's* and *its?*
- Have I followed the prescribed guidelines for formatting my manuscript?

Having revised and edited your essay, you are ready to print your final copy. Be sure to proofread your work before submitting it to your instructor. Even though you may have used your computer's spell checker, you might find that you have typed *worm* instead of *word,* or *form* instead of *from.* Also check to see that your essay is properly line spaced and that the text is legible.

The following essay was written by Rebekah Sandlin while she was a student at Miami University in Oxford, Ohio. After Rebekah read the essays in the chapter on prejudice, stereotypes, and language, her instructor, Linda Parks, asked her to write about a personal experience with biased language and how that language affected her. Rebekah vividly remembered an experience she had in the third grade, when she used the phrase "just like a nigger" to mock a classmate. Using that experience as the starting point of her essay, she then traces a series of subsequent encounters she had with the word *nigger* and recounts her resulting personal growth. By the end of her essay, Rebekah makes it clear to her readers why she felt compelled to tell her story.

Sandlin 1

Rebekah Sandlin

English 111 sec. BD

October 23, 2011

Paper #3

The "Negro Revolt" in Me

She said "seven" when the answer was clearly "ten." We were in the third grade and had been studying multiplication for a few weeks. Our teacher, Mrs. Jones, reminded Monica that "we are multiplying now, not adding. Five times two will always be ten" I laughed at Monica. How did she not know the answer to five times two? We had been over it and practiced it so many times. My laughter encouraged the other kids in the class to join in with me. Within seconds the laughing had escalated into pointing fingers and calling her stupid. That's when "it" happened. That's when I said what I will always regret for the rest of my life. I said, "Just like a nigger."

Playing on her weaknesses in math, laughing at her, encouraging the rest of the class to point at her, and calling her the most degrading word in history still eats at my insides. The class stopped laughing. Monica cried. Mrs. Jones gasped and yanked me into the hallway where she scolded me for a good half an hour. That is how I learned that language could be used as a dangerous tool. That's when I learned about prejudice and its effects on people. That's how it happened. This is how it has affected my life.

Mrs. Jones sent me home with a note explaining my "behavior" in class. I remember being terribly afraid to give that note to my mom. I felt guilty, confused, and embarrassed, but I wasn't sure why I felt that way. No one had taken the time to explain to me why the word had such a negative connotation. No one told me that blacks were once treated terribly wrong or that they were used as slaves. No one told me about the interracial rapes that occurred on plantations or about the children being taken and sold to rich white landowners. No one told me about them being denied an education and proper shelter. No one told me. I was just a small white girl living in a predominately white city and going to a predominately white school. I knew nothing about diversity and equal rights for everyone. I knew nothing.

My mom sat me down at the kitchen table and asked me how I could have said such a terrible thing. "Where did you learn that word?" she asked. She sounded furious and embarrassed. She kept asking me where I had heard the word and who taught it to me. Before I had a chance to respond she knew the answer. My dad was on the phone in the next room talking to his father. He was laughing and he said, "just like a nigger." My mom lowered her head and whispered, "go to your room." I quietly got up and obeyed her command. I'm not sure what she said to him, but I could hear their mumbled fighting through the vents. I pressed my ear to the vent on the floor to try and make sense of my mother's cries. It was no use. Two hours later they came upstairs to give me one of their "you did something wrong" speeches. Except this speech was different from most. It began with an apology and an attempt to justify my father's words.

It started with a story. My dad grew up on a tobacco farm in southern Georgia. His family hired blacks to work out in the fields. "No," he reassured, "they weren't slaves. We paid them." His family was prejudiced toward blacks. Their language and actions rubbed off onto my dad. The only difference was that my dad learned that what he said and how he treated blacks was wrong. Through growing up and living in integrated working environments, he learned how "not to act" in the presence of a black person. However, when he talked to his father he still acted and talked like he was prejudiced. He said that he didn't understand why he did it other than he desperately wanted to be accepted by his own father. He admitted that he was wrong and told me that I was lucky because I was going to learn the "real way" to treat people. He promised to never use the word again as long as I promised to do the same thing. I agreed.

I was in the fifth grade the next time I heard the word used. Ironically, I was in a math class again. Except this time I didn't say it, someone else did. Unlike Monica, this girl didn't cry. Instead, she gave an evil glare. I was the one that stood up to say something in her defense. I yelled at Dan and told him that what he had said was rude and degrading. "How would you like it if someone called you honky?"

I screamed. He hauled off and hit me right in the arm! He called me a "nigger-lover."

The teacher broke it up, and we were sent to the principal's office. I was suspended for using vulgar language. I had used the word "honky." Dan was given a warning and sent back to class. I had plenty of time to think about what I had done wrong while I waited in the office for my mom to come and pick me up. No matter how hard I tried, I couldn't see what I had done wrong. That girl did not want to be called a nigger. I was just trying to show him what it would feel like if someone had said something like that to him. My mom did not agree with me. I learned an important lesson that day. Using bad words to stop other bad words is like using violence to stop violence — it doesn't work. My mom was supportive and said that she respected what I was trying to do but next time I should use better sense. I didn't want there to be a next time.

WRITING WITH SOURCES

WHAT DOES IT MEAN TO WRITE WITH SOURCES?

Some of the writing you do in college will be experiential—that is, based on your personal experiences—but many of your college assignments will call upon you to do some research, to write with sources. While most of us have had some experience with basic research practices—locating and evaluating print and online sources, taking notes from those sources, and documenting those sources—we have not learned how to integrate these sources effectively and purposefully into our papers. (For more information on basic research and documentation practices, see Chapter 15, "A Brief Guide to Writing a Research Paper," pp. 543–568.) Your purpose in writing with sources is not to present a collection of quotations that show you can report what others have said about your topic. Your goal is to analyze, evaluate, and synthesize the materials you have researched so that you can take ownership of your topic. You learn how to view the results of research from your own perspective and arrive at an informed opinion of your topic. In short, you become a participant in a conversation with your sources about your topic.

To help you on your way, this chapter provides advice on (1) summarizing, paraphrasing, and quoting sources, (2) integrating summaries, paraphrases, and quotations into the text of your paper using signal phrases, and (3) avoiding plagiarism when writing with sources. In addition, one student paper models different ways of engaging meaningfully with outside sources and of reflecting that engagement in writing.

WRITE WITH SOURCES

Each time that you introduce an outside source into your paper be sure that you are using that source in a purposeful way. Outside sources can be used to

- support your thesis and main points with statements from noted authorities,
- offer memorable wording of key terms or ideas,
- extend your ideas by introducing new information, and
- articulate opposing positions for you to argue against.

Consider Joseph P. Kahn's use of two outside sources in the following passage from his May 5, 2011, article in the *Boston Globe* entitled "What Does Friend Mean Now?":

> What we mean when we talk about friends and friendships these days has many of us baffled. Experts who track the changing meaning of language agree that our common reference points are becoming less fixed as the lines blur between the virtual and the real, the face-to-face and Facebooked. Between what may feel good to hear — or quantify, in the case of online connections — and what squares with the reality of interpersonal relationships. "The meanings of words derive from how we use them — and clearly as the world changes, we apply words in different ways," says Lera Boroditsky, a Stanford University psychology professor and language expert. Before online interaction became a routine part of daily life, she adds, "You saw friends in person or spoke to them on the phone. Today there's a real change in how we interact, and our language is struggling to keep up."
>
> MIT sociologist Sherry Turkle, who studies technology and its cultural impact, maintains that "friend" has become "contested terrain" linguistically as social media sites alter the term's very DNA. "It calls into question how many friends we have and what they are," says Turkle, author of *Alone Together: Why We Expect More from Technology and Less from Each Other*. "You can have 3,000 friends who look at your photos and what you've published, but only 100 who know about your heart." The challenge, she contends, is to avoid confusing virtual friendship with the real deal. "Friendship is about letting something happen between two people that's surprising and new," says Turkle, whereas social networking "gives the illusion of companionship without the demands of intimacy. It's friendship on demand, when I want it."

Here Kahn quotes two language authorities — Lera Boroditsky of Stanford University and Sherry Turkle of MIT — to support his main point that the meaning of *friends* and *friendships* "are becoming less fixed as the lines blur between the virtual and the real."

In the following passage from "Why the U.S. Needs an Official Language," Mauro E. Mujica uses outside sources to present the position that he will ultimately argue against.

> Historically, the need to speak and understand English has served as an important incentive for immigrants to learn the language and assimilate into the mainstream of American society. For the last 30 years, this idea has been turned on its head. Expecting immigrants to learn English has been called "racist." Marta Jimenez, an attorney for the Mexican American Legal Defense and Educational Fund, speaks of "the historical use of English in the United States as a tool of oppression."
>
> Groups such as the National Association for Bilingual Education complain about the "restrictive goal" of having immigrant children learn in English. The former mayor of Miami, Maurice Ferre, dismissed the idea of even a bilingual future for the city. "We're talking about Spanish

as a main form of communication, as an official language," he averred. "Not on the way to English."

Perhaps this change is best illustrated in the evolving views of the League of United Latin American Citizens (LULAC). Started in 1929, the group was originally pro-English and pro-assimilation. One of the founding aims and purposes of LULAC was "to foster the acquisition and facile use of the Official Language of our country that we may hereby equip ourselves and our families for the fullest enjoyment of our rights and privileges and the efficient discharge of our duties and obligations to this, our country." By the 1980s the executive director of LULAC Arnoldo Torres, could proudly proclaim, "We cannot assimilate and we won't!"

By letting the opposition articulate their position themselves, Mujica reduces the possibility of being criticized for misrepresenting his opponents while at the same time sets himself up to give strong voice to his belief that the United States should declare English its official language.

Sometimes source material is too long and detailed to be quoted directly in its entirety. In such cases, a writer will choose to summarize or paraphrase the material in his or her own words before introducing it in an essay. For example, notice how Janet Holmes summarizes two lengthy reports about male-female discourse in the workplace for use in her essay "Women Talk Too Much" that appeared in *Language Myths* in 1999.

> Despite the widespread belief that women talk more than men, most of the available evidence suggests just the opposite. When women and men are together, it is the men who talk most. Two Canadian researchers, Deborah James and Janice Drakich, reviewed sixty-three studies which examined the amount of talk used by American women and men in different contexts. Women talked more than men in only two studies.
>
> In New Zealand, too, research suggests that men generally dominate the talking time. Margaret Franken compared the amount of talk used by female and male "experts" assisting a female TV host to interview well-known public figures. In a situation where each of three interviewers was entitled to a third of the interviewers' talking time, the men took more than half on every occasion.

Here Holmes introduces each summary with a signal phrase — "Two Canadian researchers, Deborah James and Janice Drakich, reviewed" and "Margaret Franken compared." Holmes concludes each summary with a pointed statement of the researchers' conclusion.

Finally, the following passage comes from the article "Creeper! Rando! Sketchball!" that appeared in *The New York Times* on October 29, 2010. Here writer Ben Zimmer uses representative quotations from three University of North Carolina students, all enrolled in a grammar of current English class, to speak to his claim that "terms like *creeper, rando,* and *sketchball* come in handy as women deal with men who may try to give them unwanted attention."

In interviews I conducted with [Professor Connie C.] Eble's students, one recurring theme that emerged was the impact of technology and social media on the need to patrol social boundaries. "With Facebook and texting," Natasha Duarte said, "it's easier to contact someone you're interested in, even if you only met them once and don't really know them. To the person receiving them, these texts and Facebook friend requests or wall posts can seem premature and unwarranted, or sketchy."

Facebook in particular lends itself to "stalkerish" behavior, Christina Clark explained, and indeed the compound verb *Facebook stalk* (meaning "excessively or surreptitiously peruse another's Facebook profile") shows up in the latest slang lists. "People put things on Facebook a lot of the time to show off pictures of themselves and to meet new people, but some of these new people are undesirables," Clark said. "Unfortunately, it can be hard to filter these people out without feeling unkind, so this information is available to them, and often it is alarming if they seem to be looking through pictures or constantly trying to find out what you're up to. These people then become stalkers or 'creepers.'"

Lilly Kantarakias said she believes that the shift to technologically mediated exchanges among students is leading to a "loss of intimacy" and that this failure to engage in human contact is responsible for the rise in all of the "sketchy" talk. "People have lost both their sense of communication and social-interaction skills," Kantarakias said. "We know only how to judge people off of a Facebook page or we easily misinterpret texts or e-mails. You can see it in the way people walk around campus, texting on their cells, being completely oblivious to the hundreds of people surrounding them. We've become lazy with our speech and our social profiling of fellow human beings."

By letting the three representative female students articulate their own views on the impact of technology and social media on one's social boundaries, Zimmer demonstrates that he is not discussing an isolated problem. Each student is able to speak to the issue from personal experience. Collectively, they help Zimmer make his point convincingly.

LEARN TO SUMMARIZE, PARAPHRASE, AND QUOTE FROM YOUR SOURCES.

When taking notes from your sources, you must decide whether to summarize, paraphrase, or quote directly. The approach you take is largely determined by the content of the source passage and the way you envision using it in your paper. Each of these techniques—summarizing, paraphrasing, and quoting—will help you better incorporate source material into your essays. Making use of all three of these techniques, rather than relying on only one or two, will keep your text varied and interesting. In most cases it is better to summarize or paraphrase material from sources—which by definition means using your own words—instead of quoting verbatim (word for word). Capturing an idea in your own words ensures that you have thought about and understood what your source is saying. All the examples in the following discussion are taken from essays in *Language Awareness* unless otherwise noted, and page numbers refer to pages in this text.

Summary

When you *summarize* material from one of your sources, you capture in condensed form the essential idea of a passage, an article, or an entire chapter. Summaries are particularly useful when you are working with lengthy, detailed arguments or long passages of narrative or descriptive background information in which the details are not germane to the overall thrust of your paper. You simply want to capture the essence of the passage because you are confident that your readers will readily understand the point being made or do not need to be convinced about its validity. Because you are distilling information, a summary is always shorter than the original; often a chapter or more can be reduced to a paragraph, or several paragraphs to a sentence or two. Remember in writing a summary you should use your own wording.

Consider the following paragraphs in which Gordon Allport discusses the prejudicial power of the labels humans use to describe one another.

> Some labels such as "blind man," are exceedingly salient and powerful. They tend to prevent alternative classification, or even cross-classification. Ethnic labels are often of this type, particularly if they refer to some highly visible feature, e.g., Negro, Oriental. They resemble the labels that point to some outstanding incapacity—*feeble-minded, cripple, blind man*. Let us call such symbols "labels of primary potency." These symbols act like shrieking sirens, deafening us to all finer discriminations that we might otherwise perceive. Even though the blindness of one man and the darkness of pigmentation of another may be defining attributes for some purposes, they are irrelevant and "noisy" for others.
>
> Most people are unaware of this basic law of language—that every label applied to a given person refers properly only to one aspect of his nature. You may correctly say that a certain man is *human, a philanthropist, a Chinese, a physician, an athlete*. A given person may be all of these; but the chances are that *Chinese* stands out in your mind as the symbol of primary potency. Yet neither this nor any other classificatory label can refer to the whole of a man's nature. (Only his proper name can do so.)
>
> —GORDON ALLPORT, *The Nature of Prejudice*, page 179

A student wishing to capture the gist of Allport's point without repeating his detailed explanation wrote the following summary on page 48.

> **Labels of primacy potency**
>
> Allport warns about the dangers
> of using labels — especially ethnic
> labels — because of their power to
> distort our perceptions of other
> human beings.
>
> Allport, 179

Paraphrase

When you *paraphrase* material from a source, you restate the information in your own words instead of quoting directly. Unlike a summary, which gives a brief overview of the essential information in the original, a paraphrase seeks to maintain the same level of detail as the original to aid readers in understanding or believing the information presented. A paraphrase presents the original information in approximately the same number of words but with different wording. To put it another way, your paraphrase should accurately present ideas in the original, but it should not use the same words or sentence structure as the original. Even though you are using your own words in a paraphrase, it's important to remember that you are borrowing ideas and therefore must acknowledge the source of these ideas with a citation.

How would you paraphrase the following passage from "Selection, Slanting, and Charged Language" by Newman P. and Genevieve B. Birk, which appears on pages 223–233 of this text?

> When we put our knowledge into words, a second process of selection, the process of slanting, takes place. Just as there is something, a rather mysterious principle of selection, which chooses for us what we will notice, and what will then become our knowledge, there is also a principle which operates, with or without our awareness, to select certain facts and feelings from our store of knowledge, and to choose the words and the emphasis that we shall use to communicate our meaning.

The following note card illustrates how one student paraphrased this passage:

PARAPHRASE NOTE CARD

Slanting

Every time we communicate information and ideas, we engage in a secondary process known as slanting. An even earlier selection process, that of acquiring knowledge, remains something of a mystery because who can say why we notice what we do and why it becomes a part of what we know. Slanting, a conscious or subconscious process, further selects the facts and emotions we convey; it finds not only the words we use but also the way we emphasize them when we communicate.

Newman P. Birk, Genevieve B. Birk, "Selection, Slanting, and Charged Language," 224

Notice how carefully the student captures the essence of the Birks' ideas in her own words as well as her own sentence structures. Capturing an idea in your own words demonstrates that you have thought about and understood what your source is saying.

Direct Quotation

When you *quote* a source directly, you copy the words of your source exactly, putting all quoted material in quotation marks. When you make a quotation note card, check the passage carefully for accuracy, including punctuation and capitalization. Be selective about what you choose to quote. Reserve direct quotation for important ideas stated memorably, for especially clear explanations by authorities, and for arguments by proponents of a particular position in their own words.

Consider, for example, the following passage quoted directly from William Zinsser's essay "Simplicity," on page 201 of this text, emphasizing the importance—and current rarity—of clear, concise writing.

QUOTATION NOTE CARD

Wordiness

"Clutter is the disease of American writing. We are a society strangling in unnecessary words, circular constructions, pompous frills, and meaningless jargon."

William Zinsser, "Simplicity," 201

On occasion you'll find a useful passage with some memorable wording in it. Avoid the temptation to quote the whole passage; instead, try combining summary or paraphrase with direct quotation.

Consider the following paragraph from Martin Luther King Jr.'s "Letter from Birmingham Jail" (p. 87), addressed ostensibly to eight white clergymen who had published a letter about civil disorder in the Birmingham *Post-Herald*.

> You express a great deal of anxiety over our willingness to break laws. This is certainly a legitimate concern. Since we so diligently urge people to obey the Supreme Court's decision of 1954 outlawing segregation in the public schools, at first glance it may seem rather paradoxical for us consciously to break laws. One may well ask: "How can you advocate breaking some laws and obeying others?" The answer lies in the fact that there are two types of laws: just and unjust. I would be the first to advocate obeying just laws. One has not only a legal but moral responsibility to obey just laws. Conversely, one has a moral responsibility to disobey unjust laws. I would agree with St. Augustine that "an unjust law is no law at all."

Notice how the student's note on the following page has quotation marks carefully added around all the words that were borrowed directly.

INTEGRATE BORROWED MATERIAL INTO YOUR TEXT

Being familiar with the material in your notes will help you decide how to integrate your sources into your drafts. Though it is not necessary to use all of your notes, nor to use them all at once in your first draft, you do need to know which ones support your thesis, extend your ideas, offer

QUOTATION AND SUMMARY NOTE CARD

Just and unjust laws

MLK is quick to answer his fellow clergy who question his "willingness to break laws." He addresses their concerns by explaining that there are "just and unjust" laws. King strongly believes that we all have a "legal" and "moral responsibility to obey just laws" as well as "a moral responsibility to disobey unjust laws."

Martin Luther King Jr., "Letter from Birmingham Jail," 87

better wording of your ideas, and reveal the opinions of noted authorities. Occasionally you will want to use notes that include ideas contrary to your own so that you can rebut them in your own argument. Once you have analyzed your notes, you may even alter your thesis slightly in light of the information and ideas you have discovered.

Whenever you want to use borrowed material, be it a quotation, a paraphrase, or summary, your goal always is to integrate these sources smoothly and logically so as not to disrupt the flow of your paper or confuse your readers. It is best to introduce borrowed material with a *signal phrase*, which alerts readers that borrowed information is about to be presented.

SELECTING APPROPRIATE SIGNAL PHRASES.   A signal phrase minimally consists of the author's name and a verb (e.g., *Michael Pollan contends*). Signal phrases help readers better follow your train of thought. When you integrate a quote, paraphrase, or summary into your paper, vary your signal phrases and choose verbs for the signal phrases that accurately convey the tone and intent of the writer you are citing. If a writer is arguing, use the verb *argues* (or *asserts*, *claims*, or *contends*); if a writer is contesting a particular position or fact, use the verb *contests* (or *denies*, *disputes*, *refutes*, or *rejects*). Verbs that are specific to the situation in your paper will bring your readers into the intellectual debate (and avoid the monotony of all-purpose verbs like *says* or *writes*). The following examples illustrate how you can vary signal phrases to add precision and interest to your writing:

Malcolm X confesses that "trying to write simple English, I not only wasn't articulate, I wasn't even functional" (p. 68).

Using a series of vivid examples, Stephen Pinker reminds us why "we sheathe our words in politeness and innuendo and other forms of doublespeak" (p. 115).

Anne Lamott encourages aspiring writers to give up their fears of first drafts because "few writers really know what they are doing until they've done it" (p. 190).

"Hate, like much of human feeling, is not rational," argues Andrew Sullivan, "but it usually has its reasons. And it cannot be understood, let alone condemned, without knowing them" (p. 313).

Gloria Naylor asserts that "Words themselves are innocuous; it is the consensus that gives them true power" (p. 336).

Myriam Marquez explains that English is not her family's official language because "it's a matter of respect for our parents and comfort in our cultural roots" (p. 496).

Other verbs that you should keep in mind when constructing signal phrases include the following:

acknowledges	compares	grants	reasons
adds	confirms	implies	reports
admits	declares	insists	responds
believes	endorses	points out	suggests

Well-chosen signal phrases help you integrate quotations, paraphrases, and summaries into the flow of your paper. Besides, signal phrases let your reader know who is speaking and, in the case of summaries and paraphrases, exactly where your ideas end and someone else's begin. Never confuse your reader with a quotation that appears suddenly without introduction. Unannounced quotations leave your reader wondering how the quoted material relates to the point you are trying to make. Look at the following example from the first draft of a student's paper on the pros and cons of social networking on Facebook. The quotation is from Daniel Lyons' article "The High Price of Facebook," which appeared in the May 15, 2010, issue of *Newsweek.com.*

Unannounced Quotation

Many Facebook users worry that the privacy settings are not clear enough to protect people. "I also suspect that whatever Facebook has done so far to invade our privacy, it's only the beginning. Which is why I'm considering deactivating my account. Facebook is a handy site, but I'm freaked out by the idea that my information is in the hands of people I don't trust. That's too high a price to pay" (Lyons). But we should remember that every time a privacy setting is changed, Web sites like Gizmodo.com and Slate.com alert users to the changes. Viral copy-and-paste status updates start circulating on Facebook notifying users of the privacy changes and the need to make updates to your profile if necessary. All of the criticisms Facebook is subjected to due to its rapid growth and evolution are overblown because users who are not satisfied with their level of privacy can simply delete personal information from their profiles, or routinely check their privacy settings.

In the following revision, the student integrates the quotation into the text by means of a signal phrase and in a number of other ways as well. By giving the name of the writer being quoted, referring to his authority on the subject, and noting that the writer is speaking from experience, the student provides more context so that the reader can better understand how this quotation fits into the discussion.

Integrated Quotation

Many Facebook users worry that the privacy settings are not clear enough to protect people. Tech-savvy commentator Daniel Lyons, a senior editor at *Forbes* magazine, has joined the chorus of critics. He warns, "I also suspect that whatever Facebook has done so far to invade our privacy, it's only the beginning. Which is why I'm considering deactivating my account. Facebook is a handy site, but I'm freaked out by the idea that my information is in the hands of people I don't trust. That's too high a price to pay" (Lyons). But we should remember that every time a privacy setting is changed, Web sites like Gizmodo.com and Slate.com alert users to the changes. Viral copy-and-paste status updates start circulating on Facebook notifying users of the privacy changes and the need to make updates to your profile if necessary. All of the criticisms Facebook is subjected to due to its rapid growth and evolution are overblown because users who are not satisfied with their level of privacy can simply delete personal information from their profiles or routinely check their privacy settings.

AVOID PLAGIARISM

The importance of honesty and accuracy in working with outside sources—whether print, digital, or personal interview or correspondence—cannot be stressed enough. In working closely with the ideas and words of others, intellectual honesty demands that we distinguish between what we borrow—acknowledging it with a citation—and what is our own. Any material borrowed word for word must be placed within quotation marks and be properly cited. Any idea, explanation, or argument you have paraphrased or summarized must be properly cited, and it must be clear where the paraphrase or summary begins and ends. In short, to use someone else's ideas, whether in their original form or in an altered form, without proper acknowledgment is to be guilty of **plagiarism**.

You must acknowledge and document the source of your information whenever you do any of the following:

- quote a source exactly, word for word
- paraphrase or summarize information and ideas from a source
- cite statistics, tables, charts, graphs, or other visuals

You do *not* need to document the following types of information:

- your own observations, experiences, ideas, and opinions
- factual information available in a number of reference works (information known as "common knowledge")
- proverbs, sayings, or familiar quotations

For a discussion of MLA style for in-text documentation practices, see pages 555–556.

The Council of Writing Program Administrators offers the following helpful definition of *plagiarism* in academic settings for administrators, faculty, and students: "In an instructional setting, plagiarism occurs when a writer deliberately uses someone else's language, ideas, or other (not common knowledge) material without acknowledging its source."

Accusations of plagiarism can be upheld even if plagiarism is unintentional. A little attention and effort can help to eliminate this possibility. While taking notes, check and recheck all direct quotations against the wording of the original, and be sure you've labeled them clearly as quotations. Double-check your paraphrases to be sure that you have not used the writer's wording or sentence structure.

While writing your paper, make sure that you put quotation marks around material taken verbatim, and double-check the text against your note card—or, better yet, against the original—to make sure that the quotation is accurate. When using paraphrases or summaries, be sure to cite the source.

To learn more about how you can avoid plagiarism, go to the "Tutorial on Avoiding Plagiarism" at bedfordstmartins.com/plagiarismtutorial. There you will find information on the consequences of plagiarism, tutorials explaining what sources to acknowledge, how to keep good notes, how to organize your research, and how to appropriately integrate sources. Exercises are included throughout the tutorial to help you practice skills like integrating sources and recognizing acceptable paraphrases and summaries.

The sections that follow provide examples of appropriate use of quotation, paraphrase, and summary.

USING QUOTATION MARKS FOR LANGUAGE BORROWED DIRECTLY. Again, when you use another person's exact words or sentences, you must enclose the borrowed language in quotation marks. Even if you cite the source, you are guilty of plagiarism if you fail to use quotation marks. The following example demonstrates both plagiarism and a correct citation for a direct quotation.

Original Source

In the last decade, Standards departments have become more tolerant of sex and foul language, but they have cracked down on violence and become more insistent about the politically correct presentation of minorities. Lately, however, they seem to be swinging wildly back and forth between allowing everything and allowing nothing.

> —TAD FRIEND, "You Can't Say That: The Networks Play Word Games," *New Yorker* Nov. 19, 2001, page 45.

Plagiarism

In the last decade, Standards departments have become more tolerant of sex and foul language, but, according to social commentator Tad Friend, they have cracked down on violence and become more insistent about the politically correct presentation of minorities. Lately, however, they seem to be swinging wildly back and forth between allowing everything and allowing nothing (45).

Correct Citation of Borrowed Words in Quotation Marks

"In the last decade, Standards departments have become more tolerant of sex and foul language," according to social commentator Tad Friend, "but they have cracked down on violence and become more insistent about the politically correct presentation of minorities. Lately, however, they seem to be swinging wildly back and forth between allowing everything and allowing nothing" (45).

USING YOUR OWN WORDS IN PARAPHRASE AND SUMMARY. When summarizing or paraphrasing a source, you must use your own language. It is not enough simply to change a word here or there; you must restate the idea(s) from the original *in your own words*, using your own style and sentence structure. In the following example, notice how plagiarism can occur when care is not taken in the wording or sentence structure of a paraphrase.

Original Source

Stereotypes are a kind of gossip about the world, a gossip that makes us prejudge people before we ever lay eyes on them. Hence it is not surprising that stereotypes have something to do with the dark world of prejudice. Explore most prejudices (note that the word means prejudgment) and you will find a cruel stereotype at the core of each one.

> —ROBERT L. HEILBRONER, "Don't Let Stereotypes Warp Your Judgment," *Reader's Digest* Jan. 1962, page 254.

Unacceptably Close Wording

According to Heilbroner, we prejudge other people even before we have seen them when we think in stereotypes. That stereotypes are related to the ugly world of prejudice should not surprise anyone. If you explore the heart of most prejudices — beliefs that literally prejudge — you will discover a mean stereotype lurking (254).

Unacceptably Close Sentence Structure

Heilbroner believes that stereotypes are images of people, images that enable people to prejudge other people before they have seen them. Therefore, no one should find it surprising that stereotypes are somehow related to the ugly world of prejudice. Examine most prejudices (the word literally means prejudgment) and you will uncover a vicious stereotype at the center of each (254).

Acceptable Paraphrase

Heilbroner believes that there is a link between stereotypes and the hurtful practice of prejudice. Stereotypes make for easy conversation, a kind of shorthand that enables people to find fault with others before ever meeting them. Most human prejudices, according to Heilbroner, have an ugly stereotype lurking somewhere inside them (254).

Preventing Plagiarism

Questions to Ask about Direct Quotations

- Do quotation marks clearly indicate the language that I borrowed verbatim (word for word)?
- Is the language of the quotation accurate, with no missing or misquoted words or phrases?
- Do the brackets or ellipsis marks clearly indicate any changes or omissions I have introduced?
- Does a signal phrase naming the author introduce each quotation? If not, is the author's name in the parenthetical citation?
- Does a parenthetical page citation follow each quotation?

Questions to Ask about Summaries and Paraphrases

- Is each summary and paraphrase written in my own words and style?
- Does each summary and paraphrase accurately represent the opinion, position, or reasoning of the original writer?
- Does each summary and paraphrase start with a signal phrase so that readers know where my borrowed material begins?
- Does each summary and paraphrase conclude with a parenthetical page citation?

Questions to Ask about Facts and Statistics

- Do I use a signal phrase or some other marker to introduce each fact or statistic that is not common knowledge so that readers know where the borrowed material begins?
- Is each fact or statistic that is not common knowledge clearly documented with a parenthetical page citation?

Finally, as you proofread your final draft, check your citations one last time. If at any time while you are taking notes or writing your paper you have a question about plagiarism, consult your instructor for clarification and guidance before proceeding.

A SAMPLE STUDENT ESSAY USING LIBRARY AND INTERNET SOURCES

Jake Jamieson wrote the following essay while he was a student at the University of Vermont and has updated it for inclusion in this book. His assignment was to write an argument, and he was free to choose his own topic from among the language issues covered in class. After considering a number of possible topics and doing some preliminary searches on several of them, Jamieson decided to tackle the issue of legislating English as the official language for the United States. As one who believes in the old axiom "if it isn't broken, don't fix it," Jamieson was intrigued by the supporters of the Official English movement, who feel the need to fix a system that seems to be working just fine. As you read, notice how he uses outside sources to set out the various pieces of the Official English position and then uses his own thinking and examples as well as experts who support him to undercut that position. Throughout his essay Jamieson uses MLA-style in-text citations together with a list of works cited.

Jake Jamieson

Professor A. Rosa

Written Expression 001

12 April 2012

The "Official English" Movement:

Can America Proscribe Language with a Clear Conscience?

Many people think of the United States as a giant cultural "melting pot" where people from other countries come together and bathe in the warm waters of assimilation. In this scenario the newly arrived immigrants readily adopt American cultural ways and learn to speak English. For others, however, this serene picture of the melting pot analogy does not ring true. These people see the melting pot as a giant cauldron into which immigrants are tossed; here their cultures, values, and backgrounds are boiled away in the scalding waters of discrimination. At the center of the discussion about immigrants and assimilation is language: Should immigrants be required to learn English or should accommodations be made so they can continue to use their native languages?

Those who argue that the melting pot analogy is valid believe that immigrants who come to America do so willingly and should be expected to become a part of its culture instead of hanging on to their past. For them, the expectation that immigrants will celebrate this country's holidays, dress as Americans dress, embrace American values, and, most importantly, speak English is not unreasonable. They believe that assimilation offers the only way for everyone in this country to live together in harmony and the only way to dissipate the tensions that inevitably arise when cultures clash. One major problem with this argument, however, is that there is no agreement on what exactly constitutes the "American way" of doing things.

Title: Writer introduces subject and provides focus.

Writer sets context for discussion, identifies central problem of the "Official English" language debate.

Thesis question: Writer states the key question to be addressed in paper.

Writer introduces a major problem with assimilation model.

Jamieson 2

Not everyone in America is of the same religious persuasion or has the same set of values, and different people affect vastly different styles of dress. There are so many sets of variables that it would be hard to defend the argument that there is only one culture in the United States. Currently, the one common denominator in America is that the overwhelming majority of us speak English, and because of this a major movement is being staged in favor of making English the country's "official" language while it is still the country's national and common language. Making English America's "official" language would change the ground rules and expectations surrounding immigrant assimilation. According to columnist and social commentator Charles Krauthammer, making English the "official" language has important implications:

> "Official" means the language of the government and its institutions. "Official" makes clear our expectations of accultura-tion. "Official" means that every citizen, upon entering America's most sacred political space, the voting booth, should minimally be able to identify the words President and Vice President and county commissioner and judge. The immigrant, of course, has the right to speak whatever he wants. But he must understand that when he comes to the U.S., swears allegiance and accepts its bounty, he undertakes to join its civic culture. In English. (495)

Many reasons are given to support the notion that making English the official language of the land is a good idea and that it is exactly what this country needs, especially in the face of the growing diversity of languages in metropolitan areas. Economics is a major reason. As Mauro E. Mujica, chairman and CEO of U.S. English, reports, "Los Angeles County spent $3.3 million, 15 percent of the entire election budget, to print election ballots in seven languages and hire multilingual poll workers for the March 2002 primary. The county also spends $265 per day for each of the 420 full-time court interpreters" (par. 16).

Marginal annotations:

Opposition argument: English as the common denominator in America—time to act.

Quotation: Writer quotes Krauthammer to present the "Official English" perspective.

Writer indents long quotation according to MLA style.

Writer uses MLA in-text citation format which includes introductory signal phrase and parenthetical paragraph number to integrate a quotation about the economic impact of not having English as the nation's official language.

Jamieson 3

Supporters of Official English contend that all government communication must be in English. Because communication is absolutely necessary for democracy to survive, they believe that the only way to ensure the existence of our nation is to make sure a common language exists. Making English official would ensure that all government business, from ballots to official forms to judicial hearings, would have to be conducted in English. From this vantage point championing English as our national language is not hostile at all because as Mujica asserts, "Parents around the world know that English is the global language and that their children need to learn it to succeed. English is the language of business, higher education, diplomacy, aviation, the Internet, science, popular music, entertainment, and international travel" (par. 3). Political and cultural commentator Greg Lewis echoes Mujica's sentiments when he boldly states, "to succeed in America . . . it's important to speak, read, and understand English as most Americans speak it. There's nothing cruel or unfair in that; it's just the way it is" (par. 5).

> Writer presents the opposition argument favoring Official English.

For those who do not subscribe to this way of thinking, however, this type of legislation is anything but a welcoming act or invitation to participate. Many of them, like Myriam Marquez, readily acknowledge the importance of English but fear that "talking in Spanish — or any other language, for that matter — is some sort of litmus test used to gauge American patriotism" (497). Others suggest that anyone attempting to regulate language is treading dangerously close to the First Amendment and must have a hidden agenda of some type. Why, it is asked, make a language official when it is already firmly entrenched and widely used in this country without legislation to mandate it? For many, the answer is plain and simple — discrimination.

> Writer introduces the anti-Official English position.

This tendency of Official English proponents to put down other languages is one that shows up again and again, even though they maintain that they have nothing against other languages or the people

Jamieson 4

who speak them. If there is no malice intended toward other languages, why is the use of any language other than English tantamount to lunacy according to an almost constant barrage of literature and editorial opinion? Ed Morales, the author of *Living in Spanglish*, reports that the mayor of Bogota, New Jersey, called for a boycott of McDonald's restaurants after the "company displayed a billboard advertising a new iced coffee drink in Spanish," calling "the ad . . . 'offensive' and 'divisive' because it sends a message that Hispanic immigrants do not need to learn English" (par. 2–3). Now, according to this mindset, not only is speaking any language other than English offensive, but it is also irrational and bewildering. What is this world coming to when businesses want to attract new customers using Spanish or people just want to speak and make transactions in their native language? Why do they refuse to change and become more like us? Why can't immigrants see that speaking English is quite simply the right way to go? These and many other questions like them are implied by Official English proponents when they discuss the issue.

> Quotation: Writer cites author Morales to support claim about official English proponents.

> Writer asks a series of rhetorical questions.

The scariest prospect of all is that this opinion is quickly gaining popularity all around the country. It appears to be most prevalent in areas with high concentrations of Spanish-speaking residents. To date the English Language Unity Act and one amendment to the Constitution have been proposed in the House and Senate. There are more than twenty-eight states — including Arizona, Missouri, North Dakota, Florida, California, Virginia, and New Hampshire — that have made English their official language, and more are debating the issue at this time. An especially disturbing fact about this debate — and it was front and center in 2010 during the discussions and protests about what to do with America's over 12.5 million illegal immigrants — is that Official English laws always seem to be linked to anti-immigration legislation, such as proposals to limit immigration or to restrict government benefits to immigrants.

> Writer updates readers on the status of Official English legislation.

Jamieson 5

Although Official English proponents maintain that their bid for

language legislation is in the best interest of immigrants, the facts

tend to show otherwise. University of Texas professor Robert D. King

strongly believes that "language does not threaten American unity." He

recommends that "we relax and luxuriate in our linguistic richness and

our traditional tolerance of language differences" (492). A decision has

to be made in this country about what kind of message we will send

to the rest of the world. Do we plan to allow everyone in this country

the freedom of speech that we profess to cherish, or will we decide to

reserve it only for those who speak English? Will we hold firm to our

belief that everyone is deserving of life, liberty, and the pursuit of

happiness in this country? Or will we show the world that we believe

in these things only when they pertain to ourselves and people like us?

"The irony," as Hispanic columnist Myriam Marquez observes, "is that

English-only laws directed at government have done little to change the

inevitable multi-cultural flavor of America" ("English-Only Laws" A10).

Writer cites University of Texas professor to assure readers that the United States does not need to make English the nation's official language.

Writer concludes with an observation by an Hispanic journalist about the impact of English-only legislation to date.

Jamieson 6

Works Cited

"'English Language Unity Act' Will Encourage Common Language."

　　EnglishFirst.org. 18 Mar. 2011. Web. 22 Feb. 2012.

King, Robert D. "Should English Be the Law?" *Language Awareness*. 11th

　　ed. Eds. Paul Eschholz, Alfred Rosa, and Virginia Clark. Boston:

　　Bedford, 2013. 483-92. Print.

Krauthammer, Charles. "In Plain English: Let's Make It Official." *Language*

　　Awareness. 11th ed. Eds. Paul Eschholz, Alfred Rosa, and Virginia

　　Clark. Boston: Bedford, 2013. 493-95. Print.

Lewis, Greg. "An Open Letter to Diversity's Victims." *WashingtonDispatch*

　　.com. 12 Aug. 2003. Web. 22 Feb. 2012.

Marquez, Myriam. "English-Only Laws Serve to Appease Those Who Fear

　　the Inevitable." *Orlando Sentinel* 10 July 2000: A10. Print.

---. "Why and When We Speak Spanish in Public." *Language Awareness*.

　　11th ed. Eds. Paul Eschholz, Alfred Rosa, and Virginia Clark. Boston:

　　Bedford, 2013. 496-97. Print.

Morales, Ed. "English-only Debate Turns Absurd." *Progressive.org*. 19 July

　　2006. Web. 23 Feb. 2012.

Mujica, Mauro E. "Why the U.S. Needs an Official Language." *WorldandI*

　　.com. Dec. 2003. Web. 23 Feb. 2012.

The heading *Works Cited* is centered at the top on page.

Writer uses MLA style for his list of works cited. The list begins on a new page. Entries are presented in alphabetical order by authors' last names. The first line of each entry begins at the left margin; subsequent lines are indented five spaces. Double space within entries as well as between entries.

The correct MLA forms for various other kinds of publications are given on pages 555–567.

4

UNDERSTANDING THE POWER
OF LANGUAGE

Most of us accept language as we accept the air we breathe; we cannot get along without it, and we take it for granted almost all of the time. Many days we find ourselves on language overload, bombarded by a steady stream of verbal and written messages—some invited, others not—but how much do we really know about language? How well do we understand how language works? Few of us are aware of the extent to which language is used to mislead and manipulate. Still fewer of us are fully conscious of the ways, subtle and not, in which our use of language may affect others. And even fewer of us recognize that our very perceptions of the world are influenced, and our thoughts at least partially shaped, by language. However, we are also the beneficiaries of language far more than we are its victims. Language is one of humankind's greatest achievements and most important resources, and it is a subject endlessly fascinating in itself.

If it is true that we are all in some sense prisoners of language, it is equally true that liberation begins with an awareness of that fact. Chapter 4, "Understanding the Power of Language," presents five essays in which individuals tell of their language struggles and their triumphs. In "Coming to an Awareness of Language," Malcolm X relates how he came to understand the power of words while serving time in the Norfolk Prison Colony. He remembers his frustration and feelings of inadequacy when he recognized the limitations of his slang-filled street talk. Not one to sit around and drown in self-pity, Malcolm X charted a course that empowered and liberated his mind. Next, we read the inspiring story of Helen Keller, a woman who broke the chains of blindness and deafness and connected to the world around her. In "The Day Language Came into My Life," Keller recounts the day she, with the help of her teacher Anne Mansfield Sullivan, discovered "everything had a name, and each name gave birth to a new thought." In the third essay, "On Being 17, Bright, and Unable to Read," David Raymond describes what it is like to be a dyslexic high school student, and how he met his language challenge. In the fourth essay, "Writing to Change the World," Mary Pipher tells of her first reading *The Diary of Anne Frank* as an adolescent. She uses this experience as a jumping-off point to discuss the power of the written word to advance social, political, and economic change. And in the final selection, "Letter from

Birmingham Jail," Martin Luther King Jr. demonstrates the power of written language. Through carefully crafted emotional and logical appeals, King argues that nonviolent direct action can put an end to prejudice, hatred, and bigotry in the United States. Many historians credit King's letter with changing the course of the civil rights movement in the 1960s, successfully culminating in the landmark Civil Rights Act of 1964 and the Voting Rights Act of 1965. In the e-Pages (available online at bedfordstmartins .com/languageawareness/epages), a video of Barack Obama's rousing speech "Don't Tell Me Words Don't Matter" offers a look at the effects of hopeful language on political and social change.

Coming to an Awareness of Language

MALCOLM X

On February 21, 1965, Malcolm X, the Black Muslim leader, was shot to death as he addressed an afternoon rally in Harlem. He was thirty-nine years old. In the course of his brief life, he had risen from a world of thieving, pimping, and drug pushing to become one of the most articulate and powerful African Americans in the United States during the early 1960s. In 1992 his life was reexamined in Spike Lee's film *Malcolm X*. With the assistance of the late Alex Haley, the author of *Roots,* Malcolm X told his story in *The Autobiography of Malcolm X* (1964), a moving account of his search for fulfillment. This selection is taken from the *Autobiography*.

All of us have been in situations in which we have felt somehow betrayed by our language, unable to find just the right words to express ourselves. "Words," as lexicographer Bergen Evans has said, "are the tools for the job of saying what you want to say." As our repertoire of words expands so does our ability to express ourselves—to articulate clearly our thoughts, feelings, hopes, fears, likes, and dislikes. Frustration at not being able to express himself in the letters he wrote drove Malcolm X to the dictionary, where he discovered the power of words.

WRITING TO DISCOVER: *Write about a time when someone told you that it is important to have a good vocabulary. What did you think when you heard this advice? Why do you think people believe that vocabulary is important? How would you assess your own vocabulary?*

I've never been one for inaction. Everything I've ever felt strongly about, I've done something about. I guess that's why, unable to do anything else, I soon began writing to people I had known in the hustling world, such as Sammy the Pimp, John Hughes, the gambling house owner, the thief Jumpsteady, and several dope peddlers. I wrote them all about Allah and Islam and Mr. Elijah Muhammad. I had no idea where most of them lived. I addressed their letters in care of the Harlem or Roxbury bars and clubs where I'd known them.

I never got a single reply. The average hustler and criminal was too uneducated to write a letter. I have known many slick sharp-looking hustlers, who would have you think they had an interest in Wall Street; privately, they would get someone else to read a letter if they received one. Besides, neither would I have replied to anyone writing me something as wild as "the white man is the devil."

What certainly went on the Harlem and Roxbury wires was that Detroit Red was going crazy in stir,[1] or else he was trying some hype to shake up the warden's office.

---

1. Slang for being in jail.

During the years that I stayed in the Norfolk Prison Colony, never did any official directly say anything to me about those letters, although, of course, they all passed through the prison censorship. I'm sure, however, they monitored what I wrote to add to the files which every state and federal prison keeps on the conversion of Negro inmates by the teachings of Mr. Elijah Muhammad.

But at that time, I felt that the real reason was that the white man   5 knew that he was the devil.

Later on, I even wrote to the Mayor of Boston, to the Governor of Massachusetts, and to Harry S. Truman. They never answered; they probably never even saw my letters. I handscratched to them how the white man's society was responsible for the black man's condition in this wilderness of North America.

It was because of my letters that I happened to stumble upon starting to acquire some kind of homemade education.

I became increasingly frustrated at not being able to express what I wanted to convey in letters that I wrote, especially those to Mr. Elijah Muhammad. In the street, I had been the most articulate hustler out there—I had commanded attention when I said something. But now, trying to write simple English, I not only wasn't articulate, I wasn't even functional. How would I sound writing in slang, the way I would *say* it, something such as, "Look daddy, let me pull your coat about a cat. Elijah Muhammad—"

Many who today hear me somewhere in person, or on television, or those who read something I've said, will think I went to school far beyond the eighth grade. This impression is due entirely to my prison studies.

It had really begun back in the Charlestown Prison, when Bimbi first   10 made me feel envy of his stock of knowledge. Bimbi had always taken charge of any conversation he was in, and I had tried to emulate him. But every book I picked up had few sentences which didn't contain anywhere from one to nearly all of the words that might as well have been in Chinese. When I just skipped those words, of course, I really ended up with little idea of what the book said. So I had come to the Norfolk Prison Colony still going through only book-reading motions. Pretty soon, I would have quit even these motions, unless I had received the motivation that I did.

I saw that the best thing I could do was get hold of a dictionary—to study, to learn some words. I was lucky enough to reason also that I should try to improve my penmanship. It was sad. I couldn't even write in a straight line. It was both ideas together that moved me to request a dictionary along with some tablets and pencils from the Norfolk Prison Colony school.

Anyone who has read a great deal can imagine the new world that opened.

I spent two days just rifling uncertainly through the dictionary's pages. I'd never realized so many words existed! I didn't know *which* words I needed to learn. Finally, just to start some kind of action, I began copying.

In my slow, painstaking, ragged handwriting, I copied into my tablet everything printed on that first page, down to the punctuation marks.

I believe it took me a day. Then, aloud, I read back, to myself, everything I'd written on the tablet. Over and over, aloud, to myself, I read my own handwriting.

I woke up the next morning, thinking about those words—immensely 15 proud to realize that not only had I written so much at one time, but I'd written words that I never knew were in the world. Moreover, with a little effort, I also could remember what many of these words meant. I reviewed the words whose meanings I didn't remember. Funny thing, from the dictionary's first page right now, that "aardvark" springs to my mind. The dictionary had a picture of it, a long-tailed, long-eared, burrowing African mammal, which lives off termites caught by sticking out its tongue as an anteater does for ants.

I was so fascinated that I went on—I copied the dictionary's next page. And the same experience came when I studied that. With every succeeding page, I also learned of people and places and events from history. Actually the dictionary is like a miniature encyclopedia. Finally the dictionary's A section had filled a whole tablet—and I went on into the B's. That was the way I started copying what eventually became the entire dictionary. It went a lot faster after so much practice helped me pick up handwriting speed. Between what I wrote in my tablet, and writing letters, during the rest of my time in prison I would guess I wrote a million words.

I suppose it was inevitable that as my word-base broadened, I could for the first time pick up a book and read and now begin to understand what the book was saying. Anyone who has read a great deal can imagine the new world that opened. Let me tell you something: from then until I left that prison, in every free moment I had, if I was not reading in the library, I was reading on my bunk. You couldn't have gotten me out of books with a wedge. Between Mr. Muhammad's teachings, my correspondence, my visitors . . . and my reading of books, months passed without my even thinking about being imprisoned. In fact, up to then, I never had been so truly free in my life.

THINKING CRITICALLY ABOUT THE READING

1. What motivated Malcolm X "to acquire some kind of homemade education" (7)?

2. Malcolm X narrates his experience as a prisoner using the first-person pronoun *I*. Why is the first person particularly appropriate? What would be lost or gained had he told his story using the third-person pronoun *he*? (Glossary: *Point of View*)

3. For many, *vocabulary building* means learning strange, multisyllabic, difficult-to-spell words. But acquiring an effective vocabulary does not need to be any of these things. What, for you, constitutes an effective vocabulary? How would you characterize Malcolm X's vocabulary in this selection? Do you find his word choice appropriate for his purpose? (Glossary: *Purpose*) Explain.

4. In paragraph 8, Malcolm X remembers thinking how he would "sound writing in slang" and feeling inadequate because he recognized how slang or street talk limited his options. (Glossary: *Slang*) In what kinds of situations is slang useful and appropriate? When is Standard English more appropriate? (Glossary: *Standard English*)

5. In paragraph 8, Malcolm X describes himself as having been "the most articulate hustler out there" but in writing he says he "wasn't even functional." What differences between speaking and writing could account for such a discrepancy? How does the tone of this essay help you understand Malcolm X's dilemma? (Glossary: *Tone*)

6. What is the nature of the freedom that Malcolm X refers to in the final sentence? In what sense is language liberating? Is it possible for people to be "prisoners" of their own language? Explain.

LANGUAGE IN ACTION

Many newspapers carry regular vocabulary-building columns, and the *Reader's Digest* has for many years included a section called "It Pays to Enrich Your Word Power." You might enjoy taking the following quiz, which is excerpted from *Reader's Digest*.

It Pays to Enrich Your Word Power

Zeus and his thunderbolts, Thor and his hammer, Medusa and her power to turn flesh into stone: these are all fascinating figures in mythology and folklore. Associated with such legends are words we use today, including the 10 selected below.

1. **panic** *n.*—A: pain. B: relief. C: mess. D: fear.
2. **bacchanal** (*BAK ih NAL*) *n.*—A: drunken party. B: graduation ceremony. C: backache remedy. D: victory parade.
3. **puckish** *adj.*—A: wrinkly. A: B: quirky. C: quarrelsome. D: mischievous.
4. **cyclopean** (*SIGH klo PEA en*) *adj.*—A: wise. B: gigantic. C: wealthy. D: repetitious.
5. **hector** *v.*—A: to curse. B: bully. C: disown. D: injure.
6. **cupidity** (*kyoo PID ih tee*) *n.*—A: thankfulness. B: ignorance. C: abundance. D: desire.
7. **mnemonic** (*knee MON ik*) *adj.*—pertaining to A: memory. B: speech. C: hearing. D: sight.
8. **stygian** (*STIJ ee an*) *adj.*—A: stingy. B: hellish. C: uncompromising. D: dirty.
9. **narcissistic** *adj.*—A: indecisive. B: very sleepy. C: very vain. D: just.
10. **zephyr** (*ZEF er*) *n.*—A: breeze. B: dog. C: horse. D: tornado.

ANSWERS:

1. **panic** — *[D]* Fear; widespread terror; as, An outbreak of Ebola led to *panic* in the small village. *Pan*, frightening Greek god of nature.

2. **bacchanal** — *[A]* Drunken party; orgy; as, Complaints to the police broke up the *bacchanal. Bacchus*, Roman god of wine.

3. **puckish** — *[D]* Mischievous; prankish. *Puck*, a trickloving sprite or fairy.

4. **cyclopean** — *[B]* Gigantic; huge; as, the *cyclopean* home runs of Mark McGwire. *Cyclopes*, a race of fierce, oneeyed giants.

5. **hector** — *[B]* To bully; threaten. *Hector*, Trojan leader slain by Achilles and portrayed as a bragging menace in some dramas.

6. **cupidity** — *[D]* Strong desire. *Cupid*, Roman god of love.

7. **mnemonic** — *[A]* Pertaining to memory; as, "Spring forward and fall back" is a *mnemonic* spur to change time twice a year. *Mnemosyne*, Greek goddess of memory.

8. **stygian** — *[B]* Hellish; dark and gloomy. *Styx*, a river in Hades.

9. **narcissistic** — *[C]* Very vain; self-loving; as, The *narcissistic* actress preened for the photographers. *Narcissus*, a youth who fell in love with his own reflection.

10. **zephyr** — *[A]* Soft breeze; as, The storm tapered off to a *zephyr. Zephyrus*, gentle Greek god of the west wind.

Are you familiar with most of the words on the quiz? Did some of the answers surprise you? In your opinion, is the level of difficulty appropriate for the *Reader's Digest* audience? What does the continuing popularity of vocabulary-building features suggest about the attitudes of many Americans toward language?

WRITING SUGGESTIONS

1. All of us have been in situations in which our ability to use language seemed inadequate — for example, when taking an exam; being interviewed for a job; giving directions; or expressing sympathy, anger, or grief. Write a brief essay in which you recount one such frustrating incident in your life. Before beginning to write, review your reactions to Malcolm X's frustrations with his limited vocabulary. Share your experiences with your classmates.

2. Malcolm X solved the problem of his own illiteracy by carefully studying the dictionary. Would this be a viable solution to the national problem of illiteracy? Are there more practical alternatives to Malcolm X's approach? What, for example, is being done in your community to combat illiteracy? What are some of the more successful approaches being used in other parts of the country? Write a brief essay about the problem of illiteracy. In addition to using your library for research, you may want to check out the Internet to see what it has to offer.

The Day Language Came into My Life

HELEN KELLER

Helen Keller (1880–1968) became blind and deaf at the age of eighteen months as a result of a disease. As a child, then, Keller became accustomed to her limited world, for it was all that she knew. She experienced only certain fundamental sensations, such as the warmth of the sun on her face, and few emotions, such as anger and bitterness. It wasn't until she was almost seven years old that her family hired Anne Sullivan, a young woman who would turn out to be an extraordinary teacher, to help her. As Keller learned to communicate and think, the world opened up to her. She recorded her experiences in an autobiography, *The Story of My Life* (1903), from which the following selection is taken.

Helen Keller is in a unique position to remind us of what it is like to pass from the "fog" of prethought into the world where "everything had a name, and each name gave birth to a new thought." Her experiences as a deaf and blind child also raise a number of questions about the relationship between language and thought, emotions, ideas, and memory. Over time, Keller's acquisition of language allowed her to assume all the advantages of her birthright. Her rapid intellectual and emotional growth as a result of language suggests that we, too, have the potential to achieve a greater measure of our humanity by further refining our language abilities.

WRITING TO DISCOVER: *Consider what your life would be like today if you had been born without the ability to understand language or speak or if you had suddenly lost the ability to use language later in life. Write about those aspects of your life that you think would be affected most severely.*

The most important day I remember in all my life is the one on which my teacher, Anne Mansfield Sullivan, came to me. I am filled with wonder when I consider the immeasurable contrast between the two lives which it connects. It was the third of March 1887, three months before I was seven years old.

On the afternoon of that eventful day, I stood on the porch, dumb, expectant. I guessed vaguely from my mother's signs and from the hurrying to and fro in the house that something unusual was about to happen, so I went to the door and waited on the steps. The afternoon sun penetrated the mass of honeysuckle that covered the porch and fell on my upturned face. My fingers lingered almost unconsciously on the familiar leaves and blossoms which had just come forth to greet the sweet southern spring. I did not know what the future held of marvel or surprise for me. Anger and bitterness had preyed upon me continually for weeks and a deep languor had succeeded this passionate struggle.

Have you ever been at sea in a dense fog, when it seemed as if a tangible white darkness shut you in, and the great ship, tense and anxious, groped her way toward the shore with plummet and sounding-line, and you waited with beating heart for something to happen? I was like that ship before my education began, only I was without compass or sounding-line and had no way of knowing how near the harbor was. "Light! give me light!" was the wordless cry of my soul, and the light of love shone on me in that very hour.

I felt approaching footsteps. I stretched out my hand as I supposed to my mother. Someone took it, and I was caught up and held close in the arms of her who had come to reveal all things to me, and, more than all things else, to love me.

The morning after my teacher came she led me into her room and gave me a doll. The little blind children at the Perkins Institution had sent it and Laura Bridgman had dressed it; but I did not know this until afterward. When I had played with it a little while, Miss Sullivan slowly spelled into my hand the word "d-o-l-l." I was at once interested in this finger play and tried to imitate it. When I finally succeeded in making the letters correctly I was flushed with childhood pleasure and pride. Running downstairs to my mother I held up my hand and made the letters for doll. I did not know that I was spelling a word or even that words existed; I was simply making my fingers go in monkeylike imitation. In the days that followed I learned to spell in this uncomprehending way a great many words, among them *pin, hat, cup* and a few verbs like *sit, stand* and *walk*. But my teacher had been with me several weeks before I understood that everything has a name.

One day, while I was playing with my new doll, Miss Sullivan put my big rag doll into my lap also, spelled "d-o-l-l" and tried to make me understand that "d-o-l-l" applied to both. Earlier in the day we had had a tussle over the words "m-u-g" and "w-a-t-e-r." Miss Sullivan had tried to impress it upon me that "m-u-g" is *mug* and that "w-a-t-e-r" is *water,* but I persisted in confounding the two. In despair she had dropped the subject for the time, only to renew it at the first opportunity. I became impatient at her repeated attempts and, seizing the new doll, I dashed it upon the floor. I was keenly delighted when I felt the fragments of the broken doll at my feet. Neither sorrow nor regret followed my passionate outburst. I had not loved the doll. In the still, dark world in which I lived there was no strong sentiment or tenderness. I felt my teacher sweep the fragments to one side of the hearth, and I had a sense of satisfaction that the cause of my discomfort was removed. She brought me my hat, and I knew I was going out into the warm sunshine. This thought, if a wordless sensation may be called a thought, made me hop and skip with pleasure.

We walked down the path to the well-house, attracted by the fragrance of the honeysuckle with which it was covered. Some one was drawing water and my teacher placed my hand under the spout. As the cool stream gushed over one hand she spelled into the other the word *water,* first slowly, then rapidly. I stood still, my whole attention fixed upon the motions of her fingers. Suddenly I felt a misty consciousness as of

I knew then that "w-a-t-e-r" meant the wonderful cool something that was flowing over my hand.

something forgotten — a thrill of returning thought; and somehow the mystery of language was revealed to me. I knew then that "w-a-t-e-r" meant the wonderful cool something that was flowing over my hand. The living word awakened my soul, gave it light, hope, joy, set it free! There were barriers still, it is true, but barriers that could in time be swept away.

I left the well-house eager to learn. Everything had a name, and each name gave birth to a new thought. As we returned to the house every object which I touched seemed to quiver with life. That was because I saw everything with the strange, new sight that had come to me. On entering the door I remembered the doll I had broken. I felt my way to the hearth and picked up the pieces. I tried vainly to put them together. Then my eyes filled with tears; for I realized what I had done, and for the first time I felt repentance and sorrow.

I learned a great many new words that day. I do not remember what they all were; but I do know that *mother, father, sister, teacher* were among them — words that were to make the world blossom for me, "like Aaron's rod, with flowers." It would have been difficult to find a happier child than I was as I lay in my crib at the close of that eventful day and lived over the joys it had brought me, and for the first time longed for a new day to come.

THINKING CRITICALLY ABOUT THE READING

1. In paragraph 6, Keller writes, "One day, while I was playing with my new doll, Miss Sullivan put my big rag doll into my lap also, spelled 'd-o-l-l' and tried to make me understand that 'd-o-l-l' applied to both." Why do you think Miss Sullivan placed a different doll in her lap? What essential fact about language did the action demonstrate to Keller?

2. In paragraph 6, Keller also tells us that in trying to learn the difference between "m-u-g" and "w-a-t-e-r" she "persisted in confounding the two" terms. In a letter to her home institution, Sullivan elaborated on this confusion, revealing that it was caused by Keller thinking that both words meant "drink." How in paragraph 7 does Keller finally come to understand these words? What does she come to understand about the relationship between them?

3. In paragraph 8, after the experience at the well, Keller comes to believe that "everything had a name, and each name gave birth to a new thought." Reflect on that statement. Does she mean that the process of naming leads to thinking?

4. Keller realized that over time words would make her world open up for her. Identify the parts of speech of her first words. In what ways do these parts of speech open up one's world? Explain how these words or parts of speech provide insights into the nature of writing. How does Keller's early language use compare with her use of English in her essay?

5. While it is fairly easy to see how Keller could learn the names of concrete items, it may be more difficult for us to understand how she learned about her emotions. What does her difficulty in coming to terms with abstractions—such as love, bitterness, frustration, repentance, sorrow—tell us as writers about the strategies we need to use to effectively convey emotions and feelings to our readers? In considering your answer, examine the diction Keller uses in her essay. (Glossary: *Diction*)

LANGUAGE IN ACTION

In paragraph 3, Keller uses figurative language—the metaphor of being lost in a fog—to explain her feeling of helplessness and her frustration at not being able to communicate. (Glossary: *Figures of Speech*) Metaphors and similes—brief, imaginative comparisons that highlight the similarities between things that are basically dissimilar—can be extremely helpful when trying to communicate a new concept or a strange or difficult feeling. Create a metaphor (implied comparison) or a simile (implicit comparison introduced by *like* or *as*) that would be helpful in describing each item in the following list. The first one has been completed for you to illustrate the process.

1. Skyscraper: The skyscraper sparkled in the sunlight like a huge glass needle. (Simile)

   The skyscraper, a huge glass needle, sparkled in the sunlight. (Metaphor)

2. Sound of an explosion
3. Happy person
4. Greasy French fries
5. Disagreeable roommate
6. Cold wind
7. Crowded elevator
8. Loneliness
9. Slow-moving car
10. Rainy day

Compare your metaphors and similes with those written by other members of your class. Which metaphors and similes for each item on the list seem to work best? Why? Do any seem tired or clichéd?

WRITING SUGGESTIONS

1. It could be said that we process our world in terms of our language. Using a variety of examples from your own experience, write an essay illustrating the validity of this observation. For example, aside from the photographs you took on your last vacation, your trip exists only in the words you use to describe it, whether in conversations or in writing.

2. Helen Keller explains that she felt no remorse when she shattered her doll. "In the still, dark world in which I lived there was no strong sentiment or

tenderness" (6) she recalls. However, once she understood that things had names, Keller was able to feel repentance and sorrow. In your own words, try to describe why you think her feelings changed. Before you begin to write, you may want to reread your Writing to Discover entry for the Keller article. You may also want to discuss this issue with classmates or your instructor and do some research of your own into the ways language alters perception among people who are blind or deaf.

On Being 17, Bright, and Unable to Read

DAVID RAYMOND

David Raymond was born in 1959 in Connecticut. When the following article appeared in the *New York Times* in 1976, Raymond was a junior in high school. In 1981, Raymond graduated from Curry College in Milton, Massachusetts, one of the few colleges with learning-disability programs at the time. He and his family now live in Fairfield, Connecticut, where he works as a builder.

In his essay, Raymond shares his story of being language challenged in a world of readers. Even though testing revealed that Raymond had above-average intelligence, he always felt "dumb" in school. In his plea for understanding other dyslexic children, he poignantly discusses the emotionally charged difficulties his own dyslexia caused and the many problems he experienced in school as a result.

WRITING TO DISCOVER: *One of the fundamental language arts skills that we are supposed to learn in school is how to read. How do you rate yourself as a reader? How dependent are you on reading in your everyday life? How would your life change if you were unable to read?*

One day a substitute teacher picked me to read aloud from the textbook. When I told her "No, thank you," she came unhinged. She thought I was acting smart, and told me so. I kept calm, and that got her madder and madder. We must have spent 10 minutes trying to solve the problem, and finally she got so red in the face I thought she'd blow up. She told me she'd see me after class.

Maybe someone like me was a new thing for that teacher. But she wasn't new to me. I've been through scenes like that all my life. You see, even though I'm 17 and a junior in high school, I can't read because I have dyslexia. I'm told I read "at a fourth-grade level," but from where I sit, that's not reading. You can't know what that means unless you've been there. It's not easy to tell how it feels when you can't read your homework assignments or the newspaper or a menu in a restaurant or even notes from your own friends.

> **It's not easy to tell how it feels when you can't read your homework assignments or the newspaper or a menu in a restaurant or even notes from your own friends.**

My family began to suspect I was having problems almost from the first day I started school. My father says my early years in school were the worst years of his life. They weren't so good for me, either. As I look back on it now, I can't find the words to express how bad it really was. I wanted to die. I'd come home from school screaming, "I'm dumb. I'm dumb—I wish I were dead!"

I guess I couldn't read anything at all then—not even my own name—and they tell me I didn't talk as good as other kids. But what I remember about those days is that I couldn't throw a ball where it was supposed to go, I couldn't learn to swim, and I wouldn't learn to ride a bike, because no matter what anyone told me, I knew I'd fail.

Sometimes my teachers would try to be encouraging. When I couldn't   5
read the words on the board they'd say, "Come on, David, you know that word." Only I didn't. And it was embarrassing. I just felt dumb. And dumb was how the kids treated me. They'd make fun of me every chance they got, asking me to spell "cat" or something like that. Even if I knew how to spell it, I wouldn't; they'd only give me another word. Anyway, it was awful, because more than anything I wanted friends. On my birthday when I blew out the candles I didn't wish I could learn to read; what I wished for was that the kids would like me.

With the bad reports coming from school, and with me moaning about wanting to die and how everybody hated me, my parents began looking for help. That's when the testing started. The school tested me, the child-guidance center tested me, private psychiatrists tested me. Everybody knew something was wrong—especially me.

It didn't help much when they stuck a fancy name onto it. I couldn't pronounce it then—I was only in second grade—and I was ashamed to talk about it. Now it rolls off my tongue, because I've been living with it for a lot of years—dyslexia.

All through elementary school it wasn't easy. I was always having to do things that were "different," things the other kids didn't have to do. I had to go to a child psychiatrist, for instance.

One summer my family forced me to go to a camp for children with reading problems. I hated the idea, but the camp turned out pretty good, and I had a good time. I met a lot of kids who couldn't read and somehow that helped. The director of the camp said I had a higher I.Q. than 90 percent of the population. I didn't believe him.

About the worst thing I had to do in fifth and sixth grade was go to a   10
special education class in another school in our town. A bus picked me up, and I didn't like that at all. The bus also picked up emotionally disturbed kids and retarded kids. It was like going to a school for the retarded. I always worried that someone I knew would see me on that bus. It was a relief to go to the regular junior high school.

Life began to change a little for me then, because I began to feel better about myself. I found the teachers cared; they had meetings about me and I worked harder for them for a while. I began to work on the potter's wheel, making vases and pots that the teachers said were pretty good. Also, I got a letter for being on the track team. I could always run pretty fast.

At high school the teachers are good, and everyone is trying to help me. I've gotten honors some marking periods, and I've won a letter on the cross-country team. Next quarter I think the school might hold a show of my pottery. I've got some friends. But there are still some embarrassing times. For instance, every time there is writing in the class, I get up and go to the special education room. Kids ask me where I go all the time. Sometimes I say, "to Mars."

Homework is a real problem. During free periods in school I go into the special ed room and staff members read assignments to me. When I get home my mother reads to me. Sometimes she reads an assignment into a tape recorder, and then I go into my room and listen to it. If we have a novel or something like that to read, she reads it out loud to me. Then I sit down with her and we do the assignment. She'll write, while I talk my answers to her. Lately I've taken to dictating into a tape recorder, and then someone—my father, a private tutor, or my mother—types up what I've dictated. Whatever homework I do takes someone else's time, too. That makes me feel bad.

We had a big meeting in school the other day—eight of us, four from the guidance department, my private tutor, my parents, and me. The subject was me. I said I wanted to go to college, and they told me about colleges that have facilities and staff to handle people like me. That's nice to hear.

As for what happens after college, I don't know and I'm worried about that. How can I make a living if I can't read? Who will hire me? How will I fill out the application form? The only thing that gives me any courage is the fact that I've learned about well-known people who couldn't read or had other problems and still made it. Like Albert Einstein, who didn't talk until he was 4 and flunked math. Like Leonardo da Vinci, who everyone seems to think had dyslexia.

I've told this story because maybe some teacher will read it and go easy on a kid in the classroom who has what I've got. Or, maybe some parent will stop nagging his kid, and stop calling him lazy. Maybe he's not lazy or dumb. Maybe he just can't read and doesn't know what's wrong. Maybe he's scared, like I was.

THINKING CRITICALLY ABOUT THE READING

1. What is dyslexia? Is it essential for an understanding of the essay that we know more about dyslexia than Raymond tells us? Explain.

2. Before being diagnosed dyslexic, Raymond remembers feeling "dumb" and the other kids treating him as though he were. How intelligent do you think Raymond is? What evidence did you use to arrive at your conclusion? Explain.

3. What does Raymond's story tell us about the importance of our early childhood experiences, especially within our educational system?

4. Raymond uses many colloquial and idiomatic expressions, such as "she came unhinged" and "she got so red in the face I thought she'd blow up" (1). (Glossary: *Colloquial Expression*) Identify other examples of such diction. How do they affect your reaction to the essay?

5. How has Raymond organized his story? (Glossary: *Organization*)
6. Raymond reveals the purpose of his story in the final paragraph. Why do you suppose he did not announce his intention earlier in the essay? (Glossary: *Purpose*)

LANGUAGE IN ACTION

To help teachers recognize students who might be dyslexic, *Dyslexia Teacher* has posted the following list of dyslexia symptoms on its Web site, www .dyslexia-teacher.com:

- a noticeable difference between the pupil's ability and their actual achievement;
- a family history of learning difficulties;
- difficulties with spelling;
- confusion over left and right;
- writing letters or numbers backwards;
- difficulties with math/science;
- difficulties with organizing themselves;
- difficulty following 2- or 3-step instructions.

Spelling gets singled out as one area that is important to look at when diagnosing dyslexia. According to *Dyslexia Teacher*,

> Spelling is the activity which causes most difficulty for dyslexic children. The observation of spelling errors in short, simple words is the way in which most dyslexic children first come to our attention. Examples of words which cause particular difficulty are: *any, many, island, said, they, because, enough,* and *friend.*
>
> Other words will sometimes be spelt in the way that you would expect them to be spelt if our spelling system were rational, for example, *does/dus, please/pleeze, knock/nock, search/serch, journey/jerney,* etc.
>
> Dyslexic children also experience difficulties with "jumbled spellings." These are spelling attempts in which all the correct letters are present, but are written in the wrong order. Examples include *dose/ does, freind/friend, siad/said, bule/blue, becuase/because,* and *wores/ worse.* "Jumbled spellings" show that the child is experiencing difficulty with visual memory. Nondyslexic children and adults often use their visual memory when trying to remember a difficult spelling: they write down two or three possible versions of the word on a spare piece of paper and see which spelling "looks right." They are relying on their visual memory to help them, but the visual memory of a dyslexic child may not be adequate for this task.

After hearing of the difficulties that dyslexic children and adults experience, are you better able to empathize with David Raymond's experiences? Imagine you are dyslexic and discuss with your class what it would feel like for you to exhibit some or all of the symptoms described.

WRITING SUGGESTIONS

1. Using your response to the Writing to Discover prompt for the Raymond selection as a starting point, write an essay about the importance of reading and literacy in your life.

2. Imagine that you are away at school. Recently you were caught in a speed trap—you were going seventy miles per hour in a fifty-mile-per-hour zone—and have just lost your license; you will not be able to drive home this coming weekend, as you had planned. Write two letters in which you explain why you will not be able to go home, one to your parents and the other to your best friend. Your audience is different in each case, so be sure to choose your diction accordingly. Try to imitate Raymond's informal yet serious and sincere tone in one of your letters.

Writing to Change the World

MARY PIPHER

Psychologist, educator, author, and family therapist, Mary Pipher was born in 1947 in Springfield, Missouri, and grew up in Beaver City, Nebraska. She did her undergraduate work in cultural anthropology at the University of California, Berkeley, graduating in 1969, and received her Ph.D. in clinical psychology from the University of Nebraska in 1977. Pipher is the author of eight books including the hugely popular *Hunger Pains: The Modern Woman's Tragic Quest for Thinness* (1997); *Reviving Ophelia: Saving the Selves of Adolescent Girls* (1994); *The Shelter of Each Other: Rebuilding Our Families to Enrich Our Lives* (1996); and *Seeking Peace: Chronicles of the Worst Buddhist in the World* (2009).

In the following selection taken from *Writing to Change the World* (2006), Pipher uses the epiphany she had while first reading *The Diary of Anne Frank* as a twelve-year-old to launch into an exploration of the truly incredible power of the written word. Pipher's reflections on the power of writing to change the world gives readers a fresh take on the old adage, "The pen is mightier than the sword."

WRITING TO DISCOVER: *Name two or three of the most memorable books you have read. What about these books moved you or made such an impression upon you? Did any of these books change the way you view the world? If so, explain how.*

The first book to change my view of the universe was *The Diary of Anne Frank*. I read Anne's diary when I was a twelve-year-old, in Beaver City, Nebraska. Before I read it, I had been able to ignore the existence of evil. I knew a school had burned down in Chicago, and that children had died there. I had seen grown-ups lose their tempers, and I had encountered bullies and nasty school-mates. I had a vague sense that there were criminals—jewel thieves, bank robbers, and Al Capone–style gangsters—in Kansas City and Chicago. After reading the diary, I realized that there were adults who would systematically kill children. My comprehension of the human race expanded to include a hero like Anne, but also to include the villains who killed her. When I read Anne Frank's diary, I lost my spiritual innocence.

In September 2003, when I was fifty-five years old, I visited the Holocaust Museum, in Washington, D.C., to view the Anne Frank exhibit. I looked at the cover of her little plaid diary, and at the pages of her writing, at her family pictures. Miep Gies, Otto Frank's employee who brought food to the family, spoke on video about the people who hid in the attic. She said that Anne had always wanted to know the truth about what was going on.

Others would believe the sugarcoated version of Miep's stories, but Anne would follow her to the door and ask, "What is really happening?"

The museum showed a short film clip of Anne dressed in white, her long hair dark and shiny. She is waving exuberantly from a balcony at a wedding party that is parading down the street. There are just a few seconds of film, captured by a filmmaker at the wedding who must have been entranced by her enthusiasm. The footage is haunting. Anne's wave seems directed at all of us, her small body casting a shadow across decades.

At the end of the exhibit, attendees hear the voice of a young girl reading Anne's essay, "Give," a piece inspired by her experience of passing beggars on the street. She wonders if people who live in cozy houses have any idea of the life of beggars. She offers hope: "How wonderful it is that no one has to wait, but can start right now to gradually change the world." She suggests action: "Give whatever you have to give, you can always give something, even if it is a simple act of kindness." And she ends with "The world has plenty of room, riches, money and beauty. God has created enough for each and every one of us. Let us begin by dividing it more fairly."

Even though Anne Frank was ultimately murdered, she managed, in   5
her brief and circumscribed life, to tell the truth and bequeath the gift of hope. She searched for beauty and joy even in the harsh, frightened world of the attic in which her family hid from the Nazis. Her writing has lived on to give us all a sense of the potential largesse of the human soul, even in worst-case scenarios. It also reminds us that, behind the statistics about war and genocide, there are thousands of good people who have a responsibility to help.

All writing is designed to change the world, at least a small part of the world, or in some small way, perhaps a change in a reader's mood or in his or her appreciation of a certain kind of beauty. Writing to improve the world can be assessed by the goals of its writers and/or by its effects on the world. Most likely, Mary Oliver did not write her poem "Wild Geese" to inspire environmental activists and yet environmentalists have found it inspirational. Bob Dylan claims he had no intention of composing a protest song when he penned "Blowin' in the Wind," but it became the anthem for many of the causes of the last half of the twentieth century. On the other hand, musicians like Tori Amos, the Indigo Girls, and the band Ozomatli do hope to influence their listeners in specific ways, and they succeed. Looking back, Rachel Carson, in *Silent Spring,* satisfies both intent and effect: she wrote the book to stop the use of certain pesticides, and, following its publication, DDT was banned in the United States.

My dad told me about a rule that he and other soldiers followed in the Pacific during World War II. It was called the Law of 26, and it postulates that for every result you expect from an action there will be twenty-six results you do not expect. Certainly this law applies to writing. Sometimes a book intended to have one effect has quite another.

For example, Upton Sinclair wrote *The Jungle* to call attention to the exploitation of the immigrant labor force and their working conditions in factories, yet it led to an outcry over unsanitary conditions in the meat industry and helped establish uniform standards for beef processing and inspection nationwide.

All writing to effect change need not be great literature. Some of it is art, of course, such as Walt Whitman's "I Hear America Singing" or Abraham Lincoln's Gettysburg Address. Some of it is relatively straightforward such as *Rampage: The Social Roots of School Shooting* by Katherine Newman, David Harding, and Cybelle Fox. And some of it is both artful and straightforward. For example, in *The Age of Missing Information*, Bill McKibben has a clever idea that he executes beautifully: he compares what he learns from a week in the mountains to what he learns from watching a week's worth of cable television. On the mountaintop, McKibben experiences himself as small yet connected to something large and awe-inspiring. He comes down from the mountain calm and clear-thinking. Watching cable for a week, he hears over and over that he has unmet needs, that he is grossly inadequate, yet he still is the center of the universe, deserving of everything he wants. McKibben ended the week feeling unfocused, agitated, and alone.

Good writing astonishes its writer first.

Many effective writers are not stylists, but they manage to convey a very clear message. Their writing is not directed toward sophisticates or literary critics. It is designed to influence cousin Shirley, farmer Dale, coworker Jan, Dr. Lisa, neighbor Carol, businessman Carl, or voter Sylvia. Expository writing for ordinary people calls for a variety of talent —storytelling skills, clarity, and the ability to connect. Whether they are working on an op-ed piece, a speech, or a poem, skilled writers exercise creativity and conscious control. They labor to make the important interesting, and even compelling, to readers.

Change writers hope that readers will join them in what Charles   10
Johnson calls "an invitation to struggle." Whereas writers of propaganda encourage readers to accept certain answers, writers who want to transform their readers encourage the asking of questions. Propaganda invites passive agreement; change writing invites original thought, openheartedness, and engagement. Change writers trust that readers can handle multiple points of view, contradictions, unresolved questions, and nuance. If, as André Gide wrote, "Tyranny is the absence of complexity," then change writers are founders of democracies.

Good writing astonishes its writer first. My favorite example of this phenomenon is Leo Tolstoy's *Anna Karenina*. Tolstoy planned to write a novel that condemned adultery, and his intention was to make the adulteress an unsympathetic character. But when he came to truly understand Anna as he wrote the book, he fell in love with her, and, a hundred years later, so do his readers. Empathy can turn contempt into love.

THINKING CRITICALLY ABOUT THE READING

1. What do you think Pipher means when she says, "I lost my spiritual innocence" while reading *The Diary of Anne Frank* as a twelve-year-old?
2. In paragraphs 2 through 4 Pipher tells of visiting the Holocaust Museum in Washington, D.C., to view the Anne Frank exhibit. Why do you suppose Pipher chose to tell her readers about the parts of the exhibit that she does? What insights into Anne's character does Pipher give us?
3. Pipher believes that "all writing is designed to change the world" (6). What examples does she provide to support her claim? Did you find her examples convincing?
4. According to Pipher, what talents do writers of good expository prose possess? Do you agree? How well does Pipher exhibit these talents in this essay? Explain.
5. What are the key differences between change writing and propaganda? What accounts for the power of each of these types of writing?

LANGUAGE IN ACTION

Over the years, communities throughout the United States have banned or censored many classic works of literature. Consider, for example, the following list of frequently banned books, many of which you have probably heard of if not read:

The Scarlet Letter—Nathaniel Hawthorne
The Adventures of Huckleberry Finn—Mark Twain
The Catcher in the Rye—J. D. Salinger
To Kill a Mockingbird—Harper Lee
Bridge to Terabithia—Katherine Paterson
The Lord of the Flies—William Golding
Anne Frank: The Diary of a Young Girl—Anne Frank
The Grapes of Wrath—John Steinbeck
The Color Purple—Alice Walker
Harry Potter series—J. K. Rowling
Slaughterhouse Five—Kurt Vonnegut
The Bluest Eye—Toni Morrison
The Prince of Tides—Pat Conroy
Blubber—Judy Blume
I Know Why the Caged Bird Sings—Maya Angelou

What do you think motivates communities to ban books from libraries and schools? Select one of the titles from the list above that you have read and explain what people might have found objectionable about the book. Share your analysis with your class. What do book banning and censorship tell us about the power of the written word?

WRITING SUGGESTIONS

1. In her opening sentence Pipher tells us that "the first book to change my view of the universe was *The Diary of Anne Frank*." What was the first book that caused you to view the world differently? Write an essay about that book, describing in detail the impact that it had on you when you first read it as well as your thoughts on it now. You may find it helpful to review what you wrote in response to the Writing to Discover prompt for this selection before starting to write.

2. In his memoir *Growing Up*, newspaper reporter and columnist Russell Baker recalls a moment during his eleventh-grade English class when he discovered that "my words had the power to make people laugh." Baker's teacher Mr. Fleagle wanted to make a point about essay writing by reading a student paper to the class. As Fleagle started to read, Baker—prepared for the worst—was suddenly surprised: "He was reading *my words* out loud to the entire class. What's more, the entire class was listening. Listening attentively. Then somebody laughed, then the entire class was laughing, and not in contempt and ridicule, but with open-hearted enjoyment." Have you ever considered that your writing has the power to inform, to entertain, to educate, or to persuade your peers? Write an essay in which you recount when you, or someone close to you, discovered that writing has power.

Letter from Birmingham Jail

MARTIN LUTHER KING JR.

Martin Luther King Jr. was born in 1929 in Atlanta, Georgia. The son of a Baptist minister, he was himself ordained at the age of eighteen and went on to study at Morehouse College, Crozer Theological Seminary, Boston University, and Chicago Theological Seminary. He first came to prominence in 1955, in Montgomery, Alabama, when he led a successful boycott against the city's segregated bus system. As the first president of the Southern Christian Leadership Conference, King promoted a policy of massive but nonviolent resistance to racial injustice, organized and led many civil rights demonstrations, and spoke out against the military draft and the Vietnam War. In 1964 he was awarded the Nobel Peace Prize. King's books include *Stride Toward Freedom* (1958) and *Why We Can't Wait* (1964). America lost a powerfully articulate and gifted leader when he was assassinated in Memphis, Tennessee, in 1968.

On Good Friday in 1963, the Reverend Martin Luther King Jr. led a march into downtown Birmingham, Alabama, to protest racial segregation by Birmingham's city government and local retailers. King and his fellow marchers met fierce opposition from the local police. They were arrested and jailed. King was detained for eight days. During this time King wrote his now-landmark letter from Birmingham Jail in response to a published statement by eight moderate white clergymen from Alabama who were horrified by the trouble in the streets and disagreed with King's fundamental strategy of nonviolent direct action. Historians agree that King's "Letter from Birmingham Jail" changed the political landscape in America, effectively marking a turning point of the civil rights movement and continuing to provide inspiration to the struggle for equal rights everywhere.

WRITING TO DISCOVER: *If you were to encounter an injustice in your world, how would you deal with it? Would you take direct action to confront the injustice? Would you seek some legal solution to the problem? Or would you ignore the injustice in hopes that it would go away? Is there any scenario you can imagine in which you would resort to violence? Explain.*

My Dear Fellow Clergymen:

While confined here in the Birmingham city jail, I came across your recent statement calling my present activities "unwise and untimely." Seldom do I pause to answer criticism of my work and ideas. If I sought to answer all the criticisms that cross my desk, my secretaries would have little time for anything other than such correspondence in the course of the day, and I would have no time for constructive work. But since I feel that you are men of genuine good will and that your criticisms are sincerely set forth, I want to try to answer your statement in what I hope will be patient and reasonable terms.

I think I should indicate why I am here in Birmingham, since you have been influenced by the view which argues against "outsiders coming in." I have the honor of serving as president of the Southern Christian Leadership Conference, an organization operating in every southern state, with headquarters in Atlanta, Georgia. We have some eighty-five affiliated organizations across the South, and one of them is the Alabama Christian Movement for Human Rights. Frequently we share staff, educational, and financial resources with our affiliates. Several months ago the affiliate here in Birmingham asked us to be on call to engage in a nonviolent direct-action program if such were deemed necessary. We readily consented, and when the hour came we lived up to our promise. So I, along with several members of my staff, am here because I was invited here. I am here because I have organizational ties here.

Injustice anywhere is a threat to justice everywhere.

But more basically, I am in Birmingham because injustice is here. Just as the prophets of the eighth century B.C. left their villages and carried their "thus saith the Lord" far beyond the boundaries of their home towns, and just as the Apostle Paul left his village of Tarsus and carried the gospel of Jesus Christ to the far corners of the Greco-Roman world, so am I compelled to carry the gospel of freedom beyond my own home town. Like Paul, I must constantly respond to the Macedonian call for aid.

Moreover, I am cognizant of the interrelatedness of all communities and states. I cannot sit idly by in Atlanta and not be concerned about what happens in Birmingham. Injustice anywhere is a threat to justice everywhere. We are caught in an inescapable network of mutuality, tied in a single garment of destiny. Whatever affects one directly, affects all indirectly. Never again can we afford to live with the narrow, provincial, "outside agitator" idea. Anyone who lives inside the United States can never be considered an outsider anywhere within its bounds.

You deplore the demonstrations taking place in Birmingham. But your statement, I am sorry to say, fails to express a similar concern for the conditions that brought about the demonstrations. I am sure that none of you would want to rest content with the superficial kind of social analysis that deals merely with effects and does not grapple with underlying causes. It is unfortunate that demonstrations are taking place in Birmingham, but it is even more unfortunate that the city's white power structure left the Negro community with no alternative.

In any nonviolent campaign there are four basic steps: collection of the facts to determine whether injustices exist; negotiation; self-purification; and direct action. We have gone through all these steps in Birmingham. There can be no gainsaying the fact that racial injustice engulfs this

5

community. Birmingham is probably the most thoroughly segregated city in the United States. Its ugly record of brutality is widely known. Negroes have experienced grossly unjust treatment in courts. There have been more unsolved bombings of Negro homes and churches in Birmingham than in any other city in the nation. These are the hard, brutal facts of the case. On the basis of these conditions, Negro leaders sought to negotiate with the city fathers. But the latter consistently refused to engage in good-faith negotiation.

Then, last September, came the opportunity to talk with leaders of Birmingham's economic community. In the course of the negotiations, certain promises were made by the merchants—for example, to remove the stores' humiliating racial signs. On the basis of these promises, the Reverend Fred Shuttlesworth and the leaders of the Alabama Christian Movement for Human Rights agreed to a moratorium on all demonstrations. As the weeks and months went by, we realized that we were the victims of a broken promise. A few signs, briefly removed, returned; the others remained.

As in so many past experiences, our hopes had been blasted, and the shadow of deep disappointment settled upon us. We had no alternative except to prepare for direct action, whereby we would present our very bodies as means of laying our case before the conscience of the local and the national community. Mindful of the difficulties involved, we decided to undertake a process of self-purification. We began a series of workshops on nonviolence, and we repeatedly asked ourselves: "Are you able to accept blows without retaliating?" "Are you able to endure the ordeal of jail?" We decided to schedule our direct-action program for the Easter season, realizing that except for Christmas, this is the main shopping period of the year. Knowing that a strong economic-withdrawal program would be the by-product of direct action, we felt that this would be the best time to bring pressure to bear on the merchants for the needed change.

Then it occurred to us that Birmingham's mayoral election was coming up in March, and we speedily decided to postpone action until after election day. When we discovered that the Commissioner of Public Safety, Eugene "Bull" Connor, had piled up enough votes to be in the run-off, we decided again to postpone action until the day after the run-off so that the demonstrations could not be used to cloud the issues. Like many others, we waited to see Mr. Connor defeated, and to this end we endured postponement after postponement. Having aided in this community need, we felt that our direct-action program could be delayed no longer.

You may well ask, "Why direct action? Why sit-ins, marches, and so forth? Isn't negotiation a better path?" You are quite right in calling for negotiation. Indeed, this is the very purpose of direct action. Nonviolent direct action seeks to create such a crisis and foster such a tension that a community which has constantly refused to negotiate is forced to confront the issue. It seeks so to dramatize the issue that it can no longer be ignored.   10

My citing the creation of tension as part of the work of the nonviolent-resister may sound rather shocking. But I must confess that I am not afraid of the word "tension." I have earnestly opposed violent tension, but there is a type of constructive, nonviolent tension which is necessary for growth. Just as Socrates[1] felt that it was necessary to create a tension in the mind so that individuals could rise from the bondage of myths and half-truths to the unfettered realm of creative analysis and objective appraisal, so must we see the need for nonviolent gadflies to create the kind of tension in society that will help men rise from the dark depths of prejudice and racism to the majestic heights of understanding and brotherhood.

The purpose of our direct-action program is to create a situation so crisis-packed that it will inevitably open the door to negotiation. I therefore concur with you in your call for negotiation. Too long has our beloved Southland been bogged down in a tragic effort to live in monologue rather than dialogue.

One of the basic points in your statement is that the action that I and my associates have taken in Birmingham is untimely. Some have asked: "Why didn't you give the new city administration time to act?" The only answer that I can give to this query is that the new Birmingham administration must be prodded about as much as the outgoing one, before it will act. We are sadly mistaken if we feel that the election of Albert Boutwell as mayor will bring the millennium to Birmingham. While Mr. Boutwell is a much more gentle person than Mr. Connor, they are both segregationists, dedicated to maintenance of the status quo. I have hoped that Mr. Boutwell will be reasonable enough to see the futility of massive resistance to desegregation. But he will not see this without pressure from devotees of civil rights. My friends, I must say to you that we have not made a single gain in civil rights without determined legal and nonviolent pressure. Lamentably, it is an historical fact that privileged groups seldom give up their privileges voluntarily. Individuals may see the moral light and voluntarily give up their unjust posture; but, as Reinhold Niebuhr[2] has reminded us, groups tend to be more immoral than individuals.

We know through painful experience that freedom is never voluntarily given by the oppressor; it must be demanded by the oppressed. Frankly, I have yet to engage in a direct-action campaign that was "well timed" in the view of those who have not suffered unduly from the disease of segregation. For years now I have heard the word "Wait!" It rings in the ear of every Negro with piercing familiarity. This "Wait" has almost always meant "Never." We must come to see, with one of our distinguished jurists, that "justice too long delayed is justice denied."

---

1. The greatest of the ancient Greek philosphers, Socrates was sentenced to death because he persisted in raising difficult questions of authority.

2. Niebuhr (1892–1971), an American theologian, attempted to establish a practical code of social ethics based in religious conviction.

We have waited for more than 340 years for our constitutional and God-given rights. The nations of Asia and Africa are moving with jetlike speed toward gaining political independence, but we still creep at horse-and-buggy pace toward gaining a cup of coffee at a lunch counter. Perhaps it is easy for those who have never felt the stinging darts of segregation to say, "Wait." But when you have seen vicious mobs lynch your mothers and fathers at will and drown your sisters and brothers at whim; when you have seen hate-filled policemen curse, kick, and even kill your black brothers and sisters; when you see the vast majority of your twenty million Negro brothers smothering in an airtight cage of poverty in the midst of an affluent society; when you suddenly find your tongue twisted and your speech stammering as you seek to explain to your six-year-old daughter why she can't go to the public amusement park that has just been advertised on television, and see tears welling up in her eyes when she is told that Funtown is closed to colored children, and see ominous clouds of inferiority beginning to form in her little mental sky, and see her beginning to distort her personality by developing an unconscious bitterness toward white people; when you have to concoct an answer for a five-year-old son who is asking, "Daddy, why do white people treat colored people so mean?"; when you take a cross-country drive and find it necessary to sleep night after night in the uncomfortable corners of your automobile because no motel will accept you; when you are humiliated day in and day out by nagging signs reading "white" and "colored"; when your first name becomes "nigger," your middle name becomes "boy" (however old you are) and your last name becomes "John," and your wife and mother are never given the respected title "Mrs."; when you are harried by day and haunted by night by the fact that you are a Negro, living constantly at tiptoe stance, never quite knowing what to expect next, and are plagued with inner fears and outer resentments; when you are forever fighting a degenerating sense of "nobodiness"—then you will understand why we find it difficult to wait. There comes a time when the cup of endurance runs over, and men are no longer willing to be plunged into the abyss of despair. I hope, sirs, you can understand our legitimate and unavoidable impatience.

You express a great deal of anxiety over our willingness to break laws. 15 This is certainly a legitimate concern. Since we so diligently urge people to obey the Supreme Court's decision of 1954 outlawing segregation in the public schools, at first glance it may seem rather paradoxical for us consciously to break laws. One may well ask: "How can you advocate breaking some laws and obeying others?" The answer lies in the fact that there are two types of laws: just and unjust. I would be the first to advocate obeying just laws. One has not only a legal but a moral responsibility to obey just laws. Conversely, one has a moral responsibility to disobey unjust laws. I would agree with St. Augustine[3] that "an unjust law is no law at all."

---

3. An early bishop of the Christian church, St. Augustine (354–430) is considered the founder of theology.

Now, what is the difference between the two? How does one determine whether a law is just or unjust? A just law is a manmade code that squares with the moral law or the law of God. An unjust law is a code that is out of harmony with the moral law. To put it in the terms of St. Thomas Aquinas[4]: An unjust law is a human law that is not rooted in eternal law and natural law. Any law that uplifts human personality is just. Any law that degrades human personality is unjust. All segregation statutes are unjust because segregation distorts the soul and damages the personality. It gives the segregator a false sense of superiority and the segregated a false sense of inferiority. Segregation, to use the terminology of the Jewish philosopher Martin Buber, substitutes an "I-it" relationship for an "I-thou" relationship and ends up relegating persons to the status of things. Hence segregation is not only politically, economically, and sociologically unsound, it is morally wrong and sinful. Paul Tillich[5] has said that sin is separation. Is not segregation an existential expression of man's tragic separation, his awful estrangement, his terrible sinfulness? Thus it is that I can urge men to obey the 1954 decision of the Supreme Court, for it is morally right; and I can urge them to disobey segregation ordinances, for they are morally wrong.

Let us consider a more concrete example of just and unjust laws. An unjust law is a code that a numerical or power majority group compels a minority group to obey but does not make binding on itself. This is *difference* made legal. By the same token, a just law is a code that a majority compels a minority to follow and that it is willing to follow itself. This is *sameness* made legal.

Let me give another explanation. A law is unjust if it is inflicted on a minority that, as a result of being denied the right to vote, had no part in enacting or devising the law. Who can say that the legislature of Alabama which set up that state's segregation laws was democratically elected? Throughout Alabama all sorts of devious methods are used to prevent Negroes from becoming registered voters, and there are some counties in which, even though Negroes constitute a majority of the population, not a single Negro is registered. Can any law enacted under such circumstances be considered democratically structured?

Sometimes a law is just on its face and unjust in its application. For instance, I have been arrested on a charge of parading without a permit. Now, there is nothing wrong in having an ordinance which requires a permit for a parade. But such an ordinance becomes unjust when it is used to maintain segregation and to deny citizens the First Amendment privilege of peaceful assembly and protest.

---

4. The wide-embracing Christian teachings of medieval philosopher St. Thomas Aquinas (1225–1274) have been applied to every realm of human activity.

5. Tillich (1886–1965) and Buber (1878–1965) are both important figures in twentieth-century religious thought.

I hope you are able to see the distinction I am trying to point out.   20
In no sense do I advocate evading or defying the law, as would the rabid
segregationist. That would lead to anarchy. One who breaks an unjust law
must do so openly, lovingly, and with a willingness to accept the penalty.
I submit that an individual who breaks a law that conscience tells him is
unjust, and who willingly accepts the penalty of imprisonment in order
to arouse the conscience of the community over its injustice, is in reality
expressing the highest respect for law.

Of course, there is nothing new about this kind of civil disobedience. It was evidenced sublimely in the refusal of Shadrach, Meshach, and
Abednego to obey the laws of Nebuchadnezzar,[6] on the ground that a
higher moral law was at stake. It was practiced superbly by the early Christians, who were willing to face hungry lions and the excruciating pain of
chopping blocks rather than submit to certain unjust laws of the Roman
Empire. To a degree, academic freedom is a reality today because Socrates
practiced civil disobedience. In our own nation, the Boston Tea Party represented a massive act of civil disobedience.

We should never forget that everything Adolf Hitler did in Germany
was "legal" and everything the Hungarian freedom fighters[7] did in Hungary was "illegal." It was "illegal" to aid and comfort a Jew in Hitler's
Germany. Even so, I am sure that, had I lived in Germany at the time, I
would have aided and comforted my Jewish brothers. If today I lived in
a Communist country where certain principles dear to the Christian faith
are suppressed, I would openly advocate disobeying that country's anti-
religious laws.

I must make two honest confessions to you, my Christian and Jewish brothers. First, I must confess that over the past few years I have been
gravely disappointed with the white moderate. I have almost reached the
regrettable conclusion that the Negro's great stumbling block in his stride
toward freedom is not the White Citizen's Counciler[8] or the Ku Klux
Klanner, but the white moderate, who is more devoted to "order" than
to justice; who prefers a negative peace which is the absence of tension to
a positive peace which is the presence of justice; who constantly says, "I
agree with you in the goal you seek, but I cannot agree with your methods
of direct action"; who paternalistically believes he can set the timetable
for another man's freedom; who lives by a mythical concept of time and
who constantly advises the Negro to wait for a "more convenient season."
Shallow understanding from people of good will is more frustrating than

---

6. When Shadrach, Meshach, and Abednego refused to worship an idol, King Nebuchadnezzar had them cast into a roaring furnace; they were saved by God. [See Daniel 1:7–3:30]

7. In 1956 Hungarian nationalists revolted against Communist rule, but were quickly
put down with a violent show of Soviet force.

8. Such councils were organized in 1954 to oppose school desegregation.

absolute misunderstanding from people of ill will. Lukewarm acceptance is much more bewildering than outright rejection.

I had hoped that the white moderate would understand that law and order exist for the purpose of establishing justice and that when they fail in this purpose they become the dangerously structured dams that block the flow of social progress. I had hoped that the white moderate would understand that the present tension in the South is a necessary phase of the transition from an obnoxious negative peace, in which the Negro passively accepted his unjust plight, to a substantive and positive peace, in which all men will respect the dignity and worth of human personality. Actually, we who engage in nonviolent direct action are not the creators of tension. We merely bring to the surface the hidden tension that is already alive. We bring it out in the open, where it can be seen and dealt with. Like a boil that can never be cured so long as it is covered up but must be opened with all its ugliness to the natural medicines of air and light, injustice must be exposed, with all the tension its exposure creates, to the light of human conscience and the air of national opinion, before it can be cured.

In your statement you assert that our actions, even though peaceful, must be condemned because they precipitate violence. But is this a logical assertion? Isn't this like condemning a robbed man because his possession of money precipitated the evil act of robbery? Isn't this like condemning Socrates because his unswerving commitment to truth and his philosophical inquiries precipitated the act by the misguided populace in which they made him drink hemlock? Isn't this like condemning Jesus because his unique God-consciousness and never-ceasing devotion to God's will precipitated the evil act of crucifixion? We must come to see that, as the federal courts have consistently affirmed, it is wrong to urge an individual to cease his efforts to gain his basic constitutional rights because the quest may precipitate violence. Society must protect the robbed and punish the robber.

I had also hoped that the white moderate would reject the myth concerning time in relation to the struggle for freedom. I have just received a letter from a white brother in Texas. He writes: "All Christians know that the colored people will receive equal rights eventually, but it is possible that you are in too great a religious hurry. It has taken Christianity almost two thousand years to accomplish what it has. The teachings of Christ take time to come to earth." Such an attitude stems from a tragic misconception of time, from the strangely irrational notion that there is something in the very flow of time that will inevitably cure all ills. Actually, time itself is neutral; it can be used either destructively or constructively. More and more I feel that the people of ill will have used time much more effectively than have the people of good will. We will have to repent in this generation not merely for the hateful words and actions of the bad people, but for the appalling silence of the good people. Human progress never rolls in on wheels of inevitability; it comes through the tireless efforts of men willing to be coworkers with

God, and without this hard work, time itself becomes an ally of the forces of social stagnation. We must use time creatively, in the knowledge that the time is always ripe to do right. Now is the time to make real the promise of democracy and transform our pending national elegy into a creative psalm of brotherhood. Now is the time to lift our national policy from the quicksand of racial injustice to the solid rock of human dignity.

You speak of our activity in Birmingham as extreme. At first I was rather disappointed that fellow clergymen would see my nonviolent efforts as those of an extremist. I began thinking about the fact that I stand in the middle of two opposing forces in the Negro community. One is a force of complacency, made up in part of Negroes who, as a result of long years of oppression, are so drained of self-respect and a sense of "somebodiness" that they have adjusted to segregation; and in part of a few middle-class Negroes who, because of a degree of academic and economic security and because in some ways they profit by segregation, have become insensitive to the problems of the masses. The other force is one of bitterness and hatred, and it comes perilously close to advocating violence. It is expressed in the various black nationalist groups that are springing up across the nation, the largest and best-known being Elijah Muhammad's Muslim movement. Nourished by the Negro's frustration over the continued existence of racial discrimination, this movement is made up of people who have lost faith in America, who have absolutely repudiated Christianity, and who have concluded that the white man is an incorrigible "devil."

I have tried to stand between these two forces, saying that we need emulate neither the "do-nothingism" of the complacent nor the hatred and despair of the black nationalist. For there is the more excellent way of love and nonviolent protest. I am grateful to God that, through the influence of the Negro church, the way of nonviolence became an integral part of our struggle.

If this philosophy had not emerged, by now many streets of the South would, I am convinced, be flowing with blood. And I am further convinced that if our white brothers dismiss as "rabble-rousers" and "outside agitors" those of us who employ nonviolent direct action, and if they refuse to support our nonviolent efforts, millions of Negroes will, out of frustration and despair, seek solace and security in black-nationalist ideologies—a development that would inevitably lead to a frightening racial nightmare.

Oppressed people cannot remain oppressed forever. The yearning for   30
freedom eventually manifests itself, and that is what has happened to the American Negro. Something within has reminded him of his birthright of freedom, and something without has reminded him that it can be gained. Consciously or unconsciously, he has been caught up by the *Zeitgeist*,[9] and with his black brothers of Africa and his brown and yellow brothers of Asia, South America, and the Caribbean, the United States Negro is moving with a sense of great urgency toward the promised land of racial

---

9. *Zeitgeist:* German word for "the spirit of the times."

justice. If one recognizes this vital urge that has engulfed the Negro community, one should readily understand why public demonstrations are taking place. The Negro has many pent-up resentments and latent frustrations, and he must release them. So let him march; let him make prayer pilgrimages to the city hall; let him go on freedom rides—and try to understand why he must do so. If his repressed emotions are not released in nonviolent ways, they will seek expression through violence; this is not a threat but a fact of history. So I have not said to my people, "Get rid of your discontent." Rather, I have tried to say that this normal and healthy discontent can be channeled into the creative outlet of nonviolent direct action. And now this approach is being termed extremist.

But though I was initially disappointed at being categorized as an extremist, as I continued to think about the matter I gradually gained a measure of satisfaction from the label. Was not Jesus an extremist for love: "Love your enemies, bless them that curse you, do good to them that hate you, and pray for them which despitefully use you, and persecute you." Was not Amos an extremist for justice: "Let justice roll down like waters and righteousness like an ever-flowing stream." Was not Paul an extremist for the Christian gospel: "I bear in my body the marks of the Lord Jesus." Was not Martin Luther an extremist: "Here I stand; I cannot do otherwise, so help me God." And John Bunyan: "I will stay in jail to the end of my days before I make a butchery of my conscience." And Abraham Lincoln: "This nation cannot survive half slave and half free." And Thomas Jefferson: "We hold these truths to be self-evident, that all men are created equal. . . ." So the question is not whether we will be extremists, but what kind of extremists we will be. Will we be extremists for hate or for love? Will we be extremists for the preservation of injustice or for the extension of justice? In that dramatic scene on Calvary's hill three men were crucified. We must never forget that all three were crucified for the same crime—the crime of extremism. Two were extremists for immorality, and thus fell below their environment. The other, Jesus Christ, was an extremist for love, truth, and goodness, and thereby rose above his environment. Perhaps the South, the nation, and the world are in dire need of creative extremists.

I had hoped that the white moderate would see this need. Perhaps I was too optimistic; perhaps I expected too much. I suppose I should have realized that few members of the oppressor race can understand the deep groans and passionate yearnings of the oppressed race, and still fewer have the vision to see that injustice must be rooted out by strong, persistent, and determined action. I am thankful, however, that some of our white brothers in the South have grasped the meaning of this social revolution and committed themselves to it. They are still all too few in quantity, but they are big in quality. Some—such as Ralph McGill, Lillian Smith, Harry Golden, James McBride Dabbs, Ann Braden, and Sarah Patton Boyle—have written about our struggle in eloquent and prophetic terms. Others have marched with us down nameless streets of the South. They have languished in filthy, roach-infested jails, suffering the abuse and brutality of policemen who view them as "dirty nigger-lovers." Unlike so many of their moderate brothers and sisters, they have recognized the urgency of the moment and sensed the need for powerful "action" antidotes to combat the disease of segregation.

Let me take note of my other major disappointment. I have been so greatly disappointed with the white church and its leadership. Of course, there are some notable exceptions. I am not unmindful of the fact that each of you has taken some significant stands on this issue. I commend you, Reverend Stallings, for your Christian stand on this past Sunday, in welcoming Negroes to your worship service on a nonsegregated basis. I commend the Catholic leaders of this state for integrating Spring Hill College several years ago.

But despite these notable exceptions, I must honestly reiterate that I have been disappointed with the church. I do not say this as one of those negative critics who can always find something wrong with the church. I say this as a minister of the gospel, who loves the church; who was nurtured in its bosom; who has been sustained by its spiritual blessings and who will remain true to it as long as the cord of life shall lengthen.

When I was suddenly catapulted into the leadership of the bus protest in Montgomery, Alabama, a few years ago, I felt we would be supported by the white church. I felt that the white ministers, priests, and rabbis of the South would be among our strongest allies. Instead, some have been outright opponents, refusing to understand the freedom movement and misrepresenting its leaders; all too many others have been more cautious than courageous and have remained silent behind the anesthetizing security of stained-glass windows. 35

In spite of my shattered dreams, I came to Birmingham with the hope that the white religious leadership of this community would see the justice of our cause and, with deep moral concern, would serve as the channel through which our just grievances could reach the power structure. I had hoped that each of you would understand. But again I have been disappointed. . . .

There was a time when the church was very powerful—in the time when the early Christians rejoiced at being deemed worthy to suffer for what they believed. In those days the church was not merely a thermometer that recorded the ideas and principles of popular opinion; it was a thermostat that transformed the mores of society. Whenever the early Christians entered a town, the people in power became disturbed and immediately sought to convict the Christians for being "disturbers of the peace" and "outside agitators." But the Christians pressed on, in the conviction that they were "a colony of heaven," called to obey God rather than man. Small in number, they were big in commitment. They were too God-intoxicated to be "astronomically intimidated." By their effort and example they brought an end to such ancient evils as infanticide and gladitorial contests.

Things are different now. So often the contemporary church is a weak, ineffectual voice with an uncertain sound. So often it is an arch-defender of the status quo. Far from being disturbed by the presence of the church, the power structure of the average community is consoled by the church's silent—and often even vocal—sanction of things as they are.

But the judgment of God is upon the church as never before. If today's church does not recapture the sacrificial spirit of the early church, it will lose its authenticity, forfeit the loyalty of millions, and be dismissed as an irrelevant social club with no meaning for the twentieth century. Every day I meet young people whose disappointment with the church has turned into outright disgust.

Perhaps I have once again been too optimistic. Is organized reli-   40
gion too inextricably bound to the status quo to save our nation and the world? Perhaps I must turn my faith to the inner spiritual church, the church within the church, as the true *ekklesia*[10] and the hope of the world. But again I am thankful to God that some noble souls from the ranks of organized religion have broken loose from the paralyzing chains of conformity and joined us as active partners in the struggle for free-dom. They have left their secure congregations and walked the streets of Albany, Georgia, with us. They have gone down the highways of the South on torturous rides for freedom. Yes, they have gone to jail with us. Some have been dismissed from their churches, have lost the support of their bishops and fellow ministers. But they have acted in the faith that right defeated is stronger than evil triumphant. Their witness has been the spiritual salt that has preserved the true meaning of the gospel in these troubled times. They have carved a tunnel of hope through the dark mountain of disappointment.

I hope the church as a whole will meet the challenge of this decisive hour. But even if the church does not come to the aid of justice, I have no despair about the future. I have no fear about the outcome of our struggle in Birmingham, even if our motives are at present misunderstood. We will reach the goal of freedom in Birmingham and all over the nation, because the goal of America is freedom. Abused and scorned though we may be, our destiny is tied up with America's destiny. Before the pilgrims landed at Plymouth, we were here. Before the pen of Jefferson etched the majestic words of the Declaration of Independence across the pages of history, we were here. For more than two centuries our forebears labored in this coun-try without wages; they made cotton king; they built the homes of their masters while suffering gross injustice and shameful humiliation—and yet out of a bottomless vitality they continued to thrive and develop. If the inex-pressible cruelties of slavery could not stop us, the opposition we now face will surely fail. We will win our freedom because the sacred heritage of our nation and the eternal will of God are embodied in our echoing demands.

---

10. *ekklesia:* word referring to the early Church and its spirit; from the Greek New Testament.

Before closing I feel impelled to mention one other point in your statement that has troubled me profoundly. You warmly commended the Birmingham police force for keeping "order" and "preventing violence." I doubt that you would have so warmly commended the police force if you had seen its dogs sinking their teeth into unarmed, nonviolent Negroes. I doubt that you would so quickly commend the policemen if you were to observe their ugly and inhumane treatment of Negroes here in the city jail; if you were to watch them push and curse old Negro women and young Negro girls; if you were to see them slap and kick old Negro men and young boys; if you were to observe them, as they did on two occasions, refuse to give us food because we wanted to sing our grace together. I cannot join you in your praise of the Birmingham police department.

It is true that the police have exercised a degree of discipline in handling the demonstrators. In this sense they have conducted themselves rather "nonviolently" in public. But for what purpose? To preserve the evil system of segregation. Over the past few years I have consistently preached that nonviolence demands that the means we use must be as pure as the ends we seek. I have tried to make clear that it is wrong to use immoral means to attain moral ends. But now I must affirm that it is just as wrong, or perhaps even more so, to use moral means to preserve immoral ends. Perhaps Mr. Connor and his policemen have been rather nonviolent in public, as was Chief Pritchett in Albany, Georgia, but they have used the moral means of nonviolence to maintain the immoral end of racial injustice. As T. S. Eliot has said, "The last temptation is the greatest treason: To do the right deed for the wrong reason."

I wish you had commended the Negro sit-inners and demonstrators of Birmingham for their sublime courage, their willingness to suffer, and their amazing discipline in the midst of great provocation. One day the South will recognize its real heroes. They will be the James Merediths,[11] with the noble sense of purpose that enables them to face jeering and hostile mobs, and with the agonizing loneliness that characterizes the life of the pioneer. They will be old, oppressed, battered Negro women, symbolized in a seventy-two-year-old woman in Montgomery, Alabama, who rose up with a sense of dignity and with her people decided not to ride segregated buses, and who responded with ungrammatical profundity to one who inquired about her weariness: "My feets is tired, but my soul is at rest." They will be the young high school and college students, the young ministers of the gospel and a host of their elders, courageously and nonviolently sitting in at lunch counters and willingly going to jail for conscience' sake. One day the South will know that when these disinherited children of God sat down at lunch counters, they were in reality standing up for what is best in the American dream and for the most sacred values in our Judaeo-Christian

---

11. In 1961 James Meredith became the first black student to enroll at the University of Mississippi, sparking considerable controversy and confrontation.

heritage, thereby bringing our nation back to those great wells of democracy which were dug deep by the founding fathers in their formulation of the Constitution and the Declaration of Independence.

Never before have I written so long a letter. I'm afraid it is much too long to take your precious time. I can assure you that it would have been much shorter if I had been writing from a comfortable desk, but what else can one do when he is alone in a narrow jail cell, other than write long letters, think long thoughts, and pray long prayers?   45

If I have said anything in this letter that overstates the truth and indicates an unreasonable impatience, I beg you to forgive me. If I have said anything that understates the truth and indicates my having a patience that allows me to settle for anything less than brotherhood, I beg God to forgive me.

I hope this letter finds you strong in the faith. I also hope that circumstances will soon make it possible for me to meet each of you, not as an integrationist or a civil-rights leader but as a fellow clergyman and a Christian brother. Let us all hope that the dark clouds of racial prejudice will soon pass away and the deep fog of misunderstanding will be lifted from our fear-drenched communities, and in some not too distant tomorrow the radiant stars of love and brotherhood will shine over our great nation with all their scintillating beauty.

Yours for the cause of Peace and Brotherhood,
MARTIN LUTHER KING, JR.

THINKING CRITICALLY ABOUT THE READING

1. King's letter was written in response to a published statement by eight white clergymen. What specific criticism did these men level at King and his followers? How does King respond to each objection?

2. King says that he advocates nonviolent resistance. What are the four basic steps of any nonviolent campaign? Why does King believe that the time for negotiations has passed?

3. According to King, what does the word *wait* (13) mean to the black community?

4. What does King see as the key difference between just and unjust laws? Explain.

5. The white clergy label King an *extremist* (30). What does this word mean to you? How does King turn being labeled an "extremist" to his advantage?

6. Why is King disappointed with the white church? What does he want the white clergy to do? In what ways has the church skirted its responsibilities to African Americans?

7. King says that he "stand[s] in the middle of two opposing forces in the Negro community" (27). What are those forces, and why does he see himself between them?

LANGUAGE IN ACTION

In paragraph 1, King explains that he seldom responds to criticism of his work, but in the case of the eight white clergymen, he has decided to answer. "Since I feel that you are men of genuine good will and that your criticisms are sincerely set forth, I want to try to answer your statement in what I hope will be patient and reasonable terms." To discover what it is about King's use of language that enables him to argue this contentious, emotional, and painful issue with such candor, reason, and thoughtfulness, reread paragraphs 14 and 44, circling or underlining words and phrases that you consider well chosen. What words or phrases help King make real for his readers the Negro community's "legitimate and unavoidable impatience" in paragraph 14 and the courage and discipline of the movement's "real heroes" in paragraph 44? How does King use language that enables him to be true to his position without alienating his audience? What insights into the power of language do these two paragraphs give you? Explain.

WRITING SUGGESTIONS

1. In paragraph 4, King boldly states, "Injustice anywhere is a threat to justice everywhere. We are caught in an inescapable network of mutuality, tied in a single garment of destiny. Whatever affects one directly, affects all indirectly." Write an essay in which you explore the truth in King's statement, using social and economic injustices that you see around you as examples.

2. King advocates nonviolent resistance as a way of confronting oppression. What other means of confronting oppression were available to him? What are the strengths and weaknesses of those alternatives? Write an essay in which you assess the effectiveness of nonviolent resistance in the light of its alternatives. Is nonviolent direct action still realistic or viable today? You may find it helpful to review what you wrote in response to the Writing to Discover prompt for this selection.

5

LANGUAGE ESSENTIALS

In "Language Essentials," six writers explore some language fundamentals that give us a greater understanding and appreciation for the miracle of language that we all share. In "Language and Thought," philosopher Susanne K. Langer explains how language separates humans from the rest of the animal kingdom. She demonstrates the power of language and shows "without it anything properly called 'thought' is impossible." While we might celebrate the remarkable resilience and flexibility of the English language, it can also tie us in knots, as Steven Pinker explains in "Words Don't Mean What They Mean." Pinker's essay is full of examples of how we all participate in an elaborate "linguistic dance" with each other whenever we try to communicate.

The following four selections are written by a new generation of scholars and researchers, all about forty years old. Their works attest to an endless fascination we have for language study and to a recognition of how much still needs to be done filling in the gaps in our understanding. In "Chunking," Ben Zimmer explains the theory that instead of learning the lexicon, or word-horde, of a language word by word as we assume is normal practice, we may in fact learn it in chunks or groups of words. The theory is somewhat controversial, but we're already applying it to the pedagogy of learning a second language. Erin McKean, a lexicographer, shows us in "Neologizing 101" some of the ways new words are created in English and how we can do it ourselves, if we are so inclined. Michael Erard in "An Uh, Er, Um Essay" addresses what we find so annoying in our speech and in the speech of others that we listen to — the use of filled pauses, such as *like* and *you know*. He argues that these disfluencies may not be such a bad thing, after all. Finally, Lera Boroditsky, in "Lost in Translation," reexamines one of the oldest and most intriguing of all theories of the interaction of language and the brain, the Sapir-Whorf hypothesis, also known as the linguistic relativity hypothesis. She and her fellow researchers have found new evidence that sheds light on the question: Does the language we speak shape reality, or does reality shape our language? Or, does it work both ways? Surely you will find her international explorations and the examples she brings to bear on the question fascinating.

In the e-Pages (available online at bedfordstmartins.com/languageaware ness/epages), Eric Sonstroem's audio piece "Play and Language" highlights the connection between children's play and language development.

Language and Thought

Susanne K. Langer

Susanne K. Langer was born in New York City in 1895 and attended Radcliffe College. There she studied philosophy, an interest she maintained until her death in 1985. She stayed in Cambridge, Massachusetts, as a tutor at Harvard University from 1927 to 1942. Langer then taught at the University of Delaware, Columbia University, and Connecticut College, where she remained from 1954 until the end of her distinguished teaching career. Her books include *Philosophy in a New Key: A Study of the Symbolism of Reason, Rite, and Art* (1942), *Feeling and Form* (1953), and *Mind: An Essay in Human Feeling* (1967).

In the following essay, which originally appeared in *Ms.* magazine, Langer explores how language separates humans from the rest of the animal kingdom. She contends that the use of symbols—in addition to the use of signs that animals also use—frees humans not only to react to their environment but also to think about it. Moreover, symbols allow us to create imagery and ideas not directly related to the real world, so that we can plan, imagine, and communicate abstractions—to do, in essence, the things that make us human.

WRITING TO DISCOVER: *Young children must often communicate—and be communicated to—without the use of language. To a child, for example, a danger sticker on a bottle can mean "don't touch," and a green traffic light might mean "the car will start again." Think back to your own childhood experiences. Write about how communication took place without language. What associations were you able to make?*

A symbol is not the same thing as a sign; that is a fact that psychologists and philosophers often overlook. All intelligent animals use signs; so do we. To them as well as to us sounds and smells and motions are signs of food, danger, the presence of other beings, or of rain or storm. Furthermore, some animals not only attend to signs but produce them for the benefit of others. Dogs bark at the door to be let in; rabbits thump to call each other; the cooing of doves and the growl of a wolf defending his kill are unequivocal signs of feelings and intentions to be reckoned with by other creatures.

We use signs just as animals do, though with considerably more elaboration. We stop at red lights and go on green; we answer calls and bells, watch the sky for coming storms, read trouble or promise or anger in each other's eyes. That is animal intelligence raised to the human level. Those of us who are dog lovers can probably all tell wonderful stories of how high our dogs have sometimes risen in the scale of clever sign interpretation and sign using.

A sign is anything that announces the existence or the imminence of some event, the presence of a thing or a person, or a change in the state of affairs. There are signs of the weather, signs of danger, signs of future good or evil, signs of what the past has been. In every case a sign is closely bound up with something to be noted or expected in experience. It is always a part of the situation to which it refers, though the reference may be remote in space and time. In so far as we are led to note or expect the signified event we are making correct use of a sign. This is the essence of rational behavior, which animals show in varying degrees. It is entirely realistic, being closely bound up with the actual objective course of history—learned by experience, and cashed in or voided by further experience.

If man had kept to the straight and narrow path of sign using, he would be like the other animals, though perhaps a little brighter. He would not talk, but grunt and gesticulate the point. He would make his wishes known, give warnings, perhaps develop a social system like that of bees and ants, with such a wonderful efficiency of communal enterprise that all men would have plenty to eat, warm apartments—all exactly alike and perfectly convenient—to live in, and everybody could and would sit in the sun or by the fire, as the climate demanded, not talking but just basking, with every want satisfied, most of his life. The young would romp and make love, the old would sleep, the middle-aged would do the routine work almost unconsciously and eat a great deal. But that would be the life of a social, superintelligent, purely sign-using animal.

To us who are human, it does not sound very glorious. We want to go places and do things, own all sorts of gadgets that we do not absolutely need, and when we sit down to take it easy we want to talk. Rights and property, social position, special talents and virtues, and above all our ideas, are what we live for. We have gone off on a tangent that takes us far away from the mere biological cycle that animal generations accomplish; and that is because we can use not only signs but symbols.

A symbol differs from a sign in that it does not announce the presence of the object, the being, condition, or whatnot, which is its meaning, but merely *brings this thing to mind*. It is not a mere "substitute sign" to which we react as though it were the object itself. The fact is that our reaction to hearing a person's name is quite different from our reaction to the person himself. There are certain rare cases where a symbol stands directly for its meaning: in religious experience, for instance, the Host is not only a symbol but a Presence. But symbols in the ordinary sense are not mystic. They are the same sort of thing that ordinary signs are; only they do not call our attention to something necessarily present or to be physically dealt with—they call up merely a conception of the thing they "mean."

The difference between a sign and a symbol is, in brief, that a sign causes us to think or act *in face* of the thing signified, whereas a symbol causes us to think *about* the thing symbolized. Therein lies the great importance of symbolism for human life, its power to make this life so different from any other animal biography that generations of men have found it incredible to suppose that they were of purely zoological origin. A sign is always embedded in reality, in a present that emerges from the actual past and stretches to the future; but a symbol may be divorced from reality altogether. It may refer to what is not the case, to a mere idea, a figment, a dream. It serves, therefore, to liberate thought from the immediate stimuli of a physically present world; and that liberation marks the essential difference between human and nonhuman mentality. Animals think, but they think *of* and *at* things; men think primarily *about* things. Words, pictures, and memory images are symbols that may be combined and varied in a thousand ways. The result is a symbolic structure whose meaning is a complex of all their respective meanings, and this kaleidoscope of *ideas* is the typical product of the human brain that we call the "stream of thought."

The process of transforming all direct experience into imagery or into that supreme mode of symbolic expression, language, has so completely taken possession of the human mind that it is not only a special talent but a dominant, organic need. All our sense impressions leave their traces in our memory not only as signs disposing our practical reactions in the future but also as symbols, images representing our *ideas* of things; and the tendency to manipulate ideas, to combine and abstract, mix and extend them by playing with symbols, is man's outstanding characteristic. It seems to be what his brain most naturally and spontaneously does. Therefore his primitive mental function is not judging reality, but *dreaming his desires.*

Dreaming is apparently a basic function of human brains, for it is free and unexhausting like our metabolism, heartbeat, and breath. It is easier to dream than not to dream, as it is easier to breathe than to refrain from breathing. The symbolic character of dreams is fairly well established. Symbol mongering, on this ineffectual, uncritical level, seems to be instinctive, the fulfillment of an elementary need rather than the purposeful exercise of a high and difficult talent.

The special power of man's mind rests on the evolution of this special activity, not on any transcendently high development of animal intelligence. We are not immeasurably higher than other animals; we are different. We have a biological need and with it a biological gift that they do not share.

Because man has not only the ability but the constant need of *conceiving* what has happened to him, what surrounds him, what is demanded of him—in short, of symbolizing nature, himself, and his hopes and fears—he has a constant and crying need of *expression*. What he cannot express, he cannot conceive; what he cannot conceive is chaos, and fills him with terror.

If we bear in mind this all-important craving for expression, we get a new picture of man's behavior; for from this trait spring his powers and his weaknesses. The process of symbolic transformation that all our experiences undergo is nothing more nor less than the process of *conception,* underlying the human faculties of abstraction and imagination.

When we are faced with a strange or difficult situation, we cannot react directly, as other creatures do, with flight, aggression, or any such simple instinctive pattern. Our whole reaction depends on how we manage to conceive the situation—whether we cast it in a definite dramatic form, whether we see it as a disaster, a challenge, a fulfillment of doom, or a fiat of the Divine Will. In words or dreamlike images, in artistic or religious or even in cynical form, we must *construe* the events of life. There is great virtue in the figure of speech, "I can *make* nothing of it," to express a failure to understand something. Thought and memory are processes of *making* the thought content and the memory image; the pattern of our ideas is given by the symbols through which we express them. And in the course of manipulating those symbols we inevitably distort the original experience, as we abstract certain features of it, embroider and reinforce those features with other ideas, until the conception we project on the screen of memory is quite different from anything in our real history.

Conception is a necessary and elementary process; what we do with our conceptions is another story. That is the entire history of human culture—of intelligence and morality, folly and superstition, ritual, language, and the arts—all the phenomena that set man apart from, and above, the rest of the animal kingdom. As the religious mind has to make all human history a drama of sin and salvation in order to define its own moral attitudes, so a scientist wrestles with the mere presentation of "the facts" before he can reason about them. The process of *envisaging* facts, values, hopes, and fears underlies our whole behavior pattern; and this process is reflected in the evolution of an extraordinary phenomenon found always, and only, in human societies—the phenomenon of language.

Language is the highest and most amazing achievement of the symbolistic human mind. The power it bestows is almost inestimable, for without it anything properly called "thought" is impossible. The birth of language is the dawn of humanity. The line between man and beast—between the highest ape and the lowest savage—is the language line. Whether the primitive Neanderthal man was anthropoid or human depends less on his cranial capacity, his upright posture, or even his use of tools and fire, than on one issue we shall probably never be able to settle—whether or not he spoke.

In all physical traits and practical responses, such as skills and visual judgments, we can find a certain continuity between animal and human

15

mentality. Sign using is an ever evolving, ever improving function through-out the whole animal kingdom, from the lowly worm that shrinks into his hole at the sound of an approaching foot, to the dog obeying his master's command, and even to the learned scientist who watches the movements of an index needle.

The continuity of the sign-using talent has led psychologists to the belief that language is evolved from the vocal expressions, grunts and coos and cries, whereby animals vent their feelings or signal their fellows; that man has elaborated this sort of communion to the point where it makes a perfect exchange of ideas possible.

I do not believe that this doctrine of the origin of language is correct. The essence of language is symbolic, not signific; we use it first and most vitally to formulate and hold ideas in our own minds. Conception, not social control, is its first and foremost benefit.

The essence of language is symbolic, not signific; we use it first and most vitally to formulate and hold ideas in our own minds.

Watch a young child, who is learning to speak, play with a toy; he says the name of the object, e.g.: "Horsey! horsey! horsey!" over and over again, looks at the object, moves it, always saying the name to himself or to the world at large. It's quite a time before he talks to anyone in par-ticular; he talks first of all to himself. This is his way of forming and fixing the *conception* of the object in his mind, and around this conception all his knowledge of it grows. *Names* are the essence of language; for the *name* is what abstracts the conception of the horse from the horse itself, and lets the mere idea recur at the speaking of the name. This permits the conception gathered from one horse experience to be exemplified again by another instance of a horse, so that the notion embodied in the name is a general notion.

To this end, the baby uses a word long before he *asks* for the object; when he wants his horsey he is likely to cry and fret, because he is reacting to an actual environment, not forming ideas. He uses the animal language of *signs* for his wants; talking is still a purely symbolic process—its prac-tical value has not really impressed him yet.

Language need not be vocal; it may be purely visual, like written lan-guage, or even tactual, like the deaf-mute system of speech; but it *must be denotative*. The sounds, intended or unintended, whereby animals com-municate do not constitute a language because they are signs, not names. They never fall into an organic pattern, a meaningful syntax of even the most rudimentary sort, as all language seems to do with a sort of driving necessity. That is because signs refer to actual situations, in which things have obvious relations to each other that require only to be noted; but symbols refer to ideas, which are not physically there for inspection, so their connections and features have to be represented. This gives all true

20

language a natural tendency toward growth and development, which seems almost like a life of its own. Languages are not invented; they grow with our need for expression.

In contrast, animal "speech" never has a structure. It is merely an emotional response. Apes may greet their ration of yams with a shout of "Nga!" But they do not say "Nga" between meals. If they could *talk about* their yams instead of just saluting them, they would be the most primitive men instead of the most anthropoid of beasts. They would have ideas, and tell each other things true and false, rational or irrational; they would make plans and invent laws and sing their own praises, as men do.

THINKING CRITICALLY ABOUT THE READING

1. What is Langer's thesis in this essay? Where does she state it? (Glossary: *Thesis*)

2. Define what Langer refers to as a *sign*. Define *symbol*. (Glossary: *Definition* and *Symbol*) Why is the distinction between the two so important?

3. What examples of signs and symbols does Langer provide? (Glossary: *Examples*) How effective do you find her examples? What examples of signs and symbols can you provide?

4. What is the essential difference between the way animals "think" and the way humans think? How has that changed human mental function at an organic level? How has the biological change affected our development in relation to animals?

5. In paragraph 11, Langer states: "What [man] cannot express, he cannot conceive; what he cannot conceive is chaos, and fills him with terror." Review the first ten paragraphs of the essay. How does Langer prepare the reader to accept this abstract and bold statement? (Glossary: *Concrete/Abstract* and *Organization*)

6. What does Langer mean when she says, "In words or dreamlike images . . . we must *construe* the events of life" (13)? How does this claim relate to the process of conception?

LANGUAGE IN ACTION

Review what Langer has to say about signs and symbols, particularly the differences she draws between them in paragraphs 6 and 7. Then examine the following graphics. What does each graphic mean? Which ones are signs, and which are symbols? Be prepared to defend your conclusions in a classroom discussion.

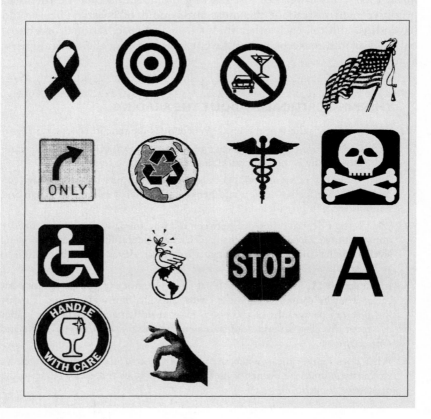

WRITING SUGGESTIONS

1. Using symbols for expression need not involve explicit use of language. Within the framework of a particular society, many methods of symbolic communication are possible. When you walk across campus, for example, what do you want to communicate to others even if you do not speak to anyone? How do you communicate this message? For instance, how does your facial expression, clothing, hairstyle, or jewelry serve as a symbol? Write an essay in which you describe and analyze the nonlanguage symbols you use to communicate.

2. It has often been said that language reveals the character of the person using it. Write an essay in which you analyze the character of a particular writer based on his or her use of language. You may want to comment on a writer in this text whose article you have read, such as Langer. Consider such areas as vocabulary range, sentence variety, slang, correct grammar, technical language, and tone. What do these elements tell you about the character of the person? (Glossary: *Slang, Technical Language,* and *Tone*)

3. Research recent experiments involving animal communication. Some experiments, for example, reveal the gorilla's use of sign language; others show that dolphins have complex communication systems that we are only beginning to understand. Write a paper in which you summarize the research and discuss how it relates to Langer's ideas about human and animal use of signs and symbols. Did you find any evidence that certain animals can use basic symbols? Is there a possibility that gorillas and dolphins can think *about* things rather than simply *of* and *at* them?

Words Don't Mean What They Mean

STEVEN PINKER

Internationally recognized language and cognition scholar and re-searcher Steven Pinker was born in Montreal, Canada, in 1954. He immi-grated to the United States shortly after receiving his B.A. from McGill University in 1976. After earning a doctorate from Harvard University in 1979, Pinker taught psychology at Harvard, Stanford University, and the Massachusetts Institute of Technology, where he directed the Center for Cognitive Neuroscience. Currently, he is professor of psychology at Harvard University. Since publishing *Language Learnability and Language Development* in 1984, Pinker has written extensively on language development in children. He has what one critic writing in the *New York Times Book Review* calls "that facility, so rare among scientists, of making the most difficult material . . . accessible to the average reader." The pop-ularity of Pinker's books *The Language Instinct* (1994), *How the Mind Works* (1997), *Words and Rules: The Ingredients of Language* (1999), *The Blank Slate: The Modern Denial of Human Nature* (2002), *The Stuff of Thought: Language As a Window into Human Nature* (2007), and *The Better Angels of Our Nature: Why Violence Has Declined* (2011) attests to the public's genuine interest in human nature and language.

In the following article, adapted from *The Stuff of Thought* and first published in the September 6, 2007, issue of *Time,* Pinker discusses how phrases convey different meanings in different contexts and how this flex-ibility can both help and hinder human communication and relationships. Pinker uses a number of examples from a wide range of endeavors to illustrate his points about words and the ways they work.

WRITING TO DISCOVER: *Have you ever found yourself in a conversation in which the words that were being spoken to you didn't mean what you supposed they meant? For example, if someone were to say "That's really nice" sarcastically, and you missed the sarcastic tone, you'd miss the meaning entirely. Describe such a situation that you've been in, and explain the difference in meaning between the words being spoken and the intended meaning.*

In the movie *Tootsie,* the character played by Dustin Hoffman is dis-guised as a woman and is speaking to a beautiful young actress played by Jessica Lange. During a session of late-night girl talk, Lange's character says, "You know what I wish? That a guy could be honest enough to walk up to me and say, 'I could lay a big line on you, but the simple truth is I find you very interesting, and I'd really like to make love to you.' Wouldn't that be a relief?"

Later in the movie, a twist of fate throws them together at a cocktail party, this time with Hoffman's character dressed as a man. The actress doesn't recognize him, and he tries out the speech on her. Before he can even finish, she throws a glass of wine in his face and storms away.

When people talk, they lay lines on each other, do a lot of role playing, sidestep, shilly-shally and engage in all manner of vagueness and innuendo. We do this and expect others to do it, yet at the same time we profess to long for the plain truth, for people to say what they mean, simple as that. Such hypocrisy is a human universal.

Sexual come-ons are a classic example. "Would you like to come up and see my etchings?" has been recognized as a double entendre for so long that by 1939, James Thurber could draw a cartoon of a hapless man in an apartment lobby saying to his date, "You wait here, and I'll bring the etchings down."

The veiled threat also has a stereotype: the Mafia wiseguy offering   5
protection with the soft sell, "Nice store you got there. Would be a real shame if something happened to it." Traffic cops sometimes face not-so-innocent questions like, "Gee, Officer, is there some way I could pay the fine right here?" And anyone who has sat through a fund-raising dinner is familiar with euphemistic schnorring like, "We're counting on you to show leadership."

Why don't people just say what they mean? The reason is that conversational partners are not modems downloading information into each other's brains. People are very, very touchy about their relationships. Whenever you speak to someone, you are presuming the two of you have a certain degree of familiarity—which your words might alter. So every sentence has to do two things at once: convey a message and continue to negotiate that relationship.

The clearest example is ordinary politeness. When you are at a dinner party and want the salt, you don't blurt out, "Gimme the salt." Rather, you use what linguists call a whimperative, as in "Do you think you could pass the salt?" or "If you could pass the salt, that would be awesome."

Taken literally, these sentences are inane. The second is an overstatement, and the answer to the first is obvious. Fortunately, the hearer assumes that the speaker is rational and listens between the lines. Yes, your point is to request the salt, but you're doing it in such a way that first takes care to establish what linguists call "felicity conditions," or the prerequisites to making a sensible request. The underlying rationale is that the hearer not be given a command but simply be asked or advised about one of the necessary conditions for passing the salt. Your goal is to have your need satisfied without treating the listener as a flunky who can be bossed around at will.

Warm acquaintances go out of their way not to look as if they are presuming a dominant-subordinate relationship but rather one of equals. It works the other way too. When people are in a subordinate relationship (like a driver with police), they can't sound as if they are presuming anything more than that, so any bribe must be veiled. Fund raisers, simulating an atmosphere of warm friendship with their donors, also can't break the spell with a bald businesslike proposition.

It is in the arena of sexual relationships, however, that the linguistic   10
dance can be its most elaborate. In an episode of *Seinfeld,* George is asked by his date if he would like to come up for coffee. He declines, explaining that caffeine keeps him up at night. Later he slaps his forehead: " 'Coffee' doesn't mean coffee! 'Coffee' means sex!" The moment is funny, but it's also a reminder of just how carefully romantic partners must always tread. Make too blatant a request, as in *Tootsie,* and the hearer is offended; too subtle, as in *Seinfeld,* and it can go over the hearer's head.

In the political arena, miscalibrated speech can lead to more serious consequences than wine in the face or a slap on the forehead. In 1980, Wanda Brandstetter, a lobbyist for the National Organization for Women (NOW), tried to get an Illinois state representative to vote for the Equal Rights Amendment (ERA) by handing him a business card on which she had written, "Mr. Swanstrom, the offer for help in your election, plus $1,000 for your campaign for the pro-ERA vote." A prosecutor called the note a "contract for bribery," and the jury agreed.

So how do lobbyists in Gucci Gulch bribe legislators today? They do it with innuendo. If Brandstetter had said, "As you know, Mr. Swanstrom, NOW has a history of contributing to political campaigns. And it has contributed more to candidates with a voting record that is compatible with our goals. These days one of our goals is the ratification of the ERA," she would have avoided a fine, probation and community service.

Indirect speech has a long history in diplomacy, too. In the wake of the Six-Day War in 1967, the U.N. Security Council passed its famous Resolution 242, which called for the "withdrawal of Israeli armed forces from territories occupied in the recent conflict." The wording is ambiguous. Does it mean "some of the territories" or "all of the territories"? In some ways it was best not to ask, since the phrasing was palatable to Israel and its allies only under the former interpretation and to concerned Arab states and their allies only under the latter. Unfortunately, for 40 years partisans have been debating the semantics of Resolution 242, and the Israeli-Arab conflict remains unresolved, to put it mildly.

That's not to say such calculated ambiguity never works for diplomats. After all, the language of an agreement has to be acceptable not just to leaders but to their citizens. Reasonable leaders might thus come to an understanding between themselves, while each exploits the ambiguities of the deal to sell it to their country's more bellicose factions. What's more, diplomats can gamble that times will change and circumstances will bring the two sides together, at which point they can resolve the vagueness amicably.

When all else fails, as it often does, nations can sort out their problems   15
without any words at all—and often without fighting either. In these cases, they may fall back on communicating through what's known as

authority ranking, also known as power, status, autonomy and dominance. The logic of authority ranking is "Don't mess with me." Its biological roots are in the dominance hierarchies that are widespread in the animal kingdom. One animal claims the right to a contested resource based on size, strength, seniority or allies, and the other animal cedes it when the outcome of the battle can be predicted and both sides have a stake in not getting bloodied in a fight whose winner is a forgone conclusion. Such sword-rattling gestures as a larger military power's conducting "naval exercises" in the waters off the coast of a weaker foe are based on just this kind of preemptive reminder of strength.

> **Words let us say the things we want to say and also things we would be better off not having said.**

People often speak of indirect speech as a means of saving face. What we're referring to is not just a matter of hurt feelings but a social currency with real value. The expressive power of words helps us guard this prized asset, but only as long as we're careful. Words let us say the things we want to say and also things we would be better off not having said. They let us know the things we need to know, and also things we wish we didn't. Language is a window into human nature, but it is also a fistula, an open wound through which we're exposed to an infectious world. It's not surprising that we sheathe our words in politeness and innuendo and other forms of doublespeak.

THINKING CRITICALLY ABOUT THE READING

1. Pinker opens his essay with an extended example from the movie *Tootsie*. What point about language does this example illustrate?

2. Pinker creates a number of categories for the ways in which people "lay lines on each other, do a lot of role playing, sidestep, shilly-shally and engage in all manner of vagueness and innuendo" (3). Explain these categories and provide an example of your own for each. In your opinion, do any of the categories overlap?

3. What do you think Pinker means when he says, "Such hypocrisy is a human universal" (3)? Do you believe that this hypocrisy is necessary? What would need to change for us to speak the "plain truth" to each other?

4. Why, according to Pinker, do people have so much trouble conversing? How is a conversation between two humans different from a conversation between two modems?

5. What are "felicity conditions" (8)? Describe several situations in which you have used "felicity conditions." Have you ever tried but failed to establish these conditions? Explain what happened.

6. Explain what "indirect speech" (13) is. Why do you think people resort to indirect speech? Why is it not surprising that indirect speech has a long history in the arenas of politics and diplomacy?

LANGUAGE IN ACTION

Read the following English folktale, which is taken from Joseph Jacob's 1890 book *English Fairy Tales*. What do you learn about the nature of words from this story? Explain. How do you think Steven Pinker would respond to this folktale?

From "Master of all Masters"

A girl once went to a fair to be hired as a servant. At last a funny-looking old gentleman engaged her and took her home to his house. When she got there he told her he had something to teach her for in his house he had his own names for things.

He said to her: "What will you call me?"
"Master or Mister or whatever you please, sir."
"You must call me 'Master of Masters.' And what would you call this?" pointing to his bed.
"Bed or couch or whatever you please, sir."
"No, that's my 'barnacle.' And what do you call these?" said he, pointing to his pants.
"Breeches or trousers or whatever you please, sir."
"You must call them 'squibs and crackers.' And what do you call her?" pointing to the cat.
"Kit or cat or whatever you please, sir."
"You must call her 'white-faced simminy.' And this now," showing the fire, "what would you call this?"
"Fire or flame or whatever you please, sir."
"You must call it 'hot cockalorum,' and what this?" he went on, pointing to the water.
"Water or wet or whatever you please, sir."
"No, 'pandalorum' is its name. And what do you call this?" asked he, as he pointed to the house.
"House or cottage or whatever you please, sir."
"You must call it 'high topper mountain.'"

That very night the servant woke her master up in a fright and said: "Master of all masters, get out of your barnacle and put on your squibs and crackers. For white-face simminy has got a spark of hot cockalorum on its tail, and unless you get some pandalorum high topper mountain will be all on hot cockalorum." . . . That's all.

WRITING SUGGESTIONS

1. According to Pinker, "It is in the arena of sexual relationships . . . that the linguistic dance can be most elaborate." He supports this claim with examples from an episode of *Seinfeld* and the movie *Tootsie*. What exactly is the "linguistic dance" to which he refers? Does your own experience or that

of your friends with the language used in any dating relationship support or contradict Pinker's claim? How would you characterize conversations in these relationships? Write an essay in which you examine the language between partners in dating relationships. You may find it helpful to compare their language with that of other relationships; for example, is their language as indirect as that of nondating friends?

2. What does Pinker mean when he says, "Language is a window into human nature, but it is also a fistula, an open wound through which we're exposed to an infectious world" (16)? In what ways can language be considered an "open wound"? Why do you suppose that Pinker is not surprised "that we sheathe our words in politeness and innuendo and other forms of doublespeak" (16)? What evidence does he provide to justify his lack of surprise? Are you convinced? Why or why not? Write a paper in which you explore the meaning of Pinker's concluding remarks about language.

Chunking

BEN ZIMMER

Ben Zimmer was born in 1971 and graduated from Yale University in 1992 with a B.A. in linguistics. He has also studied linguistic anthropology at the University of Chicago. From 2006 to 2008 Zimmer was an editor for American dictionaries for Oxford University Press and was a consultant to the *Oxford English Dictionary*. From March 2010 to February 2011, he wrote the "On Language" column made popular by the late William Safire. Zimmer is now the executive producer of the *Visual Thesaurus* and *Vocabulary.com*. Zimmer's work has been reprinted in two blog anthologies, *Far from the Madding Gerund* (2006) and *Ultimate Blogs* (2008). He has also written for *Slate* and the *Boston Globe* and can be followed on Twitter.

In the following selection, which first appeared in the *New York Times* on September 16, 2010, Zimmer describes the language acquisition theory known as "chunking." As Zimmer says, however, "not everyone is on board" with the theory and how it is now being used by some instructors to teach English as a second language.

WRITING TO DISCOVER: *Some people complain that when we run into a friend and ask, "Hey, how are you?," we really don't ask that question to find out how the person is, that we don't mean the question literally and that we are simply using a canned phrase as a way of saying hello. Have you found yourself using similarly prefabricated phrases as a shorthand method of speaking and writing? If so, what kind of response do you usually receive?*

My ebullient 4-year-old son, Blake, is a big fan of the CDs and DVDs that the band They Might Be Giants recently produced for the kiddie market. He'll gleefully sing along to "Seven," a catchy tune from their 2008 album "Here Come the 123s" that tells of a house overrun by anthropomorphic number sevens. The first one is greeted at the door: "Oh, there's the doorbell. Let's see who's out there. Oh, it's a seven. Hello, Seven. Won't you come in, Seven? Make yourself at home."

Despite the song's playful surrealism (more and more sevens arrive, filling up the living room), the opening lines are routine and formulaic. The polite ritual of answering the door and inviting a guest into your house relies on certain fixed phrases in English: "Won't you come in?" "Make yourself at home."

As Blake learned these pleasantries through the song and its video, I wondered how much—or how little—his grasp of basic linguistic etiquette is grounded in the syntactical rules that structure how words are combined in English. An idiom like "Make yourself at home" is rather tricky if you stop to think about it: the imperative verb "make" is followed by a second-person reflexive pronoun ("yourself") and an adverbial phrase ("at home"), but it's difficult to break the phrase into its components. Instead, we grasp the whole thing at once.

Ritualized moments of everyday communication—greeting someone, answering a telephone call, wishing someone a happy birthday—are full of these canned phrases that we learn to perform with rote precision at an early age. Words work as social lubricants in such situations, and a language learner like Blake is primarily getting a handle on the pragmatics of set phrases in English, or how they create concrete effects in real-life interactions. The abstract rules of sentence structure are secondary.

In recent decades, the study of language acquisition and instruction has increasingly focused on "chunking": how children learn language not so much on a word-by-word basis but in larger "lexical chunks" or meaningful strings of words that are committed to memory. Chunks may consist of fixed idioms or conventional speech routines, but they can also simply be combinations of words that appear together frequently, in patterns that are known as "collocations." In the 1960s, the linguist Michael Halliday pointed out that we tend to talk of "strong tea" instead of "powerful tea," even though the phrases make equal sense. Rain, on the other hand, is much more likely to be described as "heavy" than "strong."

A native speaker picks up thousands of chunks like "heavy rain" or "make yourself at home" in childhood, and psycholinguistic research suggests that these phrases are stored and processed in the brain as individual units. As the University of Nottingham linguist Norbert Schmitt has explained, it is much less taxing cognitively to have a set of ready-made lexical chunks at our disposal than to have to work through all the possibilities of word selection and sequencing every time we open our mouths.

Cognitive studies of chunking have been bolstered by computer-driven analysis of usage patterns in large databases of texts called "corpora." As linguists and lexicographers build bigger and bigger corpora (a major-league corpus now contains billions of words, thanks to readily available online texts), it becomes clearer just how "chunky" the language is, with certain words showing undeniable attractions to certain others.

> **It becomes clearer just how "chunky" the language is, with certain words showing undeniable attractions to certain others.**

Many English-language teachers have been eager to apply corpus findings in the classroom to zero in on salient chunks rather than individual vocabulary words. This is especially so among teachers of English as a second language, since it's mainly the knowledge of chunks that allows nonnative speakers to advance toward nativelike fluency. In his 1993 book,

5

The Lexical Approach, Michael Lewis set out a program of action, and the trend has continued in such recent works as *From Corpus to Classroom: Language Use and Language Teaching* and *Teaching Chunks of Language: From Noticing to Remembering.*

Not everyone is on board, however. Michael Swan, a British writer on language pedagogy, has emerged as a prominent critic of the lexical-chunk approach. Though he acknowledges, as he told me in an e-mail, that "high-priority chunks need to be taught," he worries that "the 'new toy' effect can mean that formulaic expressions get more attention than they deserve, and other aspects of language—ordinary vocabulary, grammar, pronunciation and skills—get sidelined."

Swan also finds it unrealistic to expect that teaching chunks will produce nativelike proficiency in language learners. "Native English speakers have tens or hundreds of thousands—estimates vary—of these formulae at their command," he says. "A student could learn 10 a day for years and still not approach native-speaker competence."   10

Besides, Swan warns, "overemphasizing 'scripts' in our teaching can lead to a phrase-book approach, where formulaic learning is privileged and the more generative parts of language—in particular the grammatical system—are backgrounded." Formulaic language is all well and good when talking about the familiar and the recurrent, he argues, but it is inadequate for dealing with novel ideas and situations, where the more open-ended aspects of language are paramount.

The methodology of the chunking approach is still open to this type of criticism, but data-driven reliance on corpus research will most likely dominate English instruction in coming years. Lexical chunks have entered the house of language teaching, and they're making themselves at home.

THINKING CRITICALLY ABOUT THE READING

1. What do the terms "chunking" and "collocation" mean in your own words? With what "lexical chunks" are you familiar?
2. What are "corpora" and how do they help teachers of English as a second language?
3. What are the arguments against using chunking as an approach to teaching a language? Do you agree or disagree with those arguments? Why or why not?
4. Does Zimmer think that the opponents of lexical chunking will prevail or does he believe that the chunking approach to language acquisition will dominate in the years ahead? Explain.
5. Why was the chunking approach to teaching and learning a language not available until recently? Explain.

LANGUAGE IN ACTION

Linguists tell us that we cannot identify expressions as chunks with any certainty unless we have corpora at our disposal to check their validity. We can, however, use our intuition and perhaps come close to identifying chunks in the language used around us. Try, for example, to identify chunks used in the following passage by bracketing them. Compare your choices with others in your class and discuss your choices.

> The basketball game was a stunning success for our team. We had endured devastating injuries in the previous contests this season and we weren't sure how our team would rise to the occasion on Saturday night. Playing as a team made all the difference, however, as did Coach Taylor's strategy for the game. By cleverly using his bench and making timely player substitutions he was able to keep the Wildcats off balance throughout most of the game. Coach Taylor's use of the clock in the waning moments of the game deserves special attention and may be the explanation of how we finally snatched victory from the jaws of defeat.

WRITING SUGGESTIONS

1. Write an essay in support of or opposition to the use of chunking as a way of teaching vocabulary to students of English as a second language. You might want to begin your research with the two writers that Zimmer cites, Michael Lewis and Michael Swan, and go into more depth about the specific goals and strategies of teachers using chunking.

2. In his famous essay "Politics and the English Language" (pp. 234–247), George Orwell took a critical approach to the use of prefabricated phrases of the kind that we now refer to as "chunks," particularly in political speeches and texts. Read his essay and write one of your own in which you analyze his concerns in light of what you now know about teaching vocabulary using such prefabricated expressions.

Neologizing 101

ERIN MCKEAN

Erin McKean is a lexicographer, or maker of dictionaries. She was born in Charlotte, North Carolina, in 1971. In 1993 she graduated from the University Chicago with a dual A.B./M.A. degree in linguistics but, as a profile in the *University of Chicago Magazine* explains, she "has been trying to figure out how the language works since she was eight years old." McKean began her professional career as a student working on the Oriental Institute's Akkadian dictionary and later interned at Thorndike-Barnhart Publishers creating children's dictionaries, all the while bringing up something about dictionaries in every class she took at Chicago. She was the editor-in-chief of the *New Oxford American Dictionary,* Second Edition (2005), and she has gathered both new words that don't make it into the dictionary and old words that may be falling out of usage into three books, *Weird and Wonderful Words* (2002), *More Weird and Wonderful Words* (2003), and *Totally Weird and Wonderful Words* (2006). McKean is also the founder of *Wordnik.com.* Most recently she published her first novel, *The Secret Lives of Dresses* (2011). Asked what observations about being a lexicographer she would like to share with her readers, McKean offered the following: "If there's anything I've learned in twenty years as a lexicographer, it's that the urge to create new words is both inexhaustible and awe-inspiring. Every time I encounter a new word I marvel at the inventive power of English and English speakers."

In "Neologizing 101," which first appeared in the *New York Times* on August 25, 2002, McKean explains how new words are created in English and the principles you should adhere to should you want to create your own new words.

WRITING TO DISCOVER: *Have you ever wondered where the words we use come from? Have you ever thought that at some point in history every word had to be created by someone? Have you also wondered how those words enter our dictionaries?*

If you've ever heard yourself saying, "He was, I don't know, squidgeral," or thought, "I wish there were a word for 'needing more than two hands to operate,'" you are probably a closet neologist. Neologizing, the practice of coining new words, may seem to be an arcane, specialized activity, but it's everywhere—and the skillful employment of neologism is what gives English much of its verve. Each word in English had to start with a person trying to express a thought. For most words, the neologizer (or neologizers—new words, like *teenage trends* or the *calculus,* are likely to pop up at the same time in very different places) is anonymous, although there are some exceptions. The humorist Gelett Burgess coined the word *blurb* in 1907. *Yester-year,* which sounds ancient, was in fact coined in 1870 by Dante Gabriel Rossetti, who wanted to translate a French word for which he couldn't find a suitable English equivalent. Paul Lewis, a professor of English at Boston College, invented the word *Frankenfood* ("genetically modified food") in a letter to *The Times* in 1992. New words are being invented every day, and some of them even make it into the dictionary.

Neologizing, the practice of coining new words, may seem to be an arcane, specialized activity, but it's everywhere—and the skillful employment of neologism is what gives English much of its verve.

Although English has no committee or academy or board that reviews new words for suitability, there are a few loose guidelines that will help you become a successful neologist.

The most important rule is unwritten but not unspoken. It is the rule of pronounceability. Sure, xzyqt looks grand, but how do you say it? If Pat Sajak has taught us anything, it is this: be sure to buy enough vowels. If the pronunciation doesn't come trippingly off your tongue, move unfriendly tongue-twister consonants farther apart. English is pretty forgiving of the "uh" sound (often called *schwa*) and can insert it almost anywhere. Can't say dreklistic easily? Try drekilistic.

Avoid spellings that have too many possible sounds. Consider mallough: is it "maloo" or "maluff"? No one likes a silent letter, even when deployed for humorous or allusive reasons. (Old joke. Q: How do you pronounce Hen3ry? A: HEN-ree. The "3" is silent.) If your word is too difficult to spell, people will avoid it out of fear or irritation. Tied in with spelling is the ease of writing. Internal punctuation (like ca!met or we?zem) is a nearly insurmountable obstacle as well as a pronunciation problem. Unless you are a major pop star (or even if), don't invent your own alphabetic characters. Very few people will want to add a new character to their fonts just for your word.

You don't have to build your word from scratch; there are many lists   5
of word parts (roots and affixes) available on the Internet and in bookstores (thank SAT prep for that). Either choose your meaning and look for parts or choose your parts and look for meaning. If you're dying to have a new word that means "overly eager to speak," you might look for roots acer- ("fierce, eager") and dict- ("speak") and then add a suffix that makes adjectives, like -ous, to get acerdictous. (Take care that your suffixes correspond to the part of speech you want. Acerdictous doesn't look like a noun, so it would be odd in a sentence like "I saw a purple acerdictous today." It's much better in a sentence like "He was so acerdictous that he took over the whole meeting.")

If you are fond of the parts bathy- ("relating to depth") and -ster ("a person engaged in or associated with a particular activity or thing"), you might go through ideas until you got bathyster, "a particularly deep person." If you don't find parts for your meaning, find a dictionary with good etymologies and look up related words. Avoid ordinary words. If you're looking for a part that means "angry," don't look up angry. Look up irate. That gets you the Latin root ira ("anger"). Can't think of a fancier word for what you want? Use a thesaurus.

Finicky word purists might tell you that your new word is macaronic. Do they mean it's cheesy? No, just that it uses roots from two or more languages, like the Latin root and Greek prefix in automobile. (In the word-coining world, words derived from just one language are seen as more sincere. However, this didn't stop automobile, and it shouldn't stop you.)

If the grandeur of Greek and the glory of Latin roots aren't inspiring enough, you may have just as much success merging ordinary words together. Humongous (probably from huge and monstrous) and ginormous (gigantic and enormous) are two similar and fairly recent blends of everyday words.

Be practical in choosing your meanings. It's easier for a new word to gain acceptance if it denotes something for which we don't already have a handy word. Trying to persuade people to use your word kwillum instead of the already accepted wall won't work. If kwillum means "wall being fought over by neighbors," you have a better chance. Invented the perfect word yesterday and want it in the dictionary tomorrow? Be patient. It can take years or decades for a new word to be accepted. You may not ever see your creation in a dictionary, especially if it was a word created for just one use or publication. The joy of having created a word of your very own should be enough. Set on seeing squidgeral between squid and squiffed? Sending a letter to dictionary editors demanding inclusion isn't the way. Try to get your word used in major media sources (for example, a major newspaper — not just on the Internet or in local or specialist publications) more than a dozen times, by people other than yourself, over a period of several years. (Or push it on your sitcom-writing friends and hope for a Seinfeldian sociological phenomenon.) Even that's not a guarantee; it just gets your word to the starting line. If your word isn't having much luck finding its way to mouths and pens, well, you can always coin another one. And another one after that.

THINKING CRITICALLY ABOUT THE READING

1. Why is the "uh" sound useful to neologists, according to McKean?
2. In paragraph 1, McKean tells us that Paul Lewis created the word *Frankenfood*. Why do you think he chose that name for "genetically altered food"?
3. By what different means were the words *automobile* and *ginormous* formed?
4. McKean says that in the "coining world" words made from parts of one rather than several languages is more sincere. Why do you suppose that's so?

5. Why does McKean write that it's hard for a new word to make it into the dictionary? What advice does she give for increasing the chances of that happening, especially if you are a neologist looking to make history?

LANGUAGE IN ACTION

Another way of making new words that McKean does not examine in her essay is the use of acronyms, or words made from the initials of the words in phrases, such as *laser* for *light amplification through the stimulated emission of radiation*. Discuss in class what the following acronyms stand for (you may also want to add some acronyms of your own):

NATO

scuba

OPEC

Interpol

Necco

AIDS

radar

loran

Initialisms are yet other neologisms. They are sounded out as letters and perhaps even more frequently written. Discuss in class the meanings of these popular texting initialisms (you may also want to add some initialisms of your own):

IMO

b/c

BTW

OMG

ICYMI

LOL

FB

LMAO

WRITING SUGGESTIONS

1. Write an essay explaining what the practice of neologizing says about the English language, the people who speak it, their culture, their history, or any other implications that you see in our desire to make new words.

2. McKean examines several ways we add new words to the English language. The Language in Action exercise above examines acronyms and initialisms, two other ways we neologize. Write an essay in which you describe and illustrate with examples other ways in which new words are added: borrowing, coinage, clipping, eponymy, and functional shift. Of course, any well-written essay would not only lay out the processes with examples but would also frame it within a thesis.

An Uh, Er, Um Essay

Michael Erard

Michael Erard graduated from Williams College and has graduate degrees in linguistics and rhetoric from the University of Texas at Austin. He has lived in South America and Asia and has written about languages and linguistics for a number of publications, including *Science, Seed, Wired,* the *Atlantic,* the *New York Times,* and *New Scientist,* and he has been a contributing writer for the *Texas Observer* and *Design Observer.* His first book was *Um . . . : Slips, Stumbles, and Verbal Blunders, and What They Mean* (2008), which he published to rave notices, among them this one from the reviewer for the *Louisville Courier-Journal:* "You can feel when an author is enjoying himself, and Erard's survey of these most common dysfunctions in our dysfunctional society is written with unexpected humor, grace and high spirits." In his second book, *Babel No More: The Search for the World's Most Extraordinary Language Learners* (2012), Erard examines the world's greatest hyperpolyglots, especially Giuseppe Cardinal Mezzofanti, who in the nineteenth century had an expert command of thirty-nine languages.

In the following essay, which was first published in *Slate* on July 26, 2011, Erard discusses the "uhs," "ers," and "ums" that pepper most people's speech and reveals a new attitude toward their use based on his research.

WRITING TO DISCOVER: *Do you insert "uhs," "ers," and "ums" at intervals in your speech? Most of us do, but have you ever wished you didn't use them? Have you wondered what function they serve? Do they annoy you when you speak? Do they annoy you when others insert them into their speech?*

Modish public speaking coaches will tell you that it's OK to say "uh" or "um" once in a while, but the prevailing wisdom is that you should avoid such "disfluencies" or "discourse particles" entirely. It's thought that they repel listeners and make speakers appear unprepared, unconfident, stupid, or anxious (or all of these together). Perhaps the biggest foe of "uh" and "um" is Toastmasters International, which charges speakers a nickel for every "filled" pause (that is, for every pause that's not silent). Each of their 12,500 clubs around the world has an official "ah" counter.

But "uh" and "um" don't deserve eradication; there's no good reason to uproot them. People have been pausing and filling their pauses with a neutral vowel (or sometimes with an actual word) for as long as we've had language, which is about 100,000 years. If listeners are so naturally repelled by "uhs" and "ums," you'd think those sounds would have been eliminated long before now. The opposite is true: Filled pauses appear in all of the world's languages, and the anti-ummers have no way to explain, if they're so ugly, what "euh" in French, or "äh" and "ähm" in German, or "eto" and "ano" in Japanese are doing in human language at all.

In the history of oratory and public speaking, the notion that good speaking requires umlessness is actually a fairly recent, and very American, invention. It didn't emerge as a cultural standard until the early twentieth century, when the phonograph and radio suddenly held up to speakers' ears all the quirks and warbles that, before then, had flitted by. Another development was the codification of public speaking as an academic subject. Counting "ums" and noting perfect fluency gave teachers something to score.

> **If listeners are so naturally repelled by "uhs" and "ums," you'd think those sounds would have been eliminated long before now.**

What's more, "uhs" and "ums" do not necessarily damage a speaker's standing. Recently, a University of Michigan research team turned their attention to phone survey interviewers. They found that the most successful interviewers—the ones who convinced respondents to stay on the line and answer questions—spoke moderately fast and paused occasionally, either silently or with a filler "uh" or "um." "If interviewers made no pauses at all," the lead researcher, Jose Benki, told *Science Daily*, "they had the lowest success rates getting people to agree to do the survey. We think that's because they sound too scripted." Speaking with a certain number of "uhs" and "ums," it seems, may actually enhance a speaker's credibility.

Blithely unaware of the evidence, some parents—call them linguistic tiger moms—strive to keep filled pauses out of their kids' mouths. In April, Sarah Groves wrote an essay in the *Christian Science Monitor* about training her children to be umless. Her son was torturing her with questions like, "That man, um, not Hector, um er that man, not Paris, um, that man, not . . ." After discussing the situation with her husband ("I want to love them by teaching them to be articulate"), she told her son, "Before you speak you must think, 'This is what I'm going to say,' and then when you start to speak you mustn't think about anything else except what you decided you were going to say. Then you say it, quick and clear, with no um's and no er's." Apparently the 5-year-old mastered umlessness in two days.

Yet studies suggest that "uh" and "um" play an active role in how we learn language and communicate. A University of Rochester lab published a paper this spring showing that kids over 2 were more likely to pay attention to an unfamiliar object if the speaker said "uh" before stating its name. Presumably, this tactic gives children a leg up on parsing an adult's speech. Take the example of the mother who says to her child, "No, that wasn't the telephone, honey. That was the, uh, timer." The "uh" indicates that there's a word coming up that might be new and unfamiliar, so extra attention is required.

Of course, "uh" and "um" don't have some magic monopoly on focusing a listener's attention. In a study published in PLoS ONE last May, Martin Corley and Robert J. Hartsuiker reported that listeners' recognition benefits from any delay before a word, whether it's a silent pause, a filled pause, or a musical tone. The delay "attunes the attention."

In the Rochester study, kids *under* 2 didn't respond to "uh" at all—they didn't seem to tune out or tune in—which probably means they hadn't yet learned to interpret "uh" as a clue to adults' intentions. The authors suggest this ability appears at some point in the second year. They don't say anything about when kids start to *say* "um," which must happen on a different time line, because my 20-month-old son recently uttered his first. Given my fascination with filled pauses, it was a happy day, and I considered sending out greeting cards to celebrate the accomplishment.

The momentous exchange went something like this:

Grandfather: Hey, Iver, how's it hanging?
Iver: Um . . . wheels?

THINKING CRITICALLY ABOUT THE READING

1. What is Erard's thesis? Do you agree with it? Why or why not?
2. With what information does Erard support his thesis?
3. What are "linguistic tiger moms"? Why do you think they are so named?
4. What point is Erard making by describing the different way kids over two and under two years old responded in the Rochester study?
5. What significance do you see in the way Iver responded to his grandfather's question?

LANGUAGE IN ACTION

Discuss in class the following statement by Lisa B. Marshall, a public speaking coach:

> Recently I attended a training course in New York City and at the start of the course each of us introduced ourselves. The senior executive sitting next to me said, and I quote, "I, like, work for a big bank, like, a large banking institution. I work, um, in technology, and head up a group of like, 500 people, right. I do, like, technology risk assessment, right, and create, um, processes, to, like, reduce risk, right."
>
> I was shocked.

Are you shocked?

WRITING SUGGESTIONS

1. Write an essay modeled on Erard's in which you, too, delve into the subject of disfluencies. Base your essay on research in the field and be sure to provide a strong thesis with plenty of evidence, especially illustrative examples, to support your argument.

2. One of the most frequently used, and most frequently maligned, disfluencies in English is the use of the word *like*. Parents, teachers, grammarians, and literary critics such as the late Christopher Hitchens rail against the use of *like* as a filler. Still others call those very commentators conservative stuffed shirts, who can't or won't acknowledge that language changes. What do you think? Is the use of the word as a filler annoying, improper, unstoppable, useless, helpful, natural? Write an essay arguing for your point of view. You may want to begin by reading Christopher Hitchens' "The *Other* L-Word" in the January 13, 2010, issue of *Vanity Fair*, which is available online. You will also want to reflect on the discussion of the use of *like* if your class did the Language in Action exercise above.

Lost in Translation

LERA BORODITSKY

Lera Boroditsky was born about 1976 in Belarus. She earned her B.A. degree with honors from Northwestern University in 1996 and her doctorate in cognitive psychology from Stanford University in 2001. She focuses her research on a very old question in language study: whether or not the languages we speak shape the way we think, often referred to as the Sapir-Whorf hypothesis. She has found evidence that suggests that the differing ways people think and see the world may stem from the differing syntactical and lexical structures of their languages. For her work, Boroditsky has been awarded a National Science Foundation Career Award and the Marr Prize from the Cognitive Science Society. In 2002 she was named a Searle Scholar in a program administered by the Kinship Foundation, and in 2011 she was named an *Utne Reader* visionary.

"Lost in Translation," first published in the *Wall Street Journal* on July 24, 2010, explains the work she and her colleagues are now doing to reexamine the Sapir-Whorf hypothesis, or linguistic relativity hypothesis, that language might indeed shape reality, an idea she says "was for a long time considered untestable at best and more often simply crazy and wrong."

WRITING TO DISCOVER: *Do you think you shape your language or your language shapes you? Or both? What do you mean by "shape"? What if you speak more than one language?*

Do the languages we speak shape the way we think? Do they merely express thoughts, or do the structures in languages (without our knowledge or consent) shape the very thoughts we wish to express?

Take "Humpty Dumpty sat on a . . . ." Even this snippet of a nursery rhyme reveals how much languages can differ from one another. In English, we have to mark the verb for tense; in this case, we say "sat" rather than "sit." In Indonesian you need not (in fact, you can't) change the verb to mark tense.

In Russian, you would have to mark tense and also gender, changing the verb if Mrs. Dumpty did the sitting. You would also have to decide if the sitting event was completed or not. If our ovoid hero sat on the wall for the entire time he was meant to, it would be a different form of the verb than if, say, he had a great fall.

In Turkish, you would have to include in the verb how you acquired this information. For example, if you saw the chubby fellow on the wall with your own eyes, you'd use one form of the verb, but if you had simply read or heard about it, you'd use a different form.

Do English, Indonesian, Russian and Turkish speakers end up attend-   5
ing to, understanding, and remembering their experiences differently
simply because they speak different languages?

These questions touch on all the major controversies in the study of
mind, with important implications for politics, law and religion. Yet very
little empirical work had been done on these questions until recently. The
idea that language might shape thought was for a long time considered
untestable at best and more often simply crazy and wrong. Now, a flurry
of new cognitive science research is showing that in fact, language does
profoundly influence how we see the world.

The question of whether languages shape the way we think goes back
centuries; Charlemagne proclaimed that "to have a second language is to
have a second soul." But the idea went out of favor with scientists when
Noam Chomsky's theories of language gained popularity in the 1960s
and '70s. Dr. Chomsky proposed that there is a universal grammar for all
human languages — essentially, that languages don't really differ from one
another in significant ways. And because languages didn't differ from one
another, the theory went, it made no sense to ask whether linguistic differences led to differences in thinking.

The search for linguistic universals yielded interesting data on languages, but after decades of work, not a single proposed universal has
withstood scrutiny. Instead, as linguists probed deeper into the world's
languages (7,000 or so, only a fraction of them analyzed), innumerable
unpredictable differences emerged.

Of course, just because people talk differently doesn't necessarily
mean they think differently. In the past decade, cognitive scientists have
begun to measure not just how people talk, but also how they think,
asking whether our understanding of even such fundamental domains
of experience as space, time and causality could be constructed by
language.

For example, in Pormpuraaw, a remote Aboriginal community in   10
Australia, the indigenous languages don't use terms like "left" and "right."
Instead, everything is talked about in terms of absolute cardinal directions (north, south, east, west), which means you say things like, "There's
an ant on your southwest leg." To say hello in Pormpuraaw, one asks,
"Where are you going?," and an appropriate response might be, "A long
way to the south-southwest. How about you?" If you don't know which
way is which, you literally can't get past hello.

About a third of the world's languages (spoken in all kinds of physical
environments) rely on absolute directions for space. As a result of this constant linguistic training, speakers of such languages are remarkably good
at staying oriented and keeping track of where they are, even in unfamiliar
landscapes. They perform navigational feats scientists once thought were
beyond human capabilities. This is a big difference, a fundamentally different way of conceptualizing space, trained by language.

Differences in how people think about space don't end there. People rely on their spatial knowledge to build many other more complex or abstract representations including time, number, musical pitch, kinship relations, morality and, emotions. So if Pormpuraawans think differently about space, do they also think differently about other things, like time?

To find out, my colleague Alice Gaby and I traveled to Australia and gave Pormpuraawans sets of pictures that showed temporal progressions (for example, pictures of a man at different ages, or a crocodile growing, or a banana being eaten). Their job was to arrange the shuffled photos on the ground to show the correct temporal order. We tested each person in two separate sittings, each time facing in a different cardinal direction. When asked to do this, English speakers arrange time from left to right. Hebrew speakers do it from right to left (because Hebrew is written from right to left).

Pormpuraawans, we found, arranged time from east to west. That is, seated facing south, time went left to right. When facing north, right to left. When facing east, toward the body, and so on. Of course, we never told any of our participants which direction they faced. The Pormpuraawans not only knew that already, but they also spontaneously used this spatial orientation to construct their representations of time. And many other ways to organize time exist in the world's languages. In Mandarin, the future can be below and the past above. In Aymara, spoken in South America, the future is behind and the past in front.

In addition to space and time, languages also shape how we understand causality. For example, English likes to describe events in terms of agents doing things. English speakers tend to say things like "John broke the vase" even for accidents. Speakers of Spanish or Japanese would be more likely to say "the vase broke itself." Such differences between languages have profound consequences for how their speakers understand events, construct notions of causality and agency, what they remember as eyewitnesses and how much they blame and punish others.

In studies conducted by Caitlin Fausey at Stanford, speakers of English, Spanish and Japanese watched videos of two people popping balloons, breaking eggs, and spilling drinks either intentionally or accidentally. Later everyone got a surprise memory test: For each event, can you remember who did it? She discovered a striking cross-linguistic difference in eyewitness memory. Spanish and Japanese speakers did not remember the agents of accidental events as well as did English speakers. Mind you, they remembered the agents of intentional events (for which their language would mention the agent) just fine. But for accidental events, when one wouldn't normally mention the agent in Spanish or Japanese, they didn't encode or remember the agent as well.

In another study, English speakers watched the video of Janet Jackson's infamous "wardrobe malfunction" (a wonderful nonagentive coinage introduced into the English language by Justin Timberlake), accompanied by one of two written reports. The reports were identical except in the last sentence where one used the agentive phrase "ripped the costume" while the other said "the costume

The languages we speak not only reflect or express our thoughts, but also shape the very thoughts we wish to express.

ripped." Even though everyone watched the same video and witnessed the ripping with their own eyes, language mattered. Not only did people who read "ripped the costume" blame Justin Timberlake more, they also levied a whopping 53 percent more in fines.

Beyond space, time and causality, patterns in language have been shown to shape many other domains of thought. Russian speakers, who make an extra distinction between light and dark blues in their language, are better able to visually discriminate shades of blue. The Piraha, a tribe in the Amazon in Brazil, whose language eschews number words in favor of terms like few and many, are not able to keep track of exact quantities. And Shakespeare, it turns out, was wrong about roses: Roses by many other names (as told to blindfolded subjects) do not smell as sweet.

Patterns in language offer a window on a culture's dispositions and priorities. For example, English sentence structures focus on agents, and in our criminal-justice system, justice has been done when we've found the transgressor and punished him or her accordingly (rather than finding the victims and restituting appropriately, an alternative approach to justice). So does the language shape cultural values, or does the influence go the other way, or both?

Languages, of course, are human creations, tools we invent and hone to suit our needs. Simply showing that speakers of different languages think differently doesn't tell us whether it's language that shapes thought or the other way around. To demonstrate the causal role of language, what's needed are studies that directly manipulate language and look for effects in cognition.   20

One of the key advances in recent years has been the demonstration of precisely this causal link. It turns out that if you change how people talk, that changes how they think. If people learn another language, they inadvertently also learn a new way of looking at the world. When bilingual people switch from one language to another, they start thinking differently, too. And if you take away people's ability to use language in what should be a simple nonlinguistic task, their performance can change dramatically, sometimes making them look no smarter than rats or infants. (For example, in recent studies, MIT students were shown dots on a screen and asked to say how many there were. If they were allowed to count normally, they did great. If they simultaneously did a nonlinguistic task—like banging out rhythms—they still did great. But if they did a verbal task when shown the dots—like repeating the words spoken in a news report—their counting fell apart. In other words, they needed their language skills to count.)

All this new research shows us that the languages we speak not only reflect or express our thoughts, but also shape the very thoughts we wish to express. The structures that exist in our languages profoundly shape how we construct reality, and help make us as smart and sophisticated as we are.

Language is a uniquely human gift. When we study language, we are uncovering in part what makes us human, getting a peek at the very nature of human nature. As we uncover how languages and their speakers differ from one another, we discover that human natures too can differ dramatically, depending on the languages we speak. The next steps are to understand the mechanisms through which languages help us construct the incredibly complex knowledge systems we have. Understanding how knowledge is built will allow us to create ideas that go beyond the currently thinkable. This research cuts right to the fundamental questions we all ask about ourselves. How do we come to be the way we are? Why do we think the way we do? An important part of the answer, it turns out, is in the languages we speak.

THINKING CRITICALLY ABOUT THE READING

1. Why according to Boroditsky is it difficult to believe in Chomsky's theory of language universals?

2. In paragraph 10 Boroditsky discusses some language-thought peculiarities (for us as English speakers) that exist in the Pormpuraaw community of Australia. In what areas of human experience do researchers find differences?

3. What relationship does Boroditsky point to between English speakers' priority for an agent-based language structure and our criminal justice system? Does knowing about this connection make you more or less optimistic about the recent turn to giving more attention to victims' rights in our society? Explain.

4. Boroditsky says in paragraph 20, "Simply showing that speakers of different languages think differently doesn't tell us whether it's language that shapes thought or the other way around." What does she say researchers now need to do?

5. Why are people who speak more than one language important to language-thought researchers?

6. In your own words, explain why the language-thinking connection is so important for us to understand.

LANGUAGE IN ACTION

Those in the class who know more than one language may want to offer for discussion instances or examples of where the languages they know differ in structure and/or meaning when referring to the same things, ideas, people, and experiences. For example, the Italian term *allegro* ("lively, brisk, rapid") is a musical direction used to indicate a passage that should be played fast and musicians know that it should not be played as fast as a passage marked *presto* ("fast, rapid"). *Allegro ma non troppo* ("fast but not too fast") makes yet another distinction. Musicians learn these terms and there is a common understanding of just how fast the music should be played, although the musicians might agree to make even finer adjustments for particular compositions and passages within them. Here is an example of how a native Czech speaker used the syntax of his language but superimposed it on English: "He talked behind my back right in front of me," which might mean "he talked critically of me but in a way that I could hear."

WRITING SUGGESTIONS

1. The larger context for Boroditsky's research is the linguistic relativity hypothesis, also known as the Sapir-Whorf hypothesis. Write an essay explaining the hypothesis and its development throughout history. Who were Edward Sapir and Benjamin Lee Whorf, and what differing views did they have on the idea that language shapes reality? What impact did Noam Chomsky's ideas about language universals have on the theory and what positions have prominent linguists taken in the last three to four decades? Be sure to offer your own evaluation of the hypothesis.

2. Write an essay describing the major arguments linguists have made for and against the linguistic relativity hypothesis. How are younger linguists, in addition to Lera Boroditsky, now seeking to prove or disprove the hypothesis?

6

LANGUAGE COMMUNITIES

We reveal ourselves—where we come from, who we are, and who we'd like to be—in the language we use every day. At the same time, our use of language shapes us: In writing, speaking, or text messaging, we evolve as individuals in communication with other language users, exchanging signs and meanings and exploring new ways of defining ourselves and our place in the world. In this chapter we offer a collection of five readings that provide different perspectives on the speech communities to which we belong and how these communities, in turn, shape how we use language.

In the first reading Paul Roberts writes about how speech communities form based on such factors as age, geography, and social class, and how the language patterns we learn in our speech communities affect how the world perceives (and receives) us. In "All-American Dialects," Richard Lederer focuses on the regional varieties or dialects of English that are spoken throughout the United States. Specifically, he explores the current state of these geographical speech communities, which he and others believe are rapidly disappearing because of the pressure from the homogenizing effects of mass media. In "If Black English Isn't a Language, Then Tell Me, What Is?" James Baldwin discusses the origin of black English and argues that it is essential to understanding the black experience, the black identity, and the black speech community in America. In "Two Ways to Belong in America," Bharati Mukherjee reflects on her experience coming to America from India and how she chose to become an American citizen. In contrast to her expatriate Indian sister, Mukherjee needed "to put roots down, to vote and make the difference that I can." In time she realized that "the price that the immigrant willingly pays, and that the exile avoids, is the trauma of self-transformation." In "Mother Tongue," Amy Tan recounts her experiences growing up in a bilingual world, with one foot firmly planted in the English-speaking community of school and books and the other in her neighborhood community where she heard Chinese as well as the limited or "broken" English spoken by her immigrant mother. Finally, in her video "21 Accents" (available online at bedfordstmartins .com/languageawareness/epages), actress Amy Walker demonstrates the differences in pronunciation across 21 varieties of the English language.

-topics
- Details of the topic (Description)
? -vocabs?
P#s - Paragraphs numbers

Speech Communities

PAUL ROBERTS

Paul Roberts (1917–1967) was a linguist, teacher, and writer. Born in California, he received his B.A. from San Jose State University and his M.A. and Ph.D. from the University of California at Berkeley. After teaching at San Jose State and then Cornell University, Roberts became director of language at the Center of American Studies in Rome. His books include *Understanding Grammar* (1954), *Patterns of English* (1956), *Understanding English* (1958), *English Sentences* (1962), and *English Syntax* (1964).

In the following selection from *Understanding English*, Roberts writes about the development of speech variations within the United States that are based on what he identifies as "speech communities." These communities — which sometimes have their own dialects, their own jargon, and their own codes, meanings, and pronunciations — are formed by a variety of factors, according to Roberts, including "age, geography, education, occupation, social position."

WRITING TO DISCOVER: *Think about your own way of speaking. What factors do you believe are the most powerful influences on your own use of English — for example, your family, the region you grew up in, your peers? Do you have more than one way of speaking, depending on whom you are with or where you are?*

P1 & P2 talks about speech commu. of age how young and oldsters
oldsters don't understand the way they speak (old/new generation)

P1 Imagine a village of a thousand people all speaking the same language and never hearing any language other than their own. As the decades pass and generation succeeds generation, it will not be very apparent to the speakers of the language that any considerable language change is going on. Oldsters may occasionally be conscious of and annoyed by the speech forms of youngsters. They will notice new words, new expressions, "bad" pronunciations, but will ordinarily put these down to the irresponsibility of youth, and decide piously that the language of the younger generation will revert to decency when the generation grows up.

P2 It doesn't revert, though. The new expressions and the new pronunciations persist, and presently there is another younger generation with its own new expressions and its own pronunciations. And thus the language changes. If members of the village could speak to one another across five hundred years, they would probably find themselves unable to communicate.

Now suppose that the village divides itself and half the people move away. They move across the river or over a mountain and form a new village. Suppose the separation is so complete that the people of New Village have no contact with the people of Old Village. The language of both

138

villages will change, drifting away from the language of their common ancestors. But the drift will not be in the same direction. In both villages there will be new expressions and new pronunciations, but not the same ones. In the course of time the languages of Old Village and New Village will be mutually unintelligible with the language they both started with. They will also be mutually unintelligible with one another.

An interesting thing—and one for which there is no perfectly clear explanation—is that the rate of change will not ordinarily be the same for both villages. The language of Old Village changes faster than the language of New Village. One might expect that the opposite would be true—that the emigrants, placed in new surroundings and new conditions, would undergo more rapid language changes. But history reports otherwise. American English, for example, despite the violence and agony and confusion to which the demands of a new continent have subjected it, is probably essentially closer to the language of Shakespeare than London English is.

Suppose one thing more. Suppose Old Village is divided sharply into   5
an upper class and a lower class. The sons and daughters of the upper class go to preparatory school and then to the university; the children of the lower class go to work. The upper-class people learn to read and write and develop a flowering literature; the lower-class people remain illiterate. Dialects develop, and the speech of the two classes steadily diverges. One might suppose that most of the change would go on among the illiterate, that the upper-class people, conscious of their heritage, would tend to preserve the forms and pronunciations of their ancestors. Not so. The opposite is true. In speech, the educated tend to be radical and the uneducated conservative. In England one finds Elizabethan forms and sounds not among Oxford and Cambridge graduates but among the people of backward villages.

A village is a fairly simple kind of speech community—a group of people steadily in communication with one another, steadily hearing one another's speech. But the village is by no means the basic unit. Within the simplest village there are many smaller units—groupings based on age, class, occupation. All these groups play intricately on one another and against one another, and a language that seems at first a coherent whole will turn out on inspection to be composed of many differing parts. Some forces tend to make these parts diverge, other forces hold them together. Thus the language continues in tension.

THE SPEECH COMMUNITIES OF THE CHILD

The child's first speech community is ordinarily his family. The child learns whatever kind of language the family speaks—or, more precisely, whatever kind of language it speaks to him. The child's language learning, now and later, is governed by two obvious motives: the desire to communicate and the desire to be admired. He imitates what he hears. More or less successful imitations usually bring action and reward and tend to be repeated. Unsuccessful ones usually don't bring action and reward and tend to be discarded.

But since language is a complicated business it is sometimes the unsuccessful imitations that bring the reward. The child, making a stab at the word *mother*, comes out with *muzzer*. The family decides that this is just too cute for anything and beams and repeats *muzzer*, and the child, feeling that he's scored a bull's eye, goes on saying *muzzer* long after he has mastered *other* and *brother*. Baby talk is not so much invented by the child as sponsored by the parent.

Eventually the child moves out of the family and into another speech community—other children of his neighborhood. He goes to kindergarten and immediately encounters speech habits that conflict with those he has learned. If he goes to school and talks about his *muzzer*, it will be borne in on him by his colleagues that the word is not well chosen. Even *mother* may not pass muster, and he may discover that he gets better results and is altogether happier if he refers to his female parent as his ma or even his old lady.

Children coming together in a kindergarten class bring with them language that is different because it is learned in different homes. It is all to some degree unsuccessfully learned, consisting of not quite perfect imitations of the original. In school all this speech coalesces, differences tend to be ironed out, and the result differs from the original parental speech and differs in pretty much the same way.

.   The pressures on the child to conform to the speech of his age group, his speech community, are enormous. He may admire his teacher and love his mother, he may even—and even consciously—wish to speak as they do. But he *has* to speak like the rest of the class. If he does not, life becomes intolerable.

The speech changes that go on when the child goes to school are often most distressing to parents. Your little Bertram, at home, has never heard anything but the most elegant English. You send him to school, and what happens? He comes home saying things like "I done real good in school today, Mom." But Bertram really has no choice in the matter. If Clarence and Elbert and the rest of the fellows customarily say "I done real good," then Bertram might as well go around with three noses as say things like "I did very nicely."

Individuals differ of course, and not all children react to the speech community in the same way. Some tend to imitate and others tend to force imitation. But all to some degree have their speech modified by forces over which neither they nor their parents nor their teachers have any real control.

Individuals differ too in their sensitivity to language. For some, language is always a rather embarrassing problem. They steadily make boners, saying the right thing in the wrong place or the wrong way. They have a hard time fitting in. Others tend to change their language slowly, sticking stoutly to their way of saying things, even though their way differs from that of the majority. Still others adopt new language habits almost automatically, responding quickly to whatever speech environment they encounter.

Indeed some children of five or six have been observed to speak two   15
or more different dialects without much awareness that they are doing so. Most commonly, they will speak in one way at home and in another on the playground. At home they say, "I did very nicely" and "I haven't any"; these become at school, "I done real good" and "I ain't got none."

THE CLASS AS A SPEECH COMMUNITY

Throughout the school years, or at least through the American secondary school, the individual's most important speech community is his age group, his class. Here is where the real power lies. The rule is conformity above all things, and the group uses its power ruthlessly on those who do not conform. Language is one of the chief means by which the school group seeks to establish its entity, and in the high school this is done more or less consciously. The obvious feature is high school slang, picked up from the radio, from other schools, sometimes invented, changing with bewildering speed. Nothing is more satisfactory than to speak today's slang; nothing more futile than to use yesterday's.

There can be few tasks more frustrating than that of the secondary school teacher charged with the responsibility of brushing off and polishing up the speech habits of the younger generation. Efforts to make *real* into *really*, *ain't* into *am not*, *I seen him* into *I saw him*, *he don't* into *he doesn't* meet at best with polite indifference, at worst with mischievous counterattack.

The writer can remember from his own high school days when the class, a crashingly witty bunch, took to pronouncing the word *sure* as *sewer*. "Have you prepared your lesson, Arnold?" Miss Driscoll would ask. "Sewer, Miss Driscoll," Arnold would reply. "I think," said Miss Driscoll, who was pretty quick on her feet too, "that you must mean 'sewerly,' since the construction calls for the adverb not the adjective." We were delighted with the suggestion and went about saying "sewerly" until the very blackboards were nauseated. Miss Driscoll must have wished often that she had let it lay.

CONFRONTING THE ADULT WORLD

When the high school class graduates, the speech community disintegrates as the students fit themselves into new ones. For the first time in the experience of most of the students the speech ways of adult communities begin to exercise real force. For some people the adjustment is a relatively simple one. A boy going to work in a garage may have a good deal of new lingo to pick up, and he may find that the speech that seemed so racy and won such approval in the corridors of Springfield High leaves his more adult associates merely bored. But a normal person will adapt himself without trouble.

For others in other situations settling into new speech communities   20
may be more difficult. The person going into college, into the business world, into scrubbed society may find that he has to think about and work on his speech habits in order not to make a fool of himself too often.

College is a particularly complicated problem. Not only does the freshman confront upperclassmen not particularly disposed to find the speech of Springfield High particularly cute, but the adult world, as represented chiefly by the faculty, becomes increasingly more immediate. The problems of success, of earning a living, of marriage, of attaining a satisfactory adult life loom larger, and they all bring language problems with them. Adaptation is necessary, and the student adapts.

The student adapts, but the adult world adapts too. The thousands of boys and girls coming out of the high schools each spring are affected by the speech of the adult communities into which they move, but they also affect that speech. The new pronunciation habits, developing grammatical features, different vocabulary do by no means all give way before the disapproval of elders. Some of them stay. Elders, sometimes to their dismay, find themselves changing their speech habits under the bombardment of those of their juniors. And then of course the juniors eventually become the elders, and there is no one left to disapprove.

THE SPACE DIMENSION

Speech communities are formed by many features besides that of age. Most obvious is geography. Our country was originally settled by people coming from different parts of England. They spoke different dialects to begin with and as a result regional speech differences existed from the start in the different parts of the country. As speakers of other languages came to America and learned English, they left their mark on the speech of the sections in which they settled. With the westward movement, new pioneers streamed out through the mountain passes and down river valleys, taking the different dialects west and modifying them by new mixtures in new environments.

Today we are all more or less conscious of certain dialect differences in our country. We speak of the "southern accent," the "Brooklyn accent," the "New England accent." Until a few years ago it was often said that American English was divided into three dialects: Southern American (south of the Mason-Dixon line); Eastern American (east of the Connecticut River); and Western American. This description suggests certain gross differences all right, but recent research shows that it is a gross oversimplification.

The starting point of American dialects is the original group of colonies.   25 We had a New England settlement, centering in Massachusetts; a Middle Atlantic settlement, centering in Pennsylvania; a southern settlement, centering in Virginia and the Carolinas. These colonies were different in speech to begin with, since the settlers came from different parts of England. Their differences were increased as the colonies lived for a century and a half or so with only thin communication with either Mother England or each other. By the time of the Revolution the dia-

> **We speak of America as the melting pot, but the speech communities of this continent are very far from having melted into one.**

lects were well established. Within each group there were of course subgroups. Richmond speech differed markedly from that of Savannah. But Savannah and Richmond were more like each other than they were like Philadelphia or Boston.

The Western movement began shortly after the Revolution, and dialects followed geography. The New Englanders moved mostly into upper New York State and the Great Lakes region. The Middle Atlantic colonists went down the Shenandoah Valley and eventually into the heart of the Midwest. The southerners opened up Kentucky and Tennessee, later the lower Mississippi Valley, later still Texas and much of the Southwest. Thus new speech communities were formed, related to the old ones of the seaboard, but each developing new characteristics as lines of settlement crossed.

New complications were added before and after the Revolution by the great waves of immigration of people from countries other than England: Swedes in Delaware, Dutch in New York, Germans and Scots-Irish in Pennsylvania, Irish in New England, Poles and Greeks and Italians and Portuguese. The bringing in of black slaves had an important effect on the speech of the South and later on the whole country. The Spanish in California and the Southwest added their mark. In [the twentieth and twenty-first centuries], movement of peoples goes on: the trek of southern blacks to northern and western cities, the migration of people from Arkansas, Oklahoma, and Texas to California. All these have shaped and are shaping American speech.

We speak of America as the melting pot, but the speech communities of this continent are very far from having melted into one. Linguists today can trace very clearly the movements of the early settlers in the still-living speech of their descendants. They can follow an eighteenth century speech community west, showing how it crossed this pass and followed that river, threw out an offshoot here, left a pocket there, merged with another group, halted, split, moved on once more. If all other historical evidence were destroyed, the history of the country could still be reconstructed from the speech of modern America.

SOCIAL DIFFERENCES

The third great shaper of speech communities is social class. This has been, and is, more important in England than in America. In England, class differences have often been more prominent than those of age or place. If you were the blacksmith's boy, you might know the son of the local baronet, but you didn't speak his language. You spoke the language of your social group, and he that of his, and over the centuries these social dialects remained widely separated.

England in the twentieth century has been much democratized, but   30
the language differences are far from having disappeared. One can still tell much about a person's family, his school background, his general position in life by the way he speaks. Social lines are hard to cross, and language is perhaps the greatest barrier. You may make a million pounds and own several cars and a place in the country, but your vowels and consonants and nouns and verbs and sentence patterns will still proclaim to the world that you're not a part of the upper crust.

In America, of course, social distinctions have never been so sharp as they are in England. We find it somewhat easier to rise in the world, to move into social environments unknown to our parents. This is possible, partly, because speech differences are slighter; conversely, speech differences are slighter because this is possible. But speech differences do exist. If you've spent all your life driving a cab in Philly and, having inherited a fortune, move to San Francisco's Nob Hill, you will find that your language is different, perhaps embarrassingly so, from that of your new acquaintances.

Language differences on the social plane in America are likely to correlate with education or occupation rather than with birth—simply because education and occupation in America do not depend so much on birth as they do in other countries. A child without family connection can get himself educated at Harvard, Yale, or Princeton. In doing so, he acquires the speech habits of the Ivy League and gives up those of his parents.

Exceptions abound. But in general there is a clear difference between the speech habits of the college graduate and those of the high-school graduate. The cab driver does not talk like the Standard Oil executive, the college professor like the carnival pitch man, or an Illinois merchant like a sailor shipping out of New Orleans. New York's Madison Avenue and

Third Avenue are only a few blocks apart, but they are widely separated in language. And both are different from Broadway.

It should be added that the whole trend of modern life is to reduce rather than to accentuate these differences. In a country where college education becomes increasingly everybody's chance, where executives and refrigerator salesmen and farmers play golf together, where a college professor may drive a cab in the summertime to keep his family alive, it becomes harder and harder to guess a person's education, income, and social status by the way he talks. But it would be absurd to say that language gives no clue at all.

GOOD AND BAD

Speech communities, then, are formed by many features: age, geography, education, occupation, social position. Young people speak differently from old people, Kansans differently from Virginians, Yale graduates differently from Dannemora graduates. Now let us pose a delicate question: aren't some of these speech communities better than others? That is, isn't better language heard in some than in others? 35

Well, yes, of course. One speech community is always better than all the rest. This is the group in which one happens to find oneself. The writer would answer unhesitatingly that the noblest, loveliest, purest English is that heard in the Men's Faculty Club of San Jose State College, San Jose, California. He would admit, of course, that the speech of some of the younger members leaves something to be desired; that certain recent immigrants from Harvard, Michigan, and other foreign parts need to work on the laughable oddities lingering in their speech; and that members of certain departments tend to introduce a lot of queer terms that can only be described as jargon. But in general the English of the Faculty Club is ennobling and sweet.

As a practical matter, good English is whatever English is spoken by the group in which one moves contentedly and at ease. To the bum on Main Street in Los Angeles, good English is the language of other L.A. bums. Should he wander onto the campus of UCLA, he would find the talk there unpleasant, confusing, and comical. He might agree, if pressed, that the college man speaks "correctly" and he doesn't. But in his heart he knows better. He wouldn't talk like them college jerks if you paid him.

If you admire the language of other speech communities more than you do your own, the reasonable hypothesis is that you are dissatisfied with the community itself. It is not precisely other speech that attracts you but the people who use this speech. Conversely, if some language strikes you as unpleasant or foolish or rough, it is presumably because the speakers themselves seem so.

To many people, the sentence "Where is he at?" sounds bad. It is bad, they would say, in and of itself. The sounds are bad. But this is very hard to prove, If "Where is he at?" is bad because it has bad sound combinations, then presumably "Where is the cat?" or "Where is my hat?" are just as bad, yet no one thinks them so. Well, then, "Where is he at?" is bad because it uses too many words. One gets the same meaning from "Where is he?" so why add the *at*? True. Then "He going with us?" is a better sentence than "Is he going with us?" You don't really need the *is*, so why put it in?

Certainly there are some features of language to which we can apply   40 the terms *good* and *bad*, *better* and *worse*. Clarity is usually better than obscurity; precision is better than vagueness. But these are not often what we have in mind when we speak of good and bad English. If we like the speech of upper-class Englishmen, the presumption is that we admire upper-class Englishmen — their characters, culture, habits of mind. Their sounds and words simply come to connote the people themselves and become admirable therefore. If we heard the same sounds and words from people who were distasteful to us, we would find the speech ugly.

This is not to say that correctness and incorrectness do not exist in speech. They obviously do, but they are relative to the speech community — or communities — in which one operates. As a practical matter, correct speech is that which sounds normal or natural to one's comrades. Incorrect speech is that which evokes in them discomfort or hostility or disdain.

THINKING CRITICALLY ABOUT THE READING

1. Why does Roberts begin with a discussion of "the village"? Is he referring literally to villages, or does "the village" stand for something else? What does his extended example of "Old Village" and "New Village" (3–5) illustrate? (Glossary: *Beginnings and Endings; Examples*)

2. Roberts writes: "Baby talk is not so much invented by the child as sponsored by the parent" (8). Explain what he means by this. What are the most basic, and motivational, factors in a child's language learning?

3. When children go to school, they move into an entirely new speech community, where, according to Roberts, their speech is modified "by forces over which neither they nor their parents nor their teachers have any real control" (13). What are these forces? What are some of the ways in which the new speech community asserts itself and establishes its own identity?

4. "We speak of America as the melting pot, but the speech communities of this continent are very far from having melted into one" (28), writes Roberts. What factors have contributed to, and continue to foster, the multiplicity of speech communities across the United States?

5. According to Roberts, the impact in England of social class on shaping speech communities differs considerably from the impact of class on speech communities in the United States. What factors contribute to this difference? Do you think these differences are as relevant today as Roberts assumed they were when he wrote *Understanding English*?

6. Roberts asks the provocative question: "Aren't some of these speech communities better than others?" (35). What do you think he means by this? Is he referring to the language of the community, or the community members themselves? What kind of value judgments do you think we make about others based on their particular way of speaking?

LANGUAGE IN ACTION

In his 1995 memoir, *Dreams from My Father: A Story of Race and Inheritance,* then senator Barack Obama writes:

> I learned to slip back and forth between my black and white worlds, understanding that each possessed its own language and customs and structures of meaning, convinced that with a bit of translation on my part the two worlds would eventually cohere. Still, the feeling that something wasn't quite right stayed with me, a warning that sounded whenever a white girl mentioned in the middle of conversation how much she liked Stevie Wonder or when a woman in the supermarket asked me if I played basketball; or when the school principal told me I was cool. I did like Stevie Wonder, I did love basketball, and I tried my best to be cool at all times. So why did such comments set me on edge?

Why do you think Obama was "set on edge" by the kinds of comments he mentions toward the end of the passage? Can you sympathize with his position? Do you believe that it's possible to make different language communities to which one belongs "eventually cohere"? Why or why not?

WRITING SUGGESTIONS

1. We are often simultaneous members of more than one speech community, especially as we move into young adulthood and are introduced to groups outside of our family. Each of these groups can have its own demands, rules of membership, culture, and identity, to which we must adapt with chameleonlike skill. Write about your own experience moving between or among groups, identifying the most influential groups on your life and what demands were made on you in order to belong. What did you have to do to adapt to each group? How did the groups differ? Were they mutually exclusive, or did they overlap on occasion? Do you consider any one of the groups to be superior to the other, or were they simply equal, but different? If it helps you organize your thinking, make a sketch or a map of your communities. Write an essay in which you discuss what you discover.

2. Roberts writes:

> If you admire the language of other speech communities more than you do your own, the reasonable hypothesis is that you are dissatisfied with the community itself. It is not precisely the other speech that attracts you but the people who use this speech. Conversely, if some language strikes you as unpleasant or foolish or rough, it is presumably because the speakers themselves seem so (38).

Write an essay that supports or refutes his argument, providing examples from your own experience as evidence.

All-American Dialects

Born in 1938, Richard Lederer has been a lifelong student of language. He holds degrees from Haverford College, Harvard University, and the University of New Hampshire and for twenty-seven years taught English at St. Paul's School in Concord, New Hampshire. Anyone who has read one of his over thirty books will understand why he has been referred to as "Conan the Grammarian" and "America's wittiest verbalist." Lederer loves language and enjoys writing about its marvelous richness and about how Americans use language. He has written over thirty-five books including *Anguished English* (1987), *Crazy English* (1989), *The Play of Words* (1990), *Adventures of a Verbivore* (1994), *Nothing Risque, Nothing Gained* (1995), *The Bride of Anguished English* (2002), *A Man of My Words: Reflections on the English Language* (2003), *Word Wizard: Super Bloopers, Rich Reflections, and Other Acts of Word Magic* (2006), and *Presidential Trivia: The Feats, Fates, Families, Foibles, and Firsts of Our American Presidents* (2007). In addition to writing books, Lederer pens a weekly syndicated column called "Looking at Language" for newspapers and magazines throughout the country. He is the "Grammar Grappler" for *Writer's Digest*, the language commentator for National Public Radio, and cohost of *A Way with Words*, a weekly radio program out of San Diego, where he currently lives.

The following essay was first published in *USA Today* magazine in July 2009. Lederer discusses, using multiple examples, regional dialects or speech communities and how they differ one from another in vocabulary, pronunciation, and grammar. Like John Steinbeck before him, Lederer fears that regional speech is rapidly disappearing. He fervently hopes that "American English does not turn into a bland, homogenized, pasteurized, assembly line product."

WRITING TO DISCOVER: *What part of the country did you grow up in? Do you think of yourself as speaking English with a regional "accent"? Are you proud of the way you and your friends and neighbors speak? How do you view speakers from other parts of the United States? Do you readily recognize regional differences in the way English is spoken?*

I have tongue and will travel, so I run around the country speaking to groups of teachers, students, librarians, women's clubbers, guild professionals, and corporate clients. These good people go to all the trouble of putting together meetings and conferences, and I walk in, share my thoughts about language in their lives, and imbibe their collective energy and synergy. I will go anywhere to spread the word about words and, in venturing from California to Manhattan Island, from the redwood forest to the Gulf Stream waters, I hear America singing. We are teeming nations within a nation, a country that is like a world. We talk in melodies of infinite variety; we dance to their sundry measure and lyrics.

Midway through John Steinbeck's epic *The Grapes of Wrath*, young Ivy observes, "Ever'body says words different. Arkansas folks says 'em different, and Oklahomy folks says 'em different, and we seen a lady from Massachusetts, an' she said 'em differentest of all. Couldn't hardly make out what she was sayin'."

One aspect of American rugged individualism is that not all of us say the same word in the same way. Sometimes, we do not even use the same name for the same object. I was born and grew up in Philadelphia a coon's age, a blue moon, a month of Sundays ago—when Hector was a pup. Phillufia, or Philly, which is what we kids called the city, was where the epicurean delight made with cold cuts, cheese, tomatoes, pickles, and onions stuffed into a long, hard-crusted Italian bread loaf was invented. The creation of that sandwich took place in the Italian pushcart section of the city, known as Hog Island. Some linguists contend that it was but a short leap from Hog Island to hoagie, while others claim that the label hoagie arose because only a hog had the appetite or technique to eat one properly.

As a young man, I moved to northern New England (N'Hampsha, to be specific), where the same sandwich designed to be a meal in itself is called a grinder—because you need a good set of grinders to chew it. Yet, my travels around the country have revealed that the hoagie or grinder is called at least a dozen other names—a bomber, Garibaldi (after the Italian liberator), hero, Italian sandwich, rocket, sub, submarine (which is what they call it in California, where I now live), torpedo, wedge, wedgie, and, in the deep South, a poor-boy (usually pronounced poh-boy).

In Philadelphia, we washed down our hoagies with soda. In New   5
England, we did it with tonic and, by that word, I do not mean medicine. Soda and tonic in other parts are known as pop, soda pop, a soft drink, Coke, and quinine.

In northern New England, they take the term milk shake quite literally. To many residing in that corner of the country, a milk shake consists of milk mixed with flavored syrup—and nothing more—shaken up until foamy. If you live in Rhode Island or in southern Massachusetts and you want ice cream in your milk drink, you ask for a cabinet (named after the square wooden cabinet in which the mixer was encased). If you live farther north, you order a velvet or a frappe (from the French *frapper*, "to ice").

Clear—or is it clean or plumb?—across the nation, Americans sure do talk different. What do you call those flat, doughy things you often eat for breakfast—battercakes, flannel cakes, flapjacks, fritters, griddle cakes, or pancakes? Is that simple strip of grass between the street and the sidewalk a berm, boulevard, boulevard strip, city strip, devil strip, green belt, the parking, the parking strip, parkway, sidewalk plot, strip, swale, tree bank, or tree lawn? Is the part of the highway that separates the northbound from the southbound lanes the centerline, center strip, mall, medial strip, median strip, medium strip, or neutral ground? Is it a cock horse, dandle, hicky horse, horse, horse tilt, ridy horse, seesaw, teeter, teeterboard, teetering board, teetering horse, teeter-totter, tilt, tilting board, tinter, tinter board, or tippity bounce? Do fishermen employ an angledog, angleworm, baitworm, earthworm, eaceworm, fishworm, mudworm, rainworm, or redworm? Is a larger worm a dew worm, night crawler, night walker, or town worm? Is it a crabfish, clawfish, craw, crawdab, crawdad, crawdaddy, crawfish, crawler, crayfish, creekcrab, crowfish, freshwater lobster, ghost shrimp, mudbug, spiny lobster, or yabby? Depends where you live and who or whom it is you are talking to.

I figger, figure, guess, imagine, opine, reckon, and suspect that my being bullheaded, contrary, headstrong, muley, mulish, ornery, otsny, pigheaded, set, sot, stubborn, or utsy about this whole matter of dialects makes you sick to, in, or at your stomach. I assure you, though, that when it comes to American dialects, I'm not speaking fahdoodle, flumadiddle, flummydiddle, or flurriddiddle—translation, nonsense. I am no all-thumbs-and-no-fingers, all-knees-and-elbows, all-left-feet, antigoddling, bumfuzzled, discombobulated, flusterated, or foozled bumpkin, clodhopper, country jake, hayseed, hick, hillbilly, hoosier, jackpine savage, mossback, mountain-boomer, pumpkin-husker, rail-splitter, rube, sodbuster, stump farmer, swamp angel, yahoo, or yokel.

The biblical book of Judges tells of how one group of speakers used the word *shibboleth*, Hebrew for "stream," as a military password. The Gileadites had defeated the Ephraimites in battle and were holding some narrow places on the Jordan River that the fleeing Ephraimites had to cross to get home. In those days, it was hard to tell one kind of soldier from another because they did not wear uniforms. The Gileadites knew that the Ephraimites spoke a slightly different dialect of Hebrew and could be recognized by their inability to pronounce an initial "sh" sound. Thus, each time a soldier wanted to cross the river, "the men of Gilead said unto him, Art thou an Ephraimite? If he said, Nay, then they said unto him, Say now Shibboleth, and he said Sibboleth: for he could not frame to pronounce it right. Then they took him and slew him at the passages of Jordan: and there fell at that time of the Ephraimites forty and two thousand."

During World War II, some American officers adapted the strategy of the Old Testament Gileadites. Knowing that many Japanese have difficulty pronouncing the letter "L," these officers instructed their sentries to use only passwords that had L's in them, such as lallapalooza. The closest the Japanese got to the sentries was rarraparooza.

10

These days, English speakers do not get slaughtered for pronouncing their words differently from other English speakers, but the way those words sound can be labeled "funny" or "quaint" or "out of touch." In the George Bernard Shaw play "Pygmalion," Prof. Henry Higgins rails at Liza Doolittle and her cockney accent: "A woman who utters such depressing and disgusting sounds has no right to be anywhere—no right to live. Remember that you are a human being with a soul and the divine gift of articulate speech: that your native language is the language of Shakespeare and Milton and the Bible; and don't sit there crooning like a bilious pigeon!"

Most of us are aware that large numbers of people in the U.S. speak very differently than we do. Most of us tend to feel that the way "we" talk is right, and the way "they" talk is weird. "They," of course, refers to anyone who differs from "us." If you ask most adults what a dialect is, they will tell you it is what somebody else in another region passes off as English. These regions tend to be exotic places like Mississippi or Texas—or Brooklyn, where oil is a rank of nobility and earl is a black, slippery substance.

It is reported that many Southerners reacted to the elections of Jimmy Carter (Georgia) and Bill Clinton (Arkansas) by saying, "Well, at last we have a president who talks without an accent." Actually, Southerners, like everyone else, do speak with an accent, as witness these tongue-in-cheek entries in our Dictionary of Southernisms: ah (organ for seeing); are (60 minutes); arn (ferrous metal); ass (frozen water); ast (questioned); bane (small, kidney-shaped vegetable); bar (seek and receive a loan); bold (heated in water); card (one who lacks courage); farst (a lot of trees); fur (distance); har (to employ); hep (to assist); hire yew (a greeting); paw tree (verse); rat (opposite of lef); reckanize (to see); tarred (exhausted); t'mar (the day following t'day); thang (item); thank (to cogitate); and y'all (a bunch of "you's").

When I visited Alexandria, Louisiana, a local pastor offered me proof that y'all has biblical origins, especially in the letters of the apostle Paul: "We give thanks to God always for you all, making mention of you in our prayers" (First Epistle to the Thessalonians, 1:2) and "First, I thank my God through Jesus Christ for you all" (First Epistle to the Romans, 1:8). "Obviously," the good reverend told me, "Saint Paul was a Southerner," before adding, "Thank you, Yankee visitor, for appreciating our beloved Southernspeak. We couldn't talk without it."

An anonymous poem that I came upon in Louisville, Kentucky, clari- 15
fies the plural use of the one-syllable pronoun y'all:

Y'all gather 'round from far and near,
Both city folk and rural,
And listen while I tell you this:
The pronoun y'all is plural.

If I should utter, "Y'all come down,
Or we-all shall be lonely,"
I mean at least a couple of folks
And not one person only.

If I should say to Hiram Jones,
"I think that y'all are lazy,"
Or "Will y'all let me use y'all's knife?"
He'd think that I was crazy.

Don't think I mean to criticize
Or that I'm full of gall,
But when we speak of one alone,
We all say "you," not "y'all."

We all have accents. Many New Englanders drop the r in cart and farm and say "caht" and "fahm." Thus, the Midwesterner's "park the car in Harvard Yard" becomes the New Englander's "pahk the cah in Hahvahd Yahd." Those r's, though, are not lost. A number of upper Northeasterners, including the famous Kennedy family of Massachusetts, add "r" to words, such as "idear" and "Cuber," when those words come before a vowel or at the end of a sentence.

I.D. BY SPEECH PATTERN

When an amnesia victim appeared at a truck stop in Missouri in the fall of 1987, authorities tried in vain to discover her identity. Even after three months, police "ran into a brick wall," according to the *Columbia Daily Tribune*. Then, linguist Donald Lance of the University of Missouri-Columbia was called in to analyze her speech. After only a few sentences, Lance recognized the woman's West Pennsylvania dialect, and, within one month, police in Pittsburgh located her family. Among the clues used to pinpoint the woman's origin was the West Pennsylvanian use of "greezy" instead of "greasy," and "teeter-totter" rather than "seesaw." Dialectologists know that people who pronounce the word as "greezy" usually live south of a line that wiggles across the northern parts of New Jersey, Pennsylvania, Ohio, Indiana, and Illinois.

Linguist Roger Shuy writes about the reactions of Illinois residents in a 1962 survey of regional pronunciations, including the soundings of "greasy": "The northern Illinois informants felt the southern pronunciation was crude and ugly; it made them think of a very messy, dirty, sticky, smelly frying pan. To the southern and midland speakers, however, the northern pronunciation connoted a messy, dirty, sticky, smelly skillet."

Using the tools of his trade, Shuy was able to profile accurately Ted Kaczynski, the elusive Unabomber who terrorized the nation through the 1990s. Culling linguistic evidence from Kaczynski's "Manifesto," published in *The New York Times*, and the notes and letters accompanying the bombs, Shuy deduced the Unabomber's geographical origin, religious background, age, and education level.

Among the clues were the Unabomber's use of "sierras" to mean   20
"mountains," an indication that the writer had spent some time living in Northern California. In his manifesto, Kaczynski used expressions common to a person who was a young adult in the 1960s — "Holy Robots," "working stiff," and "playing footsy." His employment of sociological terms, such as "other directed," and his many references to "individual drives" suggested an acquaintance with the sociology in vogue during that decade, particularly that of David Reisman. The complexity of Kaczynski's sentence structure, including the subjunctive mood, and the learned-ness of his vocabulary, such as the words "surrogate," "sublimate," "overspecialization," and "tautology," pointed to someone highly educated.

All these conclusions were verified when Kaczynski was captured: He was in his early 50s, had grown up in Chicago and lived for a time in Northern California, and was well educated, having once been a university professor.

Face facts; we all speak some sort of dialect. When you learn language, you learn it as a dialect; if you do not speak a dialect, you do not speak. Dialect is not a label for careless, unlettered, nonstandard speech. A dialect is not something to be avoided or cured. Each language is a great pie. Each slice of that pie is a dialect, and no single slice is the language. Do not try to change your language into the kind of English that nobody really speaks. Be proud of your slice of the pie.

> **When you learn language, you learn it as a dialect; if you do not speak a dialect, you do not speak.**

In the early 1960s, writer John Steinbeck decided to rediscover America in a camper with his French poodle, Charlie. He reported on his observations in a book called *Travels with Charlie* and included these thoughts on dialects: "One of my purposes was to listen, to hear speech, accent, speech rhythms, overtones, and emphasis. For speech is so much more than words and sentences. I did listen everywhere. It seemed to me that regional speech is in the process of disappearing, not gone but going. Forty years of radio and twenty years of television must have this impact. Communications must destroy localness by a slow, inevitable process."

I can remember a time when I almost could pinpoint a man's place of origin by his speech. That is growing more difficult and, in some foreseeable future, will become impossible. It is a rare house or building that is not rigged with spiky combers of the air. Radio and television speech becomes standardized, perhaps better English than we ever have used. Just as our bread—mixed and baked, packaged, and sold without benefit of accident or human frailty—is uniformly good and uniformly tasteless, so will our speech become one speech.

Forty years have passed since Steinbeck's trip, and the hum and buzz of electronic voices have since permeated almost every home across our nation. Formerly, the psalmist tells us, "The voice of the turtle was heard in the land"—now, though, it is the voice of the broadcaster, with his or her immaculately groomed diction. Let us hope that American English does not turn into a bland, homogenized, pasteurized, assembly line product. May our bodacious language remain tasty and nourishing—full of flavor, variety, and local ingredients.

25

THINKING CRITICALLY ABOUT THE READING

1. How does Lederer use the writer John Steinbeck to introduce the subject of his essay? How does he bring the essay full circle by returning to Steinbeck in his conclusion? Did you find this beginning and ending effective? Explain why or why not.

2. What function do paragraphs 3 through 8 serve in the context on Lederer's essay? Why do you suppose that Lederer provides as many examples of vocabulary differences as he does?

3. How does Lederer illustrate the idea that Americans don't all sound the same when they speak, that there are pronunciation differences? Which examples of these pronunciation differences did you find most effective and interesting? Explain why.

4. Lederer explains how linguist Roger Shuy was able to profile correctly the Unabomber Ted Kaczynski. What did you find most interesting about Shuy's contextual analysis of Kaczynski's "Manifesto"? Explain.

5. How effective did you find Lederer's pie analogy to explain a language and its various dialects?

6. According to Lederer, what accounts for the gradual disappearance of regional speech differences? What do we risk losing as American English becomes more uniform and homogenized?

LANGUAGE IN ACTION

In paragraphs 3 through 7, Lederer identifies a number of everyday items—a large sandwich designed to be a meal in itself, a carbonated drink, the part of a highway that separates the northbound from the southbound lanes, a worm used for bait, and a freshwater shellfish with claws, for example—that are called by different names in different parts of the country.

To see what your vocabulary may reveal about your regional or cultural origins, age, sex, and occupation, let's do a mini-dialect vocabulary survey similar to much longer ones used by field investigators preparing the *Linguistic Atlas of New England* and other regional atlases. For each of the following familiar, everyday items, circle the word or words you actually use (don't circle words you've heard used by your parents, grandparents, or friends). If the word you use is not listed, provide it in the space alongside the item. Before beginning, please list the places where you have lived as well as the length of time you lived in each location.

1. Round, flat confection with hole in center, made with baking powder: *crull, cruller, doughnut, fatcake, fried cake, cake doughnut, raised doughnut,* _____

2. Center of a peach: *pit, seed, stone, kernel, heart,* _____

3. Large open plastic container for scrub water: *pail, bucket,* _____

4. Family word for mother: *ma, mama, mammy, maw, mom, mommer, mommy, mother,* _____

5. Over a sink: *faucet, hydrant, spicket, spigot, tap,* _____

6. Policeman: *cop, policeman, copper, fuzz, dick, officer, bull,* _____

7. Place where packaged groceries can be purchased: *grocery store, general store, supermarket, store, delicatessen, grocery, market, food market, food store, supermart,* _____

8. A white lumpy cheese: *clabber cheese, cottage cheese, curd cheese, curd(s), Dutch cheese, homemade cheese, pot cheese, smearcase, cream cheese,* _____

9. Holds small objects together: *rubber band, rubber binder, elastic binder, gum binder, elastic band,* _____

10. Become ill with a cold: *catch a cold, catch cold, get a cold, take cold, take a cold, come down with a cold,* _____

Discuss your answers with your classmates. Did you discover any regional patterns of usage among your classmates? Did other patterns emerge? Were there any items for which you use a different word or words than either your parents or grandparents?

WRITING SUGGESTIONS

1. As Lederer points out, "Most of us are aware that large numbers of people in the U.S. speak very differently than we do. Most of us tend to feel that the way 'we' talk is right, and the way 'they' talk is weird" (12). Do you agree with Lederer? Write an essay in which you discuss how you feel about the way you and your family, friends, and neighbors speak English. In what ways is the way you speak English tied up with your identity, who you are? Before you start writing you may find it helpful to review your response to the journal prompt for this selection.

2. Lederer notes that in the early 1960s author John Steinbeck bemoaned the fact that "regional speech is in the process of disappearing, not gone but going" (23). Lederer himself dreads the day when "our speech [will] become one speech" (24). What do you think would be lost if there were no dialects in the United States? What, if anything, would be gained? If you could wave a wand and make every person in the United States a speaker of Standard American dialect, the uninflected speech of radio and television news anchors that casts an aura of authority and refinement, would you? Write an essay in which you argue for or against Lederer's hope that "American English does not turn into a bland, homogenized, pasteurized, assembly line product. May our bodacious language remain tasty and nourishing—full of flavor, variety, and local ingredients" (25).

If Black English Isn't a Language, Then Tell Me, What Is?

JAMES BALDWIN

American novelist, essayist, playwright, poet, and social critic, James
Baldwin (1924–1987) grew up in Harlem, New York. He attended the
DeWitt Clinton High School in the Bronx where he worked as literary editor on the school magazine alongside student Richard Avedon, an aspiring young photographer. After high school Baldwin pursued his studies
at The New School. It was during these years that Baldwin recognized his
own homosexuality, and in 1948, disillusioned by Americans' prejudice
against blacks and homosexuals, he immigrated to Paris, France, where
he lived as an expatriate for most of his adult life. Baldwin's first novel,
Go Tell It on the Mountain, a semi-autobiographical coming-of-age story
appeared in 1953. It was followed quickly by *Notes of a Native Son* (1955),
a collection of essays; *The Amen Corner* (1954), a play; and *Giovanni's
Room* (1956), a controversial homoerotic novel. Baldwin's other books
include the books of essays *The Fire Next Time* (1963), *No Name in the
Street* (1972), *The Evidence of Things Not Seen* (1985), and *The Price of
the Ticket* (1985); *Going to Meet the Man* (1965), a volume of short stories; the novels *Tell Me How Long the Train's Been Gone* (1968), *If Beale
Street Could Talk* (1974), and *Just Above My Head* (1979); and a book
of poems, *Jimmy's Blues* (1983). A prominent member of the African
American community, Baldwin returned to the United States during the
1960s, working for civil rights as a member of the Congress of Racial
Equality. He appeared on the cover of *Time* magazine in 1963. Later
Baldwin was disheartened by the untimely loss of his personal friends
Medgar Evers, Malcolm X, and Martin Luther King Jr.

In the following essay, which first appeared on July 29, 1979, in the
New York Times, Baldwin joined the debate about black English that was
raging in America at the time and takes white America to task for not
acknowledging the reality and validity of black English as a language and
its importance to the black community.

WRITING TO DISCOVER: *What are your thoughts when you hear the phrase
"black English"? What does black English sound like? Who have you heard use
black English? For you, how does black English differ from standard English?*

St. Paul de Vence, France — The argument concerning the use, or the
status, or the reality, of black English is rooted in American history and
has absolutely nothing to do with the question the argument supposes
itself to be posing. The argument has nothing to do with language itself
but with the *role* of language. Language, incontestably, reveals the speaker.

Language, also, far more dubiously, is meant to define the other—and, in this case, the other is refusing to be defined by a language that has never been able to recognize him.

People evolve a language in order to describe and thus control their circumstances, or in order not to be submerged by a reality that they cannot articulate. (And, if they cannot articulate it, they *are* submerged.) A Frenchman living in Paris speaks a subtly and crucially different language from that of the man living in Marseilles; neither sounds very much like a man living in Quebec; and they would all have great difficulty in apprehending what the man from Guadeloupe, or Martinique, is saying, to say nothing of the man from Senegal—although the "common" language of all these areas is French. But each has paid, and is paying, a different price for this "common" language, in which, as it turns out, they are not saying, and cannot be saying, the same things: They each have very different realities to articulate, or control.

What joins all languages, and all men, is the necessity to confront life, in order, not inconceivably, to outwit death: The price for this is the acceptance, and achievement, of one's temporal identity. So that, for example, though it is not taught in the schools (and this has the potential of becoming a political issue) the south of France still clings to its ancient and musical Provençal, which resists being described as a "dialect." And much of the tension in the Basque countries, and in Wales, is due to the Basque and Welsh determination not to allow their languages to be destroyed. This determination also feeds the flames in Ireland for many indignities the Irish have been forced to undergo at English hands is the English contempt for their language.

It goes without saying, then, that language is also a political instrument, means, and proof of power. It is the most vivid and crucial key to identity: It reveals the private identity, and connects one with, or divorces one from, the larger, public, or communal identity. There have been, and are, times, and places, when to speak a certain language could be dangerous, even fatal. Or, one may speak the same language, but in such a way that one's antecedents are revealed, or (one hopes) hidden. This is true in France, and is absolutely true in England: The range (and reign) of accents on that damp little island make England coherent for the English and totally incomprehensible for everyone else. To open your mouth in England is (if I may use black English) to "put your business in the street": You have confessed your parents, your youth, your school, your salary, your self-esteem, and, alas, your future.

Now, I do not know what white Americans would sound like if there   5 had never been any black people in the United States, but they would not sound the way they sound. *Jazz*, for example, is a very specific sexual term, as in *jazz me, baby*, but white people purified it into the Jazz Age. *Sock it to me*, which means, roughly, the same thing, has been adopted by Nathaniel Hawthorne's descendants with no qualms or hesitations at all, along with *let it all hang out* and *right on! Beat to his socks* which was once the black's most total and despairing image of poverty, was transformed into a thing called the Beat Generation, which phenomenon was, largely, composed of *uptight*, middle-class white people, imitating poverty, trying to *get down*, to get *with it*, doing their *thing*, doing their despairing best to be *funky*, which we, the blacks, never dreamed of doing—we *were* funky, baby, like *funk* was going out of style.

Now, no one can eat his cake, and have it, too, and it is late in the day to attempt to penalize black people for having created a language that permits the nation its only glimpse of reality, a language without which the nation would be even more *whipped* than it is.

I say that the present skirmish is rooted in American history, and it is. Black English is the creation of the black diaspora. Blacks came to the United States chained to each other, but from different tribes: Neither could speak the other's language. If two black people, at that bitter hour of the world's history, had been able to speak to each other, the institution of chattel slavery could never have lasted as long as it did. Subsequently, the slave was given, under the eye, and the gun, of his master, Congo Square,[1] and the Bible—or in other

If this absolutely unprecedented journey does not indicate that black English is a language, I am curious to know what definition of language is to be trusted.

words, and under these conditions, the slave began the formation of the black church, and it is within this unprecedented tabernacle that black English began to be formed. This was not, merely, as in the European example, the adoption of a foreign tongue, but an alchemy that transformed ancient elements into a new language: *A language comes into existence by means of brutal necessity, and the rules of the language are dictated by what the language must convey.*

There was a moment, in time, and in this place, when my brother, or my mother, or my father, or my sister, had to convey to me, for example, the danger in which I was standing from the white man standing just behind me, and to convey this with a speed, and in a language, that the white man could not possibly understand, and that, indeed, he cannot understand, until today. He cannot afford to understand it. This understanding would reveal to him too much about himself, and smash that mirror before which he has been frozen for so long.

Now, if this passion, this skill, this (to quote Toni Morrison) "sheer intelligence," this incredible music, the mighty achievement of having brought a people utterly unknown to, or despised by "history"—to have brought this people to their present, troubled, troubling, and unassailable

---

1. Congo Square: A gathering place in New Orleans where slaves, starting in the eighteenth century, would set up a market, sing, dance, and play music on Sundays.

and unanswerable place—if this absolutely unprecedented journey does not indicate that black English is a language, I am curious to know what definition of language is to be trusted.

A people at the center of the Western world, and in the midst of so   10 hostile a population, has not endured and transcended by means of what is patronizingly called a "dialect." We, the blacks, are in trouble, certainly, but we are not doomed, and we are not inarticulate because we are not compelled to defend a morality that we know to be a lie.

The brutal truth is that the bulk of white people in America never had any interest in educating black people, except as this could serve white purposes. It is not the black child's language that is in question, it is not his language that is despised: It is his experience. A child cannot be taught by anyone who despises him, and a child cannot afford to be fooled. A child cannot be taught by anyone whose demand, essentially, is that the child repudiate his experience, and all that gives him sustenance, and enter a limbo in which he will no longer be black, and in which he knows that he can never become white. Black people have lost too many black children that way.

And, after all, finally, in a country with standards so untrustworthy, a country that makes heroes of so many criminal mediocrities, a country unable to face why so many of the nonwhite are in prison, or on the needle, or standing, futureless, in the streets—it may very well be that both the child, and his elder, have concluded that they have nothing whatever to learn from the people of a country that has managed to learn so little.

THINKING CRITICALLY ABOUT THE READING

1. How does Baldwin define *language*? In what ways is his definition central to his argument? Explain.

2. What does Baldwin mean when he says, "The argument [about black English] has nothing do with language itself but with the *role* of language" (1)?

3. In paragraph 2, Baldwin introduces the example of French and how that language is used in different parts of the world. What light, if any, does this discussion shed on Baldwin's point about black English?

4. According to Baldwin, what is the origin of black English? In what ways is black English "a language that permits the nation its only glimpse of reality, a language without which the nation would be even more *whipped* than it is" (6)?

5. What do you think Baldwin fears has happened and will continue to happen if black children are required to learn standard English? Do you see any problems with using black English for the instruction of black children? Explain.

LANGUAGE IN ACTION

Psychiatrist Thomas Szasz has written extensively on the power of language to define, to impose one's world view on another.

> The struggle for definition is veritably the struggle for life itself. In the typical Western two men fight desperately for the possession of a gun that has been thrown to the ground: whoever reaches the weapon first, shoots and lives; his adversary is shot and dies. In ordinary life, the struggle is not for guns but for words: whoever first defines the situation is the victor; his adversary, the victim. For example, in the family, husband and wife, mother and child do not get along; who defines whom as troublesome or mentally sick? Or, in the apocryphal story about Emerson visiting Thoreau in jail; Emerson asks: "Henry, what are you doing over there?" Thoreau replies: "Ralph, what are you doing over there?" In short, he who first seizes the word imposes reality on the other: he who defines thus dominates and lives; and he who is defined is subjugated and may be killed.
>
> — *The Second Sin*, 1973

Discuss how this "struggle for definition" is played out in our daily lives. How do we use words to define ourselves as well as those around us?

WRITING SUGGESTIONS

1. At the center of Baldwin's argument about black English is the question of the *role* of language. What, for you, is the role of language within a given speech community? What does Baldwin mean when he states, "Language, incontestably, reveals the speaker. Language, also, far more dubiously, is meant to define the other—and, in this case, the other is refusing to be defined by a language that has never been able to recognize him" (1)? Write an essay in which you discuss the important role that black English played historically within the African American speech community. You may find it helpful to review the key points brought to light in the discussion of the Language in Action activity for this selection before you start writing.

2. In the mid-1990s, the Oakland, California, school system created a firestorm of controversy by proposing to teach Ebonics (also known as Vernacular Black English or African American Vernacular English [AAVE]) in the city's schools. In 1997 the Linguistic Society of America issued the following carefully crafted academic response to this very emotional and volatile issue.

Linguistics Society of America (LSA) Resolution on
the Oakland "Ebonics" Issue

Whereas there has been a great deal of discussion in the media and among the American public about the 18 December 1996 decision of the Oakland School Board to recognize the language variety spoken by many African American students and to take it into account in teaching Standard English, the Linguistic Society of America, as a society of scholars engaged in the scientific study of language, hereby resolves to make it known that:

a. The variety known as "Ebonics," "African American Vernacular English" (AAVE), and "Vernacular Black English," and by other names is systematic and rule-governed like all natural speech varieties. In fact, all human linguistic systems — spoken, signed, and written — are fundamentally regular. The systematic and expressive nature of the grammar and pronunciation patterns of the African American vernacular has been established by numerous scientific studies over the past thirty years. Characterizations of Ebonics as "slang," "mutant," "lazy," "defective," "ungrammatical," or "broken English" are incorrect and demeaning.

b. The distinction between "languages" and "dialects" is usually made more on social and political grounds than on purely linguistic ones. For example, different varieties of Chinese are popularly regarded as "dialects," though their speakers cannot understand each other, but speakers of Swedish and Norwegian, which are regarded as separate "languages," generally understand each other. What is important from a linguistic and educational point of view is not whether AAVE is called a "language" or a "dialect" but rather that its systematicity be recognized.

c. As affirmed in the LSA Statement of Language Rights (June 1996), there are individual and group benefits to maintaining vernacular speech varieties and there are scientific and human advantages to linguistic diversity. For those living in the United States there are also benefits in acquiring Standard English and resources should be made available to all who aspire to mastery of Standard English. The Oakland School Board's commitment to helping students master Standard English is commendable.

d. There is evidence from Sweden, the U.S., and other countries that speakers of other varieties can be aided in their learning of the standard variety by pedagogical approaches which recognize the legitimacy of the other varieties of a language. From this perspective, the Oakland School Board's decision to recognize the vernacular of African American students in teaching them Standard English is linguistically and pedagogically sound.

How do you think Baldwin would have responded to the LSA's statement? What techniques do the authors use to define the issue and present their position? How do they avoid entering the broader — and very contentious — societal debate over the use of Ebonics? Where do you stand on this issue? Write an essay in which you look at both the "individual and group benefits to maintaining vernacular speech varieties" as well as the "benefits in acquiring Standard English." Should people be forced to choose between their vernacular speech and Standard English, or can the two coexist comfortably?

Two Ways to Belong in America

BHARATI MUKHERJEE

The prominent Indian American writer and university professor Bharati Mukherjee was born into an aristocratic family in Calcutta (now Kolkata), India, in 1940. After India's independence, her family relocated to England because of her father's work. She returned to India in the 1950s where she earned her bachelor's degree at the University of Calcutta in 1959 and a master's degree from the University of Baroda in 1961. Later she pursued her long-held desire to become a writer by earning a master of fine arts degree at the University of Iowa and eventually a doctorate in English and comparative literature. After she married an American, Clark Blaise, the couple moved to Canada, where they lived for fourteen years until legislation there against South Asians led them to move back to the United States. Before joining the faculty at the University of California, Berkeley, Mukherjee taught at McGill University, Skidmore College, Queens College, and City University of New York. Currently her work centers on writing and the themes of immigration, particularly concerning women, immigration policy, immigrant communities, and cultural alienation. With her husband, she has authored *Days and Nights in Calcutta* (1977) and *The Sorrow and the Terror: The Haunting Legacy of the Air India Tragedy* (1987). In addition, she has published seven novels including *The Tiger's Daughter* (1971), *Wife* (1975), *Darkness* (1985), *Jasmine* (1989), *The Holder of the World* (1993), and *The Tree Bride* (2004); two collections of short stories, *Darkness* (1985) and *The Middleman and Other Stories* (1988), for which she won the National Book Critics Circle Award; and two works of nonfiction, *Political Culture and Leadership in India* (1991) and *Regionalism in Indian Perspective* (1992).

The following essay was first published in the *New York Times* in 1996 in response to new legislation championed by the then vice president, Al Gore, that gave expedited citizenship for legal immigrants living in the United States. As you read Mukherjee's essay, notice the way she has organized her presentation of the contrasting views that she and her sister have toward the various aspects of living as either a legal immigrant or a citizen in the United States.

WRITING TO DISCOVER: *The word* immigrant *has many connotations. What associations does the word have for you? If you were to move to another country, how do you think it would feel to be considered an immigrant?*

This is a tale of two sisters from Calcutta, Mira and Bharati, who have lived in the United States for some thirty-five years, but who find themselves on different sides in the current debate over the status of immigrants. I am an American citizen and she is not. I am moved that thousands of long-term residents are finally taking the oath of citizenship. She is not.

Mira arrived in Detroit in 1960 to study child psychology and pre-school education. I followed her a year later to study creative writing at the University of Iowa. When we left India, we were almost identical in appearance and attitude. We dressed alike, in saris; we expressed identical views on politics, social issues, love and marriage in the same Calcutta convent-school accent. We would endure our two years in America, secure our degrees, then return to India to marry the grooms of our father's choosing.

Instead, Mira married an Indian student in 1962 who was getting his business administration degree at Wayne State University. They soon acquired the labor certifications necessary for the green card of hassle-free residence and employment.

Mira still lives in Detroit, works in the Southfield, Michigan, school system, and has become nationally recognized for her contributions in the fields of preschool education and parent-teacher relationships. After thirty-six years as a legal immigrant in this country, she clings passionately to her Indian citizenship and hopes to go home to India when she retires.

In Iowa City in 1963, I married a fellow student, an American of   5
Canadian parentage. Because of the accident of his North Dakota birth, I bypassed labor-certification requirements and the race-related "quota" system that favored the applicant's country of origin over his or her merit. I was prepared for (and even welcomed) the emotional strain that came with marrying outside my ethnic community. In thirty-three years of marriage, we have lived in every part of North America. By choosing a husband who was not my father's selection, I was opting for fluidity, self-invention, blue jeans and T-shirts, and renouncing three thousand years (at least) of caste-observant, "pure culture" marriage in the Mukherjee family. My books have often been read as unapologetic (and in some quarters overenthusiastic) texts for cultural and psychological "mongreliza-tion." It's a word I celebrate.

Mira and I have stayed sisterly close by phone. In our regular Sunday morning conversations, we are unguardedly affectionate. I am her only blood relative on this continent. We expect to see each other through the looming crises of aging and ill health without being asked. Long before Vice President Gore's "Citizenship USA" drive, we'd had our polite arguments over the ethics of retaining an overseas citizenship while expecting the permanent protection and economic benefits that come with living and working in America.

Like well-raised sisters, we never said what was really on our minds, but we probably pitied one another. She, for the lack of structure in my life, the erasure of Indianness, the absence of an unvarying daily core.

I, for the narrowness of her perspective, her uninvolvement with the mythic depths or the superficial pop culture of this society. But, now, with the scapegoating of "aliens" (documented or illegal) on the increase, and the targeting of long-term legal immigrants like Mira for new scrutiny and new self-consciousness, she and I find ourselves unable to maintain the same polite discretion. We were always unacknowledged adversaries, and we are now, more than ever, sisters.

"I feel used," Mira raged on the phone the other night. "I feel manipulated and discarded. This is such an unfair way to treat a person who was invited to stay and work here because of her talent. My employer went to the INS and petitioned for the labor certification. For over thirty years, I've invested my creativity and professional skills into the improvement of *this* country's preschool system. I've obeyed all the rules, I've paid my taxes, I love my work, I love my students, I love the friends I've made. How dare America now change its rules in midstream? If America wants to make new rules curtailing benefits of legal immigrants, they should apply only to immigrants who arrive after those rules are already in place."

> **In one family, from two sisters alike as peas in a pod, there could not be a wider divergence of immigrant experience.**

To my ears, it sounded like the description of a long-enduring, comfortable yet loveless marriage, without risk or recklessness. Have we the right to demand, and to expect, that we be loved? (That, to me, is the subtext of the arguments by immigration advocates.) My sister is an expatriate, professionally generous and creative, socially courteous and gracious, and that's as far as her Americanization can go. She is here to maintain an identity, not to transform it.

I asked her if she would follow the example of others who have decided to become citizens because of the anti-immigration bills in Congress. And here, she surprised me. "If America wants to play the manipulative game, I'll play it too," she snapped. "I'll become a U.S. citizen for now, then change back to Indian when I'm ready to go home. I feel some kind of irrational attachment to India that I don't to America. Until all this hysteria against legal immigrants, I was totally happy. Having my green card meant I could visit any place in the world I wanted to and then come back to a job that's satisfying and that I do very well."

In one family, from two sisters alike as peas in a pod, there could not be a wider divergence of immigrant experience. America spoke to me—I married it—I embraced the demotion from expatriate aristocrat to immigrant nobody, surrendering those thousands of years of "pure culture," the saris, the delightfully accented English. She retained them all. Which of us is the freak?

Mira's voice, I realize, is the voice not just of the immigrant South Asian community but of an immigrant community of the millions who have stayed rooted in one job, one city, one house, one ancestral culture, one cuisine, for the entirety of their productive years. She speaks for greater numbers than I possibly can. Only the fluency of her English and the anger, rather than fear, born of confidence from her education, differentiate her from the seamstresses, the domestics, the technicians, the shop owners, the millions of hardworking but effectively silenced documented immigrants as well as their less fortunate "illegal" brothers and sisters.

Nearly twenty years ago, when I was living in my husband's ancestral homeland of Canada, I was always well-employed but never allowed to feel part of the local Quebec or larger Canadian society. Then, through a Green Paper that invited a national referendum on the unwanted side effects of "nontraditional" immigration, the Government officially turned against its immigrant communities, particularly those from South Asia.

I felt then the same sense of betrayal that Mira feels now. I will never forget the pain of that sudden turning, and the casual racist outbursts the Green Paper elicited. That sense of betrayal had its desired effect and drove me, and thousands like me, from the country.

Mira and I differ, however, in the ways in which we hope to interact   15 with the country that we have chosen to live in. She is happier to live in America as an expatriate Indian than as an immigrant American. I need to feel like a part of the community I have adopted (as I tried to feel in Canada as well). I need to put roots down, to vote and make the difference that I can. The price that the immigrant willingly pays, and that the exile avoids, is the trauma of self-transformation.

THINKING CRITICALLY ABOUT THE READING

1. What is Mukherjee's thesis? (Glossary: *Thesis*) Where does she present it? How has Mukherjee organized her essay? (Glossary: *Comparison and Contrast*)

2. What arguments does Mukherjee make for becoming an American citizen? What arguments does her sister make for retaining her Indian citizenship? Which sister do you think made the "right" decision? Explain.

3. Mukherjee chooses to let her sister Mira speak for herself in this essay. What do you think would have been lost had she spoken for her sister, simply reporting what Mira felt and believed as an immigrant in the United States? Explain. Why do you think Mukherjee's sister feels "used" by attempts to change American laws regarding social security benefits for noncitizens?

4. Mukherjee uses the word *mongrelization* in paragraph 5. What do you think she means by this word, and why does she celebrate it?

5. What do you think Mukherjee's sister means when she says in paragraph 10, "If America wants to play the manipulative game, I'll play it too"? How do you react to her decision and to her possible plans if and when she eventually returns to India? Explain.

6. At the end of paragraph 11 Mukherjee asks a question. How does she answer it? How would you answer it? Do you, like Mukherjee, "need to feel like a part of the community I have adopted" (15). What does Mukherjee mean when she says in paragraph 15, "The price that the immigrant willingly pays, and that the exile avoids, is the trauma of self-transformation"?

LANGUAGE IN ACTION

In recent years, the issue of immigration has been closely tied to the learning of English. Many people believe that English should be declared America's "official" language and that the business of the government ought to be carried out in English. They believe that people should be strongly urged—if not required—to learn English and that a common language would be a unifying force in a country that is growing increasingly diverse. Others believe that there is no need to legislate English as the country's official language and that immigrants should be encouraged to maintain traditional culture, cuisine, and language. The case of the Mukherjee sisters sheds some interesting light on this complex issue of immigration and language. As a class, brainstorm a list of the three most compelling reasons for encouraging/requiring new immigrants to learn English. What are three important reasons for not encouraging/requiring new immigrants to learn the dominant language? How do you think each of the sisters would respond to the following Jeff Parker cartoon?

"THEY SAY THEY'RE BUILDING A WALL BECAUSE TOO MANY OF US ENTER ILLEGALLY AND WON'T LEARN THEIR LANGUAGE OR ASSIMILATE INTO THEIR CULTURE..."

WRITING SUGGESTIONS

1. In paragraph 7 Mukherjee writes about the relationship that she had with her sister by saying that "we never said what was really on our minds, but we probably pitied one another." These types of differences are played out on a larger scale when immigrants who have transformed themselves into Americans are confronted by those who have chosen to retain their ethnic identity,

and these tensions often lead to name-calling and aggressive prejudice. Such situations exist within the Latino, African American, and Southeast Asian American communities and perhaps among all immigrant groups. Write an essay comparing and contrasting the choices of lifestyle that members of an ethnic or cultural community you are familiar with make as they try to find a comfortable place in American society.

2. Mukherjee presents her sister's reasons for not becoming a citizen and supports them with statements that her sister has made. Imagine that you are Mira Mukherjee. Write a counterargument to the one presented by your sister that gives your reasons for remaining an Indian citizen. Consider that you have already broken with tradition by marrying a man "not of your father's choosing" but also that the "trauma of self-transformation" that your sister raises in the conclusion of her essay is much deeper and more complicated than she has represented it. Can you say that you are holding on to tradition when you are not? Can you engage in a challenging self-transformation if it is not genuinely motivated?

Mother Tongue

AMY TAN

Amy Tan was born in Oakland, California, in 1952, to Chinese immigrant parents. Growing up in a bilingual world, Tan became interested in languages at an early age. At San Jose State University she earned a B.A. in English in 1973 and a master's in linguistics the following year. Tan worked as a child language development specialist and a freelance speech writer for corporate executives before she began writing stories for her own personal enjoyment and therapy. These stories resulted in her first book, *The Joy Luck Club* (1989), a tightly woven novel about four Chinese mothers and their American-born daughters. This novel was a finalist for the National Book Award and later adapted into a commercially successful film. Tan has written five other novels including *The Kitchen God's Wife* (1991), *The Hundred Secret Senses* (1995), *The Bonesetter's Daughter* (2001), *Saving Fish from Drowning* (2005), and *The Valley of Amazement* (2012); a collection of nonfiction essays *The Opposite of Fate: A Book of Musings* (2003); and two children's books, *The Moon Lady* (1992) and *Sagwa, the Chinese Siamese Cat* (1994). Tan currently resides in Sausalito, California.

The following essay was first delivered as a speech and later published in the fall 1990 issue of the *Threepenny Review*. Here Tan explains how she wrote *The Joy Luck Club* and communicated with her mother, using "all the Englishes I grew up with." She explores the limitations of growing up in a household where she heard "broken" English spoken by her immigrant parents.

WRITING TO DISCOVER: *What is your cultural identity? Do you consider yourself an American, or do you identify with another culture? To what extent is your cultural identity tied to language? Explain.*

I am not a scholar of English or literature. I cannot give you much more than personal opinions on the English language and its variations in this country or others.

I am a writer. And by that definition, I am someone who has always loved language. I am fascinated by language in daily life. I spend a great deal of my time thinking about the power of language — the way it can evoke an emotion, a visual image, a complex idea, or a simple truth. Language is the tool of my trade. And I use them all — all the Englishes I grew up with.

Recently, I was made keenly aware of the different Englishes I do use. I was giving a talk to a large group of people, the same talk I had already given to half a dozen other groups. The nature of the talk was about my writing, my life, and my book *The Joy Luck Club*. The talk was going along well enough, until I remembered one major difference that made the whole talk sound wrong. My mother was in the room. And it was perhaps the first time she had heard me give a lengthy speech, using the kind of English I have never used with her. I was saying things like "The intersection of memory upon imagination" and "There is an aspect of my fiction that relates to thus-and-thus"—a speech filled with carefully wrought grammatical phrases, burdened, it suddenly seemed to me, with nominalized forms, past perfect tenses, conditional phrases, all the forms of standard English that I had learned in school and through books, the forms of English I did not use at home with my mother.

Just last week, I was walking down the street with my mother, and I again found myself conscious of the English I was using, the English I do use with her. We were talking about the price of new and used furniture and I heard myself saying this: "Not waste money that way." My husband was with us as well, and he didn't notice any switch in my English. And then I realized why. It's because over **Language is the tool of my trade. And I use them all—all the Englishes I grew up with.** the twenty years we've been together I've often used that same kind of English with him, and sometimes he even uses it with me. It has become our language of intimacy, a different sort of English that relates to family talk, the language I grew up with.

So you'll have some idea of what this family talk I heard sounds like, I'll quote what my mother said during a recent conversation which I videotaped and then transcribed. During this conversation, my mother was talking about a political gangster in Shanghai who had the same last name as her family's, Du, and how the gangster in his early years wanted to be adopted by her family, which was rich by comparison. Later, the gangster became more powerful, far richer than my mother's family, and one day showed up at my mother's wedding to pay his respects. Here's what she said in part:

"Du Yusong having business like fruit stand. Like off the street kind. He is Du like Du Zong—but not Tsung-ming Island people. The local people call putong, the river east side, he belong to that side local people. That man want to ask Du Zong father take him in like become own family. Du Zong father wasn't look down on him, but didn't take seriously, until that man big like become a mafia. Now important person, very hard to inviting him. Chinese way, came only to show respect, don't stay for dinner. Respect for making big celebration, he shows up. Mean gives lots of respect. Chinese custom. Chinese social life that way. If too important won't have to stay too long. He come to my wedding. I didn't see, I heard it. I gone to boy's side, they have YMCA dinner. Chinese age I was nineteen."

You should know that my mother's expressive command of English belies how much she actually understands. She reads the *Forbes* report, listens to *Wall Street Week*, converses daily with her stockbroker, reads all

5

of Shirley MacLaine's books with ease—all kinds of things I can't begin to understand. Yet some of my friends tell me they understand 50 percent of what my mother says. Some say they understand 80 to 90 percent. Some say they understand none of it, as if she were speaking pure Chinese. But to me, my mother's English is perfectly clear, perfectly natural. It's my mother tongue. Her language, as I hear it, is vivid, direct, full of observation and imagery. That was the language that helped shape the way I saw things, expressed things, made sense of the world.

Lately, I've been giving more thought to the kind of English my mother speaks. Like others, I have described it to people as "broken" or "fractured" English. But I wince when I say that. It has always bothered me that I can think of no way to describe it other than "broken," as if it were damaged and needed to be fixed, as if it lacked a certain wholeness and soundness. I've heard other terms used, "limited English," for example. But they seem just as bad, as if everything is limited, including people's perceptions of the limited English speaker.

I know this for a fact, because when I was growing up, my mother's "limited" English limited *my* perception of her. I was ashamed of her English. I believed that her English reflected the quality of what she had to say. That is, because she expressed them imperfectly her thoughts were imperfect. And I had plenty of empirical evidence to support me: the fact that people in department stores, at banks, and at restaurants did not take her seriously, did not give her good service, pretended not to understand her, or even acted as if they did not hear her.

My mother has long realized the limitations of her English as well. When I was fifteen, she used to have me call people on the phone to pretend I was she. In this guise, I was forced to ask for information or even to complain and yell at people who had been rude to her. One time it was a call to her stockbroker in New York. She had cashed out her small portfolio and it just so happened we were going to go to New York the next week, our very first trip outside California. I had to get on the phone and say in an adolescent voice that was not very convincing, "This is Mrs. Tan."

And my mother was standing in the back whispering loudly, "Why he don't send me check, already two weeks late. So mad he lie to me, losing me money."

And then I said in perfect English, "Yes, I'm getting rather concerned. You had agreed to send the check two weeks ago, but it hasn't arrived."

Then she began to talk more loudly. "What he want, I come to New York tell him front of his boss, you cheating me?" And I was trying to calm her down, make her be quiet, while telling the stockbroker, "I can't tolerate any more excuses. If I don't receive the check immediately, I am going to have to speak to your manager when I'm in New York next week." And sure enough, the following week there we were in front of this astonished stockbroker, and I was sitting there red-faced and quiet, and

10

my mother, the real Mrs. Tan, was shouting at his boss in her impeccable broken English.

We used a similar routine just five days ago, for a situation that was far less humorous. My mother had gone to the hospital for an appointment, to find out about a benign brain tumor a CAT scan had revealed a month ago. She said she had spoken very good English, her best English, no mistakes. Still, she said, the hospital did not apologize when they said they had lost the CAT scan and she had come for nothing. She said they did not seem to have any sympathy when she told them she was anxious to know the exact diagnosis, since her husband and son had both died of brain tumors. She said they would not give her any more information until the next time and she would have to make another appointment for that. So she said she would not leave until the doctor called her daughter. She wouldn't budge. And when the doctor finally called her daughter, me, who spoke in perfect English—lo and behold—we had assurances the CAT scan would be found, promises that a conference call on Monday would be held, and apologies for any suffering my mother had gone through for a most regrettable mistake.

I think my mother's English almost had an effect on limiting my possibilities in life as well. Sociologists and linguists probably will tell you that a person's developing language skills are more influenced by peers. But I do think that the language spoken in the family, especially in immigrant families which are more insular, plays a large role in shaping the language of the child. And I believe that it affected my results on achievement tests, IQ tests, and the SAT. While my English skills were never judged as poor, compared to math, English could not be considered my strong suit. In grade school I did moderately well, getting perhaps B's, sometimes B-pluses, in English and scoring perhaps in the sixtieth or seventieth percentile on achievement tests. But those scores were not good enough to override the opinion that my true abilities lay in math and science, because in those areas I achieved A's and scored in the ninetieth percentile or higher. 15

This was understandable. Math is precise; there is only one correct answer. Whereas, for me at least, the answers on English tests were always a judgment call, a matter of opinion and personal experience. Those tests were constructed around items like fill-in-the-blank sentence completion, such as "Even though Tom was____ , Mary thought he was____." And the correct answer always seemed to be the most bland combinations of thoughts, for example, "Even though Tom was shy, Mary thought he was charming," with the grammatical structure "even though" limiting the correct answer to some sort of semantic opposites, so you wouldn't get answers like, "Even though Tom was foolish, Mary thought he was ridiculous." Well, according to my mother, there were very few limitations as to what Tom could have been and what Mary might have thought of him. So I never did well on tests like that.

The same was true with word analogies, pairs of words, in which you were supposed to find some sort of logical, semantic relationship—for example, " 'sunset' is to 'nightfall' as____ is to____." And here you would be presented with a list of four possible pairs, one of which showed the same kind of relationship: "red" is to "stoplight," "bus" is to "arrival," "chills" is to "fever," "yawn" is to "boring." Well, I could never think that way. I knew what the tests were asking, but I could not block out of my mind the images already created by the first pair, "sunset is to nightfall"—and I would see a burst of colors against a darkening sky, the moon rising, the lowering of a curtain of stars. And all the other pairs of words—red, bus, stoplight, boring—just threw up a mass of confusing images, making it impossible for me to sort out something as logical as saying: "A sunset precedes nightfall" is the same as "a chill precedes a fever." The only way I would have gotten that answer right would have been to imagine an associative situation, for example, my being disobedient and staying out past sunset, catching a chill at night, which turns into feverish pneumonia as punishment, which indeed did happen to me.

I have been thinking about all this lately, about my mother's English, about achievement tests. Because lately I've been asked, as a writer, why there are not more Asian Americans represented in American literature. Why are there few Asian Americans enrolled in creative writing programs? Why do so many Chinese students go into engineering? Well, these are broad sociological questions I can't begin to answer. But I have noticed in surveys—in fact, just last week—that Asian students, as a whole, always do significantly better on math achievement tests than in English. And this makes me think that there are other Asian-American students whose English spoken in the home might also be described as "broken" or "limited." And perhaps they also have teachers who are steering them away from writing and into math and science, which is what happened to me.

Fortunately, I happen to be rebellious in nature and enjoy the challenge of disproving assumptions made about me. I became an English major my first year in college, after being enrolled as pre-med. I started writing nonfiction as a freelancer the week after I was told by my former boss that writing was my worst skill and I should hone my talents toward account management.

But it wasn't until 1985 that I finally began to write fiction. And at 20 first I wrote using what I thought to be wittily crafted sentences, sentences that would finally prove I had mastery over the English language. Here's an example from the first draft of a story that later made its way into *The Joy Luck Club*, but without this line: "That was my mental quandary in its nascent state." A terrible line, which I can barely pronounce.

Fortunately, for reasons I won't get into today, I later decided I should envision a reader for the stories I would write. And the reader I decided upon was my mother, because these were stories about mothers.

So with this reader in mind — and in fact she did read my early drafts — I began to write stories using all the Englishes I grew up with: the English I spoke to my mother, which for lack of a better term might be described as "simple"; the English she used with me, which for lack of a better term might be described as "broken"; my translation of her Chinese, which could certainly be described as "watered down"; and what I imagined to be her translation of her Chinese if she could speak in perfect English, her internal language, and for that I sought to preserve the essence, but neither an English nor a Chinese structure. I wanted to capture what language ability tests can never reveal: her intent, her passion, her imagery, the rhythms of her speech and the nature of her thoughts.

Apart from what any critic had to say about my writing, I knew I had succeeded where it counted when my mother finished reading my book, and gave me her verdict: "So easy to read."

THINKING CRITICALLY ABOUT THE READING

1. How effectively do the first two paragraphs function as an introduction to this essay? What are your expectations about the essay after Tan reveals her qualifications with language and literature?

2. What specifically are the different Englishes that Tan grew up with? How was each English used?

3. To give readers some idea of what the "family talk" Tan heard while growing up sounded like, Tan quotes her mother's story in paragraph 6. What did you think of Tan's mother after reading this paragraph? Did you understand everything the first time you read it, or did you have to reread portions to make sure you got it?

4. Why do you suppose Tan recounts the story of her mother's stockbroker and her mother's dealings with the hospital in paragraphs 10 through 14?

5. What does Tan mean when she writes, "I think my mother's English almost had an effect on limiting my possibilities in life" (15)?

6. In paragraphs 16 and 17 Tan discusses her difficulties with questions on English tests that called for "fill-in-the-blank sentence completion" and facility with "word analogies." Why do you suppose such questions vexed her? Explain.

LANGUAGE IN ACTION

When we listen to people speak, we readily notice if someone is using nonstandard English. We also recognize conversational or informal standard English. On occasion, we hear people using what might be called hyper- or super-standard English, speech that sounds too formal or proper for everyday conversation. In the following sets of sentences, classify each sentence as being (1) nonstandard English, (2) informal standard English, or (3) super-standard English.

1. a. If I was going to do that, I would start right now.
   b. If I were going to do that, I would start right now.
   c. Were I to do that, I would start right now.
   d. I would start right now, if I was going to do that.
2. a. He's not as smart as she.
   b. He's not so smart as she.
   c. He ain't as smart as her.
   d. He not as smart as her.

Discuss what words or word forms in the sentences that helped you label each one.

WRITING SUGGESTIONS

1. Do you believe that the English spoken at home while you were growing up had any effect on how well you did in school or in your community at large? Using Tan's essay as a model, write an essay exploring the "Englishes" you grew up with and how they affected your performance in and out of school.

2. Write an essay in which you explore the main differences between public language — that is, language used in school, workplace, and government settings — and private language — that is, language used in familial or other intimate relationships.

7

WRITERS ON WRITING

Learning to write well is a demanding and difficult pursuit, but the ability to express exactly what you mean is one of the most enjoyable and rewarding skills you can possess. And, as with any sought-after goal, there is plenty of help available for the aspiring writer. In this chapter, we have gathered some of the best of that advice, offered by professional writers and respected teachers of writing.

The essays included in this chapter are based on current research and thinking on how writers go about their work. We begin with best-selling author Stephen King's "Reading to Write," wherein he supports the need to be an active and critical reader, much as we have done in Chapter 1, if you wish to become an effective writer. The rest of the essays in this section look more deeply into the writer's tool bag. Linda Flower analyzes what we mean by audience: "The goal of the writer is to create a momentary common ground between the reader and the writer." She explains that in order to communicate effectively writers should know as much about their readers' knowledge, attitudes, and needs as possible. Popular novelist and teacher of writing Anne Lamott recognizes that even though writers may start out with firm purpose and clear thinking, rough drafts are inevitably messy affairs. In "The Maker's Eye: Revising Your Own Manuscripts," the late Donald M. Murray recognizes the need to produce a first draft, no matter how messy, so as to move to the real job of writing. For him, as for almost all practicing writers, writing is revising. Next, we offer another take on the need to achieve clarity in your writing. In his essay "Simplicity," one of America's leading experts on writing, William Zinsser, offers the following support: "Writing is hard work. A clear sentence is no accident. Very few sentences come out right the first time, or even the third time. Remember this in moments of despair. If you find that writing is hard, it's because it *is* hard." Finally, a video with Stephen King Amis (available online at bedfordstmartins.com/languageawareness/epages) shows the renowned author discussing the importance of reading widely and writing constantly in a talk at Yale University. All these writing experts are worth reading not just once but again and again as you develop your own skills, confidence, and authority as a writer.

Reading to Write

STEPHEN KING

Born in 1947, Stephen King is a 1970 graduate of the University of Maine. He worked as a janitor in a knitting mill, a laundry worker, and a high school English teacher before he struck it big with his writing. Today, many people consider King's name synonymous with the macabre; he is, beyond dispute, the most successful writer of horror fiction today. He has written dozens of novels and hundreds of short stories, novellas, and screenplays, among other works. His books have sold well over 300 million copies worldwide, and many of his novels have been made into popular motion pictures, including *Stand by Me, Misery, The Green Mile*, and *Dreamcatcher*. His fiction, starting with *Carrie* in 1974, includes *Salem's Lot* (1975), *The Shining* (1977), *The Dead Zone* (1979), *Christine* (1983), *Pet Sematary* (1983), *The Dark Half* (1989), *The Girl Who Loved Tom Gordon* (1999), *From a Buick 8* (2002), *Everything's Eventual: Five Dark Tales* (2002), *The Colorado Kid* (2005), *Cell* (2006), *Lisey's Story* (2006), *Duma Key* (2008), *Under the Dome* (2009), *11/22/63* (2011), *The Wind Through the Keyhole* (2012), and *Mile 81* (2012). Other works include *Danse Macabre* (1980), a nonfiction look at horror in the media, and *On Writing: A Memoir of the Craft* (2000).

In the following passage taken from *On Writing*, King discusses the importance of reading in learning to write. Reading, in his words, "offers you a constantly growing knowledge of what has been done and what hasn't, what is trite and what is fresh, what works and what just lies there dying (or dead) on the page."

WRITING TO DISCOVER: *In your opinion, are reading and writing connected in some way? If the two activities are related, what is the nature of that relationship? Do you have to be a reader to be a good writer, or is writing an activity that can be learned quite apart from reading?*

If you want to be a writer, you must do two things above all others: Read a lot and write a lot. There's no way around these two things that I'm aware of, no shortcut.

I'm a slow reader, but I usually get through seventy or eighty books a year, mostly fiction. I don't read in order to study the craft; I read because I like to read. It's what I do at night, kicked back in my blue chair. Similarly, I don't read fiction to study the art of fiction, but simply because I like stories. Yet there is a learning process going on. Every book you pick up has its own lesson or lessons, and quite often the bad books have more to teach than the good ones.

When I was in the eighth grade, I happened upon a paperback novel by Murray Leinster, a science fiction pulp writer who did most of his work during the forties and fifties, when magazines like *Amazing Stories* paid a penny a word. I had read other books by Mr. Leinster, enough to know that the quality of his writing was uneven. This particular tale, which was about mining in the asteroid belt, was one of his less successful efforts. Only that's too kind. It was terrible, actually, a story populated by paper-thin characters and driven by outlandish plot developments. Worst of all (or so it seemed to me at the time), Leinster had fallen in love with the word *zestful*. Characters watched the approach of ore-bearing asteroids with *zestful smiles*. Characters sat down to supper aboard their mining ship with *zestful anticipation*. Near the end of the book, the hero swept the large-breasted, blonde heroine into a *zestful embrace*. For me, it was the literary equivalent of a smallpox vaccination: I have never, so far as I know, used the word *zestful* in a novel or a story. God willing, I never will.

Asteroid Miners (which wasn't the title, but that's close enough) was an important book in my life as a reader. Almost everyone can remember losing his or her virginity, and most writers can remember the first book he/she put down thinking: *I can do better than this, Hell, I* am *doing better than this!* What could be more encouraging to the struggling writer than to realize his/her work is unquestionably better than that of someone who actually got paid for his/her stuff?

> **If you want to be a writer, you must do two things above all others: Read a lot and write a lot.**

One learns most clearly what not to do by reading bad prose—one   5
novel like *Asteroid Miners* (or *Valley of the Dolls, Flowers in the Attic,* and *The Bridges of Madison County,* to name just a few) is worth a semester at a good writing school, even with the superstar guest lecturers thrown in.

Good writing, on the other hand, teaches the learning writer about style, graceful narration, plot development, the creation of believable characters, and truth-telling. A novel like *The Grapes of Wrath* may fill a new writer with feelings of despair and good old-fashioned jealousy—"I'll never be able to write anything that good, not if I live to be a thousand"—but such feelings can also serve as a spur, goading the writer to work harder and aim higher. Being swept away by a combination of great story and great writing—of being flattened, in fact—is part of every writer's necessary formation. You cannot hope to sweep someone else away by the force of your writing until it has been done to you.

So we read to experience the mediocre and the outright rotten; such experience helps us to recognize those things when they begin to creep into our own work, and to steer clear of them. We also read in order to measure ourselves against the good and the great, to get a sense of all that can be done. And we read in order to experience different styles.

You may find yourself adopting a style you find particularly exciting, and there's nothing wrong with that. When I read Ray Bradbury as a kid, I wrote like Ray Bradbury—everything green and wondrous and seen through a lens smeared with the grease of nostalgia. When I read James M. Cain, every-thing I wrote came out clipped and stripped and hard-boiled. When I read Lovecraft, my prose became luxurious and Byzantine. I wrote stories in my teenage years where all these styles merged, creating a kind of hilarious stew. This sort of stylistic blending is a necessary part of developing one's own style, but it doesn't occur in a vacuum. You have to read widely, constantly refining (and redefining) your own work as you do so. It's hard for me to believe that people who read very little (or not at all in some cases) should presume to write and expect people to like what they have written, but I know it's true. If I had a nickel for every person who ever told me he/she wanted to become a writer but "didn't have time to read," I could buy myself a pretty good steak dinner. Can I be blunt on this subject? If you don't have time to read, you don't have the time (or the tools) to write. Simple as that.

Reading is the creative center of a writer's life. I take a book with me everywhere I go, and find there are all sorts of opportunities to dip in. The trick is to teach yourself to read in small sips as well as in long swallows. Waiting rooms were made for books — of course! But so are theater lobbies before the show, long and boring checkout lines, and everyone's favorite, the john. You can even read while you're driving, thanks to the audiobook revolution. Of the books I read each year, anywhere from six to a dozen are on tape. As for all the wonderful radio you will be missing, come on — how many times can you listen to Deep Purple sing "Highway Star"?

Reading at meals is considered rude in polite society, but if you expect to succeed as a writer, rudeness should be the second-to-least of your con-cerns. The least of all should be polite society and what it expects. If you intend to write as truthfully as you can, your days as a member of polite society are numbered, anyway.   10

Where else can you read? There's always the treadmill, or whatever you use down at the local health club to get aerobic. I try to spend an hour doing that every day, and I think I'd go mad without a good novel to keep me company. Most exercise facilities (at home as well as outside it) are now equipped with TVs, but TV — while working out or anywhere else — really is about the last thing an aspiring writer needs. If you feel you must have the news analyst blowhards on CNN while you exercise, or the stock market blowhards on MSNBC, or the sports blowhards on ESPN, it's time for you to question how serious you really are about becoming a writer. You must be prepared to do some serious turning inward toward the life of the imagi-nation, and that means, I'm afraid, that Geraldo, Keith Olbermann, and Jay Leno must go. Reading takes time, and the glass teat takes too much of it.

Once weaned from the ephemeral craving for TV, most people will find they enjoy the time they spend reading. I'd like to suggest that turning off that endlessly quacking box is apt to improve the quality of your life as well as the quality of your writing. And how much of a sacrifice are we talking about here? How many *Frasier* and *ER* reruns does it take to make one American life complete? How many Richard Simmons infomercials? How many whiteboy/fatboy Beltway insiders on CNN? Oh man, don't get me started. Jerry-Springer-Dr.-Dre-Judge-Judy-Jerry-Falwell-Donny-and-Marie, I rest my case.

When my son Owen was seven or so, he fell in love with Bruce Springsteen's E Street Band, particularly with Clarence Clemons, the band's burly sax player. Owen decided he wanted to learn to play like Clarence. My wife and I were amused and delighted by this ambition. We were also hopeful, as any parent would be, that our kid would turn out to be talented, perhaps even some sort of prodigy. We got Owen a tenor saxophone for Christmas and lessons with Gordon Bowie, one of the local music men. Then we crossed our fingers and hoped for the best.

Seven months later I suggested to my wife that it was time to discontinue the sax lessons, if Owen concurred. Owen did, and with palpable relief—he hadn't wanted to say it himself, especially not after asking for the sax in the first place, but seven months had been long enough for him to realize that, while he might love Clarence Clemons's big sound, the saxophone was simply not for him—God had not given him that particular talent.

I knew, not because Owen stopped practicing, but because he was practicing only during the periods Mr. Bowie had set for him: half an hour after school four days a week, plus an hour on the weekends. Owen mastered the scales and the notes—nothing wrong with his memory, his lungs, or his eye-hand coordination—but we never heard him taking off, surprising himself with something new, blissing himself out. And as soon as his practice time was over, it was back into the case with the horn, and there it stayed until the next lesson or practice time. What this suggested to me was that when it came to the sax and my son, there was never going to be any real playtime; it was all going to be rehearsal. That's no good. If there's no joy in it, it's just no good. It's best to go on to some other area, where the deposits of talent may be richer and the fun quotient higher.

Talent renders the whole idea of rehearsal meaningless; when you find something at which you are talented, you do it (whatever *it* is) until your fingers bleed or your eyes are ready to fall out of your head. Even when no one is listening (or reading, or watching), every outing is a bravura performance, because you as the creator are happy. Perhaps even ecstatic. That goes for reading and writing as well as for playing a musical instrument, hitting a baseball, or running the four-forty. The sort of strenuous reading and writing program I advocate—four to six hours a day, every day—will not seem strenuous if you really enjoy doing these things and have an aptitude for them; in fact, you may be following such a program already. If you feel you need permission to do all the reading and writing your little heart desires, however, consider it hereby granted by yours truly.

The real importance of reading is that it creates an ease and intimacy with the process of writing; one comes to the country of the writer with one's papers and identification pretty much in order. Constant reading will pull you into a place (a mind-set, if you like the phrase) where you can

15

write eagerly and without self-consciousness. It also offers you a constantly growing knowledge of what has been done and what hasn't, what is trite and what is fresh, what works and what just lies there dying (or dead) on the page. The more you read, the less apt you are to make a fool of yourself with your pen or word processor.

THINKING CRITICALLY ABOUT THE READING

1. What does King mean when he writes that reading a bad novel is "worth a semester at a good writing school, even with the superstar guest lecturers thrown in" (5)? Do you take his observation seriously? Why or why not?

2. In paragraph 3, King berates the author Murray Leinster for his repeated use of the word *zestful*. He says he himself has, as far as he knows, never used the word. Why do you suppose he doesn't like the word? Have you ever used it in your own writing? Explain. (Glossary: *Diction*)

3. In paragraph 7 King says that "we read in order to experience different styles." What examples does he use to support this statement? If you have learned from someone else's style, what exactly was it that you learned? (Glossary: *Evidence*)

4. Authors, especially those as famous as King, are very much sought after as guests on television shows, at writing conferences, and at celebrity and charity events. Why does King believe that it is incompatible for one to be both a member of polite society and an author? Do you agree with him? Why or why not?

5. King does not like TV. What does he find wrong with it, especially for writers?

6. Admittedly, not everyone who wants to write well also aspires to be a great novelist. What value, if any, does King's advice about reading and writing have for you as a college student? Explain.

LANGUAGE IN ACTION

King claims in paragraph 7 that "we read in order to experience different styles." Style is, however, an elusive term. It's a difficult term to define and understand. Begin a brainstorming classroom discussion of what we mean by the word style by first turning to your glossary in *Language Awareness*. While it is a good place to start, the definition we give is necessarily limited because the term also encompasses the concepts of tone, attitude, diction, voice, and point of view, among other terms also found in your glossary. With your instructor's guidance and as time allows, develop a more detailed and informative definition of style.

WRITING SUGGESTIONS

1. King shares with his readers both his reading and writing experiences and the way they have influenced and shaped his development as a writer. Each of us has also been influenced by the reading and writing we have done. Some of us have done a lot of reading and writing in and out of school while others

have not done as much as we would have liked. Write an essay explaining what your experiences have been with reading and writing and especially how your reading has influenced your writing and vice versa. Here are some of the many questions you might want to address in your essay: What writers have you envied and wanted to imitate? What subjects have interested you? What style of writing do you favor? What style annoys you? Have your tastes changed? What particular texts have had a great influence on your thinking and outlook?

2. King seems to be especially averse to watching television. Is it the medium, the types of programs aired, or a combination that annoys him? After all, consider that movies and miniseries made from his novels have appeared on television. Why do you suppose he finds pleasure in reading and not television? Does the same relationship between reading and writing take place between watching television and writing? Write an essay in which you argue against his rejection of television or in which you, like King, take issue with it and with those programs you find a waste of time.

Writing for an Audience

LINDA FLOWER

Linda Flower is professor of rhetoric at Carnegie Mellon University, where she directed the Business Communication program for a number of years. She has been a leading researcher on the composing process, and the results of her investigations have shaped and informed her influential writing texts *Problem-Solving Strategies for Writing* (1993) and *The Construction of Negotiated Meaning* (1994).

In this selection, which is taken from *Problem-Solving Strategies for Writing*, Flower's focus is on audience — the people for whom we write. She believes that writers must establish a "common ground" between themselves and their readers, one that lessens their differences in knowledge, attitudes, and needs. Although we can never be certain who might read what we write, it is nevertheless important for us to have a target audience in mind. Many of the decisions that we make as writers are influenced by our real or imagined readers.

WRITING TO DISCOVER: *Imagine for a moment that you just received a speeding ticket for going sixty-five miles per hour in a thirty-mile-per-hour zone. How would you describe the episode to your best friend? To your parents? To the judge in court? Sketch out the three versions, and then in several paragraphs write about how the three versions of your story differ. How do you account for these differences?*

The goal of the writer is to create a momentary common ground between the reader and the writer. You want the reader to share your knowledge and your attitude toward that knowledge. Even if the reader eventually disagrees, you want him or her to be able for the moment to *see things as you see them*. A good piece of writing closes the gap between you and the reader.

ANALYZE YOUR AUDIENCE

The first step in closing that gap is to gauge the distance between the two of you. Imagine, for example, that you are a student writing your parents, who have always lived in New York City, about a wilderness survival expedition you want to go on over spring break. Sometimes obvious differences such as age or background will be important, but the critical differences for writers usually fall into three areas: the reader's *knowledge* about the topic, his or her *attitude* toward it, and his or her personal or professional *needs*. Because these differences often exist, good writers do more than simply express their meaning; they pinpoint the critical differences between themselves and their reader and design their writing to reduce those differences. Let us look at these areas in more detail.

KNOWLEDGE. This is usually the easiest difference to handle. What does your reader need to know? What are the main ideas you hope to teach? Does your reader have enough background knowledge to really understand you? If not, what would he or she have to learn?

ATTITUDES. When we say a person has knowledge, we usually refer to his conscious awareness of explicit facts and clearly defined concepts. This kind of knowledge can be easily written down or told to someone else. However, much of what we "know" is not held in this formal, explicit way. Instead it is held as an attitude or image—as a loose cluster of associations. For instance, my image of lakes includes associations many people would have, including fishing, water

> **A good piece of writing closes the gap between you and the reader.**

skiing, stalled outboards, and lots of kids catching night crawlers with flashlights. However, the most salient or powerful parts of my image, which strongly color my whole attitude toward lakes, are thoughts of cloudy skies, long rainy days, and feeling generally cold and damp. By contrast, one of my best friends has a very different cluster of associations: to him a lake means sun, swimming, sailing, and happily sitting on the end of a dock. Needless to say, our differing images cause us to react quite differently to a proposal that we visit a lake. Likewise, one reason people often find it difficult to discuss religion and politics is that terms such as "capitalism" conjure up radically different images.

As you can see, a reader's image of a subject is often the source of   5
attitudes and feelings that are unexpected and, at times, impervious to mere facts. A simple statement that seems quite persuasive to you, such as "Lake Wampago would be a great place to locate the new music camp," could have little impact on your reader if he or she simply doesn't visualize a lake as a "great place." In fact, many people accept uncritically any statement that fits in with their own attitudes—and reject, just as uncritically, anything that does not.

Whether your purpose is to persuade or simply to present your perspective, it helps to know the image and attitudes that your reader already holds. The more these differ from your own, the more you will have to do to make him or her *see* what you mean.

NEEDS. When writers discover a large gap between their own knowledge and attitudes and those of the reader, they usually try to change the reader in some way. Needs, however, are different. When you analyze a reader's needs, it is so that you, the writer, can adapt to him. If you ask a friend majoring in biology how to keep your fish tank from clouding, you don't want to hear a textbook recitation on the life processes of algae. You expect a friend to adapt his or her knowledge and tell you exactly how to solve your problem.

The ability to adapt your knowledge to the needs of the reader is often crucial to your success as a writer. This is especially true in writing done on a job. For example, as producer of a public affairs program for a television station, 80 percent of your time may be taken up planning the details of new shows, contacting guests, and scheduling the taping sessions. But when you write a program proposal to the station director, your job is to show how the program will fit into the cost guidelines, the FCC requirements for relevance, and the overall programming plan for the station. When you write that report your role in the organization changes from producer to proposal writer. Why? Because your reader needs that information in order to make a decision. He may be *interested* in your scheduling problems and the specific content of the shows, but he *reads* your report because of his own needs as station director of the organization. He has to act.

In college, where the reader is also a teacher, the reader's needs are a little less concrete but just as important. Most papers are assigned as a way to teach something. So the real purpose of a paper may be for you to make connections between two historical periods, to discover for yourself the principle behind a laboratory experiment, or to develop and support your own interpretation of a novel. A good college paper doesn't just rehash the facts; it demonstrates what your reader, as a teacher, needs to know—that you are learning the thinking skills his or her course is trying to teach.

Effective writers are not simply expressing what they know, like a   10
student madly filling up an examination bluebook. Instead they are *using* their knowledge: reorganizing, maybe even rethinking their ideas to meet the demands of an assignment or the needs of their reader.

THINKING CRITICALLY ABOUT THE READING

1. How, according to Flower, does a competent writer achieve the goal of closing the gap between himself or herself and the reader? How does a writer determine what a reader's "personal or professional needs" (2) are?

2. What, for Flower, is the difference between knowledge and attitude? Why is it important for writers to understand this difference?

3. Flower wrote this selection for college students. How well did she assess your knowledge, attitude, and needs about the subject of a writer's audience? Does Flower's use of language and examples show a sensitivity to her audience? Provide specific examples to support your view. (Glossary: *Examples*)

4. In paragraph 4, Flower discusses the fact that many words have both positive and negative associations. How do you think words come to have associations? (Glossary: *Connotation/Denotation*) Consider, for example, such words as *home, anger, royalty, welfare, politician,* and *strawberry shortcake.*

5. What does Flower believe constitutes a "good college paper" (9)? Do you agree with her assessment? Why or why not?

6. Flower notes in paragraph 4 that many words often have "a loose cluster of associations." Explain how you can use this fact to advantage when writing an argument, a personal essay, or an informative piece.

7. When using technical language in a paper on a subject you have thoroughly researched or are already familiar with, why is it important for you to know your audience? (Glossary: *Audience*) What language strategies might you use to adapt your knowledge to your audience? Explain. How could your classmates, friends, or parents help you?

LANGUAGE IN ACTION

Analyze the Web site language for Cambridge Chemical Technologies (cambchemtech.com/services/technology-definition-and-transfer/). Based on your own familiarity with this industry's language, identify those words you consider jargon. (Glossary: *Technical Language*) Which words are appropriate for a general audience? An expert audience? For what kind of audience do you think this page was written? Explain.

cambridge
CHEMICAL TECHNOLOGIES

625 Mount Auburn Street
Cambridge, MA 02138
phone:617 868 0670
fax:617 868 0672
info@cambchemtech.com

Home   About Us   People   Services   Expertise   Projects   News   Contact

Cambridge Chemical Technologies, Inc. > Services > Technology Definition Package

Technology Definition Package
Conveys the Design While Protecting the Client's IP

Services
> Basic Engineering Package
> Technology Definition Package
> Technology Transfer
> Custom Solutions

Tailored to provide critical process details.

CCTI offers a technology definition package when a technology owner is building a new plant or licensing technology to others. Working with the technology owner, we tailor the package content so that the key elements of the technology are conveyed to the Engineering, Procurement, and Construction (EPC) contractor while protecting the owner's intellectual property.

CCTI can provide this service because we are experienced not only in process development but also in the work systems of large EPC contractors. The technology package clearly defines the technical scope of work for the EPC contractor, resulting in greater overall efficiency.

Unlike a relatively standardized Basic Engineering Package, the level of detail in a technology package differs project by project. Units well within the design capabilities of the EPC are more broadly described, while those containing subtle design parameters are described in greater detail. The technology definition package becomes a pre-FEED or pre-BEP package.

The technology definition includes deliverables such as:

✓ Physical Property Compilation
✓ Process Description
✓ Critical Operating Conditions
✓ Process Flow Diagrams
✓ Design Basis
✓ Design Guidelines
✓ Critical Equipment Process Specification
✓ Critical Equipment Mechanical Design

WRITING SUGGESTIONS

1. Write an essay in which you discuss the proposition that honesty is a prerequisite of good writing. Ask yourself what it means to write honestly. What does dishonest writing look and sound like? Do you have a responsibility to be an honest writer? How is honesty in writing related to questions of audience? Be sure to illustrate your essay with examples from your own experiences.

2. In order to write well, a writer has to identify his or her audience. Choose a topic that is important to you and, taking into account what Flower calls your audience's knowledge, attitude, and needs, write a letter about that topic to your best friend. Then write a letter on the same topic to your instructor. How does your message differ from letter to letter? How does your diction change? (Glossary: *Diction*) What conclusions about audience can you draw from your two letters? How successful do you think you were in closing "the gap between you and the reader" in each letter?

Shitty First Drafts

ANNE LAMOTT

Born in San Francisco in 1954, Anne Lamott is a graduate of Goucher College in Baltimore and is the author of six novels, including *Rosie* (1983), *Crooked Little Heart* (1997), *All New People* (2000), and *Blue Shoes* (2002). She has also been the food reviewer for *California* magazine, a book reviewer for *Mademoiselle*, and a regular contributor to *Salon's* "Mothers Who Think." Her nonfiction books include *Operating Instructions: A Journal of My Son's First Year* (1993), in which she describes her adventures as a single parent; *Traveling Mercies: Some Thoughts on Faith* (1999), in which she charts her journey toward faith in God; *Plan B: Further Thoughts on Faith* (2005); and *Grace (Eventually): Thoughts on Faith* (2007); and with her son Sam, *Some Assembly Required: A Journal of My Son's First Son* (2012).

In the following selection, taken from Lamott's popular book about writing, *Bird by Bird* (1994), she argues for the need to let go and write those "shitty first drafts" that lead to clarity and sometimes brilliance in our second and third drafts.

WRITING TO DISCOVER: *Many professional writers view first drafts as something they have to do before they can begin the real work of writing — revision. How do you view the writing of your first drafts? What patterns, if any, do you see in your writing behavior when working on first drafts? Is the work liberating? Restricting? Pleasant? Unpleasant? Explain in a paragraph or two.*

Now, practically even better news than that of short assignments is the idea of shitty first drafts. All good writers write them. This is how they end up with good second drafts and terrific third drafts. People tend to look at successful writers, writers who are getting their books published and maybe even doing well financially, and think that they sit down at their desks every morning feeling like a million dollars, feeling great about who they are and how much talent they have and what a great story they have to tell; that they take in a few deep breaths, push back their sleeves, roll their necks a few times to get all the cricks out, and dive in, typing fully formed passages as fast as a court reporter. But this is just the fantasy of the uninitiated. I know some very great writers, writers you love who write beautifully and have made a great deal of money, and not one of them sits down routinely feeling wildly enthusiastic and confident. Not one of them writes elegant first drafts. All right, one of them does, but we do not like her very much. We do not think that she has a rich inner life or that God likes her or can even stand her. (Although when I mentioned this to my priest friend Tom, he said you can safely assume you've created God in your own image when it turns out that God hates all the same people you do.)

Very few writers really know what they are doing until they've done it. Nor do they go about their business feeling dewy and thrilled. They do not type a few stiff warm-up sentences and then find themselves bounding along like huskies across the snow. One writer I know tells me that he sits down every morning and says to himself nicely, "It's not like you don't have a choice, because you do—you can either type or kill yourself." We all often feel like we are pulling teeth, even those writers whose prose ends up being the most natural and fluid. The right words and sentences just do not come pouring out like ticker tape most of the time. Now, Muriel Spark is said to have felt that she was taking dictation from God every morning—sitting there, one supposes, plugged into a Dictaphone, typing away, humming. But this is a very hostile and aggressive position. One might hope for bad things to rain down on a person like this.

Very few writers really know what they are doing until they've done it.

For me and most of the other writers I know, writing is not rapturous. In fact, the only way I can get anything written at all is to write really, really shitty first drafts.

The first draft is the child's draft, where you let it all pour out and then let it romp all over the place, knowing that no one is going to see it and that you can shape it later. You just let this childlike part of you channel whatever voices and visions come through and onto the page. If one of the characters wants to say, "Well, so what, Mr. Poopy Pants?," you let her. No one is going to see it. If the kid wants to get into really sentimental, weepy, emotional territory, you let him. Just get it all down on paper, because there may be something great in those six crazy pages that you would never have gotten to by more rational, grown-up means. There may be something in the very last line of the very last paragraph on page six that you just love, that is so beautiful or wild that you now know what you're supposed to be writing about, more or less, or in what direction you might go—but there was no way to get to this without first getting through the first five and a half pages.

I used to write food reviews for *California* magazine before it folded.   5
(My writing food reviews had nothing to do with the magazine folding, although every single review did cause a couple of canceled subscriptions. Some readers took umbrage at my comparing mounds of vegetable puree with various ex-presidents' brains.) These reviews always took two days to write. First I'd go to a restaurant several times with a few opinionated, articulate friends in tow. I'd sit there writing down everything anyone said that was at all interesting or funny. Then on the following Monday I'd sit down at my desk with my notes, and try to write the review. Even after I'd been doing this for years, panic would set in. I'd try to write a lead, but instead I'd write a couple of dreadful sentences, XX them out, try again, XX everything out, and then feel despair and worry settle on my chest like an x-ray apron. It's over, I'd think, calmly. I'm not going to be able to get the magic to work this time. I'm ruined. I'm through. I'm toast. Maybe, I'd think, I can get my old job back as a clerk-typist. But probably not.

I'd get up and study my teeth in the mirror for a while. Then I'd stop, remember to breathe, make a few phone calls, hit the kitchen and chow down. Eventually I'd go back and sit down at my desk, and *sigh* for the next ten minutes. Finally I would pick up my one-inch picture frame, stare into it as if for the answer, and every time the answer would come: all I had to do was to write a really shitty first draft of, say, the opening paragraph. And no one was going to see it.

So I'd start writing without reining myself in. It was almost just typing, just making my fingers move. And the writing would be terrible. I'd write a lead paragraph that was a whole page, even though the entire review could only be three pages long, and then I'd start writing up descriptions of the food, one dish at a time, bird by bird, and the critics would be sitting on my shoulders, commenting like cartoon characters. They'd be pretending to snore, or rolling their eyes at my overwrought descriptions, no matter how hard I tried to tone those descriptions down, no matter how conscious I was of what a friend said to me gently in my early days of restaurant reviewing. "Annie," she said, "it is just a piece of *chicken*. It is just a bit of *cake*."

But because by then I had been writing for so long, I would eventually let myself trust the process—sort of, more or less. I'd write a first draft that was maybe twice as long as it should be, with a self-indulgent and boring beginning, stupefying descriptions of the meal, lots of quotes from my black-humored friends that made them sound more like the Manson girls than food lovers, and no ending to speak of. The whole thing would be so long and incoherent and hideous that for the rest of the day I'd obsess about getting creamed by a car before I could write a decent second draft. I'd worry that people would read what I'd written and believe that the accident had really been a suicide, that I had panicked because my talent was waning and my mind was shot.

The next day, though, I'd sit down, go through it all with a colored pen, take out everything I possibly could, find a new lead somewhere on the second page, figure out a kicky place to end it, and then write a second draft. It always turned out fine, sometimes even funny and weird and helpful. I'd go over it one more time and mail it in.

Then, a month later, when it was time for another review, the whole process would start again, complete with the fears that people would find my first draft before I could rewrite it.

THINKING CRITICALLY ABOUT THE READING

1. What is Lamott's thesis, and where is her statement of the thesis? (Glossary: *Thesis*)

2. Lamott says that the perceptions most people have of how writers work is different from the reality of the work itself. She refers to this in paragraph 1 as "the fantasy of the uninitiated." What does she mean?

3. In paragraph 7 Lamott refers to a time when, through experience, she "eventually let [herself] trust the process—sort of, more or less." She is referring

to the writing process, of course, but why "more or less"? Do you think her wariness is personal, or is she speaking for all writers in this regard? Explain.

4. From what Lamott has to say, is writing a first draft more about content or psychology? Do you agree in regard to your own first drafts? Explain.

5. Lamott adds humor to her argument for "shitty first drafts." Give some examples. Do her attempts at humor add or detract from the points she makes? Explain.

6. In paragraph 5, Lamott offers a narrative of her experiences writing a food review in which she refers to an almost ritualistic set of behaviors. What is her purpose in telling her readers this story and the difficulties she has? (Glossary: *Narration*) Is it helpful for us to know this information? Explain.

7. What do you think of Lamott's use of the word *shitty* in her title and in the essay itself? Is it in keeping with the tone of her essay? (Glossary: *Tone*) Are you offended by her use of the word? Why or why not? What would be lost or gained if she used a different word?

LANGUAGE IN ACTION

In his 1990 book *The Play of Words*, Richard Lederer presents the following activity called "Verbs with Verve." What do you learn about the power of verbs from this exercise? Explain.

Researchers showed groups of test subjects a picture of an automobile accident and then asked this question: "How fast were the cars going when they———?" The blank was variously filled in with *bumped*, *contacted*, *hit*, *collided*, or *smashed*. Groups that were asked "How fast were the cars going when they smashed?" responded with the highest estimates of speed.

All of which proves that verbs create specific images in the mind's eye. Because verbs are the words in a sentence that express action and movement, they are the spark plugs of effective style. The more specific the verbs you choose in your speaking and writing, the more sparky will be the images you flash on the minds of your listeners and readers.

Suppose you write, "'No,' she said and left the room." Grammatically there is nothing wrong with this sentence. But because the verbs *say* and *leave* are among the most general and colorless in the English language, you have missed the chance to create a vivid word picture. Consider the alternatives:

Said		*Left*	
apologized	jabbered	backed	sauntered
asserted	minced	bolted	skipped
blubbered	mumbled	bounced	staggered
blurted	murmured	crawled	stamped
boasted	shrieked	darted	stole
cackled	sighed	flew	strode
commanded	slurred	hobbled	strutted

drawled	snapped	lurched	stumbled
giggled	sobbed	marched	tiptoed
groaned	whispered	plodded	wandered
gurgled	whooped	pranced	whirled

If you had chosen from among these vivid verbs and had crafted the sentence "'No,' she sobbed, and stumbled out of the room," you would have created a powerful picture of someone quite distraught.

Here are brief descriptions of twenty different people. Choosing from the two lists of synonyms for *said* and *left*, fill in the blanks of the sentence "'No,' he/she _____, and _____ out of the room." Select the pair of verbs that best create the most vivid picture of each person described. Throughout your answers try to use as many different verbs as you can:

1. an angry person
2. a baby
3. a braggart
4. a child
5. a clown
6. a confused person
7. a cowboy/cowgirl
8. someone crying
9. a drunkard
10. an embarrassed person

11. an excited person
12. a frightened person
13. a happy person
14. someone in a hurry
15. an injured person
16. a military officer
17. a sneaky person
18. a timid person
19. a tired person
20. a witch

WRITING SUGGESTIONS

1. In order to become a better writer, it is essential to be conscious of what you do as a writer. In other words, you need to reflect on what you are thinking and feeling at each stage of the writing process. Lamott has done just this in writing her essay. Think about what you do at other stages of the writing process—prewriting (gathering information, selecting evidence, checking on the reliability of sources, separating facts from opinions), revising, editing, and proofreading, for example. Write an essay modeled on Lamott's in which you narrate an experience you have had with a particular type of writing or assignment.

2. Lamott's essay is about appearances versus reality. Write an essay in which you set the record straight by exposing the myths or misperceptions people have about a particular job, place, thing, or situation. Naturally, you need to ask yourself how much of an "inside story" you can reveal based on actual experiences you have had. In other words, you know that being a lifeguard is not as romantic as most people think because you have been one. Try to create the same informative but lighthearted tone that Lamott does in her essay by paying particular attention to the language you use.

The Maker's Eye: Revising Your Own Manuscripts

DONALD M. MURRAY

Born in Boston, Massachusetts, Donald M. Murray (1924–2006) taught writing for many years at the University of New Hampshire, his alma mater. He served as an editor at *Time* magazine, and he won the Pulitzer Prize in 1954 for editorials that appeared in the *Boston Globe*. Murray's published works include novels, short stories, poetry, and sourcebooks for teachers of writing, like *A Writer Teaches Writing: A Complete Revision* (1985), *The Craft of Revision* (1991), and *Learning by Teaching* (1982), in which he explores aspects of the writing process. *Write to Learn* (8th ed., 2005), a textbook for college composition courses, is based on Murray's belief that writers learn to write by writing, by taking a piece of writing through the whole process, from invention to revision. In the last decades of his life, Murray produced a weekly column entitled "Now and Then" for the *Boston Globe*.

In the following essay, first published in the *Writer* in October 1973 and later revised for this text, Murray discusses the importance of revision to the work of the writer. Most professional writers live by the maxim that "writing is rewriting." And to rewrite or revise effectively, we need to become better readers of our own work, open to discovering new meanings, and sensitive to our use of language. Murray draws on the experiences of many writers to make a compelling argument for careful revising and editing.

WRITING TO DISCOVER: *Thinking back on your education to date, what did you think you had to do when teachers asked you to revise a piece of your writing? How did the request to revise make you feel? Write about your earliest memories of revising some of your writing. What kinds of changes do you remember making?*

When students complete a first draft, they consider the job of writing done — and their teachers too often agree. When professional writers complete a first draft, they usually feel that they are at the start of the writing process. When a draft is completed, the job of writing can begin.

That difference in attitude is the difference between amateur and professional, inexperience and experience, journeyman and craftsman. Peter F. Drucker, the prolific business writer, calls his first draft "the zero draft" — after that he can start counting. Most writers share the feeling that the first draft, and all of those which follow, are opportunities to discover what they have to say and how best they can say it.

To produce a progression of drafts, each of which says more and says it more clearly, the writer has to develop a special kind of reading skill.

In school we are taught to decode what appears on the page as finished writing. Writers, however, face a different category of possibility and responsibility when they read their own drafts. To them the words on the page are never finished. Each can be changed and rearranged, can set off a chain reaction of confusion or clarified meaning. This is a different kind of reading which is possibly more difficult and certainly more exciting.

When a draft is completed, the job of writing can begin.

Writers must learn to be their own best enemy. They must accept the criticism of others and be suspicious of it; they must accept the praise of others and be even more suspicious of it. Writers cannot depend on others. They must detach themselves from their own pages so that they can apply both their caring and their craft to their own work.

Such detachment is not easy. Science-fiction writer Ray Bradbury supposedly puts each manuscript away for a year to the day and then rereads it as a stranger. Not many writers have the discipline or the time to do this. We must read when our judgment may be at its worst, when we are close to the euphoric moment of creation.   5

Then the writer, counsels novelist Nancy Hale, "should be critical of everything that seems to him most delightful in his style. He should excise what he most admires, because he wouldn't thus admire it if he weren't . . . in a sense protecting it from criticism." John Ciardi, the poet, adds, "The last act of the writing must be to become one's own reader. It is, I suppose, a schizophrenic process, to begin passionately and to end critically, to begin hot and to end cold; and, more important, to be passion-hot and critic-cold at the same time."

Most people think that the principal problem is that writers are too proud of what they have written. Actually, a greater problem for most professional writers is one shared by the majority of students. They are overly critical, think everything is dreadful, tear up page after page, never complete a draft, see the task as hopeless.

The writer must learn to read critically but constructively, to cut what is bad, to reveal what is good. Eleanor Estes, the children's book author, explains: "The writer must survey his work critically, coolly, as though he were a stranger to it. He must be willing to prune, expertly and hard-heartedly. At the end of each revision, a manuscript may look . . . worked over, torn apart, pinned together, added to, deleted from, words changed and words changed back. Yet the book must maintain its original freshness and spontaneity."

Most readers underestimate the amount of rewriting it usually takes to produce spontaneous reading. This is a great disadvantage to the student writer, who sees only a finished product and never watches the craftsman who takes the necessary step back, studies the work carefully, returns to the task, steps back, returns, steps back, again and again. Anthony Burgess, one of the most prolific writers in the English-speaking world, admits, "I might revise a page twenty times." Roald Dahl, the popular children's writer, states, "By the time I'm nearing the end of a story, the first part will have been reread and altered and corrected at least 150 times. . . . Good writing is essentially rewriting. I am positive of this."

Rewriting isn't virtuous. It isn't something that ought to be done. It is   10 simply something that most writers find they have to do to discover what they have to say and how to say it. It is a condition of the writer's life.

There are, however, a few writers who do little formal rewriting, primarily because they have the capacity and experience to create and review a large number of invisible drafts in their minds before they approach the page. And some writers slowly produce finished pages, performing all the tasks of revision simultaneously, page by page, rather than draft by draft. But it is still possible to see the sequence followed by most writers most of the time in rereading their own work.

Most writers scan their drafts first, reading as quickly as possible to catch the larger problems of subject and form, and then move in closer and closer as they read and write, reread and rewrite.

The first thing writers look for in their drafts is *information*. They know that a good piece of writing is built from specific, accurate, and interesting information. The writer must have an abundance of information from which to construct a readable piece of writing.

Next writers look for *meaning* in the information. The specifics must build to a pattern of significance. Each piece of specific information must carry the reader toward meaning.

Writers reading their own drafts are aware of *audience*. They put them-   15 selves in the reader's situation and make sure that they deliver information which a reader wants to know or needs to know in a manner which is easily digested. Writers try to be sure that they anticipate and answer the questions a critical reader will ask when reading the piece of writing.

Writers make sure that the *form* is appropriate to the subject and the audience. Form, or genre, is the vehicle which carries meaning to the reader, but form cannot be selected until the writer has adequate information to discover its significance and an audience which needs or wants that meaning.

Once writers are sure the form is appropriate, they must then look at the *structure*, the order of what they have written. Good writing is built on a solid framework of logic, argument, narrative, or motivation which runs through the entire piece of writing and holds it together. This is the time when many writers find it most effective to outline as a way of visualizing the hidden spine by which the piece of writing is supported.

The element on which writers may spend a majority of their time is *development*. Each section of a piece of writing must be adequately developed. It must give readers enough information so that they are satisfied. How much information is enough? That's as difficult as asking how much garlic belongs in a salad. It must be done to taste, but most beginning writers underdevelop, underestimating the reader's hunger for information.

As writers solve development problems, they often have to consider questions of *dimension*. There must be a pleasing and effective proportion among all the parts of the piece of writing. There is a continual process of subtracting and adding to keep the piece of writing in balance.

Finally, writers have to listen to their own voices. *Voice* is the force which drives a piece of writing forward. It is an expression of the writer's authority and concern. It is what is between the words on the page, what glues the piece of writing together. A good piece of writing is always marked by a consistent, individual voice.   20

As writers read and reread, write and rewrite, they move closer and closer to the page until they are doing line-by-line editing. Writers read their own pages with infinite care. Each sentence, each line, each clause, each phrase, each word, each mark of punctuation, each section of white space between the type has to contribute to the clarification of meaning.

Slowly the writer moves from word to word, looking through language to see the subject. As a word is changed, cut, or added, as a construction is rearranged, all the words used before that moment and all those that follow that moment must be considered and reconsidered.

Writers often read aloud at this stage of the editing process, muttering or whispering to themselves, calling on the ear's experience with language. Does this sound right — or that? Writers edit, shifting back and forth from eye to page to ear to page. I find I must do this careful editing in short runs, no more than fifteen or twenty minutes at a stretch, or I become too kind with myself. I begin to see what I hope is on the page, not what actually is on the page.

This sounds tedious if you haven't done it, but actually it is fun. Making something right is immensely satisfying, for writers begin to learn what they are writing about by writing. Language leads them to meaning, and there is the joy of discovery, of understanding, of making meaning clear as the writer employs the technical skills of language.

Words have double meanings, even triple and quadruple meanings. Each word has its own potential of connotation and denotation. And when writers rub one word against the other, they are often rewarded with a sudden insight, an unexpected clarification.   25

The maker's eye moves back and forth from word to phrase to sentence to paragraph to sentence to phrase to word. The maker's eye sees the need for variety and balance, for a firmer structure, for a more appropriate form. It peers into the interior of the paragraph, looking for coherence, unity, and emphasis, which make meaning clear.

I learned something about this process when my first bifocals were prescribed. I had ordered a larger section of the reading portion of the glass because of my work, but even so, I could not contain my eyes within this new limit of vision. And I still find myself taking off my glasses and bending my nose toward the page, for my eyes unconsciously flick back and forth across the page, back to another page, forward to still another, as I try to see each evolving line in relation to every other line.

When does this process end? Most writers agree with the great Russian writer Tolstoy, who said, "I scarcely ever reread my published writings, if by chance I come across a page, it always strikes me: all this must be rewritten; this is how I should have written it."

The maker's eye is never satisfied, for each word has the potential to ignite new meaning. This article has been twice written all the way through the writing process. . . . Now it is to be republished in a book. The editors made a few small suggestions, and then I read it with my maker's eye. Now it has been re-edited, re-revised, re-read, and re-re-edited, for each piece of writing to the writer is full of potential and alternatives.

A piece of writing is never finished. It is delivered to a deadline, torn   30
out of the typewriter on demand, sent off with a sense of accomplishment and shame and pride and frustration. If only there were a couple more days, time for just another run at it, perhaps then. . . .

THINKING CRITICALLY ABOUT THE READING

1. What are the essential differences between revising and editing? What types of language concerns are dealt with at each stage? Why is it important to revise before editing?

2. According to Murray, at what point(s) in the writing process do writers become concerned about the individual words they are using? What do you think Murray means when he says in paragraph 24 that "language leads [writers] to meaning"?

3. How does Murray define *information* and *meaning* (13–14)? Why is the distinction between the two terms important?

4. The phrase "the maker's eye" appears in Murray's title and in several places throughout the essay. What do you suppose he means by this? Consider how the maker's eye could be different from the reader's eye.

5. According to Murray, when is a piece of writing finished? What, for him, is the function of deadlines?

6. What does Murray see as the connection between reading and writing? How does reading help the writer? What should writers be looking for in their reading? What kinds of writing techniques or strategies does Murray use in his essay? Why should we read a novel or magazine article differently than we would a draft of one of our own essays?

7. According to Murray, writers look for information, meaning, audience, form, structure, development, dimension, and voice in their drafts. What rationale or logic do you see, if any, in the way Murray has ordered these items? Are these the kinds of concerns you have when reading your drafts? Explain.

8. Murray notes that writers often reach a stage in their editing where they read aloud, "muttering or whispering to themselves, calling on the ear's experience with language" (23). What exactly do you think writers are listening for when

they read aloud? Try reading several paragraphs of Murray's essay aloud. Explain what you learned about his writing. Have you ever read your own writing aloud? If so, what did you discover?

LANGUAGE IN ACTION

Carefully read the opening four paragraphs of Annie Dillard's "Living Like Weasels," which is taken from *Teaching a Stone to Talk* (1982). Using two different color pens, first circle the subject and underline the verb in each main clause in one color, and then circle the subject and underline the verb in each subordinate clause with the other. What does this exercise reveal about Dillard's diction (nouns and verbs) and sentence structure? (Glossary: *Diction*)

A weasel is wild. Who knows what he thinks? He sleeps in his underground den, his tail draped over his nose. Sometimes he lives in his den for two days without leaving. Outside, he stalks rabbits, mice, muskrats, and birds, killing more bodies than he can eat warm, and often dragging the carcasses home. Obedient to instinct, he bites his prey at the neck, either splitting the jugular vein at the throat or crunching the brain at the base of the skull, and he does not let go. One naturalist refused to kill a weasel who was socketed into his hand deeply as a rattlesnake. The man could in no way pry the tiny weasel off, and he had to walk half a mile to water, the weasel dangling from his palm, and soak him off like a stubborn label.

And once, says Ernest Thompson Seton—once, a man shot an eagle out of the sky. He examined the eagle and found the dry skull of a weasel fixed by the jaws to his throat. The supposition is that the eagle had pounced on the weasel and the weasel swiveled and bit as instinct taught him, tooth to neck, and nearly won. I would like to have seen that eagle from the air a few weeks or months before he was shot: was the whole weasel still attached to his feathered throat, a fur pendant? Or did the eagle eat what he could reach, gutting the living weasel with his talons before his breast, bending his beak, cleaning the beautiful airborne bones?

I have been reading about weasels because I saw one last week. I startled a weasel who startled me, and we exchanged a long glance.

Twenty minutes from my house, through the woods by the quarry and across the highway, is Hollins Pond, a remarkable piece of shallowness, where I like to go at sunset and sit on a tree trunk. Hollins Pond is also called Murray's Pond; it covers two acres of bottomland near Tinker Creek with six inches of water and six thousand lily pads. In winter, brown-and-white steers stand in the middle of it, merely dampening their hooves; from the distant shore they look like miracle itself, complete with miracle's nonchalance. Now, in summer, the steers are gone. The water lilies have blossomed and spread to a green horizontal plane that is terra firma to plodding blackbirds, and tremulous ceiling to black leeches, crayfish, and carp.

WRITING SUGGESTIONS

1. Why do you suppose teachers report that revision is the most difficult stage in the writing process for their students? What is it about revision that makes it difficult, or at least makes people perceive it as being difficult? Write an essay in which you explore your own experiences with revision. You may find it helpful to review what you wrote for the Writing to Discover prompt at the beginning of this essay.

2. Writing about pressing social issues usually requires a clear statement of a particular problem and the precise definition of critical terms. For example, if you were writing about the increasing number of people being kept alive by machines, you would need to examine the debate surrounding the legal and medical definitions of the word *death*. Debates continue about the meanings of other controversial terms, such as *morality, minority* (ethnic), *alcoholism, racism, sexual harassment, life* (as in the abortion issue), *pornography, liberal, gay, censorship, conservative, remedial, insanity, literacy, political correctness, assisted suicide, lying, high crimes and misdemeanors,* and *kidnapping* (as in custody disputes). Select one of these words or one of your own. After carefully researching some of the controversial people, situations, and events surrounding your word, write an essay in which you discuss the problems associated with the term and its definition.

Simplicity

WILLIAM ZINSSER

Born in New York City in 1922, William Zinsser was educated at Princeton University. After serving in the Army in World War II, he worked at the *New York Herald Tribune* as an editor, writer, and critic. During the 1970s he taught a popular course in nonfiction at Yale University, and from 1979 to 1987 he was general editor of the Book-of-the-Month Club. Zinsser has written more than a dozen books, including *The City Dwellers* (1962), *Pop Goes America* (1966), and *Spring Training* (1989), and three widely used books on writing: *Writing with a Word Processor* (1983), *Writing to Learn* (1993), and *On Writing Well* (2006). Currently, he teaches journalism at Columbia University, and his freelance writing regularly appears in some of our leading magazines.

The following selection is taken from *On Writing Well*. This book grew out of Zinsser's many years of experience as a professional writer and teacher. In this essay, Zinsser exposes what he believes is the writer's number one problem — "clutter." He sees Americans "strangling in unnecessary words, circular constructions, pompous frills, and meaningless jargon." His solution is simple: Writers must know what they want to say and must be thinking clearly as they start to compose. Then self-discipline and hard work are necessary to achieve clear, simple prose. No matter what your experience as a writer has been, you will find Zinsser's observations sound and his advice practical.

WRITING TO DISCOVER: *Some people view writing as "thinking on paper." They believe that by seeing something written on a page they are better able to "see what they think." Write about the relationship, for you, between writing and thinking. Are you one of those people who likes to "see" ideas on paper while trying to work things out? Or do you like to think through ideas before writing about them?*

Clutter is the disease of American writing. We are a society strangling in unnecessary words, circular constructions, pompous frills and meaningless jargon.

Who can understand the clotted language of everyday American commerce: the memo, the corporation report, the business letter, the notice from the bank explaining its latest "simplified" statement? What member of an insurance or medical plan can decipher the brochure explaining his costs and benefits? What father or mother can put together a child's toy from the instructions on the box? Our national tendency is to inflate and thereby sound important. The airline pilot who announces that he is presently anticipating experiencing considerable precipitation wouldn't think of saying it may rain. The sentence is too simple—there must be something wrong with it.

But the secret of good writing is to strip every sentence to its cleanest components. Every word that serves no function, every long word that could be a short word, every adverb that carries the same meaning that's already in the verb, every passive construction that leaves the reader unsure of who is doing what—these are the thousand and one adulterants that weaken the strength of a sentence. And they usually occur in proportion to education and rank.

During the 1960s the president of my university wrote a letter to mollify the alumni after a spell of campus unrest. "You are probably aware," he began, "that we have been experiencing very considerable potentially explosive expressions of dissatisfaction on issues only partially related." He meant that the students had been hassling them about different things. I was far more upset by the president's English than by the students' potentially explosive expressions of dissatisfaction. I would have preferred the presidential approach taken by Franklin D. Roosevelt when he tried to convert into English his own government's memos, such as this blackout order of 1942:

> **Clear thinking becomes clear writing; one can't exist without the other.**

> Such preparations shall be made as will completely obscure all Federal buildings and non-Federal buildings occupied by the Federal government during an air raid for any period of time from visibility by reason of internal or external illumination.

"Tell them," Roosevelt said, "that in buildings where they have to keep the work going to put something across the windows."   5

Simplify, simplify. Thoreau said it, as we are so often reminded, and no American writer more consistently practiced what he preached. Open *Walden* to any page and you will find a man saying in a plain and orderly way what is on his mind:

> I went to the woods because I wished to live deliberately, to front only the essential facts of life, and see if I could not learn what it had to teach, and not, when I came to die, discover that I had not lived.

How can the rest of us achieve such enviable freedom from clutter? The answer is to clear our heads of clutter. Clear thinking becomes clear writing; one can't exist without the other. It's impossible for a muddy thinker to write good English. He may get away with it for a paragraph or two, but soon the reader will be lost, and there's no sin so grave, for the reader will not easily be lured back.

Who is this elusive creature, the reader? The reader is someone with an attention span of about 30 seconds—a person assailed by many forces competing for attention. At one time those forces were relatively few:

newspapers, magazines, radio, spouse, children, pets. Today they also include a galaxy of electronic devices for receiving entertainment and information — television, VCRs, DVDs, CDs, video games, the Internet, e-mail, cell phones, BlackBerries, iPods — as well as a fitness program, a pool, a lawn and that most potent of competitors, sleep. The man or woman snoozing in a chair with a magazine or a book is a person who was being given too much unnecessary trouble by the writer.

It won't do to say that the reader is too dumb or too lazy to keep pace with the train of thought. If the reader is lost, it's usually because the writer hasn't been careful enough. That carelessness can take any number of forms. Perhaps a sentence is so excessively cluttered that the reader, hacking through the verbiage, simply doesn't know what it means. Perhaps a sentence has been so shoddily constructed that the reader could read it in several ways. Perhaps the writer has switched pronouns in mid-sentence, or has switched tenses, so the reader loses track of who is talking or when the action took place. Perhaps Sentence B is not a logical sequel to Sentence A; the writer, in whose head the connection is clear, hasn't bothered to provide the missing link. Perhaps the writer has used a word incorrectly by not taking the trouble to look it up.

Faced with such obstacles, readers are at first tenacious. They blame themselves — they obviously missed something, and they go back over the mystifying sentence, or over the whole paragraph, piecing it out like an ancient rune, making guesses and moving on. But they won't do that for long. The writer is making them work too hard, and they will look for one who is better at the craft.   10

Writers must therefore constantly ask: what am I trying to say? Surprisingly often they don't know. Then they must look at what they have written and ask: have I said it? Is it clear to someone encountering the subject for the first time? If it's not, some fuzz has worked its way into the machinery. The clear writer is someone clearheaded enough to see this stuff for what it is: fuzz.

I don't mean that some people are born clearheaded and are therefore natural writers, whereas others are naturally fuzzy and will never write well. Thinking clearly is a conscious act that writers must force on themselves, as if they were working on any other project that requires logic: making a shopping list or doing an algebra problem. Good writing doesn't come naturally, though most people seem to think it does. Professional writers are constantly bearded by people who say they'd like to "try a little writing sometime" — meaning when they retire from their real profession, like insurance or real estate, which is hard. Or they say, "I could write a book about that." I doubt it.

Writing is hard work. A clear sentence is no accident. Very few sentences come out right the first time, or even the third time. Remember this in moments of despair. If you find that writing is hard, it's because it *is* hard.

THINKING CRITICALLY ABOUT THE READING

1. What exactly is clutter? When do words qualify as clutter, and when do they not?

2. In paragraph 2, Zinsser states that "Our national tendency is to inflate and thereby sound important." What do you think he means by *inflate*? Provide several examples to illustrate how people use language to inflate.

3. In paragraph 9, Zinsser lists some of the language-based obstacles that a reader may encounter in carelessly constructed prose. Which of these problems most tries your patience? Why?

4. One would hope that education would help in the battle against clutter, but, as Zinsser notes, wordiness "usually occur[s] in proportion to education and rank" (3). Do your own experiences or observations support Zinsser's claim? Discuss.

5. What assumptions does Zinsser make about readers? According to Zinsser, what responsibilities do writers have to readers? How do these responsibilities manifest themselves in Zinsser's writing? How do you think Linda Flower (pp. 184–186) would respond to what Zinsser says about audience? (Glossary: *Audience*) Explain.

6. Zinsser believes that writers need to ask themselves two questions — "What am I trying to say?" and "Have I said it?" — constantly as they write (11). How would these questions help you eliminate clutter from your own writing? Give some examples from one of your essays.

7. In order "to strip every sentence to its cleanest components," we need to be sensitive to the words we use and know how they function within our sentences. For each of the "adulterants that weaken the strength of a sentence," which Zinsser identifies in paragraph 3, provide an example from your own writing.

8. Zinsser knows that sentence variety is an important feature of good writing. Locate several examples of the short sentences (seven or fewer words) he uses in this essay, and explain how each relates in length, meaning, and impact to the sentences around it.

LANGUAGE IN ACTION

The following two pages show a passage from Zinsser's final manuscript for this essay as it was published in the first edition of *On Writing Well*. Carefully study the manuscript, and discuss how Zinsser eliminated clutter in his own prose. Then, using Zinsser as a model, judiciously eliminate the clutter from several paragraphs in one of your papers.

5 --

is too dumb or too lazy to keep pace with the train of thought. My sympathies are with him. If the reader is lost, it is generally because the writer has not been careful enough to keep him on the path.

This carelessness can take any number of forms. Perhaps a sentence is so excessively cluttered that the reader, hacking his way through the verbiage, simply doesn't know what it means. Perhaps a sentence has been so shoddily constructed that the reader could read it in any of several ways. Perhaps the writer has switched pronouns in mid-sentence, or has switched tenses, so the reader loses track of who is talking or when the action took place. Perhaps Sentence B is not a logical sequel to Sentence A -- the writer, in whose head the connection is clear, has not bothered to provide the missing link. Perhaps the writer has used an important word incorrectly by not taking the trouble to look it up. He may think that "sanguine" and "sanguinary" mean the same thing, but the difference is a bloody big one. The reader can only infer (speaking of big differences) what the writer is trying to imply.

Faced with these obstacles, the reader is at first a remarkably tenacious bird. He blames himself. He obviously missed something, and he goes back over the mystifying sentence, or over the whole paragraph, piecing it out like an ancient rune, making guesses and moving on. But he won't do this for long. The writer is making him work too hard — harder than he should have to work — and the reader will look for one who is better at his craft.

6 --

The writer must therefore constantly ask himself: What am I trying to say? ~~in this sentence?~~ (Surprisingly often, he doesn't know.) ~~And~~ Then he must look at what he has ~~just~~ written and ask: Have I said it? Is it clear to someone encountering ~~who is coming upon~~ the subject for the first time? If it's not, ~~clear,~~ it is because some fuzz has worked its way into the machinery. The clear writer is a person ~~who is~~ clear-headed enough to see this stuff for what it is: fuzz.

I don't mean ~~to suggest~~ that some people are born clear-headed and are therefore natural writers, whereas others ~~other people~~ are naturally fuzzy and will ~~therefore~~ never write well. Thinking clearly is a ~~an entirely~~ conscious act that the writer must force ~~keep forcing~~ upon himself, just as if he were embarking ~~starting out~~ on any other ~~kind of~~ project that requires ~~calls for~~ logic: adding up a laundry list or doing an algebra problem ~~or playing chess.~~ Good writing doesn't ~~just~~ come naturally, though most people obviously think it does ~~it's as easy as walking.~~ The professional

WRITING SUGGESTIONS

1. Each of the essays in Chapter 7, "Writers on Writing," is concerned with the importance of writing well, of using language effectively and responsibly. Write an essay in which you explore one of the common themes (audience, revision, diction, simplicity) that is emphasized in two or more of the selections.

2. Zinsser begins his essay with the following claim: "Clutter is the disease of American writing. We are a society strangling in unnecessary words, circular constructions, pompous frills and meaningless jargon." Write an essay supporting or refuting his claim. Most important, document his view, and yours, with examples drawn from contemporary nonfiction writing—essays, advertisements, academic writing, and other forms of public prose. Try to use examples that have been published recently.

8

LANGUAGE THAT MANIPULATES: POLITICS, PROPAGANDA, AND DOUBLESPEAK

Political language can be deliberately manipulated to mislead, deceive, or cover up. In the wake of the war in Vietnam, the Watergate scandal and subsequent resignation of President Nixon, the Iran-Contra affair, the Clinton-Lewinsky scandal, and the wars in Iraq and Afghanistan, Americans have grown cynical about their political leaders' promises and programs. As presidential campaigns seem to get started earlier and earlier, we are fed a daily diet of political language. Political speech saturates print and electronic media, in an ever-shorter news cycle (and perhaps the disappearance of a news cycle altogether). Fiery sound bites and seemingly spontaneous one-liners are presented as though they contained an entire argument or philosophy. Our politicians are savvy about the time constraints in news media, and their speechwriters make sure that long speeches have at least a few headline-grabbing quotes that might win them wide, albeit brief, coverage. But in the end, we are left wondering what we can believe and who we can trust among our politicians if they don't uphold the promises they make.

In "Language That Manipulates: Politics, Propaganda, and Doublespeak," we present five essays to help you think critically about the political language that you hear every day so that you can function as a responsible citizen. In the first essay, "Propaganda: How Not to Be Bamboozled," Donna Woolfolk Cross takes the mystery out of the oft-misunderstood word *propaganda* as she identifies and defines thirteen of the rhetorical devices the propagandist uses to manipulate language for political purposes. Her examples and advice, in turn, will help you to detect those nasty "tricks" and not to be misled by the silver tongues of politicians. In "Selection, Slanting, and Charged Language," Newman and Genevieve Birk give us a crash course on how the language people use subtly shapes perceptions. They introduce us to three simple but powerful concepts — selecting, slanting, and charging — that when understood, will change forever the way we view political speech. George Orwell, in his classic essay "Politics and the English Language," picks up where Cross leaves off. Orwell knows that language is power, and he argues for a clear, simplified English that everyone can understand. He takes politicians to task for language that he claims is "designed to make lies sound truthful and

murder respectable, and to give an appearance of solidarity to pure wind."
In "The World of Doublespeak," political watchdog and language expert
William Lutz examines the language of the government and corporate
bureaucrat, "language which pretends to communicate but doesn't."
His examples illustrate how language can be used deliberately to "mislead, distort, deceive, inflate, circumvent, obfuscate." In "Language That
Silences," Jason Stanley brings the idea of silencing into view. He argues
that one of the most insidious and harmful types of propaganda is that
which makes counterarguments difficult or impossible to mount. When
debate is stifled and trust lost, we are all rendered helpless and faith in
our institutions is lost. Finally, in "Tracking the Language of the Environment" (available online at bedfordstmartins.com/languageawareness/
epages), *Good* editor Ben Jervey tracks the use of various environmental
terms over several recent decades. His charts and commentary illustrate
how specific terms have influenced—and been influenced by—politicians
and political rhetoric.

Propaganda: How Not to Be Bamboozled

Donna Woolfolk Cross

Donna Woolfolk Cross graduated from the University of Pennsylvania in 1969 and went on to receive her M.A. from the University of California, Los Angeles. A professor of English at Onondaga Community College in Syracuse, New York, Cross has written extensively about language that manipulates, including the books *Mediaspeak: How Television Makes Up Your Mind* (1981) and *Word Abuse: How the Words We Use Use Us* (1979), which won an award from the National Council of Teachers of English. Her early work as a writer of advertising copy influences her teaching and writing. In an interview she remarked, "I was horrified to discover that first-year college students were completely unaware of—and, therefore, unable to defend themselves against—the most obvious ploys of admen and politicians. . . . We tend to think of language as something we use; we are much less often aware of the way we are used by language. The only defense is to become wise to the ways of words."

Although most people are against propaganda in principle, few know exactly what it is and how it works. In the following essay, which first appeared in *Speaking of Words: A Language Reader* (1977), Cross takes the mystery out of propaganda. She starts by providing a definition of it, and then she classifies the tricks of the propagandist into thirteen major categories. Cross's essay is chock-full of useful advice on how not to be manipulated by propaganda.

WRITING TO DISCOVER: *What do you think of when you hear the word propaganda? What kinds of people, organizations, or issues do you associate with it? Write about why you think people use propaganda.*

Propaganda. If an opinion poll were taken tomorrow, we can be sure that nearly everyone would be against it because it *sounds* so bad. When we say, "Oh, that's just propaganda," it means, to most people, "That's a pack of lies." But really, propaganda is simply a means of persuasion and so it can be put to work for good causes as well as bad—to persuade people to give to charity, for example, or to love their neighbors, or to stop polluting the environment.

For good or evil, propaganda pervades our daily lives, helping to shape our attitudes on a thousand subjects. Propaganda probably determines the brand of toothpaste you use, the movies you see, the candidates you elect when you get to the polls. Propaganda works by tricking us, by momentarily distracting the eye while the rabbit pops out from beneath the cloth. Propaganda works best with an uncritical audience. Joseph Goebbels, propaganda minister in Nazi Germany, once defined his work as "the conquest of the masses." The masses would not have been conquered, however, if they had known how to challenge and to question, how to make distinctions between propaganda and reasonable argument.

People are bamboozled mainly because they don't recognize propaganda when they see it. They need to be informed about the various devices that can be used to mislead and deceive—about the propagandist's overflowing bag of tricks. The following, then, are some common pitfalls for the unwary.

I. NAME-CALLING

As its title suggests, this device consists of labeling people or ideas with words of bad connotation, literally, "calling them names." Here the propagandist tries to arouse our contempt so we will dismiss the "bad name" person or idea without examining its merits.

Bad names have played a tremendously important role in the history   5 of the world. They have ruined reputations and ended lives, sent people to prison and to war, and just generally made us mad at each other for centuries.

Name-calling can be used against policies, practices, beliefs and ideals, as well as against individuals, groups, races, nations. Name-calling is at work when we hear a candidate for office described as a "foolish idealist" or a "two-faced liar" or when an incumbent's policies are denounced as "reckless," "reactionary," or just plain "stupid." Some of the most effective names a public figure can be called are ones that may not denote anything specific: "Congresswoman Jane Doe is a *bleeding heart*!" (Did she vote for funds to help paraplegics?) or "The senator is a *tool of Washington*!" (Did he happen to agree with the president?) Senator Yakalot uses name-calling when he denounces his opponent's "radical policies" and calls them (and him) "socialist," "pinko," and part of a "heartless plot." He also uses it when he calls cars "puddle-jumpers," "can openers," and "motorized baby buggies."

For good or evil, propaganda pervades our daily lives, helping to shape our attitudes on a thousand subjects.

The point here is that when the propagandist uses name-calling, he doesn't want us to think—merely to react, blindly, unquestioningly. So the best defense against being taken in by name-calling is to stop and ask, "Forgetting the bad name attached to it, what are the merits of the idea itself? What does this name really mean, anyway?"

2. GLITTERING GENERALITIES

Glittering generalities are really name-calling in reverse. Name-calling uses words with bad connotations; glittering generalities are words with good connotations—"virtue words," as the Institute for Propaganda

Analysis has called them. The Institute explains that while name-calling tries to get us to *reject* and *condemn* someone or something without examining the evidence, glittering generalities try to get us to *accept* and *agree* without examining the evidence.

We believe in, fight for, live by "virtue words" which we feel deeply about: "justice," "motherhood," "the American way," "our Constitutional rights," "our Christian heritage." These sound good, but when we examine them closely, they turn out to have no specific, definable meaning. They just make us feel good. Senator Yakalot uses glittering generalities when he says, "I stand for all that is good in America, for our American way and our American birthright." But what exactly *is* "good for America"? How can we define our "American birthright"? Just what parts of the American society and culture does "our American way" refer to?

We often make the mistake of assuming we are personally unaffected by   10
glittering generalities. The next time you find yourself assuming that, listen to a political candidate's speech on TV and see how often the use of glittering generalities elicits cheers and applause. That's the danger of propaganda; it *works.* Once again, our defense against it is to ask questions: Forgetting the virtue words attached to it, what are the merits of the idea itself? What does "Americanism" (or "freedom" or "truth") really *mean* here? . . .

Both name-calling and glittering generalities work by stirring our emotions in the hope that this will cloud our thinking. Another approach that propaganda uses is to create a distraction, a "red herring," that will make people forget or ignore the real issues. There are several different kinds of "red herrings" that can be used to distract attention.

3. PLAIN-FOLKS APPEAL

"Plain folks" is the device by which a speaker tries to win our confidence and support by appearing to be a person like ourselves—"just one of the plain folks." The plain-folks appeal is at work when candidates go around shaking hands with factory workers, kissing babies in supermarkets, and sampling pasta with Italians, fried chicken with Southerners, bagels and blintzes with Jews. "Now I'm a businessman like yourselves" is a plain-folks appeal, as is "I've been a farm boy all my life." Senator Yakalot tries the plain-folks appeal when he says, "I'm just a small-town boy like you fine people." The use of such expressions once prompted Lyndon Johnson to quip, "Whenever I hear someone say, 'I'm just an old country lawyer,' the first thing I reach for is my wallet to make sure it's still there."

The irrelevancy of the plain-folks appeal is obvious: even if the man *is* "one of us" (which may not be true at all), that doesn't mean that his ideas and programs are sound—or even that he honestly has our best interests at heart. As with glittering generalities, the danger here is that we may mistakenly assume we are immune to this appeal. But propagandists wouldn't use it unless it had been proved to work. You can protect yourself by asking, "Aside from his 'nice guy next door' image, what does this man stand for? Are his ideas and his past record really supportive of my best interests?"

4. *ARGUMENTUM AD POPULUM* (STROKING)

Argumentum ad populum means "argument to the people" or "telling the people what they want to hear." The colloquial term from the Watergate era is "stroking," which conjures up pictures of small animals or children being stroked or soothed with compliments until they come to like the person doing the complimenting—and, by extension, his or her ideas.

We all like to hear nice things about ourselves and the group we   15
belong to—we like to be liked—so it stands to reason that we will respond warmly to a person who tells us we are "hard-working taxpayers" or "the most generous, free-spirited nation in the world." Politicians tell farmers they are the "backbone of the American economy" and college students that they are the "leaders and policy makers of tomorrow." Commercial advertisers use stroking more insidiously by asking a question which invites a flattering answer: "What kind of a man reads *Playboy?*" (Does he really drive a Porsche and own $10,000 worth of sound equipment?) Senator Yakalot is stroking his audience when he calls them the "decent law-abiding citizens that are the great pulsing heart and the life blood of this, our beloved country," and when he repeatedly refers to them as "you fine people," "you wonderful folks."

Obviously, the intent here is to sidetrack us from thinking critically about the man and his ideas. Our own good qualities have nothing to do with the issue at hand. Ask yourself, "Apart from the nice things he has to say about me (and my church, my nation, my ethnic group, my neighbors), what does the candidate stand for? Are his or her ideas in my best interests?"

5. *ARGUMENTUM AD HOMINEM*

Argumentum ad hominem means "argument to the man" and that's exactly what it is. When a propagandist uses *argumentum ad hominem*, he wants to distract our attention from the issue under consideration with personal attacks on the people involved. For example, when Lincoln issued the Emancipation Proclamation, some people responded by calling him the "baboon." But Lincoln's long arms and awkward carriage had nothing to do with the merits of the Proclamation or the question of whether or not slavery should be abolished.

Today *argumentum ad hominem* is still widely used and very effective. You may or may not support the Equal Rights Amendment, but you should be sure your judgment is based on the merits of the idea itself, and not the result of someone's denunciation of the people who support the ERA as "fanatics" or "lesbians" or "frustrated old maids." Senator Yakalot is using *argumentum ad hominem* when he dismisses the idea of using smaller automobiles with a reference to the personal appearance of one of its supporters, Congresswoman Doris Schlepp. Refuse to be waylaid by *argumentum ad hominem* and ask, "Do the personal qualities of the person being discussed have anything to do with the issue at hand? Leaving him or her aside, how good is the idea itself?"

6. TRANSFER (GUILT OR GLORY BY ASSOCIATION)

In *argumentum ad hominem,* an attempt is made to associate negative aspects of a person's character or personal appearance with an issue or idea he supports. The transfer device uses this same process of association to make us accept or condemn a given person or idea.

A better name for the transfer device is guilt (or glory) by association.   20
In glory by association, the propagandist tries to transfer the positive feelings of something we love and respect to the group or idea he wants us to accept. "This bill for a new dam is in the best tradition of this country, the land of Lincoln, Jefferson, and Washington," is glory by association at work. Lincoln, Jefferson, and Washington were great leaders that most of us revere and respect, but they have no logical connection to the proposal under consideration—the bill to build a new dam. Senator Yakalot uses glory by association when he says full-sized cars "have always been as American as Mom's apple pie or a Sunday drive in the country."

The process works equally well in reverse, when guilt by association is used to transfer our dislike or disapproval of one idea or group to some other idea or group that the propagandist wants us to reject and condemn. "John Doe says we need to make some changes in the way our government operates; well, that's exactly what the Ku Klux Klan has said, so there's a meeting of great minds!" That's guilt by association for you; there's no logical connection between John Doe and the Ku Klux Klan apart from the one the propagandist is trying to create in our minds. He wants to distract our attention from John Doe and get us thinking (and worrying) about the Ku Klux Klan and its politics of violence. (Of course, there are sometimes legitimate associations between the two things; if John Doe had been a *member* of the Ku Klux Klan, it would be reasonable and fair to draw a connection between the man and his group.) Senator Yakalot tries to trick his audience with guilt by association when he remarks that "the words 'community' and 'communism' look an awful lot alike!" He does it again when he mentions that Mr. Stu Pott "sports a Fidel Castro beard."

How can we learn to spot the transfer device and distinguish between fair and unfair associations? We can teach ourselves to *suspend judgment* until we have answered these questions: "Is there any legitimate connection between the idea under discussion and the thing it is associated with? Leaving the transfer device out of the picture, what are the merits of the idea by itself?"

7. BANDWAGON

Ever hear of the small, ratlike animal called the lemming? Lemmings are arctic rodents with a very odd habit: periodically, for reasons no one entirely knows, they mass together in a large herd and commit suicide by rushing into deep water and drowning themselves. They all run in together, blindly, and not one of them ever seems to stop and ask, "*Why* am I doing this? Is this really what I want to do?" and thus save itself from destruction. Obviously, lemmings are driven to perform their strange mass suicide rites by common instinct. People choose to "follow the herd" for more complex reasons, yet we are still all too often the unwitting victims of the bandwagon appeal.

Essentially, the bandwagon urges us to support an action or an opinion because it is popular—because "everyone else is doing it." This call to "get on the bandwagon" appeals to the strong desire in most of us to be one of the crowd, not to be left out or alone. Advertising makes extensive use of the bandwagon appeal ("join the Pepsi people"), but so do politicians ("Let us join together in this great cause"). Senator Yakalot uses the bandwagon appeal when he says that "More and more citizens are rallying to my cause every day," and asks his audience to "join them—and me—in our fight for America."

One of the ways we can see the bandwagon appeal at work is in the over- 25
whelming success of various fashions and trends which capture the interest (and the money) of thousands of people for a short time, then disappear suddenly and completely. For a year or two in the fifties, every child in North America wanted a coonskin cap so they could be like Davy Crockett; no one wanted to be left out. After that there was the hula-hoop craze that helped to dislocate the hips of thousands of Americans. [In the 1970s], what made millions of people rush out to buy their very own "pet rocks"?

The problem here is obvious: just because everyone's doing it doesn't mean that *we* should too. Group approval does not prove that something is true or is worth doing. Large numbers of people have supported actions we now condemn. [Within the last century], Hitler and Mussolini rose to absolute and catastrophically repressive rule in two of the most sophisticated and cultured countries of Europe. When they came into power they were welled up by massive popular support from millions of people who didn't want to be "left out" at a great historical moment.

Once the mass begins to move—on the bandwagon—it becomes harder and harder to perceive the leader *riding* the bandwagon. So don't be a lemming, rushing blindly on to destruction because "everyone else is doing it." Stop and ask, "Where is this bandwagon headed? Never mind about everybody else, is this what is best for *me*?" . . .

As we have seen, propaganda can appeal to us by arousing our emotions or distracting our attention from the real issues at hand. But there's a third way that propaganda can be put to work against us—by the use of faulty logic. This approach is really more insidious than the others because it gives the appearance of reasonable, fair argument. It is only when we look more closely that the holes in the logical fiber show up. The following are some of the devices that make use of faulty logic to distort and mislead.

8. FAULTY CAUSE AND EFFECT

As the name suggests, this device sets up a cause-and-effect relationship that may not be true. The Latin name for this logical fallacy is *post hoc ergo propter hoc,* which means "after this, therefore because of this." But just because one thing happened after another doesn't mean that one *caused* the other.

An example of false cause-and-effect reasoning is offered by the story 30 (probably invented) of the woman aboard the ship *Titanic*. She woke up from a nap and, feeling seasick, looked around for a call button to summon the steward to bring her some medication. She finally located a small button on one of the walls of her cabin and pushed it. A split second later, the *Titanic* grazed an iceberg in the terrible crash that was to send the entire ship to its destruction. The woman screamed and said, "Oh, God, what have I done? What have I done?" The humor of that anecdote comes from the absurdity of the woman's assumption that pushing the small red button resulted in the destruction of a ship weighing several hundred tons: "It happened after I pushed it, therefore it must be *because* I pushed it"—*post hoc ergo propter hoc* reasoning. There is, of course, no cause-and-effect relationship there.

The false cause-and-effect fallacy is used very often by political candidates. "After I came to office, the rate of inflation dropped to 6 percent." But did the person do anything to cause the lower rate of inflation or was it the result of other conditions? Would the rate of inflation have dropped anyway, even if he hadn't come to office? Senator Yakalot uses false cause and effect when he says "our forefathers who made this country great never had free hot meal handouts! And look what they did for our country!" He does it again when he concludes that "driving full-sized cars means a better car safety record on our American roads today."

False cause-and-effect reasoning is terribly persuasive because it seems so logical. Its appeal is apparently to experience. We swallowed X product— and the headache went away. We elected Y official and unemployment went down. Many people think, "There *must* be a connection." But causality is an immensely complex phenomenon; you need a good deal of evidence to prove that an event that follows another in time was "therefore" caused by the first event.

Don't be taken in by false cause and effect; be sure to ask, "Is there enough evidence to prove that this cause led to that effect? Could there have been any *other* causes?"

9. FALSE ANALOGY

An analogy is a comparison between two ideas, events, or things. But comparisons can be fairly made only when the things being compared are alike in significant ways. When they are not, false analogy is the result.

A famous example of this is the old proverb "Don't change horses in   35 the middle of a stream," often used as an analogy to convince voters not to change administrations in the middle of a war or other crisis. But the analogy is misleading because there are so many differences between the things compared. In what ways is a war or political crisis like a stream? Is the president or head of state really very much like a horse? And is a nation of millions of people comparable to a man trying to get across a stream? Analogy is false and unfair when it compares two things that have little in common and assumes that they are identical. Senator Yakalot tries to hoodwink his listeners with false analogy when he says, "Trying to take Americans out of the kind of cars they love is as undemocratic as trying to deprive them of the right to vote."

Of course, analogies can be drawn that are reasonable and fair. It would be reasonable, for example, to compare the results of busing in one small Southern city with the possible results in another, *if* the towns have the same kind of history, population, and school policy. We can decide for ourselves whether an analogy is false or fair by asking, "Are the things being compared truly alike in significant ways? Do the differences between them affect the comparison?"

10. BEGGING THE QUESTION

Actually, the name of this device is rather misleading, because it does not appear in the form of a question. Begging the question occurs when, in discussing a questionable or debatable point, a person assumes as already established the very point that he is trying to prove. For example, "No thinking citizen could approve such a completely unacceptable policy as this one." But isn't the question of whether or not the policy *is* acceptable the very point to be established? Senator Yakalot begs the question when he announces that his opponent's plan won't work "because it is unworkable."

We can protect ourselves against this kind of faulty logic by asking, "What is assumed in this statement? Is the assumption reasonable, or does it need more proof?"

11. THE TWO-EXTREMES FALLACY (FALSE DILEMMA)

Linguists have long noted that the English language tends to view reality in sets of two extremes or polar opposites. In English, things are either black or white, tall or short, up or down, front or back, left or right, good or bad, guilty or not guilty. We can ask for a "straightforward yes-or-no answer" to a question, the understanding being that we will not accept or consider anything in between. In fact, reality cannot always be dissected along such strict lines. There may be (usually are) *more* than just two possibilities or extremes to consider. We are often told to "listen to both sides of the argument." But who's to say that every argument has only two sides? Can't there be a third—even a fourth or fifth—point of view?

The two-extremes fallacy is at work in this statement by Lenin, the great Marxist leader: "You cannot eliminate *one* basic assumption, one substantial part of this philosophy of Marxism (it is as if it were a block of steel), without abandoning truth, without falling into the arms of bourgeois-reactionary falsehood." In other words, if we don't agree 100 percent with every premise of Marxism, we must be placed at the opposite end of the political-economic spectrum—for Lenin, "bourgeois-reactionary falsehood." If we are not entirely *with* him, we must be against him; those are the only two possibilities open to us. Of course, this is a logical fallacy; in real life there are any number of political positions one can maintain *between* the two extremes of Marxism and capitalism. Senator Yakalot uses the two-extremes fallacy in the same way as Lenin when he tells his audience that "in this world a man's either for private enterprise or he's for socialism."

One of the most famous examples of the two-extremes fallacy in recent history is the slogan, "America: Love it or leave it," with its implicit suggestion that we either accept everything just as it is in America today without complaint—or get out. Again, it should be obvious that there is a whole range of action and belief between those two extremes.

Don't be duped; stop and ask, "Are those really the only two options I can choose from? Are there other alternatives not mentioned that deserve consideration?"

12. CARD STACKING

Some questions are so multifaceted and complex that no one can make an intelligent decision about them without considering a wide variety of evidence. One selection of facts could make us feel one way and another selection could make us feel just the opposite. Card stacking is a device of propaganda which selects only the facts that support the propagandist's point of view, and ignores all the others. For example, a candidate could be made to look like a legislative dynamo if you say, "Representative McNerd introduced more new bills than any other member of the Congress," and neglect to mention that most of them were so preposterous that they were laughed off the floor.

Senator Yakalot engages in card stacking when he talks about the proposal to use smaller cars. He talks only about jobs without mentioning the cost to the taxpayers or the very real—though still denied—threat of depletion of resources. He says he wants to help his countrymen keep their jobs, but doesn't mention that the corporations that offer the jobs will also make large profits. He praises the "American chrome industry," overlooking the fact that most chrome is imported. And so on.

The best protection against card stacking is to take the "Yes, but . . ." 45 attitude. This device of propaganda is not untrue, but then again it is not the *whole* truth. So ask yourself, "Is this person leaving something out that I should know about? Is there some other information that should be brought to bear on this question?" . . .

So far, we have considered approaches that the propagandist can use to influence our thinking: appealing to our emotions, distracting our attention, and misleading us with logic that may appear to be reasonable but is in fact faulty and deceiving. But there is another approach that is probably the most common propaganda trick of them all.

13. TESTIMONIAL

The testimonial device consists in having some loved or respected person give a statement of support (testimonial) for a given product or idea. The problem is that the person being quoted may *not* be an expert in the field; in fact, he may know nothing at all about it. Using the name of a man who is skilled and famous in one field to give a testimonial for something in another field is unfair and unreasonable.

Senator Yakalot tries to mislead his audience with testimonial when he tells them that "full-sized cars have been praised by great Americans like John Wayne and Jack Jones, as well as by leading experts on car safety and comfort."

Testimonial is used extensively in TV ads, where it often appears in such bizarre forms as Joe Namath's endorsement of a pantyhose brand. Here, of course, the "authority" giving the testimonial not only is no expert about pantyhose, but obviously stands to gain something (money!) by making the testimonial.

When celebrities endorse a political candidate, they may not be mak-   50
ing money by doing so, but we should still question whether they are in
any better position to judge than we ourselves. Too often we are willing
to let others we like or respect make our decisions *for us,* while we follow
along acquiescently. And this is the purpose of testimonial—to get us to
agree and accept *without* stopping to think. Be sure to ask, "Is there any
reason to believe that this person (or organization or publication or whatever) has any more knowledge or information than I do on this subject?
What does the idea amount to on its own merits, without the benefit of
testimonial?"

The cornerstone of democratic society is reliance upon an informed
and educated electorate. To be fully effective citizens we need to be able
to challenge and to question wisely. A dangerous feeling of indifference
toward our political processes exists today. We often abandon our right, our
duty, to criticize and evaluate by dismissing *all* politicians as "crooked,"
all new bills and proposals as "just more government bureaucracy." But
there are important distinctions to be made, and this kind of apathy can
be fatal to democracy.

If we are to be led, let us not be led blindly, but critically, intelligently,
with our eyes open. If we are to continue to be a government "by the
people," let us become informed about the methods and purposes of propaganda, so we can be the masters, not the slaves of our destiny.

THINKING CRITICALLY ABOUT THE READING

1. According to Cross, what is propaganda? Who uses propaganda? Why is it used? (Glossary: *Propaganda*)

2. Why does Cross believe that it is necessary for people in a democratic society to become informed about the methods and practices of propaganda? What is her advice for dealing with propaganda?

3. What is a "red herring," and why do people use this technique? What is "beg-ging the question"? (Glossary: *Logical Fallacies*)

4. What, according to Cross, is the most common propaganda trick? Provide some examples of it from your own experience.

5. How does Cross use examples in her essay? (Glossary: *Examples*) What do you think of the examples from Senator Yakalot? What, if anything, does this hypothetical senator add to the essay? Which other examples do you find most effective? Least effective? Explain why.

6. In her discussion of the bandwagon appeal (23–28), Cross uses the analogy of the lemmings. How does the analogy work? Why is it not a false analogy? (Glossary: *Analogy*) How do analogies help you, as a writer, explain your subject to readers?

LANGUAGE IN ACTION

At the beginning of her essay, Cross claims that propaganda "can be put to work for good causes as well as bad." Consider the following advertisements for the U.S. Postal Service's breast-cancer-stamp campaign and for the University of Vermont's Direct Service Programs. How would you characterize the appeal of each? What propaganda techniques does each use? Do you ever find appeals such as these objectionable? Why or why not? In what situations do you think it would be acceptable for you to use propaganda devices in your own writing?

When you purchase Breast Cancer Research stamps, your United States Postal Service will donate all net proceeds to breast cancer research.* It's that simple. Doing something as ordinary as buying stamps can actually help save lives. So the next time you need to send cards, invitations, or even mail your bills, use the stamps that help stamp out breast cancer. Help us Fund the Fight to Find a Cure. To order Breast Cancer Research stamps, call **1 800 STAMP-24**, visit www.stampsonline.com, or ask for them at your local post office.

*Each stamp is valid for postage at the current First-Class letter rate. Net proceeds over First-Class letter rate go directly to fund breast cancer research at the National Institutes of Health and the Medical Research Program of the Department of Defense.
©1999 USPS

UNITED STATES POSTAL SERVICE®

Women Helping Battered Women

Summer or Fall Semester

Internships

Join the fight against domestic violence! You will work in a friendly, supportive environment. You will do challenging work for a worthwhile cause. You will have lots of learning opportunities. We need reliable people who are committed to social justice. You will need good communication skills, an open mind, and the ability to work somewhat independently.

We are now accepting applications.

Internships will be offered in the following programs:

Shelter Services
Hotline Program
Children's Shelter Services
Children's Playgroup Program
Development and Fundraising

Work Study Positions available in all the above programs as well as in the financial and administrative programs.

All interns in Direct Service Programs have to complete the full Volunteer Training. The next trainings will be in May and September. Call now for more information: 658-3131.

WRITING SUGGESTIONS

1. Using several of the devices described by Cross, write a piece of propaganda. You may want to persuade your classmates to join a particular campus organization, support a controversial movement or issue, or vote for a particular candidate in an election.

2. Cross acknowledges in paragraph 1 that propaganda is "simply a means of persuasion," but she quickly cautions that people need to recognize propaganda and be alert to its potential to mislead or deceive. Write an essay for your campus newspaper arguing for a "short course" on propaganda recognition at your school. You might want to consider the following questions in your essay: How do propaganda and argumentation differ? Do both always

have the same intended effect? What could happen to people who don't recognize or understand propaganda when they encounter it?

3. Using Cross's list of propaganda devices, write an essay analyzing several newspaper editorials, political speeches, public-service advertising campaigns, or comparable examples of contemporary prose. What did you learn about the people or organizations as a result of your analysis? How were their positions on issues or their purposes expressed? Which propaganda devices did they use? After reading Cross's essay, did you find yourself "buying" the propaganda or recognizing and questioning it? Submit the original editorials, speeches, or advertisements with your essay.

Selection, Slanting, and Charged Language

Newman P. Birk and Genevieve B. Birk

The more we learn about language and how it works, the more abundantly clear it becomes that our language shapes our perceptions of the world. Because most people have eyes to see, ears to hear, noses to smell, tongues to taste, and skin to feel, it seems as though our perceptions of reality should be pretty similar. We know, however, that this is not the case, and language, it seems, makes a big difference in how we perceive our world. In effect, language acts as a filter, heightening certain perceptions, dimming others, and totally voiding still others.

In the following selection from their book *Understanding and Using Language* (1972), Newman and Genevieve Birk discuss how we use words, especially the tremendous powers that slanted and charged language wields. As a writer, you will be particularly interested to learn just how important your choice of words is. After reading what the Birks have to say, you'll never read another editorial, watch another commercial, or listen to another politician in quite the same way.

WRITING TO DISCOVER: *Choose three different people and write a description of a person, an object, or an event from each of their perspectives. Consider how each would relate to the subject you chose, what details each would focus on, and the attitude each would have toward that subject.*

A. THE PRINCIPLE OF SELECTION

Before it is expressed in words, our knowledge, both inside and outside, is influenced by the principle of selection. What we know or observe depends on what we notice; that is, what we select, consciously or unconsciously, as worthy of notice or attention. As we observe, the principle of selection determines which facts we take in.

Suppose, for example, that three people, a lumberjack, an artist, and a tree surgeon, are examining a large tree in the forest. Since the tree itself is a complicated object, the number of particulars or facts about it that one could observe would be very great indeed. Which of these facts a particular observer will notice will be a matter of selection, a selection that is determined by his interests and purposes. A lumberjack might be interested in the best way to cut the tree down, cut it up and transport it to the lumber mill. His interest would then determine his principle of selection in observing and thinking about the tree. The artist might consider painting a picture of the tree, and his purpose would furnish his principle of selection. The tree surgeon's professional interest in the physical health of the tree might establish a principle of selection for him. If each man were now required to write an exhaustive, detailed report on everything he observed about the tree, the facts supplied by each would differ, for each would report those facts that his particular principle of selection led him to notice.[1]

The principle of selection holds not only for the specific facts that people observe but also for the facts they remember. A student suddenly embarrassed may remember nothing of the next ten minutes of class discussion but may have a vivid recollection of the sensation of the blood mounting, as he blushed, up his face and into his ears. In both noticing and remembering, the principle of selection applies, and it is influenced not only by our special interest and point of view but by our whole mental state of the moment.

The principle of selection then serves as a kind of sieve or screen through which our knowledge passes before it becomes our knowledge. Since we can't notice everything about a complicated object or situation or action or state of our own consciousness, what we do notice is determined by whatever principle of selection is operating for us at the time we gain the knowledge.

It is important to remember that what is true of the way the principle   5
of selection works for us is true also for the way it works for others. Even before we or other people put knowledge into words to express meaning, that knowledge has been screened or selected. Before an historian or an economist writes a book, or before a reporter writes a news article, the facts that each is to present have been sifted through the screen of a principle of selection. Before one person passes on knowledge to another, that knowledge has already been selected and shaped, intentionally or unintentionally, by the mind of the communicator.

B. THE PRINCIPLE OF SLANTING

When we put our knowledge into words, a second process of selection, the process of slanting, takes place. Just as there is something, a rather mysterious principle of selection, which chooses for us what we will notice, and what will then become our knowledge, there is also a principle which operates, with or without our awareness, to select certain facts and feelings from our store of knowledge, and to choose the words and emphasis that we shall use to communicate our meaning.[2] Slanting may be defined as the process of selecting (1) knowledge — factual and attitudinal; (2) words; and (3) emphasis, to achieve the intention of the

---

1. Of course, all three observers would probably report a good many facts in common — the height of the tree, for example, and the size of the trunk. The point we wish to make is that each observer would give us a different impression of the tree because of the different principle of selection that guided his observation.

2. Notice that the "principle of selection" is at work as *we take in* knowledge, and that slanting occurs *as we express* our knowledge in words.

communicator. Slanting is present in some degree in all communication: one may *slant for* (favorable slanting), *slant against* (unfavorable slanting), or *slant both ways* (balanced slanting). . . .

C. SLANTING BY USE OF EMPHASIS

Slanting by use of the devices of emphasis is unavoidable,[3] for emphasis is simply the giving of stress to subject matter, and so indicating what is important and what is less important. In speech, for example, if we say that Socrates was *a wise old man,* we can give several slightly different meanings, one by stressing *wise,* another by stressing *old,* another by giving equal stress to *wise* and *old,* and still another by giving chief stress to *man.* Each different stress gives a different slant (favorable or unfavorable or balanced) to the statement because it conveys a different attitude toward Socrates or a different judgment of him. Connectives and word order also slant by the emphasis they give: consider the difference in slanting or emphasis produced by *old but wise, old and wise, wise but old.* In writing, we cannot indicate subtle stresses on words as clearly as in speech, but we can achieve our emphasis and so can slant by the use of more complex patterns of word order, by choice of connectives, by underlining heavily stressed words, and by marks of punctuation that indicate short or long pauses and so give light or heavy emphasis. Question marks, quotation marks, and exclamation points can also contribute to slanting.[4] It is impossible either in speech or in writing to put two facts together without giving some slight emphasis or slant. For example, if we have in mind only two facts about a man, his awkwardness and his strength, we subtly slant those facts favorably or unfavorably in whatever way we may choose to join them.

More Favorable Slanting	*Less Favorable Slanting*
He is awkward and strong.	He is strong and awkward.
He is awkward but strong.	He is strong but awkward.
Although he is somewhat awkward, he is very strong.	He may be strong, but he's very awkward.

With more facts and in longer passages it is possible to maintain a delicate balance by alternating favorable emphasis and so producing a balanced effect.

---

3. When emphasis is present—and we can think of no instance in the use of language in which it is not—it necessarily influences the meaning by playing a part in the favorable, unfavorable, or balanced slant of the communicator. We are likely to emphasize by voice stress, even when we answer *yes* or *no* to simple questions.

4. Consider the slanting achieved by punctuation in the following sentences: He called the Senator an honest man? *He* called the Senator an honest man? He called the Senator an honest man! He said one more such "honest" senator would corrupt the state.

All communication, then, is in some degree slanted by the *emphasis* of the communicator.

D. SLANTING BY SELECTION OF FACTS

To illustrate the technique of slanting by selection of facts, we shall examine three passages of informative writing which achieve different effects simply by the selection and emphasis of material. Each passage is made up of true statements or facts about a dog, yet the reader is given three different impressions. The first passage is an example of objective writing or balanced slanting, the second is slanted unfavorably, and the third is slanted favorably.

1. Balanced Presentation

Our dog, Toddy, sold to us as a cocker, produces various reactions in various people. Those who come to the back door she usually growls and barks at (a milkman has said that he is afraid of her); those who come to the front door, she whines at and paws; also she tries to lick people's faces unless we have forestalled her by putting a newspaper in her mouth. (Some of our friends encourage these actions; others discourage them. Mrs. Firmly, one friend, slaps the dog with a newspaper and says, "I know how hard dogs are to train.") Toddy knows and responds to a number of words and phrases, and guests sometimes remark that she is a "very intelligent dog." She has fleas in the summer, and she sheds, at times copiously, the year round. Her blonde hairs are conspicuous when they are on people's clothing or on rugs or furniture. Her color and her large brown eyes frequently produce favorable comment. An expert on cockers would say that her ears are too short and set too high and that she is at least six pounds too heavy.

The passage above is made up of facts, verifiable facts,[5] deliberately   10
selected and emphasized to produce a *balanced* impression. Of course not all the facts about the dog have been given—to supply *all* the facts on any subject, even such a comparatively simple one, would be an almost impossible task. Both favorable and unfavorable facts are used, however, and an effort has been made to alternate favorable and unfavorable details so that neither will receive greater emphasis by position, proportion, or grammatical structure.

---

5. *Verifiable facts* are facts that can be checked and agreed upon and proved to be true by people who wish to verify them. That a particular theme received a failing grade is a verifiable fact; one needs merely to see the theme with the grade on it. That the instructor should have failed the theme is not, strictly speaking, a verifiable fact, but a matter of opinion. That women on the average live longer than men is a verifiable fact; that they live better is a matter of opinion, *a value judgment.*

2. Facts Slanted Against

That dog put her paws on my white dress as soon as I came in the door, and she made so much noise that it was two minutes before she had quieted down enough for us to talk and hear each other. Then the gas man came and she did a great deal of barking. And her hairs are on the rug and on the furniture. If you wear a dark dress they stick to it like lint. When Mrs. Firmly came in, she actually hit the dog with a newspaper to make it stay down, and she made some remark about training dogs. I wish the Birks would take the hint or get rid of that noisy, short-eared, overweight "cocker" of theirs.

This unfavorably slanted version is based on the same facts, but now these facts have been selected and given a new emphasis. The speaker, using her selected facts to give her impression of the dog, is quite possibly unaware of her negative slanting.

Now for a favorably slanted version:

3. Facts Slanted For

What a lively and responsible dog! When I walked in the door, there she was with a newspaper in her mouth, whining and standing on her hind legs and wagging her tail all at the same time. And what an intelligent dog. If you suggest going for a walk, she will get her collar from the kitchen and hand it to you, and she brings Mrs. Birk's slippers whenever Mrs. Birk says she is "tired" or mentions slippers. At a command she catches balls, rolls over, "speaks," or stands on her hind feet and twirls around. She sits up and balances a piece of bread on her nose until she is told to take it; then she tosses it up and catches it. If you are eating something, she sits up in front of you and "begs" with those big dark brown eyes set in that light, buff-colored face of hers. When I got up to go and told her I was leaving, she rolled her eyes at me and sat up like a squirrel. She certainly is a lively and intelligent dog.

Speaker 3, like Speaker 2, is selecting from the "facts" summarized in balanced version 1, and is emphasizing his facts to communicate his impression.

All three passages are examples of *reporting* (i.e., consist only of verifiable facts), yet they give three very different impressions of the same dog because of the different ways the speakers slanted the facts. Some people say that figures don't lie, and many people believe that if they have the "facts," they have the "truth." Yet if we carefully examine the ways of thought and language, we see that any knowledge that comes to us through words has been subjected to the double screening of the principle of selection and the slanting of language. . . .

Wise listeners and readers realize that the double screening that is produced by the principle of selection and by slanting takes place even when people honestly try to report the facts as they know them. (Speakers 2 and 3,   15 for instance, probably thought of themselves as simply giving information about a dog and were not deliberately trying to mislead.) Wise listeners and readers know too that deliberate manipulators of language, by mere selection and emphasis, can make their slanted facts appear to support almost any cause.

In arriving at opinions and values we cannot always be sure that the facts that sift into our minds through language are representative and relevant and true. We need to remember that much of our information about politics, governmental activities, business conditions, and foreign affairs comes to us selected and slanted. More than we realize, our opinions on these matters may depend on what newspaper we read or what news commentator we listen to. Worthwhile opinions call for knowledge of reliable facts and reasonable arguments for and against—and such opinions include beliefs about morality and truth and religion as well as about public affairs. Because complex subjects involve knowing and dealing with many facts on both sides, reliable judgments are at best difficult to arrive at. If we want to be fairminded, we must be willing to subject our opinions to continual testing by new knowledge, and must realize that after all they *are* opinions, more or less trustworthy. Their trustworthiness will depend on the representativeness of our facts, on the quality of our reasoning, and on the standard of values that we choose to apply.

We shall not give here a passage illustrating the unscrupulous slanting of facts. Such a passage would also include irrelevant facts and false statements presented as facts, along with various subtle distortions of fact. Yet to the uninformed reader the passage would be indistinguishable from a passage intended to give a fair account. If two passages (2 and 3) of casual and unintentional slanting of facts about a dog can give such contradictory impressions of a simple subject, the reader can imagine what a skilled and designing manipulation of facts and statistics could do to mislead an uninformed reader about a really complex subject. An example of such manipulation might be the account of the United States that Soviet propaganda has supplied to the average Russian. Such propaganda, however, would go beyond the mere slanting of the facts: it would clothe the selected facts in charged words and would make use of the many other devices of slanting that appear in charged language.

E. SLANTING BY USE OF CHARGED WORDS

In the passages describing the dog Toddy, we were illustrating the technique of slanting by the selection and emphasis of facts. Though the facts selected had to be expressed in words, the words chosen were as factual as possible, and it was the selection and emphasis of facts and not of words that was mainly responsible for the two distinctly different impressions of the dog. In the passages below we are demonstrating another way of slanting—by the use of charged words. This time the accounts are very similar in the facts they contain; the different impressions of the subject, Corlyn, are produced not by different facts but by the subtle selection of charged words.

The passages were written by a clever student who was told to choose as his subject a person in action, and to write two descriptions, each using the "same facts." The instructions required that one description be slanted positively and the other negatively, so that the first would make the reader favorably inclined toward the person and the action, and the second would make him unfavorably inclined.

Here is the favorably charged description. Read it carefully and form   20
your opinion of the person before you go on to read the second description.

Corlyn

Corlyn paused at the entrance to the room and glanced about. A well-cut black dress draped subtly about her slender form. Her long blonde hair gave her chiseled features the simple frame they required. She smiled an engaging smile as she accepted a cigarette from her escort. As he lit it for her she looked over the flame and into his eyes. Corlyn had that rare talent of making every male feel that he was the only man in the world.

She took his arm and they descended the steps into the room. She walked with an effortless grace and spoke with equal ease. They each took a cup of coffee and joined a group of friends near the fire. The flickering light danced across her face and lent an ethereal quality to her beauty. The good conversation, the crackling logs, and the stimulating coffee gave her a feeling of internal warmth. Her eyes danced with each leap of the flames.

Taken by itself this passage might seem just a description of an attractive girl. The favorable slanting by use of charged words has been done so skillfully that it is inconspicuous. Now we turn to the unfavorable slanted description of the "same" girl in the "same" actions:

Corlyn

Corlyn halted at the entrance to the room and looked around. A plain black dress hung on her thin frame. Her stringy bleached hair accentuated her harsh features. She smiled an inane smile as she took a cigarette from her escort. As he lit it for her she stared over the lighter and into his eyes. Corlyn had a habit of making every male feel that he was the last man on earth.

She grasped his arm and they walked down the steps and into the room. Her pace was fast and ungainly, as was her speed. They each reached for some coffee and broke into a group of acquaintances near the fire. The flickering light played across her face and revealed every flaw. The loud talk, the fire, and the coffee she had gulped down made her feel hot. Her eyes grew more red with each leap of the flames.

When the reader compares these two descriptions, he can see how charged words influence the reader's attitude. One needs to read the two descriptions several times to appreciate all the subtle differences between them. Words, some rather heavily charged, others innocent-looking but lightly charged, work together to carry to the reader a judgment of a person and a situation. If the reader had seen only the first description of Corlyn, he might well have thought that he had formed his "own judgment on the basis of the facts." And the examples just given only begin to suggest the techniques that may be used in heavily charged language. For one thing, the two descriptions of Corlyn contain no really good example of the use of charged abstractions; for another, the writer was obliged by the assignment to use the same set of facts and so could not slant by selecting his material.

F. SLANTING AND CHARGED LANGUAGE

. . . When slanting of facts, or words, or emphasis, or any combination of the three *significantly influences* feelings toward, or judgments about, a subject, the language used is charged language. . . .

Of course communications vary in the amount of charge they carry and in their effect on different people; what is very favorably charged for one person may have little or no charge, or may even be adversely charged, for others. It is sometimes hard to distinguish between charged and uncharged expression. But it is safe to say that whenever we wish to convey any kind of inner knowledge—feelings, attitudes, judgments, values—we are obliged to convey that attitudinal meaning through the medium of charged language; and when we wish to understand the inside knowledge of others, we have to interpret the charged language that they choose, or are obliged to use. Charged language, then, is the natural and necessary medium for the communication of charged or attitudinal meaning. At times we have difficulty in living with it, but we should have even greater difficulty in living without it.

Some of the difficulties in living with charged language are caused   25
by its use in dishonest propaganda, in some editorials, in many political speeches, in most advertising, in certain kinds of effusive salesmanship, and in blatantly insincere, or exaggerated, or sentimental expressions of emotion. Other difficulties are caused by the misunderstandings and misinterpretations that charged language produces. A charged phrase misinterpreted in a love letter; a charged word spoken in haste or in anger; an acrimonious argument about religion or politics or athletics or fraternities; the frustrating uncertainty produced by the effort to understand the complex attitudinal meaning in a poem or play or a short story—these troubles, all growing out of the use of charged language, may give us the feeling that Robert Louis Stevenson expressed when he said, "The battle goes sore against us to the going down of the sun."

But however charged language is abused and whatever misunderstandings it may cause, we still have to live with it—and even by it. It shapes our attitudes and values even without our conscious knowledge; it gives purpose to, and guides, our actions; through it we establish and maintain relations with other people and by means of it we exert our greatest influence on them. Without charged language, life would be but half life. The relatively uncharged language of bare factual statement, though it serves its informative purpose well and is much less open to abuse and to misunderstanding, can describe only the bare land of factual knowledge; to communicate knowledge of the turbulencies and the calms and the deep currents of the sea of inner experience we must use charged language.

THINKING CRITICALLY ABOUT THE READING

1. What is the Birks's purpose in this essay? (Glossary: *Purpose*) Do they seem more intent on explaining or on arguing their position? Point to specific language they use that led you to your conclusion. (Glossary: *Diction*)

2. How do the Birks organize their essay? (Glossary: *Organization*) Do you think the organizational pattern is appropriate given their subject matter and purpose? Explain.

3. According to the Birks, how is slanting different from the principle of selection? What devices can a speaker or writer use to slant knowledge? When is it appropriate, if at all, to slant language?

4. Do you find the examples about Toddy the dog and Corlyn particularly helpful? (Glossary: *Examples*) Why or why not? What would have been lost, if anything, had the examples not been included?

5. Why is it important for writers and others to be aware of charged words? What can happen if you use charged language unknowingly? What are some of the difficulties in living in a world with charged language?

6. The Birks wrote this essay in 1972, when people were not as sensitive to sexist language as they are today. (Glossary: *Sexist Language*) Reread several pages of their essay, paying particular attention to the Birks's use of pronouns and to the gender of the people in their examples. Suggest ways in which the Birks's diction could be changed so as to eliminate any sexist language.

LANGUAGE IN ACTION

According to the editors of *Newsweek*, the March 8, 1999, "Voices of the Century: Americans at War" issue "generated more than two hundred passionate responses from civilians and veterans." The following five letters are representative of those the editors received and published in the issue of March 29, 1999. Carefully read each letter, looking for slanting and charged language. Point out the verifiable facts you find. How do you know these facts are verifiable?

Kudos for your March 8 issue, "Voices of the Century: Americans at War." This issue surely ranks among the best magazines ever published. As a military historian, I gained a better perspective of this turbulent century from this single issue than from many other sources combined. The first-person accounts are the genius of the issue. And your selection of storytellers was truly inspired. The "Voices of the Century" is so powerful that I will urge all of my friends to read it, buying copies for those who are not subscribers. Many persons today, especially those born after WWII, do not comprehend or appreciate the defining events of this century. How can we be more confident that they will be aware of our vital past when making important social and political decisions during the next century? I have great confidence in the American spirit and will, but this missing perspective is my principal concern as I leave this nation to the ministry of my daughters, my grandchildren, and their generation. Why not publish "Voices of the Century" as a booklet and make it readily available to all young people? Why not urge every school system to make it required reading prior to graduation from high school?

—ALAN R. McKIE, Springfield, VA

Your March 8 war issue was a powerfully illustrated essay of the men and women who have served our country and the people of other lands in so many capacities. But it was the photos that touched my soul and made me cry all over again for the human loss, *my* loss. As I stared at the pictures of the injured, dead, dying, and crying, I felt as though I were intruding on their private hell. God bless all of them, and my sincere thanks for a free America.

—DEBORAH AMES, Sparks, NV

I arrived in this country at 15 as a Jewish refugee from Nazism. I became an American soldier at 19 and a U.S. Foreign Service officer at 29. As a witness to much of the history covered in your special issue, I wanted to congratulate *Newsweek* on a superb job. In your excellent introduction, I found only one word with which I take issue: that "after the war Rosie and her cohort *happily* went back to the joys of motherhood and built the baby boom." Rosie and her cohort were forced back into their traditional gender roles, and it took the women's movement another generation or two to win back the gains achieved during the war.

—LUCIAN HEICHLER, Frederick, MD

Editor's note: The word "happily" was carefully chosen. Contemporary surveys indicated that most of the American women who joined the work force because of World War II were glad to get back to family life when it was over.

On the cover of your "Americans at War" issue, you have the accompanying text "From WWI to Vietnam: The Grunts and the Great Men—In Their Own Words." In each of these wars, the grunts *were* the great men.

—PAULA S. McGUIRE, Charlotte, NC

Your March 8 issue was painful for me and other members of my family as a result of the photograph you included on page 62 showing a wounded soldier being dragged from the line of fire during the Tet Offensive. My family had previously confirmed with the photographer that the soldier was my youngest brother, Marine Cpl. Robert Mack Harrelson. His bullet-riddled body fought hard to survive and, with the assistance of many excellent, caring members of our U.S. Military Medical Staff, he was able to regain some degree of normalcy after his return. But the injuries he received were too great to overcome, resulting in the military funeral he had requested. The rekindled grief brought on by your photo is keenly felt throughout our large family, and especially so by our dear 85-year-old mother, who still speaks of Bob as though he might reappear at any time. In spite of the photo, I sincerely congratulate your fine publication for reminding the world of the tragedy of war.

—LOWELL L. HARRELSON, Bay Minette, AL

WRITING SUGGESTIONS

1. Describe a day at your school or university. Begin with details that help you create a single dominant impression. Be careful to select only details that support the attitude and meaning you wish to convey. Once you've finished, compare your essay with those of your peers. In what ways do the essays differ? How are they the same? How does this writing exercise reinforce the Birks's discussion of the principle of selection?

2. When used only positively or only negatively, charged words can alienate the reader and bring the author's reliability into question. Consider the Birks's two examples of Corlyn. In the first example Corlyn can do no wrong, and in the second she can do nothing right. Using these two examples as a guide, write your own multiparagraph description of a person you know well. Decide on the overall impression you want to convey to your readers, and use charged words—both positive and negative—to create that impression.

3. Find a newspaper or magazine editorial on a subject that you have strong opinions about. Analyze the writer's selection of facts and use of charged language. How well does the writer present different viewpoints? Is the editorial convincing? Why or why not? After researching the topic further in your library or on the Internet, write a letter to the editor in response to the editorial. In your letter, use information from your research to make a point about the subject. Also comment on any charged or slanted language the editor used. Mail your letter to the editor.

Politics and the English Language

GEORGE ORWELL

George Orwell (1903–1950), one of the most brilliant social critics of the twentieth century, grew up in England and received a traditional education at Eton. Instead of going on to a university, he joined the civil service and was sent to Burma at the age of nineteen as an assistant superintendent of police. Disillusioned with British imperialism, Orwell resigned in 1929 and began a decade of studying social and political issues firsthand and then writing about them in such works as *Down and Out in Paris and London* (1933) and *The Road to Wigan Pier* (1937). His most famous books are *Animal Farm* (1945), a satire of the Russian Revolution, and *1984* (1949), a chilling novel set in an imagined totalitarian state of the future.

In *1984*, the government has imposed on its subjects a simplified language, Newspeak, which is continually revised to give them fewer words with which to express themselves. Words like *terrible, abhorrent,* and *evil,* for example, have been replaced by the single expression *double-plus-ungood.* The way people use language, Orwell maintains, is a result of the way they think as well as an important influence on their thought. This is also the point of his classic essay "Politics and the English Language." Even though it was published in 1946, the essay is as accurate and relevant now as it was more than sixty years ago. Indeed, during the wars in Vietnam, Kosovo, and Iraq, various American officials were still using euphemisms such as *pacification, transfer of population,* and *ethnic cleansing*—words and phrases Orwell had exposed as doubletalk. Orwell, however, goes beyond exposé in this essay. He holds up to public view and ridicule some choice examples of political language at its worst, but he also offers a few short and effective rules for those who want to write more clearly.

WRITING TO DISCOVER: *Have you ever stopped to think about what clichéd phrases like* toe the line, walk the straight and narrow, sharp as a tack, *and* fly off the handle *really mean? Jot down the clichés that you find yourself or hear others using. What images come to mind when you hear them? Are these words and phrases effective expressions, or are they a kind of verbal shorthand that we automatically depend on? Explain.*

Most people who bother with the matter at all would admit that the English language is in a bad way, but it is generally assumed that we cannot by conscious action do anything about it. Our civilization is decadent and our language—so the argument runs—must inevitably share in the general collapse. It follows that any struggle against the abuse of language is a sentimental archaism, like preferring candles to electric light or hansom cabs to aeroplanes. Underneath this lies the half-conscious belief that language is a natural growth and not an instrument which we shape for our own purposes.

Now, it is clear that the decline of a language must ultimately have political and economic causes: it is not due simply to the bad influence of this or that individual writer. But an effect can become a cause, reinforcing the original cause and producing the same effect in an intensified form, and so on indefinitely. A man may take to drink because he feels himself to be a failure, and then fail all the more completely because he drinks. It is rather the same thing that is happening to the English language. It becomes ugly and inaccurate because our thoughts are foolish, but the slovenliness of our language makes it easier for us to have foolish thoughts. The point is that the process is reversible. Modern English, especially written English, is full of bad habits which spread by imitation and which can be avoided if one is willing to take the necessary trouble. If one gets rid of these habits one can think more clearly, and to think clearly is a necessary first step towards political regeneration: so that the fight against bad English is not frivolous and is not the exclusive concern of professional writers. I will come back to this presently, and I hope that by that time the meaning of what I have said here will have become clearer. Meanwhile here are five specimens of the English language as it is now habitually written.

These five passages have not been picked out because they are especially bad—I could have quoted far worse if I had chosen—but because they illustrate various of the mental vices from which we now suffer. They are a little below the average, but are fairly representative samples. I number them so that I can refer back to them when necessary:

(1) I am not, indeed, sure whether it is not true to say that the Milton who once seemed not unlike a seventeenth-century Shelley had not become, out of an experience ever more bitter in each year, more alien [*sic*] to the founder of that Jesuit sect which nothing could induce him to tolerate.

—PROFESSOR HAROLD LASKI (Essay in *Freedom of Expression*)

(2) Above all, we cannot play ducks and drakes with a native battery of idioms which prescribes such egregious collocations of vocables as the basic *put up with* for *tolerate* or *put at a loss* for *bewilder*.

—PROFESSOR LANCELOT HOGBEN (*Interglossa*)

(3) On the one side we have the free personality: by definition it is not neurotic, for it has neither conflict nor dream. Its desires, such as they are, are transparent, for they are just what institutional approval keeps in the forefront of consciousness; another institutional pattern would alter their number and intensity; there is little in them that is natural, irreducible, or culturally dangerous. But *on the other side,* the social bond itself is nothing but the mutual reflection of these self-secure integrities. Recall the definition of love. Is not this the very picture of a small academic? Where is there a place in this hall of mirrors for either personality or fraternity?

—Essay on psychology in *Politics* (New York)

(4) All the "best people" from the gentlemen's clubs, and all the frantic fascist captains, united in common hatred of Socialism and bestial horror of the rising tide of the mass revolutionary movement, have turned to acts of provocation, to foul incendiarism, to medieval legends of poisoned wells, to legalize their own destruction of proletarian organizations, and rouse the agitated petty-bourgeoisie to chauvinistic fervor on behalf of the fight against the revolutionary way out of the crisis.

—Communist pamphlet

(5) If a new spirit *is* to be infused into this old country, there is one thorny and contentious reform which must be tackled, and that is the humanization and galvanization of the B.B.C. Timidity here will bespeak canker and atrophy of the soul. The heart of Britain may be sound and of strong beat, for instance, but the British lion's roar at present is like that of Bottom in Shakespeare's *Midsummer Night's Dream*—as gentle as any sucking dove. A virile new Britain cannot continue indefinitely to be traduced in the eyes or rather ears, of the world by the effete languors of Langham Place, brazenly masquerading as "standard English." When the voice of Britain is heard at nine o'clock, better far and infinitely less ludicrous to hear aitches honestly dropped than the present priggish, inflated, inhibited, school-ma'amish arch braying of blameless bashful mewing maidens!

—Letter in *Tribune*

Each of these passages has faults of its own, but, quite apart from avoidable ugliness, two qualities are common to all of them. The first is staleness of imagery; the other is lack of precision. The writer either has a meaning and cannot express it, or he inadvertently says something else, or he is almost indifferent as to whether his words mean anything or not. This mixture of vagueness and sheer incompetence is the most marked characteristic of modern English prose, and especially of any kind of political writing. As soon as certain topics are raised, the concrete melts into the abstract and no one seems able to think of turns of speech that are not hackneyed: prose consists less and less of *words* chosen for the sake of their meaning, and more and more of *phrases* tacked together like the sections of a prefabricated henhouse. I list below, with notes and examples, various of the tricks by means of which the work of prose-construction is habitually dodged:

DYING METAPHORS.   A newly invented metaphor assists thought by   5
evoking a visual image, while on the other hand a metaphor which is technically "dead" (e.g., *iron resolution*) has in effect reverted to being an ordinary word and can generally be used without loss of vividness. But in between these two classes there is a huge dump of worn-out metaphors which have lost all evocative power and are merely used because they save people the trouble of inventing phrases for themselves. Examples are: *ring the changes on, take up the cudgels for, toe the line, ride roughshod over, stand*

shoulder to shoulder with, play into the hands of, no axe to grind, grist to the mill, fishing in troubled waters, on the order of the day, Achilles' heel, swan song, hotbed. Many of these are used without knowledge of their meaning (what is a "rift," for instance?), and incompatible metaphors are frequently mixed, a sure sign that the writer is not interested in what he is saying. Some metaphors now current have been twisted out of their original meaning without those who use them even being aware of the fact. For example, *toe the line* is sometimes written *tow the line.* Another example is the *hammer and the anvil,* now always used with the implication that the anvil gets the worst of it. In real life it is always the anvil that breaks the hammer, never the other way about: a writer who stopped to think what he was saying would be aware of this, and would avoid perverting the original phrase.

OPERATORS OR VERBAL FALSE LIMBS. These save the trouble of picking out appropriate verbs and nouns, and at the same time pad each sentence with extra syllables which give it an appearance of symmetry. Characteristic phrases are *render inoperative, militate against, make contact with, be subjected to, give rise to, give grounds for, have the effect of, play a leading part (role) in, make itself felt, take effect, exhibit a tendency to, serve the purpose of,* etc., etc. The keynote is the elimination of simple verbs. Instead of being a single word, such as *break, stop, spoil, mend, kill,* a verb becomes a *phrase,* made up of a noun or adjective tacked on to some general-purpose verb such as *prove, serve, form, play, render.* In addition, the passive voice is wherever possible used in preference to the active, and noun constructions are used instead of gerunds (*by examination of* instead of *by examining*). The range of verbs is further cut down by means of the *-ize* and *de-* formations, and the banal statements are given an appearance of profundity by means of the *not un-* formation. Simple conjunctions and prepositions are replaced by such phrases as *with respect to, having regard to, the fact that, by dint of, in view of, in the interests of, on the hypothesis that;* and the ends of sentences are saved from anticlimax by such resounding common-places as *greatly to be desired, cannot be left out of account, a development to be expected in the near future, deserving of serious consideration, brought to a satisfactory conclusion,* and so on and so forth.

PRETENTIOUS DICTION. Words like *phenomenon, element, individual* (as noun), *objective, categorical, effective, virtual, basic, primary, promote, constitute, exhibit, exploit, utilize, eliminate, liquidate,* are used to dress up simple statements and give an air of scientific impartiality to biased judgments. Adjectives like *epoch-making, epic, historic, unforgettable, triumphant, age-old, inevitable, inexorable, veritable,* are used to dignify the sordid processes of international politics, while writing that aims at glorifying war usually takes on an archaic color, its characteristic words being: *realm, throne, chariot, mailed fist, trident, sword, shield, buckler, banner, jackboot, clarion.*

Foreign words and expressions such as *cul de sac, ancien régime, deus ex machina, mutatis mutandis, status quo, gleichschaltung, weltanschauung,* are used to give an air of culture and elegance. Except for the useful abbreviations *i.e., e.g.,* and *etc.,* there is no real need for any of the hundreds of foreign phrases now current in English. Bad writers, and especially scientific, political, and sociological writers, are nearly always haunted by the notion that Latin or Greek words are grander than Saxon ones, and unnecessary words like *expedite, ameliorate, predict, extraneous, deracinated, clandestine, subaqueous* and hundreds of others constantly gain ground from their Anglo-Saxon opposite numbers.[1] The jargon peculiar to Marxist writing (*hyena, hangman, cannibal, petty bourgeois, these gentry, lacquey, flunkey, mad dog, White Guard,* etc.) consists largely of words and phrases translated from Russian, German, or French; but the normal way of coining a new word is to use a Latin or Greek root with the appropriate affix and, where necessary, the -*ize* formation. It is often easier to make up words of this kind (*deregionalize, impermissible, extramarital, non-fragmentary,* and so forth) than to think up the English words that will cover one's meaning. The result, in general, is an increase in slovenliness and vagueness.

MEANINGLESS WORDS.   In certain kinds of writing, particularly in art criticism and literary criticism, it is normal to come across long passages which are almost completely lacking in meaning.[2] Words like *romantic, plastic, values, human, dead, sentimental, natural, vitality,* as used in art criticism, are strictly meaningless, in the sense that they not only do not point to any discoverable object, but are hardly ever expected to do so by the reader. When one critic writes, "The outstanding feature of Mr. X's work is its living quality," while another writes, "The immediately striking thing about Mr. X's work is its peculiar deadness," the reader accepts this as a simple difference of opinion. If words like *black* and *white* were involved, instead of the jargon words *dead* and *living,* he would see at once that language was being used in an improper way. Many political words are similarly abused. The word *Fascism* has now no meaning except in so far as it signifies "something not desirable." The words *democracy, freedom, patriotic, realistic, justice,* have each of them several different meanings

---

1. An interesting illustration of this is the way in which the English flower names which were in use till very recently are being ousted by Greek ones, *snapdragon* becoming *antirrhinum, forget-me-not* becoming *myosotis,* etc. It is hard to see any practical reason for this change of fashion: it is probably due to an instinctive turning-away from the more homely word and a vague feeling that the Greek word is scientific.

2. Example: "Comfort's catholicity of perception and image, strangely Whitmanesque in range, almost the exact opposite in esthetic compulsion, continues to evoke that trembling atmospheric accumulative hinting at a cruel, an inexorably serene timelessness. . . . Wrey Gardiner scores by aiming at simple bull's-eyes with precision. Only they are not so simple, and through this contented sadness runs more than the surface bittersweet of resignation." (*Poetry Quarterly*)

which cannot be reconciled with one another. In the case of a word like *democracy*, not only is there no agreed definition, but the attempt to make one is resisted from all sides. It is almost universally felt that when we call a country democratic we are praising it: consequently the defenders of every kind of regime claim that it is a democracy, and fear that they might have to stop using the word if it were tied down to any one meaning. Words of this kind are often used in a consciously dishonest way. That is, the person who uses them has his own private definition, but allows his hearer to think he means something quite different. Statements like, *Marshal Pétain was a true patriot, The Soviet Press is the freest in the world, the Catholic Church is opposed to persecution,* are almost always made with intent to deceive. Other words used in variable meanings, in most cases more or less dishonestly, are: *class, totalitarian, science, progressive, reactionary, bourgeois, equality.*

Now that I have made this catalogue of swindles and perversions, let me give another example of the kind of writing that they lead to. This time it must of its nature be an imaginary one. I am going to translate a passage of good English into modern English of the worst sort. Here is a well-known verse from *Ecclesiastes:*

> I returned and saw under the sun, that the race is not to the swift, nor the battle to the strong, neither yet bread to the wise, nor yet riches to men of understanding, nor yet favour to men of skill; but time and chance happeneth to them all.

Here it is in modern English: 10

> Objective consideration of contemporary phenomena compels the con-clusion that success or failure in competitive activities exhibits no ten-dency to be commensurate with innate capacity, but that a considerable element of the unpredictable must invariably be taken into account.

This is a parody, but a very gross one. Exhibit (3), above, for instance, contains several patches of the same kind of English. It will be seen that I have not made a full translation. The beginning and ending of the sentence follow the original meaning fairly closely, but in the middle the concrete illustrations—race, battle, bread—dissolve into the vague phrase "success or failure in competitive activities." This had to be so, because no modern writer of the kind I am discussing—no one capable of using phrases like "objective consideration of contemporary phenomena"—would ever tab-ulate his thoughts in that precise and detailed way. The whole tendency of modern prose is away from concreteness. Now analyze these two sentences a little more closely. The first contains forty-nine words but only sixty syl-lables, and all its words are those of everyday life. The second contains thirty-eight words of ninety syllables: eighteen of its words are from Latin roots, and one from Greek. The first sentence contains six vivid images, and only one phrase ("time and chance") that could be called vague. The second contains not a single fresh, arresting phrase, and in spite of its ninety syllables it gives only a shortened version of the meaning contained in the first. Yet without a doubt it is the second kind of sentence that is gaining ground in modern English. I do not want to exaggerate. This kind of writing is not yet universal, and outcrops of simplicity will occur here and there in the worst-written page. Still, if you or I were told to write a few lines on the uncertainty of human fortunes, we should probably come much nearer to my imaginary sentence than to the one from *Ecclesiastes*.

As I have tried to show, modern writing at its worst does not consist in picking out words for the sake of their meaning and inventing images in order to make the meaning clearer. It consists in gumming together long strips of words which have already been set in order by someone else, and making the results presentable by sheer humbug. The attraction of this way of writing is that it is easy. It is easier—even quicker, once you have the habit—to say *In my opinion it is not an unjustifiable assumption that* than to say *I think*. If you use ready-made phrases, you not only don't have to hunt about for words; you also don't have to bother with the rhythms of your sentences, since these phrases are generally so arranged as to be more or less euphonious. When you are composing in a hurry—when you are dictating to a stenographer, for instance, or making a public speech—it is natural to fall into a pretentious, Latinized style. Tags like *a consideration which we should do well to bear in mind* or *a conclusion to which all of us would readily assent* will save many a sentence from coming down with a bump. By using stale metaphors, similes, and idioms, you save much mental effort, at the cost of leaving your meaning vague, not only for your reader but for yourself. This is the significance of mixed metaphors. The sole aim of a metaphor is to call up a visual image. When these images clash—as in *The Fascist octopus has sung its swan song, the jackboot is thrown into the melting pot*—it can be taken as certain that the writer is not seeing a mental image of the objects he is naming; in other words he is not really thinking. Look again at the examples I gave at the beginning of this essay. Professor Laski (1) uses five negatives in fifty-three words. One of these is superfluous, making nonsense of the whole passage, and in addition there is the slip *alien* for *akin*, making further nonsense, and several avoidable pieces of clumsiness which increase the general vagueness. Professor Hogben (2) plays ducks and drakes with a battery which is able to write prescriptions, and, while disapproving of the everyday phrase *put up with*, is unwilling to look *egregious* up in the dictionary and see what it means; (3), if one takes an uncharitable attitude towards it, is simply meaningless: probably one could work out its intended meaning by reading the whole of the article in which it occurs. In (4), the writer knows more or less what he wants to say, but an accumulation of stale phrases chokes him like tea leaves blocking a sink. In (5), words and meaning have almost parted company. People who write in this manner usually have a general emotional meaning—they dislike one thing and want to express solidarity with another—but they are not interested in the detail of what they are saying. A scrupulous writer, in every sentence that he writes, will ask himself at least four questions, thus: What am I trying to say? What words will express it? What image or idiom will make it clearer? Is this image fresh enough to have an effect? And he will probably ask himself two more: Could I put it more shortly? Have I said anything that is avoidably ugly? But you are not obliged to go to all this trouble. You can shirk it by simply throwing your mind open and letting the ready-made phrases come crowding in. They will construct your sentences for you—even think your thoughts for you, to a certain extent—and at need they will perform the important service of partially concealing your meaning even from yourself. It is at this point that the special connection between politics and the debasement of language becomes clear.

In our time it is broadly true that political writing is bad writing. Where it is not true, it will generally be found that the writer is some kind of rebel, expressing his private opinions and not a "party line." Orthodoxy, of whatever color, seems to demand a lifeless, imitative style. The political dialects to be found in pamphlets, leading articles,

> **In our time, political speech and writing are largely the defense of the indefensible.**

manifestos, White Papers, and the speeches of under-secretaries do, of course, vary from party to party, but they are all alike in that one almost never finds in them a fresh, vivid, homemade turn of speech. When one watches some tired hack on the platform mechanically repeating the familiar phrases—*bestial atrocities, iron heel, bloodstained tyranny, free peoples of the world, stand shoulder to shoulder*—one often has a curious feeling that one is not watching a live human being but some kind of dummy: a feeling which suddenly becomes stronger at moments when the light catches the speaker's spectacles and turns them into blank discs which seem to have no eyes behind them. And this is not altogether fanciful. A speaker who uses that kind of phraseology has gone some distance towards turning himself into a machine. The appropriate noises are coming out of his larynx, but his brain is not involved as it would be if he were choosing his words for himself. If the speech he is making is one that he is accustomed to make over and over again, he may be almost unconscious of what he is saying, as one is when one utters the responses in church. And this reduced state of consciousness, if not indispensable, is at any rate favorable to political conformity.

In our time, political speech and writing are largely the defense of the indefensible. Things like the continuance of British rule in India, the Russian purges and deportations, the dropping of the atom bombs on Japan, can indeed be defended, but only by arguments which are too brutal for most people to face, and which do not square with the professed aims of political parties. Thus political language has to consist largely of euphemism, question-begging, and sheer cloudy vagueness. Defenseless villages are bombarded from the air, the inhabitants driven out into the countryside, the cattle machine-gunned, the huts set on fire with incendiary bullets: this is called *pacification*. Millions of peasants are robbed of their farms and sent trudging along the roads with no more than they can carry: this is called *transfer of population* or *rectification of frontiers*. People are imprisoned for years without trial, or shot in the back of the neck or sent to die of scurvy in Arctic lumber camps: this is called *elimination of unreliable elements*. Such phraseology is needed if one wants to name things without calling up mental pictures of them. Consider for instance some comfortable English professor defending Russian totalitarianism. He cannot say outright, "I believe in killing off your opponents when you can get good results by doing so." Probably, therefore, he will say something like this:

> While freely conceding that the Soviet régime exhibits certain features which the humanitarian may be inclined to deplore, we must, I think, agree that a certain curtailment of the right to political opposition is an unavoidable concomitant of transitional periods, and that the rigors which the Russian people have been called upon to undergo have been amply justified in the sphere of concrete achievement.

The inflated style is itself a kind of euphemism. A mass of Latin words   15
falls upon the facts like soft snow, blurring the outlines and covering up all the details. The great enemy of clear language is insincerity. When there is a gap between one's real and one's declared aims, one turns as it were instinctively to long words and exhausted idioms, like a cuttlefish squirting out ink. In our age there is no such thing as "keeping out of politics." All issues are political issues, and politics itself is a mass of lies, evasions, folly, hatred, and schizophrenia. When the general atmosphere is bad, language must suffer. I should expect to find—this is a guess which I have not sufficient knowledge to verify—that the German, Russian, and Italian languages have all deteriorated in the last ten or fifteen years, as a result of dictatorship.

But if thought corrupts language, language can also corrupt thought. A bad usage can spread by tradition and imitation, even among people who should and do know better. The debased language that I have been discussing is in some ways very convenient. Phrases like *a not unjustifiable assumption, leaves much to be desired, would serve no good purpose, a consideration which we should do well to bear in mind,* are a continuous temptation, a packet of aspirins always at one's elbow. Look back through this essay, and for certain you will find that I have again and again committed the very faults I am protesting against. By this morning's post I have received a pamphlet dealing with conditions in Germany. The author tells me that he "felt impelled" to write it. I open it at random, and here is almost the first sentence that I see: "[The Allies] have an opportunity not only of achieving a radical transformation of Germany's social and political structure in such a way as to avoid a nationalistic reaction in Germany itself, but at the same time of laying the foundations of a cooperative and unified Europe." You see, he "feels impelled" to write—feels, presumably, that he has something new to say—and yet his words, like cavalry horses answering the bugle, group themselves automatically into the familiar dreary pattern. The invasion of one's mind by ready-made phrases (*lay the foundations, achieve a radical transformation*) can only be prevented if one is constantly on guard against them, and every such phrase anesthetizes a portion of one's brain.

I said earlier that the decadence of our language is probably curable. Those who deny this would argue, if they produced an argument at all, that language merely reflects existing social conditions, and that we cannot influence its development by any direct tinkering with words and constructions. So far as the general tone or spirit of a language goes, this may be true, but it is not true in detail. Silly words and expressions have often disappeared, not through any evolutionary process but owing to the conscious action of a minority. Two recent examples were *explore every avenue* and *leave no stone unturned*, which were killed by the jeers of a few journalists. There is a long list of fly-blown metaphors which could similarly be got rid of if enough people would interest themselves in the job; and it should also be possible to laugh the *not un-* formation out of existence,[3] to reduce the amount of Latin and Greek in the average sentence, to drive out foreign phrases and strayed scientific words, and, in general, to make pretentiousness unfashionable. But all these are minor points. The defense of the English language implies more than this, and perhaps it is best to start by saying what it does *not* imply.

To begin with, it has nothing to do with archaism, with the salvaging of obsolete words and turns of speech, or with the setting up of a "standard English" which must never be departed from. On the contrary, it is especially concerned with the scrapping of every word or idiom which has outworn its usefulness. It has nothing to do with correct grammar and syntax, which are of no importance so long as one makes one's meaning clear, or with the avoidance of Americanisms, or with having what is called a "good prose style." On the other hand it is not concerned with fake simplicity and the attempt to make written English colloquial. Nor does it even imply in every case preferring the Saxon word to the Latin one, though it does imply using the fewest and shortest words that will cover one's meaning. What is above all needed is to let the meaning choose the word, and not the other way about. In prose, the worst thing one can do with words is to surrender to them. When you think of a concrete object, you think wordlessly, and then, if you want to describe the thing you have been visualizing you probably hunt about till you find the exact words that seem to fit it. When you think of something abstract you are more inclined to use words from the start, and unless you make a conscious effort to prevent it, the existing dialect will come rushing in and do the job for you, at the expense of blurring or even changing your

---

3. One can cure oneself of the *not un-* formation by memorizing this sentence: *A not unblack dog was chasing a not unsmall rabbit across a not ungreen field.*

meaning. Probably it is better to put off using words as long as possible and get one's meaning as clear as one can through pictures or sensations. Afterwards one can choose—not simply *accept*—the phrases that will best cover the meaning, and then switch round and decide what impression one's words are likely to make on another person. This last effort of the mind cuts out all stale or mixed images, all prefabricated phrases, needless repetitions, and humbug and vagueness generally. But one can often be in doubt about the effect of a word or a phrase, and one needs rules that one can rely on when instinct fails. I think the following rules will cover most cases:

1. Never use a metaphor, simile, or other figure of speech which you are used to seeing in print.
2. Never use a long word where a short one will do.
3. If it is possible to cut a word out, always cut it out.
4. Never use the passive where you can use the active.
5. Never use a foreign phrase, a scientific word, or a jargon word if you can think of an everyday English equivalent.
6. Break any of these rules sooner than say anything outright barbarous.

These rules sound elementary, and so they are, but they demand a deep change of attitude in anyone who has grown used to writing in the style now fashionable. One could keep all of them and still write bad English, but one could not write the kind of stuff that I quoted in those five specimens at the beginning of this article.

I have not here been considering the literary use of language, but   20 merely language as an instrument for expressing and not for concealing or preventing thought. Stuart Chase and others have come near to claiming that all abstract words are meaningless, and have used this as a pretext for advocating a kind of political quietism. Since you don't know what Fascism is, how can you struggle against Fascism? One need not swallow such absurdities as this, but one ought to recognize that the present political chaos is connected with the decay of language, and that one can probably bring about some improvement by starting at the verbal end. If you simplify your English, you are freed from the worst follies of orthodoxy. You cannot speak any of the necessary dialects, and when you make a stupid remark its stupidity will be obvious, even to yourself. Political language—and with variations this is true of all political parties, from Conservatives to Anarchists—is designed to make lies sound truthful and murder respectable, and to give an appearance of solidity to pure wind. One cannot change this all in a moment, but one can at least change one's own habits, and from time to time one can even, if one jeers loudly enough, send some worn-out and useless phrase—some *jackboot, Achilles' heel, hotbed, melting pot, acid test, veritable inferno,* or other lump of verbal refuse—into the dustbin where it belongs.

THINKING CRITICALLY ABOUT THE READING

1. In your own words, summarize Orwell's argument in this essay. (Glossary: *Argument*) Do you agree or disagree with him? Explain why.

2. For what audience do you think Orwell wrote this essay? (Glossary: *Audience*) What in his diction leads you to this conclusion? (Glossary: *Diction*)

3. Grammarians and usage experts have long objected to mixed metaphors (for example, "Politicians who have their heads in the sand are leading the country over the precipice") because they are inaccurate. For Orwell, a mixed metaphor is symptomatic of a greater problem (12). What is that problem?

4. What are dead and dying metaphors (5)? (Glossary: *Figures of Speech*) Why do dying metaphors disgust Orwell?

5. Following are some of the metaphors and similes that Orwell uses in his essay. (Glossary: *Figures of Speech*) Explain how each one works and comment on its effectiveness.

   a. "Prose consists less and less of *words* chosen for the sake of their meaning, and more and more of *phrases* tacked together like the sections of a prefabricated henhouse" (4).

   b. "But in between these two classes there is a huge dump of worn-out metaphors which have lost all evocative power" (5).

   c. "The writer knows more or less what he wants to say, but an accumulation of stale phrases chokes him like tea leaves blocking a sink" (12).

   d. "A mass of Latin words falls upon the facts like soft snow, blurring the outlines and covering up all the details" (15).

   e. "When there is a gap between one's real and one's declared aims, one turns . . . instinctively to long words and exhausted idioms, like a cuttlefish squirting out ink" (15).

   f. "He . . . feels, presumably, that he has something new to say—and yet his words, like cavalry horses answering the bugle, group themselves automatically into the familiar dreary pattern" (16).

6. According to Orwell, what are four important questions scrupulous writers ask themselves before they begin to write (12)?

7. Orwell says that one of the evils of political language is question-begging (14). What does he mean? Why, according to Orwell, has political language deteriorated? Do you agree with him that "the decadence of our language is probably curable" (17)? Why or why not?

8. In this essay, Orwell moves from negative arguments (criticisms) to positive ones (proposals). Where does he make the transition from criticisms to proposals? (Glossary: *Transitions*) Do you find the organization of his argument effective? (Glossary: *Organization*) Explain.

LANGUAGE IN ACTION

Read Robert Yoakum's "Everyspeech," a parody that first appeared in the *New York Times* in November 1994. Yoakum was a speechwriter for John F. Kennedy's successful 1960 campaign. As you read, identify the features of political speech that are the butt of Yoakum's humor. Does he point out the same language abuses that Orwell criticizes in his essay? What propaganda devices does Yoakum use (see Cross's essay on pp. 209–219)?

Everyspeech

Ladies and gentlemen. I am delighted to see so many friends from the Third Congressional District. And what better site for some straight talk than at this greatest of all state fairs, where ribbons reward American individual enterprise, whether for the biggest beets or the best bull?

Speaking of bull, my opponent has said some mighty dishonest things about me. But what can you expect from a typical politician? I want to address some fundamental issues that set me apart from my opponent and his failed party—the party of gutlessness and gridlock.

The American people are ready for straight talk, although don't count on the press to report it straight. The press, like my opponent, has no respect for the public.

This democracy must return to its roots or it will perish, and its roots are you—the honest, hard-working, God-fearing people who made this the greatest nation on earth. Yes, we have problems. But what problems would not be solved if the press and politicians had faith in the people?

Take crime, for example. Rampant, brutal crime. My rival in this race believes that redemption and rehabilitation are the answers to the lawlessness that is tearing our society apart.

Well, if R and R is what you want for those robbers and rapists, don't vote for me. If pampering the punks is what you want, vote for my opponent.

Do I believe in the death penalty? You bet! Do I believe in three strikes and you're out? No, I believe in *two* strikes and you're out! I believe in three strikes and you're *dead*!

You can count on me to crack down on crime, but I won't ignore the other big C word: character. Character made our nation great. Character, and respect for family values. A belief in children and parents. In brothers and sisters and grandparents.

Oh, sure, that sounds corny. Those cynical inside-the-Beltway journalists will ridicule me tomorrow, but I would rather be guilty of a corny defense of family values than of coddling criminals.

While I'm making myself unpopular with the press and a lot of politicians, I might as well alienate even more Washington wimps by telling you frankly how I feel about taxes. I'm against them! Not just in an election year, like my adversary, but every year!

I'm in favor of slashing wasteful welfare, which is where a lot of your hard-earned tax dollars go. The American people have said "enough!" to welfare, but inside the Beltway they don't give a hoot about the industrious folks I see before me today. They're too busy with their cocktail parties, diplomatic functions, and society balls.

My opponent loves those affairs, but I'd rather be with my good friends here than with those fork-tongued lawyers, cookie-pushing State Department fops, and high-priced lobbyists. I promise that when elected, my main office will be right here in the Third District. My branch office will be in D.C. And I promise you this: I shall serve only two terms and then return to live with the folks I love.

So on Nov. 8, if you want someone with an independent mind and the courage to change — *to change back to good old American values* — if you've had enough and want someone tough, vote for me. Thank you, and God bless America.

WRITING SUGGESTIONS

1. Orwell claims that political speech is filled with such words as *patriotism, democracy, freedom, realistic,* and *justice,* words that have "several different meanings which cannot be reconciled with one another" (8). Why is Orwell so uneasy about these words? What do these words mean to you? How do your meanings differ from those of others? For example, someone who has served in the armed forces, been a political prisoner, or served as a juror may attach distinct meanings to the words *patriotism, freedom,* or *justice.* In a brief essay, recount an experience that gave you real insight into the meaning of one of these words or a word similar to them.

2. Collect examples of bureaucratic writing on your campus. How would you characterize most of this writing? Who on your campus seems to be prone to manipulative language — college administrators, student leaders, or faculty? Use information from the Orwell and Cross articles in this chapter to analyze the writing you collect. Then write an essay in which you assess the health of the English language at your school.

The World of Doublespeak

WILLIAM LUTZ

Born in Racine, Wisconsin, in 1940, William Lutz has been a professor of English at Rutgers University since 1991 and was editor of the
Quarterly Review of Doublespeak for fourteen years. Through his book
Doublespeak: From Revenue Enhancement to Terminal Living (1980),
Lutz first awakened Americans to how people in important positions
were manipulating language. As chair of the National Council of Teachers of English's Committee on Public Doublespeak, Lutz has been a
watchdog of public officials who use language to "mislead, distort,
deceive, inflate, circumvent, obfuscate." Each year the committee presents the Orwell Awards, recognizing the most outrageous uses of public doublespeak in the worlds of government and business. Lutz's recent
books are *The New Doublespeak: Why No One Knows What Anyone's Saying Anymore* (1997) and *Doublespeak Defined: Cut through the Bull*****
and Get to the Point (1999).

In the following essay, which first appeared in Christopher Ricks's
and Leonard Michaels's anthology *State of the Language* (1990), Lutz
examines doublespeak, "language which pretends to communicate but
doesn't, language which makes the bad seem good, the negative appear
positive, the unpleasant attractive, or at least tolerable." He identifies the
various types of doublespeak and cautions us about the possible serious
effects that doublespeak can have on our thinking.

WRITING TO DISCOVER: *Have you ever heard or read language that you
thought was deliberately evasive, language that manipulated your perception of
reality, or, worse yet, language that communicated nothing? Jot down your thoughts
about such language. For example, what kinds of language do people use to talk
about death, cancer, mental illness, firing a person, killing someone, or ending a relationship? Do you think evasive or manipulative language is ever justified? Explain.*

Farmers no longer have cows, pigs, chickens, or other animals on their
farms; according to the U.S. Department of Agriculture, farmers have
"grain-consuming animal units" (which, according to the Tax Reform
Act of 1986, are kept in "single-purpose agricultural structures," not pig
pens and chicken coops). Attentive observers of the English language also
learned recently that the multibillion dollar stock market crash of 1987
was simply a "fourth quarter equity retreat"; that airplanes don't crash,
they just have "uncontrolled contact with the ground"; that janitors are
really "environmental technicians"; that it was a "diagnostic misadventure
of a high magnitude" which caused the death of a patient in a Philadelphia hospital, not medical malpractice; and that President Reagan wasn't
really unconscious while he underwent minor surgery, he was just in a

"non-decision-making form." In other words, doublespeak continues to spread as the official language of public discourse.

Doublespeak is a blanket term for language which pretends to communicate but doesn't, language which makes the bad seem good, the negative appear positive, the unpleasant attractive, or at least tolerable. It is language which avoids, shifts, or denies responsibility, language which is at variance with its real or its purported meaning. It is language which conceals or prevents thought. Basic to doublespeak is incongruity, the incongruity between what is said, or left unsaid, and what really is: between the word and the referent, between seem and be, between the essential function of language, communication, and what doublespeak does— mislead, distort, deceive, inflate, circumvent, obfuscate.

When shopping, we are asked to check our packages at the desk "for our convenience," when it's not for our convenience at all but for the store's "program to reduce inventory shrinkage." We see advertisements for "pre-owned," "experienced," or "previously distinguished" cars, for "genuine imitation leather," "virgin vinyl," or "real counterfeit diamonds." Television offers not reruns but "encore telecasts." There are no slums or ghettos, just the "inner city" or "substandard housing" where the "disadvantaged," "economically nonaffluent," or "fiscal underachievers" live. Nonprofit organizations don't make a profit, they have "negative deficits" or "revenue excesses." In the world of doublespeak dying is "terminal living."

> **In other words, doublespeak continues to spread as the official language of public discourse.**

We know that a toothbrush is still a toothbrush even if the advertisements on television call it a "home plaque removal instrument," and even that "nutritional avoidance therapy" means a diet. But who would guess that a "volume-related production schedule adjustment" means closing an entire factory in the doublespeak of General Motors, or that "advanced downward adjustments" means budget cuts in the doublespeak of Caspar Weinberger, or that "energetic disassembly" means an explosion in a nuclear power plant in the doublespeak of the nuclear power industry?

The euphemism, an inoffensive or positive word or phrase designed to avoid a harsh, unpleasant, or distasteful reality, can at times be doublespeak. But the euphemism can also be a tactful word or phrase; for example, "passed away" functions not just to protect the feelings of another person but also to express our concern for another's grief. This use of the euphemism is not doublespeak but the language of courtesy. A euphemism used to mislead or deceive, however, becomes doublespeak. In 1984, the U.S. State Department announced that in its annual reports on the status of human rights in countries around the world it would no longer use the word "killing." Instead, it would use the phrase "unlawful or arbitrary deprivation of life." Thus the State Department avoids discussing

5

government-sanctioned killings in countries that the United States supports and has certified as respecting human rights.

The Pentagon also avoids unpleasant realities when it refers to bombs
and artillery shells which fall on civilian targets as "incontinent ordnance"
or killing the enemy as "servicing the target." In 1977 the Pentagon tried
to slip funding for the neutron bomb unnoticed into an appropriations bill
by calling it an "enhanced radiation device." And in 1971 the CIA gave
us that most famous of examples of doublespeak when it used the phrase
"eliminate with extreme prejudice" to refer to the execution of a suspected
double agent in Vietnam.

Jargon, the specialized language of a trade or profession, allows colleagues to communicate with each other clearly, efficiently, and quickly.
Indeed, it is a mark of membership to be able to use and understand
the group's jargon. But it can also be doublespeak—pretentious, obscure,
and esoteric terminology used to make the simple appear complex, and
not to express but impress. In the doublespeak of jargon, smelling something becomes "organoleptic analysis," glass becomes "fused silicate," a
crack in a metal support beam becomes a "discontinuity," conservative
economic policies become "distributionally conservative notions."

Lawyers and tax accountants speak of an "involuntary conversion"
of property when discussing the loss or destruction of property through
theft, accident, or condemnation. So if your house burns down, or
your car is stolen or destroyed in an accident, you have, in legal jargon,
suffered an "involuntary conversion" of your property. This is a legal
term with a specific meaning in law and all lawyers can be expected to
understand it. But when it is used to communicate with a person outside
the group who does not understand such language, it is doublespeak.
In 1978 a National Airlines 727 airplane crashed while attempting to
land at the Pensacola, Florida, airport, killing three passengers, injuring
twenty-one others, and destroying the airplane. Since the insured value
of the airplane was greater than its book value, National made an after-
tax insurance benefit of $1.7 million on the destroyed airplane, or an
extra eighteen cents a share. In its annual report, National reported that
this $1.7 million was due to "the involuntary conversion of a 727," thus
explaining the profit without even hinting at the crash and the deaths of
three passengers.

Gobbledygook or bureaucratese is another kind of doublespeak. Such
doublespeak is simply a matter of overwhelming the audience with technical, unfamiliar words. When asked why U.S. forces lacked intelligence
information on Grenada before they invaded the island in 1983, Admiral
Wesley L. McDonald told reporters that "We were not micromanaging
Grenada intelligence-wise until about that time frame."

Some gobbledygook, however impressive it may sound, doesn't even   10
make sense. During the 1988 presidential campaign, vice presidential
candidate Senator Dan Quayle explained the need for a strategic defense

initiative by saying: "Why wouldn't an enhanced deterrent, a more stable peace, a better prospect to denying the ones who enter conflict in the first place to have a reduction of offensive systems and an introduction to defensive capability. I believe this is the route the country will eventually go."

In 1974, Alan Greenspan, then chairman of the President's Council of Economic Advisors, was testifying before a Senate Committee and was in the difficult position of trying to explain why President Nixon's economic policies weren't effective in fighting inflation: "It is a tricky problem to find the particular calibration in timing that would be appropriate to stem the acceleration in risk premiums created by falling incomes without prematurely aborting the decline in the inflation-generated risk premiums." In 1988, when speaking to a meeting of the Economic Club of New York, Mr. Greenspan, [later] Federal Reserve chairman, said, "I guess I should warn you, if I turn out to be particularly clear, you've probably misunderstood what I've said."

The investigation into the *Challenger* disaster in 1986 revealed the gobbledygook and bureaucratese used by many involved in the shuttle program. When Jesse Moore, NASA's associate administrator, was asked if the performance of the shuttle program had improved with each launch or if it had remained the same, he answered, "I think our performance in terms of the liftoff performance and in terms of the orbital performance, we knew more about the envelope we were operating under, and we have been pretty accurately staying in that. And so I would say the performance has not by design drastically improved. I think we have been able to characterize the performance more as a function of our launch experience as opposed to it improving as a function of time."

A final kind of doublespeak is simply inflated language. Car mechanics may be called "automotive internists," elevator operators "members of the vertical transportation corps," and grocery store checkout clerks "career associate scanning professionals," while television sets are proclaimed to have "nonmulticolor capability." When a company "initiates a career alternative enhancement program" it is really laying off five thousand workers; "negative patient care outcome" means that the patient died; and "rapid oxidation" means a fire in a nuclear power plant.

The doublespeak of inflated language can have serious consequences. The U.S. Navy didn't pay $2,043 a piece for steel nuts; it paid all that money for "hexiform rotatable surface compression units," which, by the way, "underwent catastrophic stress-related shaft detachment." Not to be outdone, the U.S. Air Force paid $214 apiece for Emergency Exit Lights, or flashlights. This doublespeak is in keeping with such military doublespeak as "preemptive counterattack" for first strike, "engage the enemy on all sides" for ambush, "tactical redeployment" for retreat, and "air support" for bombing. In the doublespeak of the military, the 1983 invasion of Grenada was conducted not by the U.S. Army, Navy, Air Force, and Marines but by the "Caribbean Peace Keeping Forces." But then according to the Pentagon it wasn't an invasion, it was a "predawn vertical insertion."

These last examples of doublespeak should make it clear that double-   15
speak is not the product of careless language or sloppy thinking. Indeed, serious doublespeak is the product of clear thinking and is carefully designed and constructed to appear to communicate but in fact to mislead. Thus, it's not a tax increase but "revenue enhancement," "tax base broadening," or "user fees," so how can you complain about higher taxes? It's not acid rain, it's just "poorly buffered precipitation," so don't worry about all those dead trees. That isn't the Mafia in Atlantic City, those are just "members of a career-offender cartel," so don't worry about the influence of organized crime in the city. The Supreme Court justice wasn't addicted to the painkilling drug he was taking, it's just that the drug had simply "established an interrelationship with the body, such that if the drug is removed precipitously, there is a reaction," so don't worry that his decisions might have been influenced by his drug addiction. It's not a Titan II nuclear-armed, intercontinental, ballistic missile 630 times more powerful than the atomic bomb dropped on Hiroshima, it's just a "very large, potentially disruptive reentry system," so don't worry about the threat of nuclear destruction. Serious doublespeak is highly strategic, and it breeds suspicion, cynicism, distrust, and, ultimately, hostility.

In his famous and now-classic essay "Politics and the English Language," which was published in 1946, George Orwell wrote that the "great enemy of clear language is insincerity. When there is a gap between one's real and one's declared aims, one turns as it were instinctively to long words and exhausted idioms, like a cuttlefish squirting out ink." For Orwell, language was an instrument for "expressing and not for concealing or preventing thought." In his most biting comment, Orwell observes that "in our time, political speech and writing are largely the defense of the indefensible. . . . Political language has to consist largely of euphemism, question-begging, and sheer cloudy vagueness. . . . Political language . . . is designed to make lies sound truthful and murder respectable, and to give an appearance of solidity to pure wind."

Orwell understood well the power of language as both a tool and a weapon. In the nightmare world of his novel *1984*, he depicted language as one of the most important tools of the totalitarian state. Newspeak, the official state language in *1984*, was designed not to extend but to *diminish* the range of human thought, to make only "correct" thought possible and all other modes of thought impossible. It was, in short, a language designed to create a reality which the state wanted.

Newspeak had another important function in Orwell's world of *1984*. It provided the means of expression for doublethink, which Orwell described in his novel as "the power of holding two contradictory beliefs in one's mind simultaneously, and accepting both of them." The classic example of doublethink in Orwell's novel is the slogan "War is Peace."

And lest you think doublethink is confined only to Orwell's novel, you need only recall the words of Secretary of State Alexander Haig when he testified before a Congressional Committee in 1982 that a continued weapons build-up by the United States is "absolutely essential to our hopes for meaningful arms reduction." Or the words of Senator Orrin Hatch in 1988: "Capital punishment is our society's recognition of the sanctity of human life."

The more sophisticated and powerful uses of doublespeak can at times be difficult to identify. On 27 July 1981, President Ronald Reagan said in a television speech: "I will not stand by and see those of you who are dependent on Social Security deprived of the benefits you've worked so hard to earn. You will continue to receive your checks in the full amount due you." This speech had been billed as President Reagan's position on Social Security, a subject of much debate at the time. After the speech, public opinion polls recorded the great majority of the public as believing that President Reagan had affirmed his support for Social Security and that he would not support cuts in benefits. Five days after the speech, however, White House spokesperson David Gergen was quoted in the press as saying that President Reagan's words had been "carefully chosen." What President Reagan did mean, according to Gergen, was that he was reserving the right to decide who was "dependent" on those benefits, who had "earned" them, and who, therefore, was "due" them.

During the 1982 Congressional election campaign, the Republican National Committee sponsored a television advertisement which pictured an elderly, folksy postman delivering Social Security checks "with the 7.4 percent cost-of-living raise that President Reagan promised." Looking directly at his audience, the postman then adds that Reagan "promised that raise and he kept his promise, in spite of those sticks-in-the-mud who tried to keep him from doing what we elected him to do." 20

The commercial was deliberately misleading. The cost-of-living increases had been provided automatically by law since 1975, and President Reagan had tried three times to roll them back or delay them but was overruled by congressional opposition. When these discrepancies were pointed out to an official of the Republican National Committee, he called the commercial "inoffensive" and added, "Since when is a commercial supposed to be accurate? Do women really smile when they clean their ovens?"

In 1986, with the *Challenger* tragedy and subsequent investigation, we discovered that doublespeak seemed to be the official language of NASA, the National Aeronautics and Space Administration, and of the contractors engaged in the space shuttle program. The first thing we learned is that the *Challenger* tragedy wasn't an accident. As Kay Parker of NASA said, experts were "working in the anomaly investigation." The "anomaly" was the explosion of the *Challenger*.

When NASA reported that it was having difficulty determining how or exactly when the *Challenger* astronauts died, Rear Admiral Richard Truly reported that "whether or not a cabin rupture occurred prior to water impact has not yet been determined by a superficial examination of the recovered components." The "recovered components" were the bodies of the astronauts. Admiral Truly also said that "extremely large forces were imposed on the vehicle as evidenced by the immediate breakup into many pieces." He went on to say that "once these forces have been accurately determined, if in fact they can be, the structural analysts will attempt to estimate the effect on the structural and pressure integrity of the crew module." NASA referred to the coffins of the astronauts as "crew transfer containers."

Arnold Aldrich, manager of the national space transportation systems program at Johnson Space Center, said that "the normal process during the countdown is that the countdown proceeds, assuming we are in a go posture, and at various points during the countdown we tag up on the operational loops and face to face in the firing room to ascertain the facts that project elements that are monitoring the data and that are understanding the situation as we proceed are still in the go condition."

In testimony before the commission investigating the *Challenger*   25
accident, Allen McDonald, an engineer for Morton Thiokol (the maker of the rocket), said he had expressed concern about the possible effect of cold weather on the booster rocket's O-ring seals the night before the launch: "I made the comment that lower temperatures are in the direction of badness for both O-rings, because it slows down the timing function."

Larry Mulloy, manager of the space shuttle solid rocket booster program at Marshall Space Flight Center, responded to a question assessing whether problems with the O-rings or with the insulation of the liner of the nozzle posed a greater threat to the shuttle by saying, "The criticality in answering your question, sir, it would be a real foot race as to which one would be considered more critical, depending on the particular time that you looked at your experience with that."

After several executives of Rockwell International, the main contractor to build the shuttle, had testified that Rockwell had been opposed to launching the shuttle because of the danger posed by ice formation on the launch platform, Martin Cioffoletti, vice president for space transportation at Rockwell, said: "I felt that by telling them we did not have a sufficient data base and could not analyze the trajectory of the ice, I felt he understood that Rockwell was not giving a positive indication that we were for the launch."

Officials at Morton Thiokol, when asked why they reversed earlier decisions not to launch the shuttle, said the reversal was "based on the reevaluation of those discussions." The Presidential commission investigating the accident suggested that this statement could be translated to mean there was pressure from NASA.

One of the most chilling uses of doublespeak occurred in 1981 when then Secretary of State Alexander Haig was testifying before congressional committees about the murder of three American nuns and a Catholic lay worker in El Salvador. The four women had been raped and then shot at close range, and there was clear evidence that the crime had been committed by soldiers of the Salvadoran government. Before the House Foreign Affairs Committee, Secretary Haig said, "I'd like to suggest to you that some of the investigations would lead one to believe that perhaps the vehicle the nuns were riding in may have tried to run a roadblock, or may accidentally have been perceived to have been doing so, and there'd been an exchange of fire and then perhaps those who inflicted the casualties sought to cover it up. And this could have been at a very low level of both competence and motivation in the context of the issue itself. But the facts on this are not clear enough for anyone to draw a definitive conclusion."

The next day, before the Senate Foreign Relations Committee, Secre-   30
tary Haig claimed that press reports on his previous testimony were inaccurate. When Senator Claiborne Pell asked whether Secretary Haig was suggesting the possibility that "the nuns may have run through a roadblock," Secretary Haig replied, "You mean that they tried to violate . . . ? Not at all, no, not at all. My heavens! The dear nuns who raised me in my parochial schooling would forever isolate me from their affections and respect." When Senator Pell asked Secretary Haig, "Did you mean that the nuns were firing at the people, or what did 'an exchange of fire' mean?" Secretary Haig replied, "I haven't met any pistol-packing nuns in my day, Senator. What I meant was that if one fellow starts shooting, then the next thing you know they all panic." Thus did the Secretary of State of the United States explain official government policy on the murder of four American citizens in a foreign land.

The congressional hearings for the IranContra affair produced more doublespeak. During his second day of testimony before the Select Committee on Secret Military Assistance to Iran and the Nicaraguan Opposition, Oliver North admitted that he had on different occasions lied to the Iranians, his colleague Maj. Gen. Richard Secord, congressional investigators, and the Congress, and that he had destroyed evidence and created false documents. North then asserted to the committee that everything he was about to say would be the truth.

North used the words "residuals" and "diversions" to refer to the millions of dollars which were raised for the contras by overcharging Iran for arms. North also said that he "cleaned" and "fixed" things up, that he was "cleaning up the historical record," and that he "took steps to ensure" that things never "came out"—meaning he lied, destroyed official government documents, and created false documents. Some documents weren't destroyed; they were "non-log[ged]" or kept "out of the system so that outside knowledge would not necessarily be derived from having the documents themselves."

North was also careful not to "infect other people with unnecessary knowledge." He explained that the Nicaraguan Humanitarian Assistance Office provided humanitarian aid in "mixed loads," which, according to North, "meant . . . beans and Band-Aids and boots and bullets." For North, people in other countries who helped him were "assets." "Project Democracy" was a "euphemism" he used at the time to refer to the organization that was building an airfield for the contras.

In speaking of a false chronology of events which he helped construct, North said that he "was provided with additional input that was radically different from the truth. I assisted in furthering that version." He mentions "a different version from the facts" and calls the chronology "inaccurate." North also testified that he and William Casey, then head of the C.I.A., together falsified the testimony that Casey was to give to Congress. "Director Casey and I fixed that testimony and removed the offensive portions. We fixed it by omission. We left out—it wasn't made accurate, it wasn't made fulsome, it was fixed by omission." Official lies were "plausible deniability."

While North admitted that he had shredded documents after being   35
informed that officials from the Attorney General's office wanted to inspect some of the documents in his office, he said, "I would prefer to say that I shredded documents that day like I did on all other days, but perhaps with increased intensity."

North also preferred to use the passive to avoid responsibility. When asked "Where are the non-logged documents?" he replied, "I think they were shredded." Again, when asked on what authority he agreed to allow Secord to make a personal profit off the arms sale to Iran, North replied with a long, wordy response filled with such passive constructions as "it was clearly indicated," "it was already known," and "it was recognized." But he never answered the question.

For North, the whole investigation by Congress was just an attempt "to criminalize policy differences between coequal branches of government and the Executive's conduct of foreign affairs." Lying to Congress, shredding official documents, violating laws, conducting unauthorized activities were all just "policy differences" to North. But North was generous with the committee: "I think there's fault to go on both sides. I've said that repeatedly throughout my testimony. And I have accepted the responsibility for my role in it." While North accepts responsibility, he does not accept accountability.

This final statement of North's bears close reading for it reveals the subtlety of his language. North states as fact that Congress was at fault, but at fault for what he doesn't specify. Furthermore, he does not accept responsibility for any specific action, only for his "role," whatever that may have been, in "it." In short, while he may be "responsible" (not guilty) for violating the law, Congress shares in that responsibility for having passed the law.

In Oliver North's doublespeak, then, defying a law is complying with it, noncompliance is compliance. North's doublespeak allowed him to help draft a letter to Congress saying that "we are complying with the letter and spirit" of the Boland Amendment, when what the letter really meant, North later admitted, was that "Boland doesn't apply to us and so we're complying with its letter and spirit."

Contrary to his claim that he was a "stand up guy" who would tell all   40
and take whatever was coming to him, North disclaimed all responsibility for his actions: "I was authorized to do everything that I did." Yet when he was asked who gave him authorization, North replied, "My superiors." When asked which superior, he replied: "Well, who—look who sign—I didn't sign those letters to the—to this body." And North's renowned steel-trap memory went vague or forgetful again.

After North had testified, Admiral John Poindexter, North's superior, testified before the committee. Once again, doublespeak flourished. In the world of Admiral John Poindexter, one does not lie but "misleads" or "withholds information." Likewise, one engages in "secret activities" which are not the same as covert actions. In Poindexter's world, one can "acquiesce" in a shipment of weapons while at the same time not authorize the shipment. One can transfer millions of dollars of government money as a "technical implementation" without making a "substantive decision." One can also send subordinates to lie to congressional committees if one does not "micromanage" them. In Poindexter's world, "outside interference" occurs when Congress attempts to fulfill its constitutional function of passing legislation.

For Poindexter, withholding information was not lying. When asked about Col. North's testimony that he had lied to a congressional committee and that Poindexter had known that North intended to lie, Poindexter replied, "there was a general understanding that he [North] was to withhold information. . . . I . . . did not expect him to lie to the committee. I expected him to be evasive. . . . I'm sure they [North's answers] were very carefully crafted, nuanced. The total impact, I am sure, was one of withholding information from the Congress, but I'm still not convinced . . . that he lied."

Yet Poindexter protested that it is not "fair to say that I have misinformed Congress or other Cabinet officers. I haven't testified to that. I've testified that I withheld information from Congress. And with regard to the Cabinet officers, I didn't withhold anything from them that they didn't want withheld from them." Poindexter did not explain how it is possible to withhold information that a person wants withheld.

The doublespeak of Alexander Haig, Oliver North, and John Poindexter occurred during their testimony before congressional committees. Perhaps their doublespeak was not premeditated but just happened to be the way they spoke, and thought. President Jimmy Carter in 1980 could call the aborted raid to free the American hostages in Tehran an "incomplete success" and really believe that he had made a statement that clearly communicated with the American public. So too could President Ronald Reagan say in 1985 that "ultimately our security and our hopes for success at the arms reduction talks hinge on the determination that we show here to continue our program to rebuild and refortify our defenses" and really believe that greatly increasing the amount of money spent building new weapons will lead to a reduction in the number of weapons in the world. If we really believe that we understand such language and that such language communicates and promotes clear thought, then the world of *1984* with its control of reality through language is upon us.

THINKING CRITICALLY ABOUT THE READING

1. What, according to Lutz, is doublespeak? What are its essential characteristics?

2. What is a euphemism? Are all euphemisms examples of doublespeak? Explain.

3. In his discussion of Oliver North's testimony during the Iran-Contra hearings, Lutz states, "While North accepts responsibility, he does not accept accountability" (37). Explain what Lutz means here. What differences do you draw between responsibility and accountability?

4. Why, according to Lutz, does "doublespeak continue to spread as the official language of public discourse" (1)? In your opinion, is doublespeak as widespread today as it was when Lutz wrote his article? What examples can you provide to back up your opinion?

5. Lutz discusses four basic types or categories of doublespeak—euphemism, jargon, gobbledygook, and inflated language. In what ways does this classification serve to clarify not only the concept of doublespeak but also its many uses? (Glossary: *Classification*)

6. Lutz is careful to illustrate each of the basic types of doublespeak with examples. Why is it important to use plenty of examples in an essay like this? (Glossary: *Examples*) What do his many examples reveal about Lutz's expertise on the subject?

7. Why does Lutz believe that we must recognize doublespeak for what it is and voice our dissatisfaction with those who use it?

LANGUAGE IN ACTION

In an article called "Public Doublespeak," Terence Moran presents the following list of recommended language, which school administrators in Brooklyn gave their elementary school teachers to use when discussing students with their parents.

For Parent Interviews and Report Cards

Harsh Expression (Avoid)	*Acceptable Expression (Use)*
Does all right if pushed	Accomplishes tasks when interest is stimulated.
Too free with fists	Resorts to physical means of winning his point or attracting attention.

Lies (Dishonest)	Shows difficulty in distinguishing between imaginary and factual material.
Cheats	Needs help in learning to adhere to rules and standards of fair play.
Steals	Needs help in learning to respect the property rights of others.
Noisy	Needs to develop quieter habits of communication.
Lazy	Needs ample supervision in order to work well.
Is a bully	Has qualities of leadership but needs help in learning to use them democratically.
Associates with "gangs"	Seems to feel secure only in group situations; needs to develop sense of independence.
Disliked by other children	Needs help in learning to form lasting friendships.

What are your reactions to these recommendations? Why do you suppose the school administrators made up this list? What purpose does such language serve? Do you believe the "acceptable" language belongs in our nation's schools? Why or why not?

WRITING SUGGESTIONS

1. Think of the ways that you encounter doublespeak every day, whether in school or at work, or while reading a newspaper or watching television. How does it affect you? What do you suppose the speakers' or writers' motives are in using doublespeak? Using your own experiences and observations, write an essay in which you explore the reasons why people use doublespeak. Before starting to write, you may find it helpful to review your Writing to Discover response to the Lutz essay.

2. In his concluding paragraph Lutz states, "If we really believe that we understand [doublespeak] and that such language communicates and promotes clear thought, then the world of *1984* with its control of reality through language is upon us." In an essay, discuss whether or not Lutz is overstating the case and being too pessimistic and whether or not the American public is really unaware of — or apathetic about — how doublespeak manipulates and deceives. Consider also whether or not the American public has reacted to doublespeak with, as Lutz suggests, "suspicion, cynicism, distrust, and, ultimately, hostility."

3. Using resources in your library or on the Internet, write a paper about the language of funeral directors, stockbrokers, college professors, health-care professionals, or some other occupation of your choice. How pervasive is doublespeak in the occupation you selected? Based on the results of your research, why do you think people with this type of job use such language? Do you find this language troublesome? If so, what can be done to change the situation?

Language That Silences

JASON STANLEY

> Jason Stanley is a philosopher who specializes in the philosophy of lan-
> guage and linguistics, as well as questions involving cognition, context-
> dependence, and fallibilism, or the philosophical principle that we could
> be wrong about our beliefs. Stanley was born in 1969 and earned his B.A.
> in philosophy and linguistics at the State University of New York at Stony
> Brook in 1990 and his Ph.D. at the Massachusetts Institute of Technology
> in 1995. Stanley has taught at a number of colleges and universities
> and is currently professor of philosophy at Rutgers University. He has
> written three books: *Know How* (2011), *Language in Context: Selected
> Essays* (2007), and *Knowledge and Practical Interests* (2005).
>
> In "The Ways of Silencing," first published in the *New York Times*
> on June 25, 2011, Stanley examines the ways in which language may be
> supposed to further discussion or shed light on issues but is gradually
> manipulated and snuffs out the trust necessary for its very existence.

WRITING TO DISCOVER: *Do you think that most news outlets report the
news objectively without any biases, or do you think they either give intentionally
or unintentionally biased reports? On what evidence do you base your views? Cite
examples where possible.*

We might wish politicians and pundits from opposing parties to
engage in reasoned debate about the truth, but as we know, this is not the
reality of our political discourse.

Instead we often encounter bizarre and improbable claims about public
figures. Words are misappropriated and meanings twisted. I believe that
these tactics are not really about making substantive claims, but rather play
the role of silencing. They are, if you will, linguistic strategies for stealing
the voices of others. These strategies have always been part of the arsenal of
politics. But since they are so widely used today, it is worth examining their
underlying mechanisms, to make apparent their special dangers.

The feminist scholar Catharine MacKinnon famously declared, "Pornography silences women." In the 1990s, the philosophers of language
Jennifer Hornsby and Rae Langton developed an account of the mechanisms of silencing that could substantiate MacKinnon's claim. But their
basic ideas extend beyond the examples they chose, and can inform us
about silencing in our political discourse today.

In her 1993 paper, "Speech Acts and Pornography," Hornsby used
an example, credited to Langton: Suppose that men are led to believe that
when women refuse a sexual advance they don't mean it. Women, then,
will not be understood to be refusing, even when they are. If certain kinds
of pornography lead men to think that women are not sincere when they

utter the word "no," and women are aware that men think this, those kinds of pornography would rob women of the ability to refuse. Using "no" to refuse a sexual advance is what is known as a speech act — a way of doing something by using words. Hornsby and Langton's work raises the possibility that a medium may undermine the ability of a person or group — in this case, women — to employ a speech act by representing that person or group as insincere in their use of it.

Silencing extends to politics when outlandish claims are made about public figures. Suppose that President Obama really was a secret Islamist agent, or born in Kenya. In that case, he would be grossly insincere. We would have no reason to believe what he said in any situation. The function of disseminating such claims about the president is not to object to his specific arguments or agenda. It is to undermine the public's trust in him, so that nothing he says can be taken at face value.

There are multiple purposes to political speech, only one of which is to assert truths. Nevertheless, we expect a core of sincerity from our leaders. We do not expect a Muammar el-Qaddafi. It is belief in this core of sincerity that bizarre claims about the president are intended to undermine.

Silencing in the sense described by Hornsby and Langton robs others of the ability to engage in speech acts, such as assertion. But there is another kind of silencing familiar in the political domain, not discussed by these authors. It is possible to silence people by denying them access to the vocabulary to express their claims.

> **It is possible to silence people by denying them access to the vocabulary to express their claims.**

One of the best investigations of propaganda was presented by Victor Klemperer, in his book *The Language of the Third Reich*. The data for Klemperer's claims was the language used by the Third Reich. But the points he makes are applicable to propaganda in the service of much more mundane endeavors, be it to pass health care reform or to increase or decrease taxes. The use of propaganda is not limited to a single political affiliation or intent.

As Klemperer writes in *The Language of the Third Reich*, propaganda "changes the value of words and the frequency of their occurrence . . . it commandeers for the party that which was previously common property and in the process steeps words and groups of words and sentence structures in its poison." When writing these words, Klemperer was thinking of the incessant use of the term "heroisch" ("heroic") to justify the military adventures of the National Socialist state. Obviously, the mechanism described by Klemperer is not used for such odious purposes today. Nevertheless, there has been a similar appropriation of the term "freedom" in American political discourse.

Most would agree that heroism and freedom are fundamentally good things. But the terms "heroisch" and "freedom" have been appropriated for purposes that do not have much connection with the virtues of their original meanings. Whatever one thinks of the wisdom of the 2003 invasion of Iraq, it is difficult to have a reasoned debate about its costs and benefits when the invasion itself is called "Operation Iraqi Freedom." Similarly, whatever one thinks of tax cuts, or the estate tax, it is difficult to engage in reasoned debate when they have been respectively relabeled "tax relief" and "the death tax." It is difficult to have a reasoned debate about the costs and benefits of a policy when one side has seized control of the linguistic means to express all the positive claims. It is easy to say "a tax cut is not always good policy," but considerably more difficult to say "tax relief is not always good policy," even though "tax relief" is just a phrase invented to mean the same as "tax cut."

Silencing is by no means limited to its target. The Fox channel engages in silencing when it describes itself as "fair and balanced" to an audience that is perfectly aware that it is neither. The effect is to suggest that there is no such thing as fair and balanced — that there is no possibility of balanced news, only propaganda. The result is the silencing of every news organ, by suggesting a generalized gross insincerity.

The effects of a belief in general gross insincerity are apparent in societies in which the state media delivers only propaganda. Citizens who grow up in a state in which the authorities deliver propaganda have no experience with trust. So even if the members of that society have access to reliable news, say via the Internet, they do not trust it. They are trained to be suspicious of any organ marketing itself as news.

Silencing is only one kind of propaganda. In silencing, one removes the ability of a target person or group to communicate. As a philosopher of language I am less qualified to make a judgment about the wisdom of Plato, Machiavelli, and Leo Strauss than I am to comment about their favored political tool. However, I do think that given our current environment — of oppression, revolution, intervention, war, pseudo-war and ever-present human power relations — it is worthwhile bearing in mind the dangers of the manipulation of language. What may begin as a temporary method to circumvent reasoned discussion and debate for the sake of a prized political goal may very well end up permanently undermining the trust required for its existence.

THINKING CRITICALLY ABOUT THE READING

1. What is silencing? In your own terms, why does Stanley consider silencing propaganda?

2. Stanley quotes Catharine MacKinnon's statement: "Pornography silences women." What do you think MacKinnon meant by her statement?

3. Does Stanley himself engage in silencing? Explain.

4. Is Stanley an unbiased commentator on the question of silencing?

5. If silencing comes from the right as Stanley seems to believe, can you think of any examples of silencing that have come from the left?

LANGUAGE IN ACTION

Soon after Jason Stanley's article appeared in the *New York Times* the *Times* published Stanley's response ("Media and Mistrust: A Response," *New York Times*, July 18, 2011) to readers who wrote to the *Times* to comment on his original article. Reprinted below are several of the readers' comments. Choose one for discussion and evaluate its merits.

All of the networks and newspapers engage in some kind of silencing. Some years ago a reporter on a large newspaper explained to me that they [sic] would not report on "extremist" activities such as rallies, meetings and speeches because it help them [sic] get publicity for their message. On the other hand, he admitted, causes that passed muster would be covered and even promoted. He didn't regard this as any kind of censorship but just serving a civic responsibility.

This kind of double standard is everywhere in the media. It's in the *New York Times, Washington Post*, and all other newspapers. It's in NBC, Fox News and all the networks. Virtually everyone who complains about the bias of one media outlet ignores or rationalizes the same behavior in others, and that was the case with the original article by Mr. Stanley. He's clearly and obviously partisan on behalf of a point of view. To excoriate Fox News without similarly excoriating MSNBC is simply another form of distortion.

LAIRD WILCOX, Kansas

＊＊＊＊＊

I read the opinion pages of the local newspaper with a different eye today after having read this. There seem to be some attempts to use language to silence as you have described in this and the previous post, and now I have some tools to help me identify it. Before I was just aware that some words made me uncomfortable, and now I understand why.

Thank you.

GARY, North Carolina

＊＊＊＊＊

So we should not trust Fox News, but we should trust Rutgers University philosophy professors? Why, exactly? Speaking of trust, how about having a little bit of faith in us news consumers—we know every news writer/broadcaster has his/her own biases that influence their work, and that every news consumer has his own biases that filter what we [sic] read/hear. In the end, it generally balances out.

MORGAN, Philadelphia

WRITING SUGGESTIONS

1. Stanley makes some interesting references in his article to other scholars (e.g., Jennifer Hornsby, Rae Langton, and Victor Klemperer) who have addressed the importance of silencing as a propaganda strategy. Write an essay on silencing based on ideas and examples that you draw from their writings. Be careful to develop an effective thesis, to focus your work, and to include examples of your own in your essay, wherever possible.

2. Some of Stanley's readers have argued that he is guilty in his essay of the same kind of silencing to which he is opposed. Does he write with a political bias? If so, how? Do you find any problems with his examples? Do you also believe that the times we live in are more treacherous than times past, as he argues in paragraph 13? A larger question: Isn't all argumentative writing biased to an extent, even if the writer takes into account opponents' arguments as a way of countering them? Is it possible to write in a totally unbiased manner? Address some of these questions, and others that arise from these questions, in writing an essay on these important issues. You may want to reference comments made by Stanley's readers as well as the comments he has made in response at opinionator.blogs.nytimes.com/2011/07/18/media-and-mistrust-a-response/

9

LANGUAGE THAT
MADE A DIFFERENCE

Political language is powerful; it is persuasive. At its best political language inspires people and challenges them to make a difference, offering the hope that in working together, we can create a better world. We have all heard stories of how, with powerful words, Franklin D. Roosevelt and Winston Churchill energized and rallied their nations to defeat Nazi Germany during World War II and how Mahatma Gandhi, Martin Luther King Jr., and Nelson Mandela championed nonviolence in leading the fight against oppression and racism in India, America, and South Africa. Few things are more inspiring than a good speech given by an eloquent speaker. A skilled orator is a performer, much like a musician. Instead of a beat, though, the speaker gives words and phrases emphasis and makes them resonate. Like a melody, the speaker's language communicates rich images and compelling thoughts. The words of a speaker are more alive than those of a writer because the speaker can directly communicate the passion and conviction of the words to his or her audience. Nevertheless, the transcript of a good speech can still capture our attention and imagination.

In this chapter, "Language That Made a Difference," we include six selections from very different times and places. Despite the widely divergent contexts and issues they address, these writers rely on many of the same rhetorical techniques and strategies to give depth and resonance to their messages. As you read these six selections, look for the writers' use of parallelism, repetition, dramatic short sentences, biblical allusions, and memorable diction to give power and energy to their messages. Expressing real passion and dedication for her work in rural Africa, Wangari Maathai delivered a call for action to confront the ongoing assault on our environment in "Planting the Seeds of Peace," her acceptance speech for the 2004 Nobel Prize for Peace. She challenged the world to join her and perhaps use the Green Belt Movement model to make a difference for communities throughout the world: "The extreme global inequities and prevailing consumption patterns continue at the expense of the environment and peaceful co-existence. The choice is ours." Martin Luther King Jr.'s "I Have a Dream" speech uses brilliant, rich images and compelling logic to insist on equality for all Americans. Delivered on the steps of the Lincoln Memorial in 1963 during the height of the civil rights movement, this speech is considered by many to be one of the greatest speeches of the last century, and it is now part of our cultural consciousness.

John F. Kennedy, in his "Inaugural Address" in 1961, ushered in a new era of optimism, hope, and exploration. He boldly called upon Americans and the citizens of the world to work together for peace and the freedom of all peoples. As the youngest person elected to serve in the White House, President Kennedy energized the office and willingly accepted the mantle of leadership. Almost a century earlier, Abraham Lincoln, in his "Second Inaugural Address," chose to look beyond the imminent conclusion of the war that had been raging for four long years. He used tempered, well-chosen language to call on all Americans—Northerners and Southerners alike—in the closing days of the Civil War to "bind up the nation's wounds" and "with malice toward none, with charity for all, . . . achieve and cherish a just and lasting peace." In a remarkable speech delivered in the years leading up to the Civil War, the illiterate preacher and abolitionist Sojourner Truth used her simple eloquence to blunt the prejudice and fear of her foes in "And Ain't I a Woman?" Language was her weapon, and her intelligence, dignity, and conviction still resonate from her words as she demanded equal rights for women. In "A Modest Proposal," Jonathan Swift uses his wit to attack the wealthy English landlords who were, in his eyes, responsible for the widespread homelessness and poverty among sharecroppers in Ireland. In this classic essay, Swift's narrator uses a logical argument to propose a satiric solution to Ireland's problem: infanticide and cannibalism.

Planting the Seeds of Peace: 2004 Nobel Prize for Peace Speech

Wangari Maathai

Environmental and political activist Wangari Maathai was born in 1940 in Ihithe village in what was then the colony of Kenya. Educated in Catholic schools in Kenya, Maathai came to the United States on scholarship to study at Mount St. Scholastica—now Benedictine College—in Atchison, Kansas, as part of an international program sponsored by the Joseph P. Kennedy Jr. Foundation. She graduated in 1964 with a major in biology and pursued a master's degree in the biological sciences at the University of Pittsburgh. It was at Pittsburgh that she was first introduced to the concept of environmental restoration. After graduating in 1966, she returned to Kenya where she took a position as research assistant at University College of Nairobi. Maathai was encouraged to pursue graduate study in Germany, and eventually she earned a Ph.D. in anatomy in 1971 from the University College of Nairobi, which became the University of Nairobi a year later. During the 1970s she taught at the University of Nairobi and at the same time joined a number of civic and professional organizations including the Kenya Red Cross Society, the Kenya Association of University Women, and the National Council of Women of Kenya. It was during these years that Maathai came to realize that environmental degradation was central to any discussion of Kenya's social and economic problems. On June 5, 1977, as part of World Environment Day, Maathai helped plant seven trees honoring historically significant community leaders. This was the first so-called "Green Belt" and marked the beginning of the Green Belt Movement. With support from the Norwegian Forestry Society and the United Nations Voluntary Fund for Women, Maathai and her fledgling Green Belt Movement flourished in spite of a lack of cooperation from the Kenyan government. In 2004 Maathai was recognized for her contributions to "sustainable development, democracy and peace" in Kenya and throughout Africa with the Nobel Peace Prize. In announcing the award the Nobel Committee said: "Maathai stood up courageously against the former oppressive regime in Kenya. Her unique forms of action have contributed to drawing attention to political oppressions—nationally and internationally. She has served as an inspiration for many in the fight for democratic rights and has especially encouraged women to better their situation." Maathai died on September 25, 2011, in Nairobi, Kenya.

Wangari Maathai received the Nobel Peace Prize on December 10, 2004. In her acceptance speech, she traces the history and work of her Green Belt Movement and discusses the often overlooked importance of strong environmental stewardship in building democracy and promoting lasting peace. She concludes with an impassioned call to action for the global community to adopt "the holistic approach to development, as exemplified by the Green Belt Movement."

WRITING TO DISCOVER: *Some of today's world leaders are concerned with promoting a sustainable environment through sustainable energy sources, sustainable agriculture, sustainable business practices, and sustainable development. What does the word* sustainable *mean to you? Do you think that it is important for us to work toward the goal of a sustainable environment? Explain why or why not.*

Your Majesties
Your Royal Highnesses
Honorable Members of the Norwegian Nobel Committee
Excellencies
Ladies and Gentlemen
I stand before you and the world humbled by this recognition and uplifted by the honor of being the 2004 Nobel Peace Laureate.

As the first African woman to receive this prize, I accept it on behalf of the people of Kenya and Africa, and indeed the world. I am especially mindful of women and the girl child. I hope it will encourage them to raise their voices and take more space for leadership. I know the honor also gives a deep sense of pride to our men, both old and young. As a mother, I appreciate the inspiration this brings to the youth and urge them to use it to pursue their dreams.

Although this prize comes to me, it acknowledges the work of countless individuals and groups across the globe. They work quietly and often without recognition to protect the environment, promote democracy, defend human rights and ensure equality between women and men. By so doing, they plant seeds of peace. I know they, too, are proud today. To all who feel represented by this prize I say use it to advance your mission and meet the high expectations the world will place on us.

This honor is also for my family, friends, partners and supporters throughout the world. All of them helped shape the vision and sustain our work, which was often accomplished under hostile conditions. I am also grateful to the people of Kenya—who remained stubbornly hopeful that democracy could be realized and their environment managed sustainably. Because of this support, I am here today to accept this great honor. 5

I am immensely privileged to join my fellow African Peace laureates, Presidents Nelson Mandela and F.W. de Klerk, Archbishop Desmond Tutu, the late Chief Albert Luthuli, the late Anwar el-Sadat, and the UN Secretary General, Kofi Annan.

I know that African people everywhere are encouraged by this news. My fellow Africans, as we embrace this recognition, let us use it to intensify our commitment to our people, to reduce conflicts and poverty and thereby improve their quality of life. Let us embrace democratic governance, protect human rights, and protect our environment. I am confident that we shall rise to the occasion. I have always believed that solutions to most of our problems must come from us.

In this year's prize, the Norwegian Nobel Committee has placed the critical issue of environment and its linkage to democracy and peace before the world. For their visionary action, I am profoundly grateful. Recognizing that sustainable development, democracy and peace are indivisible is an idea whose time has come. Our work over the past 30 years has always appreciated and engaged these linkages.

My inspiration partly comes from my childhood experiences and observations of Nature in rural Kenya. It has been influenced and nurtured by the formal education I was privileged to receive in Kenya, the United States and Germany. As I was growing up, I witnessed forests being cleared and replaced by commercial plantations, which destroyed local biodiversity and the capacity of the forests to conserve water.

Excellencies, ladies and gentlemen,   10

In 1977, when we started the Green Belt Movement, I was partly responding to needs identified by rural women, namely lack of firewood, clean drinking water, balanced diets, shelter and income.

Throughout Africa, women are the primary caretakers, holding significant responsibility for tilling the land and feeding their families. As a result, they are often the first to become aware of environmental damage as resources become scarce and incapable of sustaining their families.

The women we worked with recounted that unlike in the past, they were unable to meet their basic needs. This was due to the degradation of their immediate environment as well as the introduction of commercial farming, which replaced the growing of household food crops. But international trade controlled the price of the exports from these small-scale farmers and a reasonable and just income could not be guaranteed. I came to understand that when the environment is destroyed, plundered or mismanaged, we undermine our quality of life and that of future generations.

Tree planting became a natural choice to address some of the initial basic needs identified by women. Also, tree planting is simple, attainable, and guarantees quick, successful results within a reasonable amount of time. This sustains interest and commitment.

So, together, we have planted over 30 million trees that provide fuel,   15 food, shelter, and income to support their children's education and household needs. The activity also creates employment and improves soils and watersheds. Through their involvement, women gain some degree of power over their lives, especially their social and economic position and relevance in the family. This work continues.

Initially, the work was difficult because historically our people have been persuaded to believe that because they are poor, they lack not only capital, but also knowledge and skills to address their challenges. Instead they are conditioned to believe that solutions to their problems must come from "outside." Further, women did not realize that meeting their needs depended on their environment being healthy and well managed. They were also unaware that a degraded environment leads to a scramble for scarce resources and may culminate in poverty and even conflict. They were also unaware of the injustices of international economic arrangements.

In order to assist communities to understand these linkages, we developed a citizen education program, during which people identify their problems, the causes and possible solutions. They then make connections between their own personal actions and the problems they witness in the environment and in society. They learn that our world is confronted with a litany of woes: corruption, violence against women and children, disruption and breakdown of families, and disintegration of cultures and communities. They also identify the abuse of drugs and chemical substances, especially among young people. There are also devastating diseases that are defying cures or occurring in epidemic proportions. Of particular concern are HIV/AIDS, malaria and diseases associated with malnutrition.

On the environment front, they are exposed to many human activities that are devastating to the environment and societies. These include widespread destruction of ecosystems, especially through deforestation, climatic instability, and contamination in the soils and waters that all contribute to excruciating poverty.

In the process, the participants discover that they must be part of the solutions. They realize their hidden potential and are empowered to overcome inertia and take action. They come to recognize that they are the primary custodians and beneficiaries of the environment that sustains them.

Entire communities also come to understand that while it is necessary to hold their governments accountable, it is equally important that in their own relationships with each other, they exemplify the leadership values they wish to see in their own leaders, namely justice, integrity, and trust.   20

Although initially the Green Belt Movement's tree planting activities did not address issues of democracy and peace, it soon became clear that responsible governance of the environment was impossible without democratic space. Therefore, the tree became a symbol for the democratic struggle in Kenya. Citizens were mobilized to challenge widespread abuses of power, corruption, and environmental mismanagement. In Nairobi's Uhuru Park, at Freedom Corner, and in many parts of the country, trees of peace were planted to demand the release of prisoners of conscience and a peaceful transition to democracy.

Through the Green Belt Movement, thousands of ordinary citizens were mobilized and empowered to take action and effect change. They learned to overcome fear and a sense of helplessness and moved to defend democratic rights.

In time, the tree also became a symbol for peace and conflict resolution, especially during ethnic conflicts in Kenya when the Green Belt Movement used peace trees to reconcile disputing communities. During the ongoing

re-writing of the Kenyan constitution, similar trees of peace were planted
in many parts of the country to promote a culture of peace. Using trees
as a symbol of peace is in keeping with a widespread African tradition. For
example, the elders of the Kikuyu carried a staff from the *thigi* tree that,
when placed between two disputing sides, caused them to stop fighting and
seek reconciliation. Many communities in Africa have these traditions.

Such practices are part of an extensive cultural heritage, which contributes both to the conservation of habitats and to cultures of peace.
With the destruction of these cultures and the introduction of new values,
local biodiversity is no longer valued or protected and as a result, it is
quickly degraded and disappears. For this reason, the Green Belt Movement explores the concept of cultural biodiversity, especially with respect
to indigenous seeds and medicinal plants.

As we progressively understood the causes of environmental degra-   25
dation, we saw the need for good governance. Indeed, the state of any
country's environment is a reflection of the kind of governance in place,
and without good governance there can be no peace. Many countries
which have poor governance systems are also likely to have conflicts and
poor laws protecting the environment.

In 2002, the courage, resilience, patience, and commitment of members of the Green Belt Movement, other civil society organizations, and
the Kenyan public culminated in the peaceful transition to a democratic
government and laid the foundation for a more stable society.

Excellencies, friends, ladies and gentlemen,

It is 30 years since we started this work. Activities that devastate the
environment and societies continue unabated. Today we are faced with a
challenge that calls for a shift in our
thinking, so that humanity stops
threatening its life-support system. We

> **Today we are faced with a challenge that calls for a shift in our thinking, so that humanity stops threatening its life-support system.**

are called to assist the Earth to heal
her wounds and in the process heal
our own—indeed, to embrace the
whole creation in all its diversity,
beauty and wonder. This will happen if we see the need to revive our sense
of belonging to a larger family of life, with which we have shared our evolutionary process.

In the course of history, there comes a time when humanity is called
to shift to a new level of consciousness, to reach a higher moral ground. A
time when we have to shed our fear and give hope to each other.

That time is now.   30

The Norwegian Nobel Committee has challenged the world to
broaden the understanding of peace: there can be no peace without equitable development; and there can be no development without sustainable
management of the environment in a democratic and peaceful space. This
shift is an idea whose time has come.

I call on leaders, especially from Africa, to expand democratic space and build fair and just societies that allow the creativity and energy of their citizens to flourish.

Those of us who have been privileged to receive education, skills, and experiences and even power must be role models for the next generation of leadership. In this regard, I would also like to appeal for the freedom of my fellow laureate Aung San Suu Kyi so that she can continue her work for peace and democracy for the people of Burma and the world at large.

Culture plays a central role in the political, economic and social life of communities. Indeed, culture may be the missing link in the development of Africa. Culture is dynamic and evolves over time, consciously discarding retrogressive traditions, like female genital mutilation (FGM), and embracing aspects that are good and useful.

Africans, especially, should re-discover positive aspects of their cul- 35 ture. In accepting them, they would give themselves a sense of belonging, identity, and self-confidence.

Ladies and Gentlemen,

There is also need to galvanize civil society and grassroots movements to catalyze change. I call upon governments to recognize the role of these social movements in building a critical mass of responsible citizens, who help maintain checks and balances in society. On their part, civil society should embrace not only their rights but also their responsibilities.

Further, industry and global institutions must appreciate that ensuring economic justice, equity, and ecological integrity are of greater value than profits at any cost.

The extreme global inequities and prevailing consumption patterns continue at the expense of the environment and peaceful co-existence. The choice is ours.

I would like to call on young people to commit themselves to activities 40 that contribute toward achieving their long-term dreams. They have the energy and creativity to shape a sustainable future. To the young people I say, you are a gift to your communities and indeed the world. You are our hope and our future.

The holistic approach to development, as exemplified by the Green Belt Movement, could be embraced and replicated in more parts of Africa and beyond. It is for this reason that I have established the Wangari Maathai Foundation to ensure the continuation and expansion of these activities. Although a lot has been achieved, much remains to be done.

Excellencies, ladies and gentlemen,

As I conclude I reflect on my childhood experience when I would visit a stream next to our home to fetch water for my mother. I would drink water straight from the stream. Playing among the arrowroot leaves I tried in vain to pick up the strands of frogs' eggs, believing they were beads. But every time I put my little fingers under them they would break. Later, I saw thousands of tadpoles: black, energetic, and wriggling through the clear water against the background of the brown earth. This is the world I inherited from my parents.

Today, over 50 years later, the stream has dried up, women walk long distances for water, which is not always clean, and children will never know what they have lost. The challenge is to restore the home of the tadpoles and give back to our children a world of beauty and wonder.

Thank you very much.   45

THINKING CRITICALLY ABOUT THE READING

1. In 2004 Wangari Maathai was honored as the Nobel Peace Laureate. What did the prize mean to her and the people of Africa?

2. Maathai started the Green Belt Movement in 1977 in response to the needs of rural African women. What exactly were the needs of these women, and what did the Green Belt Movement do to address these needs?

3. Maathai's goals are indeed laudable: She wants to encourage sustainable development, support democracy, and create lasting peace. What specific, concrete examples does she use to bring these abstract ideas to life? (Glossary: *Concrete/Abstract*)

4. Maathai believes that "sustainable development, democracy, and peace are indivisible" (8). How has the Green Belt Movement worked with communities to help them better understand how these three concepts work in concert?

5. How did the Green Belt Movement use trees to promote peace and conflict resolution during the years that Kenya was *rewriting* its constitution? In what ways did "peace trees" support African tradition and cultural heritage? How did the Green Belt Movement help pave the way for Kenya to peacefully transition to a democratic government in 2002?

6. In her conclusion, Maathai calls upon each one of us to commit to helping create and shape a "sustainable future" (40). What kinds of actions, sacrifices, and commitments are necessary to ensure such a future?

LANGUAGE IN ACTION

Writers, like Maathai, use abstract words, words that name ideas, concepts, conditions, and emotions — things that nobody can touch, see, or hear. Some abstract words are *love, wisdom, cowardice, beauty, fear,* and *liberty.* People often disagree about abstract things. You might find a forest beautiful, while someone else might find it frightening, and neither of you would be wrong. Beauty and fear are abstract ideas; they exist in your mind, not in the forest along with the trees and the owls. Writers also use concrete words, words that refer to things we can touch, see, hear, smell, and taste. *Sandpaper, soda, birch tree, smog, cow, sailboat, rocking chair,* and *pancake* are all concrete words. If you disagree with someone on a concrete issue—say, you claim that the forest is mostly oak trees, while the other person says it is mostly pine—only one of you can be right, and both of you can be wrong; the kinds of trees that grow in the forest in question are a concrete fact, not an abstract idea.

Good writing balances ideas and facts, and it also balances abstract and concrete diction. As a writer you need to know the difference. Identify each word in the following list as either abstract or concrete.

EXAMPLE: emotions: abstract

1. brilliant:
2. trophy:
3. test:
4. purple:
5. stars:
6. book:
7. weak:
8. water:
9. truth:
10. pencil:

11. honesty:
12. bright:
13. delirious:
14. puzzle:
15. tall:
16. rusty:
17. slippery:
18. apple:
19. music:
20. arrogance:

Now, analyze several paragraphs of Maathai's speech, and comment on her use of abstract and concrete diction.

WRITING SUGGESTIONS

1. So often we tend to see environmental projects as programs that simply protect the environment, never fully appreciating the impact that a healthy, sustainable environment has on all aspects of our lives. In her work as a biologist and conservationist, Maathai came to see that maintaining a sustainable environment was an important, if not essential, ingredient in her efforts "to promote democracy, defend human rights, and ensure equality between women and men" (4) in Africa. In planting trees throughout her homeland and the continent of Africa, Maathai and her followers were in fact "plant[ing] the seeds of peace" (1). "Using an environmental issue or problem in your community as your central example, write a paper in which you explore some of the positive effects that a sustainable environmental solution to the problem will have on the community.

2. Many Americans take the water they drink for granted, but good clean water is fast becoming a scarce resource worldwide as we witness the effects of both pollution and climate change. At the end of her address Maathai reflects on a childhood experience she had while fetching water for her family from a local stream. She still has a vivid memory of seeing frogs' eggs and later tadpoles in the clear, clean water. But that was fifty years ago. Today, that stream is gone, and people must travel miles for water, which is not always clean. And therein lies the challenge for Maathai. Write an essay in which you reflect on a childhood experience with water. What was the initial experience like? Could you go back and have that same experience today? Why, or why not? What would be needed to restore the environment to the condition that you found it in as a child?

I Have a Dream

MARTIN LUTHER KING JR.

Civil rights leader Martin Luther King Jr. (1929–1968) was the son of a Baptist minister in Atlanta, Georgia. Ordained at the age of eighteen, King went on to earn academic degrees from Morehouse College, Crozer Theological Seminary, Boston University, and Chicago Theological Seminary. He came to prominence in 1955 in Montgomery, Alabama, when he led a successful boycott against the city's segregated bus system. The first president of the Southern Christian Leadership Conference, King became the leading spokesman for the civil rights movement during the 1950s and 1960s, espousing a consistent philosophy of nonviolent direct action or resistance to racial injustice. He also championed women's rights and protested the Vietnam War. Named *Time* magazine's Man of the Year in 1963, King was awarded the Nobel Peace Prize in 1964. King was assassinated in April 1968 after speaking at a rally in Memphis, Tennessee.

"I Have a Dream," the keynote address for the March on Washington in 1963, has become one of the most renowned and recognized speeches of the past century. Delivered from the steps of the Lincoln Memorial to commemorate the centennial of the Emancipation Proclamation, King's speech resonates with hope even as it condemns racial oppression.

WRITING TO DISCOVER: *Most Americans have seen film clips of King delivering the "I Have a Dream" speech in Washington, D.C., on August 28, 1963. What do you know of the speech? What do you know of the events and conditions under which King presented it almost fifty years ago?*

I am happy to join with you today in what will go down in history as the greatest demonstration for freedom in the history of our nation.

Five score years ago, a great American, in whose symbolic shadow we stand today, signed the Emancipation Proclamation. This momentous decree came as a great beacon light of hope to millions of Negro slaves who had been seared in the flames of withering injustice. It came as a joyous daybreak to end the long night of their captivity. But one hundred years later, the Negro still is not free. One hundred years later, the life of the Negro is still sadly crippled by the manacles of segregation and the chains of discrimination. One hundred years later, the Negro lives on a lonely island of poverty in the midst of a vast ocean of material prosperity. One hundred years later, the Negro is still anguished in the corners of American society and finds himself in exile in his own land. And so we have come here today to dramatize a shameful condition.

In a sense we have come to our nation's capital to cash a check. When the architects of our republic wrote the magnificent words of the Constitution and the Declaration of Independence, they were signing a promissory note to which every American was to fall heir. This note was the promise that all men—yes, Black men as well as white men—would be guaranteed the inalienable rights of life, liberty, and the pursuit of happiness.

It is obvious today that America has defaulted on this promissory note insofar as her citizens of color are concerned. Instead of honoring this sacred obligation, America has given the Negro people a bad check, a check which has come back marked "insufficient funds." But we refuse to believe that the bank of justice is bankrupt. We refuse to believe that there are insufficient funds in the great vaults of opportunity of this nation; and so we have come to cash this check, a check that will give us upon demand the riches of freedom and the security of justice.

We have also come to this hallowed spot to remind America of the 5
fierce urgency of *now*. This is no time to engage in the luxury of cooling off or to take the tranquilizing drug of gradualism. *Now* is the time to make real the promises of democracy. *Now* is the time to rise from the dark and desolate valley of segregation to the sunlit path of racial justice. *Now* is the time to lift our nation from the quicksands of racial injustice to the solid rock of brotherhood. *Now* is the time to make justice a reality for all of God's children.

It would be fatal for the nation to overlook the urgency of the moment. This sweltering summer of the Negro's legitimate discontent will not pass until there is an invigorating autumn of freedom and equality. Nineteen sixty-three is not an end, but a beginning. And those who hope that the Negro needed to blow off steam and will now be content will have a rude awakening if the nation returns to business as usual. There will be neither rest nor tranquility in America until the Negro is granted his citizenship rights. The whirlwinds of revolt will continue to shake the foundations of our nation until the bright day of justice emerges.

But there is something that I must say to my people who stand on the warm threshold which leads into the palace of justice. In the process of gaining our rightful place, we must not be guilty of wrongful deeds. Let us not seek to satisfy our thirst for freedom by drinking from the cup of bitterness and hatred. We must forever conduct our struggle on the high plane of dignity and discipline. We must not allow our creative protest to degenerate into physical violence. Again and again we must rise to the majestic heights of meeting physical force with soul force. And the marvelous new militancy which has engulfed the Negro community must not lead us to a distrust of all white people; for many of our white brothers, as evidenced by their presence here today, have come to realize that their destiny is tied up with our destiny, and they have come to realize that their freedom is inextricably bound to our freedom.

We cannot walk alone. And as we walk we must make the pledge that we shall always march ahead. We cannot turn back. There are those who are asking the devotees of civil rights, "When will you be satisfied?" We can never be satisfied as long as the Negro is the victim of the unspeakable horrors of police brutality. We can never be satisfied as long as our bodies, heavy with the fatigue of travel, cannot gain lodging in the motels of the highways and the hotels of the cities. We cannot be satisfied as long as the Negro's basic mobility is from a smaller ghetto to a larger one. We can never be satisfied as long as our children are stripped of their selfhood and robbed of their dignity by signs stating "For Whites Only." We cannot be satisfied as long as the Negro in Mississippi cannot vote and a Negro in New York believes he has nothing for which to vote. No, no, we are not satisfied, and we will not be satisfied until justice rolls down like waters and righteousness like a mighty stream.

I am not unmindful that some of you have come here out of great trials and tribulations. Some of you have come fresh from narrow jail cells. Some of you have come from areas where your quest for freedom left you battered by the storms of persecution and staggered by the winds of police brutality. You have been the veterans of creative suffering. Continue to work with the faith that unearned suffering is redemptive.

Go back to Mississippi, and go back to Alabama. Go back to South   10
Carolina. Go back to Georgia. Go back to Louisiana. Go back to the slums and ghettos of our Northern cities, knowing that somehow this situation can and will be changed. Let us not wallow in the valley of despair.

I say to you today, my friends, even though we face the difficulties of today and tomorrow, I still have a dream. It is a dream deeply rooted in the American dream. I have a dream that one day this nation will rise up and live out the true meaning of its creed: "We hold these truths to be self-evident, that all men are created equal." I have a dream that one day, on the red hills of Georgia, sons of former slaves and the sons of former slave owners will be able to sit down together at the table of brotherhood. I have a dream that one day even the state of Mississippi, a state sweltering with the heat of injustice, sweltering with the heat of oppression, will be transformed into an oasis of freedom and justice. I have a dream that my four little children will one day live in a nation where they will not be judged by the color of their skin, but by the content of their character.

I have a dream that my four little children will one day live in a nation where they will not be judged by the color of their skin, but by the content of their character.

I have a dream today. I have a dream that one day down in Alabama—with its vicious racists, with its governor's lips dripping with the words of interposition and nullification—one day right there in Alabama, little Black boys and Black girls will be able to join hands with little white boys and white girls as sisters and brothers.

I have a dream today. I have a dream that one day every valley shall be exalted and every hill and mountain shall be made low, the rough places will be made plain and the crooked places will be made straight, and the glory of the Lord shall be revealed, and all flesh shall see it together.

This is our hope. This is the faith that I go back to the South with. And with this faith we will be able to hew out of the mountain of despair a stone of hope. With this faith we will be able to transform the jangling discords of our nation into a beautiful symphony of brotherhood. With this faith we will be able to work together, to pray together, to struggle together, to go to jail together, to stand up for freedom together, knowing that we will be free one day.

And this will be the day — this will be the day when all of God's chil-   15
dren will be able to sing with new meaning:

> My country, 'tis of thee,
> Sweet land of liberty,
>   Of thee I sing;
> Land where my fathers died,
> Land of the Pilgrims' pride,
> From every mountainside
>   Let freedom ring.

And if America is to be a great nation, this must become true.

And so let freedom ring from the prodigious hilltops of New Hampshire. Let freedom ring from the mighty mountains of New York. Let freedom ring from the heightening Alleghenies of Pennsylvania. Let freedom ring from the snow-capped Rockies of Colorado. Let freedom ring from the curvaceous slopes of California.

But not only that. Let freedom ring from Stone Mountain of Georgia. Let freedom ring from Lookout Mountain of Tennessee. Let freedom ring from every hill and molehill of Mississippi. "From every mountainside let freedom ring."

And when this happens — when we allow freedom to ring, when we let it ring from every village and every hamlet, from every state and every city — we will be able to speed up that day when all of God's children, Black men and white men, Jews and Gentiles, Protestants and Catholics, will be able to join hands and sing in the words of the old Negro spiritual: "Free at last! Free at last! Thank God Almighty. We are free at last!"

THINKING CRITICALLY ABOUT THE READING

1. Why does King say that the Constitution and the Declaration of Independence act as a "promissory note" (3) to the American people? In what way has America "defaulted" (4) on its promise?

2. What do you think King means when he says, "In the process of gaining our rightful place [in society] we must not be guilty of wrongful deeds" (7)? Why is this issue so important to him?

3. King uses parallel constructions and repetition throughout his speech. (Glossary: *Parallelism*) Identify the words and phrases that he emphasizes. Explain what these techniques add to the persuasiveness of his argument.

4. King makes liberal use of metaphor—and metaphorical imagery—in his speech. (Glossary: *Figures of Speech*) Choose a few examples, and examine what each adds to the speech. How do they collectively help King engage his listeners' feelings of injustice and give them hope of a better future?

5. In his final paragraph, King claims that by freeing the Negro we will all be free. What exactly does he mean? Is King simply being hyperbolic or does his claim embody an undeniable truth? Explain.

6. What, in a nutshell, is King's dream? What vision does he have for the future?

LANGUAGE IN ACTION

As Martin Luther King Jr.'s speech well demonstrates, the effectiveness of a writer's argument depends in large part on the writer's awareness of audience. For example, if a writer wished to argue for the use of more technology to solve our pressing environmental problems, that argument to a group of environmentalists would need to convince them that the technology would not cause as many environmental problems as it solves, while an argument designed for a group of industrialists might argue that the economic opportunity in developing new technologies is as important as the environmental benefits.

Consider the following proposition:

The university mascot should be changed to reflect the image of our school today. How would you argue this proposition to the following audiences?

a. the student body
b. the faculty
c. the alumni
d. the administration
e. the community at large

As a class, discuss how the consideration of audience influences the purpose, content, and language of an argument.

WRITING SUGGESTIONS

1. King portrayed an America in 1963 in which there was still systematic oppression of African Americans. What, for you, is oppression? Have you ever felt yourself—or have you known others—to be oppressed or part of a group that is oppressed? Who, if anyone, in America is oppressed today? Who are the oppressors? How can oppression be overcome? Write an essay in which you present your views on how oppression can best be combated in today's world. You may find it helpful to read Martin Luther King Jr.'s "Letter from Birmingham Jail" (87–100) before beginning to write.

2. In using the photograph on page 280 of Martin Luther King Jr. in its "Think Different" advertising campaign, Apple is relying on our cultural memory of King's "I Have a Dream" speech and of King as a person who was creative in his efforts to promote racial justice. To what extent does achieving racial equality depend on "thinking differently"? Write an essay in which you present your position.

3. Martin Luther King Jr. says that his dream is "deeply rooted in the American dream" (11). What is the American dream as you understand it? Can that dream be realized in the twenty-first century? If so, how? If not, why does the dream persist? In an essay, discuss your thoughts on the American dream and its viability today.

4. Traditionally, commencement speakers challenge our nation's high school, college, and university graduates to dream big, to think about what they contribute to making our world a better place for humankind. In 2005 Apple's iconic Steve Jobs was asked to give the commencement address at Stanford University—no small assignment for a man who was a college dropout himself. Jobs framed his talk around three instructive autobiographical stories to show the circuitous route he followed to find his passion. Jobs' message was quite simple: Trust in yourself, don't settle for something you don't love, and follow your heart and intuition no matter what the world around you is telling you to do. You can view Jobs' commencement address on *YouTube* at http://youtu.be/UF8uR6Z6KLc. After viewing Jobs' speech to the Stanford graduates—and perhaps reading the text of his address online—, ask yourself what makes his advice so alluring and yet so challenging. What, if anything, is holding you back from following your heart, doing what you love to do? Write an essay in which you explain what it is you would love to become and then discuss what it will take to achieve your dream.

Inaugural Address

JOHN F. KENNEDY

John Fitzgerald Kennedy (1917–1963), the thirty-fifth president of the United States, was assassinated in Dallas, Texas, on November 22, 1963. After attending the London School of Economics briefly in 1935, Kennedy entered Harvard College in 1936, from which he graduated with honors in 1940. Kennedy's senior thesis, an analysis of the reasons why England failed to rearm before World War II, was published as a book entitled *Why England Slept* (1940). It became an immediate best-seller. Kennedy served in the Navy during World War II as the commander of a PT boat in the South Pacific. After the war, Kennedy entered politics and in 1946 was elected to Congress as a representative from Massachusetts, a post he held until 1952 when he successfully campaigned for a seat in the Senate. A moderate liberal in the Democratic Party, Kennedy quickly emerged on the national scene. In 1960 he narrowly defeated the then vice president Richard Nixon for the presidency. During his administration, Kennedy established the Peace Corps, confronted the Soviet Union when it tried to arm Cuba, and supported black Americans in their campaign for civil rights. He was the author of the Pulitzer Prize-winning *Profiles in Courage* (1956), a collection of essays about great congressional leadership at critical moments in our nation's history, and *Strategy of Peace* (1960), a statement of his goals in foreign policy.

Kennedy, the youngest man ever elected president, was known for the youthful and hopeful image he brought to the White House and for the eloquence of his speeches. In his "Inaugural Address" Kennedy used powerful rhetoric to urge people to become involved in their country's affairs and to join the fight against the spread of communism.

WRITING TO DISCOVER: *If we know one thing about Kennedy's "Inaugural Address," it's the oft-quoted statement: "And so, my fellow Americans, ask not what your country can do for you; ask what you can do for your country." How do you think Americans would respond to such a challenge from their president today? In your opinion, what's different about Kennedy's America and the country we live in now?*

We observe today not a victory of party but a celebration of freedom, symbolizing an end as well as a beginning, signifying renewal as well as change. For I have sworn before you and Almighty God the same solemn oath our forebears prescribed nearly a century and three-quarters ago.

The world is very different now. For man holds in his mortal hands the power to abolish all forms of human poverty and all forms of human life. And yet the same revolutionary belief for which our forebears fought is still at issue around the globe, the belief that the rights of man come not from the generosity of the state but from the hand of God.

We dare not forget today that we are the heirs of that first revolution. Let the word go forth from this time and place, to friend and foe alike, that the torch has been passed to a new generation of Americans, born in this century, tempered by war, disciplined by a hard and bitter peace, proud of our ancient heritage, and unwilling to witness or permit the slow undoing of those human rights to which this nation has always been committed, and to which we are committed today at home and around the world.

Let every nation know, whether it wishes us well or ill, that we shall pay any price, bear any burden, meet any hardship, support any friend, oppose any foe to assure the survival and the success of liberty.

This much we pledge—and more.   5

To those old allies whose cultural and spiritual origins we share, we pledge the loyalty of faithful friends. United, there is little we cannot do in a host of co-operative ventures. Divided, there is little we can do, for we dare not meet a powerful challenge at odds and split asunder.

To those new states whom we welcome to the ranks of the free, we pledge our word that one form of colonial control shall not have passed away merely to be replaced by a far more iron tyranny. We shall not always expect to find them supporting our view. But we shall always hope to find them strongly supporting their own freedom, and to remember that, in the past, those who foolishly sought power by riding the back of the tiger ended up inside.

To those peoples in the huts and villages of half the globe struggling to break the bonds of mass misery, we pledge our best efforts to help them help themselves, for whatever period is required, not because the Communists may be doing it, not because we seek their votes, but because it is right. If a free society cannot help the many who are poor, it cannot save the few who are rich.

To our sister republics south of our border, we offer a special pledge: to convert our good words into good deeds, in a new alliance for progress, to assist free men and free governments in casting off the chains of poverty. But this peaceful revolution of hope cannot become the prey of hostile powers. Let all our neighbors know that we shall join with them to oppose aggression or subversion anywhere in the Americas. And let every other power know that this hemisphere intends to remain the master of its own house.

To that world assembly of sovereign states, the United Nations, our   10
last best hope in an age where the instruments of war have far outpaced the instruments of peace, we renew our pledge of support: to prevent it from becoming merely a forum for invective, to strengthen its shield of the new and the weak, and to enlarge the area in which its writ may run.

Finally, to those nations who would make themselves our adversary, we offer not a pledge but a request: that both sides begin anew the quest for peace, before the dark powers of destruction unleashed by science engulf all humanity in planned or accidental self-destruction.

We dare not tempt them with weakness. For only when our arms are sufficient beyond doubt can we be certain beyond doubt that they will never be employed.

But neither can two great and powerful groups of nations take comfort from our present course — both sides over-burdened by the cost of modern weapons, both rightly alarmed by the steady spread of the deadly atom, yet both racing to alter that uncertain balance of terror that stays the hand of mankind's final war.

So let us begin anew, remembering on both sides that civility is not a sign of weakness, and sincerity is always subject to proof. Let us never negotiate out of fear, but let us never fear to negotiate.

My fellow citizens of the world, ask not what America will do for you, but what together we can do for the freedom of man.

Let both sides explore what problems unite us instead of belaboring those problems which divide us.

Let both sides, for the first time, formulate serious and precise proposals for the inspection and control of arms, and bring the absolute power to destroy other nations under the absolute control of all nations.

Let both sides seek to invoke the wonders of science instead of its terrors. Together let us explore the stars, conquer the deserts, eradicate disease, tap the ocean depths and encourage the arts and commerce.

Let both sides unite to heed in all corners of the earth the command of Isaiah to "undo the heavy burdens . . . [and] let the oppressed go free."

And if a beachhead of co-operation may push back the jungle of suspicion, let both sides join in creating a new endeavor, not a new balance of power, but a new world of law, where the strong are just and the weak secure and the peace preserved.

All this will not be finished in the first one hundred days. Nor will it be finished in the first one thousand days, nor in the life of this Administration, nor even perhaps in our lifetime on this planet. But let us begin.

In your hands, my fellow citizens, more than mine, will rest the final success or failure of our course. Since this country was founded, each generation of Americans has been summoned to give testimony to its national loyalty. The graves of young Americans who answered the call to service surround the globe.

Now the trumpet summons us again — not as a call to bear arms, though arms we need; not as a call to battle, though embattled we are; but a call to bear the burden of a long twilight struggle, year in and year out, "rejoicing in hope, patient in tribulation," a struggle against the common enemies of men: tyranny, poverty, disease and war itself.

Can we forge against these enemies a grand and global alliance, North and South, East and West, that can assure a more fruitful life for all mankind? Will you join in that historic effort?

In the long history of the world, only a few generations have been granted the role of defending freedom in its hour of maximum danger. I do not shrink from this responsibility; I welcome it. I do not believe that any of us would exchange places with any other people or any other generation. The energy, the faith, the devotion which we bring to this endeavor will light our country and all who serve it, and the glow from that fire can truly light the world.

And so, my fellow Americans, ask not what your country can do for   25 you; ask what you can do for your country.

My fellow citizens of the world, ask not what America will do for you, but what together we can do for the freedom of man.

Finally, whether you are citizens of America or citizens of the world, ask of us here the same high standards of strength and sacrifice which we ask of you. With a good conscience our only sure reward, with history that final judge of our deeds, let us go forth to lead the land we love, asking His blessing and His help, but knowing that here on earth God's work must truly be our own.

THINKING CRITICALLY ABOUT THE READING

1. Kennedy's second paragraph begins with the statement, "The world is very different now." In what ways is the world different than what it was at our country's founding?

2. The president makes promises to several groups, not only to the citizens of the United States, but also to groups outside the country. Is it clear which groups Kennedy means? See if you can identify a few of these groups; then, explain what Kennedy gains by not "naming names."

3. Identify several examples of Kennedy's use of parallelism. (Glossary: *Parallelism*) What does this rhetorical strategy add to the strength of his speech?

4. In paragraph 23, Kennedy asks two rhetorical questions. (Glossary: *Rhetorical Questions*) What do you think his purpose is in asking these questions?

5. Kennedy makes clear what he wants to accomplish in his tenure as president; however, he doesn't say how he will achieve these goals. Do you find this problematic, or do you think this lack of specificity is appropriate in a speech of this kind?

LANGUAGE IN ACTION

Long after some speeches have been delivered and the audiences have dispersed, the speakers' words live on. Some thoughts are so compelling or are so well stated that they are quoted years after they were first written and delivered. Have you ever wondered what makes such statements by world leaders and thinkers so compelling and memorable? Carefully read and analyze the following oft-quoted statements:

If you desire many things, many things will seem few.

— BENJAMIN FRANKLIN

A friend to all is a friend to none.

— ARISTOTLE

All great things are simple and many can be expressed in single words: freedom, justice, honor, duty, mercy, hope.

—WINSTON CHURCHILL

Not everything that is faced can be changed. But nothing can be changed until it is faced.

—JAMES BALDWIN

Adopt the pace of nature: her secret is patience.

—RALPH WALDO EMERSON

They don't care how much you know until they know how much you care.

—THEODORE ROOSEVELT

Even the rich are hungry for love, for being cared for, for being wanted, for having someone to call their own.

—MOTHER TERESA

Action expresses priorities.

—MOHANDAS GANDHI

In the practice of tolerance, one's enemy is the best teacher.

—DALAI LAMA

A poem begins in delight and ends in wisdom.

—ROBERT FROST

As a class discuss what these statements have in common. Do any of them suggest or bring to mind other statements that you have heard quoted? What rhetorical techniques or strategies have these speakers used to make their statements memorable? Which ones did you find most memorable? Explain why.

WRITING SUGGESTIONS

1. Both Abraham Lincoln and John F. Kennedy were presidents renowned for the eloquence, simplicity, and brevity of their speeches. Write an essay in which you compare and contrast Lincoln's "Second Inaugural Address" (pp. 287–289) with Kennedy's "Inaugural Address."

2. Imagine that you have been elected president of the United States and that your inauguration is three weeks away. Using Kennedy's speech as a model, write an inaugural address in which you identify the chief problems and issues of today and set forth your plan for dealing with them. Consider first what approach to take—for example, you might write an inspirational address to the nation, or you may choose to describe in everyday language the problems that confront the nation and the actions you believe will solve these problems.

Second Inaugural Address

ABRAHAM LINCOLN

Born in Kentucky in 1809, Abraham Lincoln grew up in poverty and taught himself to read and write. While studying law, Lincoln worked at a variety of jobs, including postmaster, surveyor, and storekeeper, and was admitted to the bar in 1836. He was well loved in his frontier town for his honesty, strength, and sincerity. Elected to the Illinois state legislature in 1834, he served four successive terms, followed by one term in Congress, 1847–1849. In 1854 Lincoln aligned himself with the fledgling Republican Party, and in 1858 ran unsuccessfully against Stephen A. Douglas for a Senate seat from Illinois. His famous debates with Douglas did, however, win him national prominence, and in 1860 he was elected the sixteenth president of the United States. Soon after his election, the southern states seceded from the Union. The Civil War commenced with the Confederate attack on Fort Sumter on April 12, 1861. As president, Lincoln worked tirelessly to preserve the Union. Long regarding slavery as an evil injustice, he issued the "Emancipation Proclamation" in 1862. His famous "Gettysburg Address" galvanized support for the Union in 1863. Lincoln was elected to a second term in 1864 and died of an assassin's bullet only days after the Civil War ended, with Lee surrendering to Grant at Appomattox Court House in Virginia, on April 9, 1865.

The "Second Inaugural Address" was delivered on March 4, 1865, as the Civil War was drawing to its close. Many consider this his greatest speech, his legacy to a country that would have to go forward without him at the helm. In this, his last major speech before being assassinated, Lincoln asks the nation "to finish the work we are in . . . with malice toward none, with charity toward all."

WRITING TO DISCOVER: *As the day of Lincoln's second inauguration approached, people wondered what he would tell a nation still embroiled in a civil war that had lasted almost four years. Would he talk about the meaning of his own reelection, report on the progress of the victorious Union armies, lay out policies for Reconstruction and the treatment of the defeated Confederate armies, or announce programs for the liberated slaves? What would you have chosen to talk about if you were in Lincoln's shoes? Explain why.*

Fellow Countrymen:

At this second appearing to take the oath of the presidential office there is less occasion for an extended address than there was at the first. Then a statement, somewhat in detail, of a course to be pursued seemed fitting and proper. Now, at the expiration of four years, during which public declarations have been constantly called forth on every point and phase of the great contest which still absorbs the attention and engrosses the energies of the nation, little that is new could be presented. The prog-ress of our arms, upon which all else chiefly depends, is as well known to the public as to myself, and it is, I trust, reasonably satisfactory and encouraging to all. With high hope for the future, no prediction in regard to it is ventured.

On the occasion corresponding to this four years ago all thoughts were anxiously directed to an impending civil war. All dreaded it; all sought to avert it. While the inaugural address was being delivered from this place, devoted altogether to *saving* the Union without war, insurgent agents were in the city seeking to *destroy* it without war—seeking to dissolve the Union and divide effects by negotiation. Both parties dep-recated war, but one of them would *make* war rather than let the nation survive, and the other would *accept* war rather than let it perish, and the war came.

One-eighth of the whole population were colored slaves, not distrib-uted generally over the Union, but localized in the southern part of it. These slaves constituted a peculiar and powerful interest. All knew that this interest was somehow the cause of war. To strengthen, perpetuate, and extend this interest was the object for which the insurgents would rend the Union even by war, while the government claimed no right to do more than to restrict the territorial enlargement of it. Neither party expected for the war the magnitude or the duration which it has already attained. Neither antici-pated that the *cause* of the conflict might cease with or even before the conflict itself should cease. Each looked for an easier triumph, and a result less fundamental and astounding. Both read the same Bible and pray to the same God, and each invokes his aid against the other. It may seem strange that any men should dare to ask a just God's assistance in wringing their bread from the sweat of other men's faces, but let us judge not, that we be not judged. The prayers of both could not be answered. That of neither has been answered fully. The Almighty has his own purposes. "Woe unto the world because of offenses; for it must needs be that offenses come, but woe to that man by whom the offense cometh." If we shall suppose that Ameri-can slavery is one of those offenses which, in the providence of God, must needs come, but which, having continued through his appointed time, he now wills to remove, and that he gives to both North and South this ter-rible war as the woe due to those by whom the offense came, shall we dis-cern therein any departure from those divine attributes which the believers in a living God always ascribe to him? Fondly do we hope, fervently do we pray, that this mighty scourge of war may speedily pass away. Yet, if God wills that it continue until all the wealth piled by the bondsman's two hun-dred and fifty years of unrequited toil shall be sunk, and until every drop of blood drawn with the lash shall be paid by another drawn with the sword,

> **Fondly do we hope, fervently do we pray, that this mighty scourge of war may speedily pass away.**

as was said three thousand years ago, so still it must be said "the judgments of the Lord are true and righteous altogether."

With malice toward none, with charity for all, with firmness in the   5
right as God gives us to see the right, let us strive on to finish the work we are in, to bind up the nation's wounds, to care for him who shall have borne the battle and for his widow and his orphan, to do all which may achieve and cherish a just and lasting peace among ourselves and with all nations.

THINKING CRITICALLY ABOUT THE READING

1. What purpose does Lincoln's opening paragraph serve? (Glossary: *Purpose*) What tone does it set for what follows? (Glossary: *Tone*)

2. In paragraph 2, why do you think that Lincoln goes to such great lengths to show that neither side wanted war? What effect does he create by ending the paragraph with the words "and the war came"?

3. How does Lincoln reconcile or make sense of the fact that "both [sides] read the same Bible and pray to the same God, and each invokes his aid against the other" (3)?

4. Identify the four allusions Lincoln makes to the Bible. What do these allusions add to his address? What would have been lost had he not included them?

5. In what ways does Lincoln's speech provide the nation with what might be called a moral framework for reconciliation and peace? Why do you think Lincoln chose not to give a detailed plan of action for the country for the coming four years? Explain.

LANGUAGE IN ACTION

Many people are impressed by writers who use long words with seeming ease. Do you consider long words to be more intelligent than short words? Clearer? In *The Miracle of Language* (1991), Richard Lederer argues on behalf of short words. He offers his readers a sound rule for writing: "Use small, old words where you can. If a long word says just what you want to say, do not fear to use it. But know that our tongue is rich in crisp, brisk, swift, short words. Make them the spine and the heart of what you speak and write. Short words are like fast friends. They will not let you down."

As you were reading Lincoln's "Second Inaugural Address" were you aware that over two-thirds of his words were only one syllable? Analyze Lincoln's diction in his final paragraph, the paragraph that is most often quoted from this speech. What, in your opinion, makes this paragraph memorable and accounts for its power or strength? What thoughts do you have about short words now?

WRITING SUGGESTIONS

1. Columnist and political commentator Garry Wills has written that "Hemingway claimed that modern American novels are the offspring of *Huckleberry Finn*. It is no greater exaggeration to say that all modern political prose descends from the Gettysburg Address." Lincoln delivered his now-famous speech at the Gettysburg battlefield on November 19, 1863, as the Civil War raged on. It is illuminating to look again at the familiar words with their original context in mind to see how they served Lincoln's purpose, his sense of the occasion, and his larger sense of the nation's history and destiny.

Gettysburg Address

Four score and seven years ago our fathers brought forth on this continent, a new nation, conceived in Liberty, and dedicated to the proposition that all men are created equal.

Now we are engaged in a great civil war, testing whether that nation, or any nation so conceived and so dedicated, can long endure. We are met on a great battle-field of war. We have come to dedicate a portion of that field, as a final resting place for those who here gave their lives that that nation might live. It is altogether fitting and proper that we should do this.

But, in a larger sense, we can not dedicate—we can not consecrate—we can not hallow—this ground. The brave men, living and dead, who struggled here, have consecrated it, far above our poor power to add or detract. The world will little note, nor long remember what we say here, but it can never forget what they did here. It is for us the living, rather, to be dedicated here to the unfinished work which they who fought here have thus far so nobly advanced. It is rather for us to be here dedicated to the great task remaining before us—that from these honored dead we take increased devotion to that cause for which they gave the last full measure of devotion—that we here highly resolve that these dead shall not have died in vain—that this nation, under God, shall have a new birth of freedom—and that government of the people, by the people, for the people, shall not perish from the earth.

Using several of the speeches in this chapter, test Wills's claim. Write an essay in which you explore the similarities and differences you see between Lincoln's address and the speeches by Kennedy and/or King.

2. How would you characterize your own writing? Do you think of yourself as a short-word person or a long-word person? What do you think would happen if you found yourself limited to short words? Instead of thinking of it as a handicap, accept the challenge and "tap" what linguist Richard Lederer calls "the energy and eloquence of small words." Write a short composition composed entirely of one-syllable words. You may find it helpful to review the Language in Action activity for this selection before you start writing.

And Ain't I a Woman?

SOJOURNER TRUTH

Sojourner Truth was born a slave named Isabella in Ulster County, New York, in 1797. Freed by the New York State Emancipation Act of 1827, she went to New York City and underwent a profound religious transformation. She worked as a domestic servant and, in her active evangelism, tried to reform prostitutes. Adopting the name Sojourner Truth in 1843, she became a traveling preacher and abolitionist.

Although she remained illiterate, Truth's compelling presence gripped her audience as she spoke eloquently about emancipation and women's rights at conventions throughout the Northeast. Truth dictated her memoirs to Olive Gilbert and they were published as *The Narative of Sojourner Truth: A Northern Slave* (1850). After the Civil War, she worked to provide education and employment for emancipated slaves until her death in 1883.

WRITING TO DISCOVER: *What comes to mind when you hear the word speech? What are the speaking styles you respond to most, the ones that captivate you as a listener? Do you like speeches that sound reasoned and logical, or do you like ones that appeal to your emotions? Explain.*

Well, children, where there is so much racket there must be something out of kilter. I think that 'twixt the Negroes of the South and the women at the North, all talking about rights, the white men will be in a fix pretty soon. But what's all this here talking about?

That man over there says that women need to be helped into carriages, and lifted over ditches, and to have the best place everywhere. Nobody ever helps me into carriages, or over mud puddles, or gives me any best place! And ain't I a woman? Look at me! Look at my arm. I have plowed and planted, and gathered into barns, and no man could head me! And ain't I a woman? I could work as much and eat as much as a man—when I could get it—and bear the lash as well! And ain't I a woman? I have borne thirteen children, and seen them most all sold off to slavery, and when I cried out with my mother's grief, none but Jesus heard me! And ain't I a woman?

I have plowed and planted, and gathered into barns, and no man could head me! And ain't I a woman?

Then they talk about this thing in the head; what's this they call it? [Intellect, someone whispers.] That's it, honey. What's that got to do with women's rights or Negroes' rights? If my cup won't hold but a pint, and yours holds a quart, wouldn't you be mean not to let me have my little half-measure full?

Then that little man in black there, he says women can't have as much rights as men, 'cause Christ wasn't a woman! Where did your Christ come from? Where did your Christ come from? From God and a woman! Man had nothing to do with him.

If the first woman God ever made was strong enough to turn the world upside down all alone, these women together ought to be able to turn it back, and get it right side up again! And now they is asking to do it, the men better let them.   5

Obliged to you for hearing me, and now old Sojourner ain't got nothing more to say.

THINKING CRITICALLY ABOUT THE READING

1. What does Truth mean when she says, "Where there is so much racket there must be something out of kilter" (1)? Why does Truth believe that white men are going to find themselves in a "fix" (1)?

2. What does Truth put forth as her "credentials" as a woman? Why is it important for her to define what a woman is for her audience?

3. How does Truth use the comments of "that man over there" (2) and "that little man in black" (4) to help her establish her definition of woman?

4. What is the effect of Truth's repetition of the question "And ain't I a woman?" four times? What other questions does she ask? Why do you suppose Truth doesn't provide answers to questions in paragraph 3, but does for the question in paragraph 4?

5. How would you characterize Truth's tone in this speech? What phrases in the speech suggest that tone to you? (Glossary: *Tone*)

6. How does Truth counter the argument that "women can't have as much rights as men, 'cause Christ wasn't a woman" (4)?

LANGUAGE IN ACTION

Carefully read the following letter to the editor of the *New York Times*. In it Nancy Stevens, president of a small Manhattan advertising agency, argues against using the word *guys* to address women. How do you think Truth would react to the use of the word *guys* to refer to women? Do you find such usage objectionable?

WOMEN AREN'T GUYS

A young woman, a lawyer, strides into a conference room. Already in attendance, at what looks to be the start of a high-level meeting, are four smartly dressed women in their 20's and 30's. The arriving woman plunks her briefcase down at the head of the polished table and announces, "O.K., guys, let's get started."

On "Kate and Allie," a television show about two women living together with Kate's daughter and Allie's daughter and son, the dialogue often runs to such phrases as, "Hey, you guys, who wants pizza?" All of the people addressed are female, except for Chip, the young son. "Come on, you guys, quit fighting," pleads one of the daughters when there is a tiff between the two women.

Just when we were starting to be aware of the degree to which language affects people's perceptions of women and substitute "people working" for "men working" and "humankind" for "mankind," this "guy" thing happened. Just when people have started becoming aware that a 40-year-old woman shouldn't be called a girl, this "guy" thing has crept in.

Use of "guy" to mean "person" is so insidious that I'll bet most women don't notice they are being called "guys," or, if they do, find it somehow flattering to be one of them.

Sometimes, I find the courage to pipe up when a bunch of us are assembled and are called "guys" by someone of either gender. "We're not guys," I say. Then everyone looks at me funny.

One day, arriving at a business meeting where there were five women and one man, I couldn't resist. "Hello, ladies," I said. Everyone laughed embarrassedly for the blushing man until I added, "and gent." Big sigh of relief. Wouldn't want to call a guy a "gal" now, would we?

Why is it not embarrassing for a woman to be called "guy"? We know why. It's the same logic that says women look sexy and cute in a man's shirt, but did you ever try your silk blouse on your husband and send him to the deli? It's the same mentality that holds that anything male is worthy (and to be aspired toward) and anything female is trivial.

We all sit around responding, without blinking, "black with one sugar, please," when anyone asks, "How do you guys like your coffee?"

What's all that murmuring I hear?

"Come on, lighten up."

"Be a good guy."

"Nobody means anything by it."

Nonsense.

WRITING SUGGESTIONS

1. Truth spoke out against the injustice she saw around her. In arguing for the rights of women, she found it helpful to define *woman* in order to make her point. What social cause do you find most compelling today? Human rights? AIDS awareness? Domestic abuse? Alcoholism? Gay marriage? Racism? Select an issue about which you have strong feelings. Now carefully identify all key

terms that you must define before arguing your position. Write an essay in which you use definition to make your point convincingly.

2. Truth's speech holds out hope for the future. She envisioned a future in which women join together to take charge and "turn [the world] back, and get it right side up again" (5). What she envisioned has, to some extent, come to pass. Write an essay in which you speculate about how Truth would react to the world as we know it. What do you think would please her? What would disappoint her? What do you think she would want to change about our society? Explain your reasoning.

A Modest Proposal

JONATHAN SWIFT

One of the world's greatest satirists, Jonathan Swift was born in 1667 to English parents in Dublin, Ireland, and was educated at Trinity College. When his early efforts at a literary career in England met no success, he returned to Ireland in 1694 and was ordained an Anglican clergyman. From 1713 until his death in 1745, he was dean of St. Patrick's Cathedral in Dublin. A prolific chronicler of human folly, Swift is best known as the author of *Gulliver's Travels* and of the work included here, "A Modest Proposal."

In the 1720s Ireland had suffered several famines, but the English gentry, who owned most of the land, did nothing to alleviate the suffering of tenant farmers and their families; nor would the English government intervene. A number of pamphlets were circulated proposing solutions to the so-called "Irish problem." "A Modest Proposal," published anonymously in 1729, was Swift's ironic contribution to the discussion.

WRITING TO DISCOVER: *Satire is a dramatic literary art form wherein the shortcomings, foibles, abuses, and idiocies of both people and institutions are accentuated and held up for ridicule in order to shame these perpetrators into reforming themselves. Perhaps the very easiest way to see satire around us today is in the work of our political cartoonists. Make a list of individuals and institutions both here and abroad who today might make good subjects for satire. For each individual and institution on your list provide one or two traits or characteristics that might be held up for ridicule.*

A Modest Proposal for Preventing the Children of Poor People in Ireland from Being a Burden to Their Parents or Country, and for Making Them Beneficial to the Public

It is a melancholy object to those who walk through this great town, or travel in the country, when they see the streets, the roads and cabin-doors crowded with beggars of the female sex, followed by three, four, or six children, all in rags, and importuning every passenger for an alms. These mothers, instead of being able to work for their honest livelihood, are forced to employ all their time in strolling, to beg sustenance for their helpless infants, who, as they grow up, either turn thieves for want of work, or leave their dear native country to fight for the Pretender in Spain, or sell themselves to the Barbadoes.

I think it is agreed by all parties that this prodigious number of children, in the arms, or on the backs, or at the heels of their mothers, and frequently of their fathers, is in the present deplorable state of the kingdom a very great additional grievance; and therefore whoever could find out a fair, cheap, and easy method of making these children sound and useful members of the commonwealth would deserve so well of the public as to have his statue set up for a preserver of the nation.

But my intention is very far from being confined to provide only for the children of professed beggars; it is of a much greater extent, and shall take in the whole number of infants at a certain age who are born of parents in effect as little able to support them as those who demand our charity in the streets.

As to my own part, having turned my thoughts for many years upon this important subject, and maturely weighed the several schemes of other projectors, I have always found them grossly mistaken in their computation. It is true a child just dropped from its dam may be supported by her milk for a solar year with little other nourishment, at most not above the value of two shillings, which the mother may certainly get, or the value in scraps, by her lawful occupation of begging, and it is exactly at one year old that I propose to provide for them, in such a manner as, instead of being a charge upon their parents, or the parish, or wanting food and raiment for the rest of their lives, they shall, on the contrary, contribute to the feeding and partly to the clothing of many thousands.

There is likewise another great advantage in my scheme, that it will   5
prevent those voluntary abortions, and that horrid practice of women murdering their bastard children, alas, too frequent among us, sacrificing the poor innocent babes, I doubt, more to avoid the expense than the shame, which would move tears and pity in the most savage and inhuman breast.

The number of souls in Ireland being usually reckoned one million and a half, of these I calculate there may be about two hundred thousand couples whose wives are breeders, from which number I subtract thirty thousand couples who are able to maintain their own children, although I apprehend there cannot be so many under the present distresses of the kingdom; but this being granted, there will remain an hundred and seventy thousand breeders. I again subtract fifty thousand for those women who miscarry, or whose children die by accident or disease within the year. There only remain an hundred and twenty thousand children of poor parents annually born: the question therefore is, how this number shall be reared, and provided for, which as I have already said, under the present situation of affairs is utterly impossible by all the methods hitherto proposed, for we can neither employ them in handicraft or agriculture; we neither build houses (I mean in the country), nor cultivate land: they can very seldom pick up a livelihood by stealing until they arrive at six years old, except where they are of towardly parts, although I confess they learn the rudiments much earlier, during which time they can however be properly looked upon only as probationers, as I have been informed by a principal gentleman in the County of Cavan, who protested to me that he never knew above one or two instances under the age of six, even in a part of the kingdom so renowned for the quickest proficiency in that art.

I am assured by our merchants that a boy or girl before twelve years old is no salable commodity, and even when they come to this age, they will not yield above three pounds, or three pounds and half-a-crown at most on the Exchange, which cannot turn to account either to the parents or the kingdom, the charge of nutriment and rags having been at least four times that value.

I shall now therefore humbly propose my own thoughts, which I hope will not be liable to the least objection.

I have been assured by a very knowing American of my acquaintance in London, that a young healthy child well nursed is at a year old a most delicious, nourishing and wholesome food, whether stewed, roasted, baked, or boiled, and I make no doubt that it will equally serve in a fricassee, or a ragout.

I do therefore humbly offer it to public consideration, that of the hundred and twenty thousand children already computed, twenty thousand may be reserved for breed, whereof only one fourth part to be males, which is more than we allow to sheep, black-cattle, or swine, and my reason is that these children are seldom the fruits of marriage, a circumstance not much regarded by our savages, therefore one male will be sufficient to serve four females. That the remaining hundred thousand may at a year old be offered in sale to the persons of quality, and fortune, through the kingdom, always advising the mother to let them suck plentifully in the last month, so as to render them plump, and fat for a good table. A child will make two dishes at an entertainment for friends, and when the family dines alone, the fore or hind quarter will make a reasonable dish, and seasoned with a little pepper or salt will be very good boiled on the fourth day, especially in winter. 10

I have reckoned upon a medium, that a child just born will weigh twelve pounds, and in a solar year if tolerably nursed increaseth to twenty-eight pounds.

I grant this food will be somewhat dear, and therefore very proper for landlords, who, as they have already devoured most of the parents, seem to have the best title to the children.

Infant's flesh will be in season throughout the year, but more plentiful in March, and a little before and after, for we are told by a grave author, an eminent French physician, that fish being a prolific diet, there are more children born in Roman Catholic countries about nine months after Lent than at any other season; therefore reckoning a year after Lent, the markets will be more glutted than usual, because the number of Popish infants is at least three to one in this kingdom, and therefore it will have one other collateral advantage by lessening the number of Papists among us.

I have already computed the charge of nursing a beggar's child (in which list I reckon all cottagers, laborers, and four-fifths of the farmers) to be about two shillings *per annum*, rags included, and I believe no gentleman would repine to give ten shillings for the carcass of a good fat child, which, as I have said, will make four dishes of excellent nutritive meat, when he hath only some particular friend of his own family to dine with him. Thus the Squire will learn to be a good landlord and grow popular among his tenants, the mother will have eight shillings net profit, and be fit for work until she produces another child.

Those who are more thrifty (as I must confess the times require) may   15
flay the carcass; the skin of which artificially dressed, will make admirable gloves for ladies, and summer boots for fine gentlemen.

As to our city of Dublin, shambles may be appointed for this purpose, in the most convenient parts of it, and butchers we may be assured will not be wanting, although I rather recommend buying the children alive, and dressing them hot from the knife, as we do roasting pigs.

A very worthy person, a true lover of his country, and whose virtues I highly esteem, was lately pleased in discoursing on this matter to offer a refinement upon my scheme. He said that many gentlemen of this kingdom having of late destroyed their deer, he conceived that the want of venison might be well supplied by the bodies of young lads and maidens, not exceeding fourteen years of age, nor under twelve, so great a number of both sexes in every county being now ready to starve, for want of work and service: and these to be disposed of by their parents if alive, or otherwise by their nearest relations. But with due deference to so excellent a friend, and so deserving a patriot, I cannot be altogether in his sentiments. For as to the males, my American acquaintance assured me from frequent experience that their flesh was generally tough and lean, like that of our schoolboys, by continual exercise, and their taste disagreeable, and to fatten them would not answer the charge. Then as to the females, it would, I think with humble submission, be a loss to the public, because they soon would become breeders themselves: and besides, it is not improbable that some scrupulous people might be apt to censure such a practice (although indeed very unjustly) as a little bordering upon cruelty, which I confess, hath always been with me the strongest objection against any project, howsoever well intended.

But in order to justify my friend, he confessed that this expedient was put into his head by the famous Psalmanazar, a native of the island Formosa, who came from thence to London, above twenty years ago, and in conversation told my friend that in his country when any young person happened to be put to death, the executioner sold the carcass to persons of quality, as a prime dainty, and that, in his time, the body of a plump girl of fifteen, who was crucified for an attempt to poison the emperor, was sold to his Imperial Majesty's Prime Minister of State, and other great Mandarins of the Court, in joints from the gibbet, at four hundred crowns. Neither indeed can I deny that if the same use were made of several plump young girls in this town who, without one single groat to their fortunes, cannot stir abroad without a chair, and appear at the playhouse and assemblies in foreign fineries which they never will pay for, the kingdom would not be the worse.

Some persons of a desponding spirit are in great concern about that vast number of poor people, who are aged, diseased, or maimed, and I have been desired to employ my thoughts what course may be taken to ease the nation of so grievous an encumbrance. But I am not in the least pain upon that matter, because it is very well known that they are every day dying, and rotting, by cold, and famine, and filth, and vermin, as fast as can be reasonably expected. And as to the younger laborers, they are now in almost as hopeful a condition. They cannot get work, and consequently pine away from want of nourishment, to a degree that if at any time they are accidentally hired to common labor, they have not strength to perform it; and thus the country and themselves are in a fair way of being soon delivered from the evils to come.

I have too long digressed, and therefore shall return to my subject.   20
I think the advantages by the proposal which I have made are obvious and many, as well as of the highest importance.

For first, as I have already observed, it would greatly lessen the number of Papists, with whom we are yearly over-run, being the principal breeders of the nation, as well as our most dangerous enemies, and who stay at home on purpose with a design to deliver the kingdom to the Pretender, hoping to take their advantage by the absence of so many good Protestants, who have chosen rather to leave their country than stay at home and pay tithes against their conscience to an idolatrous Episcopal curate.

Secondly, the poorer tenants will have something valuable of their own, which by law may be made liable to distress, and help to pay their landlord's rent, their corn and cattle being already seized, and money a thing unknown.

Thirdly, whereas the maintenance of an hundred thousand children, from two years old, and upwards, cannot be computed at less than ten shillings a piece *per annum,* the nation's stock will be thereby increased fifty thousand pounds *per annum,* besides the profit of a new dish, introduced to the tables of all gentlemen of fortune in the kingdom, who have any refinement in taste, and the money will circulate among ourselves, the goods being entirely of our own growth and manufacture.

Fourthly, the constant breeders, besides the gain of eight shillings sterling *per annum,* by the sale of their children, will be rid of the charge of maintaining them after the first year.

Fifthly, this food would likewise bring great custom to taverns, where   25
the vintners will certainly be so prudent as to procure the best receipts for dressing it to perfection, and consequently have their houses frequented by all the fine gentlemen, who justly value themselves upon their knowledge in good eating; and a skillful cook, who understands how to oblige his guests, will contrive to make it as expensive as they please.

Sixthly, this would be a great inducement to marriage, which all wise nations have either encouraged by rewards, or enforced by laws and penalties. It would increase the care and tenderness of mothers towards their children, when they were sure of a settlement for life, to the poor babes, provided in some sort by the public to their annual profit instead of expense. We should soon see an honest emulation among the married women, which of them could bring the fattest child to the market. Men would become as fond of their wives, during the time of their pregnancy, as they are now of their mares in foal, their cows in calf, or sows when they are ready to farrow, nor offer to beat or kick them (as it is too frequent a practice) for fear of a miscarriage.

Many other advantages might be enumerated. For instance, the addition of some thousand carcasses in our exportation of barrelled beef; the propagation of swine's flesh, and improvement in the art of making good bacon, so much wanted among us by the great destruction of pigs, too frequent at our tables; which are no way comparable in taste or magnificance to a well-grown, fat yearling child, which roasted whole will make a considerable figure at a Lord Mayor's feast, or any other public entertainment. But this and many others I omit, being studious of brevity.

Supposing that one thousand families in this city would be constant customers for infants' flesh, besides others who might have it at merry meetings, particularly weddings and christenings; I compute that Dublin would take off annually about twenty thousand carcasses, and the rest of the kingdom (where probably they will be sold somewhat cheaper) the remaining eighty thousand.

I can think of no one objection that will possibly be raised against this proposal, unless it should be urged that the number of people will be thereby much lessened in the kingdom. This I freely own, and it was indeed one principal design in offering it to the world. I desire the reader will observe, that I calculate my remedy *for this one individual Kingdom of* Ireland, *and for no other that ever was, is, or, I think, ever can be upon earth.* Therefore let no man talk to me of other expedients: *Of taxing our absentees at five shillings a pound: Of using neither clothes, nor household furniture except what is of our own growth and manufacture: Of utterly rejecting the materials and instruments that promote foreign luxury: Of curing the expensiveness of pride, vanity, idleness, and gaming in our women: Of introducing a vein of parsimony, prudence, and temperance: Of learning to love our country, wherein we differ even from* Laplanders, *and the inhabitants of* Topinamboo: *Of quitting our animosities and factions, nor act any longer like the* Jews, *who were murdering one another at the very moment their city was taken: Of being a little cautious not to sell our country and consciences for nothing: Of teaching landlords to have at least one degree of mercy towards their tenants.* Lastly, *of putting a spirit of honesty, industry, and skill into our shopkeepers, who, if a resolution could now be taken to buy only our native goods, would immediately unite to cheat and exact upon us in the price, the measure and the goodness, nor could ever yet be brought to make one fair proposal of just dealing, though often and earnestly invited to it.*

Therefore I repeat, let no man talk to me of these and the like expedients, till he hath at least a glimpse of hope that there will ever be some hearty and sincere attempt to put them in practice.

But as to myself, having been wearied out for many years with offering vain, idle, visionary thoughts, and at length utterly despairing of success,

30

I fortunately fell upon this proposal, which as it is wholly new, so it hath something solid and real, of no expense and little trouble, full in our own power, and whereby we can incur no danger in disobliging England. For this kind of commodity will not bear exportation, the flesh being of too tender a consistence to admit a long continuance in salt, *although perhaps I could name a country which would be glad to eat up our whole nation without it.*

After all I am not so violently bent upon my own opinion as to reject any offer, proposed by wise men, which shall be found equally innocent, cheap, easy and effectual. But before some thing of that kind shall be advanced in contradiction to my scheme, and offering a better, I desire the author, or authors, will be pleased maturely to consider two points. First, as things now stand, how they will be able to find food and raiment for a hundred thousand useless mouths and backs? And secondly, there being a round million of creatures in human figure, throughout this kingdom, whose whole subsistence put into a common stock would leave them in debt two millions of pounds sterling; adding those who are beggars by profession, to the bulk of farmers, cottagers, and laborers with their wives and children, who are beggars in effect; I desire those politicians who dislike my overture, and may perhaps be so bold to attempt

> **I can think of no one objection that will possibly be raised against this proposal, unless it should be urged that the number of people will be thereby much lessened in the kingdom.**

an answer, that they will first ask the parents of these mortals whether they would not at this day think it a great happiness to have been sold for food at a year old, in the manner I prescribe, and thereby have avoided such a perpetual scene of misfortunes as they have since gone through, by the oppression of landlords, the impossibility of paying rent without money or trade, the want of common sustenance, with neither house nor clothes to cover them from the inclemencies of weather, and the most inevitable prospect of entailing the like, or greater miseries upon their breed for ever.

I profess in the sincerity of my heart that I have not the least personal interest in endeavoring to promote this necessary work, having no other motive than the *public good of my country, by advancing our trade, providing for infants, relieving the poor, and giving some pleasure to the rich.* I have no children by which I can propose to get a single penny; the youngest being nine years old, and my wife past child-bearing.

THINKING CRITICALLY ABOUT THE READING

1. What problem does Swift address in his proposal? What are some of the solutions that he offers? What does Swift see as the "advantages" (20) of his proposal?

2. What "other expedients" (29) are dismissed as "vain, idle, visionary thoughts" (31)? What can you infer about Swift's purpose from paragraphs 29 through 31? (Glossary: *Purpose*) Explain.

3. Describe the "author" of the proposal. Why do you suppose Swift chose such a character or persona to present this plan? At what points in the essay can you detect Swift's own voice coming through?

4. Swift entitles his essay "A Modest Proposal," and in paragraph 2 he talks of making Ireland's "children sound and useful members of the commonwealth." In what ways are Swift's title and statement ironic? Cite several other examples of Swift's irony. (Glossary: *Irony*)

5. In what ways, if any, can the argument presented in this essay be seen as logical? What is the effect, for example, of the complicated calculations in paragraph 6?

6. Satire often has a "stealth quality" about it; that is, the audience for whom it is intended often does not realize at first that the author of the satire is not being serious. At some point in the satire the audience usually catches on and then begins to see the larger issue at the center of the satire. At what point in your reading of "A Modest Proposal" did you begin to catch on to Swift's technique and larger, more important, message?

7. Toward what belief and/or action is Swift attempting to persuade his readers? How does he go about doing so? For example, did you feel a sense of outrage at any point in the essay? Did you feel that the essay was humorous at any point? If so, where and why?

LANGUAGE IN ACTION

Consider the following news item, "Global Food Summit in Rome," by P. P. Rega. The piece, which first appeared on TheSpoof.com on June 8, 2008, reports on a meeting of world leaders to "resolve the present worldwide food crisis."

GLOBAL FOOD SUMMIT IN ROME
P. P. Rega

The Global Food Crisis Summit was held in Rome, Italy, this past week. Agricultural ministers, medical experts, and political activists from around the world convened in the Eternal City to resolve the present worldwide food crisis. Below is a copy of the first day's schedule of lectures and activities that have been sponsored by the United Nation's Food and Agriculture Organization.

Program

0730–0830: Registration at the southwest entrance to The Colosseum

Cappuccino, caffè latte, biscotti anginetti, cenci alla fiorentina e cornetti a piacere

0830–0900: Introduction
0900–0930: Uganda: Dehydration, Diarrhea and Death
0930–1000: Malnutrition in Myanmar
1000–1030: Break

Gelati assortiti da Giolitti (cioccolato, nocciole, e crema) con biscotti ed acqua minerale o caffè

1030–1100: Small Farmers in Indonesia: Source of Global Salvation
1100–1200: Introduction of Rice Farming in Haiti: Is It Enough?
1200–1300: Global Epidemic: Drop in Life Expectancy among the Poor and Starving
1300–1500: Lunch at Da Piperno

L'antipasto: Carciofi alla giudia

Vino: Verdicchio di Matelica Terre di Valbona 2006

Il Primo: Risotto alla pescatore oppure zuppa napoletana
   Vino: Tommaso Bussola Amarone di Valpolicella 2002

Il Secondo: Coda alla Vaccinara

Il Contorno: Vignarola
   Vino: Cantina Nobile di Montepulciano 1999

Formaggi: Fontina Val d'Aosta, bocconcini alla panna di bufala, pecorino romano

Il Dolce: Aranci in salsa di marsala

Caffè

Sambuca siciliana con tre mosche

1500–1600: Improving Crop Production in Zimbabwe: A Lesson To Us All.
1600–1700: Fertilizer or Seeds?
1700–1730: Break

Pizza alla quattro stagione
   Birra: Nastro Azzurro alla spina
1800–1900: Keynote Speaker: Al Gore
   Topic: Doubling Global Food Production in the 21st Century
1900–2100: Dinner at La Pergola

L'antipasto: Mozzarella in carrozza
   Vino: Prosecco Superiore di Locarno 2001

(continued)

Il Primo: Gnocchetti all'amatriciana
  Vino: Recioto di Soave da Anselmi 2003

Il Secondo: Stufato di manzo con cipolline
Il Contorno: Fritto misto vegetariano
  Vino: Brunello di Montalcino 2001

Formaggi: Gorgonzola, mascarpone di bufala di Battipaglia, Parmigiano-Reggiano
Il Dolce: Cassata alla siciliana
  Caffè
  Limoncello amalfitana

What were your first impressions of Rega's story? What, for you, is Rega's point in presenting "the first day's schedule of lectures and activities"? Do you need to know Italian in order to grasp Rega's message? How do you think Swift would respond to such a meeting? What similarities do you see in the messages of Swift and Rega? Explain.

WRITING SUGGESTIONS

1. Write a modest proposal of your own to solve a difficult social or political problem of the present day or, on a smaller scale, a problem you see facing your school or community.

2. What do you think is the most effective way to bring about social change and to influence societal attitudes? Would Swift's methods work today, or would they have to be significantly modified as Rega has done in "Global Food Summit in Rome"? Write an essay in which you compare and contrast Swift's and Rega's tactics in an effort to determine how a writer can best influence public opinion today.

THE LANGUAGE OF PREJUDICE, DISCRIMINATION, AND STEREOTYPES

No single issue has absorbed our national consciousness more than prejudice and discrimination. That we are defined by and define others is an inevitability of our human condition, but the manner in which we relate to each other is a measure of our progress as a multiracial, multiethnic, and multicultural society. In a larger sense, it is a measure of our growth as a civilization. Not even the most optimistic observers of our society believe that equality is within sight or perhaps even ultimately possible, but implicit in all views of the subject is the notion that we can and must improve our appreciation of each other if we are to better our lives.

Our purpose in this chapter is to introduce you to some ideas on the sources of prejudice and to illustrate the role that language plays in the origin and perpetuation of prejudice and discrimination. We begin with Andrew Sullivan's "What's So Bad about Hate?," an in-depth inquiry into the nature of hatred and its relationship to prejudice, bias, bigotry, malice, anger, and all the emotions in between. Next we present Gordon Allport's classic essay "The Language of Prejudice," acknowledged by scholars for the past fifty years as the definitive word on the subject. Allport's concepts of "nouns that cut slices" and "verbal realism and symbol phobia" demonstrate not only how language encodes prejudice but also how we can use language to escape bias and bigotry. Next, we take a closer look at how language, culture, and prejudice interact in our society. In her essay illustrating her family and friends' repurposing of the racially charged term *nigger*, Gloria Naylor reminds us that words themselves do not exist in isolation, but are rather the product of the minds and hearts that use them. Grace Hsiang casts light on intraracial discrimination, a type of prejudice that is little known and even less talked about. We move next to Brent Staples's essay entitled "Black Men and Public Space" as he reflects on the way his presence as an African American alters public spaces and shapes the attitudes and actions of those around him. His analysis reaches into the world of body language and spatial relationships—that is, the messages we send and receive through nonverbal means. In "The 'F Word'" Firoozeh Dumas uses her wit and good sense of humor to recount what life was like growing up in America as an Iranian

306 THE LANGUAGE OF PREJUDICE, DISCRIMINATION, AND STEREOTYPES

immigrant. "All of us immigrants knew that moving to America would be fraught with challenges," she confesses, "but none of us thought that our names would be such an obstacle." How can one's name be seen as an obstacle for an immigrant? Dumas uses examples from her own experience to show how her "identifiably 'ethnic' name" left her vulnerable to taunts and name-calling incidents as a child and clear acts of prejudice and discrimination as an adult. Finally, an interview with scholar Victor Villanueva (online at bedfordstmartins.com/languageawareness /epages) connects language with a pernicious new form of racism that operates, in part, by denying that racist attitudes still exist.

What's So Bad about Hate?

ANDREW SULLIVAN

Andrew Sullivan was born in 1963 in South Godstone, Surrey, England, to Irish parents. He earned his B.A. degree in modern history at Magdalene College, Oxford, and his masters degree and Ph.D. in government at Harvard University. Sullivan began his career in journalism at the *New Republic*, later wrote for the *New York Times Magazine*, and held an editorial post at *The Atlantic*. A gay, Catholic, conservative, and often controversial commentator, Sullivan is perhaps best known for his blog *The Daily Dish*, which became very popular post-9/11 and was by 2005 receiving over 50,000 hits a day. In 2009 *The Daily Dish* won The 2008 Weblog Award for Best Blog. He has written several books: *Virtually Normal: An Argument about Homosexuality* (1995); *Love Undetectable: Notes on Friendship, Sex and Survival* (1998); and *The Conservative Soul: How We Lost It, How to Get It Back* (2006).

In "What's So Bad about Hate?," first published in the *New York Times Magazine* on September 26, 1999, Sullivan reveals how little we actually know about the emotion that lies at the base of prejudice. As he writes, "For all its emotional punch, 'hate' is far less nuanced an idea than prejudice, or bigotry, or bias, or anger, or even aversion to others."

WRITING TO DISCOVER: *Have you ever been so upset by someone that you could say that you hated the person? If so, what prompted your reaction? How would you characterize the nature of the hatred you felt? Do you think it was an uncontrollable response or a conscious one? Do you think you had your reasons and would react the same way again in similar circumstances?*

I.

I wonder what was going on in John William King's head [in 1997] when he tied James Byrd Jr.'s feet to the back of a pickup truck and dragged him three miles down a road in rural Texas. King and two friends had picked up Byrd, who was black, when he was walking home, half-drunk, from a party. As part of a bonding ritual in their fledgling white supremacist group, the three men took Byrd to a remote part of town, beat him and chained his legs together before attaching them to the truck. Pathologists at King's trial testified that Byrd was probably alive and conscious until his body finally hit a culvert and split in two. When King was offered a chance to say something to Byrd's family at the trial, he smirked and uttered an obscenity.

We know all these details now, many months later. We know quite a large amount about what happened before and after. But I am still drawn, again and again, to the flash of ignition, the moment when fear and

307

loathing became hate, the instant of transformation when King became hunter and Byrd became prey.

What was that? And what was it when Buford Furrow Jr., long-time member of the Aryan Nations, calmly walked up to a Filipino-American mailman he happened to spot, asked him to mail a letter and then shot him at point-blank range? Or when Russell Henderson beat Matthew Shepard, a young gay man, to a pulp, removed his shoes and then, with the help of a friend, tied him to a post like a dead coyote to warn off others?

For all our documentation of these crimes and others, our political and moral disgust at them, our morbid fascination with them, our sensitivity to their social meaning, we seem at times to have no better idea now than we ever had of what exactly they were about. About what that moment means when, for some reason or other, one human being asserts absolute, immutable superiority over another. About not the violence, but what the violence expresses. About what—exactly—hate is. And what our own part in it may be.

I find myself wondering what hate actually is in part because we have created an entirely new offense in American criminal law—a "hate crime"—to combat it. And barely a day goes by without someone somewhere declaring war against it. Last month President Clinton called for an expansion of hate-crime laws as "what America needs in our battle against hate." A couple of weeks later, Senator John McCain used a campaign speech to denounce the "hate" he said poisoned the land. New York's mayor, Rudolph Giuliani, recently tried to stop the Million Youth March in Harlem on the grounds that the event was organized by people "involved in hate marches and hate rhetoric."

5

For all our zeal to attack hate, we still have a remarkably vague idea of what it actually is.

The media concurs in its emphasis. In 1985, there were 11 mentions of "hate crimes" in the national media database Nexis. By 1990, there were more than a thousand. In the first six months of 1999, there were 7,000. "Sexy fun is one thing," wrote a *New York Times* reporter about sexual assaults in Woodstock '99's mosh pit. "But this was an orgy of lewdness tinged with hate." And when Benjamin Smith marked the Fourth of July this year by targeting blacks, Asians, and Jews for murder in Indiana and Illinois, the story wasn't merely about a twisted young man who had emerged on the scene. As the *Times* put it, "Hate arrived in the neighborhoods of Indiana University, in Bloomington, in the early-morning darkness."

But what exactly was this thing that arrived in the early-morning darkness? For all our zeal to attack hate, we still have a remarkably vague idea of what it actually is. A single word, after all, tells us less, not more. For all its emotional punch, "hate" is far less nuanced an idea than prejudice, or bigotry, or bias, or anger, or even mere aversion to others. Is it to stand in for all these varieties of human experience—and everything in between? If so, then the war against it will be so vast as to be quixotic. Or is "hate" to stand for a very specific idea or belief, or set of beliefs, with a very specific object or group of objects? Then waging war against it is almost certainly unconstitutional. Perhaps these kinds of questions are of no concern to those waging war on hate. Perhaps it is enough for them that they share a sentiment that there is too much hate and never enough vigilance in combating it. But sentiment is a poor basis for law, and a dangerous tool in politics. It is better to leave some unwinnable wars unfought.

II.

Hate is everywhere. Human beings generalize all the time, ahead of time, about everyone and everything. A large part of it may even be hard-wired. At some point in our evolution, being able to know beforehand who was friend or foe was not merely a matter of philosophical reflection. It was a matter of survival. And even today it seems impossible to feel a loyalty without also feeling a disloyalty, a sense of belonging without an equal sense of unbelonging. We're social beings. We associate. Therefore we disassociate. And although it would be comforting to think that the one could happen without the other, we know in reality that it doesn't. How many patriots are there who have never felt a twinge of xenophobia?

Of course, by hate we mean something graver and darker than this kind of lazy prejudice. But the closer you look at this distinction, the fuzzier it gets. Much of the time, we harbor little or no malice toward people of other backgrounds or places or ethnicities or ways of life. But then a car cuts you off at an intersection and you find yourself noticing immediately that the driver is a woman, or black, or old, or fat, or white, or male. Or you are walking down a city street at night and hear footsteps quickening behind you. You look around and see that it is a white woman and not a black man, and you are instantly relieved. These impulses are so spontaneous they are almost involuntary. But where did they come from? The mindless need to be mad at someone — anyone — or the unconscious eruption of a darker prejudice festering within?

In 1993, in San Jose, Calif., two neighbors — one heterosexual, one   10
homosexual — were engaged in a protracted squabble over grass clippings. (The full case is recounted in *Hate Crimes,* by James B. Jacobs and Kimberly Potter.) The gay man regularly mowed his lawn without a grass catcher, which prompted his neighbor to complain on many occasions that grass clippings spilled over onto his driveway. Tensions grew until one day, the gay man mowed his front yard, spilling clippings onto his neighbor's driveway, prompting the straight man to yell an obscene and common anti-gay insult. The wrangling escalated. At one point, the gay man agreed to collect the clippings from his neighbor's driveway but then later found

them dumped on his own porch. A fracas ensued with the gay man spray-
ing the straight man's son with a garden hose, and the son hitting and
kicking the gay man several times, yelling anti-gay slurs. The police were
called, and the son was eventually convicted of a hate-motivated assault,
a felony. But what was the nature of the hate: anti-gay bias, or suburban
property-owner madness?

Or take the Labor Day parade last year in Broad Channel, a small
island in Jamaica Bay, Queens. Almost everyone there is white, and in
recent years a group of local volunteer firefighters has taken to decorat-
ing a pickup truck for the parade in order to win the prize for "funniest
float." Their themes have tended toward the outrageously provocative.
Beginning in 1995, they won prizes for floats depicting "Hasidic Park,"
"Gooks of Hazzard" and "Happy Gays." Last year, they called their float
"Black to the Future, Broad Channel 2098." They imagined their community a century hence as a largely black enclave, with every stereotype
imaginable: watermelons, basketballs and so on. At one point during the
parade, one of them mimicked the dragging death of James Byrd. It was
caught on videotape, and before long the entire community was depicted
as a caldron of hate.

It's an interesting case, because the float was indisputably in bad taste
and the improvisation on the Byrd killing was grotesque. But was it hate?
The men on the float were local heroes for their volunteer work; they
had no record of bigoted activity, and were not members of any racist
organizations. In previous years, they had made fun of many other groups
and saw themselves more as provocateurs than bigots. When they were
described as racists, it came as a shock to them. They apologized for poor
taste but refused to confess to bigotry. "The people involved aren't horrible people," protested a local woman. "Was it a racist act? I don't know.
Are they racists? I don't think so."

If hate is a self-conscious activity, she has a point. The men were primarily motivated by the desire to shock and to reflect what they thought
was their community's culture. Their display was not aimed at any particular black people, or at any blacks who lived in Broad Channel—almost
none do. But if hate is primarily an unconscious activity, then the matter is
obviously murkier. And by taking the horrific lynching of a black man as a
spontaneous object of humor, the men were clearly advocating indifference
to it. Was this an aberrant excess? Or the real truth about the men's feelings toward African-Americans? Hate or tastelessness? And how on earth is
anyone, even perhaps the firefighters themselves, going to know for sure?

Or recall H. L. Mencken. He shared in the anti-Semitism of his time
with more alacrity than most and was an indefatigable racist. "It is impossible," he wrote in his diary, "to talk anything resembling discretion or
judgment into a colored woman. They are all essentially childlike, and even
hard experience does not teach them anything." He wrote at another time
of the "psychological stigmata" of the "Afro-American race." But it is also

true that, during much of his life, day to day, Mencken conducted himself with no regard to race, and supported a politics that was clearly integrationist. As the editor of his diary has pointed out, Mencken published many black authors in his magazine, *The Mercury,* and lobbied on their behalf with his publisher, Alfred A. Knopf. The last thing Mencken ever wrote was a diatribe against racial segregation in Baltimore's public parks. He was good friends with leading black writers and journalists, including James Weldon Johnson, Walter White, and George S. Schuyler, and played an underappreciated role in promoting the Harlem Renaissance.

What would our modern view of hate do with Mencken? Probably   15
ignore him, or change the subject. But, with regard to hate, I know lots of people like Mencken. He reminds me of conservative friends who oppose almost every measure for homosexual equality yet genuinely delight in the company of their gay friends. It would be easier for me to think of them as haters, and on paper, perhaps, there is a good case that they are. But in real life, I know they are not. Some of them clearly harbor no real malice toward me or other homosexuals whatsoever.

They are as hard to figure out as those liberal friends who support every gay rights measure they have ever heard of but do anything to avoid going into a gay bar with me. I have to ask myself in the same, frustrating kind of way: are they liberal bigots or bigoted liberals? Or are they neither bigots nor liberals, but merely people?

III.

Hate used to be easier to understand. When Sartre described anti-Semitism in his 1946 essay "Anti-Semite and Jew," he meant a very specific array of firmly held prejudices, with a history, an ideology and even a pseudoscience to back them up. He meant a systematic attempt to demonize and eradicate an entire race. If you go to the Web site of the World Church of the Creator, the organization that inspired young Benjamin Smith to murder in Illinois earlier this year, you will find a similarly bizarre, pseudorational ideology. The kind of literature read by Buford Furrow before he rained terror on a Jewish kindergarten last month and then killed a mailman because of his color is full of the same paranoid loopiness. And when we talk about hate, we often mean this kind of phenomenon.

But this brand of hatred is mercifully rare in the United States. These professional maniacs are to hate what serial killers are to murder. They should certainly not be ignored; but they represent what Harold Meyerson, writing in *Salon,* called "niche haters": cold blooded, somewhat deranged, often poorly socialized psychopaths. In a free society with relatively easy access to guns, they will always pose a menace.

But their menace is a limited one, and their hatred is hardly typical of anything very widespread. Take Buford Furrow. He famously issued a "wake-up call" to "kill Jews" in Los Angeles, before he peppered a Jewish community center with gunfire. He did this in a state with two Jewish female senators, in a city with a large, prosperous Jewish population, in a country where out of several million Jewish Americans, a total of 66 were reported by the F.B.I. as the targets of hate-crime assaults in 1997. However despicable Furrow's actions were, it would require a very large stretch to describe them as representative of anything but the deranged fringe of an American subculture.

Most hate is more common and more complicated, with as many varieties as there are varieties of love. Just as there is possessive love and needy love; family love and friendship; romantic love and unrequited love; passion and respect, affection and obsession, so hatred has its shadings. There is hate that fears, and hate that merely feels contempt; there is hate that expresses power, and hate that comes from powerlessness; there is revenge, and there is hate that comes from envy. There is hate that was love, and hate that is a curious expression of love. There is hate of the other, and hate of something that reminds us too much of ourselves. There is the oppressor's hate, and the victim's hate. There is hate that burns slowly, and hate that fades. And there is hate that explodes, and hate that never catches fire. 20

The modern words that we have created to describe the varieties of hate — "sexism," "racism," "anti-Semitism," "homophobia" — tell us very little about any of this. They tell us merely the identities of the victims; they don't reveal the identities of the perpetrators, or what they think, or how they feel. They don't even tell us how the victims feel. And this simplicity is no accident. Coming from the theories of Marxist and post-Marxist academics, these "isms" are far better at alleging structures of power than at delineating the workings of the individual heart or mind. In fact, these "isms" can exist without mentioning individuals at all.

We speak of institutional racism, for example, as if an institution can feel anything. We talk of "hate" as an impersonal noun, with no hater specified. But when these abstractions are actually incarnated, when someone feels something as a result of them, when a hater actually interacts with a victim, the picture changes. We find that hates are often very different phenomena one from another, that they have very different psychological dynamics, that they might even be better understood by not seeing them as varieties of the same thing at all.

There is, for example, the now unfashionable distinction between reasonable hate and unreasonable hate. In recent years, we have become accustomed to talking about hates as if they were all equally indefensible, as if it could never be the case that some hates might be legitimate, even necessary. But when some 800,000 Tutsis are murdered under the auspices of a Hutu regime in Rwanda, and when a few thousand Hutus are killed in revenge, the hates are not commensurate. Genocide is not an event like a hurricane, in which damage is random and universal; it is a planned and often merciless attack of one group upon another. The hate of the perpetrators is a monstrosity. The hate of the victims, and their survivors, is justified. What else, one wonders, were surviving Jews supposed to feel toward Germans after the Holocaust? Or, to a different degree, South African blacks after apartheid? If the victims overcome this hate, it is a supreme moral achievement. But if they don't, the victims are not as culpable as the perpetrators. So the hatred of Serbs for Kosovars today can never be equated with the hatred of Kosovars for Serbs.

Hate, like much of human feeling, is not rational, but it usually has its reasons. And it cannot be understood, let alone condemned, without knowing them. Similarly, the hate that comes from knowledge is always different from the hate that comes from ignorance. It is one of the most foolish clichés of our time that prejudice is always rooted in ignorance, and can usually be overcome by familiarity with the objects of our loathing. The racism of many Southern whites under segregation was not appeased by familiarity with Southern blacks; the virulent loathing of Tutsis by many Hutus was not undermined by living next door to them for centuries. Theirs was a hatred that sprang, for whatever reasons, from experience. It cannot easily be compared with, for example, the resilience of anti-Semitism in Japan, or hostility to immigration in areas where immigrants are unknown, or fear of homosexuals by people who have never knowingly met one.

The same familiarity is an integral part of what has become known as "sexism." Sexism isn't, properly speaking, a prejudice at all. Few men live without knowledge or constant awareness of women. Every single sexist man was born of a woman, and is likely to be sexually attracted to women. His hostility is going to be very different than that of, say, a reclusive member of the Aryan Nations toward Jews he has never met.   25

In her book *The Anatomy of Prejudices,* the psychotherapist Elisabeth Young-Bruehl proposes a typology of three distinct kinds of hate: obsessive, hysterical, and narcissistic. It's not an exhaustive analysis, but it's a beginning in any serious attempt to understand hate rather than merely declaring war on it. The obsessives, for Young-Bruehl, are those, like the Nazis or Hutus, who fantasize a threat from a minority, and obsessively try to rid themselves of it. For them, the very existence of the hated group is threatening. They often describe their loathing in almost physical terms: they experience what Patrick Buchanan, in reference to homosexuals, once described as a "visceral recoil" from the objects of their detestation. They often describe those they hate as diseased or sick, in need of a cure. Or they talk of "cleansing" them, as the Hutus talked of the Tutsis, or call them "cockroaches," as Yitzhak Shamir called the Palestinians. If you read material from the Family Research Council, it is clear that the group regards homosexuals as similar contaminants. A recent posting on its Web site about syphilis among gay men was headlined, "Unclean."

Hysterical haters have a more complicated relationship with the objects of their aversion. In Young-Bruehl's words, hysterical prejudice is a prejudice that "a person uses unconsciously to appoint a group to act out in the world forbidden sexual and sexually aggressive desires that the person has repressed." Certain kinds of racists fit this pattern. White loathing of blacks is, for some people, at least partly about sexual and physical envy. A certain kind of white racist sees in black America all those impulses he wishes most to express himself but cannot. He idealizes in "blackness" a sexual freedom, a physical power, a Dionysian release that he detests but also longs for. His fantasy may not have any basis in reality, but it is powerful nonetheless. It is a form of love-hate, and it is impossible to understand the nuances of racism in, say, the American South, or in British Imperial India, without it.

Unlike the obsessives, the hysterical haters do not want to eradicate the objects of their loathing; rather they want to keep them in some kind of permanent and safe subjugation in order to indulge the attraction of their repulsion. A recent study, for example, found that the men most likely to be opposed to equal rights for homosexuals were those most likely to be aroused by homoerotic imagery. This makes little rational sense, but it has a certain psychological plausibility. If homosexuals were granted equality, then the hysterical gay-hater might panic that his repressed passions would run out of control, overwhelming him and the world he inhabits.

A narcissistic hate, according to Young-Bruehl's definition, is sexism. In its most common form, it is rooted in many men's inability even to imagine what it is to be a woman, a failing rarely challenged by men's control of our most powerful public social institutions. Women are not so much hated by most men as simply ignored in non-sexual contexts, or never conceived of as true equals. The implicit condescension is mixed, in many cases, with repressed and sublimated erotic desire. So the unawareness of women is sometimes commingled with a deep longing or contempt for them.

Each hate, of course, is more complicated than this, and in any one person hate can assume a uniquely configured combination of these types. So there are hysterical sexists who hate women because they need them so much, and narcissistic sexists who hardly notice that women exist, and sexists who oscillate between one of these positions and another. And there are gay-bashers who are threatened by masculine gay men and gay-haters who feel repulsed by effeminate ones. The soldier who beat his fellow soldier Barry Winchell to death with a baseball bat in July had earlier lost a fight to him. It was the image of a macho gay man—and the shame of being bested by him—that the vengeful soldier had to obliterate, even if he needed a gang of accomplices and a weapon to do so. But the murderers of Matthew Shepard seem to have had a different impulse: a visceral disgust at the thought of any sexual contact with an effeminate homosexual. Their anger was mixed with mockery, as the cruel spectacle at the side of the road suggested.

In the same way, the pathological anti-Semitism of Nazi Germany was obsessive, inasmuch as it tried to cleanse the world of Jews; but also, as

30

Daniel Jonah Goldhagen shows in his book, *Hitler's Willing Executioners,* hysterical. The Germans were mysteriously compelled as well as repelled by Jews, devising elaborate ways, like death camps and death marches, to keep them alive even as they killed them. And the early Nazi phobia of interracial sex suggests as well a lingering erotic quality to the relationship, partaking of exactly the kind of sexual panic that persists among some homosexual-haters and antimiscegenation racists. So the concept of "homophobia," like that of "sexism" and "racism," is often a crude one. All three are essentially cookie-cutter formulas that try to understand human impulses merely through the one-dimensional identity of the victims, rather than through the thoughts and feelings of the haters and hated.

This is deliberate. The theorists behind these "isms" want to ascribe all blame to one group in society—the "oppressors"—and render specific others—the "victims"—completely blameless. And they want to do this in order in part to side unequivocally with the underdog. But it doesn't take a genius to see how this approach, too, can generate its own form of bias. It can justify blanket condemnations of whole groups of people—white straight males, for example—purely because of the color of their skin or the nature of their sexual orientation. And it can condescendingly ascribe innocence to whole groups of others. It does exactly what hate does: it hammers the uniqueness of each individual into the anvil of group identity. And it postures morally over the result.

In reality, human beings and human acts are far more complex, which is why these isms and the laws they have fomented are continually coming under strain and challenge. Once again, hate wriggles free of its definers. It knows no monolithic groups of haters and hated. Like a river, it has many eddies, backwaters, and rapids. So there are anti-Semites who actually admire what they think of as Jewish power, and there are gay-haters who look up to homosexuals and some who want to sleep with them. And there are black racists, racist Jews, sexist women, and anti-Semitic homosexuals. Of course there are.

IV.

Once you start thinking of these phenomena less as the "isms" of sexism/racism and "homophobia," once you think of them as independent psychological responses, it's also possible to see how they can work in a bewildering variety of ways in a bewildering number of people. To take one obvious and sad oddity: people who are demeaned and objectified in society may develop an aversion to their tormentors that is more hateful in its expression than the prejudice they have been subjected to. The F.B.I. statistics on hate crimes throws up an interesting point. In America in the 1990s, blacks were up to three times as likely as whites to commit a hate crime, to express their hate by physically attacking their targets or their property. Just as sexual abusers have often been victims of sexual abuse, and wife-beaters often grew up in violent households, so hate criminals may often be members of hated groups.

Even the Columbine murderers were in some sense victims of hate 35 before they were purveyors of it. Their classmates later admitted that Dylan Klebold and Eric Harris were regularly called "faggots" in the corridors and classrooms of Columbine High and that nothing was done to prevent or stop the harassment. This climate of hostility doesn't excuse the actions of Klebold and Harris, but it does provide a more plausible context. If they had been black, had routinely been called "nigger" in the school and had then exploded into a shooting spree against white students, the response to the matter might well have been different. But the hate would have been the same. In other words, hate-victims are often hate-victimizers as well. This doesn't mean that all hates are equivalent, or that some are not more justified than others. It means merely that hate goes both ways; and if you try to regulate it among some, you will find yourself forced to regulate it among others.

It is no secret, for example, that some of the most vicious anti-Semites in America are black, and that some of the most virulent anti-Catholic bigots in America are gay. At what point, we are increasingly forced to ask, do these phenomena become as indefensible as white racism or religious toleration of anti-gay bigotry? That question becomes all the more difficult when we notice that it is often minorities who commit some of the most hate-filled offenses against what they see as their oppressors. It was the mainly gay AIDS activist group Act Up that perpetrated the hateful act of desecrating Communion hosts at a Mass at St. Patrick's Cathedral in New York. And here is the playwright Tony Kushner, who is gay, responding to the Matthew Shepard beating in *The Nation* magazine: "Pope John Paul II endorses murder. He, too, knows the price of discrimination, having declared anti-Semitism a sin. . . . He knows that discrimination kills. But when the Pope heard the news about Matthew Shepard, he, too, worried about spin. And so, on the subject of gay-bashing, the Pope and his cardinals and his bishops and priests maintain their cynical political silence. . . . To remain silent is to endorse murder." Kushner went on to describe the Pope as a "homicidal liar."

Maybe the passion behind these words is justified. But it seems clear enough to me that Kushner is expressing hate toward the institution of the Catholic Church, and all those who perpetuate its doctrines. How else to interpret the way in which he accuses the Pope of cynicism, lying, and murder? And how else either to understand the brutal parody of religious vocations expressed by the Sisters of Perpetual Indulgence, a group of gay men who dress in drag as nuns and engage in sexually explicit performances in public? Or T-shirts with the words "Recovering Catholic" on them, hot items among some gay and lesbian activists? The implication that someone's religious faith is a mental illness is clearly an expression of contempt. If that isn't covered under the definition of hate speech, what is?

Or take the following sentence: "The act male homosexuals commit is ugly and repugnant and afterwards they are disgusted with themselves. They drink and take drugs to palliate this, but they are disgusted with the act and they are always changing partners and cannot be really happy." The thoughts of Pat Robertson or Patrick Buchanan? Actually that sentence was written by Gertrude Stein, one of the century's most notable lesbians. Or take the following, about how beating up "black boys like that made us feel good inside. . . . Every time I drove my foot into his [expletive], I felt better." It was written to describe the brutal assault of an innocent bystander for the sole reason of his race. By the end of the attack, the victim had blood gushing from his mouth as his attackers stomped on his genitals. Are we less appalled when we learn that the actual sentence was how beating up "white boys like that made us feel good inside. . . . Every time I drove my foot into his [expletive], I felt better?" It was written by Nathan McCall, an African-American who later in life became a successful journalist at the *Washington Post* and published his memoir of this "hate crime" to much acclaim.

In fact, one of the stranger aspects of hate is that the prejudice expressed by a group in power may often be milder in expression than the prejudice felt by the marginalized. After all, if you already enjoy privilege, you may not feel the anger that turns bias into hate. You may not need to. For this reason, most white racism may be more influential in society than most black racism—but also more calmly expressed.

So may other forms of minority loathing—especially hatred within minorities. I'm sure that black conservatives like Clarence Thomas or Thomas Sowell have experienced their fair share of white racism. But I wonder whether it has ever reached the level of intensity of the hatred directed toward them by other blacks? In several years of being an openly gay writer and editor, I have experienced the gamut of responses to my sexual orientation. But I have only directly experienced articulated, passionate hate from other homosexuals. I have been accused over the years by other homosexuals of being a sellout, a hypocrite, a traitor, a sexist, a racist, a narcissist, a snob. I've been called selfish, callous, hateful, self-hating, and malevolent. At a reading, a group of lesbian activists portrayed my face on a poster within the crossfires of a gun. Nothing from the religious right has come close to such vehemence.

I am not complaining. No harm has ever come to me or my property, and much of the criticism is rooted in the legitimate expression of political differences. But the visceral tone and style of the gay criticism can only be described as hateful. It is designed to wound personally, and it often does. But its intensity comes in part, one senses, from the pain of being excluded for so long, of anger long restrained bubbling up and directing itself more aggressively toward an alleged traitor than an

40

alleged enemy. It is the hate of the hated. And it can be the most hateful hate of all. For this reason, hate-crime laws may themselves be an oddly biased category—biased against the victims of hate. Racism is everywhere, but the already victimized might be more desperate, more willing to express it violently. And so more prone to come under the suspicious eye of the law.

V.

And why is hate for a group worse than hate for a person? In Laramie, Wyoming, the now-famous epicenter of "homophobia," where Matthew Shepard was brutally beaten to death, vicious murders are not unknown. In the previous 12 months, a 15-year-old pregnant girl was found east of the town with 17 stab wounds. Her 38-year-old boyfriend was apparently angry that she had refused an abortion and left her in the Wyoming foothills to bleed to death. In the summer of 1998, an 8-year-old Laramie girl was abducted, raped and murdered by a pedophile, who disposed of her young body in a garbage dump. Neither of these killings was deemed a hate crime, and neither would be designated as such under any existing hate-crime law. Perhaps because of this, one crime is an international legend; the other two are virtually unheard of.

But which crime was more filled with hate? Once you ask the question, you realize how difficult it is to answer. Is it more hateful to kill a stranger or a lover? Is it more hateful to kill a child than an adult? Is it more hateful to kill your own child than another's? Under the law before the invention of hate crimes, these decisions didn't have to be taken. But under the law after hate crimes, a decision is essential. A decade ago, a murder was a murder. Now, in the era when group hate has emerged as our cardinal social sin, it all depends.

The supporters of laws against hate crimes argue that such crimes should be disproportionately punished because they victimize more than the victim. Such crimes, these advocates argue, spread fear, hatred and panic among whole populations, and therefore merit more concern. But, of course, all crimes victimize more than the victim, and spread alarm in the society at large. Just think of the terrifying church shooting in Texas only two weeks ago. In fact, a purely random murder may be even more terrifying than a targeted one, since the entire community, and not just a part of it, feels threatened. High rates of murder, robbery, assault, and burglary victimize everyone, by spreading fear, suspicion, and distress everywhere. Which crime was more frightening to more people this summer: the mentally ill Buford Furrow's crazed attacks in Los Angeles, killing one, or Mark Barton's murder of his own family and several random day-traders in Atlanta, killing 12? Almost certainly the latter. But only Furrow was guilty of "hate."

One response to this objection is that certain groups feel fear more   45
intensely than others because of a history of persecution or intimidation.
But doesn't this smack of a certain condescension toward minorities? Why,
after all, should it be assumed that gay men or black women or Jews, for
example, are as a group more easily intimidated than others? Surely in any
of these communities there will be a vast range of responses, from panic to
concern to complete indifference. The assumption otherwise is the kind
of crude generalization the law is supposed to uproot in the first place.
And among these groups, there are also likely to be vast differences. To
equate a population once subjected to slavery with a population of Mexican immigrants or third-generation Holocaust survivors is to equate the
unequatable. In fact, it is to set up a contest of vulnerability in which one
group vies with another to establish its particular variety of suffering, a
contest that can have no dignified solution.

Rape, for example, is not classified as a "hate crime" under most existing laws, pitting feminists against ethnic groups in a battle for recognition. If, as a solution to this problem, everyone, except the white straight
able-bodied male, is regarded as a possible victim of a hate crime, then we
have simply created a two-tier system of justice in which racial profiling is
reversed, and white straight men are presumed guilty before being proven
innocent, and members of minorities are free to hate them as gleefully as
they like. But if we include the white straight male in the litany of potential victims, then we have effectively abolished the notion of a hate crime
altogether. For if every crime is possibly a hate crime, then it is simply
another name for crime. All we will have done is widened the search for
possible bigotry, ratcheted up the sentences for everyone and filled the
jails up even further.

Hate-crime-law advocates counter that extra penalties should be
imposed on hate crimes because our society is experiencing an "epidemic"
of such crimes. Mercifully, there is no hard evidence to support this
notion. The Federal Government has only been recording the incidence
of hate crimes in this decade, and the statistics tell a simple story. In 1992,
there were 6,623 hate-crime incidents reported to the F.B.I., by a total
of 6,181 agencies, covering 51 percent of the population. In 1996, there
were 8,734 incidents reported by 11,355 agencies, covering 84 percent of
the population. That number dropped to 8,049 in 1997. These numbers
are, of course, hazardous. They probably underreport the incidence of
such crimes, but they are the only reliable figures we have. Yet even if they
are faulty as an absolute number, they do not show an epidemic of "hate
crimes" in the 1990s.

Is there evidence that the crimes themselves are becoming more
vicious? None. More than 60 percent of recorded hate crimes in America involve no violent, physical assault against another human being at
all, and, again, according to the F.B.I., that proportion has not budged
much in the 1990s. These impersonal attacks are crimes against property

or crimes of "intimidation." Murder, which dominates media coverage of hate crimes, is a tiny proportion of the total. Of the 8,049 hate crimes reported to the F.B.I. in 1997, a total of eight were murders. Eight. The number of hate crimes that were aggravated assaults (generally involving a weapon) in 1997 is less than 15 percent of the total. That's 1,237 assaults too many, of course, but to put it in perspective, compare it with a reported 1,022,492 "equal opportunity" aggravated assaults in America in the same year. The number of hate crimes that were physical assaults is half the total. That's 4,000 assaults too many, of course, but to put it in perspective, it compares with around 3.8 million "equal opportunity" assaults in America annually.

The truth is, the distinction between a crime filled with personal hate and a crime filled with group hate is an essentially arbitrary one. It tells us nothing interesting about the psychological contours of the specific actor or his specific victim. It is a function primarily of politics, of special interest groups carving out particular protections for themselves, rather than a serious response to a serious criminal

> **The truth is, the distinction between a crime filled with personal hate and a crime filled with group hate is an essentially arbitrary one.**

concern. In such an endeavor, hate-crime-law advocates cram an entire world of human motivations into an immutable, tiny box called hate, and hope to have solved a problem. But nothing has been solved; and some harm may even have been done.

In an attempt to repudiate a past that treated people differently 50 because of the color of their skin, or their sex, or religion or sexual orientation, we may merely create a future that permanently treats people differently because of the color of their skin, or their sex, religion, or sexual orientation. This notion of a hate crime, and the concept of hate that lies behind it, takes a psychological mystery and turns it into a facile political artifact. Rather than compounding this error and extending even further, we should seriously consider repealing the concept altogether.

To put it another way: violence can and should be stopped by the government. In a free society, hate can't and shouldn't be. The boundaries between hate and prejudice and between prejudice and opinion and between opinion and truth are so complicated and blurred that any attempt to construct legal and political fire walls is a doomed and illiberal venture. We know by now that hate will never disappear from human consciousness; in fact, it is probably, at some level, definitive of it. We know after decades of education measures that hate is not caused merely by ignorance; and after decades of legislation, that it isn't caused entirely by law.

To be sure, we have made much progress. Anyone who argues that America is as inhospitable to minorities and to women today as it has been in the past has not read much history. And we should, of course, be vigilant that our most powerful institutions, most notably the government, do not actively or formally propagate hatred; and insure that the violent expression of hate is curtailed by the same rules that punish all violent expression.

But after that, in an increasingly diverse culture, it is crazy to expect that hate, in all its variety, can be eradicated. A free country will always mean a hateful country. This may not be fair, or perfect, or admirable, but it is reality, and while we need not endorse it, we should not delude ourselves into thinking we can prevent it. That is surely the distinction between toleration and tolerance. Tolerance is the eradication of hate; toleration is co-existence despite it. We might do better as a culture and as a polity if we concentrated more on achieving the latter rather than the former. We would certainly be less frustrated.

And by aiming lower, we might actually reach higher. In some ways, some expression of prejudice serves a useful social purpose. It lets off steam; it allows natural tensions to express themselves incrementally; it can siphon off conflict through words, rather than actions. Anyone who has lived in the ethnic shouting match that is New York City knows exactly what I mean. If New Yorkers disliked each other less, they wouldn't be able to get on so well. We may not all be able to pull off a Mencken—bigoted in words, egalitarian in action—but we might achieve a lesser form of virtue: a human acceptance of our need for differentiation, without a total capitulation to it.

Do we not owe something more to the victims of hate? Perhaps we   55
do. But it is also true that there is nothing that government can do for the hated that the hated cannot better do for themselves. After all, most bigots are not foiled when they are punished specifically for their beliefs. In fact, many of the worst haters crave such attention and find vindication in such rebukes. Indeed, our media's obsession with "hate," our elevation of it above other social misdemeanors and crimes, may even play into the hands of the pathetic and the evil, may breathe air into the smoldering embers of their paranoid loathing. Sure, we can help create a climate in which such hate is disapproved of—and we should. But there is a danger that if we go too far, if we punish it too much, if we try to abolish it altogether, we may merely increase its mystique, and entrench the very categories of human difference that we are trying to erase.

For hate is only foiled not when the haters are punished but when the hated are immune to the bigot's power. A hater cannot psychologically wound if a victim cannot psychologically be wounded. And that immunity to hurt can never be given; it can merely be achieved. The racial epithet only strikes at someone's core if he lets it, if he allows the bigot's definition of him to be the final description of his life and his person—if somewhere in his heart of hearts, he believes the hateful slur to be true. The only final answer to this form of racism, then, is not majority persecution of it, but minority indifference to it. The only permanent rebuke to homophobia is not the enforcement of tolerance, but gay equanimity in the face of prejudice. The only effective answer to sexism is not a morass of legal proscriptions, but the simple fact of female success. In this, as in so many other things, there is no solution to the problem. There is only a transcendence of it. For all our rhetoric, hate will never be destroyed. Hate, as our predecessors knew better, can merely be overcome.

THINKING CRITICALLY ABOUT THE READING

1. What does Sullivan mean when he writes in paragraph 8, "A large part of [hate] may even be hard-wired"? If he is correct, what might one conclude about attempts to legislate against hate crimes?

2. In paragraph 21, Sullivan writes that the "modern words we have created to describe the varieties of hate — 'sexism,' 'racism,' 'anti-Semitism,' 'homophobia' — tell us very little" about the different kinds of hate he delineates in the paragraph above. What does he mean by this?

3. Some argue that hatred is a result of ignorance. How does Sullivan respond to this argument?

4. What does Sullivan see as the difference between the hatred of the perpetrator and the hatred of the victim in return (24)?

5. Sullivan cites Elisabeth Young-Bruehl's typology of hate in paragraph 26. What three kinds of hate does she identify, and what characterizes each type? How helpful do you find her classification in understanding hate? (Glossary: *Classification*)

6. What problems does Sullivan see with respect to hate-crime legislation (42–56)? What arguments does he present in favor of repealing hate-crime legislation? Do you agree or disagree with his reasons?

7. What does Sullivan find interesting about the hate that has been directed at him by other gay people? How does he explain it?

LANGUAGE IN ACTION

Most of us can remember hearing the children's rhyme "Sticks and stones may break my bones / But words will never hurt me" while growing up. The implication is simple — people cannot hurt you with bad things that they say or write about you. Why then do many colleges and universities have speech codes that try to legislate against hurtful language? What exactly is hate speech? *Webster's New World Law Dictionary* (2010) defines it as follows:

> Hate speech is speech not protected by the First Amendment, because it is intended to foster hatred against individuals or groups based on race, religion, gender, sexual preference, place of national origin, or other improper classification.

What are your thoughts about hate speech? Is it as harmless as the "sticks and stones" rhyme implies, or is it potentially harmful? Put another way, when can speech be viewed as the equivalent of action? Do you think it's necessary—or even possible—to legislate how people use hurtful or prejudicial language? How would one go about policing the use of hurtful language or enforcing hate speech codes? How would one measure the fostering of hatred?

WRITING SUGGESTIONS

1. Write an essay in which you examine the various terms for hate that Sullivan uses in his essay. How might an examination of these terms help us to understand both the dynamics of prejudice and how we, as individuals and as a society, respond to these dynamics?

2. In paragraph 56, Sullivan writes: "For hate is only foiled not when the haters are punished but when the hated are immune to the bigot's power. A hater cannot psychologically wound if a victim cannot psychologically be wounded. And that immunity to hurt can never be given; it can merely be achieved." Write an essay in which you explore the implications of Sullivan's comments here. Consider in particular how what Sullivan writes here relates to the establishment of hate-crime laws.

The Language of Prejudice

GORDON ALLPORT

Gordon Allport was born in Montezuma, Indiana, in 1897. He attended Harvard College and graduated Phi Beta Kappa in 1919 with majors in philosophy and economics. During his undergraduate years, he also became interested in psychology, and a meeting with Sigmund Freud in Vienna in 1920—during which the founder of psychoanalysis failed to impress him—had a profound influence on him. After studying and teaching abroad, Allport returned to Harvard to teach social ethics and to pursue his Ph.D., which he received in 1922. He went on to become a full professor at Harvard in 1942, served as chairman of the psychology department, and received the Gold Medal Award of the American Psychological Foundation in 1963. He died in 1967.

Allport became known for his outspoken stances regarding racial prejudice, and he was hopeful about efforts being made to eradicate it. His book *The Nature of Prejudice* (1954) is still regarded as one of the most important and influential texts on the subject. The following selection from that book analyzes the connections between language and prejudice and explains some of the specific ways in which language can induce and shape prejudice.

WRITING TO DISCOVER: *While in high school and college, many students are associated with groups that bring together people of disparate racial and religious backgrounds. Labels for these groups often carry many positive or negative associations. You may have made such associations yourself without thinking twice about it, as in "He's just a jock," or "She's with the popular crowd—she'll never go out with me." To what group, if any, did you belong in high school? Briefly write about the effects on you and your classmates of cliques in your school. How did the labels associated with the different groups influence how you thought about the individual members of each group?*

Without words we should scarcely be able to form categories at all. A dog perhaps forms rudimentary generalizations, such as small-boys-are-to-be-avoided—but this concept runs its course on the conditioned reflex level, and does not become the object of thought as such. In order to hold a generalization in mind for reflection and recall, for identification and for action, we need to fix it in words. Without words our world would be, as William James said, an "empirical sand-heap."

NOUNS THAT CUT SLICES

In the empirical world of human beings there are some two and a half billion grains of sand corresponding to our category "the human race." We cannot possibly deal with so many separate entities in our thought, nor can we individualize even among the hundreds whom we encounter in our daily round. We must group them, form clusters. We welcome, therefore, the names that help us to perform the clustering.

The most important property of a noun is that it brings many grains of sand into a single pail, disregarding the fact that the same grains might have fitted just as appropriately into another pail. To state the matter technically, a noun *abstracts* from a concrete reality some one feature and assembles different concrete realities only with respect to this one feature. The very act of classifying forces us to overlook all other features, many of which might offer a sounder basis than the rubric we select. Irving Lee gives the following example:

> I knew a man who had lost the use of both eyes. He was called a "blind man." He could also be called an expert typist, a conscientious worker, a good student, a careful listener, a man who wanted a job. But he couldn't get a job in the department store order room where employees sat and typed orders which came over the telephone. The personnel man was impatient to get the interview over. "But you're a blind man," he kept saying, and one could almost feel his silent assumption that somehow the incapacity in one aspect made the man incapable in every other. So blinded by the label was the interviewer that he could not be persuaded to look beyond it.

Some labels, such as "blind man," are exceedingly salient and powerful. They tend to prevent alternative classification, or even cross-classification. Ethnic labels are often of this type, particularly if they refer to some highly visible feature, e.g., Negro, Oriental. They resemble the labels that point to some outstanding incapacity—*feeble-minded, cripple, blind man.* Let us call such symbols "labels of primary potency." These symbols act like shrieking sirens, deafening us to all finer discriminations that we might otherwise perceive. Even though the blindness of one man and the darkness of pigmentation of another may be defining attributes for some purposes, they are irrelevant and "noisy" for others.

Most people are unaware of this basic law of language—that every label applied to a given person refers properly only to one aspect of his nature.

Most people are unaware of this basic law of language—that every label applied to a given person refers properly only to one aspect of his nature. You may correctly say that a certain man is *human, a philanthropist, a Chinese, a physician, an athlete.* A given person may be all of these; but the chances are that Chinese stands out in your mind as the symbol of primary potency. Yet neither this nor any other classificatory label can refer to the whole of a man's nature. (Only his proper name can do so.)

Thus each label we use, especially those of primary potency, distracts our attention from concrete reality. The living, breathing, complex individual—the ultimate unit of human nature—is lost to sight. As in the figure, the label magnifies one attribute out of all proportion to its true significance, and masks other important attributes of the individual. . . .

A category, once formed with the aid of a symbol of primary potency, tends to attract more attributes than it should. The category labeled *Chinese* comes to signify not only ethnic membership but also reticence, impassivity, poverty, treachery. To be sure, . . . there may be genuine ethnic-linked traits, making for a certain *probability* that the member of an ethnic stock may have these attributes. But our cognitive process is not cautious. The labeled category, as we have seen, includes indiscriminately the defining attribute, probable attributes, and wholly fanciful, nonexistent attributes.

Even proper names—which ought to invite us to look at the individual person—may act like symbols of primary potency, especially if they arouse ethnic associations. Mr. Greenberg is a person, but since his name is Jewish, it activates in the hearer his entire category of Jews-as-a-whole. An ingenious experiment performed by psychologist Gregory Razran shows this point

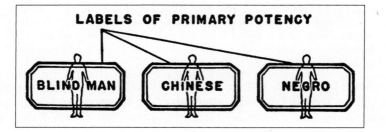

clearly, and at the same time demonstrates how a proper name, acting like an ethnic symbol, may bring with it an avalanche of stereotypes.

> Thirty photographs of college girls were shown on a screen to 150 students. The subjects rated the girls on a scale from one to five for *beauty, intelligence, character, ambition, general likability*. Two months later the same subjects were asked to rate the same photographs (and fifteen additional ones introduced to complicate the memory factory). This time five of the original photographs were given Jewish surnames (Cohen, Kantor, etc.), five Italian (Valenti, etc.), and five Irish (O'Brien, etc.); and the remaining girls were given names chosen from the signers of the Declaration of Independence and from the Social Register (Davis, Adams, Clark, etc.).
>
> When Jewish names were attached to photographs there occurred the following changes in ratings:
>
>> decrease in liking
>> decrease in character
>> decrease in beauty
>> increase in intelligence
>> increase in ambition

For those photographs given Italian names there occurred:

decrease in liking
decrease in character
decrease in beauty
decrease in intelligence

Thus a mere proper name leads to prejudgments of personal attributes. The individual is fitted to the prejudiced ethnic category, and not judged in his own right.

While the Irish names also brought about depreciated judgment, the depreciation was not as great as in the case of the Jews and Italians. The falling of likability of the "Jewish girls" was twice as great as for "Italians" and five times as great as for "Irish." We note, however, that the "Jewish" photographs caused higher ratings in *intelligence* and in *ambition*. Not all stereotypes of out-groups are unfavorable.

The anthropologist Margaret Mead has suggested that labels of primary potency lose some of their force when they are changed from nouns into adjectives. To speak of a Negro soldier, a Catholic teacher, or a Jewish artist calls attention to the fact that some other group classifications are just as legitimate as the racial or religious. If George Johnson is spoken of not only as a Negro but also as a *soldier*, we have at least two attributes to know him by, and two are more accurate than one. To depict him truly as an individual, of course, we should have to name many more attributes. It is a useful suggestion that we designate ethnic and religious membership where possible with *adjectives* rather than *nouns*.

EMOTIONALLY TONED LABELS

Many categories have two kinds of labels—one less emotional and one more emotional. Ask yourself how you feel, and what thoughts you have, when you read the words *school teacher,* and then *school marm.* Certainly the second phrase calls up something more strict, more ridiculous, more disagreeable than the former. Here are four innocent letters: m-a-r-m. But they make us shudder a bit, laugh a bit, and scorn a bit. They call up an image of a spare, humorless, irritable old maid. They do not tell us that she is an individual human being with sorrows and troubles of her own. They force her instantly into a rejective category.

In the ethnic sphere even plain labels such as Negro, Italian, Jew, Catholic, Irish-American, French-Canadian may have emotional tone for a reason that we shall soon explain. But they all have their higher key equivalents: nigger, wop, kike, papist, harp, canuck. When these labels are employed we can be almost certain that the speaker *intends* not only to characterize the person's membership, but also to disparage and reject him.

Quite apart from the insulting intent that lies behind the use of certain labels, there is also an inherent ("physiognomic") handicap in many

10

terms designating ethnic membership. For example, the proper names characteristic of certain ethnic memberships strike us as absurd. (We compare them, of course, with what is familiar and therefore "right.") Chinese names are short and silly; Polish names intrinsically difficult and outlandish. Unfamiliar dialects strike us as ludicrous. Foreign dress (which, of course, is a visual ethnic symbol) seems unnecessarily queer.

But of all of these "physiognomic" handicaps the reference to color, clearly implied in certain symbols, is the greatest. The word Negro comes from the Latin *niger* meaning black. In point of fact, no Negro has a black complexion, but by comparison with other blonder stocks, he has come to be known as a "black man." Unfortunately *black* in the English language is a word having a preponderance of sinister connotations: the outlook is black, blackball, blackguard, black-hearted, black death, blacklist, blackmail, Black Hand. In his novel *Moby Dick,* Herman Melville considers at length the remarkably morbid connotations of black and the remarkably virtuous connotations of white.

Nor is the ominous flavor of black confined to the English language. A cross-cultural study reveals that the semantic significance of black is more or less universally the same. Among certain Siberian tribes, members of a privileged clan call themselves "white bones," and refer to all others as "black bones." Even among Uganda Negroes there is some evidence for a white god at the apex of the theocratic hierarchy; certain it is that a white cloth, signifying purity, is used to ward off evil spirits and disease.

There is thus an implied value-judgment in the very concept of *white*   15 *race* and *black race.* One might also study the numerous unpleasant connotations of *yellow,* and their possible bearing on our conception of the people of the Orient.

Such reasoning should not be carried too far, since there are undoubtedly, in various contexts, pleasant associations with both black and yellow. Black velvet is agreeable, so too are chocolate and coffee. Yellow tulips are well liked; the sun and moon are radiantly yellow. Yet it is true that "color" words are used with chauvinistic overtones more than most people realize. There is certainly condescension indicated in many familiar phrases: dark as a nigger's pocket, darktown strutters, white hope (a term originated when a white contender was fought against the Negro heavyweight champion, Jack Johnson), the white man's burden, the yellow peril, black boy. Scores of everyday phrases are stamped with the flavor of prejudice, whether the user knows it or not.

We spoke of the fact that even the most proper and sedate labels for minority groups sometimes seem to exude a negative flavor. In many contexts and situations the very terms *French-Canadian, Mexican,* or *Jew,* correct and nonmalicious though they are, sound a bit opprobrious. The reason is that they are labels of social deviants. Especially in a culture where uniformity is prized, the name of *any* deviant carries with it *ipso facto* a negative value-judgment. Words like *insane, alcoholic, pervert* are presumably neutral designations of a human condition, but they are more: they are finger-pointing at a deviance. Minority groups are deviants, and for this reason, from the very outset, the most innocent labels in many situations imply a shading of disrepute. When we wish to highlight the deviance and denigrate it still further we use words of a higher emotional key: crackpot, soak, pansy, greaser, Okie, nigger, harp, kike.

Members of minority groups are often understandably sensitive to names given them. Not only do they object to deliberately insulting epithets, but sometimes see evil intent where none exists. Often the word Negro is spelled with a small *n*, occasionally as a studied insult, more often from ignorance. (The term is not cognate with white, which is not capitalized, but rather with Caucasian, which is.) Terms like "mulatto" or "octoroon" cause hard feeling because of the condescension with which they have often been used in the past. Sex differentiations are objectionable, since they seem doubly to emphasize ethnic difference: why speak of Jewess and not of Protestantess, or of Negress and not of whitess? Similar overemphasis is implied in the terms like Chinaman or Scotchman; why not American man? Grounds for misunderstanding lie in the fact that minority group members are sensitive to such shadings, while majority members may employ them unthinkingly.

THE COMMUNIST LABEL

Until we label an out-group it does not clearly exist in our minds. Take the curiously vague situation that we often meet when a person wishes to locate responsibility on the shoulders of some out-group whose nature he cannot specify. In such a case he usually employs the pronoun "they" without an antecedent. "Why don't they make these sidewalks wider?" "I hear they are going to build a factory in this town and hire a lot of foreigners." "I won't pay this tax bill; they can just whistle for their money." If asked "who?" the speaker is likely to grow confused and embarrassed. The common use of the orphaned pronoun *they* teaches us that people often want and need to designate out-groups (usually for the purpose of venting hostility) even when they have no clear conception of the out-group in question. And so long as the target of wrath remains vague and ill-defined specific prejudice cannot crystallize around it. To have enemies we need labels.

Until relatively recently [late 1940s]—strange as it may seem—there   20
was no agreed-upon symbol for *communist*. The word, of course, existed but it had no special emotional connotation, and did not designate a public enemy. Even when, after World War I, there was a growing feeling of economic and social menace in this country, there was no agreement as to the actual source of the menace.

A content analysis of the Boston *Herald* for the year 1920 turned up the following list of labels. Each was used in a context implying some threat. Hysteria had overspread the country, as it did after World War II. Someone must be responsible for the postwar malaise, rising prices, uncertainty. There must be a villain. But in 1920 the villain was impartially designated by reporters and editorial writers with the following symbols:

> alien, agitator, anarchist, apostle of bomb and torch, Bolshevik, communist, communist laborite, conspirator, emissary of false promise, extremist, foreigner, hyphenated-American, incendiary, IWW, parlor anarchist, parlor pink, parlor socialist, plotter, radical, red, revolutionary, Russian agitator, socialist, Soviet, syndicalist, traitor, undesirable.

From this excited array we note that the *need* for an enemy (someone to serve as a focus for discontent and jitters) was considerably more apparent than the precise *identity* of the enemy. At any rate, there was no clearly agreed upon label. Perhaps partly for this reason the hysteria abated. Since no clear category of "communism" existed there was no true focus for the hostility.

But following World War II this collection of vaguely interchangeable labels became fewer in number and more commonly agreed upon. The out-group menace came to be designated almost always as *communist* or *red*. In 1920 the threat, lacking a clear label, was vague; after 1945 both symbol and thing became more definite. Not that people knew precisely what they meant when they said "communist," but with the aid of the term they were at least able to point consistently to *something* that inspired fear. The term developed the power of signifying menace and led to various repressive measures against anyone to whom the label was rightly or wrongly attached.

Logically, the label should apply to specifiable defining attributes, such as members of the Communist Party, or people whose allegiance is with the Russian system, or followers, historically, of Karl Marx. But the label came in for far more extensive use.

What seems to have happened is approximately as follows. Having   25
suffered through a period of war and being acutely aware of devastating revolutions abroad, it is natural that most people should be upset, dreading to lose their possessions, annoyed by high taxes, seeing customary moral and religious values threatened, and dreading worse disasters to come. Seeking an explanation for this unrest, a single identifiable enemy is wanted. It is not enough to designate "Russia" or some other distant land. Nor is it satisfactory to fix blame on "changing social conditions." What is needed is a human agent near at hand: someone in Washington, someone in our schools, in our factories, in our neighborhood. If we *feel* an immediate threat, we reason, there must be a near-lying danger. It is, we conclude, communism, not only in Russia but also in America, at our doorstep, in our government, in our churches, in our colleges, in our neighborhood.

Are we saying that hostility toward communism is prejudice? Not necessarily. There are certainly phases of the dispute wherein realistic social conflict is involved. American values (e.g., respect for the person) and totalitarian values as represented in Soviet practice are intrinsically at odds. A realistic opposition in some form will occur. Prejudice enters only when the defining attributes of *communist* grow imprecise, when anyone who favors any form of social change is called a communist. People who fear social change are the ones most likely to affix the label to any persons or practices that seem to them threatening.

For them the category is undifferentiated. It includes books, movies, preachers, teachers who utter what for them are uncongenial thoughts. If evil befalls—perhaps forest fires or a factory explosion—it is due to communist saboteurs. The category becomes monopolistic, covering almost anything that is uncongenial. On the floor of the House of Representatives in 1946, Representative Rankin called James Roosevelt a communist. Congressman Outland replied with psychological acumen, "Apparently everyone who disagrees with Mr. Rankin is a communist."

When differentiated thinking is at a low ebb—as it is in times of social crises—there is a magnification of two-valued logic. Things are perceived as either inside or outside a moral order. What is outside is likely to be called communist. Correspondingly—and here is where damage is done—whatever is called communist (however erroneously) is immediately cast outside the moral order.

This associative mechanism places enormous power in the hands of a demagogue. For several years Senator McCarthy managed to discredit many citizens who thought differently from himself by the simple device of calling them communist. Few people were able to see through this trick and many reputations were ruined. But the famous senator has no monopoly on the device. As reported in the Boston *Herald:* on November 1, 1946, Representative Joseph Martin, Republican leader in the House, ended his election campaign against his Democratic opponent by saying, "The people will vote tomorrow between chaos, confusion, bankruptcy, state socialism or communism, and the preservation of our American life, with all its freedom and its opportunities." Such an array of emotional labels placed his opponent outside the accepted moral order. Martin was re-elected. . . .

Not everyone, of course, is taken in. Demagogy, when it goes too far, meets with ridicule. Elizabeth Dilling's book, *The Red Network,* was so exaggerated in its two-valued logic that it was shrugged off by many people with a smile. One reader remarked, "Apparently if you step off the sidewalk with your left foot you're a communist." But it is not easy in times of social strain and hysteria to keep one's balance, and to resist the tendency of a verbal symbol to manufacture large and fanciful categories of prejudiced thinking.

30

VERBAL REALISM AND SYMBOL PHOBIA

Most individuals rebel at being labeled, especially if the label is uncomplimentary. Very few are willing to be called *fascistic, socialistic,* or *anti-Semitic.* Unsavory labels may apply to others; but not to us.

An illustration of the craving that people have to attach favorable symbols to themselves is seen in the community where white people banded together to force out a Negro family that had moved in. They called themselves "Neighborly Endeavor" and chose as their motto the Golden Rule. One of the first acts of this symbol-sanctified band was to sue the man who sold property to Negroes. They then flooded the house which another Negro couple planned to occupy. Such were the acts performed under the banner of the Golden Rule.

Studies made by Stagner and Hartmann show that a person's political attitudes may in fact entitle him to be called a fascist or a socialist, and yet he will emphatically repudiate the unsavory label, and fail to endorse any movement or candidate that overtly accepts them. In short, there is a *symbol phobia* that corresponds to *symbol realism.* We are more inclined to the former when we ourselves are concerned, though we are much less critical when epithets of "fascist," "communist," "blind man," "school marm" are applied to others.

When symbols provoke strong emotions they are sometimes regarded no longer as symbols, but as actual things. The expressions "son of a bitch" and "liar" are in our culture frequently regarded as "fighting words." Softer and more subtle expressions of contempt may be accepted. But in these particular cases, the epithet itself must be "taken back." We certainly do not change our opponent's attitude by making him take back a word, but it seems somehow important that the word itself be eradicated.

Such verbal realism may reach extreme length.   35

> The City Council of Cambridge, Massachusetts, unanimously passed a resolution (December, 1939) making it illegal "to possess, harbor, sequester, introduce or transport, within the city limits, any book, map, magazine, newspaper, pamphlet, handbill, or circular containing the words Lenin or Leningrad."

Such naiveté in confusing language with reality is hard to comprehend unless we recall that word-magic plays an appreciable part in human thinking. The following examples, like the one preceding, are taken from Hayakawa.

> The Malagasy soldier must eschew kidneys, because in the Malagasy language the word for kidney is the same as that for "shot"; so shot he would certainly be if he ate a kidney.
>
> In May, 1937, a state senator of New York bitterly opposed a bill for the control of syphilis because "the innocence of children might be corrupted by a widespread use of the term. . . . This particular word creates a shudder in every decent woman and decent man."

This tendency to reify words underscores the close cohesion that exists between category and symbol. Just the mention of "communist," "Negro," "Jew," "England," "Democrats," will send some people into a panic of fear or a frenzy of anger. Who can say whether it is the word or the thing that annoys them? The label is an intrinsic part of any monopolistic category. Hence to liberate a person from ethnic or political prejudice it is necessary at the same time to liberate him from *word fetishism*. This fact is well known to students of general semantics who tell us that prejudice is due in large part to verbal realism and to symbol phobia. Therefore any program for the reduction of prejudice must include a large measure of semantic therapy.

THINKING CRITICALLY ABOUT THE READING

1. What is Allport's thesis, and where is it stated? (Glossary: *Thesis*)

2. In paragraph 2, why do you think Allport uses a metaphorical image—grains of sand—to represent people? (Glossary: *Figurative Language*) How does this metaphor help him present his point?

3. In paragraph 3, Allport uses Irving Lee's story of a blind man who was unable to get a job as an example of how powerful certain labels can be. (Glossary: *Examples*) What other quotations does he use as examples? What is the purpose of each one? Do you think they are effective? Why or why not?

4. Nouns, or names, provide an essential service in making categorization possible. Yet according to Allport, nouns are also words that "cut slices." What does he mean by that term? What is inherently unfair about nouns?

5. What are "labels of primary potency" (4)? Why does Allport equate them with "shrieking sirens"? Why are such labels important to his essay?

6. What does the experiment with the nonlabeled and labeled photos demonstrate? How do labels affect the way the mind perceives reality?

7. What does Allport mean by the "orphaned pronoun *they*" (19)? Why is it used so often in conversation?

8. What does Allport mean by *symbol phobia* (33)? How does this concept illustrate the unfairness of labeling others?

9. Allport wrote "The Language of Prejudice" in the early 1950s. Does this help explain why he devotes many paragraphs to the evolution of the label *communist*? What are the connotations of the word *communist* today? (Glossary: *Connotation/Denotation*)

LANGUAGE IN ACTION

Many people and organizations try to promote tolerance and tone down prejudice by suggesting that certain words and phrases be substituted for less respectful or insensitive ones. Consider the following examples that have been put forth in recent years.

Insensitive Words and Phrases	Respectful Alternatives
handicap	physical disability
fireman, policeman, postman	firefighter, police officer, letter carrier
illegal alien	undocumented immigrant
anti-abortion	pro-life
pro-abortion	pro-choice
unemployed	nonwaged
Indian	Native American or First Nations
uneducated	lacking formal education
Jew down	negotiate
an autistic person	a person who has autism
half-breed	multi-ethnic
blacklisted	banned
stewardess	flight attendant
old people, elderly	seniors
girls	women
gifted children	advanced learners
wheelchair-bound	a person who uses a wheelchair
BC, AD	BCE, CE
deaf	hearing impaired
mental retardation	intellectual disability
ethnic minority	persons of color
native	inhabitant
underdeveloped country	developing country

In each case, what kind of intolerance or prejudice do you think the language switch is attempting to eliminate or at least minimize? Do you think it's possible to change people's attitudes by simply requiring language changes like the ones suggested above? Discuss why or why not.

WRITING SUGGESTIONS

1. Make an extensive list of the labels that have been or could be applied to you at this time. Write an essay in which you discuss the labels that you find "truly offensive," those you can "live with," and those that you "like to be associated with." Explain your reasons for putting particular labels in each of these categories.

2. Allport states, "Especially in a culture where uniformity is prized, the name of *any* deviant carries with it *ipso facto* a negative value-judgment" (17). This was written in the 1950s. Since then, the turbulent 1960s, the political correctness movement of the 1980s and 1990s and the years since the millennium, and

the mainstreaming of "alternative" cultures have all attempted to persuade people to accept differences and be more tolerant. Write an essay in which you consider Allport's statement today. Which labels that identify someone as different still carry a negative association? Have the social movements of the past decades changed in a fundamental way how we think about others? Do you think there is more acceptance of nonconformity today, or is a nonconformist or member of a minority still subjected to negative, though perhaps more subtle, labeling? Support your conclusions with examples from your own experience and from the depiction of current events in the popular media.

3. Allport wrote *The Nature of Prejudice* before the civil rights movement began in earnest, though he did live to see it grow and reach its climax at the famous 1963 march on Washington. (See Martin Luther King Jr.'s celebrated "I Have a Dream" speech on pp. 275–278.) Obviously, part of the civil rights movement was in the arena of language, and its leaders often used impressive rhetoric to confront the language of prejudice. Write an essay in which you analyze how the kinds of labels and symbols identified by Allport were used in speeches and documents both to justify the continuation of segregation and prejudice and to decry it. How did the leaders of the civil rights movement use language to their advantage? To what emotions or ideas did the language of the opposition appeal? The Internet and your library have vast amounts of information about the movement's genesis and history, so it may be difficult at first to decide on a specific area of research. Start by looking at how language was used by both sides in the battle over civil rights.

The Meanings of a Word*

GLORIA NAYLOR

Novelist and essayist Gloria Naylor was born in New York City in 1950. She worked as a missionary for the Jehovah's Witnesses from 1967 to 1975 and then as a telephone operator until 1981, the year she graduated from Brooklyn College. Naylor later earned a master's degree in African American studies at Yale University. In her fiction, she explores the lives of African American women, drawing freely from her own experiences and those of her extended family. As Naylor has stated, "I wanted to become a writer because I felt that my presence as a black woman and my perspective as a woman in general had been underrepresented in American literature." She received the American Book Award for First Fiction for *The Women of Brewster Place* (1982), a novel that was later adapted for television. This success was followed by *Linden Hills* (1985), *Mama Day* (1988), *Bailey's Cafe* (1993), and *The Men of Brewster Place* (1998). Her most recent novel is *1996* (2005), a book that has been described as a "fictionalized memoir." Naylor's short fiction and essays have appeared widely, and she has also edited *Children of the Night: Best Short Stories by Black Writers, 1967 to the Present* (1995).

More than any other form of prejudiced language, racial slurs are intended to wound and shame. In the following essay, which first appeared in the *New York Times* in 1986, Naylor remembers a time when a third-grade classmate called her a nigger. By examining the ways in which words can take on meaning depending on who uses them and to what purpose, Naylor concludes that "words themselves are innocuous; it is the consensus that gives them true power."

WRITING TO DISCOVER: *Have you or someone you know ever been called a derogatory name? Write about how this made you feel.*

Language is the subject. It is the written form with which I've managed to keep the wolf away from the door and, in diaries, to keep my sanity. In spite of this, I consider the written word inferior to the spoken, and much of the frustration experienced by novelists is the awareness that whatever we manage to capture in even the most transcendent passages falls far short of the richness of life. Dialogue achieves its power in the dynamics of a fleeting moment of sight, sound, smell, and touch.

I'm not going to enter the debate here about whether it is language that shapes reality or vice versa. That battle is doomed to be waged whenever we seek intermittent reprieve from the chicken and egg dispute. I will simply

---

* Note from Gloria Naylor: The author wants it understood that the use of the word "nigger" is reprehensible in today's society. This essay speaks to a specific time and place when that word was utilized to empower African Americans; today it is used to degrade them even if spoken from their own mouths.

take the position that the spoken word, like the written word, amounts to a nonsensical arrangement of sounds or letters without a consensus that assigns "meaning." And building from the meanings of what we hear, we order reality. Words themselves are innocuous; it is the consensus that gives them true power.

I remember the first time I heard the word *nigger*. In my third-grade class, our math tests were being passed down the rows, and as I handed the papers to a little boy in back of me, I remarked that once again he had received a much lower mark than I did. He snatched his test from me and spit out that word. Had he called me a nymphomaniac or a necrophiliac, I couldn't have been more puzzled. I didn't know what a nigger was, but I know that whatever it meant, it was something he shouldn't have called me. This was verified when I raised my hand, and in a loud voice repeated what he had said and watched the teacher scold him for using a "bad" word. I was later to go home and ask the inevitable question that every black parent must face — "Mommy, what does *nigger* mean?"

And what exactly did it mean? Thinking back, I realize that this could not have been the first time the word was used in my presence. I was part of a large extended family that had migrated from the rural South after World War II and formed a close-knit network that gravitated around my maternal grandparents. Their ground-floor apartment in one of the buildings they owned in Harlem was a weekend mecca for my immediate family, along with countless aunts, uncles, and cousins who brought along assorted friends. It was a bustling and open house with assorted neighbors and tenants popping in and out to exchange bits of gossip, pick up an old quarrel, or referee the ongoing checkers game in which my grandmother cheated shamelessly. They were all there to let down their hair and put up their feet after a week of labor in the factories, laundries, and shipyards of New York.

Amid the clamor, which could reach deafening proportions—two or three conversations going on simultaneously, punctuated by the sound of a baby's crying somewhere in the back rooms or out on the street—there was still a rigid set of rules about what was said and how. Older children were sent out of the living room when it was time to get into the juicy details about "you-know-who" up on the third floor who had gone and gotten herself "p-r-e-g-n-a-n-t!" But my parents, knowing that I could spell well beyond my years, always demanded that I follow the others out to play. Beyond sexual misconduct and death, everything else was considered harmless for our young ears. And so among the anecdotes of the triumphs and disappointments in the various workings of their lives, the word *nigger* was used in my presence, but it was set within contexts and inflections that caused it to register in my mind as something else.

> **Words themselves are innocuous; it is the consensus that gives them true power.**

In the singular, the word was always applied to a man who had distinguished himself in some situation that brought their approval for his strength, intelligence, or drive:

"Did Johnny *really* do that?"

"I'm telling you, that nigger pulled in $6,000 of overtime last year. Said he got enough for a down payment on a house."

When used with a possessive adjective by a woman—"my nigger"—it became a term of endearment for her husband or boyfriend. But it could be more than just a term applied to a man. In their mouths it became the pure essence of manhood—a disembodied force that channeled their past history of struggle and present survival against the odds into a victorious statement of being: "Yeah, that old foreman found out quick enough—you don't mess with a nigger."

In the plural, it became a description of some group within the community that had overstepped the bounds of decency as my family defined it. Parents who neglected their children, a drunken couple who fought in public, people who simply refused to look for work, those with excessively dirty mouths or unkempt households were all "trifling niggers." This particular circle could forgive hard times, unemployment, the occasional bout of depression—they had gone through all of that themselves—but the unforgivable sin was a lack of self-respect.

A woman could never be a "nigger" in the singular, with its connotation of confirming worth. The noun *girl* was its closest equivalent in that sense, but only when used in direct address and regardless of the gender doing the addressing. *Girl* was a token of respect for a woman. The one-syllable word was drawn out to sound like three in recognition of the extra ounce of wit, nerve, or daring that the woman had shown in the situation under discussion.

"G-i-r-l, stop. You mean you said that to his face?"

But if the word was used in a third-person reference or shortened so that it almost snapped out of the mouth, it always involved some element of communal disapproval. And age became an important factor in these exchanges. It was only between individuals of the same generation, or from any older person to a younger (but never the other way around), that *girl* would be considered a compliment.

I don't agree with the argument that use of the word *nigger* at this social stratum of the black community was an internalization of racism. The dynamics were the exact opposite: the people in my grandmother's living room took a word that whites used to signify worthlessness or degradation and rendered it impotent. Gathering there together, they transformed *nigger* to signify the varied and complex human beings they knew themselves to be. If the word was to disappear totally from the mouths of even the most liberal of white society, no one in that room was naive enough to believe it would disappear from white minds. Meeting the word head-on, they proved it had absolutely nothing to do with the way they were determined to live their lives.

So there must have been dozens of times that *nigger* was spoken in front of me before I reached the third grade. But I didn't "hear" it until it was said by a small pair of lips that had already learned it could be a way to humiliate me. That was the word I went home and asked my mother about.

And since she knew that I had to grow up in America, she took me in her lap and explained.

THINKING CRITICALLY ABOUT THE READING

1. How, according to Naylor, do words get meanings?

2. Why does the boy sitting behind Naylor call her a nigger (3)? Why is she confused by this name-calling?

3. When Naylor was growing up, what two meanings did the word *girl* convey? How were those meanings defined by the speaker? In what way was age an important factor in the correct uses of *girl*?

4. Why does Naylor disagree with the notion that the use of the word *nigger* within her community was an internalization of racism?

5. Naylor begins her essay with an abstract discussion about how words derive their meaning and power. How does this introduction tie in with her anecdote and discussion of the word *nigger*? (Glossary: *Abstract/Concrete*) Why is the introduction vital to the overall message of her essay?

6. Naylor says she must have heard the word *nigger* many times while she was growing up; yet she "heard" it for the first time when she was in the third grade (15). How does she explain this seeming contradiction? (Glossary: *Paradox*)

7. Define what *nigger* means to Naylor in the context of her family. (Glossary: *Definition*) Why do you suppose she offers so little in the way of definition of her classmate's use of the word?

8. How would you characterize Naylor's tone in her essay? (Glossary: *Tone*) Is she angry, objective, cynical, or something else? Cite examples of her diction to support your answer. (Glossary: *Diction*)

LANGUAGE IN ACTION

Naylor's essay discusses how those in her community used the word *nigger* for their own purposes and "rendered it impotent" (14). Nevertheless, the word still has a lot of negative power, as revealed in the following 1995 essay by Keith Woods, which was published by the Poynter Institute for Media Studies.

The consensus to which Naylor refers—here represented by Mark Fuhrman—gives the word that power, making news organizations report it in euphemisms or as a deleted expletive. Mark Fuhrman was a Los Angeles homicide detective whose racial profiling and negative attitude toward African Americans made him one of the most controversial figures in the O.J. Simpson trial. In preparation for class discussion, think about your position on the following questions: What should be done about the word *nigger*? Should African Americans use it and try to "render it impotent" by creating their own prevailing context for it? Should the word be suppressed, forced into the fringes of racist thought, and represented in euphemisms? Or is there another way to address the word's negative power?

AN ESSAY ON A WICKEDLY POWERFUL WORD

When I heard Mark Fuhrman's voice saying the word "nigger," I heard a lynch mob. I saw the grim and gleeful faces of murderous white men. I felt the coarse, hairy rope. I smelled the sap of the hangin' tree and saw Billie Holiday's "strange fruit" dangling from its strongest limb.

What a wickedly powerful word, nigger. So many other slurs could have slithered from Fuhrman's tongue and revealed his racism without provoking those images.

Jiggaboo.

Spade.

Coon.

I hear the hatred in those words, but I don't feel the fire's heat the way I do when this white former policeman says nigger. Somewhere in that visceral reflex is the reason news organizations had to use that word this time around.

Somewhere in the sting of seeing it, hearing it, feeling it is the reason they should think hard before using it the next time.

In context, there is no other way to report what Mark Furhman said. "Racial epithet" doesn't quite get it, does it? "Spearchucker" is a racial epithet, but it doesn't make you see burnt crosses and white sheets. Just rednecks.

The "n-word" sounds silly, childish, something you'd say when you don't want your 3-year-old to know what you're talking about. And "n----?" What does that accomplish other than to allow newspapers the dubious out of saying, "Well, it's actually the reader who's saying nigger, not us."

When Mark Fuhrman or any person armed with a club or a gun or a bat or a judicial robe or a teaching certificate or any measure of power says "nigger," it's more than an insult. It summons all the historic and modern-day violence that is packed into those six letters.

Nigger is "Know your place."

Nigger is, "I am better than you."

Nigger is, "I can frame you or flunk you or beat you or kill you because . . .".

Nigger is, "I own you."

You just can't convey that definition with n-dash-dash-dash-dash-dash. You can't communicate it with bleeps or blurbs or euphemisms. The problem is that sometimes the only way to do your job as a journalist is to say or write the word that furthers the mission of racists.

I'd like to believe that there's some lessening of harm every time the word sees the light of day. I once fantasized about a day when a group of black rappers or comedians would appropriate the white sheets and hoods of the KKK and go gallivanting across MTV or HBO and forever render that image so utterly ridiculous that no self-respecting racist would ever wear it again.

But then, Richard Pryor tried to appropriate nigger, didn't he? Took it right from the white folks and turned it into a career before he thought better of it. So did the rappers NWA ("Niggas With Attitudes"). So did my friends on the streets of New Orleans. So has a generation of young black people today.

Still, the definition didn't change.

Dick Gregory tried it. In the dedication of his autobiography, "Nigger," the comedian-turned-activist wrote: "Dear Momma—Wherever you are, if ever you hear the word "nigger" again, remember they are advertising my book."

He wrote that 31 years ago, but if Lucille Gregory were here to hear Mark Fuhrman, she'd surely know he wasn't talking about her son's book. The definition doesn't change. It doesn't hurt any less after three decades. No less after three centuries.

It's the same word, spiked with the same poison, delivering the same message of inferiority, degradation, hatred, and shame. The same word whether it's Fuhrman saying it or Huck Finn or Def Comedy Jam or Snoop Doggy Dogg or my old friends from Touro Street (because, they do call themselves nigger, you know).

It hurts every time it's in the paper or on the air or in the street. Every time. Sometimes there's no way around using it in the media, but only sometimes.

Could there come a day when you see it or read it or hear it from the homeboys so much that you hardly notice? When your eyebrow doesn't arch as often or your jaw suddenly drop when the six o'clock anchor plops the word onto your living room coffee table?

Maybe. And you might even say, that day, "Oh, they're just talking about niggers again."

Are we better off then?

WRITING SUGGESTIONS

1. Write an essay in which you describe the process through which you became aware of prejudice, either toward yourself or toward another person or group of people. Did a specific event spark your awareness, such as that detailed in your Writing to Discover entry? Or did you become aware of prejudice in a more gradual way? Did you learn about prejudice primarily from your peers, your parents, or someone else? How did your new awareness affect you? How have your experiences shaped the way you think and feel about prejudice today?

2. In addition to discussing the word *nigger*, Naylor talks about the use of *girl*, a word with far less negative baggage but one that can still be offensive when used in an inappropriate context. Write an essay in which you discuss your use of a contextually sensitive word. What is its strict definition? How do you use it? In what context(s) might its use be inappropriate? Why is the word used in different ways?

"FOBs" vs. "Twinkies": The New Discrimination Is Intraracial

GRACE HSIANG

Grace Hsiang was born in San Jose, California, in 1986. In 2008 she graduated with a double major in international studies and literary journalism from the University of California, Irvine. While in college, she was a staff writer for *Jaded Magazine* and on the editorial board for *Kiosk*, a web-based magazine. Hsiang has been published in the following magazines and news services: *Alternet, Pacific News Service/New America Media, WWS Magazine, Jaded Magazine, ISM Magazine,* and *13 Minutes.* Currently, Hsiang is the director of marketing for Project by Project, a national volunteer organization of social entrepreneurs focusing on issues relating to the Asian American community.

The following selection, written when Hsiang was working as an intern for *Pacific News Service,* first appeared on April 15, 2005. When asked what inspired her to write about her community and its struggles, she wrote the following: "I think the Asian American community has made significant strides in the last century and has really carved out a presence. We are in films, fashion, and politics, and I'm proud of all the strides we've made. However, there is still a long way to go in the name of equality, and before we blame the outside or the other, we must look internally for change. I think if we face the problems within our community first it will allow us to face those outside."

WRITING TO DISCOVER: *If you are a member of a minority group, what subgroups within your community do you recognize? What tensions between members of that group are you aware of, and how do those tensions make themselves felt? Write several paragraphs describing the tensions as you understand them as well as explaining why you think they exist.*

Today in my sociology class, the teacher asked the students to volunteer our own experiences with racism or ethnic harassment. I imagined the responses would once again feature the ongoing battle between white vs. minority. Instead, to my surprise, most of the students told of being discriminated against and marginalized by members of their own ethnic group.

In the Asian community, the slurs heard most often are not terms such as "Chink" or "Jap," but rather "FOB" ("Fresh Off the Boat") or "whitewashed" (too assimilated). When Asian Americans hit puberty, they seem to divide into two camps, each highly critical of the other.

Members of the first cling to their ethnic heritage. They tend to be exclusive in their friendships, often accepting only "true Asians." They believe relationships should remain within the community, and may even opt to speak their parents' native language over English in public.

342

Members of the second group reject as many aspects of Asian culture as possible and concentrate on being seen as American. They go out of their way to refuse to date within the community, embrace friends outside their ethnic circle, and even boast to others about how un-Asian they are.

"My coworker is Vietnamese," 19-year-old Carol Lieu remarked, 5 "but she will yell at you if you speak it to her and pretend that she doesn't understand."

Second-generation Asian Americans often face pressure from their parents, who believe that the privileges we are allowed in this country make us spoiled and ungrateful. Many of us very much want to belong to our parents' community, but we cannot completely embody one culture when we are living in another.

> **Many of us very much want to belong to our parents' community, but we cannot completely embody one culture when we are living in another.**

The pressures we face force many of us to feel we must choose one culture over another. We can either cling to our parent's ideology or rebel against it and try to be "American."

The problems start when those who have made one choice discriminate against those who have made the other. I've heard ethnocentric Asians speak with disgust about Asians who wear Abercrombie and Fitch (which is viewed as the ultimate "white" brand), or make fun of those who don't know their parents' language.

This perspective even made it into the recent hit movie *Harold and Kumar Go to White Castle*. John Cho's character complains about a girl who is pursuing him despite his lack of interest: She "rambles on about her East Asian Students Club or whatever. Then I have to actually pretend that I give a s--t or she calls me a Twinkie . . . yellow on the outside, white on the inside."

"People act disappointed that I can't speak Japanese fluently," a stu- 10 dent of Mexican and Japanese ancestry in my sociology class complained this morning. "I don't see anyone giving me credit for speaking fluent Gaelic."

On the other side, second-generation kids who refuse to assimilate are called FOBs. The cars they drive are derided as "Rice Rockets," and their pastimes and ways of dressing are stereotyped as exclusively Asian. "We live in America," one freshman political science major recalls more assimilated friends telling her. "Don't bring your culture here."

Not all young Asian Americans buy into the dichotomy between "FOBs" and "Twinkies." Many, like me, understand the term "Asian American" in all its complexity, and embrace all sides of our identity. Rather than identifying with one culture or another, my friends and I accept both.

You should identify with your heritage "because that's who you are," Ricky Kim, founder of the online journal *Evil Monito,* has said. "But don't be ignorant of the culture you grew up in—that's being ungrateful."

Asian Americans grow up experiencing enough difficulties living in a predominantly white country with the face of a foreigner. The gap between races is wide enough without drawing lines within ethnicities and communities. We can avoid this internal discrimination simply by recognizing that we are of two cultures—and that in itself creates a new culture that should be fully celebrated.

THINKING CRITICALLY ABOUT THE READING

1. What surprised Hsiang when students in her class were asked to discuss their "own experiences with racism and ethnic harassment" (1)? Why did it surprise her?
2. Hsiang writes that the split in the Asian community arises when children "hit puberty" (2). Why do you suppose the split occurs at this stage of development?
3. What pressures from their parents do Asian students often face, according to Hsiang? How does this relate to her topic?
4. In "What's So Bad about Hate?" (pp. 307–323), writer Andrew Sullivan discusses other varieties of "intragroup" prejudice and concludes: "[I]ts intensity comes in part, one senses, from the pain of being excluded for so long, of anger long restrained bubbling up and directing itself more aggressively toward an alleged traitor than an alleged enemy. It is the hate of the hated." Do you think Hsiang would agree? If not, in what way(s) might she take issue with Sullivan's conclusion?
5. Does Hsiang offer any solutions to the problem she identifies? Explain.

LANGUAGE IN ACTION

Grace Hsiang discusses the growing "internal discrimination" within the Asian American community. She recognizes that "Asian Americans grow up experiencing enough difficulties living in a predominantly white country with the face of a foreigner." Torn between two cultures, the children of Asian immigrant parents experience problems with self-esteem and identity. Freelance writer and editor Caroline Hwang, the daughter of Korean immigrants, knows all too well that "children of immigrants are living paradoxes." Consider her story as a case in point.

> The moment I walked into the dry-cleaning store, I knew the woman behind the counter was from Korea, like my parents. To show her that we shared a heritage, and possibly get a fellow countryman's discount, I tilted my head forward, in shy imitation of a traditional bow.
>
> "Name?" she asked, not noticing my attempted obeisance.
>
> "Hwang," I answered.
>
> "Hwang? Are you Chinese?"
>
> Her question caught me off-guard. I was used to hearing such queries from non-Asians who think Asians all look alike, but never from one of my own people. Of course, the only Koreans I knew were

my parents and their friends, people who've never asked me where I came from, since they knew better than I.

I ransacked my mind for the Korean words that would tell her who I was. It's always struck me as funny (in a mirthless sort of way) that I can more readily say "I am Korean" in Spanish, German, and even Latin than I can in the language of my ancestry. In the end, I told her in English.

The dry-cleaning woman squinted as though trying to see past the glare of my strangeness, repeating my surname under her breath. "Oh, *Fxuang*," she said, doubling over with laughter. "You don't know how to speak your name."

I flinched. Perhaps I was particularly sensitive at the time, having just dropped out of graduate school. I had torn up my map for the future, the one that said not only where I was going but who I was. My sense of identity was already disintegrating.

When I got home, I called my parents to ask why they had never bothered to correct me. "Big deal," my mother said, sounding more flippant than I knew she intended. (Like many people who learn English in a classroom, she uses idioms that don't always fit the occasion.) "So what if you can't pronounce your name? You are American," she said.

Though I didn't challenge her explanation, it left me unsatisfied. The fact is, my cultural identity is hardly that clear-cut.

What do you think of the woman behind the counter at the dry-cleaning store? Did you find anything humorous about Caroline Hwang's predicament? In what ways does Hwang's story illustrate what Hsiang is writing about in her article? Who's the "Twinkie" and who's the "FOB"? Explain.

WRITING SUGGESTIONS

1. Hsiang's essay is important because it sheds light on a topic that is not often discussed: intraracial discrimination. Write an essay in which you express your own perspective on intraracial discrimination. Depending on your interests and experiences, you might focus on Arab American, African American, Hispanic American, or other communities within the United States. In writing your essay, consider the following questions: What role does skin color play in the discrimination exercised within a minority community? What role do different geographical origins, different levels/kinds of education, or other factors play?

2. Hsiang's essay has generated a great deal of discussion on the Web and elsewhere, especially among those who were not aware of intraracial discrimination. Write an essay based on Hsiang's in which you explore the ramifications of any intraracial discrimination you have experienced personally or have been aware of in your community. How does prejudice affect the self-esteem of the individuals involved? How does it affect the cohesion of the minority group? Does such prejudice reflect on the way the minority group as a whole is seen by the dominant culture?

Black Men and Public Space

BRENT STAPLES

Brent Staples is an important voice in American culture. He was born in 1951 in Chester, Pennsylvania, an industrial city southwest of Philadelphia. He studied at Widener University in Chester and the University of Chicago, where he earned his Ph.D. in psychology. Formerly a teacher, Staples began his newspaper career as a reporter for the *Chicago Sun-Times*. He later became a reviewer and editorial writer at the *New York Times*. Today he serves on the newspaper's editorial board and writes regularly for the Commentary section. His memoir *Parallel Time: Growing Up in Black and White* (1994) won the 1995 Anisfield-Wolff Award, also given to such notable African American writers as James Baldwin, Ralph Ellison, and Zora Neale Hurston.

"Black Men and Public Space" first appeared in 1986 in *Ms.* magazine as "Just Walk on By: A Black Man Ponders His Power to Alter Public Space." The revised version that we print here was published later the same year in *Harper's*. In the essay, Staples recounts his experiences moving through public spaces at night. After innocently scaring a woman one night, Staples writes, "It was in the echo of that terrified woman's footfalls that I first began to know the unwieldy inheritance I'd come into—the ability to alter public space in ugly ways." Since that time Staples has worked tirelessly to correct the stereotype of the "black experience" in America that is defined by poverty, violence, and crime. He believes that "black people's lives in this country are too varied to be reduced to a single term."

WRITING TO DISCOVER: *Reflect on what you know about body language. Are you aware, for example, of the messages that might be conveyed by a person's physical features, gestures, and use of space? Try observing some people around you, in your dormitory, in the school cafeteria, or at work in order to gain some appreciation of the messages that they may be sending that either support or contradict their verbal messages.*

My first victim was a woman—white, well dressed, probably in her late twenties. I came upon her late one evening on a deserted street in Hyde Park, a relatively affluent neighborhood in an otherwise mean, impoverished section of Chicago. As I swung onto the avenue behind her, there seemed to be a discreet, uninflammatory distance between us. Not so. She cast back a worried glance. To her, the youngish black man—a broad six feet two inches with a beard and billowing hair, both hands shoved into the pockets of a bulky military jacket—seemed menacingly close. After a few more quick glimpses, she picked up her pace and was soon running in earnest. Within seconds, she disappeared into a cross street.

That was more than a decade ago. I was twenty-two years old, a graduate student newly arrived at the University of Chicago. It was in the echo of that terrified woman's footfalls that I first began to know the unwieldy inheritance I'd come into—the ability to alter public space in ugly ways. It was clear that she thought herself the quarry of a mugger, a rapist, or worse. Suffering a bout of insomnia, however, I was stalking sleep, not defenseless wayfarers. As a softy who is scarcely able to take a knife to a raw chicken—let alone hold one to a person's throat—I was surprised, embarrassed, and dismayed all at once. Her flight made me feel like an accomplice in tyranny. It also made it clear that I was indistinguishable from the muggers who occasionally seeped into the area from the surrounding ghetto. The first encounter, and those that followed, signified that a vast, unnerving gulf lay between nighttime pedestrians—particularly women—and me. And I soon gathered that being perceived as dangerous is a hazard in itself. I only needed to turn a corner into a dicey situation, or crowd some frightened, armed person in a foyer somewhere, or make an errant move after being pulled over by a policeman. Where fear and weapons meet—and they often do in urban America—there is always the possibility of death.

In that first year, my first away from my hometown, I was to become thoroughly familiar with the language of fear. At dark, shadowy intersections, I could cross in front of a car stopped at a traffic light and elicit the *thunk, thunk, thunk, thunk* of the driver—black, white, male, or female—hammering down the door locks.

> **And I soon gathered that being perceived as dangerous is a hazard in itself.**

On less traveled streets after dark, I grew accustomed to but never comfortable with people crossing to the other side of the street rather than pass me. Then there were the standard unpleasantries with policemen, doormen, bouncers, cabdrivers, and others whose business it is to screen out troublesome individuals *before* there is any nastiness.

I moved to New York nearly two years ago and I have remained an avid night walker. In central Manhattan, the near-constant crowd cover minimizes tense one-on-one street encounters. Elsewhere—in SoHo, for example, where sidewalks are narrow and tightly spaced buildings shut out the sky—things can get very taut indeed.

After dark, on the warrenlike streets of Brooklyn where I live, I often 5 see women who fear the worst from me. They seem to have set their faces on neutral, and with their purse straps strung across their chests bandolier-style, they forge ahead as though bracing themselves against being tackled. I understand, of course, that the danger they perceive is not a hallucination. Women are particularly vulnerable to street violence, and young black males are drastically overrepresented among the perpetrators of that violence. Yet these truths are no solace against the kind of alienation that comes of being ever the suspect, a fearsome entity with whom pedestrians avoid making eye contact.

It is not altogether clear to me how I reached the ripe old age of twenty-two without being conscious of the lethality nighttime pedestrians attributed to me. Perhaps it was because in Chester, Pennsylvania, the small, angry industrial town where I came of age in the 1960s, I was scarcely noticeable against a backdrop of gang warfare, street knifings, and murders. I grew up one of the good boys, had perhaps a half-dozen fist-fights. In retrospect, my shyness of combat has clear sources.

As a boy, I saw countless tough guys locked away; I have since buried several, too. They were babies, really—a teenage cousin, a brother of twenty-two, a childhood friend in his mid-twenties—all gone down in episodes of bravado played out in the streets. I came to doubt the virtues of intimidation early on. I chose, perhaps unconsciously, to remain a shadow—timid, but a survivor.

The fearsomeness mistakenly attributed to me in public places often has a perilous flavor. The most frightening of these confusions occurred in the late 1970s and early 1980s, when I worked as a journalist in Chicago. One day, rushing into the office of a magazine I was writing for with a deadline story in hand, I was mistaken for a burglar. The office manager called security and, with an ad hoc posse, pursued me through the labyrinthine halls, nearly to my editor's door. I had no way of proving who I was. I could only move briskly toward the company of someone who knew me.

Another time I was on assignment for a local paper and killing time before an interview. I entered a jewelry store on the city's affluent Near North Side. The proprietor excused himself and returned with an enormous red Doberman pinscher straining at the end of a leash. She stood, the dog extended toward me, silent to my questions, her eyes bulging nearly out of her head. I took a cursory look around, nodded, and bade her good night.

Relatively speaking, however, I never fared as badly as another black   10
male journalist. He went to nearby Waukegan, Illinois, a couple of summers ago to work on a story about a murderer who was born there. Mistaking the reporter for the killer, police officers hauled him from his car at gunpoint and but for his press credentials would probably have tried to book him. Such episodes are not uncommon. Black men trade tales like this all the time.

Over the years, I learned to smother the rage I felt at so often being taken for a criminal. Not to do so would surely have led to madness. I now take precautions to make myself less threatening. I move about with care, particularly late in the evening. I give a wide berth to nervous people on subway platforms during the wee hours, particularly when I have exchanged business clothes for jeans. If I happen to be entering a building behind some people who appear skittish, I may walk by, letting them clear the lobby before I return, so as not to seem to be following them. I have been calm and extremely congenial on those rare occasions when I've been pulled over by the police.

And on late-evening constitutionals I employ what has proved to be an excellent tension-reducing measure: I whistle melodies from Beethoven and Vivaldi and the more popular classical composers. Even steely New Yorkers hunching toward nighttime destinations seem to relax, and occasionally they even join in the tune. Virtually everybody seems to sense that a mugger wouldn't be warbling bright, sunny selections from Vivaldi's *Four Seasons*.

THINKING CRITICALLY ABOUT THE READING

1. What is Staples's purpose in this essay? (Glossary: *Purpose*)

2. Staples's essay was first published in *Ms.* magazine, a publication that was very influential for young women, particularly in the beginning of the women's movement. Why is Staples's essay appropriate for that magazine? (Glossary: *Audience*)

3. Why is Staples's realization that he might cause fear in someone in a public space so surprising to him? What does he say about himself that explains the surprise he experienced?

4. Staples provides several examples to support his thesis that people have been conditioned to respond negatively to him in public spaces. (Glossary: *Evidence*) Recount several of those experiences. How effective were these examples in helping him make his case?

5. Staples never discusses his situation as an example of the racial prejudice that exists all around him. Would his essay be more or less effective if he made such statements? Explain.

6. Staples begins his essay with the words: "My first victim was a woman — white, well dressed, probably in her late twenties." What effect did this beginning have on you? (Glossary: *Beginnings and Endings*)

7. What is one of the solutions that Staples has come up with to help him deal with strangers in public spaces? Are his solutions a concession to the fact that he sees no hope of changing attitudes around him, or are they an effort to change peoples' attitudes?

LANGUAGE IN ACTION

Brent Staples's essay is in part about the concept of "territoriality" and the nonverbal messages it sends. Most of our feelings of territoriality remain unconscious until "our territory" is violated. How would you react to each of the following situations?

a. after a class has been meeting for at least three weeks, someone deliberately sat in a seat that you have been regularly occupying
b. in your library or snack bar, if someone moved your books or food and sat down while you were temporarily away
c. in an uncrowded library or classroom, someone deliberately sat right next to you
d. in your dorm room or at home, someone deliberately sat (in a chair, at a desk, etc.) that "belongs" to you or another family member

You may wish to compare your reactions with those of other members of your class. What conclusions can you draw about the way people regard invasions of their personal space?

WRITING SUGGESTIONS

1. Each of us makes an impression on those around us, either in public spaces or in more intimate surroundings. Each of us also has a more or less sensitive appreciation of the impressions we create on those around us. Describe the impression that you think you create in presenting yourself. Draw on examples of situations over time and in different settings that support the major ideas you are trying to present in your writing.

2. Write an essay that describes the various stereotypes that are created about students. What do you think of your fellow students? How do you think they regard you? How do students see themselves as a group? How does their body language reflect the way they see themselves? Do you think that most students see themselves as others do? Are the stereotypes that are applied to students fair in your judgment?

The "F Word"

FIROOZEH DUMAS

Firoozeh Dumas was born in Abadan, Iran, in 1965. When she was seven, she and her family moved to Whittier, California. Two years later, they moved back to Iran, living this time in Ahvaz and Tehran, only to return to Southern California after several years. Dumas studied at the University of California, Berkeley, where she met and, after graduation, married François Dumas, a Frenchman. In 2001, she started writing her memoir about life in Iran and the United States as a way of preserving this family history and culture for her children. *Funny in Farsi: A Memoir of Growing Up Iranian in America* was published in 2003. She builds on her first book in *Laughing Without an Accent: Adventures of an Iranian American at Home and Abroad* (2008), a collection of tender and humorous vignettes about the melding of cultures and the struggles of immigrants living in the United States.

In "The 'F Word,'" a chapter from *Funny in Farsi*, Dumas talks about the troubles she and her Iranian family and friends have had with their "identifiably 'ethnic' name[s]." She witnessed the prejudice toward immigrants that came about as a result of the Iranian hostage crisis (1979–1981) and writes about the difficulties she had getting a job interview as a college graduate with an Iranian name.

WRITING TO DISCOVER: *Do you or any of your friends have names that are identifiably ethnic? For example, are the names clearly Hispanic, Jewish, Arabic, Asian, German, Italian, Greek, or some other ethnicity? How do people react to you when they hear your family name? Describe.*

My cousin's name, Farbod, means "Greatness." When he moved to America, all the kids called him "Farthead." My brother Farshid ("He Who Enlightens") became "Fartshit." The name of my friend Neggar means "Beloved," although it can be more accurately translated as "She Whose Name Almost Incites Riots." Her brother Arash ("Giver") initially couldn't understand why every time he'd say his name, people would laugh and ask him if it itched.

All of us immigrants knew that moving to America would be fraught with challenges, but none of us thought that our names would be such an obstacle. How could our parents have ever imagined that someday we would end up in a country where monosyllabic names reign supreme, a land where "William" is shortened to "Bill," where "Susan" becomes "Sue," and "Richard" somehow evolves into "Dick"? America is a great country, but nobody without a mask and a cape has a z in his name. And have Americans ever realized the great scope of the guttural sounds they're missing? Okay, so it has to do with linguistic roots, but I do believe this

351

would be a richer country if all Americans could do a little tongue aerobics and learn to pronounce "kh," a sound more commonly associated in this culture with phlegm, or "gh," the sound usually made by actors in the final moments of a choking scene. It's like adding a few new spices to the kitchen pantry. Move over, cinnamon and nutmeg, make way for cardamom and sumac.

Exotic analogies aside, having a foreign name in this land of Joes and Marys is a pain in the spice cabinet. When I was twelve, I decided to simplify my life by adding an American middle name. This decision serves as proof that sometimes simplifying one's life in the short run only complicates it in the long run.

My name, Firoozeh, chosen by my mother, means "Turquoise" in Farsi. In America, it means "Unpronounceable" or "I'm Not Going to Talk to You Because I Cannot Possibly Learn Your Name and I Just Don't Want to Have to Ask You Again and Again Because You'll Think I'm Dumb or You Might Get Upset or Something." My father, incidentally, had wanted to name me Sara. I do wish he had won that argument.

To strengthen my decision to add an American name, I had just   5
finished fifth grade in Whittier, where all the kids incessantly called me "Ferocious." That summer, my family moved to Newport Beach, where I looked forward to starting a new life. I wanted to be a kid with a name that didn't draw so much attention, a name that didn't come with a built-in inquisition as to when and why I had moved to America and how was it that I spoke English without an accent and was I planning on going back and what did I think of America?

My last name didn't help any. I can't mention my maiden name, because:

"Dad, I'm writing a memoir."

"Great! Just don't mention our name."

Suffice it to say that, with eight letters, including a *z*, and four syllables, my last name is as difficult and foreign as my first. My first and last name together generally served the same purpose as a high brick wall. There was one exception to this rule. In Berkeley, and only in Berkeley, my name drew people like flies to baklava. These were usually people named Amaryllis or Chrysanthemum, types who vacationed in Costa Rica and to whom lentils described a type of burger. These folks were probably not the pride of Poughkeepsie, but they were refreshingly nonjudgmental.

When I announced to my family that I wanted to add an American   10
name, they reacted with their usual laughter. Never one to let mockery or good judgment stand in my way, I proceeded to ask for suggestions. My father suggested "Fifi." Had I had a special affinity for French poodles or been considering a career in prostitution, I would've gone with that one. My mom suggested "Farah," a name easier than "Firoozeh" yet still Iranian. Her reasoning made sense, except that Farrah Fawcett was at the height of her popularity and I didn't want to be associated with somebody

whose poster hung in every postpubescent boy's bedroom. We couldn't think of any American names beginning with *F*, so we moved on to *J*, the first letter of our last name. I don't know why we limited ourselves to names beginning with my initials, but it made sense at that moment, perhaps by the logic employed moments before bungee jumping. I finally chose the name "Julie" mainly for its simplicity. My brothers, Farid and Farshid, thought that adding an American name was totally stupid. They later became Fred and Sean.

That same afternoon, our doorbell rang. It was our new next-door neighbor, a friendly girl my age named Julie. She asked me my name and after a moment of hesitation, I introduced myself as Julie. "What a coincidence!" she said. I didn't mention that I had been Julie for only half an hour.

Thus I started sixth grade with my new, easy name and life became infinitely simpler. People actually remembered my name, which was an entirely refreshing new sensation. All was well until the Iranian Revolution, when I found myself with a new set of problems. Because I spoke English without an accent and was known as Julie, people assumed I was American. This meant that I was often privy to their real feelings about those "damn I-raynians." It was like having those X-ray glasses that let you see people undressed, except that what I was seeing was far uglier than people's underwear. It dawned on me that these people would have probably never invited me to their house had they known me as Firoozeh. I felt like a fake.

All of us immigrants knew that moving to America would be fraught with challenges, but none of us thought that our names would be such an obstacle.

When I went to college, I eventually went back to using my real name. All was well until I graduated and started looking for a job. Even though I had graduated with honors from UC–Berkeley, I couldn't get a single interview. I was guilty of being a humanities major, but I began to suspect that there was more to my problems. After three months of rejections, I added "Julie" to my résumé. Call it coincidence, but the job offers started coming in. Perhaps it's the same kind of coincidence that keeps African Americans from getting cabs in New York.

Once I got married, my name became Julie Dumas. I went from having an identifiably "ethnic" name to having ancestors who wore clogs. My family and non-American friends continued calling me Firoozeh, while my coworkers and American friends called me Julie. My life became one big knot, especially when friends who knew me as Julie met friends who knew me as Firoozeh. I felt like those characters in soap operas who have an evil twin. The two, of course, can never be in the same room, since they're played by the same person, a struggling actress who wears a wig to play one of the twins and dreams of moving on to bigger and better roles. I couldn't blame my mess on a screenwriter; it was my own doing.

I decided to untangle the knot once and for all by going back to my   15
real name. By then, I was a stay-at-home mom, so I really didn't care
whether people remembered my name or gave me job interviews. Besides,
most of the people I dealt with were in diapers and were in no position to
judge. I was also living in Silicon Valley, an area filled with people named
Rajeev, Avishai, and Insook.

Every once in a while, though, somebody comes up with a new per-
mutation and I am once again reminded that I am an immigrant with a
foreign name. I recently went to have blood drawn for a physical exam.
The waiting room for blood work at our local medical clinic is in the base-
ment of the building, and no matter how early one arrives for an appointment, forty coughing, wheezing people have gotten there first. Apart from
reading *Golf Digest* and *Popular Mechanics*, there isn't much to do except
guess the number of contagious diseases represented in the windowless
room. Every ten minutes, a name is called and everyone looks to see which
cough matches that name. As I waited patiently, the receptionist called
out, "Fritzy, Fritzy!" Everyone looked around, but no one stood up. Usually, if I'm waiting to be called by someone who doesn't know me, I will
respond to just about any name starting with an *F*. Having been called
Froozy, Frizzy, Fiorucci, and Frooz and just plain "Uhhhh . . . ," I am highly
accommodating. I did not, however, respond to "Fritzy" because there
is, as far as I know, no *t* in my name. The receptionist tried again, "Fritzy,
Fritzy DumbAss." As I stood up to this most linguistically original version
of my name, I could feel all eyes upon me. The room was momentarily
silent as all of these sick people sat united in a moment of gratitude for
their own names.

Despite a few exceptions, I have found that Americans are now far
more willing to learn new names, just as they're far more willing to try
new ethnic foods. Of course, some people just don't like to learn. One
mom at my children's school adamantly refused to learn my "impossible"
name and instead settled on calling me "F Word." She was recently transferred to New York where, from what I've heard, she might meet an immigrant or two and, who knows, she just might have to make some room in
her spice cabinet.

THINKING CRITICALLY ABOUT THE READING

1. Dumas confesses that "all of us immigrants knew that moving to America would
   be fraught with challenges, but none of us thought that our names would be
   such an obstacle" (2). What did she and her friends discover was the problem
   with Iranian names like Farbod, Farshid, Neggar, Arash, and Firoozeh?

2. How did Firoozeh reinvent herself when she and her family moved from
   Whittier to Newport Beach, California? How did she happen upon her new
   "American name" (10)?

3. Why do you think that Firoozeh couldn't mention her maiden name? What does she tell you about her last name? What would her last name reveal about her? In what ways did Dumas's "first and last name together generally [serve] the same purpose as a high brick wall" (9)?

4. During the Iranian Revolution, Firoozeh witnessed firsthand some pretty ugly anti-Iranian feelings expressed. Why wasn't she the target of these anti-Iranian sentiments?

5. Why do you think Firoozeh had trouble getting a job interview after graduating from the University of California, Berkeley? What is the problem with "having an identifiably 'ethnic' name" (353)? Explain.

6. Dumas writes about an extremely sensitive subject—personal names and prejudice—with humor. Did you find her humor appropriate for this subject and her audience? Cite several examples where she uses humor effectively.

LANGUAGE IN ACTION

Have you ever thought about changing your name? If so, why? Interestingly, show-business people often change their names to further their careers. Here are the professional names and the original names of a number of celebrities, past and present. Discuss with your classmates any significant associations that the original names might have and the reasons these names might have been changed.

Original Names	*Professional Names*
Demetria Guynes	Demi Moore
Michael Philip	Mick Jagger
Norma Jean Baker	Marilyn Monroe
Madonna Louise Ciccone	Madonna
Eleanor Gow	Elle MacPherson
Caryn Johnson	Whoopi Goldberg
Robert Zimmerman	Bob Dylan
Doris von Kappelhoff	Doris Day
Frederick Austerlitz	Fred Astaire
Marion Michael Morrison	John Wayne
Cassius Marcellus Clay Jr.	Muhammad Ali
Annemaria Italiano	Anne Bancroft
Maurice J. Micklewhite	Michael Caine
Thomas Mapother IV	Tom Cruise
Carlos Ray	Chuck Norris
Leonard Sly	Roy Rogers
Benjamin Kubelsky	Jack Benny

How do you think Firoozeh Dumas would react to some of these name changes? What celebrity name changes can you add to this list?

WRITING SUGGESTIONS

1. Is your surname very common in American society, very rare, or somewhere in between? Do others have difficulty pronouncing or spelling it? What does your surname reveal about your background or family history? Write an essay in which you reflect on the way your surname has affected your life and the way people react to you. Be sure to give examples of the role your name plays in day-to-day life.

2. Do a study of the names of the people in your dormitory or in one of your social groups. Analyze the names in light of Firoozeh Dumas's essay. In your opinion, are any of the names unusual? Why? Do they sound strange to you or others? Do they represent a culture different from your own? Do they remind you of another word that you find humorous? How do each of the people feel about their names? What insights, if any, do these names give you into the state of cultural diversity on your campus? Write an essay in which you discuss your findings. Make sure that you do not simply describe the names you found. Instead, build a context for your essay and provide a thesis for your comments. (Glossary: *Thesis*)

3. Write an essay in which you compare and contrast the experiences that Henry Louis Gates Jr. ("What's in a Name?, p. 14) and Dumas had with names. How did each of them feel when others named and thus defined them? What insights into oppression—namely racial, religious, or ethnic—do their experiences give you?

11

LANGUAGE AND TECHNOLOGY

Much has happened in recent years at the intersection of language and technology, and the promise of the future is that we will see even more inventions and developments that dramatically change our lives. More advancements are coming our way but their accelerating rate of turnover will test our ability to adjust to them technically, psychologically, intellectually, and behaviorally. The authors of the readings in this chapter have already begun to assess how we and our language are responding and adjusting, preferring quite naturally to focus on the perceived problems rather than obvious benefits of the new technologies. After all, we all know what cell phones and texting are doing for us. What they are doing *to* us still needs to be examined.

The first four readings in this chapter are concerned with how technology, and texting and social media in particular, may be changing the way we communicate with each other. We begin with a lengthy, detailed argument by noted British linguist David Crystal in which he exposes the rumors and myths promoted mostly by journalists that texting is degrading the English language, promoting poor spelling, sloppy writing, and inarticulateness in general. Crystal finds evidence for such claims surprisingly nonexistent for the most part or weak at best where in question. The idea that students become so accustomed to using texting language that they subconsciously let that language slip into their school essays and into their written exams is simply not borne out by his rigorous research and logical analysis. Students know the difference between formal and informal speech and writing and certainly understand where it is appropriate to use each form of discourse. Rather than a cause for alarm from those self-proclaimed experts who charge themselves with the responsibility of protecting our language, texting is not a new language, Crystal concludes. It is just another variety of language and the most recent evidence that our language is continuing to evolve.

While the new communication technology—e-mail, SMS (Short Message Service), and texting—has provided us with many benefits, not the least of them being relatively low cost, ease of use, portability, focused rapid contact and response, and privacy, there is still concern for some of the troubling side effects apparent to most users. Alison Stein Wellner

357

in "Lost in Translation" describes, for example, how much we have lost when face-to-face communication is supplanted by the new technologies. Joseph P. Kahn in "What Does 'Friend' Mean Now?" bemoans the loss of the old meaning of the word *friend* now that Facebook has blurred the lines between the real world and the virtual world. In short, what do we mean when we say someone is a friend? Indeed, have the new social media made it impossible to have any real friends? And has the new technology made it possible for us to be rude to each other in yet new ways? Journalist David Carr thinks so. In "Keep Your Thumbs Still When I'm Talking to You" he expresses his disbelief and dismay at people who decide to text or talk to someone on the phone when they are presumably having a conversation with him. What message is actually being sent when one chooses to talk to someone who isn't there over the person who is standing two feet away? Anand Giridharadas uses technology to analyze the *Corpus of Historical American English*, a massive database of our discourse over the past two hundred years. Interestingly, he finds evidence in the database that leads him to contend that as a people we have undergone a revealing change in our values over the past two hundred years. Finally, *The Visual Thesaurus* provides an example of how a new technology can both improve and complicate our use of that time-tested writing tool, the thesaurus. (See www.bedfordstmartins.com/languageawareness/epages.)

Texting: Why All the Fuss?

David Crystal

British linguist David Crystal was born in 1941 in Northern Ireland. He received his B.A. from the University of London in 1962 and his Ph.D. in 1966, and taught at the University of Reading (England) as a professor of linguistics until 1985. He is now Honorary Professor of Linguistics at the University of Wales, Bangor, and is internationally known as a leading authority on languages, particularly the English language. Crystal is the author or editor of over one hundred books but is best known for *The Cambridge Encyclopedia of Language* (1987) and *The Cambridge Encyclopedia of the English Language* (1995). In addition to his work as an author, lecturer, and reference-book editor, Crystal currently serves as the director of the Ucheldre Center, a multipurpose arts and exhibition center.

In "Texting: Why All the Fuss?" a chapter from his very popular and readable *Txtng: The Gr8 Db8* (2008), Crystal puts forth the insightful argument in favor of texting as another variety of language and the latest evidence of language evolving, while artfully putting to rest all the rumors and myths about how it is destroying our precious language, arguments promoted by what one might call the grumpy old prescriptivists who zealously seek to preserve English as it once was.

WRITING TO DISCOVER: *What arguments have you heard against texting? What do you think of them? Do you think it is destroying the English language? Do you know students who use text language inappropriately as has been charged by some critics of the new medium?*

A remarkable number of doom-laden prophecies arose during the opening years of the new millennium, all relating to the linguistic evils which would be unleashed by texting. The prophecies went something like this:

- Texting uses new and nonstandard orthography.
- This will inevitably erode children's ability to spell, punctuate, and capitalize correctly—an ability already thought to be poor.
- They will inevitably transfer these new habits into the rest of their schoolwork.
- This will inevitably give them poorer marks in examinations.
- A new generation of adults will inevitably grow up unable to write proper English.
- Eventually the language as a whole will inevitably decline.

There was never any clear evidence supporting these assertions, but that did not stop them being made. And when someone found a piece of writing which did seem to support the argument—the child who supposedly wrote her essay entirely in a texting style—it was immediately publicized as being typical of a generation. The one extract from that essay was reproduced in hundreds of newspapers and websites all over the world. The full essay, if it existed, was never presented. And no other examples of this kind have since been found. Every time I talk to groups of teachers and examiners, I ask them whether they have encountered anything remotely similar. None of them ever has.

In 2007 I had the opportunity to work with some groups of teenagers studying for A-levels at various schools in the UK. They all texted. I asked them whether they would use text abbreviations in their schoolwork. They looked at me with blank incomprehension. One said, "Why would you ever want to do that?" They were perfectly clear in their minds that texting was for mobile phones and not for other purposes. "You'd have to be pretty stupid not to see the difference," said another. The point was affirmed many times in a BBC forum which followed the report on the child's essay in 2003, such as this comment from 11-year-old Charlotte:[1]

> I write all my notes in txt, like from a video, if I were going 2 do an essay on it (which I do in normal language), but I wouldn't do it for proper work, ESPECIALLY IN EXAMS.

Or this one from 15-year-old Terri:

> I have never heard of anyone using "text language" for an essay or anything, and if I did, I'd probably hurt them horribly. But, it's not my problem if you get horrendous grades for something ridiculously stupid you did if you happen to use it. I don't understand how people can't tell the difference between what CAN be used in English (which is correct English, duh) and what can't, like text language or whatever.

Doubtless there are some children who can't "tell the difference," and who therefore introduce the occasional text spelling or abbreviation into their written work. Teachers and examiners have told me of cases, and I have seen some examples of work in which a few abbreviations appear. But the instances were few and sporadic, evidence of carelessness or lack of thought rather than a systematic inability to spell and punctuate. I also got the impression, from the general appearance of the handwriting, that some of the writers were simply in a hurry, and in their rush to get ideas down and complete a paper in time used some abbreviations in much the same way as anyone might replace *for example* by *e.g.* or use an *etc.* to replace some items in a list.

The formal examination reports are not much help, for they present an unclear picture, and their conclusions are distorted by media hype. For example, in 2006, the chief examiner's report of the Irish State

1. http://news.bbc.co.uk/cbbcnews/hi/chat/your_comments/newsid_2814000/2814357.stm.

Examination Commission drew attention to a concern over one section of the Junior Certificate:[2]

> Expertise in text messaging and email in particular would appear to have affected spelling and punctuation. Text messaging, with its use of phonetic spelling and little or no punctuation, seems to pose a threat to traditional conventions in writing.

The comment was made in relation to the "Personal Writing" section of the examination; no similar comments were made in relation to the other six sections of the exam. The conclusion in the second sentence—even allowing for its cautious phrasing—hardly seems warranted, therefore. But it takes very little to rouse the prophets of doom.[3] And not surprisingly it was the "threat" which motivated all the headlines, in which the language of possibility was transformed into the language of definite fact:

> Shock: text messages blamed for declining standards in written language (*Mobile Digest*)
> Text messages destroying our language (*The Daily Opinion*)

Also in 2006, the Scottish Qualifications Authority commented that text abbreviations were appearing, but only in a "very small" percentage of exam papers.[4] In relation to the task of "Folio Writing," they comment on things that some candidates found "demanding":

> observance of the conventions of written expression and, in a few cases, the avoidance of the inappropriate use of the informalities of talk and, occasionally, "text language"

It was a comment made for the Standard Grade only, not for the Intermediate 1 and 2, Higher, or Advanced Higher. Note the qualifications: "few cases," "occasionally." This was not enough to stop adverse political reaction and media comment about the language being "murdered" (to take a headline from *The Sunday Times*).[5]

Tim Shortis, a former chief examiner for English language A-level at the exam board AQAB, said he had rarely seen textisms used in A-level papers, though they were more common at GCSE[6] level. He commented:[7]

---

2. http://www.examinations.ie/archive/examiners_reports/cer_2006/JC_English _2006.pdf.

3. For an excellent collection of media quotations along these lines, see the paper by Thurlow referred to in Chapter 1 (note 8).

4. http://www.sqa.org.uk/files_ccc/CourseReportEnglish2006.pdf.
   http://www.sqa.org.uk/files_ccc/PAReportEnglishStandardGrade2006.pdf.

5. Katie Grant, "Our language is being murdered," *The Sunday Times*, 5 November 2006. http://www.timesonline.co.uk/tol/newspapers/sunday_times/scotland/ariticle624235 .ece.

6. General Certificate of Secondary Education (GCSE) is a qualifying examination for secondary school students (ages 14–16) and is taken in a number of specific subjects.

7. http://www.tes.co.uk/search/story/?story_id = 2341958.

There's a moral panic about young people and language, a populist alarm. But the examples you see in the media are rarely used. You get initialisms such as *LOL* for "laugh out loud" and letter and number homophones such as *r* and *2*, but they are not as widespread as you think. There are also remarkably few casual misspellings.

It would be strange if it were otherwise. As we have seen in earlier chapters, very few words in a language are abbreviated by texters—we are talking about a few dozen common words and phrases, and certainly not hundreds. Not all young texters use the abbreviated forms. And those who do use them do not use them very much—in as few as 6 percent of messages, in the Norwegian study reported earlier. People who talk of texting as a "new language," implying that the whole of the writing system is altered, are inculcating a myth.

None of this is to doubt the frequently reported observation that there   5
are many instances of poor written work in schools. But it is crucial to rec-ognize the various causes of inadequate literacy. There are indeed children who are weak at writing, poor spellers, and bad punctuators. There always have been. Possibly up to 10 percent of the child population have learning difficulties (such as dyslexia) in which reading and writing are specifically affected. The problems facing these children are increasingly being recog-nized. But there is nothing new about them. They were there long before texting was invented.

Another group of children are said to be poor writers and spellers, compared with previous generations, for a whole host of other reasons— too much television, too many video games, too much internet, not enough reading . . . It is not my purpose in this book to explore these issues. All I want to point out is that these reasons pre-date texting. The claim that there has been a decline in writing skills, whatever its merits, goes back decades. It is the theme of the opening pages of the Bullock Report on English.[8] That was in 1975. This report quoted several firms complaining about the poor levels of spoken and written English in their employees. One firm said that they were having "great difficulty in obtain-ing junior clerks who can speak and write English clearly and correctly, especially those aged from 15 to 16 years." That was in 1921.

I do not see how texting could be a significant factor when discussing children who have real problems with literacy. If you have difficulty with reading and writing, you are hardly going to be predisposed to use a tech-nology which demands sophisticated abilities in reading and writing. And if you do start to text, I would expect the additional experience of writing to be a help, rather than a hindrance.

There is a curious ambivalence around. Complaints are made about children's poor literacy, and then, when a technology arrives that provides fresh and motivating opportunities to read and write, such as email, chat,

---

8. *A Language for Life* (London: HMSO, 1975).

blogging, and texting, complaints are made about that. The problems associated with the new medium—such as new abbreviation styles—are highlighted and the potential benefits ignored. I heard someone recently complaining that "children don't keep diaries any more." The speaker was evidently unaware of the fact that the online diary—the blog—is one of the most popular areas of internet activity among young people.

A couple of axioms might be usefully affirmed at this point. I believe that any form of writing exercise is good for you. I also believe that any form of tuition which helps develop your awareness of the different properties, styles, and effects of writing is good for you. It helps you become a better reader, more sensitive to nuance, and a better writer, more sensitive to audience. Texting language is no different from other innovative forms of written expression that have emerged in the past. It is a type of language whose communicative strengths and weaknesses need to be appreciated. If it were to take its place alongside other kinds of writing in school curricula, students would soon develop a strong sense of when it is appropriate to use it and when it is not. It is not as if the school would be teaching them something totally new. Many websites are already making texters aware that there are some situations in which it is inappropriate to use texting abbreviations, because they might not be understood.

This might seem to be self-evident, yet when a text-messaging unit   10
was included as an option in the English curriculum in schools in Victoria, Australia, for students in years 8 to 10, it was condemned by no less a person than the federal minister of education.[9] The students were being taught to translate SMS texts, write glossaries of abbreviations, and compare the language of texting with that of formal written English. Stylistic comparisons of this kind have long proved their worth in English classes; their value is repeatedly asserted in the documents which led to the UK English National Curriculum, for example, and the comparative study of standard and nonstandard varieties of language is now a regular event in the English classroom—and not only in the UK.[10] The minister was reported as urging a return to "basics." But what could be more basic, in terms of language acquisition, than to focus on students' developing sense of linguistic appropriateness?

The knee-jerk antagonism to texting as a variety of language is fostered by the misinformation about it in the media. For example, on 9 November 2006 Wikipedia accepted an entry which was headed "New Zealand students able to use txt language in exams."[11] It began:

---

9. http://www.abc.net.au/worldtoday/content/2006/s1760068.htm.
10. For example, in the Kingman Report (London: HMSO, 1988), section 4.29, and many other places.
11. http://en.wikinews.org/wiki/New_Zealand_students_able_to_use_txt_language _in_exams.

> The New Zealand Qualifications Authority (NZQA) has announced that a shorter version of English known as txt language will be acceptable in the external end of year exams.

This seems absolutely clear-cut, and if it were true—given the widespread suspicion of texting—likely to provoke an outcry. But the NZQA site the next day told a very different story:[12]

> The Qualifications Authority is actively discouraging candidates in NCEA exams from using abbreviations, including text-style abbreviations. Deputy Chief Executive, Qualifications, Bali Haque said there had been no change in the Authority's policy in regard to use of abbreviations in examinations. Where an examination requires candidates to demonstrate language use—i.e. sentence structure, grammar, spelling—they would be penalized for using abbreviations, Mr Haque said . . . [because] use of abbreviations creates a risk of answers not being understood.

Far more people find the Wikipedia site than the NZQA one, of course, so the error lives on.

Misinformation of this kind can be crushed only by solid research findings. And research is slowly beginning to show that texting actually benefits literacy skills. The studies are few, with small numbers of children, so we must be cautious; but a picture is emerging that texting does not harm writing ability and may even help it. Here are the findings of some recent studies:

- Veenal Raval, a speech and language therapist working at the City University in London, compared a group of 11- to 12-year-old texters with a similar group of non-texters.[13] She found that neither group had noticeably worse spelling or grammar than the other, but that both groups made some errors. She also noted that text abbreviations did not appear in their written work.
- A team of Finnish researchers found that the informal style of texting was an important motivating factor, especially among teenage boys, and provided fresh opportunities for linguistic creativity.[14]
- In a series of studies carried out in 2006–7, Beverly Plester, Clare Wood, and others from Coventry University found strong positive links between the use of text language and the skills underlying success in standard English in a group of pre-teenage children.[15]

---

12. http://www.nzqa.govt.nz/news/releases/2006/101106.html.

13. http://www.city.ac.uk/marketing/dps/Citynews/email_bulletin/0060%20Citynews%20email%20bulletin%20-%2010%20January%202005.pdf.

14. E.-L. Kasesniemi and P. Rautiainen (2002), "Mobile culture of children and teenagers in Finland," in J. E. Katz and M. Aakhus (eds.), *Perpetual Contact: Mobile Communication, Private Talk and Public Performance* (Cambridge: Cambridge University Press), 170–92.

15. Beverly Plester, Clare Wood, and Victoria Bell (2006), "Txt msg n school literacy: does mobile phone use adversely affect children's literacy attainment?" and Beverly Plester, Clare Wood, and Puja Joshi (2007), "Exploring the relationship between children's knowledge of text message abbreviations and school literacy outcomes," both Coventry University Psychology Department.

The children were asked to compose text messages that they might write in a particular situation—such as texting a friend to say that they had missed their bus and they were going to be late. The more text abbreviations they used in their messages, the higher they scored on tests of reading and vocabulary. The children who were better at spelling and writing used the most texting abbreviations. Also interesting was the finding that the younger the children received their first phone, the higher their scores.

These results surprise some people. But why should one be surprised? Children could not be good at texting if they had not already developed considerable literacy awareness. Before you can write abbreviated forms effectively and play with them, you need to have a sense of how the sounds of your language relate to the letters. You need to know that there are such things as alternative spellings. You need to have a good visual memory and good motor skills. If you are aware that your texting behavior is different, you must have already intuited that there is such a thing as a standard. If you are using such abbreviations as *lol* ("laughing out loud") and *brb* ("be right back"), you must have developed a sensitivity to the communicative needs of your textees, because these forms show you are responding to them. If you are using *imho* ("in my humble opinion") or *afaik* ("as far as I know"), you must be aware of the possible effect your choice of language might have on them, because these forms show you are self-critical. Teenage texters are not stupid nor are they socially inept within their peer group. They know exactly what they are doing.

What teenagers are not good at is fully understanding the consequences of what they are doing, in the eyes of society as a whole. And this is where teaching (in the broadest sense of the word) comes in. They need to know when it would be appropriate to text and when it would not be. They need to know when textisms are effective and when they are not. They need to appreciate the range of social reactions which texting, in its various forms, can elicit. This knowledge is slowly acquired from parents, peers, text etiquette websites, and (in the narrow sense) teachers. Teenagers have to learn to manage this new behavior, as indeed do we all. For one thing is certain: texting is not going to go away, in the foreseeable future.

These arguments are not unique to texting. They apply equally to the other "literacies" which children need to acquire if they are to achieve a fluent command of their language as readers and writers. Here are three sentences from the previous paragraph, but with the texting terminology replaced by terms relating to a different variety of language:

> They need to know when it would be appropriate to use scientific language and when it would not be. They need to know when scientific jargon is effective and when it is not. They need to appreciate the range of social reactions which scientific jargon, in its various forms, can elicit.

You could replace "scientific language" by many other terms: "literary language," "poetic language," "journalistic language," "advertising language," "nonstandard language," "regional dialect" . . . The aim of language education is to put all these literacies under the confident control of the student, so that when they leave school they are able to cope with the linguistic demands made upon them.

Texting is just another variety of language, which has arisen as a result 15 of a particular technology. It takes its place alongside the other mediums of electronic communication which have resulted from the internet revolution. Texting is not alone, and many of its linguistic properties are shared by other kinds of computer-mediated communication. For example, text messages are short; but so are several other forms of electronic expression. In fact they are not the most succinct form: that record is held by instant messaging. A comparative study by Richard Ling and Naomi Baron showed that almost 60 percent of text messages contained more than one sentence while only 34 percent of instant messages did.[16] Sentences were longer in texting and there were more characters per message. Texts are more autonomous. This is unsurprising: it would be awkward and uneconomical to continue a lengthy chat dialogue by mobile phone. Because each text message has an individual cost, messages tend to be fuller and more self-contained. Instant messaging, by contrast, readily spreads the content of a message serially over several transmissions, with no cost implications, so that individual transmissions tend to be short and incomplete in character.

> **Texting is just another variety of language, which has arisen as a result of a particular technology.**

In the end, whatever the strengths and weaknesses of texting as a variety of language, it is in the classroom that matters need to be managed. If there are children who are unaware of the difference between texting and standard English, then it is up to teachers to make them aware. If there are children whose discourse skills are being hampered by texting, then it is up to teachers to show them how to improve. Some methods will work well and some will not. As the old song might have said, it's not what you teach but the way that you teach it. The point is made succinctly by Jill Attewell in a paper for *Literacy Today* in 2003.[17]

there are reports of examiners finding SMS abbreviations and slang in GCSE English papers. This is worrying, although enquiries should perhaps focus on how teachers have prepared their pupils for the examinations rather than on the students' use of mobile phones.

16. Naomi Baron and Richard Ling, "IM and SMS: a linguistic comparison," paper given at the International Conference of the Association of Internet Researchers, Toronto, October 2003.

17. http://www.literacytrust.org.uk/Pubs/attewell.html.

It would indeed be worrying if students entered an examination hall unaware of the difference between formal and informal English, or between standard and nonstandard English. Fortunately, all the evidence from examiners and others suggests that the vast majority of students are well aware of the difference, and do not use textisms in their writing.

The research findings are promising, but we do not yet know if the positive results will be replicated across all ability levels of children and all aspects of linguistic structure. And the emergence of these findings does not mean that we can be blasé about maintaining a balance between texting and other aspects of linguistic behavior. For example, the use of the phone keypad, along with the ready availability of predictive texting, reinforces the point made in the 1990s that the internet is reducing the opportunities, and thus the ability, of children to use handwriting. Teachings—and examining—needs to take this into account. The need to maintain a clear and fluent handwriting style is of great importance—and not only to guard against the day when there is a power-cut.

Research reports also repeatedly draw attention to the reduced grammatical complexity of text messages—as indeed of some other kinds of electronic communication, such as chat and instant messaging. Text messages are quite short, compared with emails, blogging, and other kinds of forum activity, and certainly much shorter than most traditional forms of written expression, such as the letter, diary entry, or essay. The sentences are also shorter, making use of elliptical constructions in the manner of conversational speech (e.g. *Getting the 4 pm bus* rather than *I'm getting the 4 pm bus*). Grammatical words are often omitted, in the manner of a telegram (*bus arriving 7.10*). The danger here, it is suggested, is that the constraint to write in short sentences might make children think in correspondingly short bursts, so that they become less able to handle notions which require more complex elucidation. One of Veenal Raval's findings was that texters wrote less than non-texters when asked to describe a picture. If this turns out to be a genuine effect—that text messaging is fostering a reduction in discourse skills—then this is certainly something which needs to be compensated for in classroom activity. But findings are mixed. One research team found considerable collaborative discourse activity in using mobile phones, with young people often sitting together and exchanging text content in what they refer to as "gift-giving rituals."[18] And another study concluded that texting actually helps the development of communication skills such as the ability to summarize and express oneself concisely. [19] The same study also suggested that texting motivates people to sharpen their diplomatic skills, for, as with all written activity, it allows more time to formulate thoughts and express them carefully.

---

18. A. S. Taylor and R. Harper, "Age-old practices in the 'new world': a study of gift giving between teenage mobile phone users," paper given at the Conference on Human Factors and Computing Systems, Minneapolis, April 2002.

19. Kate Fox, "Evolution, alienation and gossip: the role of mobile telecommunications in the 21st century," *Social Issues Research Centre, 2001.* www.sirc.org/publik/gossip.shtml.

As with any new technology, people have to learn to manage it. There are undoubtedly problems in relation to the use of texting, but they seem to be social or physiological, not linguistic, in character. For example, one report, by Jan Van den Bulck from the Catholic University of Leuven in Belgium, found that text messages interrupted the sleep of most adolescents.[20] Among 13-year-olds, 13.4 percent reported being woken up one to three times a month, 5.8 percent were woken up once a week, 5.3 percent were woken up several times a week, and 2.2 percent were woken up every night. Among 16-year-olds, the interference was greater: 20.8 percent were woken up between one and three times a month, 10.8 percent were woken up at least once a week, 8.9 percent were woken up several times a week, and 2.9 percent were woken up every night. This is an issue that goes well beyond the linguistic.

The issues raised by texting also go well beyond children in schools. Another report, by Glenn Wilson from the University of London, commissioned by technology firm Hewlett Packard, identified problems of reduced concentration, productivity, and even IQ among employees who spent too much time texting while at work.[21] The practice was evidently also causing some harm to personal relations: half the employees said they always responded immediately to a message—notwithstanding the fact that most people think it highly discourteous to read or answer a text message or email during a face-to-face meeting. The problems carried over into the outside world, with most employees reporting that they checked work-related text messages and emails even when at home or on holiday.

The press have made much use of the term "addiction," when reporting such findings; and indeed, there have been reports of people booking themselves into clinics for help. In 2003 the Priory clinics were reporting a sharp rise in "technology addiction," with some people evidently texting up to seven hours a day.[22] There have also been reports of undesirable physical effects. Physiotherapists have begun to notice cases of text message injury (TMI), a form of repetitive stress injury caused by excessive use of the thumb to type text messages.[23] There is also a risk of damage to the hand, wrist, and arm. They advise texters to use both hands when texting, to hold the phone higher up and as close to the body as possible to avoid neck and shoulder strain, to keep the phone as close to the body as possible to avoid extra strain on the arms, and to take regular breaks. Anything which reduces the number of keystrokes is seen as a good thing, such as predictive texting—or, of course, abbreviating.

20. Jan Van den Bulck, "Text messaging as a cause of sleep interruption in adolescents, evidence from a cross-sectional study," *Journal of Sleep Research* 12 (2003), 263.

21. http://www.timesonline.co.uk/tol/life_and_style/education/student/news/article 384086.ece.

22. Report in http://news.bbc.co.uk/1/hi/uk/3165546.stm.

23. http://www.csp.org.uk/director/newsandevents/news.cfm?item_id = 117F52FA BA0EFD81E11F1670148A480C.

At the same time, other reports are more positive. Texting has proved valuable in giving children a discreet way of reporting when they are being bullied.[24] Several teachers have stories of reserved, introverted, or nervous pupils who have had their expressive confidence boosted by their use of texting. The point has long been appreciated with reference to the use of the internet to provide chat forums in distance learning;[25] and it seems to be just as relevant here.

A national survey carried out by Kate Fox in 2001 for the Social Issues Research Centre in the UK drew attention to the important role played by texting as part of the "gossip" of a speech community.[26] Most of her focus-group participants saw texting as an important means of maintaining contact in a large social network:

> they found texting an ideal way to keep in touch with friends and family when they did not have the time, energy, inclination or budget for a "proper" phone conversation or visit.

Her main conclusion in relation to the teenagers she interviewed supported the point made above:

> texting can help them to overcome their awkwardness and develop their social and communication skills: they communicate with more people, and communicate more frequently, than they did before having access to mobile texting.

Fox's conclusions about texting formed part of a larger study of the important role of gossip in maintaining social networks. Texting dialogue reminded her of village-green conversations where little content may be exchanged but personal connections are made. And the supporting technology for mobile phones has a similar social effect in other parts of the world. In Africa, for example, limited electricity supply has brought people together in an unexpected way.[27]

> In the town center there is one phone shop that sells airtime and phones. This is where many people also charge their phones. Many have to wait for their phones because there have been incidents of phones disappearing, and there are no guarantees or insurances . . . It is common to find mostly professionals, like teachers, chatting near the shop as they wait because their schools do not have electricity; new social networks develop from this; discussions range from sharing expertise, development issues to politics . . .

---

24. http://www.bteducation.org/news/newsitem.ikml?id=376&PHPSESSID=13a3584ee0.
25. For example, by Boyd H. Davis and Jeutonne P. Brewer, *Electronic Discourse: Linguistic Individuals in Virtual Space* (Albany: State University of New York Press, 1997).
26. See Fox (note 18).
27. C. N. Adeya, "Wireless technologies and development in Africa," in *Wireless Communication and Development: a Global Perspective*, 2005. http://arnic.info/workshop05.php.

[in another village] I have observed a few people who come specifically to charge their phones, mostly retirees who do not want to walk to the village shop, maybe to save their money and airtime. They are not charged for this but I have seen them discuss issues from their experience with those in the vicinity and others working in the compound like veterinarians and children. From a cultural aspect, it reminds me of how the old used to sit around the fire with the young and impart knowledge. This culture has gradually died in many communities but maybe this charging of mobile phones may partially replace it.

Texting is one of the most innovative linguistic phenomena of modern times, and perhaps that is why it has generated such strong emotions— "a kind of laziness," "an affectation," "ridiculous"[28]—and why we have seen the "moral panic" described in earlier chapters. Yet all the evidence suggests that belief in an impending linguistic disaster is a consequence of a mythology largely created by the media. Children's use of text abbreviations has been hugely exaggerated, and the mobile phone companies have played a part in this by emphasizing their "cool" character, compiling dictionaries, and publishing usage guides—doubtless, thereby, motivating sales.

Texting has been blamed for all kinds of evils that it could not possibly have been responsible for. Virtually any piece of nonstandard English in schoolwork is now likely to be considered the result of texting, even if the evidence is incontrovertible that the nonstandardism has been around for generations. The other day I read about someone condemning *would of* (for *would have*) as a consequence of texting. That misspelling has been around for at least 200 years. You will find it in Keats. I have encountered similar misapprehensions in Japan, Finland, Sweden, and France, and it is probably present in every country where texting has become a feature of daily communication.

> **Texting is one of the most innovative linguistic phenomena of modern times, and perhaps that is why it has generated such strong emotions.**

In a logical world, text messaging should not have survived. Imagine a pitch to a potential investor. "I have this great idea. A new way of person-to-person communication, using your phone. The users won't have a familiar keyboard. Their fingers will have trouble finding the keys. They will be able to send messages, but with no more than 160 characters at a time. The writing on the screens will be very small and difficult to read, especially if you have a visual handicap. The messages will arrive at any time, interrupting your daily routine or your sleep. Oh, and every now and again you won't be able to send or receive anything because

25

---

28. http://www.student.nada.kth.se/~ulslxvti/SPRAKT/sms.pdf.

your battery will run out. Please invest in it." What would you have done?

But, it was direct, avoiding the problem of tracking down someone over the phone. It was quick, avoiding the waiting time associated with letters and emails. It was focused, avoiding time-wasting small-talk. It was portable, allowing messages to be sent from virtually anywhere. It could even be done with one hand, making it usable while holding on to a roof-strap in a crowded bus. It was personal, allowing intimacy and secrecy, reminiscent of classroom notes under the desk. It was unnoticed in public settings, if the user turned off the ringtone. It allowed young people to overcome the spatial boundary of the home, allowing communication with the outside world without the knowledge of parents and siblings. It hugely empowered the deaf, the shared writing system reducing the gap between them and hearing people. And it was relatively cheap (though, given the quantity of messaging, some parents still had an unpleasant shock when their phone bill arrived). It wasn't surprising, therefore, that it soon became the preferred method of communication among teenagers. Youngsters valued its role both as a badge of identity, like accents and dialects, and as a ludic linguistic pastime. And in due course adults too came to value its discreetness and convenience. The interruption caused by the arrival of a text message is disregarded. To those who text, the beep heralding a new message invariably thrills, not pains.

How long will it last? It is always difficult to predict the future, when it comes to technology. Perhaps it will remain as part of an increasingly sophisticated battery of communicative methods, to be used as circumstances require. Or perhaps in a generation's time texting will seem as archaic a method of communication as the typewriter or the telegram does today, and new styles will have emerged to replace it. For the moment, texting seems here to stay, though its linguistic character will undoubtedly alter as its use spreads among the older population.

Some people dislike texting. Some are bemused by it. Some love it. I am fascinated by it, for it is the latest manifestation of the human ability to be linguistically creative and to adapt language to suit the demands of diverse settings. In texting we are seeing, in a small way, language in evolution.

THINKING CRITICALLY ABOUT THE READING

1. In your own words, what were some of the "linguistic evils" or assertions of impending doom with the advent of texting?

2. In paragraph 6, Crystal refers to influences other than texting that might account for the fact that some children are said to be poor spellers and writers. What are those influences?

3. Explain the "curious ambivalence" that Crystal refers to in paragraph 8.

4. How does Crystal answer the criticism that children don't keep diaries anymore?

5. What is "linguistic appropriateness" and why does Crystal think it's important for children to develop it?

6. What does Crystal mean when he writes in paragraph 15 that texting is another variety of language, similar to the varieties known as poetic language, journalistic language, advertising language, nonstandard language, and regional dialects?

7. In paragraph 18, Crystal suggests that while the research is not totally convincing, there may be a "reduction in discourse skills" as a result of text messaging. What, in particular, may be reduced for those who text?

8. What may be some of the benefits of texting for students? Aside from the rumors, what may be some of the actual problems of texting?

LANGUAGE IN ACTION

Comment on the appropriateness of the cartoon below in the context of Crystal's article. To which specific issues does the message of the cartoon relate?

DavidCarpenter/www.CartoonStock.com

WRITING SUGGESTIONS

1. Write an essay describing your experiences with texting. How do your experiences with texting relate to what Crystal has to say about the benefits and drawbacks of texting? For example, has texting helped you socially in any ways, has it changed the length of your sentences or your grammar to any noticeable degree? Has texting disrupted your daily schedule, made it difficult for you to get things done, altered your sleep pattern? Do you think you are "addicted" to texting to any degree? Can you be without your ability to text for very long? Has texting made your life safer?

2. The Gallaudet Research Institute at Gallaudet University reports that approximately 35 million people have some kind of hearing deficiency. Write an essay describing the way that texting has changed the lives of the hearing impaired. You may want to interview people who are deaf or have a hearing deficiency to gain a better understanding of how new technology—texting, SMS (Short Message Service), and e-mail—has made it possible, or easier, for them to communicate among themselves and with the hearing community.

3. Many people have made comments about the less-than-load-bearing nature of our text messages and that they so often convey very little of importance. Write an essay in which you reflect on the notion that texting is really less about communicating information and ideas, although undeniably useful in that respect, than it is about "gifting" each other with our presence and the recognition of our fellow humans. Is texting really about being a part of something, and that's why it is so vital particularly to young people? Is texting a minimally impacting way of building and maintaining community, something most people believe is a worthwhile endeavor?

Lost in Translation

ALISON STEIN WELLNER

Alison Stein Wellner is an award-winning writer who serves as the culinary travel editor for *About.com*, a New York Times Company-owned Web magazine for original ideas and advice. Wellner grew up in New York City and, as she puts it, "ate her way through its great neighborhoods." Passionate about traveling, eating, and writing, she revels in what she regards as the ideal life. Her writing has appeared in many publications, including *Business Week, Chicago Tribune, New York Magazine, Glamour, Ladies' Home Journal, Money, Mother Jones, The Smart Set,* the *Toronto Star,* and *USA Weekend.* Wellner is also the author of *(Like) Riding a Bike: On Learning as an Adult* (2011), a book about how at nearly thirty-four years of age she finally decided to learn to ride a bicycle. Her writing has been anthologized in *Best Women's Travel Writing 2010,* and you can follow her on Twitter.

In "Lost in Translation," first published on *Inc.com* on September 1, 2005, Wellner extols the virtues of face-to-face communication over e-mail.

WRITING TO DISCOVER: *Is it better to meet people face-to-face or simply send an e-mail, or does it depend on what you have to say? How do you decide? What are the advantages and disadvantages of meeting or e-mailing?*

When employees report to work on Fridays at Roberts Golden Consulting in San Francisco, they're greeted with a gentle reminder from president Sara Roberts: Remember, today is No E-mail Friday.

From Monday through Thursday at this management consultancy, as at most companies, e-mail reigns as the primary form of communication — whether with colleagues, clients, or suppliers. But on the fifth day of the workweek, Roberts's employees give their keyboards a rest. Too much e-mail, says Roberts, makes it harder to build rapport, and that threatens to derail effective business relationships. "People hide behind e-mail," she says. "For just one day a week, I want us to pick up the phone or talk to someone face-to-face."

Uneasiness about e-mail is almost as old as e-mail itself. But until now, most of the complaints have focused on things like e-mail overload, or the damage and embarrassment caused when messages go to the wrong people, or the need, for legal reasons, to be careful about what is put into writing. But those concerns just scratch the surface. New research indicates that overreliance on e-mail can degrade an organization's interpersonal communications. If it's not used properly, instead of making your company quicker and more efficient, too much text-based communicating can actually make it stupider.

To be sure, e-mail is not inherently evil. But it can be the kiss of death when it's used to communicate anything sensitive, important, or complicated, says Ron McMillan, who is co-author of *Crucial Conversations: Tools for Talking When Stakes Are High* and who spent 10,000 hours observing how companies nationwide communicate. As text messages fly between desktops, laptops, and hand-helds, McMillan says, they arrive without the rich stew of nonverbal information, such as tone of voice, facial expressions, and eye gaze, that we typically rely on to figure out what someone really means.

New research indicates that overreliance on e-mail can degrade an organization's interpersonal communications.

One study by UCLA psychology professor Albert Mehrabian found that 55 percent of meaning in an interaction comes from facial and body language and 38 percent comes from vocal inflection. Only 7 percent of an interaction's meaning is derived from the words themselves. Since e-mail is, by definition, just the words themselves, it's more easily misunderstood than an actual conversation. Yet managers and employees rely increasingly on text messages for nuanced conversations that really ought to be handled face-to-face, or at least voice-to-voice, says McMillan.

The results range from the merely comical to the truly horrifying, as Sara Roberts observed during a 10-year career in corporate America prior to founding her company. In one case, a colleague interacted on a near daily basis with a client over e-mail—without ever figuring out whether the person was male or female.

More seriously, text messages often touch off needless conflict. At one company, Roberts witnessed an explosive turf battle sparked when one employee left another off a "reply all" e-mail chain. Battles started over e-mail often rage longer, and more dramatically, than face-to-face disputes. People tend to be less inhibited over e-mail and more prone to conflict, according to Barry Wellman at the University of Toronto. Indeed, several studies comparing e-mail with face-to-face communication found that e-mail was more blunt and included more swearing and insults. "Everyone has an e-mail that they wish they hadn't sent," says Wellman.

That's why the 40 employees at MSCO, a marketing firm based in Purchase, N.Y., are not allowed to use e-mail or their BlackBerrys if they plan to criticize one another. It's just too easy for an exchange to escalate out of control, says CEO Mark Stevens. A few months ago, one employee complained about another's work performance via BlackBerry—and copied four others, including Stevens, on the message. "The person doing the criticizing was two offices down from the person being criticized, so what was that about?" wondered Stevens, who dropped what he was doing, sat down with the e-critic, and let him know that what he'd done was inappropriate.

Of course, there's no reason to go office to office looking deep into the eyes of every staffer whenever you send an e-mail. But periodic in-person check-ins will let you know when you need to do some damage control. In fact, if you make the time for old-fashioned face-to-face encounters on a regular basis, e-mail and IM actually may strengthen your working relationships, says University of Toronto's Wellman. "The face-to-face world and the bit-to-bit world can fit together," he says.

JoAnne Yates, a professor at MIT's Sloan School of Management who studies e-mail usage in the workplace, advises people to use electronic communication only to transmit and confirm simple information, and have actual conversations for anything that could possibly be sensitive. At the same time, flexibility is key. Sara Roberts, for example, knows she can't force her employees to ignore a message from a client who expects an immediate written response—even on No E-mail Friday. The point isn't to achieve perfect adherence, she says, but rather to remind people of the importance of communicating face-to-face. "No E-mail Friday helps us to remember we really could go over to that person sitting right over there and collaborate more," she says. In a wired world, it's worth remembering that there's still no technology more powerful than an actual meeting of minds.

ALL E-MAIL (ALL THE TIME)

Sometimes, face-to-face communication simply is not possible. That's   10
the case at Alpine Access, a provider of outsourced call-center services based in Golden, Colo. Senior executives at the company log zero face time with their 7,500 employees—including call-center agents, managers, and trainers, nearly all of whom work from their homes scattered across the country. Hiring, training, day-to-day management, and strategic planning all are handled electronically or over the phone. "There's no opportunity to look into someone's eyes to make sure they understand what's being said," says co-founder Jim Ball. So the company has developed a number of practices to compensate—practices that will boost the effectiveness of e-mail at any company.

Clarity Is Everything

Important messages, such as word that everyone needs to work harder to meet a monthly target, are vetted by several people for everything from grammar to nuance.

Trust but Verify

When employees get an e-mail, they're required to acknowledge receipt and are immediately offered the opportunity to ask questions.

Managers check back regularly to ensure that employees are on track and not missing any critical info.

Know When Not to Type

For truly difficult conversations—such as performance reviews—forget the bits and bytes. "You can be just as empathetic over the phone as you would be in person," Ball insists. "It's more difficult, but it can be done."

THINKING CRITICALLY ABOUT THE READING

1. In paragraph 2, Wellner quotes Sara Roberts as saying, "People hide behind email." What does she mean?

2. In paragraph 4, Wellner reports that Professor Mehrabian found "only 7 percent of an interaction's meaning is derived from the words themselves." Does that statistic seem accurate to you? Why or why not?

3. Wellner writes in paragraph 6 "text messages often touch off needless conflict." What evidence does she provide for her claim?

4. According to Wellner in paragraph 6, there are several studies that "found that e-mail was more blunt and included more swearing and insults." Why might that be true?

5. In paragraph 10, Wellner cites the example of Alpine Access in Golden, Colorado, where face-to-face communication is impossible. Assess the advice Alpine Access offers its employees to improve e-mail effectiveness. Do you think the company's advice could help improve communication? Explain.

LANGUAGE IN ACTION

In paragraph 13, Wellner quotes the following advice from Alpine Access (where face-to-face contact is not possible) to use the phone rather than e-mail:

> Know when not to type: For truly difficult conversations—such as performance reviews—forget the bits and bytes. "You can be just as empathetic over the phone as you would be in person," Ball insists. "It's more difficult, but it can be done."

Discuss in class the pros and cons of doing any kind of performance review over the phone.

WRITING SUGGESTIONS

1. In our culture we tend to think that any kind of personal communication can be accomplished over the phone or through texts or e-mail. If you have traveled, however, you soon realize that such might not be the case in other cultures. One student realized that when she traveled through France, Spain,

and Italy, she needed to present herself in person to discuss complicated or involved matters and that it was almost disrespectful to do otherwise. Showing up in person legitimized the discussion whereas attempting to discuss matters on the telephone trivialized them. If you have traveled abroad, write an essay describing your experiences in this regard. What cultural differences did you notice and how did you learn to communicate within them? If you have not traveled abroad, what cultural norms have you learned to abide by in this country? Would you text your history professor explaining why work on your research project is not going well? Would you call your professor at home? Would you ask permission to send a draft of your project proposal to your professor beforehand? What advice can you offer as to how to decide when and by what means and under what circumstances people should communicate with colleagues?

2. Write an essay in which you describe the particular dangers in miscommunication that can arise when using e-communication. Wellner has quoted Barry Wellman at the University of Toronto as saying, "Everyone has an e-mail that they wish they hadn't sent." What e-mail(s) do you wish you hadn't sent? Have you ever sent a traditional or snail mail letter that you wish you hadn't sent? Have you ever misaddressed a text or e-mail message? What problems arose? Of special interest when discussing this topic is what happens when you text a message and the autocorrect feature of your phone sends a message you did not intend. Such messages can be funny and appreciated for their humor or they can offend with their inadvertent crudeness. Most are easily excused as a by-product of our digital age. Does that make them all right, in your opinion? What do all miscommunications say about the need to carefully proofread?

What Does "Friend" Mean Now?

JOSEPH P. KAHN

Joseph P. Kahn comes from a family of writers and says that writing was always a topic of conversation in his family as he was growing up. His father was a famous *New Yorker* writer and the younger Kahn followed in his footsteps as a journalist. A man of diverse interests and a lot of curiosity, Kahn writes on lifestyles for the *Boston Globe* where he has treated such subjects as Henry Livingston Jr., who some believe to be the real author of *The Night Before Christmas*; Boston Public Library's renovated map repository; the contemporary architect Renzo Piano; Harvard's basketball team; origami at MIT; sex therapist Dr. Ruth Westheimer; a tattoo convention; majoring in poker in college; the increased use of profanity in our society; e-mail's lack of privacy; and what some writers think falling in love is all about.

In "What Does 'Friend' Mean Now?" first published in the *Boston Globe* on May 5, 2011, Kahn looks at how the definition of "friend" has recently evolved and expanded to cover relationships that never used to come under that label. These days a friend might even be a person you don't even know.

WRITING TO DISCOVER: *When you refer to someone as your friend, what exactly do you mean by that term? Do you use the term to mean different things depending on the person in question?*

Back in the mid-1990s, when online relationships were barely a blip on anyone's computer screen, songwriter Randy Newman earned an Oscar nod for "You've Got a Friend in Me," a jaunty, sentimental hymn to childhood fellowship. On television, the NBC sitcom *Friends* hit the ratings jackpot with its cast of young urbanites bound together by proximity and camaraderie.

These days? If not exactly a dime a dozen, friends are not what they used to be. What the term "friend" signifies seems harder to pin down, at any rate, having been Facebooked (ugh) into a transitive verb and overworked to the point where compliant preschoolers are encouraged to call everyone at school a friend (indeed) whether that label truly applies or not.

"To me, the term is constantly in flux," says Charlene DeLoach Oliver, a local blogger (*CharleneChronicles.com*) on health and fitness issues for young moms. "A teen, for instance, will have a completely different perspective on who's a friend than my grandmother will. To her, a friend is someone she sees once a week, in person. Me? I have virtual 'friends' I've never even met."

Her toddler-age son faces his own challenges in determining who's a friend and who isn't, according to Oliver. "At his daycare center, they'll say things like, 'Johnny, we don't hit a friend, do we?'" she says. "Some might say that's nice to do. But what are kids growing up to understand? It becomes a label without deeper meaning."

What we mean when we talk about friends and friendships these days   5 has many of us baffled, not just Oliver. Experts who track the changing meaning of language agree that our common reference points are becoming less fixed as the lines blur between the virtual and real, the face-to-face and Facebooked. Between what may feel good to hear—or quantify, in the case of online connections—and what squares with the reality of interpersonal relationships.

"The meanings of words derive from how we use them—and clearly as the world changes, we apply words in different ways," says Lera Boroditsky, a Stanford University psychology professor and language expert. Before online interaction became a routine part of daily life, she adds, "You saw friends in person or spoke to them on the phone. Today there's a real change in how we interact, and our language is struggling to keep up."

MIT sociologist Sherry Turkle, who studies technology and its cultural impact, maintains that "friend" has become "contested terrain" linguistically as social media sites alter the term's very DNA.

"It calls into question how many friends we have and what they are," says Turkle, author of *Alone Together: Why We Expect More from Technology and Less from Each Other.* "You can have 3,000 friends who look at your photos and what you've published, but only 100 who know about your heart."

The challenge, she contends, is to avoid confusing virtual friendship with the real deal. "Friendship is about letting something happen between two people that's surprising and new," says Turkle, whereas social networking "gives the illusion of companionship without the demands of intimacy. It's friendship on demand, when I want it."

Is there a limit to the number of real friends one can have? British   10 evolutionary anthropologist Robin Dunbar suggests there is. Based on his research into primate behavior, Dunbar posits a limit to the number of stable relationships an individual is capable of maintaining, and fixes it at around 150, a quantity widely known as Dunbar's Number. He further maintains that on average we each possess about 50 friends, 15 "good" friends, and a mere 5 that can be categorized as "intimate."

In a recent *New York Times* op-ed column, Dunbar addressed the Facebook-friending phenomenon and questioned how authentic many of these Web-based friendships really are. "Put simply," he wrote, "our minds are not designed to allow us to have more than a very limited number of people in our social world. The emotional and psychological investments that a close relationship requires are considerable, and the emotional capital we have available is limited."

Dunbar elaborated on that theme in an e-mail from his University of Oxford office. "I don't think the real nature of friendship has changed as such," he asserted. "The key contrast is between friends (and relations) and acquaintances." Real friends "require time and effort to get to know," he added, in contrast to less intimate relationships that by definition are less demanding to sustain and manage.

Differentiating between true friendship and the more superficial kind is not merely the province of academics, to be sure. As the meaning of "friend" gets stretched and changed, many admit to making conscious decisions about who fits the definition and who does not, and why.

As the meaning of "friend" gets stretched and changed, many admit to making conscious decisions about who fits the definition who does not, and why.

To Boston-based public relations consultant Caron Le Brun, friendships get complicated by factors like age and professional contacts in real-world situations. "I'm of the (over-60) generation where family and friends are your most valued possessions," Le Brun says. "In the business world, though, especially public relations, you end up being a friend to everyone — but not really."

Like Le Brun, Boston attorney Joseph Feaster formed his ideas of friendship long before Mark Zuckerberg came along. Feaster, 61, has found it useful to divide relationships into four categories: partners, meaning people he would give or do anything for; friends, or people for whom he'd do just about anything (emphasis on almost); associates, meaning those he's merely acquainted with, perhaps through his office or gym; and people he knows, but that's about it.   15

He does use social media sites like LinkedIn and Facebook, the latter a site on which he counts 200 friends. However, Feaster is selective about whom he elects to "friend" and doesn't look to social media sites to cultivate relationships he'd put in the "partner" category.

"It's too impersonal for me," he says. "I want to see, touch, feel you. I'm of the generation that would rather pick up the phone than text."

Boston University junior Sam Davidson has formulated categories of his own, divided between what he calls "primary" and "secondary" friends. The former, says Davidson, 22, are "people I'd hang out with outside class, whose phone numbers I have." The latter? "People I say hi to, or friend on Facebook, but that's about it. The reality is, in college if you're invited to a party, you can't bring all your friends along. So that narrows it to two or three."

One expert who doesn't seem overly troubled by how "friend" keeps changing is linguist and language columnist Ben Zimmer. Because words are endlessly flexible, Zimmer says, we shouldn't expect them to remain immutable but to be used in various ways for various purposes over time.

"People worry that this dilution is impacting (its meaning)," says   20
Zimmer. "I see it as the inherent flexibility of language taking on new
guises over time."

Society often focuses on these semantic shifts, he adds, as a way to
complain about larger social phenomena, such as being disconnected
geographically—and emotionally—from one's family and childhood
roots. "Words become proxies for anxieties," he says, "in this case anxiety
about connections to people" in the Facebook age.

THINKING CRITICALLY ABOUT THE READING

1. What is Kahn's thesis? Where does he state it?

2. In paragraph 8, Kahn quotes Sherry Turkle at MIT as believing "that 'friend'
    has become 'contested terrain' linguistically as social media sites alter the
    term's very DNA." What does Turkle mean?

3. What is Dunbar's Number? Why is a knowledge of Dunbar's Number critical
    to Kahn's analysis of the semantic shift that has taken place with the word
    friend?

4. Why does Kahn feel it's necessary to give the ages of some of the people he
    cites as authorities in his article?

5. Kahn and others believe that the number of true friends one can have is lim-
    ited by one's emotional capital. What is emotional capital and why do we
    consider it limited?

WRITING SUGGESTIONS

1. Write an essay in which you define what a friend is and what the term implies
    for you. To what does being someone's friend obligate you? What benefits
    might come to you as someone's friend? What would you do for a friend and
    expect a friend to do for you? Are there qualities in a friendship that do not
    have to do with favors or deeds exchanged? Include in your essay a number of
    brief anecdotes or examples of what you mean by friendship and perhaps even
    a long example to illustrate your definition.

2. Write an essay similar to Kahn's on how social media is changing our lan-
    guage. Show how words other than *friend* have been changed or influenced
    either by semantic shift or diffusion by social media. What new words have
    been added and what do they mean and how do we use them? Here are a
    few such words and word combinations that you may wish to use or that
    may get you thinking about how our language is evolving: hashtag, tweet,
    retweet, pin, community, trending, lurk or lurker, post or poster, unfriend,
    viral, timeline, webinar, Facebook me, and follow. What about symbols such
    as # and @?

LANGUAGE IN ACTION

Think about the message of the following cartoon by the Canadian cartoonist and comic Rina Piccolo, who is best known for her comic strip *Tina's Groove*. What's humorous about it? How well does the cartoon illustrate and extend the points Kahn makes?

"It says no one really knows who he is but that he has 400,000 followers on Twitter."

Keep Your Thumbs Still
When I'm Talking to You

DAVID CARR

David Carr is a journalist and author who writes about media and culture for the *New York Times*. He was born and raised in 1956 in Hopkins, Minnesota, where he attended grade school and high school. Later, he attended the University of Wisconsin–River Falls and then the University of Minnesota, all the while working at odd jobs to pay for his education. In all, as he put it in an interview for a series about unconventional educations, it took him seven years to get through college. Carr is the former editor of the *Twin Cities Reader,* and he wrote for the alternative weekly *Washington City Paper*, the *Atlantic Monthly*, and *New York Magazine* before moving to the *Times*. In addition to being one of the writers featured in *Page One: Inside the New York Times*, a documentary about how and why the *New York Times* wouldn't relinquish its esteemed position in the journalistic world to Facebook and Twitter, Carr is the author of the best-selling memoir *The Night of the Gun*. In the book he recounts the story of his own cocaine addiction by interviewing the people he associated with during that period of his life. In his review of the memoir, Corby Kummer, his former editor at the *Atlantic*, referred to Carr's "joyous peculiarity."

In "Keep Your Thumbs Still When I'm Talking to You," which was first published in the *New York Times* on April 15, 2011, Carr argues that our digital age "has made it fashionable to be rude."

WRITING TO DISCOVER: *When someone you are conversing with answers a call or takes out a phone to make a call, what has been your response? How did you feel? Unimportant? Understanding, especially if there might be an emergency? Angry or disgusted when you realized the call was trivial chit-chat? Have you changed the way you react to such situations over time?*

You are at a party and the person in front of you is not really listening to you. Yes, she is murmuring occasional assent to your remarks, or nodding at appropriate junctures, but for the most part she is looking beyond you, scanning in search of something or someone more compelling.

Here's the funny part: If she is looking over your shoulder at a room full of potentially more interesting people, she is ill-mannered. If, however, she is not looking over your shoulder, but into a smartphone in her hand, she is not only well within modern social norms, but is also a wired, well-put-together person.

Add one more achievement to the digital revolution: It has made it fashionable to be rude.

I thought about that a lot at South by Southwest Interactive, the annual campfire of the digitally interested held in Austin, Tex., the second week of March; inside, conference rooms brimmed with wireless connections, and the people on the dais competed with a screen in almost every seat: laptops, or even more commonly, tablets. In that context, the live presentation that the people in the audience had ostensibly come many miles to see was merely companion media.

But even more remarkably, once the badge-decorated horde spilled   5
into the halls or went to the hundreds of parties that mark the ritual, almost everyone walked or talked with one eye, or both, on a little screen. We were adjacent but essentially alone, texting and talking our way through what should have been a great chance to engage flesh-and-blood human beings. The wait in line for panels, badges, or food became one more chance to check in digitally instead of an opportunity to meet someone you didn't know.

I moderated a panel there called "I'm So Productive, I Never Get Anything Done," which was ostensibly about how answering e-mail and looking after various avatars on Facebook, Twitter and Tumblr left little time to do what we actually care about or get paid for. The biggest reaction in the session by far came when Anthony De Rosa, a product manager and programmer at Reuters and a big presence on Twitter and Tumblr, said that mobile connectedness has eroded fundamental human courtesies.

"When people are out and they're among other people they need to just put everything down," he said. "It's fine when you're at home or at work when you're distracted by things, but we need to give that respect to each other back."

His words brought sudden and tumultuous applause. It was sort of a moment, given that we were sitting amid some of the most digitally devoted people in the hemisphere.

Add one more achievement to the digital revolution: It has made it fashionable to be rude.

Perhaps somewhere on the way to the merger of the online and offline world, we had all stepped across a line without knowing it.

In an e-mail later, Mr. De Rosa wrote: "I'm fine with people stepping aside to check something, but when I'm standing in front of someone and in the middle of my conversation they whip out their phone, I'll just stop talking to them and walk away. If they're going to be rude, I'll be rude right back."

After the panel, one of the younger people in the audience came   10
up to me to talk earnestly about the importance of actual connection, which was nice, except he was casting sidelong glances at his iPhone while we talked. I'm not even sure he knew he was doing it. It's not just conferences full of inforati where this happens. In places all over America (theaters, sports arenas, apartments), people gather in groups only to disperse into lone pursuits between themselves and their phones.

Every meal out with friends or colleagues represents a negotiation between connectedness to the grid and interaction with those on hand. "Last year, for my friend's birthday, my gift to her was to stay off my phone at her birthday dinner," said Molly McAleer, who blogs and sends Twitter messages under the name Molls. "How embarrassing."

If South by Southwest is, as its attendees claim, an indicator of what is to come, we won't be seeing a lot of one another even if we happen to be in the same room. Anthony Breznican, a reporter for *Entertainment Weekly*, said all it takes is for one person at a dinner to excuse himself into his phone, and the race is on among everyone else.

"Instead of continuing with the conversation, we all take out our phones and check them in earnest," he said. "For a few minutes everybody is typing away. A silence falls over the group and we all engage in a mass thumb-wrestling competition between man and little machine. Then the moment passes, the BlackBerrys and iPhones are reholstered, and we return to being humans again after a brief trance."

In the instance of screen etiquette, sharing is not always caring, and sometimes, the bigger the screen, the larger the faux pas: On an elevator in the Austin Convention Center, some crazed social media promoter jammed his iPad under my nose and started demo-ing his hideously complicated social networking app that was going to change the world. I leaped to safety as soon as the door opened.

Still, many are finished apologizing for what has become a very natu-   15
ral mix of online and offline pursuits. In an essay on *TechCrunch* entitled "I Will Check My Phone at Dinner and You Will Deal With It," MG Siegler wrote, "Forgive me, but it's Dinner 2.0."

He added: "This is the way the world works now. We're always connected and always on call. And some of us prefer it that way."

It scans as progress, but doesn't always feel that way. There are a number of reasons why people at conferences and out in the world treat their phones like a Tamagotchi, the digital pet invented in Japan that died if it wasn't constantly looked after and fed.

To begin with, phones glow. It is a very normal impulse to stare at something in your hand that is emitting light.

Beyond the gadget itself, the screen offers a data stream of many people, as opposed to the individual you happen to be near. Your e-mail, Twitter, Facebook, and other online social groups all offer a data stream of many individuals, and you can choose the most interesting one, unlike the human rain delay you may be stuck with at a party. Then there is also a specific kind of narcissism that the social Web engenders. By grooming and updating your various avatars, you are making sure you remain at the popular kid's table. One of the more seductive data points in real-time media is what people think of you. The metrics of followers and retweets beget a kind of always-on day trading in the unstable currency of the self.

"My personal pet peeve is people who live-tweet every interaction,"   20
said Roxanna Asgarian, a student at the CUNY Graduate School of Journalism who attended South by Southwest this year. "I prefer to experience
the thing itself over the experience of telling people I'm doing the thing."

Still, for those of us who are afraid of missing something, having the
grid at our fingertips offers reassurance that we are in the right spot or
gives indicators of heat elsewhere.

But all is not vanity. For anybody with children, a job, or a significant other, the expectation these days is that certain special people, usually
beginning with our bosses, can reach us at any minute of any day. Every
once in a while something truly important tumbles into our in-box that
requires immediate attention.

Mobile devices do indeed make us more mobile, but that tether is also
a leash, letting everyone know that they can get you at any second, most
often to tell you they are late, but on their way. (Another bit of bad manners that the always-on world helps facilitate, by the way.)

At the conference, I saw people who waited 90 minutes to get into
a party with a very tough door, peering into their phones the whole
while, only to breach the door finally and resume staring into the same
screen and only occasionally glancing up. In that sense, the scenery
never really changes when you are riding with your digital wingman.
I saw people who were sitting on panels surfing or e-mailing during
lulls, and then were taken by surprise when it was their turn to talk.
(And it's not just those children. I was hosting a discussion at another
conference with Martha Stewart, no slouch when it comes to manners,
and she kept us all waiting while she checked "one more thing" on her
Twitter.)

I should sheepishly mention I was on highest alert for electronic   25
offense because I switched out my smartphone before South by Southwest
and was on a new Droid that I'm pretty sure could guide the next mission to Mars, but it was clunky when it came to sending texts and Twitter
messages. Digital natives (read "young people") will tell you that they can
easily toggle between online and offline. My colleague Brian Stelter can
almost pull it off, in part because he always seems to be creating media and
consuming it. And in Austin I saw Andy Carvin, NPR's one-man signal
tower of North African revolution on Twitter, sitting in front of a screen
while the British band Yuck played a killer outdoor set at Stubb's. He sent
Twitter messages about the show, and about Bahrain as well.

William Powers, the author of *Hamlet's BlackBerry*, a book about
getting control of your digital life, appeared on a panel at South by Southwest and wrote that he came away thinking he had witnessed "a gigantic
competition to see who can be more absent from the people and conversations happening right around them. Everyone in Austin was gazing into
their little devices — a bit desperately, too, as if their lives depended on not
missing the next tweet."

In a phone conversation a few weeks afterward, Mr. Powers said that he is far from being a Luddite, but that he doesn't "buy into the idea that digital natives can do both screen and eye contact."

"They are not fully present because we are not built that way," he said.

Where other people saw freedom—from the desktop, from social convention, from the boring guy in front of them—Mr. Powers saw "a kind of imprisonment."

"There is a great deal of conformity under way, actually," he added.   30

And therein lies the real problem. When someone you are trying to talk to ends up getting busy on a phone, the most natural response is not to scold, but to emulate. It's mutually assured distraction.

THINKING CRITICALLY ABOUT THE READING

1. In paragraph 4 Carr discusses his experience at the South by Southwest Interactive conference. What did he find ironic about the presentations by people on the dais? (Glossary: *Irony*)

2. Why, according to Carr, do we find it more attractive to reach for our phone than talk to the person we are with? What's the allure?

3. What does Carr mean when he writes in paragraph 19: "The metrics of followers and retweets beget a kind of always-on day trading in the unstable currency of the self"? Explain the metaphor that Carr uses in paragraph 24 when he writes: "In that sense, the scenery never really changes when you are riding with your digital wingman." (Glossary: *Figures of Speech*)

4. Author William Powers thought he had witnessed at the South by Southwest show "a gigantic competition to see who can be more absent from the people and conversations happening right around them" (27). In your opinion, is he correct? If so, what does that observation say about how we are changing as a result of the digital revolution?

5. How well does Carr's title reflect his topic and thesis? (Glossary: *Title*)

LANGUAGE IN ACTION

How do you think texting might be affecting personal relationships between partners and married people? What are the issues? Are there gender differences? What are the implications in the following cartoon?

"You have to learn how to communicate. Buy a pair of texting mobile phones and use them."

A. Bacall/www.CartoonStock.com

WRITING SUGGESTIONS

1. Carr raises the issue of rudeness. What is it, anyway? Is the possibility of rudeness always present but made more obvious by our interactive media? Or, as the population grows, are we all fighting for more recognition and a desire to be in the center of things and caring less for how we might offend each other? Write an essay in which you define rudeness and how our smartphones and the language they carry are encouraging the disrespect we see for each other wherever people gather today. Finally, if you disagree with the assumptions just presented, write an essay in which you define rudeness but argue that rudeness is not new, just made easier and more visible by recent innovations and methods of communicating.

2. Write an essay in which you examine your own behavior when talking on your cell phone or texting. Are you conscious of when and where to use your cell phone? Have your habits changed over the time you have been making calls and texting? Do you talk on the phone in public places such as restaurants, lectures, sporting events, and parties? What distinctions do you and your friends make about the proper etiquette to use in various situations? What determines the principles you abide by and how do you react to those who violate generally accepted practices?

America and the "Fun" Generation

ANAND GIRIDHARADAS

A columnist for the *New York Times* and its foreign edition the *International Herald Tribune*, Anand Giridharadas was born in Cleveland, Ohio, to parents from Bombay. He grew up in Cleveland, Paris, and the Washington, D.C., area. After studying the history of political thought at the University of Michigan, Ann Arbor; and St. Edmund Hall, Oxford; he left in 2003 to become a Bombay-based columnist. For four years he reported on the transformation of the Indian economy and society as it rose in international stature, covering such topics as terrorism, outsourcing, Bollywood (India's film industry), democracy, poverty, and how technology has altered the lives of the Indian people. In addition to his television and radio appearances and public speaking engagements, Giridharadas has written *India Calling: An Intimate Portrait of a Nation's Rebuilding* (2011). Also, in 2011 the Aspen Institute, a values-based leadership and policy conference, named Giridharadas a Henry Crown Fellow.

In "America and the 'Fun' Generation," first published in the *New York Times* on October 29, 2010, Giridharadas makes an interesting observation about America's shifting values from the 1810s to the 2000s by analyzing the *Corpus of Historical American English*, a vast database of 425 million words. Certainly, observations and research of this kind would not be possible without the use of advanced digital technology.

WRITING TO DISCOVER: *What do you mean by the words* pleasure *and* fun? *What's the difference in meaning between the two words? What would be a pleasurable experience for you? What would be a fun experience?*

From the first years of the American republic, a quiet battle has simmered over the words that denote the nation's soul. And now a count can declare the victors: "achievement" and "fun."

From the 1810s to the 2000s, the frequency of "achievement" in written American English grew elevenfold, according to a search of the *Corpus of Historical American English*, a database of 107,000 newspapers, magazines, novels, plays and film scripts. In the same period, the frequency of "fun" multiplied by more than eight times.

Meanwhile, another pair of words met an opposite fate. As talk of "achievement" soared over two centuries, the term "excellence" dropped out of favor, also elevenfold. As "fun" gained influence, mentions of "pleasure" fell by a factor of four.

In the history of language, words rise and fall. We make and remake them; they make and remake us.

The story of a word is as complex as a hurricane. It is difficult to know for sure how it catches on, meets new needs, acquires new valences. It is impossible to blame the decline of one word on the rise of another.

But in the destinies of these two pairs of words is a suggestion of a turning in American culture, and one that has influenced the world. It is a turning away from an arguably aristocratic idea of the intrinsic worth of things: from pleasure, with its sense of an internal condition of mind, to fun, so closely affiliated with outward activities; from excellence, an inner trait whose attainment is its own reward, to achievement, which comes through slogging and recognition.

> **In the history of language, words rise and fall. We make and remake them; they make and remake us.**

Merriam-Webster defines "pleasure" as "a state of gratification," while fun is "what provides amusement or enjoyment; specifically, playful, often boisterous, speech or action." It defines "excellence" as "the quality of being excellent," which in turn means "very good of its kind: eminently good." "Achievement," meanwhile, is "a result gained by effort."

The arc of American usage from "pleasure" to "fun" can be traced in the corpus's database. In an 1812 play, John Blake White wrote, "Wherefore wealth, if not to purchase pleasure? Wherefore health, if not to taste, when pleasure holds the cup and bids us drink." By 2009, this line from the novelist Hyatt Bass was more typical: "Come on. Don't you think it's fun to have a bottle of wine that was released the same month you got engaged?"

"Pleasure" carries a hint of the sublime; it speaks of a state of mind that comes organically, that need not be artificially induced.

"Fun," though almost synonymous with "pleasure" for contemporary speakers, often involves artificial inducement. You don't feel fun; you do a fun thing. And fun has no hint of elitism, whereas pleasure vaguely does.

Gushing waterfalls provide pleasure; games of paintball, in which friends playfully (and sometimes painfully) shoot one another with pellets of paint, provide fun. A long, gabby dinner party may well be a "pleasure"; a crowded, sweat-laced night at the six-deep bar is more likely to be termed "fun."

If "pleasure" comes from being and from talking through ideas, "fun" comes from doing and, often, switching off the brain. The change perhaps partly accounts for the American insistence on activities for all occasions, rather than trusting pleasure to develop on its own.

Rare is the American corporate retreat or after-Thanksgiving party that does not involve a skit or contest or session of Nintendo Wii. Where others might eat, drink, and talk, Americans often create themes and talent shows.

In *Eat, Pray, Love*, the best-selling memoir by Elizabeth Gilbert, she describes discovering the Italian idea of pleasure as if it were a buried city: "During my first few weeks in Italy, all my Protestant synapses were zinging in distress, looking for a task. I wanted to take on pleasure like a homework assignment." She concludes that "Americans have an inability to relax into sheer pleasure. Ours is an entertainment-seeking nation, but not necessarily a pleasure-seeking one."

Italians, on the other hand, have mastered *bel far niente*, the beauty of 15 doing nothing, Ms. Gilbert writes.

Then there is the arc from "excellence" to "achievement." Consider this sentence, from an 1813 poem: "would she thus a moral teach; / That man should see, but never reach, / The height of excellence, and show / The vanity of works below?"

And this one, from a 2005 biography: "the young man pursues his dream while others scoff, he undertakes a lonely journey from the country to the city in search of fulfillment, overcomes obstacles with a combination of pluck, determination, and talent, and finally rises to heights of achievement and prosperity."

"Excellence" evokes Aristotle with its overtones of virtue. Anyone can achieve, in garbage collection or neurosurgery, but how many can truly be excellent?

"The ancient Greek definition of happiness was the full use of your powers along lines of excellence," President John F. Kennedy once said.

"Achievement" is a word more likely to come from American leaders 20 today, and, like "fun," it is outward in nature. It comes in doing specific things. It is more about checking boxes than fulfilling inner potentialities.

The achievement culture permeates life today. From elementary-school testing to the incessant pressure to overschedule as a university student, educational culture emphasizes the racking up of achievements over intellectual crackle. Wall Street stumbled in part because so many chased achiever bonuses while neglecting the pursuit of excellence in their vocation. An American culture of instantaneous celebrity teaches young people that fame is an end in itself rather than an incidental symptom of excellence in craft.

The world in which "pleasure" and "excellence" roared was less equitable than our world today. It shut out vast categories of humankind. In the intervening years, those exclusions dwindled; the world opened up for so many, not least in the United States. But with that change has come another: what would seem to be a growing intolerance for merely being, and an anguished insistence on doing, doing, doing.

THINKING CRITICALLY ABOUT THE READING

1. What point is Giridharadas trying to make in his essay? How well does he make that point in your opinion?

2. In paragraph 1, Giridharadas writes: "And now a count can declare the victors: 'achievement' and 'fun.'" What did "achievement" and "fun" win out over?

3. How has Giridharadas made use of technology in his research? Explain how the technology works.

4. How would you summarize the difference between the life Italians lead and the life Americans lead, based on the evidence Giridharadas presents from Elizabeth Gilbert's book *Eat, Pray, Love*?

5. In reflecting on the arc of usage change for the two pairs of words on which he bases his article, what conclusions does Giridharadas draw and what is their significance for America and for the rest of the world?

6. Why does Giridharadas believe that the frequency of the words we use is revealing? Do you agree?

LANGUAGE IN ACTION

Discuss the following cartoon as one suggests there are varying degrees of acceptance by diners of those who are texting near them in a restaurant. Have you texted while dining? Would you ever? Does it make a difference what kind of restaurant it is? Would you text in a diner but not in a fine dining establishment, for example? What is the difference, if any? Is the cartoon's creator being serious in suggesting that soon we'll have to ask people how close they'd be willing to sit near texters in a restaurant? Or, is the situation in restaurants getting so bad that soon we'll actually have to ask the question asked by the host in the cartoon?

A. Bacall/www.CartoonStock.com

"Easily annoyed by nearby texting guests or not easily annoyed by nearby texting guests?"

Turn to page 394.

G SUGGESTIONS

1. Argue against the conclusions Giridharadas draws. Just because the words *achievement* and *fun* have become more frequent than *excellence* and *pleasure* over the nearly two hundred years covered by the database, does that mean those values themselves have changed in American culture? Is there not a presumption in his argument that the people who used the two pairs of words in the past made the same distinctions between them that he is now making? Might it be the case that we hold the same values we always have but are simply using different words for those values? After all, he himself writes that it's difficult to know, "But in the destinies of these two pairs of words is a suggestion of a turning in American culture, and one that has influenced the world" (6). He does not state it as fact.

2. In the beginning of his essay, Giridharadas writes, "From the first years of the American republic, a quiet battle has simmered over the words that denote the nation's soul." Write an essay in which you enter into that fray by describing America's soul from your perspective. What words would figure prominently in your description? You might wish to begin your essay by discussing the analysis Giridharadas engages in and the conclusions he comes to in his essay, findings that are not all positive or negative. You might not only describe the soul of our country as you see and understand it but also as you might wish it.

12

LANGUAGE AND ADVERTISING

Advertising is big business and a very real part of our daily lives. We hear a steady stream of ads on the radio; see them on television, the Web, and our phones; read them in newspapers and magazines; and even wear them on our clothing. Advertising is so ever-present in our lives that we often take it for granted, never thinking about the impact that it has on each of us every day. In the next decade American businesses will spend well over $150 billion a year on print ads and television and Internet commercials. Appealing to our fantasies of wealth, good looks, power, social acceptance, healthy living, love, and happiness, advertising tries to persuade us to purchase particular products or services. Though every business hopes that its ads will be memorable and work effectively, we know that not all of them are successful. What makes one advertisement more effective than another? To answer such a question, we need to become more sensitive to advertising language and the ways advertisers combine words and images.

The articles in this chapter cover a range of views on the power of advertising in our lives. In the opening selection, "The Hard Sell: Advertising in America," Bill Bryson provides a historical perspective and context for the world of advertising, whose roots he locates in the late nineteenth and early twentieth centuries. William Lutz challenges advertisers and their manipulative language in "Weasel Words" and exposes some of the secrets of successful advertising language and what it really means. Business consultant Frank Luntz specializes in message creation and image management. In "Be All That You Can Be: The Company Persona and Language Alignment," he takes us inside some of America's most successful companies and shows us how they create a company persona, "the sum of the corporate leadership, the corporate ethos, the products and services offered, interaction with the customer, and, most importantly, the language that ties it all together." In "Be It Ever So Homespun, There's Nothing Like Spin," food writer Kim Severson discusses the impact that the environmental green movement has had on advertising. She believes that the "green-elite food consumers" will no longer be persuaded by the instant identifiers associated with current packaging designs and folksy narratives used to describe products. Soon they will "push companies for even more information about environmental impact, labor practices, and community involvement, and mass market consumers will start reading labels instead of just searching out easy identifiers." We offer a case-in-point study of the word *natural* with Sarah Federman's "What's Natural about Our Natural Products?" Most consumers are persuaded by the connotations of words like *natural, fresh, organic, local,* and *wholesome* to believe that they are buying something that will be good for them. Not necessarily so, says Federman. We know that *natural* sounds good, but because the word is unregulated, it is never really clear what it means when attached to any given product. Finally, we provide a close look at an iconic Super Bowl commercial in "'Halftime in America' Backlash," a video commentary from *Wall Street Journal* featuring Jeff Bennett (available online at bedfordstmartins.com/languageawareness/epages). Bennett examines the ad's carefully crafted language and corporate ethos as well as the attention it received—both positive and negative.

The Hard Sell: Advertising in America

BILL BRYSON

Journalist and author Bill Bryson was born in Des Moines, Iowa, in 1951, and spent two years at Drake University before dropping out in 1972. He spent most of his adult life in Great Britain, beginning with a backpacking trip to Europe in 1973. He settled in England with his wife in 1977, where he worked as a journalist, eventually becoming chief copy editor of the business section of the *Times,* and then national news editor for the *Independent.* Bryson's interest in language is reflected in his *A Dictionary of Troublesome Words* (1987), *The Mother Tongue: English and How It Got That Way* (1990), *Shakespeare: The World as Stage* (2007), and *Bryson's Dictionary for Writers and Editors* (2008). Among his many books on travel are *The Lost Continent: Travels in Small-Town America* (1989), *Neither Here Nor There: Travels in Europe* (1992), *A Walk in the Woods: Rediscovering America on the Appalachian Trail* (1998), and *Bill Bryson's African Diary* (2002). Bryson's 2003 book on science, *A Short History of Nearly Everything,* won the prestigious Royal Society Aventis Prize for science writing. His memoir, *The Life and Times of the Thunderbolt Kid,* was published in 2006. Most recently he served as Chancellor of Durham University in Durham, England.

The following essay is a chapter in Bryson's *Made in America: An Informal History of the English Language in the United States* (1994). In it, he provides a historical perspective on advertising and explores some of the trends that have appeared over the years. It may surprise many people to learn that advertising as we know it is a modern invention, spanning only about a century. During that time, however, the influence of advertisements has grown so much that they now shape the way we see the world.

WRITING TO DISCOVER: *Reactions to advertising vary, but most people would say that ads are a necessary evil and that they ignore them whenever possible. Yet advertising is a multibillion-dollar industry, which is financed by what we buy and sell. Think about some recent TV shows you've watched or newspapers you've read. Jot down the names of the products you saw advertised. Do you buy any of these products? Write about the influences, if any, advertising seems to have on the way you spend your money.*

In 1885, a young man named George Eastman formed the Eastman Dry Plate and Film Company in Rochester, New York. It was rather a bold thing to do. Aged just thirty-one, Eastman was a junior clerk in a bank on a comfortable but modest salary of $15 a week. He had no background in business. But he was passionately devoted to photography and had become increasingly gripped with the conviction that anyone who could develop a simple, untechnical camera, as opposed to the cumbersome, outsized, fussily complex contrivances then on the market, stood to make a fortune.

Eastman worked tirelessly for three years to perfect his invention, supporting himself in the meantime by making dry plates for commercial photographers, and in June 1888 produced a camera that was positively dazzling in its simplicity: a plain black box just six and a half inches long by three and a quarter inches wide, with a button on the side and a key for advancing the film. Eastman called his device the *Detective Camera*. Detectives were all the thing—Sherlock Holmes was just taking off with American readers—and the name implied that it was so small and simple that it could be used unnoticed, as a detective might.

The camera had no viewfinder and no way of focusing. The *photographer* or *photographist* (it took a while for the first word to become the established one) simply held the camera in front of him, pressed a button on the side, and hoped for the best. Each roll took a hundred pictures. When the roll was fully exposed, the anxious owner sent the entire camera to Rochester for developing. Eventually he received the camera back, freshly loaded with film, and—assuming all had gone well—one hundred small circular pictures, two and a half inches in diameter.

Often all didn't go well. The film Eastman used at first was made of paper, which tore easily and had to be carefully stripped of its emulsion before the exposures could be developed. It wasn't until the invention of celluloid roll film by a sixty-five-year-old Episcopal minister named Hannibal Goodwin in Newark, New Jersey—this truly was the age of the amateur inventor—that amateur photography became a reliable undertaking. Goodwin didn't call his invention *film* but *photographic pellicule*, and, as was usual, spent years fighting costly legal battles with Eastman without ever securing the recognition or financial payoff he deserved—though eventually, years after Goodwin's death, Eastman was ordered to pay $5 million to the company that inherited the patent.

In September 1888, Eastman changed the name of the camera to *Kodak*—an odd choice, since it was meaningless, and in 1888 no one gave meaningless names to products, especially successful products. Since British patent applications at the time demanded a full explanation of trade and brand names, we know how Eastman arrived at his inspired name. He crisply summarized his reasoning in his patent application: "First. It is short. Second. It is not capable of mispronunciation. Third. It does not resemble anything in the art and cannot be associated with anything in the art except the Kodak." Four years later the whole enterprise was renamed the Eastman Kodak Company.

Despite the considerable expense involved—a Kodak camera sold for $25, and each roll of film cost $10, including developing—by 1895, over 100,000 Kodaks had been sold and Eastman was a seriously wealthy man. A lifelong bachelor, he lived with his mother in a thirty-seven-room mansion with twelve bathrooms. Soon people everywhere were talking about snapshots, originally a British shooting term for a hastily executed shot. Its photographic sense was coined by the English astronomer Sir John Herschel, who also gave the world the terms *positive* and *negative* in their photographic senses.

From the outset, Eastman developed three crucial strategies that have been the hallmarks of virtually every successful consumer goods company since. First, he went for the mass market, reasoning that it was better to make a little money each from a lot of people rather than a lot of money from a few. He also showed a tireless, obsessive dedication to making his products better and cheaper. In the 1890s, such an approach was widely perceived as insane. If you had a successful product, you milked it for all it was worth. If competitors came along with something better, you bought them out or tried to squash them with lengthy patent fights or other bullying tactics. What you certainly did not do was create new products that made your existing lines obsolescent. Eastman did. Throughout the late 1890s, Kodak introduced a series of increasingly cheaper, niftier cameras — the Bull's Eye model of 1896, which cost just $12, and the famous slim-line Folding Pocket Kodak of 1898, before finally in 1900 producing his eureka model: the little box Brownie, priced at just $1 and with film at 15 cents a reel (though with only six exposures per reel).

Above all, what set Eastman apart was the breathtaking lavishness of his advertising. In 1899 alone, he spent $750,000, an unheard-of sum, on advertising. Moreover, it was *good* advertising: crisp, catchy, reassuringly trustworthy. "You press the button — we do the rest" ran the company's first slogan, thus making a virtue of its shortcomings. Never mind that you couldn't load or unload the film yourself. Kodak would do it for you. In 1905, it followed with another classic slogan: "If It Isn't an Eastman, It Isn't a Kodak."

Kodak's success did not escape other businessmen, who also began to see virtue in the idea of steady product refinement and improvement. AT&T and Westinghouse, among others, set up research laboratories with the idea of creating a stream of new products, even at the risk of displacing old ones. Above all, everyone everywhere began to advertise.

Advertising was already a well-established phenomenon by the turn of the twentieth century. Newspapers had begun carrying ads as far back as the early 1700s, and magazines soon followed. (Benjamin Franklin has the distinction of having run the first magazine ad, seeking the whereabouts of a runaway slave, in 1741.) By 1850, the country had its first *advertising agency,* the American Newspaper Advertising Agency, though its function was to buy advertising space rather than come up with creative campaigns. The first advertising agency in the modern sense was N. W. Ayer & Sons of Philadelphia, established in 1869. *To advertise* originally carried the sense of to broadcast or disseminate news. Thus a nineteenth-century newspaper that called itself the *Advertiser* meant that it had lots of news, not lots of ads. By the early 1800s the term had been stretched to accommodate the idea of spreading the news of the availability of certain goods or services. A newspaper notice that read "Jos. Parker, Hatter" was essentially announcing that if anyone was in the market for hats, Jos. Parker had them. In the sense of persuading members of the public to acquire items they might not otherwise think of buying—items they didn't know they needed—advertising is a phenomenon of the modern age.

By the 1890s, advertising was appearing everywhere—in newspapers and magazines, on *billboards* (an Americanism dating from 1850), on the sides of buildings, on passing streetcars, on paper bags, even on matchbooks, which were invented in 1892 and were being extensively used as an advertising medium within three years.

Very early on, advertisers discovered the importance of a good slogan. Many of our more venerable slogans are older than you might think. Ivory Soap's "99 44/100 percent pure" dates from 1879. Schlitz has been calling itself "the beer that made Milwaukee famous" since 1895, and Heinz's "57 varieties" followed a year later. Morton Salt's "When it rains, it pours" dates from 1911, the American Florist Association's "Say it with flowers" was first used in 1912, and the "good to the last drop" of Maxwell House coffee, named for the Maxwell House Hotel in Nashville, where it was first served, has been with us since 1907. (The slogan is said to have originated with Teddy Roosevelt, who pronounced the coffee "good to the last drop," prompting one wit to ask, "So what's wrong with the last drop?")

Sometimes slogans took a little working on. Coca-Cola described itself as "the drink that makes a pause refreshing" before realizing, in 1929, that "the pause that refreshes" was rather more succinct and memorable. A slogan could make all the difference to a product's success. After advertising its soap as an efficacious way of dealing with "conspicuous nose pores," Woodbury's Facial Soap came up with the slogan "The skin you love to touch" and won the hearts of millions. The great thing about a slogan was that it didn't have to be accurate to be effective. Heinz never actually had exactly "57 varieties" of anything. The catchphrase arose simply because H. J. Heinz, the company's founder, decided he liked the sound of the number. Undeterred by considerations of verity, he had the slogan slapped on every one of the products he produced, already in 1896 far more than fifty-seven. For a time the company tried to arrange its products into fifty-seven arbitrary clusters, but in 1969 it gave up the ruse altogether and abandoned the slogan.

Early in the 1900s, advertisers discovered another perennial feature of marketing—the *giveaway,* as it was called almost from the start. Consumers soon became acquainted with the irresistibly tempting notion that if they bought a particular product they could expect a reward—the chance to receive a prize, a free book (almost always ostensibly dedicated to the general improvement of one's well-being but invariably a thinly disguised plug for the manufacturer's range of products), a free sample, or a rebate in the form of a shiny dime, or be otherwise endowed with some gratifying bagatelle. Typical of the genre was a turn-of-the-century tome called *The Vital Question Cook Book,* which was promoted as an aid to livelier meals, but which proved upon receipt to contain 112 pages of recipes all involving the use of Shredded Wheat. Many of these had a certain air of desperation about them, notably the "Shredded Wheat Biscuit Jellied Apple Sandwich" and the "Creamed Spinach on Shredded Wheat Biscuit Toast." Almost all involved nothing more than spooning some everyday food on a piece of shredded wheat and giving it an inflated name. Nonetheless the company distributed no fewer than four million copies of *The Vital Question Cook Book* to eager consumers.

The great breakthrough in twentieth-century advertising, however, came with the identification and exploitation of the American consumer's Achilles' heel: anxiety. One of the first to master the form was King Gillette, inventor of the first safety razor and one of the most relentless advertisers of the early 1900s. Most of the early ads featured Gillette himself, who with his fussy toothbrush mustache and well-oiled hair looked more like a caricature of a Parisian waiter than a captain of industry. After starting with a few jaunty words about the ease and convenience of the safety razor—"Compact? Rather!"—he plunged the reader into the heart of the matter: "When you use my razor you are exempt from the dangers that men often encounter who allow their faces to come in contact with brush, soap, and barbershop accessories used on other people."

Here was an entirely new approach to selling goods. Gillette's ads were in effect telling you that not only did there exist a product that you never previously suspected you needed, but if you *didn't* use it you would very possibly attract a crop of facial diseases you never knew existed. The combination proved irresistible. Though the Gillette razor retailed for a hefty $5—half the average workingman's weekly pay—it sold by the millions, and King Gillette became a very wealthy man. (Though only for a time, alas. Like many others of his era, he grew obsessed with the idea of the perfectibility of mankind and expended so much of his energies writing books of convoluted philosophy with titles like *The Human Drift* that he eventually lost control of his company and most of his fortune.)

By the 1920s, advertisers had so refined the art that a consumer could scarcely pick up a magazine without being bombarded with unsettling questions: "Do You Make These Mistakes in English?"; "Will Your Hair Stand Close Inspection?"; "When Your Guests Are Gone—Are You Sorry You Ever Invited Them?" (because, that is, you lack social polish); "Did Nature fail to put roses in your cheeks?"; "Will There be a Victrola in Your Home This Christmas?"[1] The 1920s truly were the Age of Anxiety. One

15

---

1. The most famous 1920s ad of them all didn't pose a question, but it did play on the reader's anxiety: "They Laughed When I Sat Down, but When I Started to Play . . ." It was originated by the U.S. School of Music in 1925.

ad pictured a former golf champion, "now only a wistful onlooker," whose career had gone sour because he had neglected his teeth. Scott Tissues mounted a campaign showing a forlorn-looking businessman sitting on a park bench beneath the bold caption "A Serious Business Handicap—These Troubles That Come from Harsh Toilet Tissue." Below the picture the text explained "65 percent of all men and women over 40 are suffering from some form of rectal trouble, estimates a prominent specialist connected with one of New York's largest hospitals. 'And one of the contributing causes,' he states, 'is inferior toilet tissue.'" There was almost nothing that one couldn't become uneasy about. One ad even asked: "Can You Buy a Radio Safely?" Distressed bowels were the most frequent target. The makers of Sal Hepatica warned: "We rush to meetings, we dash to parties. We are on the go all day long. We exercise too little, and we eat too much. And, in consequence, we impair our bodily functions—often we retain food within us too long. And when that occurs, poisons are set up—*Auto-Intoxication begins.*"

In addition to the dread of auto-intoxication, the American consumer faced a gauntlet of other newly minted maladies—*pyorrhea, halitosis* (coined as a medical term in 1874, but popularized by Listerine beginning in 1922 with the slogan "Even your best friend won't tell you"), *athlete's foot* (a term invented by the makers of Absorbine Jr. in 1928), *dead cuticles, scabby toes, iron-poor blood, vitamin deficiency* (*vitamins* had been coined in 1912, but the word didn't enter the general vocabulary until the 1920s, when advertisers realized it sounded worryingly scientific), *fallen stomach, tobacco breath,* and *psoriasis,* though Americans would have to wait until the next decade for the scientific identification of the gravest of personal disorders—*body odor,* a term invented in 1933 by the makers of Lifebuoy soap and so terrifying in its social consequences that it was soon abbreviated to a whispered *B.O.*

The white-coated technicians of American laboratories had not only identified these new conditions, but—miraculously, it seemed—simultaneously come up with cures for them. Among the products that were invented or rose to greatness in this busy, neurotic decade were *Cutex* (for those deceased cuticles), *Vick's VapoRub, Geritol, Serutan* ("Natures spelled backwards," as the voiceover always said with somewhat bewildering reassurance, as if spelling a product's name backward conferred some medicinal benefit), *Noxema* (for which read: "knocks eczema"), *Preparation H, Murine* eyedrops, and *Dr. Scholl's Foot Aids.*[2] It truly was an age of miracles—one in which you could even cure a smoker's cough by smoking, so long as it was Old Golds you smoked, because, as the slogan proudly if somewhat untruthfully boasted, they contained "Not a cough

---

2. And yes, there really was a Dr. Scholl. His name was William Scholl; he was a real doctor, genuinely dedicated to the well-being of feet, and they are still very proud of him in his hometown of La Porter, Indiana.

in a carload." (As late as 1953, L&M cigarettes were advertised as "just what the doctor ordered!")

By 1927, advertising was a $1.5-billion-a-year industry in the United States, and advertising people were held in such awe that they were asked not only to mastermind campaigns but even to name the products. An ad man named Henry N. McKinney, for instance, named *Keds* shoes, *Karo* syrup, *Meadow Gold* butter, and *Uneeda Biscuits.* 20

Product names tended to cluster around certain sounds. Breakfast cereals often ended in *-ies (Wheaties, Rice Krispies, Frosties);* washing powders and detergents tended to be gravely monosyllabic *(Lux, Fab, Tide, Duz).* It is often possible to tell the era of a product's development by its termination. Thus products dating from the 1920s and early 1930s often ended in *-ex (Pyrex, Cutex, Kleenex, Windex),* while those ending in *master (Mixmaster, Toastmaster)* generally betray a late 1930s or early-1940s genesis. The development of *Glo-Coat* floor wax in 1932 also heralded the beginning of American business's strange and long-standing infatuation with illiterate spellings, a trend that continued with *ReaLemon* juice in 1935, *Reddi-Wip* whipped cream in 1947, and many hundreds of others since, from *Tastee-Freez* drive-ins to *Toys 'Я' Us,* along with countless others with a *Kwik, E-Z,* or *U* (as in *While-U-Wait*) embedded in their titles. The late 1940s saw the birth of a brief vogue for endings in *matic,* so that car manufacturers offered vehicles with *Seat-O-Matic* levers and *Cruise-O-Matic* transmissions, and even fitted sheets came with *Ezy-Matic* corners. Some companies became associated with certain types of names. Du Pont, for instance, had a special fondness for words ending in *-on.* The practice began with *nylon*—a name that was concocted out of thin air and owes nothing to its chemical properties—and was followed with *Rayon, Dacron, Orlon,* and *Teflon,* among many others. In recent years the company has moved on to what might be called its *Star Trek* phase with such compounds as *Tyvek, Kevlar, Sontara, Condura, Nomex,* and *Zemorain.*

Such names have more than passing importance to their owners. If American business has given us a large dose of anxiety in its ceaseless quest for a healthier *bottom line* (a term dating from the 1930s, though not part of mainstream English until the 1970s), we may draw some comfort from the thought that business has suffered a great deal of collective anxiety over protecting the names of its products.

A certain cruel paradox prevails in the matter of preserving brand names. Every business naturally wants to create a product that will dominate its market. But if that product so dominates the market that the brand name becomes indistinguishable in the public mind from the product itself—when people begin to ask for a *thermos* rather than a "Thermos brand vacuum flask"—then the term has become generic and the owner faces the loss of its trademark protection. That is why advertisements and labels so often carry faintly paranoid-sounding lines like "Tabasco is the registered trademark for the brand of pepper sauce made by McIlhenny

Co." and why companies like Coca-Cola suffer palpitations when they see a passage like this (from John Steinbeck's *The Wayward Bus*):

> "Got any coke?" another character asked.
> "No," said the proprietor. "Few bottles of Pepsi-Cola. Haven't had any coke for a month. . . . It's the same stuff. You can't tell them apart."

An understandable measure of confusion exists concerning the distinction between patents and trademarks and between trademarks and trade names. A *patent* protects the name of the product and its method of manufacture for seventeen years. Thus from 1895 to 1912, no one but the Shredded Wheat Company could make shredded wheat. But because patents require manufacturers to divulge the secrets of their products—and thus make them available to rivals to copy when the patent runs out— companies sometimes choose not to seek their protection. *Coca-Cola,* for one, has never been patented. A *trademark* is effectively the name of a product, its *brand name*. A *trade name* is the name of the manufacturer. So *Ford* is a trade name, *Taurus* a trademark. Trademarks apply not just to names, but also to logos, drawings, and other symbols and depictions. The MGM lion, for instance, is a trademark. Unlike patents, trademark protection goes on forever, or at least as long as the manufacturer can protect it.

> **Few really successful brand names of today were not just as familiar to your grandparents or even great-grandparents, and a well-established brand name has a sort of self-perpetuating power.**

For a long time, it was felt that this permanence gave the holder an unfair advantage. In consequence, America did not enact its first trademark law until 1870, almost a century after Britain, and then it was declared unconstitutional by the Supreme Court. Lasting trademark protection did not begin for American companies until 1881. Today, more than a million trademarks have been issued in the United States and the number is rising by about thirty thousand a year.

A good trademark is almost incalculably valuable. Invincible-seeming brand names do occasionally falter and fade. *Pepsodent, Rinso, Chase & Sanborn, Sal Hepatica, Vitalis, Brylcreem,* and *Burma-Shave* all once stood on the commanding heights of consumer recognition but are now defunct or have sunk to the status of what the trade calls "ghost brands"—products that are still produced but little promoted and largely forgotten. For the most part, however, once a product establishes a dominant position in a market, it is exceedingly difficult to depose it. In nineteen of twenty-two categories, the company that owned the leading American brand in 1925 still has it today— *Nabisco* in cookies, *Kellogg's* in breakfast cereals, *Kodak* in film, *Sherwin Williams* in paint, *Del Monte* in canned fruit, *Wrigleys* in chewing gum, *Singer* in sewing machines, *Ivory* in soap, *Campbell's* in soup, *Gillette* in razors. Few really successful brand names of today were not just as familiar to your grandparents or even great-grandparents, and a

25

well-established brand name has a sort of self-perpetuating power. As *The Economist* has noted: "In the category of food blenders, consumers were still ranking General Electric second twenty years after the company had stopped making them."

An established brand name is so valuable that only about 5 percent of the sixteen thousand or so new products introduced in America each year bear all-new brand names. The others are variants on an existing product — *Tide with Bleach, Tropicana Twister Light Fruit Juices,* and so on. Among some types of product a certain glut is evident. At last count there were 220 types of branded breakfast cereal in America. In 1993, according to an international business survey, the world's most valuable brand was *Marlboro,* with a value estimated at $40 billion, slightly ahead of *Coca-Cola.* Among the other ten brands were *Intel, Kellogg's, Budweiser, Pepsi, Gillette,* and *Pampers. Nescafé* and *Bacardi* were the only foreign brands to make the top ten, underlining American dominance.

Huge amounts of effort go into choosing brand names. General Foods reviewed 2,800 names before deciding on *Dreamwhip.* (To put this in proportion, try to think of just ten names for an artificial whipped cream.) Ford considered more than twenty thousand possible car names before finally settling on *Edsel* (which proves that such care doesn't always pay), and Standard Oil a similar number of names before it opted for *Exxon.* Sometimes, however, the most successful names are the result of a moment's whimsy. *Betty Crocker* came in a flash to an executive of the Washburn Crosby Company (later absorbed by General Mills), who chose *Betty* because he thought it sounded wholesome and sincere and *Crocker* in memory of a beloved fellow executive who had recently died. At first the name was used only to sign letters responding to customers' requests for advice or information, but by the 1950s, Betty Crocker's smiling, confident face was appearing on more than fifty types of food product, and her loyal followers could buy her recipe books and even visit her "kitchen" at the General Foods headquarters.

Great efforts also go into finding out why people buy the brands they do. Advertisers and market researchers bandy about terms like *conjoint analysis technique, personal drive patterns, Gaussian distributions, fractals,* and other such arcana in their quest to winnow out every subliminal quirk in our buying habits. They know, for instance, that 40 percent of all people who move to a new address will also change their brand of toothpaste, that the average supermarket shopper makes fourteen impulse decisions in each visit, that 62 percent of shoppers will pay a premium for mayonnaise even when they think a cheaper brand is just as good, but that only 24 percent will show the same largely irrational loyalty to frozen vegetables.

To preserve a brand name involves a certain fussy attention to linguistic and orthographic details. To begin with, the name is normally expected to be treated not as a noun but as a proper adjective — that is, the name should be followed by an explanation of what it does: *Kleenex facial tissues,*   30

Q-Tip cotton swabs, Jell-O brand gelatin dessert, Sanka brand decaffeinated coffee. Some types of products—notably cars—are granted an exemption, which explains why General Motors does not have to advertise *Cadillac self-propelled automobiles* or the like. In all cases, the name may not explicitly describe the product's function, though it may hint at what it does. Thus *Coppertone* is acceptable; *Coppertan* would not be.

The situation is more than a little bizarre. Having done all they can to make their products household words, manufacturers must then in their advertisements do all in their power to imply that they aren't. Before trademark law was clarified, advertisers positively encouraged the public to treat their products as generics. Kodak invited consumers to "Kodak as you go," turning the brand name into a dangerously ambiguous verb. It would never do that now. The American Thermos Product Company went so far as to boast, "Thermos is a household word," to its considerable cost. Donald F. Duncan, Inc., the original manufacturer of the *Yo-Yo*, lost its trademark protection partly because it was amazingly casual about capitalization in its own promotional literature. "In case you don't know what a yo-yo is . . ." one of its advertisements went, suggesting that in commercial terms Duncan didn't. Duncan also made the elemental error of declaring, "If It Isn't a Duncan, It Isn't a Yo-Yo," which on the face of it would seem a reasonable claim, but was in fact held by the courts to be inviting the reader to consider the product generic. Kodak had long since stopped saying "If it isn't an Eastman, it isn't a Kodak."

Because of the confusion, and occasional lack of fastidiousness on the part of their owners, many dozens of products have lost their trademark protection, among them *aspirin, linoleum, yo-yo, thermos, cellophane, milk of magnesia, mimeograph, lanolin, celluloid, dry ice, escalator, shredded wheat, kerosene,* and *zipper.* All were once proudly capitalized and worth a fortune.

On July 1, 1941, the New York television station WNBT-TV interrupted its normal viewing to show, without comment, a Bulova watch ticking. For sixty seconds the watch ticked away mysteriously, then the picture faded and normal programming resumed. It wasn't much, but it was the first television *commercial.*

Both the word and the idea were already well established. The first commercial—the term was used from the very beginning—had been broadcast by radio station WEAF in New York on August 28, 1922. It lasted for either ten or fifteen minutes, depending on which source you credit. Commercial radio was not an immediate hit. In its first two months, WEAF sold only $550 worth of airtime. But by the mid-1920s, sponsors were not only flocking to buy airtime but naming their programs after their products—*The Lucky Strike Hour, The A&P Gypsies, The Lux Radio Theater,* and so on. Such was the obsequiousness of the radio networks that by the early 1930s, many were allowing the sponsors to take complete artistic and production control of the programs. Many of the most popular shows were actually written by the advertising agencies, and the agencies naturally seldom missed an opportunity to work a favorable mention of the sponsor's products into the scripts.

With the rise of television in the 1950s, the practices of the radio   35
era were effortlessly transferred to the new medium. Advertisers inserted their names into the program title — *Texaco Star Theater, Gillette Cavalcade of Sports, Chesterfield Sound-Off Time, The U.S. Steel Hour, Kraft Television Theater, The Chevy Show, The Alcoa Hour, The Ford Star Revue, Dick Clark's Beechnut Show,* and the arresting hybrid *The Lux-Schlitz Playhouse,* which seemed to suggest a cozy symbiosis between soapflakes and beer. The commercial dominance of program titles reached a kind of hysterical peak with a program officially called *Your Kaiser Dealer Presents Kaiser-Frazer "Adventures in Mystery" Starring Betty Furness in "Byline."* Sponsors didn't write the programs any longer, but they did impose a firm control on the contents, most notoriously during a 1959 *Playhouse 90* broadcast of *Judgment at Nuremberg,* when the sponsor, the American Gas Association, managed to have all references to gas ovens and the gassing of Jews removed from the script.

Where commercial products of the late 1940s had scientific-sounding names, those of the 1950s relied increasingly on secret ingredients. Gleem toothpaste contained a mysterious piece of alchemy called *GL-70.*[3] There was never the slightest hint of what GL-70 was, but it would, according to the advertising, not only rout odor-causing bacteria but "wipe out their enzymes!"

A kind of creeping illiteracy invaded advertising, too, to the dismay of many. When Winston began advertising its cigarettes with the slogan "Winston tastes good like a cigarette should," nationally syndicated columnists like Sydney J. Harris wrote anguished essays on what the world was coming to — every educated person knew it should be "as a cigarette should" — but the die was cast. By 1958, Ford was advertising that you could "travel smooth" in a Thunderbird Sunliner and the maker of Ace Combs was urging buyers to "comb it handsome" — a trend that continues today with "pantihose that fits you real comfortable" and other grammatical manglings too numerous and dispiriting to dwell on.

We may smile at the advertising ruses of the 1920s — frightening people with the threat of "fallen stomach" and "scabby toes" — but in fact such creative manipulation still goes on, albeit at a slightly more sophisticated level. The *New York Times Magazine* reported in 1990 how an advertising copywriter had been told to come up with some impressive labels for a putative hand cream. She invented the arresting and healthful-sounding term *oxygenating moisturizers* and wrote accompanying copy with

---

3. For purposes of research, I wrote to Procter & Gamble, Gleem's manufacturer, asking what GL-70 was, but the public relations department evidently thought it eccentric of me to wonder what I had been putting in my mouth all through childhood and declined to reply.

references to "tiny bubbles of oxygen that release moisture into your skin." This done, the advertising was turned over to the company's research and development department, which was instructed to come up with a product that matched the copy.

If we fall for such commercial manipulation, we have no one to blame but ourselves. When Kentucky Fried Chicken introduced "Extra Crispy" chicken to sell alongside its "Original" chicken, and sold it at the same price, sales were disappointing. But when its advertising agency persuaded it to promote "Extra Crispy" as a premium brand and to put the price up, sales soared. Much the same sort of verbal hypnosis was put to work for the benefit of the fur industry. Dyed muskrat makes a perfectly good fur, for those who enjoy cladding themselves in dead animals, but the name clearly lacks stylishness. The solution was to change the name to *Hudson seal.* Never mind that the material contained not a strand of seal fur. It sounded good, and sales skyrocketed.

Truth has seldom been a particularly visible feature of American   40 advertising. In the early 1970s, Chevrolet ran a series of ads for the Chevelle boasting that the car had "109 advantages to keep it from becoming old before its time." When looked into, it turned out that these 109 vaunted features included such items as rearview mirrors, backup lights, balanced wheels, and many other components that were considered pretty well basic to any car. Never mind; sales soared. At about the same time, Ford, not to be outdone, introduced a "limited edition" Mercury Monarch at $250 below the normal list price. It achieved this, it turned out, by taking $250 worth of equipment off the standard Monarch.

And has all this deviousness led to a tightening of the rules concerning what is allowable in advertising? Hardly. In 1986, as William Lutz relates in *Doublespeak,* the insurance company John Hancock launched an ad campaign in which "real people in real situations" discussed their financial predicaments with remarkable candor. When a journalist asked to speak to these real people, a company spokesman conceded that they were actors and "in that sense they are not real people."

During the presidential campaign [in 1982], the Republican National Committee ran a television advertisement praising President Reagan for providing cost-of-living pay increases to federal workers "in spite of those sticks-in-the-mud who tried to keep him from doing what we elected him to do." When it was pointed out that the increases had in fact been mandated by law since 1975 and that Reagan had in any case three times tried to block them, a Republican official responded: "Since when is a commercial supposed to be accurate?" Quite.

In linguistic terms, perhaps the most interesting challenge facing advertisers today is that of selling products in an increasingly multicultural society. Spanish is a particular problem, not just because it is spoken over such a widely scattered area but also because it is spoken in so many different forms. Brown sugar is *azucar negra* in New York, *azucar prieta* in

Miami, *azucar morena* in much of Texas, and *azucar pardo* pretty much everywhere else—and that's just one word. Much the same bewildering multiplicity applies to many others. In consequence, embarrassments are all but inevitable.

In mainstream Spanish, *bichos* means *insects,* but in Puerto Rico it means *testicles,* so when a pesticide maker promised to bring death to the *bichos,* Puerto Rican consumers were at least bemused, if not alarmed. Much the same happened when a maker of bread referred to its product as *un bollo de pan* and discovered that to Spanish-speaking Miamians of Cuban extraction that means a woman's private parts. And when Perdue Chickens translated its slogan "It takes a tough man to make a tender chicken" into Spanish, it came out as the slightly less macho "It takes a sexually excited man to make a chick sensual."

Never mind. Sales soared.   45

THINKING CRITICALLY ABOUT THE READING

1. Why do you think Bryson begins his essay with an extensive passage on George Eastman before even mentioning advertising, the focus of his essay? Why is this background information important to the rest of the essay? (Glossary: *Beginnings and Endings*) What do you need to consider when writing an introduction to an essay?

2. What is Bryson's purpose in this essay—to express personal thoughts and feelings, to inform his audience, or to argue a particular position? (Glossary: *Purpose*) What in his essay leads you to this conclusion?

3. Bryson peppers his essay with examples from the world of business and advertising. (Glossary: *Examples*) These examples serve not only to illustrate the points he makes but also to help establish his authority on the subject. Which examples do you find most effective? Least effective? Explain why.

4. It is important for companies to prevent their trademarks from becoming household words because they could lose their trademark protection. For example, advertisements for Kleenex and Xerox urge people to ask for a *tissue* or say they're going to *copy* a paper. Identify two or three current trademarks that you think could lose their trademark protection in the future, and explain your reasoning for choosing each trademark.

5. Bryson discusses what he calls a "creeping illiteracy" (37) that has invaded advertising. What form does this illiteracy take? In what ways might using poor English benefit advertisers?

6. In talking about the powers of advertising to persuade, Bryson discusses *commercial manipulation* and *verbal hypnosis* (39). What exactly does he mean by each term? How have advertisers used these techniques to sell their products? How do you think you as a consumer can guard against such advertising practices?

7. According to Bryson, what is one of the more interesting linguistic challenges facing today's advertisers?

LANGUAGE IN ACTION

In 1976, the Committee on Public Doublespeak (a committee of the National Council of Teachers of English) gave Professor Hugh Rank of Governors State University its Orwell Award for the Intensify/Downplay schema he developed to help people analyze public persuasion. As Rank explains, "All people *intensify* (commonly by *repetition, association, composition*) and *downplay* (commonly by *omission, diversion, confusion*) as they communicate in words, gestures, numbers, etc. But, 'professional persuaders' have more training, technology, money, and media access than the average citizen. Individuals can better cope with organized persuasion by recognizing the common ways that communication is intensified or downplayed, and by considering who is saying what to whom, with what intent and what result." Look closely at Rank's schema on page 410, listing the questions you can ask yourself about any type of advertisement.

Use Rank's schema to analyze the World War I Navy recruitment posters on pages 413–414. Find examples of intensifying and downplaying in each. Then check out today's Navy recruitment efforts at www.navy.com. Have the government's persuasive techniques changed?

WRITING SUGGESTIONS

1. Think of a product that you have used and been disappointed by, one that has failed to live up to its advertising claims. Write a letter to the manufacturer in which you describe your experience with the product and explain why you believe the company's advertisements have been misleading. Send your letter to the president of the company or to the director of marketing.

2. Many product names are chosen because of their connotative or suggestive values. (Glossary: *Connotation/Denotation*) For example, the name *Tide* for a detergent suggests the power of the ocean tides and the rhythmic surge of cleansing waters; the name *Pride* for the wax suggests how the user will feel after using the product; the name *100% Natural* for the cereal suggests that the consumer is getting nothing less than nature's best; and the name *Taurus* for the Ford car suggests the strength and durability of a bull. Test what Bryson has said about brand names by exploring the connotations of the brand names in one of the following categories: cosmetics, deodorants, candy, paint, car batteries, fast-food sandwiches, pain relievers, disposable diapers, or cat food. Report your findings in an essay.

3. In paragraph 12, Bryson reminds us that successful advertisers have always known the importance of good slogans. Some early slogans, such as the American Florist Association's "Say it with flowers," are still in use today even though they were coined years ago. Research five or six current product slogans that Bryson doesn't mention—like Microsoft's "Where do you want to go?" or Just for Men's "So natural no one can tell"—and write an essay in which you discuss the importance of slogans to advertising campaigns. How, for example, do slogans serve to focus, direct, and galvanize advertising campaigns? What do you think makes some slogans work and others fail? What

makes a slogan memorable? As you start this project, you may find it helpful to search out materials in your library or on the Internet relating to slogans in general and how they engage people.

INTENSIFY

Repetition

How often have you seen the ad? On TV? In print? Do you recognize the **brand name? trademark? logo? company? package?** What key words or images repeated within ad? Any repetition patterns *(alliteration, anaphora, rhyme)* used? Any **slogan?** Can you hum or sing the **musical theme** or **jingle?** How long has this ad been running? How old were you when you first heard it? (For information on frequency, duration, and costs of ad campaigns, see *Advertising Age.)*

Association

What **"good things"** - already loved or desired by the intended audience - are associated with the product? Any links with basic needs *(food, activity, sex, security)?* With an appeal to save or gain money? With desire for certitude or outside approval (from *religion, science,* or the *"best," "most,"* or *"average" people)?* With desire for a sense of space *(neighborhood, nation, nature)?* With desire for love and belonging *(intimacy, family, groups)?* With other human desires *(esteem, play, generosity, curiosity, creativity, completion)?* Are **"bad things"** - things already hated or feared - stressed, as in a **"scare-and-sell"** ad? Are *problems* presented, with products as *solutions?* Are the speakers (models, endorsers) **authority figures:** people you respect, admire? Or **friend figures:** people you'd like as friends, identify with, or would like to be?

Composition

Look for the basic strategy of "the pitch": Hi . . . TRUST ME . . . YOU NEED . . . HURRY . . . BUY. What are the **attention-getting (HI)** words, images, devices? What are the **confidence-building (TRUST ME)** techniques: words, images, smiles, endorsers, brand names? Is the main **desire-stimulation (YOU NEED)** appeal focused on our benefit-seeking *to get* or *to keep* a "good," or *to avoid* or *to get rid of* a "bad"? Are you the **"target audience"?** If not, who is? Are you part of an unintended audience ? When and where did the ads appear? Are **product claims** made for: *superiority, quantity, beauty, efficiency, scarcity, novelty, stability, reliability, simplicity, utility, rapidity,* or *safety?* Are any **"added values"** suggested or implied by using any of the association techniques (see above)? Is there any **urgency-stressing (HURRY)** by words, movement, pace? Or is a "soft sell" conditioning for *later* purchase? Are there specific **response-triggering** words **(BUY):** to buy, to do, to call? Or is it conditioning (image building or public relations) to make us *"feel good"* about the company, to get favorable public opinion on *its* side *(against government regulations, laws, taxes)?* **Persuaders seek some kind of response!**

Omission

What "bad" aspects, disadvantages, drawbacks, hazards, have been **omitted** from the ad? Are there some unspoken assumptions? An unsaid story? Are some things implied or suggested, but not explicitly stated? Are there concealed problems concerning the **maker,** the **materials, the design,** the **use,** or the **purpose of the product? Are there any unwanted or harmful side effects:** *unsafe, unhealthy, uneconomical, inefficient, unneeded?* Does any **"disclosure law"** exist (or is needed) requiring public warning about a concealed hazard? In the ad, what gets less time, less attention, smaller print? *(Most ads are true, but incomplete.)*

Diversion

What benefits (low cost, high speed, etc) get high priority in the ad's claim and promises? Are these **your** priorities? Significant, important to you? Is there any **"bait-and-switch"**? *(Ad stresses* low cost, *but the actual seller switches buyer's priority to* high quality.) Does ad divert focus from **key issues,** important things *(e.g., nutrition, health, safety)*? Does ad focus on **side-issues,** unmeaningful trivia *(common in parity products)*? Does ad divert attention from your other choices, other options: buy something else, use less, use less often, rent, borrow, share, do without? *(Ads need not show other choices, but* you *should know them.)*

Confusion

Are the words clear or ambiguous? Specific or vague? Are claims and promises absolute, or are there qualifying words *("may help," "some")*? Is the claim measurable? Or is it **"puffery"**? *(Laws permit most "sellers's talk" of such general praise and subjective opinions.)* Are the words common, understandable, familiar? Uncommon? Jargon? Any parts difficult to "translate" or explain to others? Are analogies clear? Are comparisons within the same kind? Are examples related? Typical? Adequate? Enough examples? Any contradictions? Inconsistencies? Errors? Are there frequent changes, variations, revisions *(in size, price, options, extras, contents, packaging)*? Is it too complex: too much, too many? Disorganized? Incoherent? Unsorted? Any confusing statistics? Numbers? Do you know exact costs? Benefits? Risks? Are **your own goals,** priorities, and desires clear or vague? Fixed or shifting? Simple or complex? *(Confusion can also exist within us as well as within an ad. If any confusion exists: slow down, take care.)*

DOWNPLAY

Weasel Words: The Art of Saying Nothing at All

WILLIAM LUTZ

William Lutz was born in 1940 in Racine, Wisconsin. An emeritus professor of English at Rutgers University at Camden, Lutz holds a Ph.D. in Victorian literature, linguistics and rhetoric, and a law degree from the Rutgers School of Law. Lutz is the author or coauthor of numerous books having to do with language, including *Webster's New World Thesaurus* (1985) and *The Cambridge Thesaurus of American English* (1994). Considered an expert on language, Lutz has worked with many corporations and government agencies to promote clear, "plain" English. A member of the Pennsylvania bar, he was awarded the Pennsylvania Bar Association Clarity Award for the Promotion of Plain English in Legal Writing in 2001.

Lutz is best known for his series of books on "doublespeak": *Doublespeak: From Revenue Enhancement to Terminal Living* (1989), *The New Doublespeak: Why No One Knows What Anyone's Saying Anymore* (1996), and *Doublespeak Defined: Cut Through the Bull**** and Get to the Point* (1999). Lutz edited the *Quarterly Review of Doublespeak* from 1980 to 1994.

The term *doublespeak* comes from the Newspeak vocabulary of George Orwell's novel *1984*. It refers to speech or writing that presents two or more contradictory ideas in such a way that an unsuspecting audience is not consciously aware of the contradiction and is likely to be deceived. As chair of the National Council of Teachers of English's Committee on Public Doublespeak, Lutz has been a watchdog of public officials and business leaders who use language to "mislead, distort, deceive, inflate, circumvent, and obfuscate." Each year the committee presents the Orwell Awards, recognizing the most outrageous uses of public doublespeak in government and business.

In the following excerpt from his book *Doublespeak*, Lutz reveals some of the ways that advertisers use language to imply great things about products and services without promising anything at all. With considerable skill, advertisers can produce ads that make us believe a certain product is better than it is without actually lying about it. Lutz's word-by-word analysis of advertising claims reveals how misleading—and ridiculous—these slogans and claims can be.

WRITING TO DISCOVER: *Imagine what it would be like if you were suddenly transported to a world in which there were no advertisements and no one trying to sell you a product. Write about how you would decide what to buy. How would you learn about new products? Would you prefer to live in such a world? Why or why not?*

WEASEL WORDS

One problem advertisers have when they try to convince you that the product they are pushing is really different from other, similar products is that their claims are subject to some laws. Not a lot of laws, but there are some designed to prevent fraudulent or untruthful claims in advertising. Even during the happy years of nonregulation under President Ronald Reagan, the FTC did crack down on the more blatant abuses in advertising claims. Generally speaking, advertisers have to be careful in what they say in their ads, in the claims they make for the products they advertise. Parity claims are safe because they are legal and supported by a number of court decisions. But beyond parity claims there are weasel words.

Advertisers use weasel words to appear to be making a claim for a product when in fact they are making no claim at all. Weasel words get their name from the way weasels eat the eggs they find in the nests of other animals. A weasel will make a small hole in the egg, suck out the insides, then place the egg back in the nest. Only when the egg is examined closely is it found to be hollow. That's the way it is with weasel words in advertising: Examine weasel words closely and you'll find that they're as hollow as any egg sucked by a weasel. Weasel words appear to say one thing when in fact they say the opposite, or nothing at all.

"Help"—The Number One Weasel Word

The biggest weasel word used in advertising doublespeak is "help." Now "help" only means to aid or assist, nothing more. It does not mean to conquer, stop, eliminate, end, solve, heal, cure, or anything else. But once the ad says "help," it can say just about anything after that because "help" qualifies everything coming after it. The trick is that the claim that comes after the weasel word is usually so strong and so dramatic that you forget the word "help" and concentrate only on the dramatic claim. You read into the ad a message that the ad does not contain. More importantly, the advertiser is not responsible for the claim that you read into the ad, even though the advertiser wrote the ad so you would read that claim into it.

The next time you see an ad for a cold medicine that promises that it "helps relieve cold symptoms fast," don't rush out to buy it. Ask yourself what this claim is really saying. Remember, "help" means only that the medicine will aid or assist. What will it aid or assist in doing? Why, "relieve" your cold "symptoms." "Relieve" only means to ease, alleviate, or mitigate, not to stop, end, or cure. Nor does the claim say how much relieving this medicine will do. Nowhere does this ad claim it will cure anything. In fact, the ad doesn't even claim it will *do* anything at all. The ad only claims that it will aid in relieving (not curing) your cold symptoms, which are probably a runny nose, watery eyes, and a headache. In other words, this medicine probably contains a standard decongestant and some aspirin. By the way, what does "fast" mean? Ten minutes, one hour, one day? What is fast to one person can be very slow to another. Fast is another weasel word.

Ad claims using "help" are among the most popular ads. One says, "Helps keep you young looking," but then a lot of things will help keep you young looking, including exercise, rest, good nutrition, and a facelift. More importantly, this ad doesn't say the product will keep you young, only "young *looking*." Someone may look young to one person and old to another.

A toothpaste ad says, "Helps prevent cavities," but it doesn't say it will actually prevent cavities. Brushing your teeth regularly, avoiding sugars in food, and flossing daily will also help prevent cavities. A liquid cleaner ad says, "Helps keep your home germ free," but it doesn't say it actually kills germs, nor does it even specify which germs it might kill.

"Help" is such a useful weasel word that it is often combined with other action-verb weasel words such as "fight" and "control." Consider the claim, "Helps control dandruff symptoms with regular use." What does it really say? It will assist in controlling (not eliminating, stopping, ending, or curing) the *symptoms* of dandruff, not the cause of dandruff nor the dandruff itself. What are the symptoms of dandruff? The ad deliberately leaves that undefined, but assume that the symptoms referred to in the ad are the flaking and itching commonly associated with dandruff. But just shampooing with *any* shampoo will temporarily eliminate these symptoms, so this shampoo isn't any different from any other. Finally, in order to benefit from this product, you must use it regularly. What is "regular use"—daily, weekly, hourly? Using another shampoo "regularly" will have the same effect. Nowhere does this advertising claim say this particular shampoo stops, eliminates, or cures dandruff. In fact, this claim says nothing at all, thanks to all the weasel words.

Look at ads in magazines and newspapers, listen to ads on radio and television, and you'll find the word "help" in ads for all kinds of products. How often do you read or hear such phrases as "helps stop . . . ," "helps overcome . . . ," "helps eliminate . . . ," "helps you feel . . . ," or "helps you look . . ."? If you start looking for this weasel word in advertising, you'll be amazed at how often it occurs. Analyze the claims in the ads using "help," and you will discover that these ads are really saying nothing.

There are plenty of other weasel words used in advertising. In fact, there are so many that to list them all would fill the rest of this book. But, in order to identify the doublespeak of advertising and understand the real meaning of an ad, you have to be aware of the most popular weasel words in advertising today.

Virtually Spotless

One of the most powerful weasel words is "virtually," a word so innocent that most people don't pay any attention to it when it is used in an advertising claim. But watch out. "Virtually" is used in advertising claims that appear to make specific, definite promises when there is no promise. After all, what does "virtually" mean? It means "in essence or effect, although not in fact." Look at that definition again. "Virtually" means *not in fact*. It does *not* mean "almost" or "just about the same as," or anything else. And before you dismiss all this concern over such a small word, remember that small words can have big consequences.

In 1971 a federal court rendered its decision on a case brought by a woman who became pregnant while taking birth control pills. She sued the manufacturer, Eli Lilly and Company, for breach of warranty. The woman lost her case. Basing its ruling on a statement in the pamphlet accompanying the pills, which stated that, "When taken as directed, the tablets offer virtually 100 percent protection," the court ruled that there was no warranty, expressed or implied, that the pills were absolutely effective. In its ruling, the court pointed out that, according to *Webster's Third New International Dictionary*, "virtually" means "almost entirely" and clearly does not mean "absolute" (*Whittington* v. *Eli Lilly and Company*, 333 F. Supp. 98). In other words, the Eli Lilly company was really saying that its birth control pill, even when taken as directed, *did not in fact* provide 100 percent protection against pregnancy. But Eli Lilly didn't want to put it that way because then many women might not have bought Lilly's birth control pills.

The next time you see the ad that says that this dishwasher detergent "leaves dishes virtually spotless," just remember how advertisers twist the meaning of the weasel word "virtually." You can have lots of spots on your dishes after using this detergent and the ad claim will still be true, because what this claim really means is that this detergent does not *in fact* leave your dishes spotless. Whenever you see or hear an ad claim that uses the word "virtually," just translate that claim into its real meaning. So the television set that is "virtually trouble free" becomes the television set that is not in fact trouble free, the "virtually foolproof operation" of any appliance becomes an operation that is in fact not foolproof, and the product that "virtually never needs service" becomes the product that is not in fact service free.

New and Improved

If "new" is the most frequently used word on a product package, "improved" is the second most frequent. In fact, the two words are almost always used together. It seems just about everything sold these days is "new and improved." The next time you're in the supermarket, try counting the number of times you see these words on products. But you'd better do it while you're walking down just one aisle, otherwise you'll need a calculator to keep track of your counting.

Just what do these words mean? The use of the word "new" is restricted by regulations, so an advertiser can't just use the word on a product or in an ad without meeting certain requirements. For example, a product is considered new for about six months during a national advertising campaign. If the product is being advertised only in a limited test market area, the word can be used longer, and in some instances has been used for as long as two years.

What makes a product "new"? Some products have been around for a   15
long time, yet every once in a while you discover that they are being advertised as "new." Well, an advertiser can call a product new if there has been "a material functional change" in the product. What is "a material functional change," you ask? Good question. In fact it's such a good question it's being asked all the time. It's up to the manufacturer to prove that the product has undergone such a change. And if the manufacturer isn't challenged on the claim, then there's no one to stop it. Moreover, the change does not have to be an improvement in the product. One manufacturer added an artificial lemon scent to a cleaning product and called it "new and improved," even though the product did not clean any better than without the lemon scent. The manufacturer defended the use of the word "new" on the grounds that the artificial scent changed the chemical formula of the product and therefore constituted "a material functional change."

Which brings up the word "improved." When used in advertising, "improved" does not mean "made better." It only means "changed" or "different from before." So, if the detergent maker puts a plastic pour spout on the box of detergent, the product has been "improved," and away we go with a whole new advertising campaign. Or, if the cereal maker adds more fruit or a different kind of fruit to the cereal, there's an improved product. Now you know why manufacturers are constantly making little changes in their products. Whole new advertising campaigns, designed to convince you that the product has been changed for the better, are based on small changes in superficial aspects of a product. The next time you see an ad for an "improved" product, ask yourself what was wrong with the old one. Ask yourself just how "improved" the product is. Finally, you might check to see whether the "improved" version costs more than the unimproved one. After all, someone has to pay for the millions of dollars spent advertising the improved product.

Of course, advertisers really like to run ads that claim a product is "new and improved." While what constitutes a "new" product may be subject to some regulation, "improved" is a subjective judgment. A manufacturer changes the shape of its stick deodorant, but the shape doesn't improve the function of the deodorant. That is, changing the shape doesn't affect the deodorizing ability of the deodorant, so the manufacturer calls it "improved." Another manufacturer adds ammonia to its liquid cleaner and calls it "new and improved." Since adding ammonia does affect the cleaning ability of the product, there has been a "material functional change" in the product, and the manufacturer can now call its cleaner "new," and "improved" as well. Now the weasel words "new and improved" are plastered all over the package and are the basis for a multimillion-dollar ad campaign. But after six months the word "new" will have to go, until someone can dream up another change in the product. Perhaps it will be adding color to the liquid, or changing the shape of the package, or maybe adding a new dripless pour spout, or perhaps a ___. The "improvements" are endless, and so are the new advertising claims and campaigns.

"New" is just too useful and powerful a word in advertising for advertisers to pass it up easily. So they use weasel words that say "new" without really saying it. One of their favorites is "introducing," as in, "Introducing improved Tide," or "Introducing the stain remover." The first is simply saying, here's our improved soap; the second, here's our new advertising campaign for our detergent. Another favorite is "now," as in, "Now there's Sinex," which simply means that Sinex is available. Then there are phrases like "Today's Chevrolet," "Presenting Dristan," and "A fresh way to start the day." The list is really endless because advertisers are always finding new ways to say "new" without really saying it. If there is a second edition of [my] book, I'll just call it the "new and improved" edition. Wouldn't you really rather have a "new and improved" edition of [my] book rather than a "second" edition?

Acts Fast

"Acts" and "works" are two popular weasel words in advertising because they bring action to the product and to the advertising claim. When you see the ad for the cough syrup that "Acts on the cough control center," ask yourself what this cough syrup is claiming to do. Well, it's just claiming to "act," to do something, to perform an action. What is it that the cough syrup does? The ad doesn't say. It only claims to perform an action or do something on your "cough control center." By the way, what and where is your "cough control center"? I don't remember learning about that part of the body in human biology class.

Ads that use such phrases as "acts fast," "acts against," "acts to pre- 20 vent," and the like are saying essentially nothing, because "act" is a word empty of any specific meaning. The ads are always careful not to specify exactly what "act" the product performs. Just because a brand of aspirin claims to "act fast" for headache relief doesn't mean this aspirin is any better than any other aspirin. What is the "act" that this aspirin performs? You're never told. Maybe it just dissolves quickly. Since aspirin is a parity product, all aspirin is the same and therefore functions the same.

Works Like Anything Else

If you don't find the word "acts" in an ad, you will probably find the weasel word "works." In fact, the two words are almost interchangeable in advertising. Watch out for ads that say a product "works against," "works like," "works for," or "works longer." As with "acts," "works" is the same meaningless verb used to make you think that this product really does something, and maybe even something special or unique. But "works," like "acts," is basically a word empty of any specific meaning.

Like Magic

Whenever advertisers want you to stop thinking about the product and to start thinking about something bigger, better, or more attractive than the product, they use that very popular weasel word "like." The word "like" is the advertiser's equivalent of a magician's use of misdirection. "Like" gets you to ignore the product and concentrate on the claim the advertiser is making about it. "For skin like peaches and cream" claims the ad for a skin cream. What is this ad really claiming? It doesn't say this cream will give you peaches-and-cream skin. There is no verb in this claim, so it doesn't even mention using the product. How is skin ever like "peaches and cream"? Remember, ads must be read literally and exactly, according to the dictionary definition of words. (Remember "virtually" in the Eli Lilly case.) The ad is making absolutely no promise or claim whatsoever for this skin cream. If you think this cream will give you soft, smooth, youthful-looking skin, you are the one who has read that meaning into the ad.

The wine that claims "It's like taking a trip to France" wants you to think about a romantic evening in Paris as you walk along the boulevard after a wonderful meal in an intimate little bistro. Of course, you don't really believe that a wine can take you to France, but the goal of the ad is to get you to think pleasant, romantic thoughts about France and not about how the wine tastes or how expensive it may be. That little word "like" has taken you away from crushed grapes into a world of your own imaginative making. Who knows, maybe the next

> The word "like" is the advertiser's equivalent of a magician's use of misdirection.

time you buy wine, you'll think those pleasant thoughts when you see this brand of wine, and you'll buy it. Or, maybe you weren't even thinking about buying wine at all, but now you just might pick up a bottle the next time you're shopping. Ah, the power of "like" in advertising.

How about the most famous "like" claim of all, "Winston tastes good like a cigarette should"? Ignoring the grammatical error here, you might want to know what this claim is saying. Whether a cigarette tastes good or bad is a subjective judgment because what tastes good to one person may well taste horrible to another. Not everyone likes fried snails, even if they are called escargot. (*De gustibus non est disputandum*, which was probably the Roman rule for advertising as well as for defending the games in the Colosseum.) There are many people who say all cigarettes taste terrible, other people who say only some cigarettes taste all right, and still others who say all cigarettes taste good. Who's right? Everyone, because taste is a matter of personal judgment.

Moreover, note the use of the conditional, "should." The complete claim is, "Winston tastes good like a cigarette should taste." But should cigarettes taste good? Again, this is a matter of personal judgment and probably depends most on one's experiences with smoking. So, the Winston ad is simply saying that Winston cigarettes are just like any   25 other cigarette: Some people like them and some people don't. On that statement R. J. Reynolds conducted a very successful multimillion-dollar advertising campaign that helped keep Winston the number-two-selling cigarette in the United States, close behind number one, Marlboro.

CAN IT BE UP TO THE CLAIM?

Analyzing ads for doublespeak requires that you pay attention to every word in the ad and determine what each word really means. Advertisers try to wrap their claims in language that sounds concrete, specific, and objective, when in fact the language of advertising is anything but. Your job is to read carefully and listen critically so that when the announcer says that "Crest can be of significant value . . ." you know immediately that this claim says absolutely nothing. Where is the doublespeak in this ad? Start with the second word.

Once again, you have to look at what words really mean, not what you think they mean or what the advertiser wants you to think they mean. The ad for Crest only says that using Crest "can be" of "significant value." What really throws you off in this ad is the brilliant use of "significant." It draws your attention to the word "value" and makes you forget that the ad only claims that Crest "can be." The ad doesn't say that Crest *is* of value, only that it is "able" or "possible" to be of value, because that's all that "can" means.

It's so easy to miss the importance of those little words, "can be." Almost as easy as missing the importance of the words "up to" in an ad. These words are very popular in sale ads. You know, the ones that say, "Up to 50% Off!" Now, what does that claim mean? Not much, because the store or manufacturer has to reduce the price of only a few items by 50 percent. Everything else can be reduced a lot less, or not even reduced. Moreover, don't you want to know 50 pecent off of what? Is it 50 percent off the "manufacturer's suggested list price," which is the highest possible price? Was the price artificially inflated and then reduced? In other ads, "up to" expresses an ideal situation. The medicine that works "up to ten times faster," the battery that lasts "up to twice as long," and the soap that gets you "up to twice as clean" all are based on ideal situations for using those products, situations in which you can be sure you will never find yourself.

UNFINISHED WORDS

Unfinished words are a kind of "up to" claim in advertising. The claim that a battery lasts "up to twice as long" usually doesn't finish the comparison — twice as long as what? A birthday candle? A tank of gas? A cheap battery made in a country not noted for its technological achievements? The implication is that the battery lasts twice as long as batteries made by other battery makers, or twice as long as earlier model batteries made by the advertiser, but the ad doesn't really make these claims. You read these claims into the ad, aided by the visual images the advertiser so carefully provides.

Unfinished words depend on you to finish them, to provide the words   30
the advertisers so thoughtfully left out of the ad. Pall Mall cigarettes were once advertised as "A longer finer and milder smoke." The question is, longer, finer, and milder than what? The aspirin that claims it contains "Twice as much of the pain reliever doctors recommend most" doesn't tell you what pain reliever it contains twice as much of. (By the way, it's aspirin. That's right; it just contains twice the amount of aspirin. And how much is twice the amount? Twice of what amount?) Panadol boasts that "nobody reduces fever faster," but, since Panadol is a parity product, this claim simply means that Panadol isn't any better than any other product in its parity class. "You can be sure if it's Westinghouse," you're told, but just exactly what it is you can be sure of is never mentioned. "Magnavox gives you more" doesn't tell you what you get more of. More value? More television? More than they gave you before? It sounds nice, but it means nothing, until you fill in the claim with your own words, the words the advertiser didn't use. Since each of us fills in the claim differently, the ad and the product can become all things to all people, and not promise a single thing.

Unfinished words abound in advertising because they appear to promise so much. More importantly, they can be joined with powerful visual images on television to appear to be making significant promises about a product's effectiveness without really making any promises. In a television ad, the aspirin product that claims fast relief can show a person with a headache taking the product and then, in what appears to be a matter of minutes, claiming complete relief. This visual image is far more powerful than any claim made in unfinished words. Indeed, the visual image completes the unfinished words for you, filling in with pictures what the words leave out. And you thought that ads didn't affect you. What brand of aspirin do you use?

Some years ago, Ford's advertisements proclaimed "Ford LTD — 700 percent quieter." Now, what do you think Ford was claiming with these unfinished words? What was the Ford LTD quieter than? A Cadillac? A Mercedes Benz? A BMW? Well, when the FTC asked Ford to substantiate this unfinished claim, Ford replied that it meant that the inside of the LTD was 700 percent quieter than the outside. How did you finish those unfinished words when you first read them? Did you even come close to Ford's meaning?

COMBINING WEASEL WORDS

A lot of ads don't fall neatly into one category or another because they use a variety of different devices and words. Different weasel words are often combined to make an ad claim. The claim, "Coffee-Mate gives coffee more body, more flavor," uses unfinished words ("more" than what?) and also uses words that have no specific meaning ("body" and "flavor"). Along with "taste" (remember the Winston ad and its claim to taste good), "body" and "flavor" mean nothing because their meaning is entirely subjective. To you, "body" in coffee might mean thick, black, almost bitter coffee, while I might take it to mean a light brown, delicate coffee. Now, if you think you understood that last sentence, read it again, because it said nothing of objective value; it was filled with weasel words of no specific meaning: "thick," "black," "bitter," "light brown," and "delicate." Each of those words has no specific, objective meaning, because each of us can interpret them differently.

Try this slogan: "Looks, smells, tastes like ground-roast coffee." So, are you now going to buy Taster's Choice instant coffee because of this ad? "Looks," "smells," and "tastes" are all words with no specific meaning and depend on your interpretation of them for any meaning. Then there's that great weasel word "like," which simply suggests a comparison but does not make the actual connection between the product and the quality. Besides, do you know what "ground-roast" coffee is? I don't, but it sure sounds good. So, out of seven words in this ad, four are definite weasel words, two are quite meaningless, and only one has clear meaning.

Remember the Anacin ad—"Twice as much of the pain reliever doctors recommend most"? There's a whole lot of weaseling going on in this ad. First, what's the pain reliever they're talking about in this ad? Aspirin, of course. In fact, any time you see or hear an ad using those words "pain reliever," you can automatically substitute the word "aspirin" for them. (Makers of acetaminophen and ibuprofen pain relievers are careful in their advertising to identify their products as nonaspirin products.) So, now we know that Anacin has aspirin in it. Moreover, we know that Anacin has twice as much aspirin in it, but we don't know twice as much as what. Does it have twice as much aspirin as an ordinary aspirin tablet? If so, what is an ordinary aspirin tablet, and how much aspirin does it contain? Twice as much as Excedrin or Bufferin? Twice as much as a chocolate chip cookie? Remember those unfinished words and how they lead you on without saying anything.

Finally, what about those doctors who are doing all that recommending? Who are they? How many of them are there? What kind of doctors are they? What are their qualifications? Who asked them about recommending pain relievers? What other pain relievers did they recommend? And there are a whole lot more questions about this "poll" of doctors to which I'd like to know the answers, but you get the point. Sometimes, when I call my doctor, she tells me to take two aspirin and call her office in the morning. Is that where Anacin got this ad?

THINKING CRITICALLY ABOUT THE READING

1. What are weasel words? How, according to Lutz, did they get their name?
2. Lutz is careful to illustrate each of the various kinds of weasel words with examples of actual usage. (Glossary: *Examples*) What do these examples add to his essay? Which ones do you find most effective? Explain.

3. According to Lutz, why is *help* the biggest weasel word used by advertisers (3–8)? In what ways does it help them present their products without having to make promises about actual performance?

4. Why is *virtually* a particularly effective weasel word (10–12)? Why can advertisers get away with using words that literally mean the opposite of what they want to convey?

5. When advertisers use the word *like,* they often create a simile — "Ajax cleans *like* a white tornado." (Glossary: *Figures of Speech*) What, according to Lutz, is the power of similes in advertising (22–24)? Explain by citing several examples of your own.

6. What kinds of claims fit into Lutz's "unfinished words" category (29–32)? Why are they weasels? What makes them so difficult to detect?

7. Lutz uses the strategy of division and classification to develop this essay. (Glossary: *Division and Classification*) Explain how he uses this strategy. Why do you suppose Lutz felt the need to create the "Combining Weasel Words" category? Did the headings in the essay help you follow his discussion? What would be lost had he not included them?

LANGUAGE IN ACTION

Select one eye-catching advertisement from a magazine. Analyze the text of the ad, identifying any words that Lutz would describe as weasels. How does recognizing such language affect your impression of the product being advertised? What would happen to the text of the ad if the weasels were eliminated? Share your analysis with others in your class.

WRITING SUGGESTIONS

1. Choose something that you own and like — a mountain bike, a CD or DVD collection, luggage, a comfortable sofa, a stereo, or anything else that you are glad you bought. Imagine that you need to sell it to raise some money for a special weekend, and to do so you need to advertise on radio. Write copy for a 30-second advertising spot in which you try to sell your item. Include a slogan or make up a product name and use it in the ad. Then write a short essay about your ad in which you discuss the features of the item you chose to highlight, the language you used to make it sound as appealing as possible, and how your slogan or name makes the advertisement more memorable.

2. Pay attention to the ads for companies that offer rival products or services (for example, Apple and IBM, Coca-Cola and Pepsi-Cola, Burger King and McDonald's, Charles Schwab and Smith Barney, and AT&T and Verizon). Focusing on a single pair of ads, analyze the different appeals that companies make when comparing their products or services to those of the competition. To what audience does each ad appeal? How many weasel words can you detect? How does each ad use Intensify/Downplay (pp. 411–412)

techniques to its product's advantage? Based on your analysis, write an essay about the advertising strategies companies use when in head-to-head competition with the products of other companies.

3. Look at several issues of one popular women's or men's magazine (such as *Cosmopolitan, Vogue, Elle, Glamour, Sports Illustrated, GQ, Playboy, Car and Driver, Field and Stream*), and analyze the advertisements they contain. What types of products or services are advertised? Which ads caught your eye? Why? Are the ads made up primarily of pictures, or do some have a lot of text? Do you detect any relationship beween the ads and the editorial content of the magazine? Write an essay in which you present the findings of your analysis.

Be All That You Can Be: The Company Persona and Language Alignment

FRANK LUNTZ

Political consultant, pollster, and Republican Party strategist, Frank Luntz was born in West Hartford, Connecticut, in 1962. He graduated from the University of Pennsylvania with a degree in history and political science and took his doctorate in politics from Oxford University. Luntz taught at the University of Pennsylvania from 1989 to 1996 and later at George Washington University and American University. He has appeared on a number of television news shows including *The Colbert Report, Good Morning America, PBS NewsHour, The O'Reilly Factor,* and *Hardball with Chris Matthews,* and his op-ed articles appear regularly in newspapers such as the *Wall Street Journal,* the *Financial Times,* and the *Washington Post.* Luntz's company, Luntz Global, LLC, specializes in message creation and image management for commercial and political clients. His clients know that he understands the world of words and that he can fashion word combinations that will help market a product or change public opinion about an issue or public figure. In 2007, Barack Obama said, "When Frank Luntz invites you to talk to his focus group, you talk to his focus group." He's that good. Luntz has authored four books: *Candidates, Consultants, and Campaigns: The Style and Substance of American Electioneering* (1988); *Words That Work: It's Not What You Say, It's What People Hear* (2007); *What Americans Really Want . . . Really* (2009); and *Win: The Key Principles to Take Your Business from Ordinary to Extraordinary* (2011).

The following essay, most recently published in *Advertising in the Digital Age* on December 13, 2010, was excerpted from *Words That Work.* Here Luntz talks about the concept of "company persona" and the marketing benefits of what he calls *language alignment*; that is, "when the message, the messenger, and recipient are all on the same page."

WRITING TO DISCOVER: *Identify two or three current advertising campaigns that you like and find effective. What is it about each one that you like? How do the advertisements grab and keep your attention? What do you feel about the products as a result of the advertising?*

It's not just CEOs and corporate spokespeople who need effective language to be the message. The most successful advertising taglines are not seen as slogans for a product. They are the product. From M&M's "melts in your mouth, not in your hand" to "Please don't squeeze the Charmin" bathroom tissue, from the "plop, plop, fizz, fizz" of Alka-Seltzer to "Fly the friendly skies of United," there is no light space between the product and its marketing. Words that work reflect "not only the soul of the brand, but the company itself and its reason for being in business," according to Publicis worldwide executive creative director David Droga.

In the same vein, advertising experts identify a common quality among the most popular and long-lasting corporate icons: Rather than selling for their companies, these characters personify them. Ronald McDonald, the Marlboro Man, Betty Crocker, the Energizer Bunny—they aren't shills trying to talk us into buying a Big Mac, a pack of smokes, a box of cake mix, a package of batteries; they don't even personalize the product. Just like the most celebrated slogans, they are the product.

Walk through any bookstore and you'll find dozens of books about the marketing and branding efforts of corporate America. The process of corporate communication has been thinly sliced and diced over and over, but what you won't find is a book about the one truly essential characteristic in our twenty-first-century world: the company persona and how words that work are used to create and sustain it.

The company persona is the sum of the corporate leadership, the corporate ethos, the products and services offered, interaction with the customer, and, most importantly, the language that ties it all together. A majority of large companies do not have a company persona, but those that do benefit significantly. Ben & Jerry's attracts customers in part because of the funky names they gave to the conventional (and unconventional) flavors they offer, but the positive relationship between corporate management and their employees also plays a role, even after Ben and Jerry sold the company. McDonald's in the 1970s and Starbucks over the past decade became an integral part of the American culture as much for the lifestyle they reflected as the food and beverages they offered, but the in-store lexicon helped by setting them apart from their competition. (Did any customers ever call the person who served them a cup of coffee a "barista" before Starbucks made the term popular?) Language is never the sole determinant in creating a company persona, but you'll find words that work associated with all companies that have one.

And when the message, messenger, and recipient are all on the same page, I call this rare phenomenon "language alignment," and it happens far less frequently than you might expect. In fact, virtually all of the companies that have hired my firm for communication guidance have found themselves linguistically unaligned.   5

This manifests itself in two ways. First, in service-oriented businesses, the sales force is too often selling with a different language than the marketing people are using. There's nothing wrong with individualizing the sales approach to each customer, but when you have your sales force promoting a message that has no similarity with the advertising campaign, it undermines both efforts. The language in the ads and promotions must match the language on the street, in the shop, and on the floor. For example, Boost Mobile, which caters to an inner city youth demographic, uses the slogan "Where you at?" Not grammatically (or politically) correct—but it's the language of their consumer.

And second, corporations with multiple products in the same space too often allow the language of those products to blur and bleed into each other. Procter & Gamble may sell a hundred different items, but even though each one fills a different need, a different space, and/or a different category, it is perfectly fine for them to share similar language. You can use some of the same verbiage to sell soap as you would to sell towels, because no consumer will confuse the products and what they do.

Not so for a company that is in a single line of work, say selling cars or selling beer, where companies use the exact same adjectives to describe very different products. In this instance, achieving linguistic alignment requires a much more disciplined linguistic segmentation. It is almost always a more effective sales strategy to divvy up the appropriate adjectives and create a unique lexicon for each individual brand.

An example of a major corporation that has confronted both of these challenges and still managed to achieve linguistic alignment, even as they are laying off thousands of workers, is the Ford Motor Company—which manages a surprisingly diverse group of brands ranging from Mazda to Aston Martin. The Ford corporate leadership recognized that it was impossible to separate the Ford name, corporate history, heritage, and range of vehicles—so why bother. They came as a package. Sure, Ford maintains individual brand identity, through national and local ad campaigns and by creating and maintaining a separate image and language for each brand. For example, "uniquely sensual styling" certainly applies when one is talking about a Jaguar S Type, but would probably not be pertinent for a Ford F 250 pickup truck. But the fact that the CEO carries the Ford name communicates continuity to the company's customers, and Bill Ford sitting in front of an assembly line talking about leadership and innovation in all of Ford's vehicles effectively puts all the individual brands into alignment.

The words he uses—"innovation," "driven," "re-committed," "dra- 10 matically," "dedicated"—represent the simplicity and brevity of effective communications, and they are wrapped around the CEO who is the fourth-generation Ford to lead the company—hence credibility. The cars are the message, Bill Ford is the messenger, the language is dead-on, and Ford is weathering the American automotive crisis far better than its larger rival General Motors. Again, the language of Ford isn't the only driver of corporate image and sales—but it certainly is a factor.

In fact, the brand-building campaign was so successful that GM jumped on board. But Ford quickly took it a step further. In early 2006, they began to leverage their ownership of Volvo (I wonder how many readers did not know that Ford bought Volvo in 1999 and purchased Jaguar a decade earlier) to communicate a corporate-wide commitment to automotive safety, across all of its individual brands and vehicles. Volvo is one of the most respected cars on the road today, and aligning all of Ford behind an industry leader is a very smart strategy indeed.

So what about the competition?

General Motors, once the automotive powerhouse of the world, has an equally diverse product line and arguably a richer history of technology and innovation, but their public message of cutbacks, buy-backs, and lay-offs was designed to appeal to Wall Street, not Main Street, and it crushed new car sales. At the time of this writing, GM is suffering through record losses, record job layoffs, and a record number of bad stories about its failing marketing efforts.

It didn't have to be this way.

The actual attributes of many of the GM product lines are more   15
appealing than the competition, but the product image itself is not. To own a GM car is to tell the world that you're so 1970s, and since what you drive is considered an extension and expression of yourself to others, people end up buying cars they actually like less because they feel the cars will say something more about them.

Think about it. Here's a company that was the first to develop a catalytic converter, the first to develop an advanced anti-tipping stabilization technology, the first to develop engines that could use all sorts of blended gasolines, and most importantly in today's market, the creator of OnStar—an incredible new-age computerized safety and tracking device. Yet most American consumers have no idea that any of these valuable innovations came from General Motors, simply because GM decided not to tell them. So instead of using its latest and greatest emerging technology to align itself with its customers, GM finds itself in a deteriorating dialogue with shareholders. No alignment = no sales.

Another problem with GM: No one knew that the various brands under the GM moniker were in fact . . . GM. Even such well-known brands as Corvette and Cadillac had become disconnected from the parent company. Worse yet, all the various brands (with the exception of Hummer, which couldn't get lost in a crowd even if the brand manager wanted it to) were using similar language, similar visuals, and a similar message—blurring the distinction between brands and turning GM vehicles into nothing more than generic American cars. Repeated marketing failures were just part of GM's recurring problems, but as that issue was completely within their control, it should have been the easiest to address. When products, services, and language are aligned, they gain another essential attribute:

> **When products, services, and language are aligned, they gain another essential attribute: authenticity.**

authenticity. In my own market research for dozens of Fortune 500 companies, I have found that the best way to communicate authenticity is to trigger personalization: Do audience members see themselves in the slogan . . . and therefore in the product? Unfortunately, achieving personalization is by no means easy.

To illustrate how companies and brands in a competitive space create compelling personas for themselves while addressing the needs of different consumer groups, let's take a look at cereals. Anyone can go out and buy a box of cereal. But different cereals offer different experiences. Watch and listen carefully to their marketing approach and the words they use.

Most cereals geared toward children sell energy, excitement, adventure, and the potential for fun—even more than the actual taste of the sugar-coated rice or wheat puffs in the cardboard box. On the other hand, cereal aimed at grown-ups is sold based on its utility to the maintenance and enhancement of health—with taste once again secondary.

Children's cereals are pitched by nonthreatening cartoon characters— tigers, parrots, chocolate-loving vampires, Cap'ns, and a tiny trio in stocking caps—never an adult or authority figure. Adult cereals come at you head-on with a not-so-subtle Food Police message, wrapped in saccharine-sweet smiles, exclaiming that this cereal is a favorite of healthy and cholesterol-conscious adults who don't want to get colon cancer! Ugghhh. Kids buy Frosted Flakes because "They're grrrreat!" Adults buy Special K because we want to be as attractive and vigorous as the actors who promote it. When it comes to cereal, about the only thing parents and kids have in common is that the taste matters only slightly more than the image, experience, and product association—and if the communication appears authentic, they'll buy.

And cereal certainly sells. From Cheerios to Cinnamon Toast Crunch, more than $6 billion worth of cold cereal was sold in the United States alone in 2005. If you were to look at the five top-selling brands, you would see a diverse list targeted to a diverse set of customers. The language used for each of these five brands is noticeably different, but in all cases totally essential.

In looking at the first and third best-selling brands of cereal, one might initially think that only a slight variation in ingredients mark their distinctions. Cheerios and Honey Nut Cheerios are both based around the same whole-grain O shaped cereal, but are in fact two very different products, beyond the addition of honey and a nutlike crunch.

The language behind Cheerios is remarkably simple and all-encompassing— "The one and only Cheerios." Could be for kids . . . could be for young adults . . . could be for parents. Actually, Cheerios wants to sell to all of them. As its Web site states, Cheerios is the right cereal for "toddlers to adults and everyone in between." The subtle heart-shaped bowl on each box suggests to the older consumer that the "whole-grain" cereal is a healthy start to a healthy day. But the Web site also has a section devoted entirely to younger adults, complete with testimonials and "tips from new parents" talking about how Cheerios has helped them to raise happy, healthy children. The language behind Cheerios works because it transcends the traditional societal boundaries of age and adds a sense of authenticity to the product.

While you could probably live a happy and healthy existence with Cheerios as your sole cereal choice, there is a substantial segment of the cereal market that demands more. For the cereal-consuming public roughly between the ages of four and fourteen, a different taste and linguistic approach is required. Buzz the Bee, the kid-friendly mascot of Honey Nut Cheerios, pitches the "irresistible taste of golden honey," selling the sweetness of the product to a demographic that craves sweet foods. While the parent knows that his or her child wants the cereal because of its sweet taste (as conveyed through the packaging), Honey Nut Cheerios must still pass the parent test. By putting such statements as "whole-grain" and "13 essential vitamins and minerals" on the box, the product gains authenticity, credibility, and the approval of the parent.

Two different messages on one common box effectively markets the same product to both children and parents alike, helping to make Honey Nut Cheerios the number three top-selling cereal in 2004. So with the addition of honey and nuts, General Mills, the producer of the Cheerios line, has filled the gap between toddlers and young adults, and completed the Cheerios cradle-to-grave lifetime hold on the consumer.   25

To take another example, if you want people to think you're hip and healthy, you make sure they see you drinking bottled water—and the fancier the better. No one walking around with a Diet Dr Pepper in hand is looking to impress anybody. These days, there's almost a feeling that soft drinks are exclusively for kids and the uneducated masses. There's a cache to the consumption of water, and expensive and exclusive brands are all the rage. Now, there may be a few people who have such extremely refined, educated taste buds that they can taste the difference between Dasani and Aquafina (I certainly can't), but the connoisseurs of modish waters are more likely than not posers (or, to continue the snobbery theme, poseurs). You won't see many people walking around Cincinnati or Syracuse clutching fancy bottled water. Hollywood, South Beach, and the Upper East Side of New York City are, as usual, another story.

There's one final aspect of being the message that impacts what we hear and how we hear it. How our language is delivered can be as important as the words themselves, and no one understands this principle better than Hollywood.

At a small table tucked away in the corner of a boutique Italian restaurant on the outskirts of Beverly Hills, I had the opportunity to dine with legendary actors Charles Durning, Jack Klugman, and Dom DeLuise. The entire dinner was a litany of stories of actors, writers, and the most memorable movie lines ever delivered. (Says Klugman, an Emmy Award winner, "A great line isn't spoken, it is delivered.") Best known for his roles in *The Odd Couple* and *Quincy*, Klugman told a story about how Spencer Tracy was practicing his lines for a movie late in his career in the presence of the film's screenwriter. Apparently not pleased with the reading, the writer said to Tracy, "Would you please pay more attention to how you are read-ing that line? It took me six months to write it," to which Tracy shot back, "It took me thirty years to learn how to say correctly the line that took you only six months to write."

Spencer Tracy knew how to be the message—and his shelf of Acad-emy Awards proved it.

THINKING CRITICALLY ABOUT THE READING

1. What does Luntz mean when he says "the most successful advertising tag-lines are not seen as slogans for a product. They are the product" (1)? What examples does he use to illustrate his point? Name an advertising tagline that you can add to his list.

2. What, for Luntz, is a company's "persona," and how is language "used to create and sustain it" (3)?

3. What is "language alignment" (5)? Why do you think it's such a rarity in the world of corporate advertising? Why does Luntz believe that "language align-ment" is so important? Explain.

4. Luntz describes two ways in which a company can be "linguistically unaligned" (5). What are the two ways that this condition manifests itself, and how can each problem be remedied?

5. According to Luntz, what is "authenticity" (17)? How does one communi-cate authenticity to consumers?

6. In paragraphs 22–25, Luntz discusses the "first and third best-selling brands of cereals . . . Cheerios and Honey Nut Cheerios." What point about market-ing and advertising does Luntz make with this example?

LANGUAGE IN ACTION

For each of the following corporate icons, identify the company or product that each represents and an advertising tagline or slogan if one comes to mind:

Tony the Tiger

Chef Boyardee

Aunt Jemima

Uncle Ben

Snap, Crackle, and Pop

Mr. Clean

Betty Crocker

Fred Flintstone

Mac and PC

Polar bear

Flo

Jolly Green Giant

Add several corporate icons of your own to this list, together with the company names and advertising taglines. Discuss the value of a corporate icon to a business's long-term marketing strategy.

WRITING SUGGESTIONS

1. David Droga, worldwide executive creative director of the Publicis Group, a French-owned communications giant, believes that the language used to describe and market a brand should capture "not only the soul of the brand, but the company itself and its reason for being in business" (1). Do you agree with Droga's position? Why do you think that Luntz values this aspect of marketing so much? To test Droga's position, analyze the language that a company like Apple or Microsoft or Dell uses to attract first-time customers and to keep them for repeat sales. How well does the company you researched meet Luntz's definitions for "company persona" and "language alignment"? Write an essay in which you present your analysis of the company's marketing program.

2. In 2010 when Luntz published this essay, General Motors was a company without direction, floundering in the uncertain economic times that had hit the nation. As he explains in paragraphs 13–17, this once proud "automotive powerhouse of the world . . . was suffering through record losses, record job layoffs, and a record number of bad stories about its failing marketing efforts" (13). Luntz holds no punches in describing how GM got itself into the difficult position that it did. Since that time, however, GM has turned its business around. What has changed? How can you account for GM's rise from the brink of bankruptcy in recent years? After studying the General Motors company Web site and analyzing several of its print and television advertisements, write an essay in which you explain how GM addressed the critical problems and shortcomings outlined by Luntz in his essay.

Be It Ever So Homespun, There's Nothing Like Spin

KIM SEVERSON

Journalist and food writer Kim Severson was born in 1961 in Eau Claire, Wisconsin. After graduating with what she calls a "state school education," she launched her career as a writer for several daily newspapers on the West Coast before landing a position as an editor and reporter for the *Anchorage Daily News* in Alaska. After seven years in Alaska, she took a position with the *San Francisco Chronicle*, where she wrote about cooking and the culture of food. In 2004 she joined the staff at the *New York Times* as a food and dining writer. Severson has been the winner of the prestigious James Beard Award for food writing on four occasions, and she received the Casey Medal for Meritorious Journalism in 2002 for a series she wrote with Meredith May on childhood obesity. Chef Mario Batali cites Severson "among the handful of American food writers with both real wit and truth in their bag." Severson has written *The Trans Fat Solution: Cooking and Shopping to Eliminate the Deadliest Fat from Your Diet* (2003) and *The New Alaska Cookbook* (2009). Her most recent book, *Spoon Fed: How Eight Cooks Saved My Life* (2010), is a memoir recounting the invaluable life lessons she learned from a generation of female cooks and chefs, lessons that were all delivered in the kitchen. Since 2010, Severson has been the bureau chief for the *New York Times* in Atlanta.

In the following article, which first appeared in the *New York Times* on January 3, 2007, Severson examines what she calls the "greenwashing" of America's grocery store shelves. She's discovered a specific type of food packaging that "makes subtle use of specific colors, images, typefaces, and the promise of what marketers call 'an authentic narrative' to sell food." What worries her is that buyers believe that when they purchase these greenwashed products they're "buying a specific set of healthy environmental and socially correct values."

WRITING TO DISCOVER: *Take a moment to reflect on your own experiences with food. How would you describe your daily diet and your eating habits? Do you try to eat a healthy, nutritionally balanced diet, or are you a junk-food junkie? What are your expectations when you see words like* natural, organic, fresh, *and* wholesome *used to describe a food product? What kinds of food packaging do you usually associate with such products? Do these products appeal to you? Why or why not?*

Something made me uneasy when I dropped a box of gluten-free EnviroKidz organic Koala Crisp cereal in my shopping cart. But it's hard to suspect a cartoon koala, so I moved on.

The unsettling sensation came back when I bought a bag of my favorite organic frozen French fries. Why did the verdant fields in the Cascadian Farm logo make me feel so smug?

Then I got really suspicious. A bag of natural Cheetos seemed so much more appealing than the classic cheese puff. Why? Was it the image of a subdued Chester Cheetah rising gently from a farm field bathed in golden sunlight?

Like clues to a murder that suddenly point to a single culprit, the mystery in my shopping cart revealed itself. Wheat sheaf by wheat sheaf, sunrise by sunrise, the grocery store shelves had been greenwashed.

And I was falling for it. 5

The kind of greenwashing I'm talking about is not just a fake environmental ethos. Greenwashing, it seems to me, can also describe a pervasive genre of food packaging designed to make sure that manufacturers grab their slice of the $25 billion that American shoppers spend each year on natural or organic food.

As a design shorthand, it makes subtle use of specific colors, images, typefaces and the promise of what marketers call "an authentic narrative" to sell food. Especially in recent years, greenwashing has spilled out well past the organic section of the grocery store. Even the snack aisle at the gas station isn't immune.

"Somebody becomes successful with a specific point of view, and the consumer begins to identify with it and it spreads like a virus," said Paula Scher, a partner in Pentagram, an international design firm. From there it's only a matter of time before Cap'n Crunch shows up in a hemp jacket, raising money to save the manatees.

Buy a greenwashed product and you're buying a specific set of healthy environmental and socially correct values.

If the package does its work, then the food inside doesn't actually 10 have to be organic, only organic-

> **If the package does its work, then the food inside doesn't actually have to be organic, only organic-ish.**

ish. The right cues on a package free mass-market consumers from doing any homework, said Elizabeth Talerman, a branding analyst. They can assume that a group she calls the green elite — those early adopters who pushed for organic food laws and who helped make Whole Foods markets a success — have done the work for them.

"The mass market wants an instant identifier," said Ms. Talerman, a longtime New York advertising consultant.

So what are the identifiers? After shopping for dozens of products in places as varied as food co-ops and convenience stores, I've uncovered the essential elements of a greenwashed product. Start with a gentle image of a field or a farm to suggest an ample harvest gathered by an honest, hardworking family. To that end, strangely oversize vegetables or fruits are good. If they are dew-kissed and nestled in a basket, all the better. A little red tractor is O.K. Pesticide tanks and rows of immigrant farm laborers bent over in the hot sun are not.

Earth's Best, a baby and toddler food company, offers a delicious example. Its whole grain rice cereal features two babies working the rice fields. One is white and one is black. (A greenwashed package would never show the black child working in the fields alone.) A sign that looks hand-hewn declares "No GMO's." There is a barn, a butterfly, and a typeface that could have come from the back room of a general store.

A good greenwashed product should show an animal displaying special skills or great emotional range. Some Organic Valley packages feature a sax-playing, environmentally friendly earthworm. Jaunty cows on Stony-field Farm yogurt wear sunglasses and headbands. The cows on Horizon's milk cartons dance a bovine jig, despite challenges by organic purists that some Horizon cows see precious little pasture.

A little family history helps, too. My Family Farm of Fort Thomas, 15 Ky., sells packaged cookies and crackers and promises to give some of the money to charity. On the back of the box is a story that begins, "With careers as licensed social workers, my sister and I are committed to improving the lives of children." A carton of Country Hen omega-3 eggs, which cost $3.69 for six, had a fuzzy black-and-white photograph inside showing the company's owner, George Bass, and the entire Country Hen family, along with their favorite eggnog recipe.

A cause is important. Nature's Path, the maker of Koala Crisp, promises that 1 percent of sales will be spent saving endangered species. Barbara's Bakery, maker of Puffins cereal, pays for the National Audubon Society's live "puffin cams" in the Gulf of Maine. Buy a box of Peace Cereal's raspberry ginger crisp, and a percentage of the profit helps pay for International Peace Prayer Day in New Mexico.

The actual health benefits of a product don't always matter. A package of organic Naturepops from College Farm shows a field of lollipops and a barn, suggesting a well-educated farmer tending her candy. The sugar might come from cane juice and tapioca syrup, but it's sugar just the same.

And although "organic" is losing its power as a code word for certain cultural values, it doesn't hurt to flaunt it if you've got it. The word appears 21 times on a box of Cascadian Farm Vanilla Almond Crunch.

Having established a design paradigm that succeeds in selling food that is often more expensive than conventional groceries, the design world should perhaps rejoice. This is not the case. Some top brand and package designers find the cartoonish animals and bad hippie typefaces as grating as a self-righteous vegan at a barbecue.

But then, they didn't like American food package design that much 20 to begin with.

"It's the bottom of the barrel," said Ms. Scher, who works in the New York office of Pentagram design.

Riskier designs, like the clean lettering and curvy bottle of Pom Wonderful pomegranate juice, are rare. Food manufacturers usually agonize over changing the size of a box or shifting the background color from teal to aquamarine.

But when a trend starts to show success, it's a design pileup. That's what happened with the natural and organic category, which makes up about 10 percent of the food at the grocery store and has been growing by more than 20 percent a year since 2000. In the grocery business, a 4 percent jump is considered a victory.

"It's aisle after aisle of design desperation," said Brian Collins, chairman and chief creative officer of the design group at Ogilvy, the international advertising and public relations company. He called the look "phony naïveté" and predicted that its demise was close because consumers are wising up. There is value in telling a story, but it must be true, he said.

Merely dressing up the package is not enough, he said. Nonetheless,   25
manufacturers are eager to project a wholesome image.

"It's the halo effect," said Caren Wilcox, executive director of the Organic Trade Association. "That's why we encourage consumers to look for the U.S.D.A. organic seal."

But even the organic seal doesn't necessarily offer assurances that the item is produced in a way that jibes with consumer expectations for something that comes in a greenwashed package.

"All the ingredients being used in items with the organic seal are produced using the organic system," Ms. Wilcox said. "It doesn't mean they don't sometimes end up in products some people think other people shouldn't eat."

Design and packaging experts fixed the start of sincerity and authenticity in food package design in the 1970s. Mo Siegel began selling Celestial Seasonings tea in boxes with sleepy bears. Tom and Kate Chappell gave up the corporate life to create Tom's of Maine toothpaste. Ben Cohen and Jerry Greenfield sold ice cream in Vermont, using goofy hand-rendered graphics to tell their story.

The trend grew in the 1980s, when corporate America entered a non-   30
corporate phase. "Companies began to try to not look like big companies," Ms. Scher said. By the late 1990s, anything with a hint of natural organic goodness sold in big numbers. Today, many companies that started with a humble story line have been purchased by larger interests. Unilever owns Ben and Jerry's, the Hain Celestial Group is traded on Nasdaq and Tom's of Maine is controlled by Colgate-Palmolive.

The kind of imagery that once marked a brand as an alternative to corporate food conglomerates has now been incorporated into Lay's potato chips. Consumers can buy classic Lay's in the shiny yellow bag, or Natural Lay's, with a thicker cut, expeller-pressed oil, and sea salt. The package has a brown harvest graphic design, old-timey typefaces, and a matte bag.

The natural chips cost about 10 cents an ounce more than the classics. A handful of either still offers 150 calories and 10 grams of fat.

"When it gets to Lay's," Ms. Scher said, "it's time to change."

Ms. Talerman, the New York advertising consultant, predicted that the fascination with what she called the green identifiers will last about five years longer. Then, she said, green-elite food consumers will push companies for even more information about environmental impact, labor practices, and community involvement, and mass market consumers will start reading labels instead of just searching out easy identifiers.

Food manufacturers might begin to copy the new nutrition-style labels that Timberland is putting on its shoe boxes. Each one lists the amount of energy it took to make the shoes, how much of that was renewable, whether child labor was used, and how many hours per pair Timberland dedicated to community service.

"As soon as the mass market starts to understand these issues more,"   35
Ms. Talerman predicted, "we'll get away from the fields and the giant vegetables and get back to better design."

THINKING CRITICALLY ABOUT THE READING

1. What about the products that Severson was putting in her shopping cart made her uneasy? What does she mean when she says "the grocery store shelves had been greenwashed" (4)?

2. According to Severson, what are the dangers of greenwashing for mass-market consumers?

3. What has Severson discovered are the "instant identifiers" of greenwashed products?

4. Why isn't the whole design world celebrating the success of the greenwashed design paradigm? What specifically do critics find fault with about greenwashed packaging? What is Severson's point in briefly recounting the history of "sincerity and authenticity in food package design" in paragraphs 29–33?

5. What kinds of information about products does advertising consultant Elizabeth Talerman believe "green-elite food consumers" will be demanding of companies in the future? Do you think mass-market consumers will start reading food labels or will they continue to search for the instant identifiers they have in the past? Explain.

LANGUAGE IN ACTION

Products and packages announcing environmental features that may influence your decision to purchase abound today. Each of us needs to be able to differentiate legitimate claims from misleading or unsubstantiated claims about the supposed environmental benefits of a product or service. Consider the following language used by advertisers in the United States:

recyclable	eco-safe
biodegradable	Earth Smart
ozone-friendly	compostable
essentially nontoxic	CFC-free
environmentally friendly	sustainable
environmentally preferable	please recycle
50% more recycled content than before	

Do you find these words and phrases helpful? What problems or issues does language like this raise for you? What does each of these words or phrases mean to you? What additional information should manufacturers or advertisers supply to make the words and phrases even more helpful to consumers?

WRITING SUGGESTIONS

1. In her conclusion, Severson states that advertising consultant Elizabeth Talerman believes that consumers' fascination with "green identifiers will last about five years longer" (33). That was in 2007. Has anything happened? To test Talerman's prediction, visit your local grocery store and examine the food packaging designs for so-called natural or organic products. What changes, if any, did you find had occurred since Severson wrote her article. Write an essay in which you report your findings.

2. Severson examines how food products have been greenwashed in America. From your own experience and observations, what other areas of American life have been or are being greenwashed by advertisers? Identify one industry that particularly interests you—energy, clothing, eco-tourism, transportation—and write an essay in which you analyze the language that is used to sell you "a specific set of healthy environmental and socially correct values" (9).

What's Natural about Our Natural Products?

SARAH FEDERMAN

A freelance writer, Sarah Federman was born in New York City in 1976. She graduated from the University of Pennsylvania in 1998, where she majored in intellectual history. A strong interest in alternative medicine led her to work at the Institute for Health and Healing at California Pacific Medical Center in San Francisco. In 2003 she returned to New York to work in media advertising. From 2008 through 2011, she worked with media software technology in Paris, France. Federman currently resides in Arlington, Virginia, pursuing a career in conflict resolution.

Federman wrote the following essay expressly for *Language Awareness*. She first became curious about the word *natural* as an undergraduate when she defended its use as a meaningful word on food labels in a debate with one of her professors. Since that time, however, Federman has had a change of heart. As she reports in her essay, the meaning of *natural* is elusive and extremely difficult to pin down.

WRITING TO DISCOVER: *What do you think you're buying when you purchase a product with the word* natural *on its label? Do you use any natural products on a regular basis? Do you think such products are better for you than their regular alternatives? Are you willing to pay more for a natural product? Why or why not?*

Whether you're picking up Nature's Energy Supplements, Natrol, Nature's Way, Naturade, Nature's Gate, or Nature's Herbs in the vitamin aisle, attending a lecture on "Natural Sleep Aids," or diving into a bowl of Quaker 100% Natural Granola, you cannot escape the hype. Variations of the words "nature" and "natural" are used for product naming to distinguish alternative medicine practitioners from their western counterparts and as slogans or names for everything from toothpaste to blue jeans. In a recent issue of *Delicious* magazine, for example, these words were used 85 times in the first 40 pages, with advertisements using them 8 times! Now pet owners can even skim through a copy of *Natural Dog* or *Natural Cat* while waiting at the vet.

Nowhere is the buzzword "natural" more prevalent than at the local grocery store where Fantastic Soups, Enrico's Pizza Sauce, Health Valley Cereals, and Celestial Seasonings tea, among others, brag unabashedly about the "naturalness" of their products. I often find myself seduced by the lure of the "natural" label on goods and services. I throw Tom's Natural Toothpaste, Pop-Secret Natural Flavored Popcorn, and Grape-Nuts Natural Wheat and Barley Cereal into my shopping cart with the utmost confidence that these natural varieties prove far superior to their "unnatural" or "less natural" counterparts. Recently, I took a closer look at the labels of my revered products only to discover the widespread abuse of the word "natural." The word "natural" has become more a marketing ploy than a way to communicate meaningful information about a product.

But this is not news. More than a decade ago the Consumers Union first sounded the alarm about "natural." The report alerted consumers to the fact that their beloved Quaker 100% Natural Cereal contained 24 percent sugar, not to mention the nine grams of fat which, according to the March 1999 *Nutrition Action Healthletter*, is the same as a small McDonald's hamburger. But despite the best efforts of the Union, nothing has changed. In fact, things have gotten worse, *especially* in the cereal aisle where 22 varieties, including Froot Loops, proclaim their commitment to "natural" ingredients. Berry Berry Kix, a brightly colored kids' cereal, promises "natural Fruit Flavors." Sure there is some grape juice, right after the sugar, partially hydrogenated oils, and corn syrup, and some strawberry juice, right after the dicalcium and trisodium phosphates. That's it for the fruits, the rest is corn meal and starch.

> The word "natural" has become more a marketing ploy than a way to communicate meaningful information about a product.

The Consumer Union's report also pointed out products using "natural" as an "indeterminate modifier," rather than as an adjective to convey some meaningful information about the product. In other words, placing the word "natural" in a slogan or product description without having it refer to anything in particular. For example, most major U.S. supermarkets sell Kraft's Natural Shredded Non-Fat Cheese, Natural Reduced Fat Swiss, and Natural Cheese Cubes. But don't dare to ask the question, What does that mean? Kraft has done nothing special with the cheese itself; "natural" in this case presumably relates to the shredding, reducing, and cubing process. What is natural cubing?

To me, a "natural" product or service suggests any or all of the following: a healthy alternative, an environmentally friendly product, vegetarian, and/or produced without synthetic chemicals. Friends and family have also taken natural to mean wholesome, pure, low-fat, healthy, organic, and, simply, better. The meanings given in one popular dictionary, however, prove less specific: 1) determined by nature, 2) of or relating to nature, 3) having normal or usual character, 4) grown without human care, 5) not artificial, 6) present in or produced by nature. Interestingly, these definitions make no value judgments. There is nothing in the dictionary meaning to suggest, for instance, that a natural banana (one grown in the wild) is healthier than one raised by banana farmers. This positive spin we add ourselves.

Unlike using "low-fat," "organic," and "vegetarian," food manufacturers can use "natural" any way they choose. The Nutritional Labeling and Education Act of 1990 (ULEA) restricted the use of the following terms on food labels: low fat, low sodium, low cholesterol, low calorie,

5

lean, extra lean, reduced, good source, less, fewer, light, and more. A calorie-free product, for example, must have fewer than 5 calories per serving, while a cholesterol-free product must have 2 milligrams or less of cholesterol per serving. *Mother Earth News* reports that products labeled "organic" must align themselves with one of the 40 sets of organic standards, most often the California Organic Foods Act of 1990. This leaves "natural" as one of the few unregulated words.

Health-food companies and mainstream producers use the word to create an aura around the product. Actually, they use the word and "we" create the aura, allowing them to get away with higher prices or simply to take up more shelf space at the supermarket. For example, every month thousands of bags of Lay's "Naturally Baked" Potato Chips travel through desert and farmland to enable us to "Ohh, ahh" and purchase these natural wonders. When first seeing this name, I had visions of organic farms and rugged, healthy farmers cultivating a much-loved product. Unfortunately, a closer look at the label served to shatter rather than support my countryside fantasy. While the ingredients reveal less fat per serving than the standard chip (1.5 grams versus 9 grams), I found nothing that explained the meaning of "naturally baked." Do you think this means they leave the chips out in the sun to crispen up? Probably not, so why does this natural process cost more per ounce (5.5 ounces for $1.99 versus 7.5 ounces) when it uses less fat?

Mott's and Del Monte use "natural" to promote a new line without knocking their standard product. Mott's applesauce has three products on the shelf of my local San Francisco market—"Apple Sauce," "Natural Apple Sauce," and "Chunky Apple Sauce." A comparison of the labels reveals that the "natural" version has no corn syrup added. Now, if they just wrote "no corn syrup added" on the label, we consumers would immediately become aware that there is, indeed, sweetener added to their standard version. Del Monte Fruit Cocktail has a two-product line-up with "Fruit Naturals" right next to "Fruit Cocktail." The natural variety costs 6 cents more and actually has *fewer* ingredients, presumably requiring less manufacturing. The natural version has no sugar and preservatives; the standard version has added corn syrup and sugar.

Fantastic, maker of dried soups and instant mixes, uses "natural" to connote something about the food and the type of person who may buy it. Under the heading Instant Black Beans, Fantastic writes "All Natural. Vegetarian." A vegetarian product, we know, means without meat. But what does "all natural" mean? Adding this phrase right before Vegetarian suggested to me that this product should appeal to vegetarians and self-proclaimed naturals. Mildly health-conscious people surely would prefer to ally themselves with natural rather than unnatural foods. Whether or not this product serves as a healthy alternative to other brands is irrelevant because the point is that Fantastic could sell you artery-clogging lard and still use the word.

Next to vitamins, bottled beverages probably use the word more than   10
any other product. Every Snapple bottle promises an "all natural" treat,
although the most natural iced tea is quite simply brewed tea with ice.
In Snapple's case, you end up paying more for tasty sugar water, but
with Hansen's Natural Soda you are outright deceived. Hansen's soda has
exactly the same ingredients as Sprite and 7-Up minus the sodium citrate.
Blue Sky Natural Soda has fructose sweetener, caramel color, and something called tartaric acid. Doesn't Blue Sky Natural Soda sound refreshing? Too bad your intestines can't distinguish it from Coca-Cola.

At least we have natural bottled water as an alternative. Or do we?
The Natural Resources Defense Council, a national environmental group,
found dangerous amounts of arsenic in Crystal Geyser's "Natural" Spring
water. A four-year study revealed that one-third of the 103 bottled waters
tested contained contaminants beyond safe federal limits. Odwalla "Natural" Spring Water, another popular beverage company, especially among
health-food lovers, had high bacteria counts in a number of bottles. Hey,
bacteria are natural so what's the problem? The problem is that natural or
not, some bacteria make us sick. So it seems you cannot win with beverages. "Natural" serves as a meaningless label, a deceptive marketing tool,
or means "contains natural critters and natural toxins that may make you
sick." Best to just purchase a "Pur" (pronounced "pure") water filter; just
don't ask what they mean by pure.

Some products come closer to meeting my expectations. The Hain
Food Group, a "natural-food producer" whose projected 1999 annual sales
are $300 million, manufactures soup called "Healthy Naturals." Although
the split peas are not certified organic, Hain uses no preservatives or MSG.
The ingredients are listed as water, split green peas, carrots, celery, onion
powder, and spices. This product lives up to my notion of natural. But
even Hain veers from their presumed commitment to health food. The 14
product "Hain Kidz" line, introduced early in 1999, includes marshmal-
low crisp cereal and snack bars, gummybear-like candy, and animal cookies.
It appears that as major brands (Kraft's, Mott's, Quaker) increasingly tout
their new-found "naturalness," health-food companies such as Hain have
started going toward more "unnatural" products.

So as the line between specialty health-food company and standard
food producer becomes more elusive, I begin to wonder why the extra
cost? Why do plain peas and carrots cost *more* than highly refined and processed soups? And how did we get to a point where we need a special label
to tell us that the product is what it says it is? Before I infuse one more
dollar into this industry, I will assuredly read the list of ingredients more
carefully and do some research at www.naturalinvesting.com and www
.naturalhomeandgarden.com.

THINKING CRITICALLY ABOUT THE READING

1. According to Federman, what is the literal meaning of the word *natural*? What connotations do consumers bring to the word? (Glossary: *Connotation/ Denotation*)

2. What restrictions does the Nutritional Labeling and Education Act of 1990 place on what manufacturers can say on food labels? How is the word *organic* regulated? What restrictions, if any, are imposed on the use of the term *natural*?

3. What does Federman point to as the two main reasons that companies use the word *natural*? What does she mean when she says companies "use the word and 'we' create the aura" (7)?

4. Why do you think Federman talks about Kraft's Natural Shredded Non-Fat Cheese and Lay's "Naturally Baked" Potato Chips? Name some other products whose labels use the word *natural* or *naturally* in an unclear or ambiguous manner.

5. Why do you suppose manufacturers charge more for their "natural" products when, in fact, these products may cost less to produce?

WRITING SUGGESTIONS

1. What, for you, are the connotations of the words *natural*, *fresh*, *organic*, *locally grown*, and *wholesome*? Do you find these words helpful when you see them on a product label, or do you believe that these words are inherently deceptive? Write an essay in which you argue for or against the regulation of such language in advertising. Before you start writing, you may find it helpful to review your response to the Writing to Discover prompt for this selection.

2. Federman claims that the word "*natural* has become more of a marketing ploy than a way to communicate meaningful information about a product" (2). Do you agree? How do you think Kim Severson (see pp. 435–440) would respond to Federman's claim? Spend some time in your local supermarket comparing price and ingredients between several "natural" products and their regular counterparts. Do price differences correlate with ingredient differences? What other factors might affect the prices of natural versus regular products? In an essay, present your analysis and conclusions.

LANGUAGE IN ACTION

What statement is the following cartoon "Sign Language" making about the influence of advertising and commercialism on our beliefs and behavior? Does the cartoon exaggerate the power of advertising in our lives? What do you find more compelling, the verbal or the visual component of an advertisement? How do you think Sarah Federman and Kim Severson (435–440) would respond to this cartoon? Discuss.

13

LANGUAGE
AND GENDER

When one considers the range of topics and the variety of approaches taken by scholars in the general field of gender studies, there is an astounding body of work that one can access and analyze, and perhaps research even further. When one adds to the mix the scholarly efforts occurring in the study of language, the conjoined field of language and gender offers one of the most vibrant and revealing areas of intellectual pursuit available today. From the various definitions of gender itself to questions of usage, stylistics, ethnography, race, power, education, sociology, folklore, communication, pragmatics, literature, queer culture, and sexuality—to name just a few areas of research in play—the intersecting studies of language and gender have offered some amazing insights into who we are and how we communicate with one another.

The essays in Language and Gender are but a small sampling of the ways gender and language interact. In "You're Wearing *That*?: Understanding Mothers and Daughters in Conversation," Deborah Tannen reflects on her relationship with her mother toward the end of her mother's life and broadens her observations into an arresting essay on the ways mothers and daughters communicate. In "He and She: What's the Real Difference?," Clive Thompson reports on a computer algorithm that can allegedly determine by analysis of the words used in a text whether the author of that text is male or female. The development of the program naturally gives rise to a whole new set of fascinating questions regarding what constitutes gendered language usage. John McWhorter, in "Missing the Nose on Our Face: Pronouns and the Feminist Revolution" looks into the fact that English does not have a gender-neutral pronoun and how we have to address the problem in our speech and writing. Next, Michael Kimmel examines the "Guy Code" that he claims prescribes what it means to be a man in our society and how language aids and abets in the formation and preservation of that strange cultural phenomenon. Martha Irvine traces the fascinating history of the word *queer* from being synonymous with "odd" or "unusual" to its use as an anti-gay insult, to its being reclaimed, redefined, and embraced by the gay community. Finally, Paul Muhlhauser and Kelly Bradbury's *How Genders Work: Producing the J. Crew Catalog*, an interactive Web text (available online at bedfordstmartins .com/languageawareness/epages), offers a satirical look at the gender-based language used in a popular retailer's catalog.

447

You're Wearing *That*?: Understanding Mothers and Daughters in Conversation

DEBORAH TANNEN

Deborah Tannen, professor of linguistics at Georgetown University, was born in 1945 in Brooklyn, New York. Tannen received her B.A. in English from the State University of New York at Binghamton in 1966 and taught English in Greece until 1968. She then earned an M.A. in English litera-ture from Wayne State University in 1970. While pursuing her Ph.D. in linguistics at the University of California, Berkeley, she received several prizes for her poetry and short fiction. Her work has appeared in *New York, Vogue,* and the *New York Times Magazine.*

As a noted linguist, Tannen has broadened the scope of the discipline by encouraging linguists to move beyond syntax and the history of lan-guage to everyday conversation. In the process, she has brought her ideas out of academia to a wider audience, publishing twenty-one books and over a hundred articles, including five best-selling books on how people's conversations affect relationships: *That's Not What I Meant!* (1986), *You Just Don't Understand* (1990), *Talking from 9 to 5* (1994), *The Argument Culture: Stopping America's War of Words* (1998), and *I Only Say This Because I Love You* (2001).

This essay, first published in the *Washington Post* on January 22, 2006, as "Oh, Mom. Oh, Honey: Why Do You Have to Say *That?,*" is based on Tannen's book *You're Wearing* That?: *Understanding Mothers and Daughters in Conversation* (2006). The period in which Tannen was researching and writing this book coincided with the end of her mother's life. According to Tannen, the time she spent with her mother during this period not only intensified their relationship, it also "transformed [her] thinking about mother-daughter relationships."

WRITING TO DISCOVER: *Think about the title of the essay. Did your mother ever manage to stop you in your tracks with the all-too-familiar: "You're wearing that?" If so, what was your response? Think of some other stop-in-your-tracks com-ments by your parents. How did they make you feel?*

The five years I recently spent researching and writing a book about mothers and daughters also turned out to be the last years of my mother's life. In her late eighties and early nineties, she gradually weakened, and I spent more time with her, caring for her more intimately than I ever had before. This experience—together with her death before I finished writing—transformed my thinking about mother-daughter relationships and the book that ultimately emerged.

All along I had in mind the questions a journalist had asked during an interview about my research. "What is it about mothers and daughters?" she blurted out. "Why are our conversations so complicated, our relationships so fraught?" These questions became more urgent and more personal, as I asked myself: What had made my relationship with my mother so volatile? Why had I often ricocheted between extremes of love and anger? And what had made it possible for my love to swell and my anger to dissipate in the last years of her life?

Though much of what I discovered about mothers and daughters is also true of mothers and sons, fathers and daughters, and fathers and sons, there is a special intensity to the mother-daughter relationship because talk—particularly talk about personal topics—plays a larger and more complex role in girls' and women's social lives than in boys' and men's. For girls and women, talk is the glue that holds a relationship together—and the explosive that can blow it apart. That's why you can think you're having a perfectly amiable chat, then suddenly find yourself wounded by the shrapnel from an exploded conversation.

Daughters often object to remarks that would seem harmless to outsiders, like this one described by a student of mine, Kathryn Ann Harrison:

"Are you going to quarter those tomatoes?" her mother asked as   5
Kathryn was preparing a salad. Stiffening, Kathryn replied, "Well, I was. Is that wrong?"

"No, no," her mother replied. "It's just that personally, I would slice them." Kathryn said tersely, "Fine." But as she sliced the tomatoes, she thought, can't I do *anything* without my mother letting me know she thinks I should do it some other way?

I'm willing to wager that Kathryn's mother thought she had merely asked a question about a tomato. But Kathryn bristled because she heard the implication, "You don't know what you're doing. I know better."

> **For girls and women, talk is the glue that holds a relationship together—and the explosive that can blow it apart.**

I'm a linguist. I study how people talk to each other, and how the ways we talk affect our relationships. My books are filled with examples of conversations that I record or recall or that others record for me or report to me. For each example, I begin by explaining the perspective that I understand immediately because I share it: in mother-daughter talk, the daughter's, because I'm a daughter but not a mother. Then I figure out the logic of the other's perspective. Writing this book forced me to look at conversations from my mother's point of view.

I interviewed dozens of women of varied geographic, racial, and cultural backgrounds, and I had informal conversations or e-mail exchanges with countless others. The complaint I heard most often from daughters was, "My mother is always criticizing me." The corresponding complaint from mothers was, "I can't open my mouth. She takes everything as criticism." Both are right, but each sees only her perspective.

One daughter said, for example, "My mother's eyesight is failing, but   10
she can still spot a pimple from across the room." Her mother doesn't
realize that her comments—and her scrutiny—make the pimple bigger.

Mothers subject their daughters to a level of scrutiny people usually
reserve for themselves. A mother's gaze is like a magnifying glass held
between the sun's rays and kindling. It concentrates the rays of imperfection on her daughter's yearning for approval. The result can be a
conflagration—*whoosh.*

This I knew: Because a mother's opinion matters so much, she has
enormous power. Her smallest comment—or no comment at all, just a
look—can fill a daughter with hurt and consequently anger. But this I
learned: Mothers, who have spent decades watching out for their children,
often persist in commenting because they can't get their adult children to
do what is (they believe) obviously right. Where the daughter sees power,
the mother feels powerless. Daughters and mothers, I found, both overestimate the other's power—and underestimate their own.

The power that mothers and daughters hold over each other derives,
in part, from their closeness. Every relationship requires a search for
the right balance of closeness and distance, but the struggle is especially
intense between mothers and daughters. Just about every woman I spoke
to used the word "close," as in "We're very close" or "We're not as close
as I'd like (or she'd like) to be."

In addition to the closeness/distance yardstick—and inextricable
from it—is a yardstick that measures sameness and difference. Mothers
and daughters search for themselves in the other as if hunting for treasure,
as if finding sameness affirms who they are. This can be pleasant: After her
mother's death, one woman noticed that she wipes down the sink, cuts
an onion and holds a knife just as her mother used to do. She found this
comforting because it meant her mother was still with her.

Sameness, however, can also make us cringe. One mother thought she   15
was being particularly supportive when she assured her daughter, "I know
what you mean," and described a matching experience of her own. But
one day her daughter cut her off: "Stop saying you know because you've
had the same experience. You don't know. This is my experience. The
world is different now." She felt her mother was denying the uniqueness
of her experience—offering *too* much sameness.

"I sound just like my mother" is usually said with distaste—as is the
wry observation, "Mirror mirror on the wall, I am my mother after all."

When visiting my parents a few years ago, I was sitting across from my
mother when she asked, "Do you like your hair long?"

I laughed, and she asked what was funny. I explained that in my
research, I had come across many examples of mothers who criticize their
daughters' hair. "I wasn't criticizing," she said, looking hurt. I let the

matter drop. A little later, I asked, "Mom, what do you think of my hair?" Without hesitation, she said, "I think it's a little too long."

Hair is one of what I call the Big Three that mothers and daughters critique (the other two are clothing and weight). Many women I talked to, on hearing the topic of my book, immediately retrieved offending remarks that they had archived, such as, "I'm so glad you're not wearing your hair in that frumpy way anymore"; another had asked, "You did that to your hair on purpose?" Yet another told her daughter, after seeing her on television at an important presidential event, "You needed a haircut."

I would never walk up to a stranger and say, "I think you'd look 20 better if you got your hair out of your eyes," but her mother might feel entitled, if not obligated, to say it, knowing that women are judged by appearance—and that mothers are judged by their daughters' appearance, because daughters represent their mothers to the world. Women must choose hairstyles, like styles of dress, from such a wide range of options, it's inevitable that others—mothers included—will think their choices could be improved. Ironically, mothers are more likely to notice and mention flaws, and their comments are more likely to wound.

But it works both ways. As one mother put it, "My daughters can turn my day black in a millisecond." For one thing, daughters often treat their mothers more callously than they would anyone else. For example, a daughter invited her mother to join a dinner party because a guest had bowed out. But when the guest's plans changed again at the last minute, her daughter simply uninvited her mother. To the daughter, her mother was both readily available and expendable.

There's another way that a mother can be a lightning rod in the storm of family emotions. Many mothers told me that they can sense and absorb their daughters' emotions instantly ("If she feels down, I feel down") and that their daughters can sense theirs. Most told me this to illustrate the closeness they cherish. But daughters sometimes resent the expectation that they have this sixth sense—and act on it.

For example, a woman was driving her mother to the airport following a visit, when her mother said petulantly, "I had to carry my own suitcase to the car." The daughter asked, "Why didn't you tell me your luggage was ready?" Her mother replied, "You knew I was getting ready." If closeness requires you to hear—and obey—something that wasn't even said, it's not surprising that a daughter might crave more distance.

Daughters want their mothers to see and value what they value in themselves; that's why a question that would be harmless in one context can be hurtful in another. For example, a woman said that she told her mother of a successful presentation she had made, and her mother asked, "What did you wear?" The woman exclaimed, in exasperation, "Who cares what I wore?!" In fact, the woman cared. She had given a lot of thought to selecting the right outfit. But her mother's focus on clothing—rather than the content of her talk—seemed to undercut her professional achievement.

Some mothers are ambivalent about their daughters' success because   25
it creates distance: A daughter may take a path her mother can't follow. And mothers can envy daughters who have taken paths their mothers would have liked to take, if given the chance. On the other hand, a mother may seem to devalue her daughter's choices simply because she doesn't understand the life her daughter chose. I think that was the case with my mother and me.

My mother visited me shortly after I had taken a teaching position at Georgetown University, and I was eager to show her my new home and new life. She had disapproved of me during my rebellious youth, and had been distraught when my first marriage ended six years before. Now I was a professor; clearly I had turned out all right. I was sure she'd be proud of me—and she was. When I showed her my office with my name on the door and my publications on the shelf, she seemed pleased and approving.

Then she asked, "Do you think you would have accomplished all this if you had stayed married?" "Absolutely not," I said. "If I'd stayed married, I wouldn't have gone to grad school to get my Ph.D."

"Well," she replied, "if you'd stayed married you wouldn't have had to." Ouch. With her casual remark, my mother had reduced all I had accomplished to the consolation prize.

I have told this story many times, knowing I could count on listeners to gasp at this proof that my mother belittled my achievements. But now I think she was simply reflecting the world she had grown up in, where there was one and only one measure by which women were judged successful or pitiable: marriage. She probably didn't know what to make of my life, which was so different from any she could have imagined for herself. I don't think she intended to denigrate what I had done and become, but the lens through which she viewed the world could not encompass the one I had chosen. Reframing how I look at it takes the sting out of this memory.

Reframing is often key to dissipating anger. One woman found that   30
this technique could transform holiday visits from painful to pleasurable. For example, while visiting, she showed her mother a new purchase: two pairs of socks, one black and one navy. The next day she wore one pair, and her mother asked, "Are you sure you're not wearing one of each color?" In the past, her mother's question would have set her off, as she wondered, "What kind of incompetent do you think I am?" This time she focused on the caring: Who else would worry about the color of her socks? Looked at this way, the question was touching.

If a daughter can recognize that seeming criticism truly expresses concern, a mother can acknowledge that concern truly implies criticism—and bite her tongue. A woman who told me that this worked for her gave me an example: One day her daughter announced, "I joined Weight Watchers and already lost two pounds." In the past, the mother would have said, "That's great" and added, "You have to keep it up." This time she replied, "That's great"—and stopped there.

Years ago, I was surprised when my mother told me, after I began a letter to her "Dearest Mom," that she had waited her whole life to hear me say that. I thought this peculiar to her until a young woman named Rachael sent me copies of e-mails she had received from her mother. In one, her mother responded to Rachael's effusive Mother's Day card: "Oh, Rachael!!!!! That was so WONDERFUL!!! It almost made me cry. I've waited 25 years, 3 months and 7 days to hear something like that . . . ."

Helping to care for my mother toward the end of her life, and writing this book at the same time, I came to understand the emotion behind these parallel reactions. Caring about someone as much as you care about yourself, and the critical eye that comes with it, are two strands that cannot be separated. Both engender a passion that makes the mother-daughter relationship perilous—and precious.

THINKING CRITICALLY ABOUT THE READING

1. Much of what Tannen discovered in researching her book on mother-daughter relationships could be applied to mothers and sons, fathers and daughters, and fathers and sons—but there is a "special intensity to the mother-daughter relationship" (3), according to Tannen. What does Tannen think creates that special intensity? What is "the glue that holds a relationship together—and the explosive that can blow it apart" (3)?

2. Tannen records many examples of everyday conversations in her work as a linguist. Explain the process that she goes through to get to a better and broader understanding of each person's perspective in the conversation. Why does Tannen feel it is important to see things from both perspectives?

3. In her countless interviews and contacts with a diverse group of women, what complaint does Tannen report that she heard most often? Does this surprise you? Why or why not?

4. Tannen writes: "Where the daughter sees power, the mother feels powerless. Daughters and mothers, I found, both overestimate the other's power—and underestimate their own" (12). What does she mean by this? How does power affect the relationships between mothers and daughters?

5. Tannen refers to a technique she uses to change a memory, conflicting view, or incident between mother and daughter from painful to pleasurable. How does she do this? How did she come to terms with her own mother's apparent disappointment at her life choices?

6. Tannen concludes her essay by talking about "two strands that cannot be separated. Both engender a passion that makes the mother-daughter relationship perilous—and precious." What is she referring to here?

LANGUAGE IN ACTION

Do you feel the scenarios related by Tannen apply only to mothers and daughters? List instances of miscommunication or miscues within your own family that parallel Tannen's examples. Compare them with those of others in a small group. Does the mother-daughter relationship seem unique to you, as Tannen claims it is?

WRITING SUGGESTIONS

1. Tannen believes strongly that linguists can use their study and scientific analysis of language to help solve communications problems in the real world: "If a daughter can recognize that seeming criticism truly expresses concern, a mother can acknowledge that concern truly implies criticism—and bite her tongue" (31). Think about your own relationship with a parent of either sex. Do the solutions Tannen suggests seem applicable? Do you think they would work? In a short essay, explain why or why not.

2. Reread Paul Roberts's "Speech Communities" (pp. 138–148) and consider how Roberts's thinking in that essay might be applied to the specific mother-daughter relationship Tannen discusses. Also, consider what ways Tannen's piece might illuminate Roberts's piece. Write an essay in which you discuss the ways that each essay expands/complicates a view of how "language gaps" arise.

He and She: What's the Real Difference?

CLIVE THOMPSON

Clive Thompson was born in 1968 in Toronto, Canada, and received a B.A. in political science and English from the University of Toronto in 1987. He began his career writing about politics, but due to his lifelong interest in computers, switched to writing primarily about science and technology. When asked to submit his biography for this book, Thompson wrote the following of this piece: "What interested me about this story was how the scientists used artificial intelligence to examine questions about male and female identity that are as old as the hills. Human philosophy and linguistics has for millennia been limited by the fact that human brains are only good at observing small collections of text at a time; when we try to think about the way language works, we rely on our knowledge of the thousands of books and articles we've read in our lifetime. But computers are able to scan millions and billions of pieces of human writing—allowing them to observe patterns that we ourselves would never be able to spot."

In 2002, Thompson began his year as a Knight Science Journalism Fellow at M.I.T. and started his blog, *Collision Detection* (www .collisiondetection.net). Since then, the blog has grown into a highly regarded and influential source of writing and research on technology and culture. Thompson is currently a contributing writer for the *New York Times Magazine* and a columnist for *Wired* magazine. He writes about gaming and technology for *Slate* and contributes regularly to *Discover, Fast Company,* and *New York* magazine, among others. Thompson edited *The Best of Technology Writing* (2008). This essay originally appeared in the *Boston Globe* on July 6, 2003.

WRITING TO DISCOVER: *Think about what we can learn about the author of a piece of writing aside from what the author tells us directly. Can you tell what a writer is like as a person, a writer's age, or if the writer is a male or female from the style of the writing? Explain how you came to your conclusions.*

Imagine, for a second, that no [author's name] is attached to this article. Judging by the words alone, can you figure out if I am a man or a woman?

Moshe Koppel can. This summer, a group of computer scientists— including Koppel, a professor at Israel's Bar-Ilan University—are publishing two papers in which they describe the successful results of a gender-detection experiment. The scholars have developed a computer algorithm that can examine an anonymous text and determine, with accuracy rates of better than 80 percent, whether the author is male or female. For centuries, linguists and cultural pundits have argued heatedly about whether men and women communicate differently. But Koppel's group is the first to create an actual prediction machine.

A rather controversial one, too. When the group submitted its first paper to the prestigious journal *Proceedings of the National Academy of Sciences,* the referees rejected it "on ideological grounds," Koppel maintains. "They said, 'Hey, what do you mean? You're trying to make some claim about men and women being different, and we don't know if that's true. That's just the kind of thing that people are saying in order to oppress women!' And I said, 'Hey—I'm just reporting the numbers.'"

When they submitted their papers to other journals, the group made a significant tweak. One of the co-authors, Anat Shimoni, added her middle name "Rachel" to her byline, to make sure reviewers knew one member of the group was female. (The third scientist is a man, Shlomo Argamon.) The papers were accepted by the journals *Literary and Linguistic Computing* and *Text,* and are appearing over the next few months. Koppel says they haven't faced any further accusations of antifeminism.

The odd thing is that the language differences the researchers dis-   5
covered would seem, at first blush, to be rather benign. They pertain not to complex, "important" words, but to the seemingly quotidian parts of speech: the ifs, ands, and buts.

For example, Koppel's group found that the single biggest difference is that women are far more likely than men to use personal pronouns—"I," "you," "she," "myself," or "yourself" and the like. Men, in contrast, are more likely to use determiners—"a," "the," "that," and "these"—as well as cardinal numbers and quantifiers like "more" or "some." As one of the papers published by Koppel's group notes, men are also more likely to use "post-head noun modification with an *of* phrase"—phrases like "garden of roses."

It seems surreal, even spooky, that such seemingly throwaway words would be so revealing of our identity. But text-analysis experts have long relied on these little parts of speech. When you or I write a text, we pay close attention to how we use the main topic–specific words—such as, in this article, the words "computer" and "program" and "gender." But we don't pay much attention to how we employ basic parts of speech, which means we're far more likely to use them in unconscious but revealing patterns. Years ago, Donald Foster, a professor of English at Vassar College, unmasked Joe Klein as the author of the anonymous book *Primary Colors,* partly by paying attention to words like "the" and "and," and to quirks in the use of punctuation. "They're like fingerprints," says Foster.

To divine these subtle patterns, Koppel's team crunched 604 texts taken from the British National Corpus, a collection of 4,124 documents assembled by academics to help study modern language use. Half of the chosen texts were written by men and half by women; they ranged from novels such as Julian Barnes's *Talking It Over* to works of nonfiction (including even some pop ephemera, such as an instant-biography of the singer Kylie Minogue). The scientists removed all the topic-specific words, leaving the non-topic-specific ones behind.

> **We don't pay much attention to how we employ basic parts of speech, which means we're far more likely to use them in unconscious but revealing patterns.**

Then they fed the remaining text into an artificial-intelligence sorting algorithm and programmed it to look for elements that were relatively unique to the women's set and the men's set. "The more frequently a word got used in one set, the more weight it got. If the word 'you' got used in the female set very often and not in the male set, you give it a stronger female weighting," Koppel explains.

When the dust settled, the researchers wound up zeroing in on barely 50 features that had the most "weight," either male or female. Not a big group, but one with ferocious predictive power: When the scientists ran their test on new documents culled from the British National Corpus, they could predict the gender of the author with over 80 percent accuracy.

It may be unnerving to think that your gender is so obvious, and so dominates your behavior, that others can discover it by doing a simple word-count. But Koppel says the results actually make a sort of intuitive sense. As he points out, if women use personal pronouns more than men, it may be because of the old sociological saw: Women talk about people, men talk about things. Many scholars of gender and language have argued this for years.

"It's not too surprising," agrees Deborah Tannen, a linguist and author of best-sellers such as *You Just Don't Understand: Women and Men in Conversation*. "Because what are [personal] pronouns? They're talking about people. And we know that women write more about people." Also, she notes, women typically write in an "involved" style, trying to forge a more intimate connection with the reader, which leads to even heavier pronoun use. Meanwhile, if men are writing more frequently about things, that would explain why they're prone to using quantity words like "some" or "many." These differences are significant enough that even when Koppel's team analyzed scientific papers—which would seem to be as content-neutral as you can get—they could still spot male and female authors. "It blew my mind," he says.

But this gender-spotting eventually runs into a $64,000 conceptual question: What the heck is gender, anyway? At a basic level, Koppel's group assumes that there are only two different states—you're either male or female. ("Computer scientists love a binary problem," as Koppel jokes.) But some theorists of gender, such as Berkeley's Judith Butler, have argued that this is a false duality. Gender isn't simply innate or biological, the argument goes; it's as much about how you act as what you are.

10

Tannen once had a group of students analyze articles from men's and women's magazines, trying to see if they could guess which articles had appeared in which class of publication. It wasn't hard. In men's magazines, the sentences were always shorter, and the sentences in women's magazines had more "feeling verbs," which would seem to bolster Koppel's findings. But here's the catch: The actual identity of the author didn't matter. When women wrote for men's magazines, they wrote in the "male" style. "It clearly was performance," Tannen notes. "It didn't matter whether the author was male or female. What mattered was whether the intended audience was male or female."

Critics charge that experiments in gender-prediction don't discover   15 inalienable male/female differences; rather, they help to create and exaggerate such differences. "You find what you're looking for. And that leads to this sneaking suspicion that it's all hardwired, instead of cultural," argues Janet Bing, a linguist at Old Dominion University in Norfolk, Virginia. She adds: "This whole rush to categorization usually works against women." Bing further notes that gays, lesbians, or transgendered people don't fit neatly into simple social definitions of male or female gender. Would Koppel's algorithm work as well if it analyzed a collection of books written mainly by them?

Koppel enthusiastically agrees it's an interesting question—but "we haven't run that experiment, so we don't know." In the end, he's hoping his group's data will keep critics at bay. "I'm just reporting the numbers," he adds, "but you can't be careful enough."

THINKING CRITICALLY ABOUT THE READING

1. Describe the gender-detection experiment performed by computer scientists at Israel's Bar-Ilan University. How was the experiment set up and carried out? What were the results?

2. What were the original concerns of the editors of *Proceedings of the National Academy of Sciences* when the researchers submitted the results of their experiment? How did the researchers respond to the concerns other editors had?

3. What words are women far more likely to use? What words are men more likely to use? Why are the words in both cases rather surprising?

4. Review paragraph 14 and explain how the research that Tannen did with her students extends the findings of the research that Koppel and his associates did. What role does audience play in the kinds of language that writers use? (Glossary: *Audience*)

5. What question(s) are not answered by Koppel's research, according to linguist Janet Bing?

6. Why do you suppose Thompson ends his article with a reiteration of the "I'm just reporting the numbers" quotation that he used earlier in his article? To what does Koppel refer when he's quoted at the end of the article by saying, "but you can't be careful enough"? (Glossary: *Beginnings and Endings*)

LANGUAGE IN ACTION

Using the tips that Thompson says are at the heart of the program developed to detect whether an author is more likely male or female, examine the following passages to see if you can make a calculated guess as to the sex of their authors. Make sure you are able to explain to your instructor or the members of your class why you could or could not make a judgment in each case. (The authors' names are found on p. 460.)

Writer 1

I was saved from sin when I was going on thirteen. But not really saved. It happened like this. There was a big revival at my Auntie Reed's church. Every night for weeks there had been much preaching, singing, praying, and shouting, and some very hardened sinners had been brought to Christ, and the membership of the church had grown by leaps and bounds. Then just before the revival ended, they held a special meeting for children, "to bring the young lambs to the fold." My aunt spoke of it for days ahead. That night I was escorted to the front row and placed on the mourners' bench with all the other young sinners, who had not yet been brought to Jesus.

My aunt told me that when you were saved you saw a light, and something happened to you inside! And Jesus came into your life! And God was with you from then on! She said you could see and hear and feel Jesus in your soul. I believed her.

Writer 2

The stealth of autumn catches one unaware. Was that a goldfinch perching in the early September woods, or just the first turning leaf? A red-winged blackbird or a sugar maple closing up shop for the winter? Keen-eyed as leopards, we stand still and squint hard, looking for signs of movement. Early-morning frost sits heavily on the grass, and turns barbed wire into a string of stars. On a distant hill, a small square of yellow appears to be a lighted stage. At last the truth dawns on us: Fall is staggering in, right on schedule, with its baggage of chilly nights, macabre holidays, and spectacular, heart-stoppingly beautiful leaves. Soon the leaves will start cringing on the trees, and roll up in clenched fists before they actually fall off. Dry seedpods will rattle like tiny gourds. But first there will be weeks of gushing color so bright, so pastel, so confettilike, that people will travel up and down the East Coast just to stare at it—a whole season of leaves.

WRITING SUGGESTIONS

1. In paragraph 13, Thompson writes of the research that Koppel's group has done: "But this gender-spotting eventually runs into a $64,000 conceptual question: What the heck is gender, anyway? At a basic level, Koppel's group assumes that there are only two different states—you're either male or female.

('Computer scientists love a binary problem,' as Koppel jokes.) But some theorists of gender, such as Berkeley's Judith Butler, have argued that this is a false duality. Gender isn't simply innate or biological, the argument goes; it's as much how you act as what you are." Write an essay in which you attempt to define the term *gender* using Thompson's essay as well as other sources that you find in your library or on the Internet.

2. If Deborah Tannen is correct, that the most important issue in word choice is the writer's intended audience, then it would seem that audience as a writer's concern is perhaps even more important than we have assumed. We are never sure who will read what we write, but we need to have an audience in mind as we write. Or do we? Is it possible to write for ourselves or for an audience so general that we don't have it clearly in mind? Write an essay in which you examine the concept of audience as it pertains to the writer's craft. Is it as important as writing teachers and theorists think? If so, why? What have writing experts said about audience that is important for us to know? You may find it helpful to read Linda Flower, "Writing for an Audience" (pp. 184–186).

Authors on page 459:
Writer 1: Langston Hughes, "Salvation"
Writer 2: Diane Ackerman, "Why Leaves Turn Color in the Fall"

Missing the Nose on Our Face: Pronouns and the Feminist Revolution

John H. McWhorter

Linguist, scholar, and cultural critic, John McWhorter was born in Philadelphia in 1965. McWhorter received a master's degree in American studies at New York University, followed by a Ph.D. in linguistics at Stanford University. He taught in the Department of Language and Linguistics at Cornell University before becoming associate professor of linguistics at the University of California, Berkeley. He is currently a senior fellow at the Manhattan Institute, where he writes for the Institute's Center for Race and Ethnicity. McWhorter is also a regular columnist for the *New York Sun* and makes frequent guest appearances on television news and discussion programs such as *20/20, All Things Considered,* and *Meet the Press.* His articles on race and cultural issues have appeared in such publications as the *Wall Street Journal,* the *New York Times,* the *Washington Post,* and the *Chronicle of Higher Education.* McWhorter is also the author of numerous books on language, linguistics, and race, including the best-seller *Losing the Race: Self-Sabotage in Black America* (2001); *The Power of Babel: A Natural History of Language* (2002); *Authentically Black: Essays on the Black Silent Majority* (2003); *Winning the Race: Beyond the Crisis in Black America* (2005); and his latest, *All About the Beat: Why Hip-Hop Can't Save Black America* (2008).

In an October 19, 2003, review in the *Washington Post* of McWhorter's *Doing Our Own Thing: The Degradation of Language and Music in America and Why We Should, Like, Care* (2003), Jonathan Yardley describes McWhorter as a "linguist of the modern school" who "believes that language is ever-evolving and that change is neither good nor bad but simply change." According to Yardley, McWhorter's own prose "too often takes a decidedly ungrammatical turn." Clearly, McWhorter practices what he preaches, even in the title of his essay, "Missing the Nose on Our Face," which is a chapter from *Word on the Street: Debunking the Myth of a "Pure" Standard English* (2001). In this essay, McWhorter discusses possible solutions to the sexism inherent in English, a language that "has no pronoun that was originally gender-neutral."

WRITING TO DISCOVER: *How conscious are you of the issue of sexism and gender-neutrality in language? Does it bother you when you hear a sentence like "Somebody left his book here," when the speaker is not sure whether the "somebody" was male or female?*

Here are three sentences of ordinary English:

Ask one of the musicians whether they lost a page of this score.

Somebody left their book here.

If a student asks for an extension, tell them no.

Thoroughly everyday pieces of English, no? And yet as unobjectionable as those mundane little utterances may seem, according to the rules of classroom grammar, they are considered wrong. *To wit,* what we are often told is that the use of *they, them,* or *their* to refer to single persons is a mistake because *they, them,* and *their* are plural words.

Yet the question is what singular pronoun we are supposed to use here. Instead of the offending plural pronouns, we have often been told by many official sources that it is better to use *he, him,* or *his*:

Ask one of the musicians whether he lost a page of this score.

Somebody left his book here.

If a student asks for an extension, tell him no.

This, however, does not sit quite right with many of us, especially in light of the profound change in the roles of women in Western societies over the past several decades. Using *he, him,* and *his* seems to imply that musicians, students, and, well, somebodies of the world are all men, or at least so often men that the occasional females are just so much static.

In older grammars, pundits often actually came right out and said that men were higher than women in the cosmic order of things, as in an admonition from 1500s to "let us keep a natural order, and set the man before the woman for maners sake," since after all, "the worthier is preferred and set before." Even by the 1700s, however, this was beginning to seem a rather bald thing to put down in black and white (if not to think), and the party line became that *he* was intended as gender-neutral, since English has no pronoun that was originally gender-neutral.

This is nonsense. To decree a pronoun gender-neutral in a book has no effect on how we link language to basic meanings, and for all of us, a sentence like *Somebody left his book here* calls up the image of a boy or man leaving the book. As a matter of fact, applying the sentence to the image of a girl or woman leaving the book seems downright inappropriate because of the obvious male connotation of *he.*

In any case, a bad odor has grown around this gender-neutral feint of late, as the feminist revolution has led a call to eliminate words and expressions from the language that promote the conception that the levers of power in society are the province of men. The commitment that has substituted *police officer* for *policeman* and *chairperson* for *chairman* has led in the pronoun department to a long overdue rethinking of the gender-neural pronoun issue. One of the most popular suggestions has been to use *he or she,* both in speech and in writing. This construction becomes more prevalent with every year:

> Ask one of the musicians whether he or she lost a page of this score.
>
> Somebody left his or her book here.
>
> If a student asks for an extension, tell him or her no.

He or she is founded upon good intentions, but ultimately it will not do. For one thing, the man is still first. Why not *she or he?* But then, two wrongs don't make a right—why should women be first either? If one argues that this would redress millennia of oppression, one might ask how we would decide exactly when the oppression had been redressed, and besides, *then* what would we do?

Moreover, as a look at the above sentences shows, *he or she* is a construction of inherently limited domain. Conscious and forced, it could never go beyond writing and formal speech. There is not a single language out of the over 5,000 on earth in which people spontaneously refer to unisex subjects as "he or she" in conversation, including English. It's one thing to use this in a paper (albeit with that nagging Why-should-men-come-first? problem), lecture, speech, or announcement. However, imagine anyone using *he or she* chewing on a mouthful of pizza while watching a football game on the tube. When we are rattling along in real time in the real world, our concern, while we juggle shopping bags and avoid offending and fix our hair, is the subject we are addressing. A cooked construction like *he or she* is not a piece of spontaneous language, but a statement of allegiance to gender-neutral speech. As laudable as this is, to genuflect to an allegiance to a broad sociopolitical position in the middle of a casual discussion of anything else is no more natural than to genuflect to any number of other noble issues outside of our topic, such as concern with injustice or love of our children. In other words, *he or she* is strictly conscious, whereas spoken language is inherently unconscious, like breathing, or walking without falling. What this means is that if our response to the *they* issue is to decree that *he or she* is the proper form, then while we have applied a Band-Aid to formal speech, we are meanwhile leaving casual speech with the same old *they* that grammarians make us feel guilty about.

One variation on this theme, particularly hip lately, is to switch between *he/him/his* and *she/her/her* in alternate sentences. This one, however, is as hopelessly conscious as *he or she.* Doing this takes a kind of close attention to one's text flow that is virtually impossible outside of writing or careful, planned speech, such as lectures. Once again, there is no language on earth in which people spontaneously alternate their pronouns like this, and there's a reason. This switching also has this disadvantage: Whether spoken or written, each particular use of the male or female pronoun calls up an image of that particular gender, which is both awkward and ends up calling attention to itself instead of to the content of the utterance. To say *he*, especially to audiences familiar with the problems with the gender-neutral fallacy, gives the little jolt of seeming sociologically unsavory; when the speaker or writer corrects this by saying *she* a while later, this usage is distracting as well because after all, women aren't the only ones referred to either. To say *she* first still creates this problem, and even when *he* is used second, it still creates the jolt, especially if the reference to *she* occurred a while ago. In any case, because of the heavy self-monitoring required, this kind of self-conscious alternation is unlikely to ever go beyond a tiny segment of society with a particularly strong interest in demonstrating their commitment to gender-neutral speech.

Of course, some might say that I lack imagination in declaring that *he or she* and the switching are alien to spontaneous speech, and that our goal ought to be to change the very nature of spontaneous speech for the future. I am the last one to dismiss idealism, but there are times when it is best described as quixotic. In that vein, we must ask how realistic it is to imagine, say, children using *he or she* or switching pronouns between sentences. Like *Billy and I went to the store* and *whom*, these devices are the kind of thing only learnable as artificial second layers. They will always flake away with two drinks, laughter, or even simple social comfort.

Then there is *s/he*, which is a complete disaster. This one makes no [10] pretense of being intended for spoken language; it is as unpronounceable as the glyph that the artist formerly known as Prince adopted. Even in writing, however, just look at it—it's too darned ugly to be used as frequently as a pronoun has to be. Imagine great literature splattered with *s/he*'s!

Why are we stuck with all of these awkward little concoctions for written English while condemned to "misusing" *they* in spoken English? The source of the problem here is that there happens to have been no originally singular gender-neutral pronoun in English. Many, many languages do not distinguish between males and females with their third person pronouns. For example, the Finnish pronoun *hän* can refer to either a man or a woman, which is why Finns new to English often mistakenly refer to a woman as *he*. This lack has even led some people to try to work up their own gender-neutral pronoun to bestow on English, but to date, proposals like *hesh, hirm, co, et, E, ho, mon, ne, po,* and *thon* have had distinctly marginal impact on English (yes, people actually have suggested that these be used!). It's not that it's impossible to introduce new words into a language, of course: words like *humongous* and *zillion* do not descend nobly from ancient roots, but were instead made up and somehow hung on. However, around the world, languages are much more resistant to accepting new words, made up or foreign, which are as central to their grammar as pronouns are. It can happen: none other than *they, them,* and *their* were actually taken from Scandinavian after Danes invaded Britain—the originals were the now impossible-looking *hi, heo,* and *hira*. Yet it is still a sometime thing, and even these pronouns entered the language gradually, without any individual commanding that it be so. It is all but impossible for such things to catch on when the introducer is a sole person brandishing a pamphlet.

"The entire question is unlikely to be resolved in the near future" intones the latest edition of the *American Heritage Dictionary*, after a fine capsule summary of the *they/he/she* or *she/s/he* conundrum. The fact is, however, that the issue has been brilliantly resolved for several centuries, if only our grammarians would wake up and realize that language is a lava lamp and not a clockworks. English has long offered a very simple solution that could neatly apply to both casual and formal speech, sail over the problems of whether men or women are to go first, and spare us the drain on the mental battery of parlor tricks like switching between sentences. Notice that in the last paragraph, I said that English has no *originally* singular gender-neutral pronoun. It does, however, have a *presently* singular gender-neutral pronoun, and that is none other than the *they*, which all of us use in this function all of the time despite the frowns of prescriptivists.

We are told that because it is a plural pronoun, *they* must not be used to refer to single persons because it "doesn't make sense." However, the fact is that today, *they* is indeed both a singular and a plural pronoun, as indicated by the fact that all English speakers use it so. *They* is singular as well as plural for the simple reason that the language has changed and made it so. The idea that *they* is only a plural pronoun is an illusion based on the fallacy of treating the English of one thousand years ago as if it was somehow hallowed, rather than just one arbitrary stage of an endless evolution over time.

I say that we know *they* can be singular because people use it that way so regularly, but it is tempting to suppose that English speakers may have just gotten lazy and infected each other with a bad habit. But once again, we gain perspective on this by looking at languages elsewhere. The French pronoun *vous* began as the plural *you*, originally used with people of the highest rank with the implication that they were such awesome personages that they were more like two

> **We are told that because it is a plural pronoun, they must not be used to refer to single persons because it "doesn't make sense."**

people, rather like a person today might facetiously refer to themselves as "we" to connote a certain aristocracy. (Note the use of *themselves* in that last sentence—does it really look like a mistake?) Over time, *vous* came to be used to refer to single people as a mark of respect, and gradually percolated down to indicating respect for ordinary people of authority or even just one's elders. Thus today, within the first month of French instruction we learn that single persons are referred to as *vous* when we are conveying respect (*Comment allez-vous?*), and no one in France or elsewhere considers this to "not make sense"—it happened, and it just is.

In the same month we are also taught that "we" is *nous,* as in *Nous* 15
prenons du café chaque matin, "We drink coffee every morning." However, once we get to France, one of the first things we learn about French
as it is actually spoken casually is that "we" is usually rendered with the
singular gender-neutral pronoun on. *On prend du café chaque matin* has
not exclusively meant "one drinks coffee every morning" for centuries,
and is so commonly used to mean "we," and not just "in the streets" but
even among educated folk, that mastering spoken French usually entails
unlearning the *nous* that textbooks emphasize. Again, the claim that this
"doesn't make sense" would be meaningless—it wouldn't have eons ago
when *on* still only meant "one," but it has long since acquired this new
meaning, to no one's objection.

Things are even more far out in Italian, where the polite form of
"you" is *lei,* which also means "she"! Thus *lei parla* means both "she
speaks" and "you speak." The reason for this is that centuries ago, noble
women were addressed as "she," and this percolated down first to women
in ordinary society, and then spread even to men! Things are similar even
in the plural—to address two people respectfully one uses *loro,* the word
which is also used for "they." One would search in vain for any Italian
newspaper editorial where someone complained that these usages don't
make sense. They wouldn't have made sense 1,500 years ago when these
changes had yet to occur, but this is today, when these changes have taken
place. These usages create no confusion and thus make perfect sense.

And then we return to English and recall once again that our own *you*
began as plural, with *thou* being the original second-person singular form.
As we saw, there were once indignant grammarians who decried the use
of *you* in the singular as illogical. Today, however, *thou* is now relegated
to the Bible and jocular imitations of archaic speech, while *you* is both
plural and singular. None of us [has] any sense of singular *you* as in any
way wrong or sloppy; and the fact that it used to be a plural word only is
something we only learn about in books like this one. In other words, the
use of *you* changed over time, and now, whatever its original use happened
to be, it has had a new one longer than anyone can now remember.

Language change is ever thus. In the beginning a word has one meaning or use. Then as the meaning or use begins to change, prescriptivist
grammarians call the new form sloppy and wrong. This sort of thing cannot stop the language from changing because nothing can. Instead it just
creates a situation where people use the new form casually when Aunt
Lucy isn't looking but avoid it in formal speech. Eventually, the new form
becomes so prevalent that it starts popping up even in formal language
(*whole nother*); the grammarians give up and jump on the latest new forms
(*Hopefully, she'll come*); and before long no one, grammarian or civilian,
even remembers that the now accepted form was even ever considered
a problem (singular *you*). The old criticisms, the trees felled to provide
the paper on which they were written, and the insecurity they sowed in

millions of people—all of it served no more purpose than throwing salt over our shoulder to ward off bad luck.

In this light, our modern grammarians' discomfort with singular *they* is nothing but this comical intermediate stage in an inevitable change, as misguided and futile as the old grumbles about singular *you*. As much as we might like pronouns to stick to their little corners and hone to a perfect model where there is one form for each person/number combination with no overlaps, the fact is that very few languages ever maintain things this way, and if they do, it's by accident. We have to be told by Aunt Lucy that *they* "cannot" refer to one person, and the reason this never occurs to us until we are told is because in Modern English, *they* indeed *can* refer to one person. That's why we use it that way and are understood when we do. We are no more wrong in allowing *they, them,* and *their* to change in this way than the French speakers were who started saying *on prend du café* or the Italians who started calling their monsignors *lei;* or the Middle English speakers who started saying *Charles, you have to do it* instead of *Charles, thou hast to do it;* or the horselike mammals who started developing longer necks on their way to evolving into giraffes. Like life forms, languages are always changing. We would no more expect one to be the way it used to be than we would expect whales to still be bearlike critters bumbling around the seashore. (Yes, this is what whales began as!) Most importantly, language change goes the whole nine yards—nothing in it is exempt, not sounds, not word order, not word meanings, and certainly not good old pronouns.

Thus English has already taken care of the unisex pronoun issue—we   20 don't need *he or she, s/he,* "Look-Ma-I'm-politically-correct" switching, *co, hesh,* or *thon;* because we have *they.* The *they* case is particularly exasperating in that singular *they* has been available to English speakers for several centuries. The only thing keeping us from taking advantage of it has been the power of the prescriptivist hoax, starting with Lowth and Murray's inevitable whacks at it back in the 1700s. The next time someone tells you that *they* must be used only to refer to plural things, ask *them* to explain why it is okay to use *you* in the singular or what's wrong with the sentence *Comment allez-vous, Guillaume?,* and see what *they* come up with.

THINKING CRITICALLY ABOUT THE READING

1. What are some of the problems with the supposedly gender-neutral use of the phrase "he or she"? Why does McWhorter call it a "cooked" construction?

2. How did the masculine *he* become the "gender-neutral" pronoun in the eighteenth century? Why does McWhorter decry this usage?

3. What are the reasons for the feminist attempt to eliminate sexist pronouns from our language?

4. McWhorter talks about the difference between "conscious" language and "unconscious" language, formal speech and casual speech, spoken language

and written language. What are the differences? When is one or the other used? Why is one deemed "proper" and the other not?

5. What does McWhorter find so objectionable about the solutions that use the construction *s/he,* or *he/him/his* and *she/her/her* in alternate sentences?

6. McWhorter says that the insistence on limiting the use of the word *they* to its plural meaning is "an illusion based on the fallacy of treating the English of one thousand years ago as if it was somehow hallowed" (13). What does he mean? What does this reveal about his perspective on the evolution of language?

LANGUAGE IN ACTION

How would you remedy the pronoun problems in McWhorter's opening examples of "ordinary English":

Ask one of the musicians whether they lost a page of this score.

Somebody left their book here.

If a student asks for an extension, tell them no.

Try some of the "awkward little constructions" McWhorter refers to. Do they work for you? In your view, do they succeed in purging the sentence of sexism, or do they simply scream: Look how politically correct I am!

WRITING SUGGESTIONS

1. Go to the library or local bookstore and examine some of the many reference books dedicated to English grammar and language usage. Look up "pronouns" in several of the books and compare their rules. Do any of the books address the issues of gender-neutrality and sexism? What reasoning seems to be behind any solutions they might recommend? Write an essay in which you discuss what you find, especially as it relates to the recommendations made by McWhorter in his essay.

2. Think about McWhorter's approach to grammar in general and his willingness, if not delight, in breaking the rules set down by traditional grammarians. Do you think that grammatical rules and regulations can have a positive impact on the language, or do you agree with McWhorter that nothing *can* stop a language from changing, and further, that nothing *should* stop its natural evolution? From your own point of view, defend or criticize McWhorter's approach.

"Bros Before Hos": The Guy Code

MICHAEL KIMMEL

Michael Kimmel has an international reputation as a researcher, lecturer, and writer on men and masculinity. Born in 1951, he earned his B.A. with distinction from Vassar College in 1972, his M.A. from Brown University in 1974, and his Ph.D. from the University of California, Berkeley, in 1981. Among his many published works are *Changing Men: New Directions in Research on Men and Masculinity* (1987), *Men Confront Pornography* (1990), *Manhood in America: A Cultural History* (1996), *The Gendered Society* (2nd ed., 2003), *The History of Men: Essays on American and British Masculinities* (2005), and *The Gender of Desire: Essays on Masculinity and Sexuality* (2005). Kimmel has taught at Bryant University, New York University, Rutgers University, the University of Oslo, and at Stony Brook University where he is presently Distinguished Professor of Sociology.

In "'Bros Before Hos': The Guy Code," taken from his book *Guyland: The Perilous World Where Boys Become Men* (2008), Kimmel defines the term "Guy Code" as a "collection of attitudes, values, and traits that together composes what it means to be a man" in American society today. Notice how language is skillfully utilized to encourage compliance with the code by its members and to discourage wandering from its demands by any independent thinkers.

WRITING TO DISCOVER: *Think about the groups that you belong to and how language has been used to unify its members and to characterize those who either do not belong or fail to conform to its requirements.*

Whenever I ask young women what they think it means to be a woman, they look at me puzzled, and say, basically, "Whatever I want." "It doesn't mean anything at all to me," says Nicole, a junior at Colby College in Maine. "I can be Mia Hamm, I can be Britney Spears, I can be Madame Curie or Madonna. Nobody can tell me what it means to be a woman anymore."

For men, the question is still meaningful—and powerful. In countless workshops on college campuses and in high-school assemblies, I've asked young men what it means to be a man. I've asked guys from every state in the nation, as well as about fifteen other countries, what sorts of phrases and words come to mind when they hear someone say, "Be a man!"

The responses are rather predictable. The first thing someone usually says is "Don't cry," then other similar phrases and ideas—never show your feelings, never ask for directions, never give up, never give in, be strong, be aggressive, show no fear, show no mercy, get rich, get even, get laid, win—follow easily after that.

Here's what guys say, summarized into a set of current epigrams. Think of it as a "Real Guy's Top Ten List."

1. "Boys Don't Cry"
2. "It's Better to Be Mad than Sad"
3. "Don't Get Mad—Get Even"
4. "Take It Like a Man"
5. "He Who Has the Most Toys When He Dies, Wins"
6. "Just Do It," or "Ride or Die"
7. "Size Matters"
8. "I Don't Stop to Ask for Directions"
9. "Nice Guys Finish Last"
10. "It's All Good"

The unifying emotional subtext of all these aphorisms involves never showing emotions or admitting to weakness. The face you must show to the world insists that everything is going just fine, that everything is under control, that there's nothing to be concerned about (a contemporary version of Alfred E. Neuman of *MAD* Magazine's "What, me worry?"). Winning is crucial, especially when the victory is over other men who have less amazing or smaller toys. Kindness is not an option, nor is compassion. Those sentiments are taboo.

This is "The Guy Code," the collection of attitudes, values, and traits that together composes what it means to be a man. These are the rules that govern behavior in Guyland, the criteria that will be used to evaluate whether any particular guy measures up. The Guy Code revisits what psychologist William Pollack called "the boy code" in his bestselling book *Real Boys*—just a couple of years older and with a lot more at stake. And just as Pollack and others have explored the dynamics of boyhood so well, we now need to extend the reach of that analysis to include late adolescence and young adulthood.

In 1976, social psychologist Robert Brannon summarized the four basic rules of masculinity:

1. "No Sissy Stuff!" Being a man means not being a sissy, not being perceived as weak, effeminate, or gay. Masculinity is the relentless repudiation of the feminine.
2. "Be a Big Wheel." This rule refers to the centrality of success and power in the definition of masculinity. Masculinity is measured more by wealth, power, and status than by any particular body part.
3. "Be a Sturdy Oak." What makes a man is that he is reliable in a crisis. And what makes him so reliable in a crisis is not that he is able to respond fully and appropriately to the situation at hand, but rather that he resembles an inanimate object. A rock, a pillar, a species of tree.

4. "Give 'em Hell." Exude an aura of daring and aggression. Live life out on the edge. Take risks. Go for it. Pay no attention to what others think.

Amazingly, these four rules have changed very little among successive generations of high-school and college-age men. James O'Neil, a developmental psychologist at the University of Connecticut, and Joseph Pleck, a social psychologist at the University of Illinois, have each been conducting studies of this normative definition of masculinity for decades. "One of the most surprising findings," O'Neil told me, "is how little these rules have changed."

BEING A MAN AMONG MEN

Where do young men get these ideas? "Oh, definitely, my dad," says Mike, a 20-year-old sophomore at Wake Forest. "He was always riding my ass, telling me I had to be tough and strong to make it in this world."

"My older brothers were always on my case," says Drew, a 24-year-old University of Massachusetts grad. "They were like, always ragging on me, calling me a pussy, if I didn't want to play football or wrestle. If I just wanted to hang out and like play my Xbox, they were constantly in my face."

"It was subtle, sometimes," says Warren, a 21-year-old at Towson, "and other times really out front. In school, it was the male teachers, saying stuff about how explorers or scientists were so courageous and braving the elements and all that. Then, other times, it was phys-ed class, and everyone was all over everyone else talking about 'He's so gay' and 'He's a wuss.'"

"The first thing I think of is my coach," says Don, a 26-year-old former football player at Lehigh. "Any fatigue, any weakness, any sign that being hit actually hurt and he was like 'Waah! [fake crying] Widdle Donny got a boo boo. Should we kiss it guys?' He'd completely humiliate us for showing anything but complete toughness. I'm sure he thought he was building up our strength and ability to play, but it wore me out trying to pretend all the time, to suck it up and just take it."

The response was consistent: Guys hear the voices of the men in their lives—fathers, coaches, brothers, grandfathers, uncles, priests—to inform their ideas of masculinity.

This is no longer surprising to me. One of the more startling things I found when I researched the history of the idea of masculinity in America for a previous book was that men subscribe to these ideals not because they want to impress women, let alone any inner drive or desire to test themselves against some abstract standards. They do it because they want to be positively evaluated by other men. American men want to be a

10

"man among men," an Arnold Schwarzenegger-like "man's man," not a Fabio-like "ladies' man." Masculinity is largely a "homosocial" experience: performed for, and judged by, other men.

Noted playwright David Mamet explains why women don't even enter the mix. "Women have, in men's minds, such a low place on the social ladder of this country that it's useless to define yourself in terms of a woman. What men need is men's approval." While women often become a kind of currency by which men negotiate their status with other men, women are for possessing, not for emulating. 15

THE GENDER POLICE

Other guys constantly watch how well we perform. Our peers are a kind of "gender police," always waiting for us to screw up so they can give us a ticket for crossing the well-drawn boundaries of manhood. As young men, we become relentless cowboys, riding the fences, checking the boundary line between masculinity and femininity, making sure that nothing slips over. The possibilities of being unmasked are everywhere. Even the most seemingly insignificant misstep can pose a threat or activate that haunting terror that we will be found out.

On the day the students in my class "Sociology of Masculinity" were scheduled to discuss homophobia, one student provided an honest and revealing anecdote. Noting that it was a beautiful day, the first day of spring after a particularly brutal Northeast winter, he decided to wear shorts to class. "I had this really nice pair of new Madras shorts," he recounted. "But then I thought to myself, these shorts have lavender and pink in them. Today's class topic is homophobia. Maybe today is not the best day to wear these shorts." Nods all around.

Our efforts to maintain a manly front cover everything we do. What we wear. How we talk. How we walk. What we eat (like the recent flap over "manwiches"—those artery-clogging massive burgers, dripping with extras). Every mannerism, every movement contains a coded gender language. What happens if you refuse or resist? What happens if you step outside the definition of masculinity? Consider the words that would be used to describe you. In workshops it generally takes less than a minute to get a list of about twenty terms that are at the tip of everyone's tongues: wimp, faggot, dork, pussy, loser, wuss, nerd, queer, homo, girl, gay, skirt, Mama's boy, pussy-whipped. This list is so effortlessly generated, so consistent, that it composes a national well from which to draw epithets and put-downs.

Ask any teenager in America what is the most common put-down in middle school or high school? The answer: "That's so gay." It's said about anything and everything—their clothes, their books, the music or TV shows they like, the sports figures they admire. "That's so gay" has become a free-floating put-down, meaning bad, dumb, stupid, wrong. It's the generic bad thing.

Listen to one of America's most observant analysts of masculinity, Eminem. Asked in an MTV interview in 2001 why he constantly used "faggot" in every one of his raps to put down other guys, Eminem told the interviewer, Kurt Loder, 20

> The lowest degrading thing you can say to a man when you're battling him is to call him a faggot and try to take away his manhood. Call him a sissy, call him a punk. "Faggot" to me doesn't necessarily mean gay people. "Faggot" to me just means taking away your manhood.

But does it mean homosexuality? Does it really suggest that you suspect the object of the epithet might actually be attracted to another guy? Think, for example, of how you would answer this question: If you see a man walking down the street, or meet him at a party, how do you "know" if he is homosexual? (Assume that he is not wearing a T-shirt with a big pink triangle on it, and that he's not already holding hands with another man.)

When I ask this question in classes or workshops, respondents invariably provide a standard list of stereotypically effeminate behaviors. He walks a certain way, talks a certain way, acts a certain way. He's well dressed, sensitive, and emotionally expressive. He has certain tastes in art and music—indeed, he has *any* taste in art and music! Men tend to focus on the physical attributes, women on the emotional. Women say they "suspect" a man might be gay if he's interested in what she's talking about, knows something about what she's talking about, or is sensitive and a good listener. One recently said, "I suspect he might be gay if he's looking at my eyes, and not down my blouse." Another said she suspects he might be gay if he shows no sexual interest in her, if he doesn't immediately come on to her.

> **Every mannerism, every movement contains a coded gender language.**

Once I've established what makes a guy "suspect," I ask the men in the room if any of them would want to be thought of as gay. Rarely does a hand go up—despite the fact that this list of attributes is actually far preferable to the restrictive one that stands in the "Be a Man" box. So, what do straight men do to make sure that no one gets the wrong idea about them?

Everything that is perceived as gay goes into what we might call the Negative Playbook of Guyland. Avoid everything in it and you'll be all right. Just make sure that you walk, talk, and act in a different way from the gay stereotype; dress terribly; show no taste in art or music; show no emotions at all. Never listen to a thing a woman is saying, but express immediate and unquenchable sexual interest. Presto, you're a real man, back in the "Be a Man" box. Homophobia—the fear that people might *misperceive* you as gay—is the animating fear of American guys' masculinity. It's what lies underneath the crazy risk-taking behaviors practiced by boys of all ages, what drives the fear that other guys will see you as weak, unmanly, frightened. The single cardinal rule of manhood, the one from which all the other characteristics—wealth, power, status, strength, physicality—are derived is to offer constant proof that you are not gay.

Homophobia is even deeper than this. It's the fear *of* other men—that other men will perceive you as a failure, as a fraud. It's a fear that others will see you as weak, unmanly, frightened. This is how John Steinbeck put it in his novel *Of Mice and Men*:   25

> "Funny thing," [Curley's wife] said. "If I catch any one man, and he's alone, I get along fine with him. But just let two of the guys get together an' you won't talk. Jus' nothin' but mad." She dropped her fingers and put her hands on her hips. "You're all scared of each other, that's what. Ever'one of you's scared the rest is goin' to get something on you."

In that sense, homosexuality becomes a kind of shorthand for "unmanliness"—and the homophobia that defines and animates the daily conversations of Guyland is at least as much about masculinity as it is about sexuality.

But what would happen to a young man if he were to refuse such limiting parameters on who he is and how he's permitted to act? "It's not like I want to stay in that box," says Jeff, a first-year Cornell student at my workshop. "But as soon as you step outside it, even for a second, all the other guys are like, 'What are you, dude, a fag?' It's not very safe out there on your own. I suppose as I get older, I'll get more secure, and feel like I couldn't care less what other guys say. But now, in my fraternity, on this campus, man, I'd lose everything."

The consistency of responses is as arresting as the list is disturbing: "I would lose my friends." "Get beat up." "I'd be ostracized." "Lose my self-esteem." Some say they'd take drugs or drink. Become withdrawn, sullen, a loner, depressed. "Kill myself," says one guy. "Kill them," responds another. Everyone laughs, nervously. Some say they'd get mad. And some say they'd get even. "I dunno," replied Mike, a sophomore at Portland State University. "I'd probably pull a Columbine. I'd show them that they couldn't get away with calling me that shit."

Guys know that they risk everything—their friendships, their sense of self, maybe even their lives—if they fail to conform. Since the stakes are so enormous, young men take huge chances to prove their manhood, exposing themselves to health risks, workplace hazards, and stress-related illnesses. Here's a revealing factoid. Men ages 19 to 29 are three times less likely to wear seat belts than women the same age. Before they turn nineteen though, young men are actually *more* likely to wear seat belts. It's as if they suddenly get the idea that as long as they're driving the car, they're completely in control, and therefore safe. Ninety percent of all driving offenses, excluding parking violations, are committed by men, and 93 percent of road ragers are male. Safety is emasculating! So they drink too much, drive too fast, and play chicken in a multitude of dangerous venues.

The comments above provide a telling riposte to all those theories of   30
biology that claim that this definition of masculinity is "hard-wired," the result of millennia of evolutionary adaptation or the behavioral response to waves of aggression-producing testosterone, and therefore inevitable. What these theories fail to account for is the way that masculinity is coerced and policed relentlessly by other guys. If it were biological, it would be as natural as breathing or blinking. In truth, the Guy Code fits as comfortably as a straightjacket.

THINKING CRITICALLY ABOUT THE READING

1. In your own words what is the "Guy Code"? Do you believe it actually exists? Explain.
2. How is language used to support the Guy Code and ward off threats to it?
3. If you are a man, what are the consequences of violating the Guy Code?
4. According to Kimmel, is the Guy Code hard-wired into us biologically or do we create it ourselves? Why is the question and how we answer it important?
5. What does Kimmel mean when he writes in paragraph 26, "In that sense, homosexuality becomes a kind of shorthand for 'unmanliness'—and the homophobia that defines and animates the daily conversations of Guyland is at least as much about masculinity as it is about sexuality"?
6. How appropriate is Kimmel's title?

LANGUAGE IN ACTION

In an essay entitled "The Common Guy" written by Audrey Bilger and published in 2002 in the feminist publication *Bitch Magazine,* she argues that women need to stop referring to groups of two or more women as "guys." Here is what Bilger has to say in the next to last paragraph of her essay:

> Most of us have probably had the experience of pointing out some type of sexist expression or behavior to acquaintances and being accused of being "too sensitive" or "too pc" and told to "lighten up." It's certainly easier just to go along with things, to avoid making people uncomfortable, to accept what we think will do no harm. If you feel this way about "you guys," you might want to consider Alice Walker's view of the expression: "I see in its use some women's obsequious need to be accepted, at any cost, even at the cost of erasing their own femaleness, and that of other women. Isn't it at least ironic that after so many years of struggle for women's liberation, women should end up calling themselves this?"

What relationship, if any, do you see between how Kimmel has characterized "Guyland" and its inhabitants and what Bilger and Alice Walker find so wrong with referring to groups of women as "guys"? Has your opinion about the use of the term changed as a result of your reading of both Kimmel and Bilger? If so, how?

WRITING SUGGESTIONS

1. Write an essay in which you describe your own experiences in growing into manhood—or growing up around men. Has Kimmel opened your eyes to what you are experiencing or observing but perhaps not realizing? Do the examples he uses to support his argument sound familiar? What examples and insights of your own can you add? Of course, even more interesting is a thesis to the contrary, one in which you paint an entirely different, perhaps more benign, picture of what it means to be a man. Most important is the role language plays in either approach to manhood. Be sure to use examples of the kind of language involved in the process, examples that shed light because they are both authentic and revealing.

2. The women's movement has sought since the nineteenth century in modern times, and most especially from the 1950s in the twentieth century to the present day, to affirm the independence of women and their desire for self-actualization. Read Audrey Bilger's essay (available online) and write an essay of your own on how the phrase "you guys" demonstrates the power of language in undermining those efforts. Why is it not such an innocuous phrase and why have women surprisingly embraced the term, sometimes willfully and happily? Is there some sense in which the phrase can be seen to be empowering but, like a Trojan Horse, is not what it's assumed to be? How can women stop trying to be the "common guy"? What advice can you offer to discourage such usage?

"Queer" Evolution: Word Goes Mainstream

MARTHA IRVINE

Martha Irvine is a graduate of the University of Michigan and the Columbia Graduate School of Journalism and began her journalism career in 1986. She has worked for publications in Australia, New Zealand, Michigan, Minnesota, and New York. She is now a national writer for the Associated Press and writes stories about issues and trends in popular culture for juveniles and young adults.

"Queer Evolution," an Associated Press article, was first published in a number of newspapers across the country on November 27, 2003. Irvine said the following about how she got the idea for the article: "The 'Queer Evolution' idea came to me after hearing more friends using the word in casual conversation—some of it tied to the television shows *Queer as Folk* and *Queer Eye for the Straight Guy,* though not exclusively so. I was aware that the word is—especially to older generations—difficult to hear, and often considered offensive. But this didn't seem to be the case with younger people, gay or straight. I wanted to see if there was a story there—and indeed, there was."

WRITING TO DISCOVER: *What role does language play when discussing sexual and gender orientations different from your own? Why might it be important for you to be informed about such matters?*

Something queer is happening to the word "queer."

Originally a synonym for "odd" or "unusual," the word evolved into an anti-gay insult in the last century, only to be reclaimed by defiant gay and lesbian activists who chanted: "We're here, we're queer, get used to it."

Now "queer" is sneaking into the mainstream—and taking on a hipster edge as a way to describe any sexual orientation beyond straight.

Jay Edwards, a 28-year-old gay man from Houston, has noticed it.

"Hey Jay," a straight co-worker recently said. "Have you met the new guy? He's really cute and queer, too. Just your type!"

It's the kind of exchange that still makes many—gay or straight—wince. That's because, in the 1920s and '30s the word "queer" became synonymous with "pansy," "sissy," and even "pervert," says Gregory Ward, a Northwestern University linguist who teaches a course on language and sexuality.

Now, Ward says, the increasing use of "queer"—as in the prime-time TV show titles *Queer Eye for the Straight Guy* and *Queer as Folk*—is changing the word's image.

"It's really losing the hurtful and quasi-violent nature it had," Ward says.

Trish McDermott, vice president of "romance" at the Match.com online dating service, says she's seeing the word appear more often in personal ads.

The title of one current ad: "Nice Guy for the Queer Guy."   10

Something queer is happening to the word "queer."

Meanwhile, a recent review in the *Chicago Tribune*'s Metromix entertainment guide defined the crowd in a new upscale bar as "model-types and young clubbers amid dressy Trixies, middle-aged Gold Coast cigar-chompers, and queer-eyed straight guys" (the latter term referring to straight men who've spiffed themselves up).

And while some in the gay community began using the word in the last decade or two as an umbrella term for "gay, lesbian, bisexual, and trans-gendered," today's young people say that "queer" encompasses even more.

"I love it because, in one word, you can refer to the alphabet soup of gay, lesbian, bisexual, questioning, 'heteroflexible,' 'omnisexual,' 'pansexual,' and all of the other shades of difference in that fluid, changing arena of human sexuality," says 27-year-old Stacy Harbaugh. She's the program coordinator for the Indiana Youth Group, a drop-in center in Indianapolis for youth who may place themselves into any of those categories.

"I find myself attracted to boy-like girls and girl-like boys," Harbaugh adds. "If 'lesbian' or 'bi' doesn't seem to fit, 'queer' certainly does."

Heteroflexible? Pansexual? The growing list of terms can be down-right boggling.   15

James Cross, a 26-year-old Chicagoan, personally likes the term "metrosexual," meant to describe straight men like him who are into designer clothes, love art and fashion, and even enjoy shopping (much like "queer-eyed straight guys").

He's also noticed the word "queer" being bandied about more often, especially at the public relations firm where he works. But he says women are "definitely more comfortable" with it.

"I hate to admit it, but I certainly wear masks with the term. When I'm at work and talking with women, I'm down with it," he says. "But when I'm out on the rugby pitch or drinking beer with my 'bros,' I'm just one of the guys."

Indeed, use of a word that carries so much baggage can cause confusion.

Andy Rohr, a 26-year-old gay man living in Boston, noted that when   20 a straight co-worker told him she liked the show *Queer Eye for the Straight Guy,* she whispered the word 'queer,' he says.

Dan Cordella says he, too, is perplexed about what he "can and can't say."

"An entire generation of suburban youth was taught to practically walk on eggshells with their wording around those that, one, chose an alternative lifestyle and, two, were of a different ethnic background," says Cordella, a 26-year-old straight man who lives in New York and grew up outside Boston.

Ward, the Northwestern linguist, says that people are wise to use "queer" carefully because it is still "very context-sensitive."

"It really matters who says it and why they're saying it," he says.

Edwards, from Houston, says he likes when straight people are com-   25
fortable using it.

"If they can say the word with as much casualness and confidence as my gay friends, it lets me know that they are comfortable with who I am," he says.

Rohr, from Boston, is less sure about its use in everyday conversation but says it works with the *Queer Eye* title because its use is "archaic and unexpected."

"The bottom line is, I think the term has lost its political potency, if it ever had any, and has just become campy," he says.

Others, especially those with strong memories of the word as an insult, still find its use hurtful. "I believe this word continues to marginalize us," says Robin Tyler, a California-based activist and lesbian who's in her sixties.

THINKING CRITICALLY ABOUT THE READING

1. What does the evolution of the word *queer* suggest about the flexibility of the English language? Do other words go through similar evolutions in meaning? Can you think of some examples of such words?

2. Why might the word *queer* show a greater speed of evolution than other words in our vocabulary? Is the word of greater service today than it used to be? If so, why?

3. How are people who live alternative lifestyles reclaiming the word *queer*? What have they done to its earlier meanings?

4. Why does Gregory Ward, the Northwestern University linguist, think that people should still be careful how they use the word *queer*?

5. What does Irvine mean by claiming that *queer* has taken on a "hipster edge" today (3)?

6. Irvine uses a number of sources in reporting on the evolution of *queer*. Why doesn't she just report on what she *thinks* the word means and how she *thinks* it has changed over the years?

Language in Action

"Something queer is happening to the word 'queer,'" writes Irvine in opening her essay. What, if anything, has happened to the word since 2003, when Irvine wrote her essay? Go to Google and enter the word *queer*, then do a quick scan of the ways the word is used in context in the first ten hits that are returned. How many of them use the word primarily or exclusively in the sense Irvine describes as "new"? How many incorporate older uses of the word *queer*? What, if anything, can you conclude about the way the use of the word has continued to evolve?

WRITING SUGGESTIONS

1. One of the linguists quoted in the essay urges caution in using the word *queer* because it is "very context-sensitive" (23). What does he mean by this? Are there other words that you feel comfortable using in some situations and not in others? Write an essay describing your own experience with the use of the word *queer*.

2. Do words really have as much power as described in Irvine's article? Write an essay defending or criticizing the use of certain words that have sharply divergent meanings and that in one context might be considered inflammatory, in others complimentary. Explain the difference between the use of a word to defeat its negativity, and the "abuse" of a word as a means of insult. Where does one draw the line? You may find it helpful to read Gloria Naylor's "The Meanings of a Word" (pp. 336–341) before starting to write.

14

ARGUING ABOUT LANGUAGE

SHOULD ENGLISH BE THE LAW?

Since Great Britain gained control over what is now the United States, English has been the dominant language in our country. Despite the multitude of cultures and ethnicities that comprise the United States, English has until now been a common thread linking them. It may be somewhat surprising, then, that there is no official U.S. language. Now, even as English literacy becomes a necessity for people in many parts of the world, some people in the United States believe its primacy is being threatened at home. Much of the current controversy focuses on Hispanic communities with large Spanish-speaking populations, who may feel little or no pressure to learn English. Most would agree that in order for everyone to participate in our society, some way must be found to bridge the linguistic and cultural divide.

Recent government efforts in this regard have included bilingual programs in schools, for providing emergency notices, and so on. The goal of the programs is to maintain a respect for the heritage and language of the non-English speakers while they learn the English language. The programs have come under fire, however, from those who believe that the U.S. government should conduct itself only in English. If people come here, the argument goes, they should assume the responsibility of learning the native language as quickly as possible. And, English-only proponents reason, if immigrants do not or are not willing to learn English, the government should not accommodate them in another language. Some believe that there should be a mandate that the official language of the United States is English and that the government will conduct business in no other language. Many state governments have, in fact, already made such a declaration.

The other side of the argument has two components. One is the belief that it is discriminatory to mandate English because those who do not speak it are then denied basic rights until they learn the language. The second part of this argument is that the current situation is nothing new: There have always been groups of immigrants that were slow to assimilate into American culture, but they all eventually integrated, and the controversy will resolve itself. Furthermore, English is not threatened, and its use does not need to be legislated. Indeed, according to English-only critics, declaring English the official U.S. language could create far more problems than it solves.

The first two selections address the issue head on. Robert King asks "Should English Be the Law?" in the context of our history and that of countries around the world. He notes that compared to similar situations in other countries, including the French Canadian separatist crisis just to our north, the problems here seem almost trivial. If being American still means anything unique, he concludes, we should be able to enjoy our linguistic diversity rather than be threatened by it. Charles Krauthammer's "In Plain English: Let's Make It Official" obviously comes to the opposite conclusion. Krauthammer claims, "History has blessed us, because of the accident of our origins, with a linguistic unity that brings a critically needed cohesion to a nation as diverse, multiracial and multiethnic as America." Finally, in "Why and When We Speak Spanish in Public," Myriam Marquez explains why she and her parents continue to speak Spanish when they are together, why they "haven't adopted English as our official family language." She knew that in order to get ahead in this country she had to learn English, but she contends that "[b]eing an American has very little to do with what language we use during our free time in a free country."

Should English Be the Law?

ROBERT D. KING

Scholar and teacher Robert D. King was born in Mississippi in 1936. He graduated from the Georgia Institute of Technology in 1959 with a degree in mathematics, beginning a distinguished and diverse career in academe. After a brief stint at IBM, King went to the University of Wisconsin, receiving a Ph.D. in German linguistics in 1965. He was hired by the University of Texas at Austin to teach German that same year and has spent more than three decades there teaching linguistics and Asian studies in addition to German. He also served as the dean of the College of Liberal Arts from 1979 until 1989 and currently holds the Audre and Bernard Rapoport Regents Chair of Liberal Arts. Indian and imperialism studies have captured his attention lately, and his most recent books are *Nehru and the Language Politics of India* (1997) and *The Statecraft of British Imperialism: Essays in Honor of Wm. Roger Lewis* (1999).

The language politics of the United States has become a hot topic in recent years as well. In the following selection, first published in the April 1997 issue of the *Atlantic,* King provides historical background and perspective on the English-only debate.

WRITING TO DISCOVER: *What reasons can you give in favor of not making English the official language of the United States?*

We have known race riots, draft riots, labor violence, secession, anti-war protests, and a whiskey rebellion, but one kind of trouble we've never had: a language riot. Language riot? It sounds like a joke. The very idea of language as a political force — as something that might threaten to split a country wide apart — is alien to our way of thinking and to our cultural traditions.

This may be changing. On August 1 of last year [1996] the U.S. House of Representatives approved a bill that would make English the official language of the United States. The vote was 259 to 169, with 223 Republicans and thirty-six Democrats voting in favor and eight Republicans, 160 Democrats, and one independent voting against. The debate was intense, acrid, and partisan. On March 25 of last year [1996] the Supreme Court agreed to review a case involving an Arizona law that would require public employees to conduct government business only in English. Arizona is one of several states that have passed "Official English" or "English Only" laws. The appeal to the Supreme Court followed a 6-to-5 ruling, in October of 1995, by a federal appeals court striking down the Arizona law. These events suggest how divisive a public issue language could become in America — even if it has until now scarcely been taken seriously.

Traditionally, the American way has been to make English the national language—but to do so quietly, locally, without fuss. The Constitution is silent on language: the Founding Fathers had no need to legislate that English be the official language of the country. It has always been taken for granted that English *is* the national language, and that one must learn English in order to make it in America.

To say that language has never been a major force in American history or politics, however, is not to say that politicians have always resisted linguistic jingoism. In 1753 Benjamin Franklin voiced his concern that German immigrants were not learning English: "Those [Germans] who come hither are generally the most ignorant Stupid Sort of their own Nation. . . . they will soon so out number us, that all the advantages we have will not, in My Opinion, be able to preserve our language, and even our government will become precarious." Theodore Roosevelt articulated the unspoken American linguistic-melting-pot theory when he boomed, "We have room for but one language here, and that is the English language, for we intended to see that the crucible turns our people out as Americans, of American nationality, and not as dwellers in a polyglot boarding house." And: "We must have but one flag. We must also have but one language. That must be the language of the Declaration of Independence, of Washington's Farewell address, of Lincoln's Gettysburg speech and Second Inaugural."

OFFICIAL ENGLISH

TR's linguistic tub-thumping long typified the tradition of American politics. That tradition began to change in the wake of the anything-goes attitudes and the celebration of cultural differences arising in the 1960s. A 1975 amendment to the Voting Rights Act of 1965 mandated the "bilingual ballot" under certain circumstances, notably when the voters of selected language groups reached five percent or more in a voting district. Bilingual education became a byword of educational thinking during the 1960s. By the 1970s linguists had demonstrated convincingly—at least to other academics—that black English (today called African-American vernacular English or Ebonics) was not "bad" English but a different kind of authentic English with its own rules. Predictably, there have been scattered demands that black English be included in bilingual-education programs.

It was against this background that the movement to make English the official language of the country arose. In 1981 Senator S.I. Hayakawa, long a leading critic of bilingual education and bilingual ballots, introduced in the U.S. Senate a constitutional amendment that not only would have made English the official language but would have prohibited federal and state laws and regulations requiring the use of other languages. His English Language Amendment died in the Ninety-seventh Congress.

In 1983 the organization called U.S. English was founded by Hayakawa and John Tanton, a Michigan ophthalmologist. The primary purpose of the organization was to promote English as the official language of the United States. (The best background readings on America's "neolinguisticism" are the books *Hold Your Tongue,* by James Crawford, and *Language Loyalties,* edited by Crawford, both published in 1992.) Official English initiatives were passed by California in 1986, by Arkansas, Mississippi, North Carolina, North Dakota, and South Carolina in 1987, by Colorado, Florida, and Arizona in 1988, and by Alabama in 1990. The majorities voting for these initiatives were generally not insubstantial: California's, for example, passed by 73 percent.

It was probably inevitable that the Official English (or English-only—the two names are used almost interchangeably) movement would acquire a conservative, almost reactionary undertone in the 1990s. Official English is politically very incorrect. But its cofounder John Tanton brought with him strong liberal credentials. He had been active in the Sierra Club and Planned Parenthood, and in the 1970s served as the national president of Zero Population Growth. Early advisers of U.S. English resist ideological pigeonholing: they included Walter Annenberg, Jacques Barzun, Bruno Bettelheim, Alistair Cooke, Denton Cooley, Walter Cronkite, Angier Biddle Duke, George Gilder, Sidney Hook, Norman Podhoretz, Arnold Schwarzenegger, and Karl Shapiro. In 1987 U.S. English installed as its president Linda Chávez, a Hispanic who had been prominent in the Reagan Administration. A year later she resigned her position, citing "repugnant" and "anti-Hispanic" overtones in an internal memorandum written by Tanton. Tanton, too, resigned, and Walter Cronkite, describing the affair as "embarrassing," left the advisory board. One board member, Norman Cousins, defected in 1986, alluding to the "negative symbolic significance" of California's Official English initiative, Proposition 63. The current chairman of the board and CEO of U.S. English is Mauro E. Mujica, who claims that the organization has 650,000 members.

The popular wisdom is that conservatives are pro and liberals con. True, conservatives such as George Will and William F. Buckley Jr. have written columns supporting Official English. But would anyone characterize as conservatives the present and past U.S. English board members Alistair Cooke, Walter Cronkite, and Norman Cousins? One of the strongest opponents of bilingual education is the Mexican American writer Richard Rodriguez, best known for his eloquent autobiography, *Hunger of Memory* (1982). There is a strain of American liberalism that defines itself in nostalgic devotion to the melting pot.

For several years relevant bills awaited consideration in the U.S. House 10 of Representatives. The Emerson Bill (H.R. 123), passed by the House last August, specifies English as the official language of government, and requires that the government "preserve and enhance" the official status of English. Exceptions are made for the teaching of foreign languages; for actions necessary for public health, international relations, foreign trade, and the protection of the rights of criminal defendants; and for the use of "terms of art" from languages other than English. It would, for example, stop the Internal Revenue Service from sending out income-tax forms and instructions in languages other than English, but it would not ban the use of foreign languages in census materials or documents dealing with national security. "*E Pluribus Unum*" can still appear on American money. U.S. English supports the bill.

What are the chances that some version of Official English will become federal law? Any language bill will face tough odds in the Senate, because some western senators have opposed English-only measures in the past for various reasons, among them a desire by Republicans not to alienate the growing number of Hispanic Republicans, most of whom are uncomfortable with mandated monolingualism. Texas Governor George W. Bush, too, has forthrightly said that he would oppose any English Only proposals in his state. Several of the Republican candidates for President in 1996 (an interesting exception is Phil Gramm) endorsed versions of Official English, as has Newt Gingrich. While governor of Arkansas, Bill Clinton signed into law an English-only bill. As President, he has described his earlier action as a mistake.

Many issues intersect in the controversy over Official English: immigration (above all), the rights of minorities (Spanish-speaking minorities in particular), the pros and cons of bilingual education, tolerance, how best to educate the children of immigrants, and the place of cultural diversity in school curricula and in American society in general. The question that lies at the root of most of the uneasiness is this: Is America threatened by the preservation of languages other than English? Will America, if it continues on its traditional path of benign linguistic neglect, go the way of Belgium, Canada, and Sri Lanka—three countries among many whose unity is gravely imperiled by language and ethnic conflicts?

LANGUAGE AND NATIONALITY

Language and nationalism were not always so intimately intertwined. Never in the heyday of rule by sovereign was it a condition of employment that the King be able to speak the language of his subjects. George I spoke no English and spent much of his time away from England, attempting to use the power of his kingship to shore up his German possessions. In the Middle Ages nationalism was not even part of the picture: one owed loyalty to a lord, a prince, a ruler, a family, a tribe, a church, a piece of land, but not to a nation and least of all to a nation as a language unit. The capital city of the Austrian Hapsburg empire was Vienna, its ruler a monarch with effective control of peoples of the most varied and incompatible ethnicities, and languages, throughout Central and Eastern Europe. The official language, and the lingua franca as well, was German. While it stood—and it stood for hundreds of years—the empire was an anachronistic relic of what for most of human history had been the normal relationship between country and language: none.

The marriage of language and nationalism goes back at least to Romanticism and specifically to Rousseau, who argued in his *Essay on the Origin of Languages* that language must develop before politics is possible and that language originally distinguished nations from one another. A little-remembered aim of the French Revolution—itself the legacy of Rousseau—was to impose a national language on France, where regional languages such as Provençal, Breton, and Basque were still strong competitors against standard French, the French of the Ile de France. As late as 1789, when the Revolution began, half the population of the south of France, which spoke Provençal, did not understand French. A century earlier the playwright Racine said that he had had to resort to Spanish and Italian to make himself understood in the southern French town of Uzès. After the Revolution nationhood itself became aligned with language.

In 1846 Jacob Grimm, one of the Brothers Grimm of fairy-tale fame   15 but better known in the linguistic establishment as a forerunner of modern comparative and historical linguists, said that "a nation is the totality of people who speak the same language." After midcentury, language was invoked more than any other single criterion to define nationality. Language as a political force helped to bring about the unification of Italy and of Germany and the secession of Norway from its union with Sweden in 1905. Arnold Toynbee observed—unhappily—soon after the First World War that "the growing consciousness of Nationality had attached itself neither to traditional frontiers nor to new geographical associations but almost exclusively to mother tongues."

The crowning triumph of the new desideratum was the Treaty of Versailles, in 1919, when the allied victors of the First World War began redrawing the map of Central and Eastern Europe according to nationality as best they could. The magic word was "self-determination," and none of Woodrow Wilson's Fourteen Points mentioned the word "language" at all. Self-determination was thought of as being related to "nationality," which today we would be more likely to call "ethnicity"; but language was simpler to identify than nationality or ethnicity. When it came to drawing the boundary lines of various countries—Czechoslovakia, Yugoslavia, Romania, Hungary, Albania, Bulgaria, Poland—it was principally language that guided the draftsman's hand. (The main exceptions were Alsace-Lorraine, South Tyrol, and the German-speaking parts of Bohemia and Moravia.) Almost by default language became the defining characteristic of nationality.

And so it remains today. In much of the world, ethnic unity and cultural identification are routinely defined by language. To be Arab is to speak Arabic. Bengali identity is based on language in spite of the division of Bengali-speakers between Hindu India and Muslim Bangladesh. When eastern Pakistan seceded from greater Pakistan in 1971, it named itself Bangladesh: *desa* means "country"; *bangla* means not the Bengali people or the Bengali territory but the Bengali language.

Scratch most nationalist movements and you find a linguistic grievance. The demands for independence of the Baltic states (Latvia, Lithuania, and Estonia) were intimately bound up with fears for the loss of their respective languages and cultures in a sea of Russianness. In Belgium the war between French and Flemish threatens an already weakly fused country. The present atmosphere of Belgium is dark and anxious, costive; the metaphor of divorce is a staple of private and public discourse. The lines of terrorism in Sri Lanka are drawn between Tamil Hindus and Sinhalese Buddhists—and also between the Tamil and Sinhalese languages. Worship of the French language fortifies the movement for an independent Quebec. Whether a united Canada will survive into the twenty-first century is a question too close to call. Much of the anxiety about language in the United States is probably fueled by the "Quebec problem": unlike Belgium, which is a small European country, or Sri Lanka, which is halfway around the world, Canada is our close neighbor.

Language is a convenient surrogate for nonlinguistic claims that are often awkward to articulate, for they amount to a demand for more political and economic power. Militant Sikhs in India call for a state of their own: Khalistan ("Land of the Pure" in Punjabi). They frequently couch this as a demand for a linguistic state, which has a certain simplicity about it, a clarity of motive—justice, even, because states in India are normally linguistic states. But the Sikh demands blend religion, economics, language, and retribution for sins both punished and unpunished in a country where old sins cast long shadows.

Language is an explosive issue in the countries of the former Soviet   20
Union. The language conflict in Estonia has been especially bitter. Ethnic Russians make up almost a third of Estonia's population, and most of them do not speak or read Estonian, although Russians have lived in Estonia for more than a generation. Estonia has passed legislation requiring knowledge of the Estonian language as a condition of citizenship. Nationalist groups in independent Lithuania sought restrictions on the use of Polish—again, old sins, long shadows.

In 1995 protests erupted in Moldova, formerly the Moldavian Soviet Socialist Republic, over language and the teaching of Moldovan history. Was Moldovan history a part of Romanian history or of Soviet history? Was Moldova's language Romanian? Moldovan—earlier called Moldavian—*is* Romanian, just as American English and British English are both English. But in the days of the Moldavian SSR, Moscow insisted that the two languages were different, and in a piece of linguistic nonsense required Moldavian to be written in the Cyrillic alphabet to strengthen the case that it was not Romanian.

The official language of Yugoslavia was Serbo-Croatian, which was never so much a language as a political accommodation. The Serbian and Croatian languages are mutually intelligible. Serbian is written in the Cyrillic alphabet, is identified with the Eastern Orthodox branch of the Catholic Church, and borrows its high-culture words from the east—from Russian and Old Church Slavic. Croatian is written in the Roman alphabet, is identified with Roman Catholicism and borrows its high-culture words from the west—from German, for example, and Latin. One of the first things the newly autonomous Republic of Serbia did, in 1991, was to pass a law decreeing Serbian in the Cyrillic alphabet the official language of the country. With Croatia divorced from Serbia, the Croatian and Serbian languages are diverging more and more. Serbo-Croatian has now passed into history, a language-museum relic from the brief period when Serbs and Croats called themselves Yugoslavs and pretended to like each other.

Slovakia, relieved now of the need to accommodate to Czech cosmo-politan sensibilities, has passed a law making Slovak its official language. (Czech is to Slovak pretty much as Croatian is to Serbian.) Doctors in state hospitals must speak to patients in Slovak, even if another language would aid diagnosis and treatment. Some 600,000 Slovaks—more than 10 percent of the population—are ethnically Hungarian. Even staff meet-ings in Hungarian-language schools must be in Slovak. (The government dropped a stipulation that church weddings be conducted in Slovak after heavy opposition from the Roman Catholic Church.) Language inspectors are told to weed out "all sins perpetrated on the regular Slovak language." Tensions between Slovaks and Hungarians, who had been getting along, have begun to arise.

The twentieth century is ending as it began—with trouble in the Balkans and with nationalist tensions flaring up in other parts of the globe. (Toward the end of his life Bismarck predicted that "some damn fool thing in the Balkans" would ignite the next war.) Language isn't always part of the problem. But it usually is.

UNIQUE OTHERNESS

Is there no hope for language tolerance? Some countries manage to   25
maintain their unity in the face of multilingualism. Examples are Finland, with a Swedish minority, and a number of African and Southeast Asian countries. Two others could not be more unlike as countries go: Switzerland and India.

German, French, Italian, and Romansh are the languages of Switzerland. The first three can be and are used for official purposes; all four are designated "national" languages. Switzerland is politically almost hyperstable. It has language problems (Romansh is losing ground), but they are not major, and they are never allowed to threaten national unity.

Contrary to public perception, India gets along pretty well with a host of different languages. The Indian constitution officially recognizes nineteen languages, English among them. Hindi is specified in the constitution as the national language of India, but that is a pious postcolonial fiction: outside the Hindi-speaking northern heartland of India, people don't want to learn it. English functions more nearly than Hindi as India's lingua franca.

From 1947, when India obtained its independence from the British, until the 1960s blood ran in the streets and people died because of language. Hindi absolutists wanted to force Hindi on the entire country, which would have split India between north and south and opened up other fracture lines as well. For as long as possible Jawaharlal Nehru, independent India's first Prime Minister, resisted nationalist demands to redraw the capricious state boundaries of British India according to language. By the time he capitulated, the country had gained a precious decade to prove its viability as a union.

Why is it that India preserves its unity with not just two languages to contend with, as Belgium, Canada, and Sri Lanka have, but nineteen? The answer is that India, like Switzerland, has a strong national identity. The two countries share something big and almost mystical that holds each together in a union transcending language. That something I call "unique otherness."

The Swiss have what the political scientist Karl Deutsch called "learned   30 habits, preferences, symbols, memories, and patterns of landholding": customs, cultural traditions, and political institutions that bind them closer to one another than to people of France, Germany, or Italy living just across the border and speaking the same language. There is Switzerland's traditional neutrality, its system of universal military training (the "citizen army"), its consensual allegiance to a strong Swiss franc—and fondue, yodeling, skiing, and mountains. Set against all this, the fact that Switzerland has four languages doesn't even approach the threshold of becoming a threat.

As for India, what Vincent Smith, in the *Oxford History of India*, calls its "deep underlying fundamental unity" resides in institutions and beliefs such as caste, cow worship, sacred places, and much more. Consider *dharma*, *karma*, and *maya*, the three root convictions of Hinduism; India's historical epics; Gandhi; *ahimsa* (nonviolence); vegetarianism; a distinctive cuisine and way of eating; marriage customs; a shared past; and what the Indologist Ainslie Embree calls "Brahmanical ideology." In other words, "We are Indian; we are different."

Belgium and Canada have never managed to forge a stable national identity; Czechoslovakia and Yugoslavia never did either. Unique otherness immunizes countries against linguistic destabilization. Even Switzerland and especially India have problems; in any country with as many different languages as India has, language will never *not* be a problem. However, it is one thing to have a major illness with a bleak prognosis; it is another to have a condition that is irritating and occasionally painful but not life-threatening.

History teaches a plain lesson about language and governments: there is almost nothing the government of a free country can do to change language usage and practice significantly, to force its citizens to use certain languages in preference to others, and to discourage people from speaking a language they wish to continue to speak. (The rebirth of Hebrew in Palestine and Israel's successful mandate that Hebrew be spoken and written by Israelis is a unique event in the annals of language history.) Quebec has since the 1970s passed an array of laws giving French a virtual monopoly in the province. One consequence—unintended, one wishes to believe—of these laws is that last year kosher products imported for Passover were kept off the shelves, because the packages were not labeled in French. Wise governments keep their hands off language to the extent that it is politically possible to do so.

We like to believe that to pass a law is to change behavior; but passing laws about language, in a free society, almost never changes attitudes or behavior. Gaelic (Irish) is living out a slow, inexorable decline in Ireland despite enormous government support of every possible kind since Ireland gained its independence from Britain. The Welsh language, in contrast, is alive today in Wales in spite of heavy discrimination during its history. Three out of four people in the northern and western counties of Gwynedd and Dyfed speak Welsh.

I said earlier that language is a convenient surrogate for other national problems. Official English obviously has a lot to do with concern about immigration, perhaps especially Hispanic immigration. America may be threatened by immigration; I don't know. But America is not threatened by language.

35

The usual arguments made by academics against Official English are commonsensical. Who needs a law when, according to the 1990 census, 94 percent of American residents speak English anyway? (Mauro E. Mujica, the chairman of U.S. English,

> **We like to believe that to pass a law is to change behavior; but passing laws about language, in a free society, almost never changes attitudes or behavior.**

cites a higher figure: 97 percent.) Not many of today's immigrants will see their first language survive into the second generation. This is in fact the common lament of first-generation immigrants: their children are not learning their language and are losing the culture of their parents. Spanish is hardly a threat to English, in spite of isolated (and easily visible) cases such as Miami, New York City, and pockets of the Southwest and southern California. The everyday language of south Texas is Spanish, and yet south Texas is not about to secede from America.

But empirical, calm arguments don't engage the real issue: language is a symbol, an icon. Nobody who favors a constitutional ban against flag burning will ever be persuaded by the argument that the flag is, after all, just a "piece of cloth." A draft card in the 1960s was never merely a piece of paper. Neither is a marriage license.

Language, as one linguist has said, is "not primarily a means of communication but a means of communion." Romanticism exalted language, made it mystical, sublime—a bond of national identity. At the same time, Romanticism created a monster: it made of language a means for destroying a country.

America has that unique otherness of which I spoke. In spite of all our racial divisions and economic unfairness, we have the frontier tradition, respect for the individual, and opportunity; we have our love affair with the automobile; we have in our history a civil war that freed the slaves and was fought with valor; and we have sports, hot dogs, hamburgers, and milk shakes—things big and small, noble and petty, important and trifling. "We are Americans; we are different."

If I'm wrong, then the great American experiment will fail—not   40
because of language but because it no longer means anything to be an American; because we have forfeited that "willingness of the heart" that F. Scott Fitzgerald wrote was America; because we are not long joined by Lincoln's "mystic chords of memory."

We are not even close to the danger point. I suggest that we relax and luxuriate in our linguistic richness and our traditional tolerance of language differences. Language does not threaten American unity. Benign neglect is a good policy for any country when it comes to language, and it's a good policy for America.

THINKING CRITICALLY ABOUT THE READING

1. According to King, "It has always been taken for granted that English *is* the national language, and that one must learn English in order to make it in America" (3). What has changed in recent years to make learning English a political issue?

2. What does King mean when he says, "Official English is politically very incorrect" (8)?

3. What, according to King, makes the English-only issue so controversial? What other issues complicate the decision to make English the nation's language?

4. Why do you think King takes time to explain the evolution of the relationship between language and nationality in Europe and the rest of the world? What insights into the English-only issue does this brief history of language and culture give you? Explain.

5. What does King mean by the term "unique otherness"? What do you see as America's "unique otherness"? Do you agree with King's assessment that America's "unique otherness" will help us transcend our language differences? Why or why not?

6. King concludes that "[b]enign neglect is a good policy for any country when it comes to language, and it's a good policy for America" (41). Do you share King's optimistic view?

In Plain English: Let's Make It Official

CHARLES KRAUTHAMMER

Pulitzer Prize–winning columnist and commentator Charles Krauthammer was born in 1950 in New York City to parents of French citizenship. He grew up in Montreal and graduated from McGill University in 1970. The following year he continued his studies in political science as a Commonwealth Scholar at Balliol College, Oxford. In 1972 he moved to the United States and enrolled in Harvard Medical School, earning his M.D. in psychiatry in 1975. In 1978 he joined Jimmy Carter's administration to direct planning in psychiatric research, and later he served as speechwriter for Vice President Walter Mondale and senior editor at the *New Republic*. As a journalist, Krauthammer quickly gained a reputation for his clear prose and sound arguments. He is widely recognized and respected for his political and social columns, which appear regularly in the *Washington Post, Time,* the *New Republic,* and the *Weekly Standard.* In 1985 he published *Cutting Edges: Making Sense of the Eighties,* a collection of his essays. One critic commented that "Krauthammer is at his best when he writes not so much about 'hard' politics as about political culture . . . and beyond than about the contemporary social climate in general."

In the following essay, first published in *Time* on June 12, 2006, Krauthammer presents the case for making English the official language of the United States. He strongly believes that America's unprecedented success as a nation can be traced to the unifying force of the English language.

WRITING TO DISCOVER: *Our country's elected officials are struggling with the question of whether or not to make English our official language. Make a list of the reasons why you think it should or should not be the language of the land for all official transactions.*

Growing up (as I did) in the province of Québec, you learn not just the joys but also the perils of bilingualism. A separate national identity, revolving entirely around "Francophonie," became a raging issue that led to social unrest, terrorism, threats of separation and a referendum that came within a hair's breadth of breaking up Canada.

Canada, of course, had no choice about bilingualism. It is a country created of two nations at its birth, and has ever since been trying to cope with that inherently divisive fact. The U.S., by contrast blessed with a single common language for two centuries, seems blithely and gratuitously to be ready to import bilingualism with all its attendant divisiveness and antagonisms.

One of the major reasons for America's great success as the world's first "universal nation," for its astonishing and unmatched capacity for assimilating immigrants, has been that an automatic part of acculturation was the acquisition of English. And yet during the great immigration debate now raging in Congress, the people's representatives cannot make up their minds whether the current dominance of English should be declared a national asset, worthy of enshrinement in law.

The Senate could not bring itself to declare English the country's "official language." The best it could do was pass an amendment to the immigration bill tepidly declaring English the "national language." Yet even that was too much for Senate Democratic leader Harry Reid, who called that resolution "racist."

Less hyperbolic opponents point out that granting special official   5
status to English is simply unnecessary: America has been accepting foreign-language-speaking immigrants forever—Brooklyn is so polyglot it is a veritable Babel—and yet we've done just fine. What's the great worry about Spanish?

The worry is this. Polyglot is fine. When immigrants, like those in Brooklyn, are members of a myriad of linguistic communities, each tiny and discrete, there is no threat to the common culture. No immigrant presumes to make the demand that the state grant special status to his language. He may speak it in the street and proudly teach it to his children, but he knows that his future and certainly theirs lie inevitably in learning English as the gateway to American life.

> **One of the major reasons for America's great success as the world's first "universal nation," for its astonishing and unmatched capacity for assimilating immigrants, has been that an automatic part of acculturation was the acquisition of English.**

But all of that changes when you have an enormous, linguistically monoclonal immigration as we do today from Latin America. Then you get not Brooklyn's successful Babel but Canada's restive Québec. Monoclonal immigration is new for the U.S., and it changes things radically. If at the turn of the twentieth century, Ellis Island had greeted teeming masses speaking not 50 languages but just, say, German, America might not have enjoyed the same success at assimilation and national unity that it has.

Today's monoclonal linguistic culture is far from hypothetical. Growing rapidly through immigration, it creates large communities—in some places already majorities—so overwhelmingly Spanish speaking that, in time, they may quite naturally demand the rights and official recognition for Spanish that French has in French-speaking Québec.

That would not be the end of the world—Canada is a decent place—but the beginning of a new one for the U.S., a world far more complicated and fraught with division. History has blessed us with all the freedom and advantages of multiculturalism. But it has also blessed us, because of the accident of our origins, with a linguistic unity that brings a critically needed cohesion to a nation as diverse, multiracial and multi-ethnic as America. Why gratuitously throw away that priceless asset? How mindless to call the desire to retain it "racist."

I speak three languages. My late father spoke nine. When he became a   10
naturalized American in midcentury, it never occurred to him to demand of his new and beneficent land that whenever its government had business with him—tax forms, court proceedings, ballot boxes—that it should be required to communicate in French, his best language, rather than English, his last and relatively weakest.

English is the U.S.'s national and common language. But that may change over time unless we change our assimilation norms. Making English the official language is the first step toward establishing those norms. "Official" means the language of the government and its institutions. "Official" makes clear our expectations of acculturation. "Official" means that every citizen, upon entering America's most sacred political space, the voting booth, should minimally be able to identify the words President and Vice President and county commissioner and judge. The immigrant, of course, has the right to speak whatever he wants. But he must understand that when he comes to the U.S., swears allegiance and accepts its bounty, he undertakes to join its civic culture. In English.

THINKING CRITICALLY ABOUT THE READING

1. According to Krauthammer, what has been one of the most important reasons for America's success as a nation?

2. How does Krauthammer counter those people who believe that "granting special official status to English is simply unnecessary" (5)?

3. What is "monoclonal immigration" (7)? In what ways does monoclonal immigration affect assimilation and national unity? Explain.

4. How does Krauthammer answer the question, "What's the great worry about Spanish" (5)? What do you see as his greatest fear?

5. Why does Krauthammer believe that "linguistic unity" is so important for the United States at this point in its history? Do you agree with his assessment of the situation? Explain why or why not.

6. What, for Krauthammer, is the difference between declaring English "the 'national language'" and making English the "'official language'" (4)? What does he believe the label "official" will mean for future generations?

Why and When We Speak Spanish in Public

Myriam Marquez

An award-winning columnist for the *Orlando Sentinel*, Myriam Marquez was born in Cuba in 1954 and grew up in South Florida. After graduating from the University of Maryland in 1983 with a degree in journalism and a minor in political science, she worked for United Press International in Washington, D.C., and in Maryland, covering the Maryland legislature as statehouse bureau chief. Marquez joined the editorial board of the *Sentinel* in 1987 and, since 1990, has been writing three weekly columns. Her commentaries focus on state and national politics, the human condition, civil liberties, and issues important to women and Hispanics. She is a founding board member of the YMCA Achievers program, which aims to help Hispanic students succeed in high school. Since 2000, Marquez has tutored public school children in reading. The Florida Society of Newspaper Editors awarded her its highest award for commentary in 2003.

As a Hispanic, Marquez recognizes that English is the "common language" in America but knows that being American has little if anything to do with what language one speaks. In this article, which first appeared in the *Orlando Sentinel* on July 5, 1999, she explains why she and her parents, all bilingual, continue to speak Spanish when they are together, even though they have lived in the United States for forty years.

WRITING TO DISCOVER: *How would you feel if you met a friend and her parents in a public place and they spoke a language other than English in your presence?*

When I'm shopping with my mother or standing in line with my step-dad to order fast food or anywhere else we might be together, we're going to speak to one another in Spanish.

That may appear rude to those who don't understand Spanish and overhear us in public places.

Those around us may get the impression that we're talking about them. They may wonder why we would insist on speaking in a foreign tongue, especially if they knew that my family has lived in the United States for 40 years and that my parents do understand English and speak it, albeit with difficulty and a heavy accent.

Let me explain why we haven't adopted English as our official family language. For me and most of the bilingual people I know, it's a matter of respect for our parents and comfort in our cultural roots.

It's not meant to be rude to others. It's not meant to alienate anyone or to Balkanize America. 5

It's certainly not meant to be un-American—what constitutes an "American" being defined by English speakers from North America.

Being an American has very little to do with what language we use during our free time in a free country. From its inception, this country was careful not to promote a government-mandated official language.

We understand that English is the common language of this country and the one most often heard in international business circles from Peru to Norway. We know that, to get ahead here, one must learn English.

But that ought not mean that somehow we must stop speaking in our native tongue whenever we're in a public area, as if we were ashamed of who we are, where we're from. As if talking in Spanish—or any other language, for that matter—is some sort of litmus test used to gauge American patriotism.

Throughout this nation's history, most immigrants—whether from   10
Poland or Finland or Italy or wherever else—kept their language through the first generation and, often, the second. I suspect that they spoke among themselves in their native tongue—in public. Pennsylvania even provided voting ballots written in German during much of the 1800s for those who weren't fluent in English.

In this century, Latin American immigrants and others have fought for this country in U.S.-led wars. They have participated fully in this nation's democracy by voting, holding political office, and paying taxes. And they have watched their children and grandchildren become so "American" that they resist speaking in Spanish.

> **Being an American has very little to do with what language we use during our free time in a free country.**

You know what's rude?

When there are two or more people who are bilingual and another person who speaks only English and the bilingual folks all of a sudden start speaking Spanish, which effectively leaves out the English-only speaker. I don't tolerate that.

One thing's for sure. If I'm ever in a public place with my mom or dad and bump into an acquaintance who doesn't speak Spanish, I will switch to English and introduce that person to my parents. They will respond in English, and do so with respect.

THINKING CRITICALLY ABOUT THE READING

1. How does Marquez explain the fact that she and her parents "haven't adopted English as our official family language"(4)? If you were standing next to the three of them and they were speaking Spanish, would you consider their behavior rude? Why or why not?

2. Marquez claims that "from its inception, this country was careful not to promote a government-mandated official language"(7). Why do you suppose the

U.S. government has steered clear of legislating an official language? Is there a need for such legislation now?

3. For Marquez, "being an American has very little to do with what language we use during our free time in a free country"(7). Do you think that the English-only debate gets muddied when people see language as "some sort of litmus test used to gauge American patriotism"(9)? Explain.

4. Under what circumstances would Marquez stop speaking Spanish and use English? If you were or are bilingual, would you behave the same way in similar situations? Explain.

WRITING SUGGESTIONS: DEBATING THE ISSUE

1. While it's no secret that English is the common language of the United States, few of us know, as Myriam Marquez is quick to remind us, that our country has been "careful not to promote a government-mandated official language"(7). Why do you suppose that our federal government has chosen to keep its hands off the language issue? If it has not been necessary to mandate English in the past, why do you think that people now feel a need to declare English the "official language" of the United States? Write an essay in which you give your own opinion on this issue.

2. Robert D. King explains that "[i]n much of the world, ethnic unity and cultural identification are routinely defined by language" (17). To what extent is this true in the United States? Why is it sometimes difficult for nonnative speakers of English who immigrate to the United States to take ownership of Standard English? Write an essay in which you explore what it means to take ownership of language. Does one need this ownership to succeed?

3. Myriam Marquez explains the bilingual world she shares with her parents. What insights, if any, do their personal reflections give us into the English-only debate? Where do you think she stands on the issue of English-only?

4. Write an essay in which you frame the English-only debate as a political issue, a social issue, an economic issue, or some combination of the three. In this context, what do you see as the relationship between language and power?

5. The selections from King and Krauthammer address immigrant assimilation from an academic viewpoint, but it is a highly personal subject for those who come here. After all, they must confront their English-language deficiencies right from the start. When American students study a foreign language at school, however, almost all of the speaking and instruction is in English until they progress far enough to understand instruction and detailed conversations in the other language. Think about your classroom experience in learning a foreign language. What are the most difficult challenges for you in language studies? Are you comfortable expressing yourself in the language? If you absolutely needed to communicate in that language, how well could you do it? How do you respond to people who are just learning English? Do you get impatient with them or assume that they are poorly educated? Write an essay about how well you think you would do if suddenly you had to function in another country with a different language. How would you deal with those

who were impatient with your language skills or dismissive of you? How self-conscious do you think you would be?

6. The Federal Maritime Commission has issued a clear explanation of the law with respect to the "Ability to Speak English" in its Basis for Discrimination Web site: www.fmc.gov/bureaus_offices/basis_of_discrimination.aspx. It reads as follows:

> Employers who require that their employees be able to speak English must show that fluency in English is a bona fide occupational qualification or a business necessity, for the position in question. Further, an employer's rule which requires employees to speak English at all times, including during their work break and lunch time, is one example of an employment practice which discriminates against persons whose primary language is not English.
>
> However, an employer may require employees to speak only English at certain times and this would not be discriminatory, if the employer shows that the rule is justified by business necessity. The employer must clearly inform its employees of the general circumstances under which they are required to speak only English and the consequences of violating the rule.

After considering both the cartoon above and the Maritime Commission guidelines, write an essay about the potential problems in the workplace that could arise when non–English speakers have certain jobs. Why do some employment opportunities require English while others do not? Is the double standard discriminatory or appropriate, in your opinion?

This section opens with a provocative question: Should language be censored? If you're anything like our students, you will probably immediately respond — Of course not! Before moving on to the next topic, though, you should take a minute to look at your own experience as a student and citizen of a learning community, and ask yourself: *Is* language censored at my school and in my community? If so, how, and by whom? To what extent does such censorship impede my learning? To what extent does it affect the world outside the classroom? Finally, what should we do about it?

Vigorous campus debates on the issues of speech codes, First Amendment rights, political correctness, and the virtues and sins of various kinds of free expression give students ample opportunity to examine these issues firsthand. It is imperative that as members of a learning community, we neither uncritically embrace nor thoughtlessly dismiss movements that seek to increase sensitivity to the larger problems of prejudice and discrimination in our society or that attempt to propagate moral codes and value lessons. As members of our college communities, we need to know as much as we can about these movements and to articulate in both speech and writing what we think. What you learn about censorship now, while you're in school, and how you act as a result of what you learn, will significantly affect both how you conduct yourself in the wider world and the way that world works.

This section assembles the work of four well-known writers, each arguing from a different perspective, in a debate about censorship and core values in our society. In the opening essay, "We Are Free to Be You, Me, Stupid, and Dead," Roger Rosenblatt goes to the fundamentals of language itself — "our sauntering, freewheeling, raucous, stumbling, unbridled, unregulated, unorthodox words" — to champion unbridled freedom of speech. In his essay "Pornography, Obscenity, and the Case for Censorship," conservative pundit Irving Kristol counters the liberal view by arguing for censorship of pornography and obscenity, which, in his opinion, threaten our civilization, our humanity, and our democracy. Noted American novelist Pat Conroy in his "Letter to the Editor of the *Charleston Gazette*" offers an impassioned and thoughtful response to the Charleston School Board for their attempt to reject the teaching of two of his works. In the process he comes to the defense of English teachers everywhere for their courage in facing down those who would ban and suppress the freedom to read and teach and for their dedication to the English language itself. Finally, we present an interesting case of rights in conflict in journalist Richard Pérez-Peña's article "Stutterer Speaks Up in Class; His Professor Says Keep Quiet." When Philip Garber Jr., a student who stutters, attempts to speak in his college history class his teacher thinks he takes too long to express himself and takes valuable class time away from her instructional schedule and from the other students in the class. She tries to accommodate his needs but nevertheless he is left aggrieved. We are left to wonder if it is a case of silencing or of simply ensuring equal rights.

We Are Free to Be You, Me, Stupid, and Dead

ROGER ROSENBLATT

Journalist, author, and essayist Roger Rosenblatt was born in 1940 in New York City. He received his Ph.D. in English and American literature in 1968 from Harvard University, where he also taught and directed the freshman English program. He began his career as a journalist in 1975 as literary editor for the *New Republic* before joining the *Washington Post* as a columnist. From 1980 to 1988, Rosenblatt was senior editor and essayist at *Time* magazine, where his essays won two George Polk Awards, among other major recognition. Rosenblatt currently appears regularly on the *PBS NewsHour with Jim Lehrer*, where his commentaries have won both a Peabody Award and an Emmy.

Rosenblatt's nonfiction books, which cover a wide range of social and cultural themes, include *Children at War*, which was a finalist for the National Book Critics Circle Award and won the Robert F. Kennedy Book Prize; *Witness: The World Since Hiroshima* (1985); *Life Itself: Abortion in the American Mind* (1992); *Rules for Aging* (2000); and *Anything Can Happen: Notes on My Inadequate Life and Yours* (2003). His first novel, *Lapham Rising*, was published in 2006, followed by *Beet* in 2008. He is also the author of five plays, including the 1991 play *Free Speech in America*.

"We Are Free to Be You, Me, Stupid, and Dead" comes from Rosenblatt's essay collection *Where We Stand: Thirty Reasons for Loving Our Country* (2002). In defending the right to freedom of speech given by the Constitution, Rosenblatt cites a number of colorful examples of protected speech that many of us would find objectionable, while reminding us "that the Founding Fathers . . . actually meant it when they allowed someone to do something that would outrage the rest of us."

WRITING TO DISCOVER: *Think about your personal definition of "free speech." Does it mean the freedom to say anything you want — to anyone, about anyone, using any words you please? Do you think freedom of speech can go too far? Do you set limits for yourself and others, and if so, what are they?*

Everyone loves free expression as long as it isn't exercised. Several years ago, Mahmoud Abdul-Rauf, a basketball player for the Denver Nuggets, refused to stand up for the playing of the national anthem because of personal religious convictions. The National Basketball Association greeted his decision by suspending him from the league until someone suggested that the Founding Fathers had actually meant it when they allowed someone to do something that would outrage the rest of us.

Similarly, major league baseball suspended John Rocker, the famous nut-case relief pitcher for the Atlanta Braves, when Rocker said that he did not want to ride New York City's Number 7 subway with all those single moms, queers, and illegal aliens. The court did not interfere, perhaps because the Constitution only states that government has no right to prevent free expression; it grants no affirmative licenses. I don't really get the difference between the two cases, but I know that Rocker had a perfect, or rather imperfect, right to sound like a jackass.

The rights of jackasses are more than a national staple. The strange beauty of American freedom is that it is ungovernable, that it always runs slightly ahead of human temperament. You think you know what you will tolerate. A man on a soapbox speaks out for China. Fine. An editorial calls for sympathy with the Taliban. (Gulp) okay. But then a bunch of Nazis want to march around Skokie, Illinois, or Harlem, and, hold on a minute! And what the hell is this? An art exhibit called "African-American Flag" in New Jersey. Or this? An exhibit in the Phoenix Art Museum called "What Is the Proper Way to Display the US Flag?"

Now that one was a doozie. The exhibit required observers to walk across an American flag on the floor to get to what was displayed on a wall. "That's my flag, and I'm going to defend it," said a visitor to the museum as he tried to take the flag from the floor. "No son of a bitch is going to do that."

The thing that I like best about sons of bitches doing that and worse,   5 as long as they do not cry "fire" in a crowded room, is (a) it enhances my appreciation of the wild courage of the Founders, and (b) it expands my mind, which could use some expanding. Freedom is like a legal drug. *How far will we go?* is not a rhetorical question here. Another exhibit in Chicago showed a flag with the word "think" where the stars should have been. Think. I hate it when that happens.

You think you know how far freedom will go in America, and then you meet another jackass. In the 1990s, I wrote a story for the *New York Times Magazine* about the Philip Morris company called "How Do They Live with Themselves?" The answer to that question, which came from the company executives I interviewed, turned out to be "Quite comfortably, thanks." The reason that their consciences did not seem to bother them about manufacturing an addictive lethal product was that their customers were engaging in the blessed American activity of freedom of choice. They were right—at least until new laws or lawsuits would prove them wrong. People technically had the choice of becoming addicted to cigarettes or not. I doubt that any of the Philip Morris people would ever step on the flag.

Since free is the way people's minds were made to be, it has been instructive for me to spend time in places where freedom was limited. In the Soviet Union, it was fascinating to see how many ways the workers of the world managed to squeeze free thought through the cracks of their utopian cells: the secret publication of books, the pirated music, the tricky subversive lines of poetry read at vast gatherings of tens of thousands. And the below-the-surface comedy. I was checking out of a hotel in Tbilisi. Checking out of Russian hotels was always a feat—they didn't have dollars, they didn't have rubles, no one had ever checked out before. The clerk at the desk spoke little English, and she wanted to tell me that another, more fluent, clerk would be along shortly. "Mr. Rosenblatt," she said. "Would you mind coming back in fifteen years?" We both exploded in laughter because we knew it was remotely possible.

> **The strange beauty of American freedom is that it is ungovernable, that it always runs slightly ahead of human temperament.**

The mind expands, the mind settles, then is shaken up, resists, and expands again. One of the great ongoing stupidities of the country are school boards and library committees that ban certain books they deem dangerous. On the positive side, though, the folks who do the banning offer some delightful defenses for their decisions. The three literary works most frequently banned in our country are *Macbeth*, *King Lear*, and *The Great Gatsby*. The reason school boards offer for banning *Macbeth* is that the play promotes witchcraft. Perhaps it does. One doesn't think of *Macbeth* as promoting things, but if it did, witchcraft would be it. They don't say why they want to ban *King Lear*. Promotes ingratitude, I suppose. I assume that *The Great Gatsby* promotes Long Island.

Sometimes the reasons offered for censoring certain works are obscure, thus intriguing. In Georgia, the Harry Potter books were recently burned because they were said to encourage kids to want to be sorcerers. In Spokane, Washington, they wanted to remove the children's picture book *Where's Waldo?* from the elementary school library. People objected to *Where's Waldo?*, they said, because it contains "explicit subject matter." A plea for surrealism, I imagine. In Springfield, Virginia, they banned a book called *Hitler's Hang-Ups* because it offered "explicit sexual details about Hitler's life." Given the *other* tendencies of Hitler's life, I should think the sexual details would be relatively acceptable. And, in the town of Astoria, Oregon, a book called *Wait Till Helen Comes* was challenged in an elementary school for giving "a morbid portrayal of death." Now they've gone too far.

THINKING CRITICALLY ABOUT THE READING

1. Rosenblatt opens his essay with the statement: "Everyone loves free expression as long as it isn't exercised." What does he mean by this statement? How does it apply to the two sports figures he cites as examples?
2. What is Rosenblatt getting at when he says that we "think" we know what we will tolerate? What do his examples of the Nazis in Skokie and the flag exhibit in the art museum tell us about the limits of our tolerance?

3. Rosenblatt refers to the "wild courage of the Founders" (5). Explain why he chose the phrase "wild courage."

4. Why were the Philip Morris executives comfortable with their position as purveyors of "an addictive lethal product" like cigarettes? How does this fit in with free expression as described by Rosenblatt?

5. Describe Rosenblatt's experience in the then–Soviet Union, and why it was instructive. How, according to Rosenblatt, did Soviet citizens express free thought in a repressive society? What did the desk clerk at the hotel mean when she asked, "Would you mind coming back in fifteen years"?

6. What is the central argument of Rosenblatt's essay? Does he believe that free speech should never be curtailed? Cite evidence from the essay to support your answer. (Glossary: *Argument; Evidence*)

Pornography, Obscenity, and the Case for Censorship

IRVING KRISTOL

Writer, editor, and political and social critic Irving Kristol (1920–2009) was born in New York City and educated at City College of New York, a hotbed of radical left-wing intellectualism in the 1930s and 1940s, where Kristol became involved early on in progressive movements. Upon graduating in 1940, however, Kristol gradually developed a philosophy at the opposite end of the political spectrum. Often referred to as the "godfather of neoconservatism," he was managing editor of *Commentary* (1947–1952), a magazine later called the "neocon Bible," and has written numerous books on issues of concern to conservatives, including *On the Democratic Idea in America* (1972), *Two Cheers for Capitalism* (1978), and *Reflections of a Neoconservative: Looking Back, Looking Ahead* (1983). *Neoconservatism: Autobiography of an Idea* (1995) is a collection of essays Kristol wrote over fifty years that follows the establishment of the neocon approach. Kristol's articles have appeared in the *New York Times, Harper's*, the *Atlantic, Fortune, Foreign Affairs*, and *Yale Review*, among other places, and he was a member of the board of contributors of the *Wall Street Journal* and a distinguished fellow at the American Enterprise Institute. His son is the noted neoconservative commentator William Kristol.

"Pornography, Obscenity, and the Case for Censorship" was first published on May 28, 1971, in the *New York Times Magazine*. It has since been reprinted in numerous anthologies. In it, Kristol makes a well-reasoned, highly controversial case for media censorship, saying, "For almost a century now, a great many intelligent, well-meaning, and articulate people have argued eloquently against any kind of censorship of art and entertainment. . . . Somehow, things have not worked out as they were supposed to. . . ."

WRITING TO DISCOVER: *Has any song, movie, book, or work of art ever offended you so much that you felt it should be censored? Do you think censoring art is ever justified? Why or why not?*

Being frustrated is disagreeable, but the real disasters in life begin when you get what you want. For almost a century now, a great many intelligent, well-meaning, and articulate people — of a kind generally called liberal or intellectual, or both — have argued eloquently against any kind of censorship of art and/or entertainment. And within the past 10 years, the courts and the legislatures of most Western nations have found these arguments persuasive — so persuasive that hardly a man is now alive who clearly remembers what the answers to these arguments were. Today, in the United States and other democracies, censorship has to all intents and purposes ceased to exist.

Is there a sense of triumphant exhilaration in the land? Hardly. There is, on the contrary, a rapidly growing unease and disquiet. Somehow, things have not worked out as they were supposed to, and many notable civil libertarians have gone on record as saying this was not what they meant at all. They wanted a world in which *Desire Under the Elms* could be produced, or *Ulysses* published, without interference by philistine busybodies holding public office. They have got that, of course; but they have also got a world in which homosexual rape takes place on the stage, in which the public flocks during lunch hours to witness varieties of professional fornication, in which Times Square has become little more than a hideous market for the sale and distribution of printed filth that panders to all known (and some fanciful) sexual perversions.

But disagreeable as this may be, does it really matter? Might not our unease and disquiet be merely a cultural hangover—a "hangup," as they say? What reason is there to think that anyone was ever corrupted by a book?

This last question, oddly enough, is asked by the very same people who seem convinced that advertisements in magazines or displays of violence on television do indeed have the power to corrupt. It is also asked, incredibly enough and in all sincerity, by people—e.g., university professors and school teachers—whose very lives provide all the answers one could want. After all, if you believe that no one was ever corrupted by a book, you have also to believe that no one was ever improved by a book (or a play or a movie). You have to believe, in other words, that all art is morally trivial and that, consequently, all education is morally irrelevant. No one, not even a university professor, really believes that.

To be sure, it is extremely difficult, as social scientists tell us, to trace the effects of any single book (or play or movie) on an individual reader or any class of readers. But we all know, and social scientists know it too, that the ways in which we use our minds and imaginations do shape our characters and help define us as persons. That those who certainly know this are nevertheless moved to deny it merely indicates how a dogmatic resistance to the idea of censorship can—like most dogmatism—result in a mindless insistence on the absurd. 5

I have used these harsh terms—"dogmatism" and "mindless"—advisedly. I might also have added "hypocritical." For the plain fact is that none of us is a complete civil libertarian. We all believe that there is some point at which the public authorities ought to step in to limit the "self expression" of an individual or a group, even where this might be seriously intended as a form of artistic expression, and even where the artistic transaction is between consenting adults. A playwright or theatrical director might, in this crazy world of ours, find someone willing to commit suicide on the stage, as called for by the script. We would not allow that—any more than we would permit scenes of real physical torture on the stage, even if the victim were a willing masochist. And I know of no one, no matter how free in spirit, who argues that we ought to permit gladiatorial contests in Yankee Stadium, similar to those once performed in the Colosseum at Rome—even if only consenting adults were involved.

The basic point that emerges is one that Prof. Walter Berns has powerfully argued: no society can be utterly indifferent to the ways its citizens publicly entertain themselves.* Bearbaiting and cockfighting are prohibited only in part out of compassion for the suffering animals; the main reason they were abolished was because it was felt that they debased and brutalized the citizenry who flocked to witness such spectacles. And the question we face with regard to pornography and obscenity is whether, now that they have such strong legal protection from the Supreme Court, they can or will brutalize and debase our citizenry. We are, after all, not dealing with one passing incident—one book, or one play, or one movie. We are dealing with a general tendency that is suffusing our entire culture.

> After all, if you believe that no one was ever corrupted by a book, you have also to believe that no one was ever improved by a book (or a play or a movie).

I say pornography *and* obscenity because, though they have different dictionary definitions and are frequently distinguishable as "artistic" genres, they are nevertheless in the end identical in effect. Pornography is not objectionable simply because it arouses sexual desire or lust or prurience in the mind of the reader or spectator; this is a silly Victorian notion. A great many non-pornographic works—including some parts of the Bible—excite sexual desire very successfully. What is distinctive about pornography is that, in the words of D. H. Lawrence, it attempts "to do dirt on [sex] . . . [It is an] insult to a vital human relationship."

In other words, pornography differs from erotic art in that its whole purpose is to treat human beings obscenely, to deprive human beings of their specifically human dimension. That is what obscenity is all about. It is light years removed from any kind of carefree sensuality—there is no continuum between Fielding's *Tom Jones* and the Marquis de Sade's *Justine*. These works have quite opposite intentions. To quote Susan Sontag: "What pornographic literature does is precisely to drive a wedge between one's existence as a full human being and one's existence as a sexual being—while in ordinary life a healthy person is one who prevents such a gap from opening up." This definition occurs in an essay *defending* pornography—Miss Sontag is a candid as well as gifted critic—so the definition, which I accept, is neither tendentious nor censorious.

---

*This is as good a place as any to express my profound indebtedness to Walter Berns's superb essay, "Pornography vs. Democracy," in the winter, 1971, issue of *The Public Interest*.

Along these same lines, one can point out—as C. S. Lewis pointed   10
out some years back—that it is no accident that in the history of all
literatures obscene words—the so-called "four-letter words"—have
always been the vocabulary of farce or vituperation. The reason is clear:
they reduce men and women to some of their mere bodily functions—they
reduce man to his animal component, and such a reduction is an essential
purpose of farce or vituperation.

Similarly, Lewis also suggested that it is not an accident that we have
no offhand, colloquial, neutral terms—not in any Western European language at any rate—for our most private parts. The words we do use are
either (a) nursery terms, (b) archaisms, (c) scientific terms, or (d) a term
from the gutter (i.e., a demeaning term). Here I think the genius of language is telling us something important about man. It is telling us that
man is an animal with a difference: he has a unique sense of privacy, and
a unique capacity for shame when this privacy is violated. Our "private
parts" are indeed private, and not merely because convention prescribes
it. This particular convention is indigenous to the human race. In practically all primitive tribes, men and women cover their private parts; and in
practically all primitive tribes, men and women do not copulate in public.

It may well be that Western society, in the latter half of the twentieth
century, is experiencing a drastic change in sexual mores and sexual relationships. We have had many such "sexual revolutions" in the past—and
the bourgeois family and bourgeois ideas of sexual propriety were themselves established in the course of a revolution against eighteenth-century
"licentiousness"—and we shall doubtless have others in the future. It is,
however, highly improbable (to put it mildly) that what we are witnessing
is the Final Revolution which will make sexual relations utterly unproblem-
atic, permit us to dispense with any kind of ordered relationships between
the sexes, and allow us freely to redefine the human condition. And so long
as humanity has not reached that utopia, obscenity will remain a problem.

One of the reasons it will remain a problem is that obscenity is not
merely about sex, any more than science fiction is about science. Science
fiction, as every student of the genre knows, is a peculiar vision of power:
what it is really about is politics. And obscenity is a peculiar vision of
humanity: what it is really about is ethics and metaphysics.

Imagine a man—a well-known man, much in the public eye—in a
hospital ward, dying an agonizing death. He is not in control of his bodily
functions, so that his bladder and his bowels empty themselves of their
own accord. His consciousness is overwhelmed and extinguished by pain,
so that he cannot communicate with us, nor we with him. Now, it would
be, technically, the easiest thing in the world to put a television camera in
his hospital room and let the whole world witness this spectacle. We don't
do it—at least we don't do it as yet—because we regard this as an *obscene*
invasion of privacy. And what would make the spectacle obscene is that we
would be witnessing the extinguishing of humanity in a human animal.

Incidentally, in the past our humanitarian crusaders against capital   15
punishment understood this point very well. The abolitionist literature
goes into great physical detail about what happens to a man when he is
hanged or electrocuted or gassed. And their argument was—and is—that
what happens is shockingly obscene, and that no civilized society should
be responsible for perpetrating such obscenities, particularly since in the
nature of the case there must be spectators to ascertain that this horror was
indeed being perpetrated in fulfillment of the law.

Sex—like death—is an activity that is both animal and human. There
are human sentiments and human ideals involved in this animal activity.
But when sex is public, the viewer does not see—cannot see—the sentiments and the ideals. He can only see the animal coupling. And that
is why, when men and women make love, as we say, they prefer to be
alone—because it is only when you are alone that you can make love, as
distinct from merely copulating in an animal and casual way. And that,
too, is why those who are voyeurs, if they are not irredeemably sick, also
feel ashamed at what they are witnessing. When sex is a public spectacle,
a human relationship has been debased into a mere animal connection.

It is also worth noting that this making of sex into an obscenity is
not a mutual and equal transaction, but is rather an act of exploitation
by one of the partners—the male partner. I do not wish to get into the
complicated question as to what, if any, are the essential differences—as
distinct from conventional and cultural differences—between male and
female. I do not claim to know the answer to that. But I do know—and
I take it as a sign which has meaning—that pornography is, and always
has been, a man's work; that women rarely write pornography; and that
women tend to be indifferent consumers of pornography.* My own guess,
by way of explanation, is that a woman's sexual experience is ordinarily
more suffused with human emotion than is a man's, that men are more
easily satisfied with autoerotic activities, and that men can therefore more
easily take a more "technocratic" view of sex and its pleasures. Perhaps this
is not correct. But whatever the explanation, there can be no question that
pornography is a form of "sexism," as the Women's Liberation Movement
calls it, and that the instinct of Women's Lib has been unerring in perceiv-
ing that, when pornography is perpetrated, it is perpetrated against them,
as part of a conspiracy to deprive them of their full humanity.

But even if all this is granted, it might be said—and doubtless will be
said—that I really ought not to be unduly concerned. Free competition

---

* There are, of course, a few exceptions—but of a kind that prove the rule. *L'Histoire
d'O,* for instance, written by a woman, is unquestionably the most *melancholy* work of pornography ever written. And its theme is precisely the dehumanization accomplished by
obscenity.

in the cultural marketplace—it is argued by people who have never otherwise had a kind word to say for laissez faire—will automatically dispose of the problem. The present fad for pornography and obscenity, it will be asserted, is just that, a fad. It will spend itself in the course of time; people will get bored with it, will be able to take it or leave it alone in a casual way, in a "mature way," and, in sum, I am being unnecessarily distressed about the whole business. The *New York Times*, in an editorial, concludes hopefully in this vein.

"In the end . . . the insensate pursuit of the urge to shock, carried from one excess to a more abysmal one, is bound to achieve its own antidote in total boredom. When there is no lower depth to descend to, ennui will erase the problem."

I would like to be able to go along with this line of reasoning, but I   20
cannot. I think it is false, and for two reasons, the first psychological, the second political.

The basic psychological fact about pornography and obscenity is that it appeals to and provokes a kind of sexual regression. The sexual pleasure one gets from pornography and obscenity is autoerotic and infantile; put bluntly, it is a masturbatory exercise of the imagination, when it is not masturbation pure and simple. Now, people who masturbate do not get bored with masturbation, just as sadists don't get bored with sadism, and voyeurs don't get bored with voyeurism.

In other words, infantile sexuality is not only a permanent temptation for the adolescent or even the adult—it can quite easily become a permanent, self-reinforcing neurosis. It is because of an awareness of this possibility of regression toward the infantile condition, a regression which is always open to us, that all the codes of sexual conduct ever devised by the human race take such a dim view of autoerotic activities and try to discourage autoerotic fantasies. Masturbation is indeed a perfectly natural autoerotic activity, as so many sexologists blandly assure us today. And it is precisely because it is so perfectly natural that it can be so dangerous to the mature or maturing person, if it is not controlled or sublimated in some way. That is the true meaning of Portnoy's complaint. Portnoy, you will recall, grows up to be a man who is incapable of having an adult sexual relationship with a woman; his sexuality remains fixed in an infantile mode, the prison of his autoerotic fantasies. Inevitably, Portnoy comes to think, in a perfectly *infantile* way, that it was all his mother's fault.

It is true that, in our time, some quite brilliant minds have come to the conclusion that a reversion to infantile sexuality is the ultimate mission and secret destiny of the human race. I am thinking in particular of Norman O. Brown, for whose writings I have the deepest respect. One of the reasons I respect them so deeply is that Mr. Brown is a serious thinker who is unafraid to face up to the radical consequences of his radical theories. Thus, Mr. Brown knows and says that for his kind of salvation to be achieved, humanity must annul the civilization it has created—not merely the civilization we have today, but all civilization—so as to be able to make the long descent backwards into animal innocence.

What is at stake is civilization and humanity, nothing less. The idea that "everything is permitted," as Nietzsche put it, rests on the premise of nihilism and has nihilistic implications. I will not pretend that the case against nihilism and for civilization is an easy one to make. We are here confronting the most fundamental of philosophical questions, on the deepest levels. But that is precisely my point—that the matter of pornography and obscenity is not a trivial one, and that only superficial minds can take a bland and untroubled view of it.

In this connection, I might also point out those who are primarily   25
against censorship on liberal grounds tell us not to take pornography or obscenity seriously, while those who are for pornography and obscenity, on radical grounds, take it very seriously indeed. I believe the radicals—writers like Susan Sontag, Herbert Marcuse, Norman O. Brown, and even Jerry Rubin—are right, and the liberals are wrong. I also believe that those young radicals at Berkeley, some five years ago, who provoked a major confrontation over the public use of obscene words, showed a brilliant political instinct. Once the faculty and administration had capitulated on this issue—saying: "Oh, for God's sake, let's be adult: what difference does it make anyway?"—once they said that, they were bound to lose on every other issue. And once Mark Rudd could publicly ascribe to the president of Columbia a notoriously obscene relationship to his mother, without provoking any kind of reaction, the S.D.S. had already won the day. The occupation of Columbia's buildings merely ratified their victory. Men who show themselves unwilling to defend civilization against nihilism are not going to be either resolute or effective in defending the university against anything.

I am already touching upon a political aspect of pornography when I suggest that it is inherently and purposefully subversive of civilization and its institutions. But there is another and more specifically political aspect, which has to do with the relationship of pornography and/or obscenity to democracy, and especially to the quality of public life on which democratic government ultimately rests.

Though the phrase, "the quality of life," trips easily from so many lips these days, it tends to be one of those clichés with many trivial meanings and no large, serious one. Sometimes it merely refers to such externals as the enjoyment of cleaner air, cleaner water, cleaner streets. At other times it refers to the merely private enjoyment of music, painting or literature. Rarely does it have anything to do with the way the citizen in a democracy views himself—his obligations, his intentions, his ultimate self-definition.

Instead, what I would call the "managerial" conception of democracy is the predominant opinion among political scientists, sociologists, and economists, and has, through the untiring efforts of these scholars, become the conventional journalistic opinion as well. The root idea behind this "managerial" conception is that democracy is a "political system" (as they say) which can be adequately defined in terms of—can be fully reduced to—its mechanical arrangements. Democracy is then seen as a set of rules and procedures, and *nothing but* a set of rules and procedures, whereby majority rule and minority rights are reconciled into a state of equilibrium. If everyone follows these rules and procedures, then a democracy is in working order. I think this is a fair description of the democratic idea that currently prevails in academia. One can also fairly say that it is now the liberal idea of democracy par excellence.

I cannot help but feel that there is something ridiculous about being this kind of a democrat, and I must further confess to having a sneaking sympathy for those of our young radicals who also find it ridiculous. The absurdity is the absurdity of idolatry—of taking the symbolic for the real, the means for the end. The purpose of democracy cannot possibly be the endless functioning of its own political machinery. The purpose of any political regime is to achieve some version of the good life and the good society. It is not at all difficult to imagine a perfectly functioning democracy which answers all questions except one—namely, why should anyone of intelligence and spirit care a fig for it?

There is, however, an older idea of democracy—one which was fairly   30
common until about the beginning of this century—for which the conception of the quality of public life is absolutely crucial. This idea starts from the proposition that democracy is a form of self-government, and that if you want it to be a meritorious polity, you have to care about what kind of people govern it. Indeed, it puts the matter more strongly and declares that, if you want self-government, you are only entitled to it if that "self" is worthy of governing. There is no inherent right to self-government if it means that such government is vicious, mean, squalid and debased. Only a dogmatist and a fanatic, an idolater of democratic machinery, could approve of self-government under such conditions.

And because the desirability of self-government depends on the character of the people who govern, the older idea of democracy was very solicitous of the condition of this character. It was solicitous of the individual self, and felt an obligation to educate it into what used to be called "republican virtue." And it was solicitous of that collective self which we call public opinion and which, in a democracy, governs us collectively. Perhaps in some respects it was nervously over-solicitous—that would not be surprising. But the main thing is that it cared, cared not merely about the machinery of democracy but about the quality of life that this machinery might generate.

And because it cared, this older idea of democracy had no problem in principle with pornography and/or obscenity. It censored them—and it did so with a perfect clarity of mind and a perfectly clear conscience. It was not about to permit people capriciously to corrupt themselves. Or, to put it more precisely: in this version of democracy, the people took some care not to let themselves be governed by the more infantile and irrational parts of themselves.

I have, it may be noticed, uttered that dreadful word, "censorship." And I am not about to back away from it. If you think pornography and/or obscenity is a serious problem, you have to be for censorship. I'll go even further and say that if you want to prevent pornography and/or obscenity from becoming a problem, you have to be for censorship. And lest there be any misunderstanding as to what I am saying, I'll put it as bluntly as possible: if you care for the quality of life in our American democracy, then you have to be for censorship.

THINKING CRITICALLY ABOUT THE READING

1. What is the downside, in Kristol's opinion, of unfettered, uncensored expression in arts and entertainment? What is the outcome, as he sees it, of "dogmatic resistance to the idea of censorship" (5)?

2. Explain Kristol's central argument about the power of art to improve or to corrupt lives. (Glossary: *Argument*) Do you believe that anyone has ever been corrupted by a book?

3. Kristol utilizes extreme examples, mostly hypothetical, to bolster his argument for censorship. What are some of his examples? Can you cite any examples of instances where entertainment crosses the line? (Glossary: *Examples*)

4. In Kristol's opinion, what is the purpose of pornography? Why does he find sex as "a public spectacle" (16) problematic if not abhorrent?

5. What is Kristol's theory about the "political aspect of pornography" (26)?

6. What are the issues of "quality of life" (27) that Kristol refers to? How does this notion of "quality of life" relate to American democracy?

Letter to the Editor of the *Charleston Gazette*

PAT CONROY

A celebrated southern American novelist noted for his stylistic skills, Pat Conroy credits his mother with his love of the English language. He was born in 1945 in Atlanta, Georgia, the first of seven children. His father, a United States Marine Corps pilot, was a strong disciplinarian and an abusive man, whose biggest mistake, according to Conroy, was having a novelist for a son. Conroy exposed the family's secrets and conflicts. His father insisted he enroll in the Citadel military college in Charleston, South Carolina. Conroy would later use the experience to expose the fabled institution's racism, sexism, and harsh disciplinary practices. After college Conroy became an English teacher, a career that landed him in trouble for some of his controversial attitudes and practices, such as refusing to use corporal punishment on his students. His book *The Water Is Wide* (1972) is based on his experiences as a teacher. Among his novels, some of which have been made into successful movies, are: *The Great Santini* (1976), *Lords of Discipline* (1980), *The Prince of Tides* (1986), and *Beach Music* (1995), which *Publisher's Weekly* called "sweepingly lyrical."

In response to information provided him by a high school student in Charleston, West Virginia, Conroy wrote the following letter to the *Charleston Gazette* on October 24, 2007. In the letter Conroy protests the action of the Charleston School Board for attempting to suppress the teaching of two of his works. Thankfully for us, Conroy could not resist the call for help and in response offers an eloquent defense of his work, the real and often violent world that gave rise to it, the English language itself, and English teachers everywhere.

WRITING TO DISCOVER: *Have you in your educational experience been involved in or been witness to any attempts to ban or suppress the reading and teaching of any books (or viewing of films or other media)? What were the circumstances? What was the outcome and what did you think of it?*

I received an urgent e-mail from a high school student named Makenzie Hatfield of Charleston, West Virginia. She informed me of a group of parents who were attempting to suppress the teaching of two of my novels, *The Prince of Tides* and *Beach Music*. I heard rumors of this controversy as I was completing my latest filthy, vomit-inducing work. These controversies are so commonplace in my life that I no longer get involved. But my knowledge of mountain lore is strong enough to know the dangers of refusing to help a Hatfield of West Virginia. I also do not mess with McCoys.

I've enjoyed a lifetime love affair with English teachers, just like the ones who are being abused in Charleston, West Virginia, today. My English teachers pushed me to be smart and inquisitive, and they taught me the great books of the world with passion and cunning and love. Like your English teachers, they didn't have any money either, but they lived in the bright fires of their imaginations, and they taught because they were born to teach the prettiest language in the world. I have yet to meet an English teacher who assigned a book to damage a kid. They take an unutterable joy in opening up the known world to their students, but they are dishonored and unpraised because of the scandalous paychecks they receive. In my travels around this country, I have discovered that America hates its teachers, and I could not tell you why. Charleston, West Virginia, is showing clear signs of really hurting theirs, and I would be cautious about the word getting out.

In 1961, I entered the classroom of the great Eugene Norris, who set about in a thousand ways to change my life. It was the year I read *The Catcher in the Rye*, under Gene's careful tutelage, and I adore that book to this very day. Later, a parent complained to the school board, and Gene Norris was called before the board to defend his teaching of this book. He asked me to write an essay describing the book's galvanic effect on me, which I did. But Gene's defense of *The Catcher in the Rye* was so brilliant and convincing in its sheer power that it carried the day. I stayed close to Gene Norris till the day he died. I delivered a eulogy at his memorial service and was one of the executors of his will. Few in the world have ever loved English teachers as I have, and I loathe it when they are bullied by know-nothing parents or cowardly school boards.

About the novels your county just censored: *The Prince of Tides* and *Beach Music* are two of my darlings which I would place before the altar of God and say, "Lord, this is how I found the world you made." They contain scenes of violence, but I was the son of a Marine Corps fighter pilot who killed hundreds of men in Korea, beat my mother and his seven kids whenever he felt like it, and fought in three wars. My youngest brother, Tom, committed suicide by jumping off a fourteen-story building; my French teacher ended her life with a pistol; my aunt was brutally raped in Atlanta; eight of my classmates at The Citadel were killed in Vietnam; and my best friend was killed in a car wreck in Mississippi last summer. Violence has always been a part of my world. I write about it in my books and make no apology to anyone. In *Beach Music*, I wrote about the Holocaust and lack the literary powers to make that historical event anything other than grotesque.

People cuss in my books.   5

People cuss in my real life. I cuss, especially at Citadel basketball games. I'm perfectly sure that Steve Shamblin and other teachers prepared their students well for any encounters with violence or profanity in my books just as Gene Norris prepared me for the profane language in *The Catcher in the Rye* forty-eight years ago.

The world of literature has everything in it, and it refuses to leave anything out. I have read like a man on fire my whole life because the genius of English teachers touched me with the dazzling beauty of language. Because of them I rode with Don Quixote and danced with Anna Karenina at a ball in St. Petersburg and lassoed a steer in *Lonesome Dove* and had nightmares about slavery in *Beloved* and walked the streets of Dublin in *Ulysses* and made up a hundred stories in *The Arabian Nights* and saw my mother killed by a baseball in *A Prayer for Owen Meany*. I've been in ten thousand cities and have introduced myself to a hundred thousand strangers in my exuberant reading career, all because I listened to my fabulous English teachers and soaked up every single thing those magnificent men and women had to give. I cherish and praise them and thank them for finding me when I was a boy and presenting me with the precious gift of the English language.

> **Violence has always been a part of my world. I write about it in my books and make no apology to anyone.**

The school board of Charleston, West Virginia, has sullied that gift and shamed themselves and their community. You've now entered the ranks of censors, book-banners, and teacher-haters, and the word will spread. Good teachers will avoid you as though you had cholera. But here is my favorite thing: Because you banned my books, every kid in that county will read them, every single one of them. Because book-banners are invariably idiots, they don't know how the world works—but writers and English teachers do.

I salute the English teachers of Charleston, West Virginia, and send my affection to their students. West Virginians, you've just done what history warned you against—you've riled a Hatfield.

Sincerely,
Pat Conroy

THINKING CRITICALLY ABOUT THE READING

1. Many writers do not get involved when censors and book banners attack their works. Why do you suppose that is the case? Why is it useful in this case to have Conroy write his letter?

2. The Hatfield-McCoy family feud in West Virginia that took place in the latter half of the nineteenth century has become the dominant metaphor for feuding parties of any kind in this country. How does Conroy use the metaphor in his letter?

3. Why does Conroy tell us in paragraph 4 about the violence he has known? What does it have to do with the censorship question he writes about?

4. Why does Conroy "cherish and praise . . . and thank" English teachers?

5. "Bookbanners are invariably idiots," writes Conroy in paragraph 8. Is he being unduly abusive? Why or why not?

6. Conroy becomes emotional when discussing the English language. How would you put into your own words the passion he feels?

Stutterer Speaks Up in Class; His Professor Says Keep Quiet

RICHARD PÉREZ-PEÑA

Richard Pérez-Peña has been a *New York Times* reporter since 1992 and has covered New Jersey news since 2010. He was born in Santiago, Cuba, in 1963, grew up in the Los Angeles area and studied European History at Pomona College in Claremont, California. After college he had a number of jobs as a reporter covering general assignments before arriving at the *Times* where he has covered health-care issues and politics from the Albany bureau. He has reported on the Los Angeles riots, the Branch Davidian conflict in Waco, Texas, as well as events following the World Trade Center disaster and the 2002 national election.

In the following article, first published in the *New York Times* on October 10, 2011, Pérez-Peña reports on the case of Philip Garber Jr. who was asked by his instructor not to speak in his college history class because as a stutterer he was taking too much time to ask his questions and make comments. As you read, notice that Garber was not the only one silenced as a result of his protesting his instructor's actions.

WRITING TO DISCOVER: *Have you ever been in a class where one or two people monopolized class time? How did the instructor handle the situation? How did you and the other students respond to the usurpation of your time? Was the situation allowed to stand or was it resolved in some manner? Were you happy with the solution?*

As his history class at the County College of Morris here discussed exploration of the New World, Philip Garber Jr. raised his hand, hoping to ask why China's fifteenth-century explorers, who traveled as far as Africa, had not also reached North America. He kept his hand aloft for much of the 75-minute session, but the professor did not call on him. She had already told him not to speak in class.

Philip, a precocious and confident 16-year-old who is taking two college classes this semester, has a lot to say but also a profound stutter that makes talking difficult, and talking quickly impossible. After the first couple of class sessions, in which he participated actively, the professor, an adjunct named Elizabeth Snyder, sent him an e-mail asking that he pose questions before or after class, "so we do not infringe on other students' time."

As for questions she asks in class, Ms. Snyder suggested, "I believe it would be better for everyone if you kept a sheet of paper on your desk and wrote down the answers."

Later, he said, she told him, "Your speaking is disruptive."

Unbowed, Philip reported the situation to a college dean, who sug- 5
gested he transfer to another teacher's class, where he has been asking and
answering questions again.

While Philip's case is unusual, stuttering is not: About 5 percent of
people stutter at some point, and about 1 percent stutter as adults, according to the National Institutes of Health.

His classroom experience underlines a perennial complaint among
stutterers, that society does not recognize the condition as a disability,
and touches on an age-old pedagogical—and social—theme: the balance
between the needs of an individual and the good of a group.

"As we do with all students seeking accommodations, we have taken
action to resolve Philip's concerns so he can successfully continue his
education," said Kathleen Brunet Eagan, the college's communications
director.

She would not say if Ms. Snyder, who declined to discuss the matter,
had been disciplined, but noted that the college "strives to educate faculty
and staff on how to accommodate students."

Ms. Snyder has taught history at the college for a decade, and several 10
current and former students on campus said in interviews that they had
largely positive views of her. She was one of the first students when the
college opened in 1968, then earned bachelor's and master's degrees at
Montclair State University, and taught middle school social studies for
more than 30 years.

For Philip, who has spent most of his life being home-schooled or
attending a small charter school, the teacher's attitude was a surprise
and a disappointment. "I've never experienced any kind of discrimination," he said, "so for it to happen in a college classroom was quite
shocking."

Jim McClure, a board member of the National Stuttering Association
and its spokesman, said Philip's experience is unusual—because most stutterers avoid speaking in class.

"Teachers ignore them, or have to coax them to speak out," Mr.
McClure said. "The fact that this guy wants to participate is a really healthy
sign."

Kasey Errico, who taught most of Philip's seventh- and eighth-grade
classes at the Ridge and Valley Charter School in Blairstown, N.J., noted
that there were always students who monopolized class time.

"I wonder what this professor has done with those students, the ones 15
who didn't stutter," Ms. Errico said. "If she told them the same thing she
told Philip, then I might understand."

Two students in Ms. Snyder's class, who spoke on the condition of
anonymity to avoid alienating their teacher, said that Philip did take up
more time than the other students, but not egregiously so, and that his

contributions were solid. They said they did not know what happened between him and Ms. Snyder, but did notice the day he held his hand up for most of the class and never got called on.

"What about a kid who's got a thick accent and has to repeat everything?" asked Philip's father, also named Philip, the managing editor of two small newspapers. "I don't think you'd tell that kid he can't talk."

But advocates for people who stutter say that the same people who accept a delay in a bus ride to load a disabled passenger are often less patient with those who struggle to speak clearly.

Doctors once saw stuttering as a psychological issue, but the current medical view is that its origins are physiological and hereditary, though emotions can make it worse. Last year, the National Institutes of Health identified the first genes linked to stuttering.

The outlines of Philip's experience are common: there was a family   20
history (an uncle who stuttered), the problem began before he reached school age, and he spent years going to speech therapists, some of whom did more harm than good. His most recent therapist gave Philip confidence and some techniques for managing his speech, but he decided last winter to stop going, at least for now.

"I understand that it can be hard to listen to someone who stutters, but the answer can't just be to shut him down," said his mother, Marin Martin, a nurse. As it is, she said, "there are social situations where he just can't be part of the conversation."

> **Advocates for people who stutter say that the same people who accept a delay in a bus ride to load a disabled passenger are often less patient with those who struggle to speak clearly.**

Talking with Philip requires a degree of patience—all the more so because he is remarkably uninhibited, and tends to speak in complete paragraphs, as displayed in videos on his YouTube channel. For the listener, the payoff is insight and wry wit.

He has suppressed a trait common to stutterers—bouncing all or part of the body, as if trying to force a word out. "I found it's hard to get people to listen when they think you're having a seizure," he said. An avid amateur photographer, he hopes to make a career of it, but worries that "even if nobody expects the photographer to say much, you do have to talk."

After years of speech therapy, Philip can force himself to speak fairly fluidly, but it requires such intense concentration that he cannot hold a train of thought for long while doing it.

For now, he is taking courses in history and English composition at   25
the college, home-schooling in other subjects and traveling into Manhattan once a week to work on acting and playwriting with Our Time Theater Company, a group for people who stutter.

As for Ms. Snyder, he said he might have had some sympathy for the professor's quandary if she had expressed it less harshly.

"I've been very lucky to never have been teased, bullied or anything, but some people who stutter completely stop speaking because of that kind of abuse," Philip said. "People don't think of it as a legitimate disability. They just need to learn."

THINKING CRITICALLY ABOUT THE READING

1. Do you think that Snyder acted appropriately in not letting Garber participate in her class?

2. Was Snyder's advice to Garber that he ask his questions before or after class a reasonable resolution? Why or why not?

3. If you were the instructor in Garber's class, would you have recognized a problem or simply let him speak? If you saw the situation as a problem, how would you have handled it?

4. Would you be comfortable trying to learn in Snyder's class with Garber as a fellow student?

5. To what degree was the conflict in Garber's class one of opposing rights — Garber's right to speak and the other students' right not to have the class monopolized by one student's comments, no matter how they were delivered or how cogent they were?

6. Garber's mother admits in paragraph 21 that " 'there are social situations where he just can't be a part of the conversation.' " If he is also silenced in the classroom, where can he speak?

7. Who else besides Garber was silenced? Explain.

SPECIAL NOTE ON THIS SELECTION

When a reader commented on Pérez-Peña's article saying that it was unfortunate that we don't have the instructor's side of the story, Pérez-Peña wrote the following:

> The teacher declined to respond, and the college made only a fairly general statement about accommodating Philip, declining to address the merits of the underlying dispute. I was genuinely disappointed by this, precisely because I did not want to write a one-sided article. I was not present in the classroom, so I do not know how much time Philip was taking up. But I can see that the instructor might have had legitimate concerns, no matter how inartfully she expressed them. The article makes clear that listening to him can try one's patience (as even his mother concedes), though I hope I also made clear that it's worth the wait. I do not know this teacher's history, and I would not want her to be vilified based on a brief exchange that might have been ill-advised. (If that were the standard, would anyone be immune?) We did not go into this in the article, but it struck me that technology provides ways to keep things moving along in class at a good pace, while providing a level playing field for all students. For instance, questions and answers could be submitted by e-mail or text message during class, and could even be displayed on a projector.

As a class discuss Pérez-Peña's additional reflections on the Garber case.

WRITING SUGGESTIONS: DEBATING THE ISSUE

1. Read, or reread, "Stutterer Speaks Up in Class; His Professor Says Keep Quiet" by Richard Pérez-Peña (pp. 517–520). Write an essay in which you argue your point of view in the case of Philip Garber Jr. Is he the victim of censorship? Has his teacher been "silenced"? Have other members of his class? What's your view of how the situation should have been handled? Does Garber have any recourse? Has his teacher been unfairly criticized? You may want to search for readers' comments on the case and use them to inform your own view.

2. In "Pornography, Obscenity, and the Case for Censorship," Irving Kristol poses a question to which his essay was intended to provide an answer: "What reason is there to think that anyone was ever corrupted by a book?" The question is at the heart of a debate that has been with us as long as art and entertainment—plays, books, television, movies, video games, and Internet Web sites, to name just a few kinds—have been with us. Do some research on a historical or contemporary debate on the corrupting influence of a particular work of art or entertainment. Some possibilities—drawn from a seemingly endless supply—are below:

   - *Doom* or *Mortal Kombat* (video games)
   - *Teletubbies* (television show)
   - Batman and Robin (comic book heroes)
   - *The Catcher in the Rye* (novel)
   - pinball machines

Do you believe that books—or video games, or television shows, etc.—can and do corrupt? Consider drawing on the arguments and evidence cited by Kristol and cite evidence from your research to support your position.

3. Many articles and even some books have examined censorship issues that are very close to you as a student attending a college or university here in the United States. Research both online and in your library any of the incidents that have given rise to attempts to forbid teachers, lecturers, political figures and candidates, and entertainers with controversial points of view or artistic performances from appearing on campuses. Write an essay in which you choose events to discuss, preferably those that have occurred on your campus or in your community so that you have firsthand accounts readily available to draw upon, and argue for or against the censorship that lies at the heart of the controversy. What was the event(s), who sponsored it, who was opposed to it, and for what reasons? How was the conflict resolved? Was the result fair, in your opinion? What was right or wrong with the way university officials or community leaders handled the affair?

4. In the eleventh edition of *Merriam-Webster's Collegiate Dictionary,* the phrase "politically correct" (first used in 1936) is defined as "conforming to a belief that language and practices which could offend political sensibilities (as in matters of sex or race) should be eliminated." The *Concise Oxford English Dictionary* (11th ed.) defines "political correctness" as "the careful avoidance of forms of expression or action that are perceived to exclude or insult groups of people who are socially disadvantaged or discriminated against." Research the history of "political correctness," and write an essay describing that history and discussing the factors that brought a "politically correct" standard to college campuses. Using examples from at least two of the essays in this chapter, as well as any examples you might have from your own experience, describe the relationship between "political correctness" and censorship.

5. The American Library Association (ALA) compiles lists of the authors and books that individuals, parents, or groups seek most often to remove from library shelves or keep out of the classroom. Included in their list of the top ten "most challenged" books in 2007 are Mark Twain's *The Adventures of Huckleberry Finn,* Alice Walker's *The Color Purple,* and Maya Angelou's *I Know Why the Caged Bird Sings.* The ALA takes the position that even when these objections are made with good intentions, that is, to protect children, they are still censorship: "Censorship can be subtle, almost imperceptible, as well as blatant and overt, but, nonetheless, harmful." Take a look at the ALA's data on challenges to books at http://www.ala.org/advocacy/banned/frequentlychallenged, read Diane Ravitch's take on the subject in *The Language Police* (2003), and read or reread Pat Conroy's "Letter to the Editor of the *Charleston Gazettte.*" Then, write an essay expressing your own perspective on the subject of book banning. What do you think about a community's rights when it comes to what books libraries can put on their shelves? What do you think of the ALA's warning about censorship? Are there limits to what you would consider appropriate in a school library?

6. The Web site for Parents Against Bad Books in Schools (http://www.pabbis .com/), located in the state of Virginia, is loaded with information about how to ban objectionable books from schools, including a "List of Lists" noting

books that have been found objectionable by some (and on what grounds), a "Sample Book Review Documentation Form," and links to like-minded groups and organizations. Spend some time on the site, and use the information you find there to evaluate a book read while you were in school (K–12). Would it likely pass muster? Should it? (Is it on the PABBIS "List of Lists" already?) Write an essay in which you discuss what's at stake, for groups like PABBIS and for students. Do you find the PABBIS mission sympathetic, or do you object to it? On what grounds? Use one or more of the essays in this chapter to support your position.

7. Put yourself in a hypothetical situation: You are a writer whose work revolves around documenting gang life on the streets in a big city. The language people use under these conditions is tough, often profane, abusive, and violent. In attempting to get your work published, you run into an editor who deletes and replaces words, and edits your work to the point that it loses not only its meaning but also its purpose. Write a defense of your work, explaining why the language as recorded is essential to the work. Use the arguments and evidence in one or more of the essays in this chapter to bolster your position.

8. Write an essay arguing in favor of or against Philip Garber Jr.'s right to speak in his college history class. Expand on Garber's case to address any or all of the following questions: Does any student in a course have the right to speak in that course or does the instructor decide how the course will be run and when students may speak? In other words, do the same rules apply in a structured environment as they do in other aspects of our lives? Are there other situations where you might legitimately have to refrain from speaking? Are those situations fair? Are they always legal? Does it make a difference whether you refrain from speaking voluntarily or whether silence is enforced by an authority figure? What about in a courtroom? A library? A religious service? Do we ever have a right to speak out, interrupt, or monopolize the time of someone who is speaking or performing? What are some of the potential consequences of doing so?

The four articles in this section of "Arguing about Language" focus on the word "retard," the latest in a long history of words in English that are hurtful to certain groups of people. Unlike some abusive terms that discriminate against people specifically for their sexual orientation, race, nationality, ethnicity, age, gender, religion, or occupation, "retard" cuts across all subsets of our population sparing none from the stinging pain and exclusion it causes. Many people who use the term do so in humorous contexts — telling jokes and putting down their friends — so they might be surprised to find the term gaining ground as one of those words you just don't use because it hurts people. They don't realize that using the word in any context tends to legitimize it and prolong its life as an insult. In 2004, after prompting from its athletes, the Special Olympics moved away from using the words "retard(ed)" and "mental retardation" to using the label "intellectual disabilities" instead. In 2008 the organization began calling for an end to the use of the word "retard" with a broad-based campaign at *R-word* (http://www.r-word.org). Their campaign slogan is "Spread the Word to End the Word." It is asking government agencies to stop using the term in their programs and in clinical settings. The campaign is also seeking to curtail the use of the term in all facets of popular culture — films, songs, and television programs. Supporters are also encouraged to sign the following pledge on the Web site:

> I pledge and support the elimination of the derogatory use of the r-word from everyday speech and promote the acceptance and inclusion of people with intellectual disabilities.

We present the arguments in "How Do Words Hurt?" in the order of their publication dates, beginning with Christopher M. Fairman's "The Case against Banning the Word 'Retard,'" published on February 14, 2010. Fairman's argument is a classic one in favor of freedom of expression. He explains that he is not against protecting intellectually disabled people from abusive language, but he does think that the effort simply won't work because offensive terms have a way of being replaced by yet other offensive terms. In the end, he thinks that the risk to freedom of expression far outweighs the more immediate and practical reasons to ban the term. On February 15, 2010, Timothy Shriver, the chairman and chief executive of Special Olympics, rebutted Fairman's argument. In "The Bigotry Behind the Word 'Retard'" he claims that the issue is much bigger than the word itself, admitting, however, that words are extremely important. His concern is with how we socially stigmatize those with intellectual disabilities, how few of us realize we are doing it, and the pain we inflict. On March 2, 2010, John C. McGinley, actor and comedian best known as Dr. Perry Cox in the television show *Scrubs*, weighed in with the story of his son Max, who has Down syndrome. McGinley brings to the debate an up close and personal look at someone with intellectual disabilities. He gives voice to Max: who he is, what his special gifts are, and how using the word "retard" even if not within earshot of Max creates a world that works to institutionalize his pain. Finally, Vicki Santillano, a freelance writer, reported on September 1, 2010, on yet another high-profile public use of the word "retard," this time by celebrity Jennifer Aniston. Santillano's article offers proof that not everyone has gotten the message, that there is much work still to be done in educating the public about the use of "retard," and that the debate over its use lingers on.

The Case against Banning the Word "Retard"

CHRISTOPHER M. FAIRMAN

Christopher M. Fairman is professor of law at Moritz College of Law at the Ohio State University. He received both his B.A. degree and his J.D. degree at the University of Texas in 1982 and 1994, respectively. Voted most popular professor of law and most popular law advisor by law students at Moritz College of Law, Fairman is also the author of numerous legal articles. He is very widely known as well for being the author of *Fuck: Word Taboo and Protecting Our First Amendment Liberties* (2007), one of the most often referenced legal publications ever as attested to by its number of online hits.

In "The Case against Banning the Word 'Retard,'" first published in the *Washington Post* on February 14, 2010, Fairman argues against the banning of any word. He does so while recognizing the pain and displeasure that those with intellectual disabilities suffer when the word "retard" is still so widely used by so many people. One of his fears is that the banning of any word could eventually lead to "government control of language and institutionalized word taboo."

WRITING TO DISCOVER: *Have you ever jokingly or seriously called someone a "retard"? Has someone ever used the term in reference to you? Have you ever thought about how hurtful the term might be? If you have used the term in the past, do you still use it?*

Long before Rahm Emanuel, Sarah Palin, and Rush Limbaugh made the word fodder for political controversy and late-night punch lines, a movement was underway to eliminate it from everyday conversation. Saying, irrefutably, that the word and its variations are hurtful to many, the Special Olympics is leading a campaign to end its use and is promoting a national awareness day on March 3. Nearly 60,000 people have signed on to the following promise on www.r-word.org: "I pledge and support the elimination of the derogatory use of the r-word from everyday speech and promote the acceptance and inclusion of people with intellectual disabilities."

I sympathize with the effort, but I won't be making that pledge. It's not that I've come to praise the word "retard"; I just don't think we should bury it. If the history of offensive terms in America shows anything, it is that words themselves are not the culprit; the meaning we attach to them is, and such meanings change dramatically over time and across communities. The term "mentally retarded" was itself introduced by the medical establishment in the twentieth century to supplant other terms that had been deemed offensive. Similarly, the words "gay" and "queer" and even the N-word can be insulting, friendly, identifying, or academic in different contexts.

The varied and evolving uses of such words ultimately render self-censorship campaigns unnecessary. And restricting speech of any kind comes with a potential price—needlessly institutionalized taboos, government censorship, or abridged freedom of expression—that we should be wary of paying.

The latest battle over the R-word kicked into high gear with a Jan. 26 *Wall Street Journal* report that last summer White House Chief of Staff Rahm Emanuel blasted liberal activists unhappy with the pace of health-care reform, deriding their strategies as "[expletive] retarded." Palin, the mother of a special-needs child, quickly took to Facebook to demand Emanuel's firing, likening the offensiveness of the R-word to that of the N-word. Limbaugh seized the low ground, saying he found nothing wrong with "calling a bunch of people who are retards, retards," and Palin rushed to his defense, saying Limbaugh had used the word satirically. Comedy Central's Stephen Colbert took her up on it, calling Palin an "[expletive] retard" and adding, with a smile: "You see? It's satire!"

Emanuel apologized and promised to take the R-Word.org pledge, but as March 3 nears, the word may already be an endangered species. Forty-eight states have voted to remove the term "mental retardation" from government agencies and state codes, and legislation is pending in Congress to strike it from any federal statutes that still use it, such as the Individuals With Disabilities Education Act. The largest advocacy group for the intellectually disabled, the Association for Retarded Citizens, is now simply the Arc. Similarly, the American Association of Mental Retardation is now the American Association on Intellectual and Developmental Disabilities. The Centers for Disease Control and Prevention now use "intellectual disability" in place of "mental retardation." The diagnostic manuals used by medical professionals also embrace "intellectual disability" as the official label. Behind the changes is the belief that "retardation" doesn't communicate dignity and respect.

> If the history of offensive terms in America shows anything, it is that words themselves are not the culprit.

The irony is that the use of "mental retardation" and its variants was originally an attempt to convey greater dignity and respect than previous labels had. While the verb "retard"—meaning to delay or hinder—has roots in the fifteenth century, its use in reference to mental development didn't occur until the late nineteenth and early twentieth centuries, when medical texts began to describe children with "retarded mental development," "retarded children" and "mentally retarded patients." By the 1960s, "mental retardation" became the preferred medical term, gradually replacing previous diagnostic standards such as "idiot," "imbecile" and "moron"—terms that had come to carry pejorative connotations.

As I was growing up in the 1970s, my father worked for the Texas Department of Mental Health and Mental Retardation, one of the now-renamed state agencies. The term "retardation" was common in my home and life, but it was sterile and clinical. It is only in the past generation that the medical term turned into the slang "retard" and gained power as an insult. The shift is even apparent in popular movies. There was little public controversy when Matt Dillon tried to woo Cameron Diaz in the 1998 hit comedy *There's Something About Mary* by confessing his passion: "I work with retards." (Diaz's character, Mary, had a mentally disabled brother.) But 10 years later, in the comedy *Tropic Thunder*, Robert Downey Jr.'s use of the phrase "full retard" led to picketing and calls for a boycott.

What happened to make the word a target for extinction?

All cultures have taboos. Western culture, particularly in the United States, has several taboos surrounding sexuality, grounded largely in a sub-conscious fear of the parade of horribles—adultery, unwanted pregnancy, incest, venereal disease—that might befall us because of some sexual behaviors. Sometimes the taboo extends to even uttering the words that describe certain behaviors. You can see word taboo at work in the way Emanuel's blunder was reported: "[expletive] retarded." It's still okay to print the R-word. The F-word? Forget it.

For years, I've been researching taboo language and its interaction with the law, and I have written a law review article and recently a book, both titled with the unprintable four letter F-word. The resilience of word taboos, the multiple usages and meanings of a single word, the rise of self-censorship, and the risks of institutionalized taboo and ultimately censorship are all core issues surrounding the F-word, and they help explain what is happening—and may happen still—with the R-word.

Mental disorders also carry cultural taboos. For centuries, mental illness and disability were poorly understood; as recently as the 1800s, they were thought to be the work of devils and demons. Because the origins of mental illness were a mystery, fears that such conditions could be contagious led to isolation through institutionalization. Shame was often attached to individuals and their families, and the result was stigma.

Fortunately, we've come a long way from those days. It's precisely the new enlightenment and openness about mental disabilities that allow Palin to launch the controversy over "retard." But at a subconscious level, the underlying taboo may explain why we constantly seek new terms for this type of disability, new ways to avoid the old stigmas. Invariably, negative connotations materialize around whatever new word is used; "idiot" becomes an insult and gives way to "retardation," which in turn suffers the same fate, leading to "intellectual disability." This illustrates one of the recurring follies of speech restriction: While there may be another word to use, a negative connotation eventually is found. Offense—both given and taken—is inevitable.

Whatever future offensiveness may emerge, though, are we not better off by purging today's insulting language and making our discourse a little kinder? That is the argument of self-censorship advocates such as Palin, who draws parallels between the use of the R-word and the N-word—the most powerful and insulting of all racial epithets. In some respects, the comparison seems overblown. The N-word invokes some of the foulest chapters in our nation's history; "retard," however harsh, pales in comparison. But there still may be some guidance to be gleaned.

While the N-word endures as an insult, it is so stigmatized that its use is no longer tolerated in public discourse. This is a positive step for us all, of course, but its containment does not come without costs. As Harvard law professor Randall Kennedy described in his 2002 book on the subject, stigmatizing the word has elicited new problems, including an overeagerness to detect insult where none is intended and the use of excessively harsh punishment against those who use the word wrongly.

I've coined a term for overzealous or extreme responses to insulting   15 words: "word fetish." Those under the influence of word fetish aren't content to refrain from using a certain word; they are set on eradicating any use by others. A classic example was the plight of David Howard, a white employee in the D.C. mayor's office in 1999. Howard told staff members that because of budget cuts, he would have to be "niggardly" with available funds. Wrongly believing "niggardly" was a variation of the N-word, black subordinates lobbied for his resignation. Howard ultimately resigned after public protests, though he was soon reinstated. If the campaign against "retard" is successful, an identical risk of word fetish exists. (Imagine that Emanuel had spoken of "retarding the opposition"— would that be unacceptable?)

Like virtually every word in our language, the N-word has multiple uses. While its use as an insult has decreased, there has been a resurgence of the word as a term of identification, even affection, among some African Americans. But should certain groups of people, to the exclusion of others, be allowed to reclaim certain words? If "retard" or "retarded" were similarly restricted, could intellectually disabled individuals appropriate the term for self-identification, essentially reclaiming its original use or developing a new one?

Over time, word fetish can evolve into censorship among private organizations and ultimately direct government control of language and institutionalized word taboo. During the 1980s and 1990s, for example, many colleges and universities sought to reduce discrimination by developing speech codes, often targeting racial hate speech such as the N-word. Even with the most combustible insults, however, there must be some accommodation to their continued use; freedom of expression surely embraces unpopular, even insulting, speech. Luckily, speech codes that have been challenged in court have generally lost because they violated the First Amendment.

The risk of direct government censorship of the word "retard" is real. The New Zealand chapter of the Special Olympics is already calling on the country's Broadcasting Standards Authority (equivalent to our Federal Communications Commission) to deem the word "retard" unacceptable for broadcast. This plea is based upon a single incident involving New Zealand television personality Paul Henry, who described the runner-up in the *Britain's Got Talent* competition, Susan Boyle, as retarded. It is not difficult to imagine calls for a similar broadcast ban emerging here.

The current public awareness campaign surrounding the use of the word "gay" offers better lessons and parallels for the R-word debate. Advocacy groups contend that the phrase "that's so gay" fosters homophobia and that anti-gay language is directly related to violence and harassment against homosexuals. At the same time, there is recognition that much anti-gay language is uttered carelessly and isn't necessarily intended as hurtful — as is probably the case with uses of "retard." The Ad Council and the Gay, Lesbian and Straight Education Network have developed a Web site, ThinkB4YouSpeak.com, that, much like R-Word.org, encourages the public to sign a pledge to cease using the phrase. (The slogan: "Saying that's so gay is so yesterday.") By increasing sensitivity and awareness, the campaign hopes to encourage people to think about the possible consequences of their word choices. Such reflection would presumably lead individuals to censor themselves once they understand that others can be hurt by their language.

Inherent in this idea is the realization that words have multiple meanings and that those meanings depend on the context and circumstances surrounding any particular statement. For example, "gay" is a term of identification for homosexuals, but it also can be used as an all-purpose put-down: "That's so gay." Those using it as an insult don't intend to say "that's so homosexual," nor do they necessarily make the conscious leap that homosexuality is bad. (Indeed, the success of the ThinkB4YouSpeak .com campaign depends on this distinction.) 20

Similarly, the R-word has multiple usages. When Emanuel calls fellow Democrats "retarded" for jeopardizing a legislative plan, the term is a stand-in for "stupid" or "misguided" or "dumb" — it obviously does not mean that they meet the IQ diagnostic standard for intellectual disability. It is quite another thing to look at a person with Down syndrome and call him or her a "retard." So, if there are readily identifiable alternate meanings, what is the reason for censorship?

Differing usages also give rise to reclaiming — when words that have an offensive meaning are deliberately given a new spin. The putative slur is captured, repurposed, and owned by the target of insult. We see this when an African American uses the N-word as a term of identification for his friends, or when the word "queer" is reclaimed for TV shows such as

Queer Eye for the Straight Guy and *Queer as Folk*, and for queer studies and queer theory in university courses. Reclaiming the word "retard" is an option that should involve no risk to freedom of expression.

If interest groups want to pour resources into cleaning up unintentional insults, more power to them; we surely would benefit from greater kindness to one another. But we must not let "retard" go without a requiem. If the goal is to protect intellectually disabled individuals from put-downs and prejudice, it won't succeed. New words of insult will replace old ones.

Words are ideas, and we should be reluctant to surrender any of them. Freedom of expression has come at a dear price, and it is not worth abridging, even so we can get along a little better. That's one F-word we really can't do without.

THINKING CRITICALLY ABOUT THE READING

1. What is there in his credentials that makes Fairman an authority on the use of the R-word?

2. What does Fairman mean when he writes in paragraph 2 that "words themselves are not the culprit"?

3. What irony, according to Fairman, surrounds the use of the phrase "mental retardation"?

4. What's ironic about the media's use of "[expletive] retarded"?

5. What do you think about Fairman's argument that if people don't use the R-word they will find another equally offensive term to use to label the intellectually disabled?

6. What is Fairman's definition of the phrase "word fetish"? How does his use of the phrase figure into his argument against banning the R-word?

7. What is Fairman's argument concerning the possibility of reclaiming the R-word?

The Bigotry Behind the Word "Retard"

TIMOTHY SHRIVER

Timothy Shriver is the chairman and CEO of Special Olympics. He was born in Boston, Massachusetts, in 1959 and earned his B.A. from Yale University in 1981, his M.A. in religion and religious education from the Catholic University of America in 1988, and his Ph.D. in education from the University of Connecticut in 1996. After Yale, Shriver served as a high school teacher in New Haven, Connecticut, and as a teacher in the University of Connecticut branch of the Upward Bound program. A member of the Kennedy family through his mother, Eunice Kennedy Shriver, who founded Special Olympics, Shriver has continued the family tradition of public service, addressing in particular problems that interfere with learning such as substance abuse, teen pregnancy, and violence. He took over the reins of Special Olympics in 1996 and in an October 25, 2009, article in the *New York Times* he explained his role at Special Olympics: "I've tried to shift the conversation here from what Special Olympics does to what it means. It's often seen as a service organization, but I believe that it's a civil rights movement. Volunteers might think that they're only coaching or serving water at a track and field event, for example, but they are doing far more. My mission has been to remind them that they are serving the search for human dignity and acceptance."

In "The Bigotry Behind the Word 'Retard,'" first published in the *Washington Post* on February 15, 2010, Shriver believes that Christopher M. Fairman, the author of "The Case against Banning the Word 'Retard'" (pp. 526–531), "missed the point of the campaign by people who have intellectual disabilities." Shriver argues that he is fighting for so much more than is represented by the r-word, and that is a world free of the bigotry and isolation that is visited upon people incapable of defending themselves.

WRITING TO DISCOVER: *Do you know anyone with Down syndrome, or someone who is otherwise intellectually or physically disabled? How would you describe that person's ability to function within society?*

Professor and author Christopher M. Fairman ["The Case against Banning the Word 'Retard,'" *Outlook*, Feb. 14] made good arguments about the limits of language to effect change in behavior and attitude, as well as about the nuanced ways in which words such as "retard," "queer" and "gay" can carry multiple meanings, some of which intend no insult or humiliation.

But I believe he missed the point of the campaign by people who have intellectual disabilities, their friends, advocates, and tens of thousands of individuals and dozens of organizations: We are fighting a word because it represents one of the most stubborn and persistent stigmas in history. Millions of people have a prejudice they often are not even aware of. It is much bigger than a word, but words matter. And the word "retard," whatever its history, reflects a massive problem.

Mental Disability Rights International has found evidence around the world of horrific conditions — starvation, abuse, isolation — in institutions serving people with intellectual disabilities. It happens in this country. In Texas, caregivers were recently found to be forcing residents of an institution to awake in the middle of the night and fight one another while staffers cheered and taunted. Here in Washington, repeated investigations have revealed people with intellectual disabilities as the victims of abuse, indifference, and negligent death.

Seventy to 90 percent of people with intellectual disabilities in the United States are estimated to be unemployed. Special Olympics studies reveal that more than 60 percent of Americans don't believe that children with intellectual disabilities should be educated in their child's school. Special Olympics' work with health-care providers reveals, among almost all medical professions, a shocking lack of training in the care of people with intellectual disabilities.

> **We are fighting a word because it represents one of the most stubborn and persistent stigmas in history.**

Sadly, it seems that many assume that poor health care, poor living conditions, and underemployment are inevitable. As one health insurance agent told a parent of a child with Down syndrome seeking health care, "Ma'am. We're not paying for services. Your child is retarded!"

Our coalition seeks no law to ban words and no official censorship against those who freely use "retard." Fairman is surely correct that as language evolves, new words that carry disgusting ridicule will emerge. He can study them and educate us about their evolution.

But for our part, we are trying to awaken the world to the need for a new civil rights movement — of the heart. We seek to educate people that a crushing prejudice against people with intellectual disabilities is rampant — a prejudice that assumes that people with significant learning challenges are stupid or hapless or somehow just not worth much. They're, um, "retarded." And that attitude is not funny or nuanced or satirical. It's horrific.

Last week, I tried to assuage the depression of a Special Olympics athlete, an adult, who can't stop hearing the taunt of "retard" that plagued her through school. She has few friends and struggles with a terrifying sense of isolation. Counseling and medication aren't enough. There is nowhere she feels she fits in.

Her pain is enough for me to change my language. That's only a small step and we need many more. But we're not going to get these changes until and unless we awaken our fellow citizens to the truth: Most of us look down on people with intellectual disabilities, and we don't even realize it.

And that's why this word is important: "Retard" is a symbol of a   10 pain few realize exists. Even when it's not directed at people with intellectual disabilities, it perpetuates that pain and stigma. We hope that the discussion about ending it will awaken millions to the hope of ending the discrimination it represents.

If we're successful, the world will discover the joy, hope, and sparkling individuality of millions of people. With that, real change will come.

It can't come soon enough.

THINKING CRITICALLY ABOUT THE READING

1. Does Shriver have problems with the word "retard" itself? Explain.

2. How does Shriver document the abuse that people with intellectual disabilities suffer? Were you previously aware of the information about abuse he provides?

3. Why does Shriver think it necessary to mention that his "coalition seeks no law to ban words and no official censorship against those who freely use 'retard'"?

4. Shriver uses the word "stigmas" in paragraph 2 and "stigma" in paragraph 10. What does he mean by his use of the word in this context? Is it an appropriate use of the word? Explain.

5. Why might people not want their children to be in school with intellectually disabled students? What might be done about this particular educational situation?

6. If you were standing next to a couple of teenagers who were yelling "Retard! Retard!" at each other at the self-serve checkout in your supermarket, what would you say, if anything, to them? Would you be afraid to speak to them about their use of the word "retard"? Would you consider it an infringement on their right to free speech if you were to speak to them about what they were saying? Explain.

Spread the Word to End the Word

JOHN C. MCGINLEY

John C. McGinley is perhaps best known as the actor who plays Dr. Perry
Cox on the medical comedy-drama television series *Scrubs* which aired
from 2001 to 2010. McGinley was born in New York City in 1959 and
was raised in Millburn, New Jersey. After attending Syracuse University,
McGinley transferred to New York University where he received both
his undergraduate degree and his master of fine arts degree in acting in
1984. In addition to his appearance in *Scrubs*, a role he took so that
he could be close to home for his son Max who has Down syndrome,
McGinley has appeared in over sixty films, among them *Platoon* (1986),
Wall Street (1987), *Talk Radio* (1988), and *Born on the Fourth of July*
(1989). McGinley serves as an ambassador for the National Down Syndrome Society.

In "Spread the Word to End the Word," first published on the news
Web site the *Huffington Post* on March 2, 2010, McGinley gives us an up-
close-and-personal look at his son Max. In getting to know Max and his
special attributes, and especially his capacity to bring out the joy of life
in those around him, we can gain even more appreciation for the type of
person we are hurting when we callously use the r-word for those with
intellectual disabilities.

WRITING TO DISCOVER: *Why is it important to put faces on the people who
make up groups that we refer to with generic labels, such as the elderly, kids, teenagers, politicians, nurses, professional athletes, the homeless? How does putting a face
on someone lead to greater human understanding?*

*The way you see people is the way you treat them, and the way you treat them
is what they become.*

—GOETHE

I am a father. My son's name is Max and my daughter's name is Billie
Grace. Twelve years ago Max was born with Down syndrome. His journey
has been complicated by infantile seizures, sleep apnea, dietary challenges,
and now puberty! Max has also (somehow) managed to become a medium
through whom other people are introduced to their own personal stories
of compassion and love and heretofore undiscovered capacity to revel in
joy. It is not entirely clear to me just how Max is able to perform this service. I can, however, attest to the fact that my son has made a gift of love
and presented it to countless people. I have witnessed this phenomenon
and I have been one of those people.

Twelve years ago it never occurred to me that my son would someday
be caught dead in the crosshairs of painful hate speech and insensitive

language, leveled directly at a special needs population that Max was born into. With the distinct physical markers that identify a person born with Down syndrome, my son (through no fault of his own), has inherited the unwelcome stigma that sadly accompanies the R-word.

Freedom of speech is to all Americans as oxygen is to the human condition. It is a right that has been irreversibly programmed into our hard drive. We are free to speak our minds. An artist's right to express him or herself as best suits their art is the artist's prerogative and it is guaranteed. Even if a private citizen wants to burn an American flag that person has the right to go ahead and do so. The First Amendment of the United States Constitution is a component of the Bill of Rights. Included in the First Amendment are protections that prohibit Congress from infringing on freedom of speech.

When the words we are free to speak are aimed at specific populations of people and target that group in a harmful way, there are repercussions.

Our right to speak as we see fit is sacred and not something that any of us is willing to relinquish. Nor should we.

However, when the words we   5
are free to speak are aimed at specific populations of people and target that group in a harmful way, there are repercussions. There is a "tax" that is imposed on those who choose to assault others with their hate speech.

This "duty" may be levied in the form of boycotts, marches, firings (see: Imus), or even a stiff right to the jaw! In other words, when the words that we are free to speak include racial slurs, epithets, or sexist slander, there has been and always will be blowback. Groups like the NAACP, the Anti-Defamation League, NOW, and GLAAD will respond to derisive language directed at their constituents. The price paid by those who cavalierly choose to verbally disrespect the dignity of African Americans, Jews, women, and homosexuals is steep. Those who insist on using words like nigger, kike, or faggot will most often pay with their jobs and any shred of character that they may have been pretending to assume.

It is every American's right to use words like "nigger" and "kike" and "faggot." It is also the right of those who are on the receiving end of such hate speech to object to that kind of denigration. The objections exercised by groups like African Americans, Jews, homosexuals, and women have been largely successful in disincentivizing the continued, public, widespread use of disparaging language hurled at them. You are not likely to hear Rahm Emanuel use the words "stupid f-cking niggers!" You are also not likely to hear Rush Limbaugh use the words "kikes are kikes." Nor, for that matter, are you likely to hear other media fixtures like Jon Stewart, Bill Maher, and countless others of their ilk, sprinkle their speech with words like "faggot," "wop," or "spic." If they did it once, they would be gone! It is really that simple. No questions asked.

The consequences for launching into hurtful language, aimed at powerful ethnic, religious, and gender-based groups, are profound and final (see: Michael Richards and Jimmy "The Greek"). The very real fear of a counter-punch thrown by the victimized party is usually enough to scare away almost every single one of those who would otherwise toss about slander without a care. The fear of the tax or the very real cost is a hammer that sometimes informs the speech that we are so free to express.

Verbally assaulting those who have done absolutely nothing wrong and cannot even begin to defend themselves is an exponentially more egregious transgression. Only bullies and cowards pick on the defenseless. However, it does seem fair to assume that a vast majority of people who use the R-word (i.e., "retard" and "retarded") are not even aware that their language is offensive and hurtful to members of the special needs community. And at the risk of being redundant, perhaps there is some value in setting the record straight: the R-word hurts! And it makes no difference that a person with special needs is not in earshot when the word is spoken. Using the R-word perpetuates a negative stigma that belittles people with special needs. And the casual nature in which the R-word is now thrown about only makes the impact even more insidious and the trickle-down effect more persistent. The R-word hurts.

There are two relatively simple exercises that expose the R-word for the instrument of hurt that (in its contemporary context) it has evolved into. First, is there a single instance when the R-word is used as a compliment? Do we find ourselves showering our peers with the R-word after a great triumph or a significant achievement? Is the R-word the stuff that support and elevation are made of? [10]

And secondly, whenever we are compelled to use the R-word, would the circumstances allow for substituting the N-word instead? Could the R-word just as easily be replaced by any number of pejorative slurs that would serve the same purpose? The answer to both these hypotheticals is: Not in a million years!

The First Amendment protects everyone's right to use the R-word. There is not a member of the special needs community who wishes to compromise any fellow American's freedom of speech. That is certainly not the drill here. However, armed with the knowledge that the R-word is a source of pain and that using the R-word demeans a group that is not in a position to defend itself and who definitely never did anything to merit this kind of derision, the hope is that people will exercise some degree of compassion or at least a heightened sensitivity toward the continued use of the R-word. Again, this is not an invasion of the Bill of Rights. Rather, it is a civil call to integrate a simple change into the way we treat, regard, and address the special needs population.

THINKING CRITICALLY ABOUT THE READING

1. Why is McGinley not sure how Max is able to instill love in those around him? What does his inability to understand say about Max's special gift?

2. McGinley shifts the focus of his essay as he moves from his second to his third paragraph. What is that shift and why has he made it?

3. Is McGinley trying to deny anyone's right to freedom of speech? Is he attempting to abridge anyone's right to freedom of speech? Explain.

4. What does McGinley mean when he writes that "there is a 'tax' that is imposed on those who choose to assault others with their hate speech"?

5. How does McGinley support the idea that "disincentivizing" users of slurs is a strategy that gets results? What evidence does he bring into his argument?

6. How does McGinley rebut the argument that using the R-word without malice is acceptable?

7. In your own words what are the two exercises that McGinley says "expose the R-word for the instrument of hurt that (in its contemporary context) it has evolved into"?

The Great "R-word" Debate: Is It Ever Okay to Say?

VICKI SANTILLANO

Vicki Santillano is currently a freelance writer at Dataessential, a food-industry market research company. She earned her B.A. degree in literature with highest honors at the University of California, Santa Cruz, in 2006, and now makes her home in the Los Angeles area. Prior to working at Dataessential, Santillano was a writer at *DivineCaroline: Life in Your Words*, an online magazine with stories about entertainment, beauty, style, family, home, food, relationships, parenting, money, and the world at large. Santillano has written many articles covering a wide range of subjects including health and wellness, representation of women in the media, hormones, gastronomy, and pop culture.

"The Great 'R-word' Debate: Is It Ever Okay to Say?" first appeared on *DivineCaroline.com* on September 1, 2010, shortly after popular radio show host Dr. Laura Schlessinger made racist comments involving the N-word. Santillano comments on the public's response to another unfortunate comment made by a celebrity, this time by actor Jennifer Aniston.

WRITING TO DISCOVER: *How influential do you think celebrities are when it comes to setting fashions and trends? Do you think they also influence the way we speak and the words we use? What kind of power do they have to change the way we use language?*

As if the nation weren't already shaken by Dr. Laura's wildly racist rant in August 2010, Jennifer Aniston had to go and rock the boat even more by using the word "retard" in an interview just a week later. "Yes, I play dress-up! I do it for a living, like a retard," she joked on *Live! with Regis and Kelly* on August 19. The audience laughed, but many people around the country failed to see the humor in her self-deprecating comment. That's because she used a word that's almost as divisive and contentious as the N-word. But while most people agree on the absolute inappropriateness of the N-word, the public is surprisingly divided on whether it's okay to say "retard" or "retarded" pejoratively.

Just look at the response to Aniston's offhand remark: plenty have called her insensitive and have demanded everything from a public apology to a boycott of her movies. But a sizable number of other people say it's not a big deal; they argue that the word (in noun or adjectival form) doesn't mean what it used to, that it has nothing to do with the intellectually disabled anymore. But does that make it okay?

"Retard" and "retarded" are used so often in conversations that the Special Olympics and Best Buddies International teamed up in 2009 to

539

create the "Spread the Word to End the Word" campaign, asking people to pledge not to use the R-word ever again. How can a term that's so emotionally loaded for some become an acceptable part of the vernacular for others?

SHIFTING AWAY FROM CONTROVERSY

Jennifer Aniston's R-word woes are nothing new; in the past few years, other celebrities have come under fire for their use of the word as well. A group of protestors went to the *Tropic Thunder* movie premiere in 2008 because a character uses the word "retard." More recently, the *Wall Street Journal* quoted White House chief of staff Rahm Emanuel using the word "retarded" to describe a plan suggested in a meeting. He apologized publicly to Special Olympics chairman and CEO Timothy Shriver soon after and actually took the organization's R-word pledge. Even President Obama hasn't been exempt from backlash: after describing his bowling skills as "like Special Olympics, or something" on *The Tonight Show* in 2009, Obama made a personal phone call to Shriver and apologized.

Despite the uproar surrounding them, instances like these show just   5
how casually the word is thrown around in our society. But not everyone thinks of that as a problem, especially because "retard" is used more as a synonym for "stupid" than it is to describe the intellectually disabled. It's true that the word is no longer used in many official documents and legalese; the Special Olympics made the switch from "mental retardation" to "intellectual disabilities" in 2004 at the behest of its athletes, who felt the word only fueled "playground taunts" at this point. In addition, the American Association on Mental Retardation became the American Association on Intellectual and Developmental Disabilities in 2007; one of the reasons given for the name change was that "it is less offensive to persons with disabilities." And in August 2010, the U.S. Senate passed "Rosa's Law," which will replace all references to "mental retardation" in federal laws with "intellectual disability." The Centers for Disease Control and Prevention and the World Health Organization have already made the switch.

> How can a term that's so emotionally loaded for some become an acceptable part of the vernacular for others?

"Retard" is going the way of "idiot," "imbecile," "feeble-minded," and other once-official words now considered merely negative, and that's because (like those other words) it's used too widely as an insult now. "It used to be a label used exclusively for those people with a very low IQ, and marked a division between those who had what we considered average intelligence or above, and those who would be considered mentally deficient . . . Now it seems to have become a blanket term for anyone who doesn't measure up to another person's standards, which [other teachers and I] feel is very unfortunate," says a teacher I spoke with who works with intellectually disabled students. "I don't believe most people who use the label actually think about our kids, but they should, because its use is a disservice to them."

A WEIGHTY MATTER REMAINS

When issues like these are brought to light, it really makes us step back and consider our own thoughts and actions. The R-word is but one of many terms that hit a nerve in some and are perfectly fine to others. And just as other offensive words have been phased out of acceptable public vernacular, it's possible that people won't use the R-word so flippantly in the future. In a BBC survey from a few years back, it was voted the most offensive word used to describe disabilities. And as of March 2010, the Special Olympics made its initial goal of getting one hundred thousand pledges against the R-word on its Web site—and that number's no doubt grown even more after the Aniston debacle.

It's also possible that the word's casual use will only increase after it's been completely removed from official documents and organizations. Maybe someday "retard" will carry about as much emotional weight as "stupid," and eventually it won't be an issue. A word's connotation—of which there can be many—can change over time. But as Aniston's on-air slip proves, the word's acceptability and potential for inflicting hurt are still very much up for debate.

THINKING CRITICALLY ABOUT THE READING

1. What is wrong with using the R-word, especially if you only mean it in jest?
2. Santillano writes that the public is divided about the use of the R-word. What explanation, if any, does she give for the difference of opinion?
3. Why do you think that use of the R-word persists in our vernacular? What does the fact that high government officials have recently used the word tell us about its prevalence in our society?
4. What is Rosa's Law? Have you ever heard of it? Do you think it's a good law, or is it yet another example of what might be deemed excessive political correctness?
5. Rejection of the term "retard" is indicated by the growing number of people making the "Spread the Word to End the Word" pledge. Why does Santillano say that the R-word's use may even increase after it is removed from official documents?
6. Has your thinking been changed at all by Santillano's article? How so, or why not?

WRITING SUGGESTIONS: DEBATING THE ISSUE

1. John C. McGinley uses the phrase "hate speech" in paragraph 6 of "Spread the Word to End the Word." Read or reread Andrew Sullivan's "What's So Bad about Hate?" (pp. 307–322) and write an essay in which you place the words "retard" or "retarded" in the context of hate speech. In what ways is and isn't the R-word a form of hate speech? Should the R-word be considered hate speech even—or especially—when it isn't directed at an intellectually disabled person?
2. *Delanceyplace.com* is a Web site that reprints well-written and interesting passages from important books and articles about a variety of subjects. On March 18, 2011, the editors of the site reprinted an excerpt from Kipling D. Williams's

"The Pain of Exclusion" first published in *Scientific American Mind,* January/February 2011, 30–37. Read the excerpt online and write an essay relating what you now know about how the intellectually disabled have been isolated through the use of the R-word. If possible, interview several people with intellectual disabilities and their caregivers or guardians to gain a better understanding of the way they cope with problems associated with isolation and ostracism.

3. Christopher Fairman writes in "The Case against Banning the Word 'Retard'" that "reclaiming the word 'retard' is an option that should involve no risk to the freedom of expression." Write an essay focusing on whether or not reclaiming the words "retard" and "retarded" is possible. How would such a process be put into effect? Who or what organization would attempt to reclaim and repurpose the words? Is there something about the R-word and what it represents that makes it more or less difficult to reclaim than words such as "gay" and "queer"?

4. Are you like many people who cringe and feel powerless to express your distaste for offensive language used in your presence? Write an essay offering advice on what to do if you hear someone using language inappropriately. First of all, do you even have a right to ask other people to change the way they are speaking? How do you overcome your reluctance to speak out against such language? Are you afraid someone might continue to speak inappropriately to you personally? How does one handle the situation?

5. What are the major taboo words and ideas in our culture? How do cultures (and subcultures) differ in what they consider to be taboo language and customs? Write an essay in which you place the R-word in the context of taboo language. How are Shriver, McGinley, and Santillano trying to make the R-word taboo in our culture? Will their efforts cause people to offer up alternative language that becomes just as offensive? Is the problem less with the words people use and more with the way they think when it comes to offensive and abusive language?

6. Write an essay in which you investigate the terms "euphemism" and "dysphemism" with respect to the current debate about the R-word. In what ways do we use terms like "retarded" and "intellectually disabled" as euphemisms, dysphemisms, or neutral references? What is it about a term and its connotations that establishes it as euphemistic, dysphemistic, or neutral?

7. Some people might argue that the "Spread the Word to End the Word" campaign is simply another instance of political correctness aimed at changing people's behavior, that it will do little to change the reality behind the words we use, and that it will ultimately fail. Are we indeed confusing the word with the thing to which it refers? Write an essay in which you explore the concept of reification and how it applies to the ways we think about and use the R-word. Can changing the language we use change the reality of a situation? How do we sort out the confusion?

8. A widely accepted principle of language use is that we should respect people's wishes when it comes to how they want to be referenced. Is it not what we want to call people that's important but what they want to be called, what labels they themselves find comfortable and prefer? Write an essay in which you explain and explore this rather simple language principle as a way of achieving a level of courtesy, respect, and caring as we interact with one another and carry on our daily activities.

A Brief Guide to Writing a Research Paper

The research paper is an important part of a college education for good reason. In writing such a paper, you acquire a number of indispensable research skills that you can adapt to other college assignments and, after graduation, to important life tasks.

The real value of writing a research paper, however, goes beyond acquiring basic skills; it is a unique hands-on learning experience. The purpose of a research paper is not to present a collection of quotations that show you can report what others have said about your topic. Rather, your goal is to analyze, evaluate, and synthesize the materials you research—and thereby learn how to do so with any topic. You learn how to view the results of research from your own perspective and arrive at an informed opinion of a topic.

Writing a researched essay is not very different from the other writing you will be doing in your college writing course. You will find yourself drawing heavily on what you have learned in "Writing in College and Beyond" (pp. 21–42). First you determine what you want to write about. Then you decide on a purpose, consider your audience, develop a thesis, collect your evidence, write a first draft, revise and edit, and prepare a final copy. What differentiates the researched paper from other kinds of papers is your use of outside sources and how you acknowledge them.

Your library research will involve working with print and electronic sources. Your aim is to select the most appropriate sources for your research from the many that are available on your topic. (See also Chapter 3, "Writing with Sources.")

In this chapter, you will learn some valuable research techniques:

- How to establish a realistic schedule for your research project
- How to conduct research on the Internet using directory and keyword searches
- How to evaluate sources
- How to analyze sources
- How to develop a working bibliography
- How to take useful notes
- How to acknowledge your sources using Modern Language Association (MLA) style in-text citations and a list of works cited
- How to present your research paper using MLA manuscript format

ESTABLISH A REALISTIC SCHEDULE

A research project easily spans several weeks. So as not to lose track of time and find yourself facing an impossible deadline at the last moment, establish a realistic schedule for completing key tasks. By thinking of the research paper as a multi-staged process, you avoid becoming overwhelmed by the size of the whole undertaking.

Your schedule should allow at least a few days to accommodate unforeseen needs and delays. Use the following template, which lists the essential steps in writing a research paper to plan your own research schedule:

Research Paper Schedule

Task	Completion Date
1. Choose a research topic and pose a worthwhile question.	_/_/_
2. Locate print and electronic sources.	_/_/_
3. Develop a working bibliography.	_/_/_
4. Evaluate your sources.	_/_/_
5. Read your sources, taking complete and accurate notes.	_/_/_
6. Develop a preliminary thesis and make a working outline.	_/_/_
7. Write a draft of your paper, integrating sources you have summarized, paraphrased, and quoted.	_/_/_
8. Visit your college writing center for help with your revision.	_/_/_
9. Decide on a final thesis and modify your outline.	_/_/_
10. Revise your paper and properly cite all borrowed materials.	_/_/_
11. Prepare a list of works cited.	_/_/_
12. Prepare the final manuscript and proofread.	_/_/_
13. Submit research paper.	_/_/_

LOCATE AND USE PRINT AND ONLINE SOURCES

The distinction between print sources and electronic sources is fast disappearing. Many sources that used to appear only in print are now available in electronic format as well; some, in fact, are moving entirely to electronic format, as a more efficient and in many cases less expensive means of distribution.

There are, however, still important distinctions between print sources (or their electronic equivalent) and Internet sources. Many of the sources you will find through an Internet search will not be as reliable as those that traditionally appeared in print. For this reason, in most cases you should use print sources or their electronic versions (books, newspapers, journals, periodicals, encyclopedias, pamphlets, brochures, and government publications) as your primary tools for research. These sources, unlike many Internet sources, are often reviewed by experts in the field before they are published, are generally overseen by a reputable publishing company or organization, and are examined by editors and fact checkers for accuracy and reliability. Unless you are instructed otherwise, you should try to use these sources in your research.

The best place to start any search for sources is your college library's home page. Here you will find links to the computerized catalog of book holdings, online reference works, periodical databases, electronic journals, and a list of full-text databases. You'll also find links for subject study guides and for help conducting your research.

To get started, decide on some likely search terms and try them out. (For tips on conducting and refining keyword searches, see pages 546–547.) Search through your library's reference works, electronic catalog, periodical indexes, and other databases to generate a preliminary listing of books,

magazine and newspaper articles, public documents and reports, and other sources that may be helpful in exploring your topic. At this early stage, it is better to err on the side of listing too many sources. Then, later on, you will not have to backtrack to find sources you discarded too hastily.

Sources that you find through an Internet search can also be informative and valuable additions to your research. The Internet is especially useful in providing recent data, stories, and reports. For example, you might find a just-published article from a university laboratory, or a news story in your local newspaper's online archives. Generally, however, Internet sources should be used alongside sources you access through your college library and not as a replacement for them. Practically anyone with access to a computer and an Internet connection can put text and pictures on the Internet; there is often no governing body that checks for content or accuracy. Therefore, while the Internet offers a vast number of useful and carefully maintained resources, it also contains much unreliable information. It is your responsibility to determine whether a given Internet source should be trusted. (For advice on evaluating sources, see pages 548–550.)

If you need more instruction on conducting Internet searches, go to your on-campus computer center for more information, or consult one of the many books written for Internet beginners. You can also access valuable information for searching the Internet at Diana Hacker's *Research and Documentation Online* at bedfordstmartins.com/resdoc.

Conduct Keyword Searches

When searching for sources about your topic in an electronic database, in the library's computerized catalog, or on the Internet, you should start with a keyword search. To make the most efficient use of your time, you will want to know how to conduct a keyword search that is likely to yield solid sources and leads for your research project. As obvious or simple as it may sound, the key to a successful keyword search is the quality of the keywords you generate about your topic. You might find it helpful to start a list of potential keywords as you begin your research and add to it as your work proceeds. Often you will discover combinations of keywords that will lead you right to the sources you need.

Databases and library catalogs index sources by author, title, and year of publication, as well as by subject headings assigned by a cataloger who has previewed the source. The key here is to find a keyword that matches one of the subject headings. Once you begin to locate sources that are on your topic, be sure to note the subject headings listed for each source. You can use these subject headings as keywords to lead you to additional book sources or to articles in periodicals, using full-text databases like *Info Trac, LexisNexis, Expanded Academic ASAP,* or *JSTOR* to which your library subscribes.

The keyword search process is somewhat different—more wide open—when you are searching on the Web. It is always a good idea to look for search tips on the help screens or advanced search instructions for the search engine you are using before initiating a keyword search.

When you type a keyword in the "Search" box on a search engine's home page, the search engine goes looking for Web sites that match your term. One problem with keyword searches is that they can produce tens of thousands of matches, making it difficult to locate sites of immediate value. For that reason, make your keywords as specific as you can, and make sure that you have the correct spelling. Once you start a search, you may want to narrow or broaden it depending on the number of hits, or matches, you get.

Refining Keyword Searches on the Web

While some variation in command terms and characters exists among electronic databases and popular search engines on the Internet, the following functions are almost universally accepted. If you have a particular question about refining your keyword search, seek assistance by clicking on "Help" or "Advanced Search."

- Use quotation marks or parentheses to indicate that you are searching for words in exact sequence—e.g., "bilingual education"; (college slang).
- Use AND or a plus sign (+) between words to narrow your search by specifying that all words need to appear in a document—e.g., prejudice AND Asians; doublespeak + advertisements.
- Use NOT or a minus sign (–) between words to narrow your search by eliminating unwanted words–e.g., advertisements NOT public service; natural–organic.
- Use an asterisk (*) to indicate that you will accept variations of a term—e.g., euphemism*.

Use Subject Directories to Define and Develop Your Research Topic

If you are undecided as to exactly what you want to write about, the subject directories on the home pages of search engines make it easy to browse the Web by various subjects and topics for ideas that interest you. Subject directories can also be a big help if you have a topic but are undecided about your exact research question or if you simply want to see if there is enough material to supplement your research work with print sources. Once you choose a subject area in the directory, you can select more specialized subdirectories, eventually arriving at a list of sites closely related to your topic.

The most common question students have at this stage of a Web search is, "How can I tell if I'm looking in the right place?" There is no straight answer; if more than one subject area sounds plausible, you will have to dig more deeply into each of their subdirectories, using logic and the process of elimination to determine which one is likely to produce the best leads for your topic. In most cases, it doesn't take long—usually just one or two clicks—to figure out whether you're searching in the right subject area. If you click on a subject area and none of the topics listed in its subdirectories seems to pertain even remotely to your research topic, try a different subject area. As you browse through various subject directories and subdirectories, keep a running list of keywords associated with your topic that you can use in subsequent keyword searches.

EVALUATE YOUR SOURCES

You will not have to spend much time in the library to realize that you do not have time to read every print and online source that appears relevant. Given the abundance of print and Internet sources, the key to successful research is identifying those books, articles, Web sites, and other online sources that will help you most. You must evaluate your potential sources to determine which materials you will read, which you will skim, and which you will simply eliminate. Here are some evaluation strategies and questions to assist you in identifying your most promising sources.

Strategies for Evaluating Print and Online Sources

EVALUATING A BOOK

- Read the dust jacket or cover copy for insights into the book's coverage and currency as well as the author's expertise.
- Scan the table of contents and identify any promising chapters.
- Read the author's preface, looking for his or her thesis and purpose.
- Check the index for key words or key phrases related to your research topic.
- Read the opening and concluding paragraphs of any promising chapter; if you are unsure about its usefulness, skim the whole chapter.

- Ask yourself: Does the author have a discernable bias? If so, you must be aware that this bias will color his or her claims and evidence.

EVALUATING AN ARTICLE

- Ask yourself what you know about the journal or magazine publishing the article:

  - Is the publication scholarly or popular? Scholarly journals (*American Economic Review, Journal of Marriage and the Family, The Wilson Quarterly*) publish articles about original research written by authorities in the field. Research essays always cite their sources in footnotes or bibliographies. Popular news and general interest magazines (*National Geographic, Smithsonian, Time, Ebony*), on the other hand, publish informative, entertaining, and easy-to-read articles written by editorial staff or freelance writers. Popular essays sometimes cite sources but often do not.
  - What is the reputation of the journal or magazine? Determine the publisher or sponsor. Is it an academic institution or a commercial enterprise or individual? Does the publisher or publication have a reputation for accuracy and objectivity?
  - Who are the readers of this journal or magazine?

- What are the author's credentials?
- Consider the title or headline of the article as well as the opening paragraph or two and the conclusion. Does the source appear to be too general or too technical for your needs and audience?
- For articles in journals, read the abstract (a summary of the main points) if there is one.
- Examine any photographs, charts, graphs, or other illustrations that accompany the article. Determine how useful they might be for your research purposes.

EVALUATING A WEB SITE

- Consider the type of Web site. Is this site a personal blog or a professional publication? Often the URL, especially the top-level domain name, can give you a clue about the kinds of information provided and the type of organization behind the site. Common suffixes include:

  .com — business/commercial/personal
  .edu — educational institution

.gov — government sponsored
.net — various types of networks
.org — nonprofit organization, but also some commercial/personal

- Be advised that *.org* is not regulated like *.edu* and *.gov*, for example. Most nonprofits use *.org*, but many commercial and personal sites do as well.
- Examine the home page of the site.

  - Does the content appear to be related to your research topic?
  - Is the home page well maintained and professional in appearance?
  - Is there an *About* link on the home page that takes you to background information on the site's sponsor? Is there a mission statement, history, or statement of philosophy? Can you verify whether the site is official — actually sanctioned by the organization or company?

- Identify the author of the site. What are the author's qualifications for writing on this subject?
- Determine whether a print equivalent is available. Is the Web version more or less extensive than the print version?
- Determine when the site was last updated. Is the content current enough for your purposes?

You can find sources on the Internet itself that offer useful guidelines for evaluating electronic sources. One excellent example was created by reference librarians at the Wolfgram Memorial Library of Widener University. Type *Wolfgram evaluate web pages* into a search engine to access that site. For additional guidance, go to bedfordstmartins.com/researchroom and click on "How to Evaluate Sources" or "Evaluating Online Sources: A Tutorial."

On the basis of your evaluation, select the most promising books, articles, and Web sites to pursue in depth for your research project.

ANALYZE YOUR SOURCES

Before beginning to take notes, it is essential that you carefully analyze your sources for their thesis, overall argument, amount and credibility of evidence, bias, and reliability in helping you explore your research topic. Look for the writers' main ideas, key examples, strongest arguments, and conclusions. Read critically. While it is easy to become absorbed in sources that support your own beliefs, always seek out several sources with opposing viewpoints, if only to test your own position. Look for information about the authors themselves—information that will help you determine their authority and where they position themselves in the broader conversation on the issue. You should also know the reputation and special interests of book publishers and magazines, because you are likely to get different views—conservative, liberal, international, feminist—on the same topic depending on the publication you read. Use the following checklist to assist you in analyzing your print and online sources.

Checklist for Analyzing Print and Online Sources

- What is the writer's thesis or claim?
- How does the writer support this thesis? Does the evidence seem reasonable and ample, or is it mainly anecdotal?
- Does the writer consider opposing viewpoints?
- Does the writer have any obvious political or religious biases? Is the writer associated with any special-interest groups such as Planned Parenthood, Greenpeace, Amnesty International, or the National Rifle Association?
- Is the writer an expert on the subject? Do other writers mention this author in their work?
- Does the publisher or publication have a reputation for accuracy and objectivity?
- Is important information documented through footnotes or links so that it can be verified or corroborated in other sources?
- What is the author's purpose—to inform or to argue for a particular position or action?
- Do the writer's thesis and purpose clearly relate to your research topic?
- Does the source appear to be too general or too technical for your needs and audience?
- Does the source reflect current thinking and research in the field?

DEVELOP A WORKING BIBLIOGRAPHY OF YOUR SOURCES

As you discover books, journal and magazine articles, newspaper stories, and Web sites that you think might be helpful, you need to start maintaining a record of important information about each source. This record, called a working bibliography, will enable you to know where sources are located as well as what they are when it comes time to consult them or acknowledge them in your list of works cited or final bibliography (see pp. 556–565 and 551). In all likelihood, your working bibliography will contain more sources than you actually consult and include in your list of works cited.

One method for creating a working bibliography is to make a separate bibliography card, using a 3- by 5-inch index card, for each work that you think might be helpful to your research. As your collection of cards grows, alphabetize them by the authors' last names. By using a separate card for each book, article, or Web site, you can continually edit your working bibliography, dropping sources that did not prove helpful for one reason or another and adding new ones.

With the computerization of most library resources, you now have the option to copy and paste bibliographic information from the library computer catalog and periodical indexes or from the Internet into a document on your computer that you can edit/add/delete/search throughout the research process. Or you can track your project online with the Bedford Bibliographer at bedfordstmartins.com/bibliographer. The advantage of the copy/paste option over the index card method is accuracy, especially in punctuation, spelling, and capitalization—details that are essential in accessing Internet sites.

Checklist for a Working Bibliography

FOR BOOKS

- Library call number
- Names of all authors, editors, and translators
- Title and subtitle
- Publication data:
    Place of publication (city and state)
    Publisher's name
    Date of publication
- Edition (if not first) and volume number (if applicable)

FOR PERIODICAL ARTICLES

- Names of all authors
- Name and subtitle of article
- Title of journal, magazine, or newspaper

- Publication data:
    Volume number and issue number
    Date of issue
    Page numbers

FOR INTERNET SOURCES

- Names of all authors, editors, compilers, or sponsoring agents
- Title and subtitle of the document
- Title of the longer work to which the document belongs (if applicable)
- Title of the site or discussion list
- Author, editor, or compiler of the Web site or online database
- Name of company or organization that owns the Web site
- Date of release, online posting, or latest revision
- Name and vendor of database or name of online service or network
- Medium (online, CD-ROM, etc.)
- Format of online source (Web page, .pdf, podcast)
- Date you accessed the site
- Electronic address (URL)

FOR OTHER SOURCES

- Name of author, government agency, organization, company, recording artist, personality, etc.
- Title of the work
- Format (pamphlet, unpublished diary, interview, television broadcast, etc.)
- Publication or production data:
    Name of publisher or producer
    Date of publication, production, or release
    Identifying codes or numbers (if applicable)

TAKE NOTES

As you read, take notes. You're looking for ideas, facts, opinions, statistics, examples, and other evidence that you think will be useful as you write your paper. As you read through books and articles, look for recurring themes, and notice where writers are in agreement and where they differ. Try to remember that the effectiveness of your paper is largely determined by the quality—not necessarily the quantity—of your notes. Your purpose is not to present a collection of quotes that show that you've read all the material and know what others have said about your topic.

Your goal is to analyze, evaluate, and synthesize the information you collect—in other words, to enter into the discussion of the issues and thereby take ownership of your topic. You want to view the results of your research from your own perspective and arrive at an informed opinion of your topic. (For more information on writing with sources, see Chapter 3.)

Now for some practical advice on taking notes. First, be systematic in your note-taking. As a rule, write one note on a card, and include the author's full name, the complete title of the source, and a page number indicating the origin of the note. Use cards of uniform size, preferably 4- by 6-inch index cards because they are large enough to accommodate even a long note on a single card and yet small enough to be easily handled and conveniently carried. If you keep notes electronically, consider creating a separate file for each topic or source, or using an electronic research manager like Zotero (zotero.org) or OneNote. If you keep your notes organized, when you get to the planning and writing stage, you will be able to sequence them according to the plan you have envisioned for your paper. Furthermore, should you decide to alter your organizational plan, you can easily reorder your notes—whether on cards or in digital files—to reflect those revisions.

Second, try not to take too many notes. One good way to control your note-taking is to ask yourself, "How exactly does this material help prove or disprove my thesis?" Try to envision where in your paper you will use the information. If it does not seem relevant to your thesis, don't bother to take a note.

Once you decide to take a note, you must decide whether to summarize, paraphrase, or quote directly. The approach you take should be determined by the content of the passage and the way you plan to use it in your paper. For detailed advice on summaries, paraphrases, and quotations, see Chapter 3, pages 46–57.

DOCUMENT YOUR SOURCES

Whenever you summarize, paraphrase, or quote a person's thoughts and ideas and whenever you use facts or statistics that are not commonly known or believed, you must properly acknowledge the source of your information. If you do not properly acknowledge ideas and information created by someone else, you are guilty of *plagiarism,* or using someone else's material but making it look as if it were your own. (For more information on plagiarism and how to avoid it, see pages 53–57.) You must document the source of your information whenever you do the following:

- Quote a source word for word
- Refer to information and ideas from another source that you present in your own words as either a paraphrase or a summary
- Cite statistics, table, charts, graphs, or other visuals

You do not need to document these types of information:

- Your own observations, experiences, and ideas
- Factual information available in a number of reference works (information known as "common knowledge")
- Proverbs, sayings, and familiar quotations

A reference to the source of your borrowed information is called a *citation*. There are many systems for making citations, and your citations must consistently follow one of these systems. The documentation style recommended by the Modern Language Association (MLA) is commonly used in English and the humanities and is the style used throughout this book. Another common system is the American Psychological Association (APA) style, which is generally used in the social sciences. Your instructor will probably tell you which style to use. For more information on documentation styles, consult the appropriate manual or handbook, or go to Diana Hacker's Research and Documentation Online at bedfordstmartins .com/resdoc.

There are two components of documentation. *In-text citations* are placed in the body of your paper, and the *list of works cited* provides complete publication data for your in-text citations and is placed on a separate page at the end of your paper. Both of these components are necessary for complete documentation.

In-Text Citations

In-text citations, also known as *parenthetical citations*, give the reader citation information immediately, at the point at which it is most meaningful. Rather than having to find a footnote or an endnote, the reader sees the citation as a part of the writer's text.

Most in-text citations consist of only the author's last name and a page reference. Usually the author's name is given in an introductory signal phrase at the beginning of the borrowed material, and the page reference is given in parentheses at the end. If the author's name is not given at the beginning, put it in parentheses along with the page reference. When you borrow material from two or more works by the same author, you must include the title of the work in the signal phrase or parenthetically at the end. (For examples of signal phrases and in-text citations, see pages 50–53.) The parenthetical reference signals the end of the borrowed material and directs your readers to the list of works cited should they want to pursue a particular source. Treat electronic sources as you do print sources, keeping in mind that some electronic sources use paragraph numbers instead of page numbers. Consider the following examples of in-text citations, taken from student Richard Carbeau's paper on the debate over whether or not to make English America's official language.

Many people are surprised to discover that English is not the official language of the United States. Today, even as English literacy becomes a necessity for people in many parts of the world, some people in the United States believe its primacy is being threatened right at home. Much of the current controversy focuses on Hispanic communities with large Spanish-speaking populations who may feel little or no pressure to learn English. Columnist and cultural critic Charles Krauthammer believes English should be America's official language. He notes that this country has been "blessed . . . with a linguistic unity that brings a critically needed cohesion to a nation as diverse, multiracial and multiethnic as America" and that communities such as these threaten the bond created by a common language (112). There are others, however, who think that "Language does not threaten American unity. Benign neglect is a good policy for any country when it comes to language, and it's a good policy for America" (King 64).

Citation with author's name in the signal phrase

Citation with author's name in parentheses

Works Cited

King, Robert D. "Should English Be the Law?" *The Atlantic Monthly* Apr.
    1997: 55-64. Print.
Krauthammer, Charles. "In Plain English: Let's Make It Official." *Time* 12
    June 2006: 112. Print.

In the preceding example, the student followed MLA style guidelines for his Works Cited list. When constructing the list of works cited page for your paper, consult the following MLA guidelines, based on the *MLA Handbook for Writers of Research Papers*, seventh edition (2009), where you will find model entries for periodical print publications, nonperiodical print publications, web publications, and other common sources.

List of Works Cited

In this section, you will find general MLA guidelines for creating a works cited list followed by sample entries that cover the citation situations you are most likely to encounter. Make sure that you follow the formats as they appear on the following pages. If you would like to compile your list of works cited online, try the Bedford Bibliographer at bedfordstmartins.com/bibliographer.

GUIDELINES FOR CONSTRUCTING YOUR WORKS CITED PAGE

1. Begin the list on a fresh page following the last page of text.
2. Center the title *Works Cited* at the top of the page.
3. Double-space both within and between entries on your list.
4. Alphabetize your sources by the authors' last names. If you have two or more authors with the same last name, alphabetize first by last names and then by first names.
5. If you have two or more works by the same author, alphabetize by the first word of the titles, not counting *A*, *An*, or *The*. Use the author's name in the first entry and three unspaced hyphens followed by a period in subsequent entries:

   > Twitchell, James B. *Branded Nation: When Culture Goes Pop*. New York: Simon, 2004. Print.
   >
   > ---. "The Branding of Higher Ed." *Forbes* 25 Nov. 2002: 50. Print.
   >
   > ---. *Living It Up: America's Love Affair with Luxury*. New York: Columbia UP, 2002. Print.

6. If no author is known, alphabetize by title.
7. Begin each entry at the left margin. If the entry is longer than one line, indent the second and subsequent lines five spaces or one-half inch.
8. Italicize the titles of books, journals, magazines, and newspapers. Use quotation marks with titles of periodical articles, chapters and essays within books, short stories, and poems.
9. Provide the medium of the source (i.e., Print, Web, Film, Television, Performance).

Periodical Print Publications: Journals, Magazines, and Newspapers

STANDARD INFORMATION FOR PERIODICAL PRINT PUBLICATIONS

1. Name of the author of the work; for anonymous works, begin entry with title of work
2. Title of the work, in quotation marks
3. Name of the periodical, italicized
4. Series number or name, if relevant
5. Volume number (for scholarly journals that use volume numbers)
6. Issue number (if available, for scholarly journals)

7. Date of publication (for scholarly journals, year; for other periodicals, day, month, and year, as available)

8. Page numbers

9. Medium of publication (for print sources, use *Print*)

ARTICLE IN A SCHOLARLY JOURNAL

For all scholarly journals—whether they paginate continuously throughout a given year or not—provide the volume and issue numbers (if both are given) separated by a period, the year, the page numbers, and the medium.

> Gazzaniga, Michael S. "Right Hemisphere Language Following Brain Bisection: A Twenty-Year Perspective." *American Psychologist* 38.5 (1983): 528-49. Print.

If the journal does not use volume numbers, cite the issue number alone.

> Harpham, Geoffrey Galt. "Roots, Races, and the Return to Philology." *Representations* 106 (2009): 34-62. Print.

ARTICLE IN A MAGAZINE

When citing a weekly or biweekly magazine, give the complete date (day, month, year).

> Begley, Sharon. "What's in a Word?" *Newsweek* 20 July 2009: 31. Print.

When citing a magazine published every month or every two months, provide the month or months and year.

> Bernstein, Charles. "Sounding the Word." *Harper's Magazine* Mar. 2011: 15-18. Print.

If an article in a magazine is not printed on consecutive pages—for example, an article might begin on page 45, then skip to 48—include only the first page followed by a plus sign.

ARTICLE IN DAILY OR WEEKLY NEWSPAPER

> Carney, Heather. "Unlocking English." *Naples Daily News* 18 Dec. 2011, final ed.: A1+. Print.

> Evelyn, Jamilah. "The 'Silent Killer' of Minority Enrollments." *Chronicle of Higher Education* 20 June 2003: A17-18. Print.

REVIEW (BOOK/FILM)

> Morozov, Evgeny. "Sharing It All." Rev. of *I Know Who You Are and I Saw What You Did: Social Networks and the Death of Privacy,* by Lori Andrews. *New York Times Book Review* 29 Jan. 2012: 18. Print.

> Dargis, Manohla. "The King's English, Albeit with Twisted Tongue." Rev. of *The King's Speech,* dir. Mike Leigh. *New York Times* 25 Nov. 2010, nat. ed.: AR18. Print.

If the review has no title, simply begin with *Rev.* after the author's name. If there is neither title nor author, begin with *Rev.* and alphabetize by the title of the book or film being reviewed.

ANONYMOUS ARTICLE

When no author's name is given, begin the entry with the title.

"Pompeii: Will the City Go from Dust to Dust?" *Newsweek* 1 Sept. 1997: 8. Print.

EDITORIAL (SIGNED/UNSIGNED)

Jackson, Derrick Z. "The Winner: Hypocrisy." Editorial. *Boston Globe* 6 Feb. 2004: A19. Print.

"Beginning of the End." Editorial. *New York Times* 19 Feb. 2012, national ed.: SR10. Print.

LETTER TO THE EDITOR

Lakind, Alexandra. "Constructive Criticism." Letter. *New Yorker* 13 & 20 Feb. 2012: 8. Print.

Nonperiodical Print Publications: Books, Brochures, and Pamphlets

BOOK BY A SINGLE AUTHOR

Metcalf, Allan. *OK: The Improbable Story of America's Greatest Word*. New York: Oxford UP, 2011. Print.

Use a shortened version of the publisher's name—for example, *Houghton* for Houghton Mifflin, or *Cambridge UP* for Cambridge University Press.

ANTHOLOGY

Eggers, Dave, ed. *The Best American Nonrequired Reading, 2002*. New York: Houghton, 2002. Print.

BOOK BY TWO OR MORE AUTHORS

For a book by two or three authors, list the authors in the order in which they appear on the title page.

Perry, Theresa, and Lisa Delpit. *The Real Ebonics Debate*. Ypsilanti, MI: Beacon, 1998. Print.

For a book by four or more authors, list the first author in the same way as for a single-author book, followed by a comma and the abbreviation *et al.* ("and others").

Chomsky, Noam, et al. *Acts of Aggression*. New York: Seven Stories, 1999. Print.

BOOK BY A CORPORATE AUTHOR

Carnegie Foundation for the Advancement of Teaching. *Campus Life: In Search of Community*. Princeton, NJ: Princeton UP, 1990. Print.

WORK IN AN ANTHOLOGY

Smith, Seaton. "'Jiving' with Your Teen." *The Best American Nonrequired Reading, 2002*. Ed. Dave Eggers. New York: Houghton, 2002. 217-20. Print.

ARTICLE IN A REFERENCE BOOK

Baugh, John. "Dialect." *The World Book Encyclopedia*. 2009 ed. Print.

If an article is unsigned, begin with the title.

"Dictionary of the English Language." *Benet's Reader's Encyclopedia*. 5th ed. 2008. Print.

INTRODUCTION, PREFACE, FOREWORD, OR AFTERWORD TO A BOOK

McCourt, Frank. Foreword. *Eats, Shoots & Leaves: The Zero Tolerance Approach to Punctuation*. By Lynne Truss. New York: Gotham Books, 2004. xi-xiv. Print.

TRANSLATION

Chaucer, Geoffrey. *The Canterbury Tales: A Complete Translation into Modern English*. Trans. Ronald L. Ecker and Eugene J. Crook. Palatka, FL: Hodge & Braddock, 1993. Print.

CHAPTER OR SECTION IN A BOOK

Lamott, Anne. "Shitty First Drafts." *Bird by Bird: Some Instructions on Writing and Life*. New York: Pantheon, 1994. 21-27. Print.

BOOK PUBLISHED IN A SECOND OR SUBSEQUENT EDITION

Aitchison, Jean. *Language Change: Process or Decay?* 2nd ed. Cambridge: Cambridge UP, 1991. Print.

Modern Language Association of America. *MLA Handbook for Writers of Research Papers*. 7th ed. New York: MLA, 2009. Print.

BROCHURE/PAMPHLET

Harry S. Truman Library and Museum. *Museum Guide*. Independence, MO: Truman Library, 2008. Print.

GOVERNMENT PUBLICATION

United States. Dept. of Justice. *Hate Crime Statistics, 1990: A Resource Book*. Washington: GPO. 1991. Print.

Give the government, the agency, and the title with a period and a space after each. The publisher is the Government Printing Office (GPO).

Web Publications

The following guidelines and models for citing information retrieved from the World Wide Web have been adapted from the most recent advice of the MLA, as detailed in the *MLA Handbook for Writers of Research Papers*, 7th ed. (2009), and from the "MLA Style" section on the MLA's Web site (mla.org). You will quickly notice that citations of Web publications have some common features with both print publications and reprinted works, broadcasts, and live performances. Standard information for all citations of online materials includes:

1. Name of the author, editor, or compiler of the work. The guidelines for print sources for works with more than one author, a corporate author, or unnamed author apply. For anonymous works, begin your entry with the title of the work.
2. Title of the work. Italicize the title, unless it is part of a larger work. Titles that are part of a larger work should be presented within quotation marks.
3. Title of the overall Web site in italics if this is distinct from item 2 above.
4. Version or edition of the site, if relevant.
5. Publisher or sponsor of the site. This information is often found at the bottom of the Web page. If this information is not available, use *N.p.* (for *no publisher*).
6. Date of publication (day, month, and year, if available). If no date is given, use *n.d.*
7. Medium of publication. For online sources, the medium is *Web*.
8. Date of access (day, month, and year).

MLA does not require you to include URLs in works cited entries. However, if your instructor wants you to include URLs in your citations or if you believe readers will not be able to locate the source without the URL, insert the URL as the last item in an entry, immediately after the date of access. Enclose the URL in angle brackets, followed by a period. The following example illustrates an entry with the URL included:

> Finley, Laura L. "How Can I Teach Peace When the Book Only Covers War?" *The Online Journal of Peace and Conflict Resolution* 5.1 (2003): n. pag. Web. 12 Feb. 2012. <http://www.trinstitute.org/ojpcr/5_1finley.htm>.

MLA style requires that you break URLs extending over more than one line only after a slash. Do *not* add spaces, hyphens, or any other punctuation to indicate the break.

ONLINE SCHOLARLY JOURNALS. To cite an article, review, editorial, or letter to the editor in a scholarly journal existing only in electronic form on the Web, provide the author, the title of the article, the title of the journal, the volume and issue, and the date of issue, followed by the page numbers (if available), the medium, and the date of access.

ARTICLE IN AN ONLINE SCHOLARLY JOURNAL

Donner, Jonathan. "The Rules of Beeping: Exchanging Messages Via Intentional 'Missed Calls' on Mobile Phones." *Journal of Computer-Mediated Communication* 7.1 (2007): n. pag. Web. 28 Feb. 2012.

BOOK REVIEW IN ONLINE SCHOLARLY JOURNAL

Opongo, Elias Omondi. Rev. of *Responsibility to Protect: The Global Effort to End Mass Atrocities*, by Alex J. Bellamy. *Journal of Peace, Conflict, and Development* 14.14 (2009): n. pag. Web. 7 Mar. 2011.

EDITORIAL IN ONLINE SCHOLARLY JOURNAL

"Writing Across the Curriculum and Writing Centers." Editorial. *Praxis: A Writing Center Journal* 6.2 (2009): n. pag. Web. 10 Jan. 2011.

PERIODICAL PUBLICATIONS IN ONLINE DATABASES. Here are some model entries for periodical publications collected in online databases.

JOURNAL ARTICLE FROM AN ONLINE DATABASE OR SUBSCRIPTION SERVICE

Johnstone, Barbara, and Dan Baumgardt. "'Pittsburghese' Online: Vernacular Norming in Conversation." *American Speech* 79.2 (2004): 115-45. *Project Muse*. Web. 29 Feb. 2012

McEachern, William Ross. "Teaching and Learning in Bilingual Countries: The Examples of Belgium and Canada." *Education* 123. 1 (2002): 103. *Expanded Academic ASAP Plus*. Web. 17 Mar. 2011.

MAGAZINE ARTICLE FROM AN ONLINE DATABASE OR SUBSCRIPTION SERVICE

Keizer, Garret. "Sound and Fury: The Politics of Noise in a Loud Society." *Harper's Magazine*. Mar. 2001: 39-48. *Expanded Academic ASAP Plus*. Web. 27 Mar. 2011.

NEWSPAPER ARTICLE FROM AN ONLINE DATABASE OR SUBSCRIPTION SERVICE

Sanders, Joshunda. "Think Race Doesn't Matter? Listen to Eminem." *San Francisco Chronicle* 20 July 2003. *LexisNexis*. Web. 18 Mar. 2011.

NONPERIODICAL WEB PUBLICATIONS. Nonperiodical Web publications includes all Web-delivered content that does not fit into one of the previous two categories—scholarly journal Web publications and periodical publication in an online database or subscription service.

ARTICLE IN AN ONLINE MAGAZINE

Green, Joshua. "The Elusive Green Economy." *The Atlantic.com*. Atlantic Monthly Group, July-Aug. 2009. Web. 3 Mar. 2012.

Grossman, Samantha. "British School Bans Students from Using Slang and 'Text Speak.'" *Time.com*. Time, 15 Feb. 2012. Web. 10 Mar. 2012.

Hitchings, Henry. "What's the Language of the Future?" *Salon.com*. 6 Nov. 2011. Web. 23 Feb. 2012.

ARTICLE IN AN ONLINE NEWSPAPER

Peach, Gary. "Latvians Reject Russian as an Official National Language." *Seattletimes .com*. Seattle Times, 18 Feb. 2012. Web. 22 Feb. 2012.

"Immigration and the Campaign." Editorial. *New York Times*. New York Times, 20 Feb. 2012. Web. 7 Mar. 2012.

ARTICLE IN ONLINE SCHOLARLY PROJECT

Driscoll, Dana Lynn. "Irregular Verbs." Chart. *The OWL at Purdue*. Purdue U Online Writing Lab, 13 May 2007. Web. 8 Mar. 2011.

BOOK OR PART OF A BOOK ACCESSED ONLINE

For a book available online, provide the author, the title, the editor (if any), original publication information, the name of the database or Web site, the medium (*Web*), and the date of access.

Sapir, Edward. *Language: An Introduction to the Study of Speech*. New York: Harcourt, 1921. *Bartleby.com: Great Books Online*. Web. 1 Mar. 2012.

If you are citing only part of an online book, include the title or name of the part directly after the author's name.

Johnson, Samuel, and John Walker. "Sounds of the Vowels." *Dictionary of the English Language*. London: Pickering, 1828. *Google Book Search*. Web. 15 Jan. 2012.

SPEECH, ESSAY, POEM, OR SHORT STORY FROM ONLINE SITE

Faulkner, William. "On Accepting the Nobel Prize." 10 Dec. 1950. *The History Place: Great Speeches Collection*. Web. 12 Mar. 2011.

ARTICLES AND STORIES FROM ONLINE NEWS SERVICES

Pressman, Gabe. "Eminent Domain: Let the Public Beware!" *NBCNewYork.com*. NBC New York, 5 Dec. 2009. Web. 6 Mar. 2012.

"Americans Urged to Live MLK's Ideals at Memorial Dedication." *CNN.com*. Cable News Network, 17 Oct. 2011. Web. 18 Mar. 2012.

ARTICLE IN ONLINE ENCYCLOPEDIA OR OTHER REFERENCE WORK

"Etymology." *Encyclopaedia Britannica Online*. Encyclopaedia Britannica, 2012. Web. 13 Mar. 2012.

"Semantics." *Merriam-Webster Online Dictionary*. Merriam-Webster. 2012. Web. 23 Mar. 2012.

ONLINE CHARTS, MAPS, ARTWORK, PHOTOGRAPHS, AND OTHER IMAGES

Ager, Simon. "Braille: Basic Letters." Chart. *Omniglot.com*. 12 Jan. 2007. Web.
29 Feb. 2012.

da Vinci, Leonardo. *Mona Lisa*. 1503-06. Musee du Louvre, Paris. *WebMuseum*, 19
June 2006. Web. 22 Mar. 2011.

Short, Daniel M. "World Distribution of Indo-European Languages." Map. *Danshort
.com*. 25 Sept. 2008. Web. 5 Mar. 2012.

ONLINE GOVERNMENT PUBLICATION

United States. Dept. of Justice. Federal Bureau of Investigation. *Hate Crime
Statistics, 2010*. Nov. 2011. Web. 2 Apr. 2012.

HOME PAGE FOR ACADEMIC DEPARTMENT

Dept. of English. Home page. Arizona State U, n.d. Web. 29 Mar. 2012.

WIKI ENTRY

"Sign Language." *Wikipedia*. Wikimedia Foundation. 17 Feb. 2012. Web. 4 Mar. 2012.

No author is listed for a Wiki entry because the content is written
collaboratively.

POSTING ON A BLOG

Broadway Bob. "Defining Home." *babblebob*. By Robert M. Armstrong, 24 Aug. 2009.
Web. 10 Feb. 2012.

VIDEO RECORDING POSTED ONLINE

Jeanroustan. "Alyssa Talking Backwards." *YouTube*. YouTube, 30 Jan. 2012. Web. 29
Feb. 2012.

Additional Common Sources

TELEVISION OR RADIO BROADCAST

"Everyone's Waiting." *Six Feet Under*. Dir. Alan Ball. Perf. Peter Krause, Michael C.
Hall, Frances Conroy, and Lauren Ambrose. Writ. Alan Ball. HBO. 21 Aug. 2005.
Television.

SOUND RECORDING

Muri, John T., and Ravin I. McDavid Jr. *American's Speaking*. NCTE, 1967. LP Record.

Shakespeare, William. *Macbeth*. Ed. A. R. Branmuller. New York: Voyager, 1994. CD.

FILM OR VIDEO RECORDING

The Gods Must Be Crazy, I & II. Dir. Jamie Uys. Perf. N!xau, Marius Weyers, Sandra
Prinsloo. 1990. Sony. 2004. DVD.

INTERVIEW

Handke, Peter. Interview. *New York Times Magazine* 2 July 2006: 13. Print.

For interviews that you conduct, provide the name of the person interviewed, the type of interview (personal, telephone, e-mail), and the date.

Clark, Virginia P. Telephone interview. 30 Jan. 2012.

CARTOON OR COMIC STRIP

Luckovich, Mike. Cartoon. *Atlanta Journal-Constitution* 24 Nov. 2009. Print.

ADVERTISEMENT

Rosetta Stone. Advertisement. *Smithsonian* Mar. 2012: 42. Print.

LECTURE, SPEECH, ADDRESS, READING

England, Paula. "Gender and Inequality: Trends and Causes." President's Distinguished Lecture Series. U. of Vermont. Memorial Lounge, Burlington. 12 Mar. 2012. Lecture.

LETTER, MEMO, OR E-MAIL MESSAGE

Britto, Marah. Letter to the author. 22 Jan. 2012. MS.

Macomber, Sarah. "New Online Language Options." Message to the author. 10 Feb. 2012. E-mail.

Indicate the medium using MS (handwritten manuscript), TS (typescript), or E-mail.

DIGITAL FILE

A number of different types of work can come to you as a digital file—a book, typescript, photograph, or sound recording. It is important that you record the format of the digital file in the space reserved for medium of publication (JPEG file, PDF file, Microsoft Word file, MP3 file).

Dengle, Isabella. *Eben Peck Cabin*. ca. 1891. Wisconsin Historical Society, Madison. JPEG file.

Federman, Sarah. "The Language of Conflict: Seeking Resolution." 2012. Microsoft Word file.

MLA MANUSCRIPT FORMAT

The following guidelines for formatting manuscripts have been adapted from Modern Language Association recommendations.

Paper and Type

For academic papers use 8½- by 11-inch, twenty-pound white paper, and print in black on one side of each sheet. Use a standard type style such as New Times Roman or Courier. Use a paper clip (do not staple) to secure the pages unless instructed otherwise. Finally, be sure you keep both a paper copy and an electronic copy of your paper.

Title, Name, and Course Information

Beginning at the left margin one inch from the top of the first page, type your name, your instructor's name, the name and number of the course, and the date on separate lines, double-spaced. Double-space again, and center your title. Double-space between your title and the first sentence of your paper. For example, see page 39.

Margins, Line Spacing, and Paragraph Indentation

Leave a one-inch margin on all sides of the page. Double-space the text of the paper including long, set-off quotations, information notes, and the entries on the Works Cited page. Do not justify (make even) the right-hand margin. Indent the first line of each paragraph one-half inch (or five spaces).

Page Numbers

Place your last name and the page number (e.g., DeAngelus 1) in the upper right corner of each page, approximately one-half inch from the top and one inch from the right edge of the page. Do not use the word *page* or its abbreviation *p;* do not use a period or any other mark of punctuation with your name and page number. Number all pages of your paper, including the first and last. For example, see pages 39–42.

Long Quotations

Set off prose quotations that are longer than four lines to help your reader more clearly see the quotation as a whole. Poetry quotations are set off when longer than three lines. Set-off quotations are indented ten spaces from the left margin and are double-spaced; no quotation marks are necessary because the format itself indicates that the passage is a quotation. When you are quoting two or more paragraphs from the same source, indent the first line of each paragraph three additional spaces. Note that, unlike an integrated quotation in which the parenthetical citation is inside the end punctuation, with a long, set-off quotation the parenthetical citation is placed outside the final punctuation. For example, see pages 60–61.

Spacing for Punctuation

Leave one space after a comma, colon, or semicolon and between the three periods in an ellipsis. MLA recommends one space after a period, question mark, or exclamation point at the end of a sentence. Form dashes by using two hyphens with no space between them. Do not leave a space before or after a dash. Most word processors will convert your two hyphens into a dash, as seen in the sample student paper on pages 58–63.

Web Addresses

Should you have occasion to divide a Web address at the end of a line in the text of your paper, MLA recommends that you break only after a slash. Never insert a hyphen to mark the break.

Works Cited Page

The list of works cited is placed on a separate page at the end of your paper and titled *Works Cited*. Place your last name and page number in the upper right-hand corner, one-half inch from the top and one inch from the right edge of the page. Double space and then center the words *Works Cited*. For a model works cited page from a student paper, see page 63. For the specific requirements of the format of each entry in the list of works cited, refer to the model entries on pages 556–565.

To assemble a works cited list for your paper, follow the guidelines given on page 549.

GLOSSARY OF RHETORICAL AND LINGUISTIC TERMS

Abstract   See *Concrete/Abstract*.

Accent   Characteristics of pronunciation that reflect regional or social identity.

Acronym   A word made from the initial letters (in some cases, the first few letters) of a phrase or organization; for example, NATO (North Atlantic Treaty Organization) and scuba (self-contained underwater breathing apparatus).

Allusion   A passing reference to a familiar person, place, or thing drawn from history, the Bible, mythology, or literature. An allusion is an economical way for a writer to capture the essence of an idea, atmosphere, emotion, or historical era, as in "The scandal was his Watergate," "He saw himself as a modern Job," or "Everyone there held those truths to be self-evident."

American Sign Language (ASL, Ameslan)   A system of communication used by deaf people in the United States, consisting of hand symbols that vary in the shape of the hands, the direction of their movement, and their position in relation to the body. It is different from finger spelling, in which words are signed in the order in which they are uttered, thus preserving English structure and syntax.

Analogy   A special form of comparison in which the writer explains something complex or unfamiliar by comparing it to something familiar: "A transmission line is simply a pipeline for electricity. In the case of a water pipeline, more water will flow through the pipe as water pressure increases. The same is true of a transmission line for electricity." When a subject is unobservable or abstract, or when readers may have trouble understanding it, analogy is particularly useful.

Argument   A strategy for developing an essay. To argue is to attempt to convince a reader to agree with a point of view, to make a given decision, or to pursue a particular course of action. Logical argument is based on reasonable explanations and appeals to the reader's intelligence. See also *Persuasion, Logical Fallacies, Deduction,* and *Induction.*

Attitude   A writer's opinion of a subject, which may be very positive, very negative, or somewhere between these two extremes. See also *Tone.*

Audience   The intended readership for a piece of writing. For example, the readers of a national weekly newsmagazine come from all walks of life and have diverse opinions, attitudes, and educational experiences. In contrast, the readership for an organic chemistry journal may be comprised of people with similar scientific interests and educational backgrounds. The essays in this book are intended for general readers, intelligent people who may lack specific information about the subjects being discussed.

Beginnings and Endings   A *beginning* is the sentence, group of sentences, or section that introduces an essay. Good beginnings usually identify the thesis or main idea, attempt to interest the reader, and establish a tone. Some effective ways to begin essays include (1) telling an anecdote that illustrates the thesis, (2) providing a controversial statement or opinion that engages the reader's interest, (3) presenting startling statistics or facts, (4) defining a term that is central to the discussion that follows, (5) asking thought-provoking questions, (6) providing a quotation that illustrates the thesis, (7) referring to a current event that helps to establish the thesis, or (8) showing the significance of the subject or stressing its importance to the reader.

An *ending* is the sentence or group of sentences that brings an essay to closure. Good endings are well planned; they are the natural outgrowths of the essays themselves and give readers a sense of finality or completion. Some of the techniques mentioned above for beginnings may be effective for endings as well.

Biased Language   Language that is used by a dominant group within a culture to maintain its supposed superior position and to disempower others. See also *Racist Language* and *Sexist Language*.

Bidialectalism   The use of two dialects of the same language.

Bilingual Education   Teaching in a child's primary language, which may or may not be the language of the dominant population.

Black English   A vernacular variety of English used by some black people; it may be divided into Standard Black English and Black English Vernacular (BEV). See also *Ebonics*.

Brainstorming   A discovery technique in which writers list everything they know about a topic, freely associating one idea with another. When writers brainstorm, they also make lists of questions about aspects of the topic for which they need information. See also *Clustering* and *Freewriting*.

Cause and Effect Analysis   A strategy for developing an essay. Cause and effect analysis answers the question *why*. It explains the reasons for an occurrence or the consequences of an action. Whenever a question asks *why*, answering it will require discovering a *cause* or series of causes for a particular *effect*; whenever a question asks *what if*, its answer will point out the effect or effects that can result from a particular cause.

Classification   See *Division and Classification*.

Cliché   An expression that has become ineffective through overuse, such as *quick as a flash, dry as dust, jump for joy*, and *slow as molasses*. Writers normally avoid such trite expressions and seek instead to express themselves in fresh and forceful language. See also *Figures of Speech*.

Clustering   A discovery technique in which a writer puts a topic or keyword in a circle at the center of a blank page and then generates main ideas about that topic, circling each idea and connecting it with a line to the topic in the center. Writers often repeat the process in order to add specific examples and details to each main idea. This technique allows writers to generate material and sort it into meaningful clusters at the same time. See also *Brainstorming* and *Freewriting*.

Coherence   A quality of good writing that results when all of the sentences, paragraphs, and longer divisions of an essay are naturally connected. Coherent writing is achieved through (1) a logical sequence of ideas (arranged in chronological order, spatial order, order of importance, or some other appropriate order), (2) the thoughtful repetition of keywords and ideas, (3) a pace suitable for your topic and your reader, and (4) the use of transitional words and expressions. Coherence should not be confused with unity. See also *Unity* and *Transitions.*

Colloquial Expressions   Informal expressions that are typical of a particular language. In English, phrases such as *come up with, be at loose ends,* or *get with the program* are colloquial expressions. Such expressions are acceptable in formal writing only if they are used for a specific purpose.

Comparison and Contrast   A strategy for developing an essay. In comparison and contrast, the writer points out the similarities and differences between two or more subjects in the same class or category. The function of any comparison and contrast is to clarify — to reach some conclusion about the items being compared and contrasted. An effective comparison and contrast does not dwell on obvious similarities or differences; instead, it tells readers something significant that they may not already know.

Conclusions   See *Beginnings and Endings.*

Concrete/Abstract   A *concrete word* names a specific object, person, place, or action that can be directly perceived by the senses: *car, bread, building, book, John F. Kennedy, Chicago,* or *hiking.* An *abstract word,* in contrast, refers to general qualities, conditions, ideas, actions, or relationships that cannot be directly perceived by the senses: *bravery, dedication, excellence, anxiety, friendship, thinking,* or *hatred.*

    Although writers must use both concrete and abstract language, good writers avoid using too many abstract words. Instead, they rely on concrete words to define and illustrate abstractions. Because concrete words appeal to the senses, they are easily comprehended by a reader.

Connotation/Denotation   Both terms refer to the meanings of words. *Denotation* is the dictionary meaning of a word, its literal meaning. *Connotation,* on the other hand, is a word's implied or suggested meaning. For example, the denotation of *lamb* is a "a young sheep." The connotations of lamb are numerous: *gentle, docile, weak, peaceful, blessed, sacrificial, blood, spring, frisky, pure, innocent,* and so on. Good writers are sensitive to both the denotations and the connotations of words and use these meanings to advantage in their writing.

Deduction   The process of reasoning that moves from stated premises to a conclusion that follows necessarily. This form of reasoning moves from the general to the specific. See also *Induction* and *Syllogism.*

Definition   A strategy for developing an essay. A definition, which states the meaning of a word, may be either brief or extended; it may be part of an essay or an entire essay itself.

Denotation   See *Connotation/Denotation.*

Description   A strategy for developing an essay. Description tells how a person, place, or thing is perceived by the five senses. Objective description reports these sensory qualities factually, whereas subjective description gives the writer's interpretation of them.

Descriptivism   A school of linguistic analysis that seeks to describe linguistic facts as they are. See also *Prescriptivism.*

Dialect   A variety of language, usually regional or social, that is set off from other varieties of the same language by differences in pronunciation, vocabulary, and grammar.

Diction   A writer's choice and use of words. Good diction is precise and appropriate — the words mean exactly what the writer intends, and the words are well suited to the writer's subject, intended audience, and purpose. The word-conscious writer knows, for example, that there are differences among *aged, old,* and *elderly; blue, navy,* and *azure;* and *disturbed, angry,* and *irritated.* Furthermore, this writer knows when to use each word. See also *Connotation/ Denotation.*

Direct Quotation   A writer's use of the exact words of a source. Direct quotations, which are put in quotation marks, are normally reserved for important ideas stated memorably, for especially clear explanations by authorities, and for proponents' arguments conveyed in their own words. See also *Paraphrase, Summary,* and *Plagiarism.*

Division and Classification   A strategy for developing an essay. *Division* involves breaking down a single large unit into smaller subunits, or separating a group of items into discrete categories. *Classification,* on the other hand, involves arranging or sorting people, places, or things into categories according to their differing characteristics, thus making them more manageable for the writer and more understandable for the reader. Division, then, takes apart, while classification groups together. Although the two processes can operate separately, most often they work hand in hand.

Doublespeak   According to doublespeak expert William Lutz, "Doublespeak is a blanket term for language which pretends to communicate but doesn't, language which makes the bad seem good, the negative appear positive, the unpleasant attractive, or at least tolerable. It is language which avoids, shifts, or denies responsibility."

Ebonics   A term coined in 1973 for African American Vernacular English (AAVE). Public debate centers on whether it is a dialect of English or a separate language with its own grammatical rules and rhythms. See also *Black English.*

Endings   See *Beginnings and Endings.*

English-Only Movement   The ongoing attempts, which began in the Senate in 1986, to declare English the official language of the United States. Although these attempts have failed thus far at the federal level, a number of states have passed various forms of English-only legislation.

Essay   A relatively short piece of nonfiction in which the writer attempts to make one or more closely related points. A good essay is purposeful, informative, and well organized.

Ethnocentricity   The belief that one's culture (including language) is at the center of things and that other cultures (and languages) are inferior.

Euphemism   A pleasing, vague, or indirect word or phrase that is substituted for one that is considered harsh or offensive. For example, *pacify* is a euphemism for *bomb, pavement deficiency* for *pothole, downsize* or *release from employment* for *fire.*

Evidence   The data on which a judgment or argument is based or by which proof or probability is established. Evidence usually takes the form of statistics, facts, names, examples or illustrations, and opinions of authorities.

Examples   Ways of illustrating, developing, or clarifying an idea. Examples enable writers to show and not simply to tell readers what they mean. The terms *example* and *illustration* are sometimes used interchangeably. An example may be anything from a statistic to a story; it may be stated in a few words or go on for several pages. An example should always be *relevant* to the idea or generalization it is meant to illustrate. An example should also be *representative*. In other words, it should be typical of what the writer is trying to show.

Exemplification   A strategy for developing an essay. In exemplification, the writer uses examples — facts, opinions, anecdotes, or statistics — to make ideas more vivid and understandable. Exemplification is used in all types of essays. See also *Examples*.

Fallacy   See *Logical Fallacies*.

Figures of Speech   Brief, imaginative comparisons that highlight the similarities between things that are basically dissimilar. They make writing vivid and interesting and therefore more memorable. Following are the most common figures of speech:

Simile: An implicit comparison introduced by *like* or *as*. "The fighter's hands were like stone."

Metaphor: An implied comparison that uses one thing as the equivalent of another. "All the world's a stage."

Onomatopoeia: The use of words whose sound suggests the meaning, as in *buzz, hiss,* and *meow.*

Personification: A special kind of simile or metaphor in which human traits are assigned to an inanimate object. "The engine coughed and then stopped."

Freewriting   A discovery technique that involves writing for a brief uninterrupted period of time — ten or fifteen minutes — on anything that comes to mind. Writers use freewriting to discover new topics, new strategies, and other new ideas. See also *Brainstorming* and *Clustering*.

Gobbledygook   The use of technical or unfamiliar words that confuse rather than clarify an issue for an audience.

Grammar   The system of a language including its parts and the methods for combining them.

Idiom   A word or phrase that is used habitually with a particular meaning in a language. The meaning of an idiom is not always readily apparent to nonnative speakers of that language. For example, *catch cold, hold a job, make up your mind,* and *give them a hand* are all idioms in English.

Illustration   See *Examples*.

Indo-European Languages   A group of languages descended from a supposed common ancestor and now widely spoken in Europe, North and South America, Australia, New Zealand, and parts of India.

Induction   A process of reasoning whereby a conclusion about all members of a class is reached by examining only a few members of the class. This form of reasoning moves from a set of specific examples to a general statement or principle. As long as the evidence is accurate, pertinent, complete, and sufficient to represent the assertion, the conclusion of the inductive argument can be regarded as valid; if, however, readers can spot inaccuracies in the evidence or point to contrary evidence, they have good reason to doubt the assertion as it stands. Inductive reasoning is the most common of argumentative structures. See also *Deduction.*

Introductions   See *Beginnings and Endings.*

Irony   The use of words to suggest something different from their literal meaning. A writer can use irony to establish a special relationship with the reader and to add an extra dimension or twist to the meaning.

Jargon   See *Technical Language.*

Language   Words, their pronunciation, and the conventional and systematic methods for combining them as used and understood by a community.

Lexicography   The art of dictionary-making.

Linguistic Relativity Hypothesis   The belief that the structure of a language shapes the way speakers of that language view reality. Also known as the Sapir-Whorf Hypothesis after Edward Sapir and Benjamin Lee Whorf.

Logical Fallacies   Errors in reasoning that render an argument invalid. Some of the more common logical fallacies are listed here:

Oversimplification: The tendency to provide simple solutions to complex problems. "The reason we have inflation today is that OPEC has unreasonably raised the price of oil."

Non sequitur ("It does not follow"): An inference or conclusion that does not follow from established premises or evidence. "It was the best movie I saw this year, and it should get an Academy Award."

Post hoc, ergo propter hoc ("After this, therefore because of this"): Confusing chance or coincidence with causation. Because one event comes after another one, it does not necessarily mean that the first event caused the second. "I won't say I caught cold at the hockey game, but I certainly didn't have it before I went there."

Begging the question: Assuming in a premise that which needs to be proven. "If American autoworkers built a better product, foreign auto sales would not be so high."

False analogy: Making a misleading analogy between logically unconnected ideas. "He was a brilliant basketball player; therefore, there's no question in my mind that he will be a fine coach."

Either/or thinking: The tendency to see an issue as having only two sides. "Used car salesmen are either honest or crooked."

Logical Reasoning   See *Deduction* and *Induction.*

Metaphor   See *Figures of Speech.*

Narration   A strategy for developing an essay. To narrate is to tell a story, to tell what happened. Although narration is most often used in fiction, it is also important in nonfiction, either by itself or in conjunction with other strategies. A good narrative essay has four essential features. The first is *context:* The writer makes clear when the action happened, where it happened, and to whom. The second is *point of view:* The writer establishes and maintains a consistent relationship to the action, either as a participant or as a reporter simply looking on. The third is *selection of detail:* The writer carefully chooses what to include, focusing on those actions and details that are most important to the story while merely mentioning or actually eliminating others. The fourth is *organization:* The writer organizes the events of the narrative into an appropriate sequence, often a strict chronology with a clear beginning, middle, and end.

Objective/Subjective   *Objective writing* is factual and impersonal, whereas *subjective writing,* sometimes called impressionistic writing, relies heavily on personal interpretation.

Onomastics   The study of the meaning and origins of proper names of persons and places.

Onomatopoeia   See *Figures of Speech.*

Organization   In writing, the thoughtful arrangement and presentation of one's points or ideas. Narration is often organized chronologically, whereas other kinds of essays may be organized point by point or from most familiar to least familiar. Argument may be organized from least important to most important. There is no single correct pattern of organization for a given piece of writing, but good writers are careful to discover an order of presentation suitable for their subject, audience, and purpose.

Paradox   A seemingly contradictory statement that may nonetheless be true. For example, *we little know what we have until we lose it* is a paradoxical statement.

Paragraph   A series of closely related sentences and the single most important unit of thought in an essay. The sentences in a paragraph adequately develop its central idea, which is usually stated in a topic sentence. A well-written paragraph has several distinguishing characteristics: a clearly stated or implied topic sentence, adequate development, unity, coherence, and an appropriate organizational pattern.

Paraphrase   A restatement of the information a writer is borrowing. A paraphrase closely parallels the presentation of the ideas in the original, but it does not use the same words or sentence structure. See also *Direct Quotation, Summary,* and *Plagiarism.*

Personification   See *Figures of Speech.*

Persuasion   An attempt to convince readers to agree with a point of view, to make a given decision, or to pursue a particular course of action. See also *Argument, Induction,* and *Deduction.*

Phonetics   The study of speech sounds.

Phonology   The study of sounds systems in languages.

Plagiarism   The use of someone else's ideas in their original form or in an altered form without proper documentation. Writers avoid plagiarism by (1) putting direct quotations within quotation marks and properly citing them and (2) documenting any idea, explanation, or argument that is borrowed and presented in a summary or paraphrase, making it clear where the borrowed material begins and ends. See also *Direct Quotation, Paraphrase,* and *Summary.*

Point of View   The grammatical person of the speaker in an essay. For example, a first-person point of view uses the pronoun *I* and is commonly found in autobiography and the personal essay; a third-person point of view uses the pronouns *he, she,* or *it* and is commonly found in objective writing.

Prescriptivism   A grammar that seeks to explain linguistic facts as they should be. See also *Descriptivism.*

Process Analysis   A strategy for developing an essay. Process analysis answers the question *how* and explains how something works or gives step-by-step directions for doing something.

Propaganda   Ideas, facts, or rumors purposely spread to further one's cause or to damage the cause of an opponent.

Purpose   What a writer wants to accomplish in a particular composition—his or her reason for writing. The three general purposes of writing are *to express* thoughts and feelings and lessons learned from life experiences, *to inform* readers about something about the world around them, or *to persuade* readers to accept some belief or take some action.

Racist Language   A form of biased language that makes distinctions on the basis of race and deliberately or subconsciously suggests that one race is superior to all others.

Rhetorical Questions   Questions that are asked but require no answer from the reader. "When will nuclear proliferation end?" is such a question. Writers use rhetorical questions to introduce topics they plan to discuss or to emphasize important points.

Sapir-Whorf Hypothesis   See *Linguistic Relativity Hypothesis.*

Semantics   The study of meanings in a language.

Sexist Language   A form of biased language that makes distinctions on the basis of sex and shows preference for one sex over the other.

Signal Phrase   A phrase alerting the reader that borrowed information is to follow. A signal phrase usually consists of the author's name and a verb (for example, "Keesbury argues") and helps to integrate direct quotations, paraphrases, and summaries into the flow of a paper.

Simile   See *Figures of Speech.*

Slang   The unconventional, very informal language of particular subgroups in a culture. Slang words such as *zonk, split, rap, cop,* and *stoned* are acceptable in formal writing only if they are used for a specific purpose. A writer might use slang, for example, to re-create authentic dialogue in a story.

Specific/General   *General words* name groups or classes of objects, qualities, or actions. *Specific words,* on the other hand, name individual objects, qualities, or actions within a class or group. To some extent the terms *general* and *specific* are relative. For example, *dessert* is a class of things. *Pie,* however, is more specific than *dessert* but more general than *pecan pie* or *chocolate cream pie.* Good writing judiciously balances the general with the specific. Writing with too many general words is likely to be dull and lifeless because general words do not create vivid responses in the reader's mind. On the other hand, writing that relies exclusively on specific words may lack focus and direction, which more general statements provide.

Standard English   A variety of English that is used by the government and the media and that is taught in the schools. It is often best expressed in written form.

Style   The individual manner in which a writer expresses his or her ideas. Style is created by the author's particular selection of words, construction of sentences, and arrangement of ideas.

Subjective   See *Objective/Subjective.*

Summary   A condensed form of the essential idea of a passage, article, or entire chapter. A summary is always shorter than the original. See also *Paraphrase, Direct Quotation,* and *Plagiarism.*

Syllogism   An argument that utilizes deductive reasoning and consists of a major premise, a minor premise, and a conclusion. For example,
All trees that lose leaves are deciduous. (major premise)
Maple trees lose their leaves. (minor premise)

Therefore, maple trees are deciduous. (conclusion)
See also *Deduction.*

Symbol   A person, place, or thing that represents something beyond itself. For example, the eagle is a symbol of America, and the bear is a symbol of Russia.

Syntax   The way words are arranged to form phrases, clauses, and sentences. Syntax also refers to the grammatical relationships among the words themselves.

Taboo Language   Language that is avoided in a given society. Almost all societies have language taboos.

Technical Language   The special vocabulary of a trade or profession. Writers who use technical language do so with an awareness of their audiences. If the audience is a group of peers, technical language may be used freely. If the audience is a more general one, technical language should be used sparingly and carefully so as not to sacrifice clarity. Technical language that is used only to impress, hide the truth, or cover insecurities is termed *jargon* and is not condoned. See also *Diction.*

Thesis   A statement of the main idea of an essay, the point the essay is trying to make. A thesis may sometimes be implied rather than stated directly.

Tone   The manner in which a writer relates to an audience, the "tone of voice" used to address readers. Tone may be described as friendly, serious, distant, angry, cheerful, bitter, cynical, enthusiastic, morbid, resentful, warm, playful, and so forth. A particular tone results from a writer's diction, sentence structure, purpose, and attitude toward the subject. See also *Attitude.*

Topic Sentence   The sentence that states the central idea of a paragraph and thus limits and controls the subject of the paragraph. Although the topic sentence normally appears at the beginning of the paragraph, it may appear at any other point, particularly if the writer is trying to create a special effect. See also *Paragraph.*

Transitions   Words or phrases that link the sentences, paragraphs, and larger units of an essay in order to achieve coherence. Transitional devices include parallelism, pronoun references, conjunctions, and the repetition of key ideas, as well as the many transitional expressions such as *moreover, on the other hand, in addition, in contrast,* and *therefore.* See also *Coherence.*

Unity   A quality that is achieved in an essay when all the words, sentences, and paragraphs contribute to its thesis. The elements of a unified essay do not distract the reader. Instead, they all harmoniously support a single idea or purpose.

Usage   The way in which words and phrases are actually used in a language community. See also *Descriptivism* and *Prescriptivism.*

RHETORICAL CONTENTS

e bedfordstmartins.com/languageawareness/epages

CAUSE AND EFFECT ANALYSIS

COMPARISON AND CONTRAST

DEFINITION

DESCRIPTION

DIVISION AND CLASSIFICATION

🄔 **bedfordstmartins.com/languageawareness/epages**

EXAMPLE AND ILLUSTRATION

NARRATION

PROCESS AND ANALYSIS

permission of Scribner, a Division of Simon & Schuster, Inc. All rights reserved.

Michael Kimmel, "Bros Before Hos: The Guy Code." From *Guyland: The Perilous World Where Boys Become Men.* Copyright © 2008 by Michael Kimmel. Reprinted with permission of HarperCollins Publishers.

Charles Krauthammer, "In Plain English: Let's Make It Official," *Time* Magazine, June 4, 2006. Copyright *Time* Inc. Reprinted with permission. *Time* is a registered trademark of Time Inc. All rights reserved.

Irving Kristol, "Pornography, Obscenity, and the Case for Censorship," *The New York Times*, March 28, 1971. All rights reserved. Published by permission of Irving Kristol c/o Writers Representatives, LLC, New York, NY 10011.

Anne Lamott, "Shitty First Drafts." From *Bird by Bird*. Copyright © 1994 by Anne Lamott. Reprinted with permission of Pantheon Books, a division of Random House, Inc.

Susanne Langer, "Language and Thought." From *Ms.* Magazine, 1953. Reprinted with permission of the heirs of Ms. Langer.

Richard Lederer, "All-American Dialects," *Verbivore*. Reprinted with permission of the author.

Richard Lederer, "Verbs with Verve, The Play of Words." From *The Play of Words*. Copyright © 1990 by Richard Lederer. Reprinted with the permission of Simon & Schuster, Inc. All rights reserved.

Dr. Frank Luntz, "Be All That You Can Be." From *Words the Work*. Copyright © 2006 by Dr. Frank Luntz. Reprinted with permission of Hyperion. All rights reserved.

William Lutz, "The World of Doublespeak." Copyright © 1989. "Weasel Words." Copyright © 1980. From *Doublespeak*. Reprinted with permission of William Lutz, in care of the Jean V. Naggar Literary Agency, Inc.

Wangari Maathai, "Planting the Seeds of Peace," Nobel Lecture, Oslo, December 10, 2004. © The Nobel Foundation 2004. Reprinted with permission of The Nobel Foundation.

Myriam Marquez, "Why and When We Speak Spanish in Public," *The Orlando Sentinel*, July 5, 1999. Republished with permission of *The Orlando Sentinel*, permission conveyed through Copyright Clearance Center, Inc.

Lisa B. Marshall, "Like, Eliminate Ums and Ahs, Right?" From The Public Speaker, Episode 9: February 26, 2012. Reprinted with permission of the author. Communication Strategist/Author/Speaker/Host of The Public Speaker's Quick and Dirty Tips for Improving Your Communication Skills, http://www.lisabmarshall.com.

John C. McGinley, "Spread the Word to End the Word," *Huffington Post*, March 2, 2010. Reprinted with permission of the author.

Erin McKean, "Neologizing 101," *The New York Times*, August 25, 2002. Reprinted with permission of the author.

John McWhorter, "Missing the Nose on Our Face: Pronouns and the Feminist Revolution," Word on the Street: Debunking the Myth of "Pure" Standard English. Copyright © 2001 John McWhorter. Reprinted with permission of Basic Books, a member of the Perseus Books Group.

Michael Mercier, "A Clockwork Green," *Adweek*, August 17, 2009. Copyright © 2009 *Adweek*. Reprinted with permission of Adweek via Wright's Media.

Mauro E. Mujica, "Why the U.S. Needs an Official Language." From *World and I*. Copyright © 2003. Reprinted with permission of *World and I*.

Bharati Mukherjee, "Two Ways to Belong in America." Copyright © 1996 by Bharati Mukherjee. Originally published in *The New York Times*. Reprinted with permission of the author.

Donald M. Murray, "The Maker's Eye: Revising Your Own Manuscripts." *The Writer*, 1973. Copyright © 1973 by Donald M. Murray. Reprinted with permission of The Rosenberg Group on behalf of author's estate.

Gloria Naylor, "The Meanings of a Word." Reprinted with permission of SLL/Sterling Lord Literistic, Inc. Copyright by Gloria Naylor.

George Orwell, "Politics and the English Language." From *Shooting an Elephant and Other Essays*. Copyright 1946 by Sonia Brownell Orwell. Copyright © 1974 renewed by Sonia Orwell. Reprinted with permission of Houghton Mifflin Harcourt Publishing Company. All rights reserved.

Richard Pérez-Peña, "Stutterer Speaks Up in Class; His Professor Says Keep Quiet." From *The New York Times*, October 10 © 2011 *The New York Times*. All rights reserved. Reprinted with permission and protected by the Copyright Laws of the United States. The printing, copying, redistribution, or retransmission of this Content without express written permission is prohibited.

Steven Pinker, "Words Don't Mean What They Mean." From *The Stuff of Thought*. Copyright © 2007 by Steven Pinker. Reprinted with permission of Viking Penguin, a division of Penguin Group (USA) Inc.

Mary Pipher, "Writing to Change the World." From *Writing to Change the World*. Copyright © 2006 by Mary Pipher. Reprinted with permission of Riverhead Books, an imprint of Penguin Group (USA) Inc.

Reader comments from Stanley's "Media and Distrust: A Response." From *The New York Times*, July 18 © 2011 *The New York Times*. All rights reserved. Reprinted with permission and protected by the

Malcolm X, "Coming to an Awareness of Language." From *The Autobiography of Malcolm X* by Malcolm X and Alex Haley. Copyright © 1964 by Alex Haley and Malcolm X. Copyright © 1965 by Alex Haley and Betty Shabazz. Reprinted with permission of Random House, Inc.

Robert Yoakum, "Everyspeech." Originally published in *The New York Times*, November 1994. Reprinted with permission of the author.

Ben Zimmer, "Chunking." From *The New York Times*, September 19 © 2010 *The New York Times*. All rights reserved. Reprinted with permission and protected by the Copyright Laws of the United States. The printing, copying, redistribution, or retransmission of the material without express written permission is prohibited.

Ben Zimmer, "Creeper! Rando! Sketchball!" From *The New York Times*, October 31 © 2010 *The New York Times*. All rights reserved. Reprinted with permission and protected by the Copyright Laws of the United States. The printing, copying, redistribution, or retransmission of this Content without express written permission is prohibited.

William Zinsser, "Draft of Simplicity" and "Simplicity." Reprinted with permission of the author.

PHOTO ACKNOWLEDGMENTS

6.1 By Jeff Parker, politicalcartoons.com/Cagle Cartoons, Inc.

7.1 Courtesy of Cambridge Chemical Technologies, Inc. (CCTI) http://www.cambchemtech.com

8.2 University of Vermont

9.1 David Ryan, *The Boston Globe*, Getty Images

11.1 David Carpenter/www.CartoonStock.com

11.2 Rina Piccolo's Panel Cartoon used with the permission of Rina Piccolo and the Cartoonist Group. All rights reserved.

11.3 A. Bacall/www.CartoonStock.com

11.4 A. Bacall/www.CartoonStock.com

12.1 Courtesy of The Library of Congress, lithograph 1917

12.2 Courtesy of The Library of Congress, Prints & Photographs Division.

12.5 © Carol Lay

14.1 © Mike Lester

15.1 Courtesy of the University of Vermont Libraries.

E-PAGES ACKNOWLEDGMENTS

[Chapter 4] Barack Obama. "Don't Tell Me Words Don't Matter." Used with permission from C-SPAN.

[Chapter 5] Eric Sonstroem, "Play and Language." *A Moment of Science* courtesy of WFIU Public Radio, from Indiana University in Bloomington. Copyright © The Trustees of Indiana University.

[Chapter 6] Amy Walker. "21 Accents." By Amy Walker, www.AmyWalker.com.

[Chapter 7] Stephen King. "On Writing." Video clip: Courtesy of Keith Lynn with permission from Stephen King.

[Chapter 8] Ben Jervey. "Tracking the Language of the Environment." Originally appeared on www.GOOD.is on December 23, 2010. Reprinted with permission from GOOD.

[Chapter 10] Victor Villanueva and Nick Burns. "Language and Racism." Courtesy of Nick Burns, Salt Lake Community College Communications Department.

[Chapter 11] *The Visual Thesaurus*®. Images from the *Visual Thesaurus*®. Copyright © 1998–2012 Thinkmap Inc. www.visualthesaurus.com. All rights reserved.

[Chapter 12] *Wall Street Journal.* "'Halftime in America' Backlash." Reprinted with permission of *The Wall Street Journal*, Copyright 2012, Dow Jones & Company, Inc. All rights reserved worldwide.

[Chapter 13] Paul Muhlhauser and Kelly S. Bradbury, *How Genders Work: Producing the J. Crew Catalog.* Courtesy of Paul Muhlhauser, Assistant Professor of English at McDaniel College and Kelly S. Bradbury, Assistant Professor of English at the College of Staten Island. Copyright © 2010.

INDEX OF AUTHORS AND TITLES

Missing something? To access the e-Pages that accompany this text, visit **bedfordstmartins.com/languageawareness /epages**. Students who do not buy a new book can purchase access to e-Pages at this site.

Inside the e-Pages for *Language Awareness*

Barack Obama, *Don't Tell Me Words Don't Matter* (video)

Eric Sonstroem, *Play and Language* (audio)

Amy Walker, *21 Accents* (video)

Stephen King, *Advice from Stephen King* (video)

Ben Jervey, *Tracking the Language of the Environment* (Web text)

Victor Villanueva and Nick Burns, *Language and Racism* (video)

Thinkmap Inc., *The Visual Thesaurus*® (Web site)

Wall Street Journal, *"Halftime in America" Backlash* (video)

Paul Muhlhauser and Kelly Bradbury, *How Genders Work: Producing the J. Crew Catalog* (Web text)